Intertextuality in Flavian Epic Poetry

Trends in Classics – Supplementary Volumes

Edited by
Franco Montanari and Antonios Rengakos

Associate Editors
Stavros Frangoulidis · Fausto Montana · Lara Pagani
Serena Perrone · Evina Sistakou · Christos Tsagalis

Scientific Committee
Alberto Bernabé · Margarethe Billerbeck
Claude Calame · Jonas Grethlein · Philip R. Hardie
Stephen J. Harrison · Richard Hunter · Christina Kraus
Giuseppe Mastromarco · Gregory Nagy
Theodore D. Papanghelis · Giusto Picone
Tim Whitmarsh · Bernhard Zimmermann

Volume 64

Intertextuality in Flavian Epic Poetry

Contemporary Approaches

Edited by
Neil Coffee, Chris Forstall, Lavinia Galli Milić and Damien Nelis

DE GRUYTER

ISBN 978-3-11-077701-7
e-ISBN (PDF) 978-3-11-060220-3
e-ISBN (EPUB) 978-3-11-059975-6
ISSN 1868-4785

Library of Congress Control Number: 2019945643

Bibliographic information published by the Deutsche Nationalbibliothek
The Deutsche Nationalbibliothek lists this publication in the Deutsche Nationalbibliografie;
detailed bibliographic data are available on the Internet at http://dnb.dnb.de.

© 2021 Walter de Gruyter GmbH, Berlin/Boston
This volume is text- and page-identical with the hardback published in 2020.
Editorial Office: Alessia Ferreccio and Katerina Zianna
Logo: Christopher Schneider, Laufen
Printing and binding: CPI books GmbH, Leck

www.degruyter.com

Contents

Acknowledgments —— IX

Neil Coffee/Chris Forstall/Lavinia Galli Milić/Damien Nelis
Introduction —— 1

Helen Lovatt
Meanwhile Back at the Ranch:
Narrative Transition and Structural Intertextuality in Statius *Thebaid* 1 —— 21

Tim Stover
Valerius Flaccus' *Argonautica* **3.598–725: Epic, History, and Intertextuality** —— 43

Damien Nelis
Allusive Technique in the *Argonautica* **of Valerius Flaccus** —— 65

Raymond Marks
Searching for Ovid at Cannae:
A Contribution to the Reception of Ovid in Silius Italicus' *Punica* —— 87

Michael Dewar
The Flavian Epics and the Neoterics —— 107

Federica Bessone
Allusive (Im-)Pertinence in Statius' Epic —— 133

Antony Augoustakis
Collateral Damage? *Todeskette* **in Flavian Epic** —— 169

Mark Heerink
Replaying Dido:
Elegy and the Poetics of Inversion in Valerius Flaccus' *Argonautica* —— 187

Chiara Battistella/Lavinia Galli Milić
Foreshadowing Medea: Prolepsis and Intertextuality in Valerius Flaccus —— 205

François Ripoll
Ulysses as an Inter- (and Meta-)textual Hero in the *Achilleid* of Statius —— 243

Marco Fucecchi
Constructing (Super-)characters: The Case Study of Silius' Hannibal —— 259

Gianpiero Rosati
The Redemption of the Monster, or: The 'Evil Hero' in Ancient Epic —— 283

Thomas Baier
Flavian Gods in Intertextual Perspective.
How Rulers Used Religious Practice as a Means of Communicating —— 305

Alison Keith
Palatine Apollo, Augustan Architectural Ecphrasis,
and Flavian Epic Intertextuality —— 323

Carole Newlands
Statius' Post-Vesuvian Landscapes and Virgil's Parthenope —— 349

Neil Bernstein
Quantitative and Qualitative Perspectives on the Use of Poetic Tradition in Silius Italicus' *Punica* —— 373

Peter Heslin
Lemmatizing Latin and Quantifying the *Achilleid* —— 389

Neil Coffee/James Gawley
How Rare are the Words that Make Up Intertexts?
A Study in Latin and Greek Epic Poetry —— 409

Stephen Hinds
Pre- and Post-digital Poetics of 'Transliteralism':
Some Greco-Roman Epic Incipits —— 421

List of Contributors —— 447
Index Locorum —— 451

Acknowledgments

This collection of essays arises from a research project on intertextuality in Flavian epic poetry funded by the Swiss National Science Foundation and involving the University of Geneva, Switzerland, and the University at Buffalo, SUNY, USA. All the papers were first presented at a work-in-progress seminar held at the Fondation Hardt, in Vandœuvres, on 28–30 May 2015. We would like to thank all the staff at the Fondation Hardt for hosting the event and for all their attentive kindness. Thanks also to those who helped fund the conference, the Swiss National Science Foundation and the Faculty of Arts and the 'Commission administrative' of the University of Geneva. We are very grateful to Valéry Berlincourt, Collin Osborne, Matteo Romanello, and Yannick Zanetti for precious help of various kinds. Warm thanks are also due to the staff at De Gruyter for all their assistance, to the editors of the series Trends in Classics for accepting the volume, to two anonymous readers for helpful advice, to Marco Michele Acquafredda for all his encouragement and support, and to everyone involved for their angelic patience. The final word of thanks must go to all the contributors: it was both a pleasure and an education to have the opportunity to work closely with such a generous, friendly, and talented group of scholars.

Neil Coffee, Chris Forstall, Lavinia Galli Milić, Damien Nelis

Neil Coffee/Chris Forstall/Lavinia Galli Milić/Damien Nelis
Introduction

When Julia Kristeva invented the term intertextuality, she knew very well that the definition she provided for it would create a problem for scholars involved in traditional forms of source criticism, even if she was certainly not thinking first and foremost of classical philologists. Consider three of her formulations:

> "[T]out texte se construit comme mosaïque de citations, tout texte est absorption et transformation d'un autre texte."[1]
> "Le livre renvoie à d'autres livres [...] et donne à ces livres une nouvelle façon d'être, élaborant ainsi sa propre signification."[2]
> "Le signifié poétique renvoie à des signifiés discursifs autres, de sorte que dans l'énoncé poétique plusieurs autres discours sont lisibles. Il se crée, ainsi, autour du signifié poétique, un espace textuel multiple dont les éléments sont susceptibles d'être appliqués dans le texte poétique concret. Nous appellerons cet espace intertextuel. Pris dans l'intertextualité, l'énoncé poétique est un sous-ensemble plus grand qui est l'espace des textes appliqués dans notre ensemble."[3]

Confusion between Kristeva's intended meaning and what others would make of her ideas was inevitable from the outset. And she herself, as neatly pointed out by J. Culler, was not always good at maintaining clear distinctions, when it came to the business of analyzing texts: "Anyone thinking that the point of intertextuality is to take us beyond the study of identifiable sources is brought up short by Kristeva's observation that 'in order to compare the presupposed text with the text of *Poésies II*, one needs to determine what editions of Pascal, Vauvenargues and La Rochefoucauld Ducasse could have used, for the versions vary considerably from one edition to another' ".[4] It did not take very long for Kristeva herself to become weary of confusion about what she meant by intertextuality. Already in 1974 she wrote: "Le terme d'*intertextualité* désigne cette transposition d'un (ou de plusieurs) systèmes de signes en un autre, mais puisque ce terme a souvent été entendu dans le sens banal de 'critique des sources' d'un texte, nous lui préférons celui de *transposition*."[5] It seems fair to say that her preferred alternative has not caught on.

---

1 Kristeva (1969) 85.
2 Kristeva (1969) 121.
3 Kristeva (1969) 194.
4 Culler (1981) 106.
5 Kristeva (1974) 59–60.

Leaving aside the question of exactly what Kristeva meant by her use of the term and the fact that the complexity and the incompleteness of her original formulations easily gave rise to modifications and differing applications of her ideas (e.g. by Barthes, Riffaterre, Jenny, Genette), one can easily appreciate the attractivity of a term such as intertextuality for students of Latin poetry as a whole and of Flavian epic poetry in particular. The epic poetry of Valerius Flaccus, Statius and Silius Italicus forms a corpus ideally suited to theorizing of this kind. The Flavian epic poems had always been read as imitative and derivative in nature. But by the 1970s the pressure was increasing on Latinists to come up with meaningful literary interpretations of cases of *imitatio*, rather than simply indulging in the pleasure of collecting and listing verbal similarities. When one adds in a timely dose of New Critical concern about authorial intention and, by the 1980s, an evolving sense of the metapoetic implications of many of the Latin texts' own nods to matters of literary history, belatedness and rewriting, the term intertextuality came along as a very welcome addition to the vocabulary with which one could talk about imitation and literary history. And so, in the vocabulary of Latinists it came to be added to such frequently used terms as allusion, reference, borrowing, echo, influence, and so on. When such influential anglophone scholars as Oliver Lyne and Richard Thomas began using the term in the titles of articles and books, intertextuality entered standard usage and became widely used as a catch-all way of referring to text reuse.[6] Use of the term has now become so common as to go quite unremarked. For example, in two recent volumes on Flavian epic specifically and, for the sake of comparison, one on Senecan tragedy, it is used pervasively.[7]

It is in this research context that we have used the word intertextuality in the title of this collection of essays. It is also used by many of the individual contributors, but not by all. Certainly, in organizing both this volume and the conference that gave rise to it the editors gave no guidelines whatsoever concerning terminology to the participants. And there is surely no need to offer here a detailed definition of exactly what we mean by our use of the term. Like so many scholars, we use it as a useful term for talking about the relationships between texts on a number of different levels, just as other terms such as allusion, reference, borrowing, echo, influence, and so on have been used by Latinists for a long time. Intertextuality helpfully covers the interaction between referential allusion in the

---

[6] See Lyne (1994), Thomas (1999). The conversation was of course not confined to the field of classics. See, e.g., the survey of modern theorists provided by Allen (2011) that touches *inter alia* on Barthes, Genette, Riffaterre, and Bloom.
[7] Manuwald/Voigt (2013), Augoustakis (2014), Trinacty (2014).

form of obvious verbal citation of an earlier text and the reuse of standard generic features that function on a more thematic level. It also facilitates thinking about highly complex patterns of poetic imitation that involve several texts at the same time. It seems slightly easier to say, for example, that there is an intertextual relationship between Statius, Lucan, Vergil and Homer rather than to say that Statius is alluding to Lucan, Vergil and Homer, suggesting that he has in mind all three at the same time and in the same way. In the end, both formulations can amount to exactly the same thing when it comes to arguing for the presence and meaning of a particular example of imitation or text reuse, but individual scholars can be troubled by the associations of certain terms, such as when Richard Thomas chose to use reference in preference to allusion, thinking the latter "far too frivolous to suit the process".[8] It thus seems useful to adopt a term with which a majority of scholars now seem happy and make the most of the capaciousness it offers.

Questions of terminology aside, therefore, we would like to make use of this introduction to put forward for consideration a few remarks about the current state of practice in relation to the study of intertextuality as employed by Valerius Flaccus, Statius and Silius Italicus. We have three main aims in publishing this volume: first, to offer to interested readers a selection of papers that is representative of the kinds of work currently being done on Flavian epic by providing examples of research that takes as its starting point a fundamentally intertextual approach and successfully demonstrates the centrality of this method; second, to draw attention to recent developments in digital humanities that seem certain to play an important role in the years to come; third, to suggest that a considerable amount of systematic work still remains to be done on the *Argonautica*, the *Thebaid*, the *Achilleid*, and the *Punica*.

1 Overview of Contributions

In relation to the first of these points, the papers collected here have been organized in the following way. First comes a group of four papers (Lovatt, Stover, Nelis, Marks) that deal mainly with defined sections of text and have an interest in the use of specific models as well as imitative narrative structures and allusive techniques. Then come three papers of similar type (Dewar, Bessone, Augoustakis) but with a focus on tracing wider influences and dealing also with matters of generic

---

[8] Thomas (1999) 115.

shifts and tone. The next three papers treat specific characters (Heerink, Battistella/Galli Milić, Ripoll), before the following three deal with epic character types from a wider perspective (Fucecchi, Rosati, Baier). Two papers then handle matters of space and topography (Keith, Newlands). Finally, four papers deal with digital matters (Bernstein, Heslin, Coffee/Gawley, Hinds), describing recent developments in this area and looking forward to future work. The individual contributions are as follows.

Helen Lovatt opens the first group of papers with an examination of the intertextual role of Statian scene transitions, in her essay "Meanwhile Back at the Ranch: Narrative Transition and Structural Intertextuality in Statius *Thebaid* 1." Writing against the context of the ever-increasing sophistication and pervasiveness of computational tools for detecting textual similarities at the lexical level, Lovatt observes that the limits of a word-based approach are, more than ever, as apparent as its power. Frequently, as Lovatt notes, verbal correspondences are only meaningful when their narratological context is taken into account. In this paper, Lovatt illuminates some of the complex ways in which features at different levels—scene, word, and sub-word—interact to open an intertextual space in which multiple connections, between and within works, can resonate. In particular, Lovatt demonstrates that structural intertext is more than the parallel alignment of scenes. Rather, the transitions between scenes themselves take up space on the page, and carry their own textual reminiscences. These may be code-model similarities, establishing the transition as a kind of type-scene in itself; or more directed links to specific referents. Lovatt does not treat structural connections as independent of word-level features, but shows the ways in which individual words such as *interea* ("meanwhile") or *at* ("but") may shift between semantic and structural significance.

Tim Stover demonstrates the value of intertextual evidence to a historicising reading of Valerius Flaccus in his chapter, "Valerius Flaccus' *Argonautica* 3.598–725: Epic, History, and Intertextuality." Stover's subject is a pivotal moment in the Argonauts' journey, their debate over whether to abandon the missing hero Hercules, and the resonance of this passage with the tumultuous politics of 68–69, the infamous 'Year of the Four Emperors.' Specifically, he examines the role of Valerius' Meleager, who is characterized by the poet as a perfidious demagogue even as he successfully persuades the Argonauts to depart without Hercules, asking to what degree Meleager finds a model in Tacitus' representation of the general Antonius Primus. Stover brings intertextual evidence to bear on this question in two, complementary ways. First, drawing on close verbal connections with Bacchylides, Vergil, and Ovid, he illuminates Meleager's longstanding literary rivalry with Hercules and his affinity for duplicity (evoking models in both

Ulysses and Aeneas). Second, he tackles the problem of direct intertextual connections to Tacitus' *Histories* themselves, showing not only the potential of such connections to add meaning our reading of the epic, but also some of the difficulties which must be overcome in order to thoroughly disentangle the web of literary relationships among Valerius, Tacitus, and their common sources.

In "Allusive Technique in the *Argonautica* of Valerius Flaccus", Damien Nelis takes a close look at a short passage at the opening of Valerius' fifth book. His aim is to combine study of narrative structure and verbal allusion, in order to demonstrate that the two are inseparable, given the compositional techniques of ancient epic poets. In this particular case, Nelis is able to show that Valerius Flaccus' planning of the whole structure of his epic narrative is built on close study of the intertextual relationship between Vergil's *Aeneid* and the *Argonautica* of Apollonius Rhodius. The Flavian author is thus able to indulge in a continuous process of two-tier allusion to both models, as he consistently bases his imitation of the *Aeneid* on his profound knowledge of Vergil's large debt to his key Hellenistic model.

Raymond Marks begins his paper "Searching for Ovid at Cannae: A Contribution to the Reception of Ovid in Silius Italicus' *Punica*" by pointing out that the presence of Ovid in the *Punica*—even if it is not directly signalled, as is the case with Vergil or Ennius—is especially pervasive within the narrative of the books 8–10 on the battle of Cannae. The quarrel between Paulus and Varro, the description of the Marsian contingent in the catalogue, and the story of Satricus and Solymus are some of the passages where Marks detects several striking verbal and thematic allusions to the biographical Ovid as depicted in the *Fasti*, the *Metamorphoses*, the *Tristia* and the *Ibis*. This network of references as well as some Alexandrian footnotes, an acrostic and the recurring imagery of civil strife and shipwreck allow the reader—Marks goes on to argue—to make an analogy between the self-destructive character of this battle and the construction of the biography of Ovid in exile as a "self-inflicted downfalls" (p. 103), as a ruin because of his own poetry (cf. the famous *carmen et error*). This supports the compelling idea of D. Krasne that Silius has read the *Ibis* as an invective against Ovid himself and/or the poetry that has played a part in his punishment at Tomis.

In his contribution, "The Flavian Epics and the Neoterics", Michael Dewar sets out first to establish a chain of continuity between the reading practices of the Flavian period and the literature of the middle of the first century BCE. In doing so he defends his use of the debated term 'neoterics' as a useful designation for a recognizable literary-historical phenomenon to which it is convenient for modern scholars to attach a name. He then goes on to establish that Catullus and Calvus were still being read and imitated in the Flavian period, before surveying the evidence for possible traces of the influence of a series of specific works, Cinna and his *Propempticon Pollionis*, Calvus' *Io*, and Cornificus' *Glaucus*. Overall, he reaches the conclusion that despite the highly fragmentary state of the remains of the neoteric poets, with the exception of Catullus, it is possible to argue with reasonable certainty that they were indeed read and imitated by all of the three surviving Flavian epicists. In particular Dewar singles out Statius as the Flavian poet "who is probably more familiar with recherché poetry of all kinds, Greek and Latin, than almost any Roman poet except Ovid" (p. 130).

Federica Bessone explores the range of Statius' antiphrastic intertextual modes in her chapter, "Allusive (Im-)Pertinence in Statius' Epic." Allusions that ironize, undercut, or work against the grain of their source material are for Bessone a window onto the larger landscape of Statian style. Statius' use of 'impertinent' allusions is complex, comprising a spectrum of behaviours from the comic to the grimly ironic, from the diffuse to those of cento-like density. In particular, Bessone demonstrates how Statius deploys antiphrastic intertextual material to different effects in the *Thebaid* and the *Achilleid*. So, for example, in the introduction of Oedipus at the *Thebaid*'s opening two dense constellations of allusive references—one concerning darkness and light, the other, winged predators—collide and interact to surprising effect. In the *Achilleid*, elegiac aspects of the relationship between Achilles and Deidamia are illuminated by a series of allusions that seems to dance precariously on the edge of parody. In several of these cases the key allusion is a window reference, and the tone of Statius' impertinence must be read against that of an intermediary (often Ovid). Throughout the chapter, Bessone reflects on the process of discovery and reading, documenting the diversity of textual features that signal allusion—*iuncturae*, *incipits* and *clausulae*, syntactic structures, and phonetic elements smaller than words—and noting in particular which features are amenable to computational analysis and which, with present technology, are not.

In his article, "Collateral Damage? *Todeskette* in Flavian Epic," Antony Augoustakis argues that the lists of the warriors slain by great epic chieftains that are a stock feature of epic are fashioned with considerable creativity by the Flavian poets. Augoustakis demonstrates through examples from Valerius, Statius, and Silius Italicus the depth of interplay in the names of the slain, which repurpose and combine names from the epic tradition, create irony, evoke associations of place and person, and generally provide the reader with the various pleasures of recognition and variation, up to and including the innovative catalog of burned ships supplied by Silius Italicus in book 14 of his *Punica*. Augoustakis succeeds in showing how, for their contemporary readers and for us today, epic lists of the slain are hardly rote recountings but packed with significance.

In "Replaying Dido: Elegy and the Poetics of Inversion in Valerius Flaccus' *Argonautica*," Mark Heerink takes as his starting point influential work by M. Putnam, S. Hinds and F. Cairns on the interplay between epic and elegy within Vergil's *Aeneid*. The Dido episode plays a crucial role in this approach to a poem that begins with 'arms and the man', but which must pass through the love story that dominates much of the first half of the poem before getting to Latium and the outbreak of war in book 7. Heerink goes on to show how Valerius interprets and responds to this Vergilian dynamic by means of verbal allusion and thematic and structural reworkings, looking in particular at the massacre on Lemnos and the role of Hypsipyle, the many connections between Lemnos and Colchis and their Vergilian background, and the Hylas episode. He arrives at the conclusion that the *Argonautica* is an elegized *Aeneid*. He concludes by arguing that this elegiac rewriting of the *Aeneid* plays a role in Valerius' creation of a pessimistic vision of the contemporary Roman world under Vespasian and his inability to believe in his Vergilian model's positive Augustan vision of *imperium sine fine*.

In their co-written paper "Foreshadowing Medea: Prolepsis and Intertextuality in Valerius Flaccus," Chiara Battistella and Lavinia Galli Milić explore the role of the prolepsis as an idiosyncratic device of Valerius' Medea and consider proleptic passages as strategic places for Valerius to challenge his literary predecessors. They focus on the description of the first meeting between Medea and Jason in book 5 and on the monologue delivered by Hecate in book 6. A close reading of these passages allow them to detect some new intergeneric, intra- and intertextual connexions between the Valerius' Medea and the tragic Medea as well as other female figures, Dido in particular, and Venus. Battistella and Galli Milić argue that the Flavian poet is recasting essential epic patterns (as the simile between the female character and a goddess, the reference to the beauty of the male hero) bringing into them tragic irony and proleptic undertones—that were absent from the Homeric archetype—through verbal and thematic allusions to Vergil's *Aeneid* (book 1, 4, 7), Ovid's *Metamorphoses* and Seneca's *Medea*. This tragedy, in particular, has to be taken as the textual backdrop against which Valerius shapes the sympathetic Hecate's monologue that participates in the multifaceted generic profile of Valerius' Medea.

In his article "Ulysses as an Inter-(and Meta-)textual Hero in the *Achilleid* of Statius," François Ripoll provides a new way of understanding Statius's Ulysses. While on one level the Ulysses of the *Achilleid* is fashioned from the stock features of his representation in the tradition, when seen in full with his complement of intertextual resonances, Ulysses becomes a richly meaningful character who even stands for the whole project of the *Achilleid*. Ripoll shows how Statius endows his Ulysses with three different intertextual aspects. He is at times a 'super-

Ulysses,' with his typical craftiness and eloquence highly amplified. He can be a 'proto-Ulysses,' with traits prefiguring events in his destiny after the episode on Scyros. And he can be a 'meta-Ulysses,' employed as an approving observer of the Achilleid itself. Ripoll's multi-tiered analysis not only neatly unfolds of the character of Ulysses, but also provides an exemplary case study in the complexity of Statius's intertextual artistry.

In his article "Constructing (Super-)characters: The Case Study of Silius' Hannibal," Marco Fucecchi builds upon the issue of the multiple intertextuality at work in the characterisation of Silius' Hannibal. He focuses in particular on the way Silius merges features drawn from the antagonist figures of Caesar and Pompey, as they occur in Lucan's *Civil War*. His approach is based on the close reading of the end of the *Punica* 17—where Hannibal's departure from Italy and his flight from Zama are narrated—that allows Fucecchi to illustrate the subtle intertextuality of the poem, combining Lucanian patterns for Caesar and Pompey and verbal references to passages from Ovid *Metamorphoses, Amores, Epistulae ex Ponto*, and from the *Elegy for Maecenas*. Furthermore, Fucecchi highlights that the super-character of Hannibal, as a syncretic figure of loser and winner, has been already anticipated in the extradiegetic allusion to his death in exile (end of books 2 and 13). To conclude, Fucecchi convincingly points out that the Flavian poet, by deconstructing and reassembling the material of his models, "stand[s] as a critic of a whole literary tradition" (p. 279) and invites the reader to explore deeper the relationship between the Caesar/Pompey opposition in the original Lucanian context.

In his article "The Redemption of the Monster, or: the 'Evil Hero' in Ancient Epic," Gianpiero Rosati assembles the cast of 'evil heroes' in classical epic, warriors whose martial prowess and courage are unquestionable, but whose motives, methods, and appearance put them beyond the pale. Rosati takes as his focus Statius's Capaneus, a powerful warrior who openly scorns and even physically attacks the gods. The legacy of Capaneus, Rosati argues, traces back to Homer's Cyclops, Stesichorus's Geryon, and Vergil's Mezentius. Each of these monstrous figures has at least one redeeming feature. Through the exploration of this strand of the epic tradition, Rosati demonstrates the distinctiveness of Statius's approach to endowing Capaneus, as well as even the cannibalistic Tydeus, with sympathetic virtues through the full description of the fidelity with which their wives honor them after their deaths.

Thomas Baier ("Flavian Gods in Intertextual Perspective. How Rulers Used Religious Practice as a Means of Communicating") turns his attention to religion, in particular how the interactions between humanity and the divine can be used as a means of gaining political authority. Because they provide examples of heroes in contact with the gods, epic texts can explore contemporary political concerns, simply by permitting readers to make the shift from the deeds of an epic hero to consideration of the role of a statesman who wields power in the real world. In this area as in others, the Vergilian model provides Flavian authors with much food for thought, and Baier's case studies are devoted principally to Valerius' and Statius' reactions to the *Aeneid*, with passing consideration of other texts that can teach us about the Flavian age, those of Tacitus and the Gospel of Mark. The combination of religion and power in the Augustan epic opens the way to consideration of the Flavian dynasty in both the *Argonautica* and the *Thebaid*. By drawing attention to the constant connections between *religio* and *imperium* in both Augustan and Flavian epic poetry, Baier offers yet another way of thinking about the intertextual relationship between Vergil and his Flavian successors.

Alison Keith explores the role of intertextuality in architectural ecphrasis. Starting out from Homeric precedent and quickly surveying later examples in a rich tradition of epic descriptions of buildings, she devotes her paper ("Palatine Apollo, Augustan Architectural Ecphrasis, and Flavian Epic Intertextuality") to tracing the influence of Vergil's description of the Cumaean temple to Apollo in *Aeneid* 6 and Ovid's account of the Palace of the Sun in *Metamorphoses* 2 on two architectural ecphrases in Flavian epic: the temple of the Sun at Colchis in Valerius Flaccus' *Argonautica* 5 and the temple of Apollo at Cumae in Silius Italicus' *Punica* 12. By detailed comparison and close analysis of precise patterns of verbal allusion she demonstrates just how richly intertextual these ecphrastic passages are, with a particular emphasis on the presence of many-layered allusions, combinatorial reference and intermedial poetics.

In her article "Statius' Post-Vesuvian Landscapes and Vergil's Parthenope," Carole Newlands deals with the poetic geography of the Bay of Naples in the *Silvae* as a mirror of the generic lability of the poem and as one of the ways chosen by Statius to posit himself within the literary tradition. She explores in particular how Parthenope, the mythical founder of Naples, is shaped in *Silvae* 3.1, 3.5, 4.4 and 5.3 against Vergil's Parthenope in *Georgics* 4. In a post-Vesuvian world, the local Parthenope is shown as a heroic epic figure exceeding the boundaries of pastoral poetry. Furthermore, a selective topography of the region and the recurrent idea that, here, nature is dominated by art play a part in Parthenope's myth making. Through the Siren, Newlands argues, Statius challenges the literary discourse about contemporary Campania by associating this mythical figure with the Greek tradition and by questioning Rome's cultural primacy. Finally, Newlands addresses the metaliterary implications of this figure and concludes that

Statius closely assimilates his poetic self to Parthenope in order to fashion himself as the actual successor of Greek peaceful poetry and philosophy.

Neil Bernstein opens the group of papers devoted to digital matters by exploring the productive relationship between traditional and computational philological methods in his paper, "Quantitative and Qualitative Perspectives on the Use of Poetic Tradition in Silius Italicus' *Punica*." Taking the point of view of the commentator, he demonstrates how digital search results can support the philologist's intertextual analysis at both the micro and macro scales. Work at the micro scale—i.e. traditional close reading—is illustrated by detailed studies of two images in *Punica* 2 with dense intertextual associations: the image of a woman with bared breast and shoulder, used by Vergil, Valerius Flaccus, and later Claudian to depict a host of goddesses and female warriors; and the image of light reflected on water, linking Apollonius Rhodius's Medea to Silius' Hannibal by way of Vergil, Ovid and Lucan, and connecting the inner workings of a leader's troubled mind to the physical destruction of cities. Bernstein demonstrates how digital search can aid the commentator's work of collecting and making sense of these associations by providing large numbers of candidate passages, marked by textual similarity, for evaluation. This widens the net but does not necessarily make the philologist's task easier—rather, notes Bernstein, by shifting the burden from discovery to interpretation, it "productively complicates" the work of scholarly reading (p. 386). At the macro-level, digital tools allow quantitative studies of intertextual practice that would be impossible to complete by hand, for example, to compare the intensity of intertextual relationships between a large work such as the *Punica* and every other hexameter text in the Latin corpus. An important side-effect of this kind of computational research is that the scholar must formalize the question before a computer can calculate the result. For example, Bernstein collaborates with a statistician to define in mathematical terms what it is he really means by the "intensity" of an intertextual relationship between two poems. He notes that others might define "intensity" differently. He therefore conceives of the use of computational tools as a dynamic extension of the philologist's personal intellectual practices, rather than a source of fixed standards for evaluation.

In his contribution "Lemmatizing Latin and Quantifying the Achilleid," Peter Heslin argues for statistics and macroscopic analysis as a complementary approach to the traditional close reading of Latin texts. He assumes that the Ovidianness of the Achilleid is not limited to the erotic and elegiac colour of the Scyros' episode achieved through specific references drawn from the *Amores*, the *Ars Amatoria* and the *Heroides*. Intertexts from the *Metamorphoses*, especially books 12 and 13, suggest that Statius is challenging and subverting the canonical Trojan

Homeric tradition. With this in mind, Heslin undertakes some tests of lemma similarity between the epic poems of Vergil, Ovid, and Statius, in order to demonstrate to which extent the language of the *Achilleid* is different from the language of the *Thebaid* and it is instead influenced by the *Metamorphoses*. Focusing on the problems of Latin lemmatization, the author gives an overview of some current projects for automated morphological analysis as Morpheus, Collatinus, LemLat, Classical Language Toolkit and proposes his own implementations and improvements. Subsequently he goes on to study word frequency in the R language statistical environment through word-clouds and various metrics (term-frequency/inverse-document-frequency, cosine similarity), explaining clearly how these metrics work and pointing out some caveats (for instance the bias caused by the shortness of the *Achilleid* compared to full-length epics or by editorial inconsistency and incomplete lemmatization). To conclude, Heslin emphasizes the role of statistics in highlighting places to look for literary influence and strongly reasserts the need for a better-tagged Latin corpus.

In their article "How Rare are the Words that Make Up Intertexts? A Study in Latin and Greek Epic Poetry," Neil Coffee and James Gawley attempt to provide an empirical answer to a basic question about intertextuality. Repetition of very common words, such as *aut ... aut*, is not usually thought to constitute a meaningful intertext. They support this conclusion by arguing for the inverse, finding that words identified by scholars as parts of intertexts are relatively rare in the corpus, meaning rarer than random words taken from the same texts. They base this conclusion upon the frequency of individual words in intertexts between Vergil's *Aeneid* and Lucan's *Civil War*, and between Homer's *Iliad* and Apollonius' *Argonautica*. They go on to spot a difference between Greek and Latin epic: the words in Apollonius's intertexts are relatively rarer than those in Lucan's. Their contribution is a step toward quantifying the language features that contribute to creating intertextuality and how to describe and detect them.

In "Pre- and Post-digital Poetics of 'Transliteralism': Some Greco-Roman Epic Incipits," Stephen Hinds examines the phenomenon of cross-linguistic intertextuality. He demonstrates that, in their proems, epic poems engage in highly self-reflexive ways with Greek verse. In his judgment, this self-reflexivity, and the irony and other gestures produced, remain far over the horizon of digital detection, if they will ever be reached at all. How, he asks, would a digital search detect the fact that Livius Andronicus's *versutum* was not just a translation of Homer's πολύτροπον as "experienced," but, with its connotations of "turning" and "translation," a winking acknowledgement of Livius's act of translating Homer's *Odyssey*? Hinds goes on to illustrate how the rich cross-linguistic interplay in epic proems poses a bracing challenge for those wishing to approximate human-level sensitivity to intertextuality, even as the field relies upon "that intertextual cyborg of our time, the digitally equipped historian of Greco-Roman literature" (p. 443).

2 Intertextuality and Digital Methods

This closing group of papers leads naturally to some more general considerations about the second of our three aims in this volume, that of the digital turn. The Tesserae Project (http://tesserae.caset.buffalo.edu) launched the first web tool for automatic intertextual discovery in classical texts in 2008. Now, a decade later, after the continued development of Tesserae and emergence of similar and related tools—prominent examples include Filum (www.qcrit.org/filum), Musisque Deoque (http://mqdq.it), and TRACER (https://www.etrap.eu/research/tracer/)—it is worth taking stock of how digital resources have aided and altered the field. The contributions to this volume, from a wide range of scholars on some of the most densely intertextual Latin poets, illustrate the current climate and speak to the significant impact the digital humanities have had upon intertextual study and on our understanding of classical literature more broadly in the intervening years.

A few things can be said unequivocally. Digital search has obviously expanded the comprehensiveness with which scholars can investigate instances of intertextuality, in the process shifting the goalposts with respect to what potential sources are worth considering, and what kinds of correspondences are reported. "How many times does this phrase occur in ..." is a question we now unhesitatingly ask even of unfamiliar texts. Searching for exact repetitions or slight variations of an expression across the entire classical Latin corpus takes an instant with the free PHI tool. With some of the software mentioned above, one can equally search for more subtle echoes, without necessarily knowing ahead of time exactly what one is looking for.

Indeed, digital methods have allowed us to pose entirely new questions about intertextuality. Thus, common observation suggests that, all other things being equal, a phrase with rare words is more likely to recall a previous similar passage then one with common words. But how rare does a word have to be? This is the question Coffee and Gawley take up in their contribution. Here the digital approach involves not search within primary texts, but rather the collation of intertexts from commentaries and the evaluation of the frequencies of the words within them. At the other end of the scale, Bernstein expands the scope of earlier work by Knauer and Nelis to a new order of magnitude, analyzing whole texts or even authors for their aggregate levels of intertextuality not simply with other specific texts or authors, but across an entire genre.⁹ Neither of these questions would have been realistically tractable without digital methods.

At the same time it is also unequivocal that, as much as digital tools can aid intertextual research in ways that are functionally impossible for scholars to do unassisted, they are also far from replicating what a scholar can do. The piece by Hinds in this volume points not only to the limitations in performance of current search functions, such as the ability to find intertexts across Greek and Latin, but also to the formidable challenge of interpreting the full web of context and significance surrounding a given passage in order to arrive at a satisfyingly holistic understanding of the effects of a complex and meaningful intertext. At a time when advances in natural language processing and information retrieval seem ever to be accelerating, it is futile to predict which of these challenges will eventually be met—as, for example, important hurdles to automated translation or self-driving cars have been overcome. Nevertheless, although it is certain that the tools of textual analysis will continue to improve, as it stands an autonomous, working model of the human experience of intertextual discovery and interpretation remains distant.

Amid these clearer points, there is another important one worth considering, even if it is difficult to maintain with certainty. This is the question of how far digital methods have already altered practices of intertextual research and even our theories of the nature of intertextuality. Aristarchus, were he alive today and studying intertextual resonances, would surely check his interpretations against the results provided by digital tools, just as he would consult any relevant commentaries. If we assume most living scholars already do the same, then we must wonder if the use of computational methods is affecting how they view their texts.

In general, they seem to be encouraging the *operationalization* of interpretive problems. The ongoing process of definition, modelling, breaking seemingly intuitive actions down into component steps which underpins the development of computational tools appears to be exerting a force on scholarly practices, nudging scholars toward being more explicit, or at least more conscious, of the criteria for their interpretive decisions. There is a new incentive to create definitions and identify objects and boundaries within the texts. In this volume, Lovatt places the text under a microscope by asking which linguistic or literary elements serve to demarcate scene boundaries and to signal intertextual correspondences. While her paper is not a digital study, her precise insights can be read as a response to

---

9 Knauer (1979² [1964]), Nelis (2001).

digitally-driven research. They also contribute back: Lovatt's work will be especially beneficial to efforts to extend current word-based digital tools to more abstract, structural intertextuality.

One thing we can say for certain is that digital tools present us with many more potential connections. They also therefore challenge scholars to define what they will accept (and publish) as meaningful. Before the introduction of digital tools, scholars periodically published works that disrupted standard narratives of literary inheritance, as when Nelis demonstrated that we could not skip from Homer to Vergil without accounting for the influence of Apollonius. Now, an even broader vista opens up, particularly for densely intertextual poets, proceeding down to all grades of nuance to the plain use of language. It is a landscape that brings us back to Kristeva's original, all-encompassing definition of intertextuality. As Bernstein observes, the burden is shifting from the discovery to the interpretation of intertexts. Amid this embarrassment of riches (and false positives) does the scholar's conception of intertextuality necessarily change? Does it look less like a sly game among learned authors and more like a fixed feature of language that authors sometimes elaborate? Digital methods seem like they will tilt the balance toward the latter view, though how far remains to be seen.

3 Future Work on Flavian Intertextuality

Concerning our third aim, the desire to insist on the idea that a considerable amount of work still remains to be done on Flavian intertextuality, let us look closely at a specific passage. At the beginning of the seventh book of the *Thebaid* Jupiter sends Mercury to Thrace. His aim in doing so is to speed up the Argive advance towards Thebes and so ensure a rapid outbreak of hostilities. It is to this end that Mars is called into action. Statius opens the encounter with a description of the shrine of the god of war (7.40–63). In his highly informative and deservedly influential commentary on *Thebaid* 7, J.J.L. Smolenaars begins his discussion of this passage by drawing attention to Homeric precedent, citing *Iliad* 6.152ff and 13.32ff and also Val. Fl. 4.181–186, all examples of cases where the narrative stops for a moment and there occurs a detailed description of a particular place. He then goes on to note that the position of this Statian description within a scene involving an intervention in human affairs by Jupiter corresponds to Hom. *Od.* 5.55–74 and Verg. *Aen.* 4.259–264. Next, Smolenaars points out that in terms of both structure and content Statius also has in mind Vergil's description of the palace of Latinus at *Aen.* 7.170–186, before adding that the poet is also fleshing out his description of the shrine of Mars "from 'secondary' passages in Homer, Vergil, Seneca and Valerius".[10]

As he works his way through the passage phrase by phrase and line by line, Smolenaars points out a series of further similarities between Statius and earlier texts, this time on the purely verbal level. For example, that Statius is indeed thinking of Valerius Flaccus' description of the cave of Amycus is suggested by the fact that *Theb.* 7.39 (*palla, nec Arcadii bene protegit umbra galeri*) imitates Val. Fl. 4.138 (*tempora Parrhasio patris de more galero*).[11] Similarly, Smolenaars states that Statius' triple reference to iron (*ferrea ... ferro ... ferratis*) is a deliberate variation on Vergil's triple reference to bronze (*aerea ... aere ... aenis*) in his description of Juno's temple at *Aen.* 1.448–449. For the use of verb *incumbo* with the dative case (*incumbunt tecta columnis*) he cites Verg. *Ecl.* 8.16 (*incumbens tereti ... olivae*), while also comparing *Aen.* 7.170, *tectum ... sublime columnis*. On line 45 he notes that the expression *Phoebi iubar* to refer to the radiance of the sun also occurs at Sen. *Ag.* 463 and in Statius' own *Silvae* at 2.2.46.

There is of course much more to Smolenaars' excellent commentary than this, but we have highlighted these details for two reasons: firstly, they show an expert commentator at work on a passage of Flavian epic poetry and, secondly, they are, it seems fair to say, quite typical of the ways in which modern commentators go about doing their job. If one dips into any of the major commentaries on individual books of the *Thebaid* that we now have available, we very quickly find numerous examples of exactly the same kind of procedure.[12] The key point to be made here is that the now standard approach to reading Statius' *Thebaid* is profoundly intertextual in its basic approach to the elucidation of the text. And exactly the same is true of work on the *Achilleid* and on Valerius Flaccus and Silius Italicus.[13] Of course, commentaries are not alone in this. A quick glance at some recent monographs leads to the same conclusion.[14]

This state of affairs is far from new. Already in the 19th century work on the Flavian epics was often intertextual in approach, and those scholars in turn were

---

10 Smolenaars (1994) 22.
11 The point here is that *Parrhasio* = Arcadian, while *galerus* is a very rare word in Latin epic.
12 To name but a few recent examples, see Briguglio (2017) on *Thebaid* 1, Gervais (2017) on *Thebaid* 2, Micozzi (2007) and Parkes (2012) on *Thebaid* 4, Augoustakis (2016) on *Thebaid* 8.
13 E.g. Ripoll/Soubiran (2008), Nuzzo (2012) and Uccellini (2012) on the *Achilleid*; Manuwald (2015) on *Argonautica* 3, Fucecchi (1997), Baier (2001), and Fucecchi (2006) on *Argonautica* 6, Lazzarini (2012) and Pellucchi (2012) on *Argonautica* 8; Bernstein (2017) on *Punica* 2, Littlewood (2011) on *Punica* 7 and Littlewood (2017) on *Punica* 10.
14 See, for example, Heslin (2005), Ganiban (2007), Tipping (2010), Stover (2012). The contents of several companions and collections of papers point in the same direction.

drawing on earlier work that provided massive documentation about models and imitation.¹⁵ But the very persistence of this way of reading and the impressively high quality of so much of the work done in recent years, particularly in the form of commentaries on individual books, may paradoxically give rise to some concerns, when one turns to consider the future. The theoretical debates of the 1980s and 1990s about the nature and the limits of referential allusion in Latin poetry have come to a close. There can be little doubt that a number of important contributions (e.g. by A.J. Woodman and D. West, R. Thomas, G.B. Conte, A. Barchiesi, S. Hinds, L. Edmunds, J. Farrell, D. Fowler, J. Wills, to name but a few) have greatly sharpened critical faculties, and there is good reason to believe that the study of Flavian epic has been one of the major beneficiaries of scholarly debates that were as fruitful as they were sometimes fractious.¹⁶ The resultant consensus that now seems to reign in many quarters has undoubtedly created the feeling that it is now possible to get down to the business of intertextual analysis without having to go over the much-trodden ground of theoretical considerations. Also prevalent is the related idea that most of the basic work of recovering parallels, imitations or allusions has already been done and that there is little new of any value to be discovered about the basic facts of text reuse. Both of these assumptions require further thought.

Commentators on Latin texts must be selective. They cannot comment on everything, and so difficult decisions have to be made about where the main difficulties lie, what requires comment, what can be assumed to be common knowledge, which passages require translating, how much metrical analysis is required, and so on. And while the quotation and analysis of verbal allusions seems now to be taking up more space than before, commentators still have much else to think about, with textual, and linguistic details, historical contexts, and so on all jostling for space and attention. There is a case to be made, therefore, that the standard philological commentary may no longer be the best format for detailed study of texts that are agreed by all to be fundamentally intertextual in nature.¹⁷ The capacities and interfaces offered by modern digital systems may provide greater scope for the collection of the mass of information that already exists, scattered across numerous theses, articles and monographs in addition to commentaries. They also allow for efficient visualisation and fast retrievability of what is a highly complex data set. Furthermore, new on-line tools such as Tes-

---

15 See Berlincourt (2013).
16 That said, see now Conte (2017) for a contribution that may stir things up again.
17 See Heslin (2016).

serae and Musisque Deoque, when used alongside the Classical Latin Texts database of the Packard Humanities Institute, the Biblioteca Teubneriana Latina on-line, and the Thesaurus Linguae Latinae on-line, are surely pushing open the door to a new age in the study of intertextuality.[18] A quick look at how much remains to be said even about a relatively straightforward passage so expertly handled by Smolenaars will illustrate what is at stake here. In each case, a few minutes of digital searching easily turns up new information that complements Smolenaar's findings. Statius' description of the shrine of Mars begins thus (*Theb.* 7.41–43):

> hic steriles delubra notat Mavortia silvas
> (horrescitque tuens), ubi mille furoribus illi
> cingitur averso domus inmansueta sub Haemo.

> Here he marks barren woods, Mars' shrine, and
> shudders as he looks. There under distant Haemus
> is the god's ungentle house, girt with a thousand Rages.
>
> (Trans. Shackleton Bailey)

These lines resemble Lucan 9.966–969, where Julius Caesar visits Troy:

> iam silvae steriles et putres robore trunci
> Assaraci pressere domos et templa deorum
> iam lassa radice tenent, ac tota teguntur
> Pergama dumetis: etiam periere ruinae.

> Now barren woods and trunks with rotting timber
> have submerged Assaracus' houses and, with roots now weary,
> occupy the temples of the gods, and all of Pergamum
> is veiled by thickets: even the ruins suffered oblivion.
>
> (Trans. Braund)

Lucan describes barren woods (*silvae steriles*; cf. Statius' *steriles ... silvas*) at the moment when a visitor arrives and sees the home of Assaracus (*domos*; cf. Statius' *domus*) and temples of the gods (*templa deorum*; cf. Statius' *delubra Mavortia*). In turn, Statius' expression *domus inmansueta sub Haemo* is comparable to *Aen.* 12.546, where Vergil has *domus alta sub Ida*, also closing the hexameter. In each case the patterning of *domus* followed by an adjective plus *sub* with the name of a mountain is identical. In addition, the verse-ending *sub Haemo* has already been used by Statius at both *Theb.* 1.275 (cited by Smolenaars) and 5.16

---

18 See Coffee *et al.* (2012) and Coffee (2018).

(not cited by Smolenaars). If we look at the following sentence, this kind of exercise can be easily repeated:

> ferrea compago laterum, ferro apta teruntur
> limina, ferratis incumbunt tecta columnis.
>
> The sides are of iron structure, the trodden thresholds
> are fitted with iron, the roof rests on iron-bound pillars.
>
> (Trans. Shackleton Bailey)

The combination of the nouns *compago* and *latus* first occurs at *Aen.* 1.122 *laterum compagibus*, with *laterum* in precisely the same metrical position in each case. Compare also Man. *Astr.* 1.840, *laterum compagine*. And finally to the third sentence:

> laeditur adversum Phoebi iubar, ipsaque sedem
> lux timet, et durus contristat sidera fulgor.
>
> Phoebus' opposing ray takes hurt, the very light
> fears the dwelling and a harsh glare glooms the stars.
>
> (Trans. Shackleton Bailey)

As already stated, Smolenaars notes that the expression *Phoebi iubar* to refer to the radiance of the sun occurs at Sen. *Ag.* 463 and Statius' own *Silv.* 2.2.46. He does not mention Val. Fl. 5.331 (cf. also 3.559–560 for *Phoebi* and *iubar* in close proximity, but not grammatically connected).

The aim of all this is in no way to imply criticism of any kind of Smolenaars; his is still one of the very best commentaries on any Flavian poetry book. When it comes to the accumulation and evaluation of intertextual parallels his book sets a high standard, particularly in relation to multi-tier allusion and the relationship between verbal and structural allusion, that few other commentators have attained. The point is simply that there is always more to be said than space allows and that modern digital searching has greatly facilitated work of this kind in ways Smolenaars could not even begin to imagine when he was writing his commentary. The more general point to be made is that even in terrain that has been much trodden over, there is still more to be found. And all the while, excellent new work is sharpening perspectives and opening up new visions.[19] If this volume succeeds in promoting an interest in Flavian intertextuality among a new generation of scholars, then its editors will be happy enough.

---

[19] See for example Hutchinson (2013), Feeney (2016), Lyne (2016).

Bibliography

Allen, Graham (2011²), *Intertextuality*, 2nd ed., New York.
Augoustakis, Antony (ed.) (2014), *Flavian Poetry and its Greek Past*, Leiden.
Augoustakis, Antony (2016), *Statius*, Thebaid 8, Oxford.
Baier, Thomas (2001), *Valerius Flaccus*, Argonautica, *Buch VI*, Munich.
Berlincourt, Valéry (2013), *Commenter la Thébaïde (16ᵉ–19ᵉ s.): Caspar von Barth et la tradition exégétique de Stace*, Leiden/Boston.
Bernstein, Neil W. (2017), *Silius Italicus*, Punica 2, Oxford.
Briguglio, Stefano (2017), FRATERNAS ACIES. *Saggio di commento a Stazio, Tebaide, 1, 1–389*, Alessandria.
Coffee, Neil (2018), "An Agenda for the Study of Intertextuality", in: *TAPhA* 148.1, 205–233.
Coffee, Neil/Koenig, Jean-Pierre/Poornima, Shakthi/Ossewaarde, Roelant/Forstall, Christopher/Jacobson, Sarah (2012), "Intertextuality In the Digital Age", in: *TAPhA* 142.2, 383–422.
Conte, Gian Biagio (2017), *Stealing the Club from Hercules. On Imitation in Latin Poetry*, Berlin.
Culler, Jonathan (1981), *The Pursuit of Signs. Semiotics, Literature, Deconstruction*, Ithaca, NY.
Feeney, Denis (2016), *Beyond Greek. The Beginnings of Latin Literature*, Cambridge, MA.
Fowler, Don P. (1997), "On the Shoulders of Giants: Intertextuality and Classical Studies", in: *MD* 39, 13–34 [= Don P. Fowler, *Roman Constructions: Readings in Postmodern Latin*, Oxford, 2000, 115–137].
Fucecchi, Marco (1997), *La teichoskopia e l'innamoramento di Medea. Saggio di commento a Valerio Flacco* Argonautiche 6, 427–760, Pisa.
Fucecchi, Marco (2006), *Una guerra in Colchide*. Argonautiche 6, 1–426, Pisa.
Ganiban, Randall (2007), *Statius and Virgil. The* Thebaid *and the Reinterpretation of the* Aeneid, Cambridge.
Gervais, Kyle (2017), *Statius*, Thebaid 2, Oxford.
Heslin, Peter (2005), *The transvestite Achilles: Gender and Genre in Statius' Achilleid*, Cambridge/New York.
Heslin, Peter (2016), "The Dream of a Universal Variorum. Digitizing the Commentary Tradition", in: Kraus/Stray (2016) 494–511.
Hutchinson, Gregory (2013), *Greek to Latin. Frameworks and Contexts for Intertextuality*, Oxford.
Knauer, Georg Nicolaus (1979² [1964]), *Die Aeneis und Homer. Studien zur poetischen Technik Vergils mit Listen der Homerzitate in der Aeneis*, 2nd ed., Göttingen.
Kraus, Christina/Stray, Christopher (eds.) (2016), *Classical Commentaries: Explorations in a Scholarly Genre*, Oxford.
Kristeva, Julia (1969), *Semeiotike. Recherches pour une sémanalyse*, Paris.
Kristeva, Julia (1974), *La révolution du langage poétique*, Paris.
Lazzarini, Caterina (2012), *L'addio di Medea. Valerio Flacco*, Argonautiche 8, 1–287, Pisa.
Littlewood, R. Joy (2011), *A Commentary on Silius Italicus' Punica 7*, Oxford.
Littlewood, R. Joy (2017), *A Commentary on Silius Italicus' Punica 10*, Oxford.
Lyne, R.O.A.M (1994), "Vergil's *Aeneid*: Subversion by Intertextuality, Catullus 66.39–40 and Other Examples", in: *G&R* 41, 187–204.
Lyne, Raphael (2016), *Memory and Intertextuality in Renaissance Literature*, Cambridge.
Manuwald, Gesine (2015), *Valerius Flaccus*, Argonautica, *Book III*, Cambridge.

Manuwald, Gesine/Voigt, Astrid (eds.) (2013), *Flavian Epic Interactions*, Berlin.
Micozzi, Laura (2007), *Il catalogo degli eroi. Saggio di commento a Stazio* Tebaide *4, 1–344*, Pisa.
Nelis, Damien P. (2001), *Vergil's* Aeneid *and the* Argonautica *of Apollonius Rhodius*, Leeds.
Nuzzo, Gianfranco (2012), *Publio Papinio Stazio*, Achilleide, Palermo.
Parkes, Ruth (2012), *Statius*, Thebaid 4, Oxford.
Pellucchi, Tiziana (2012), *Commento al libro VIII delle* Argonautiche *di Valerio Flacco*, Hildesheim.
Ripoll, François/Soubiran, Jean (2008), *Stace*, Achilléide, Leuven/Paris/Dudley.
Smolenaars, Johannes J.L. (1994), *Statius*, Thebaid 7, Leiden.
Stover, Timothy (2012), *Epic and Empire in Vespasianic Rome: A New Reading of Valerius Flaccus'* Argonautica, Oxford.
Tipping, Ben (2010), *Exemplary Epic: Silius Italicus'* Punica, Oxford.
Thomas, Richard (1999), *Reading Virgil and his Texts. Studies in Intertextuality*, Ann Arbor, MI.
Trinacty, Christopher (2014), *Senecan Tragedy and the Reception of Augustan Poetry*, Oxford.
Uccellini, Renée (2012), *L'arrivo di Achille a Sciro. Saggio di commento a Stazio* Achilleide *1, 1–396*, Pisa.

Helen Lovatt
Meanwhile Back at the Ranch: Narrative Transition and Structural Intertextuality in Statius *Thebaid* 1

> It is now necessary for me to use the rather hackneyed phrase 'meanwhile, back at the ranch.' The word 'hackneyed' here means 'used by so many writers that by the time Lemony Snicket uses it, it is a tiresome cliché.' 'Meanwhile, back at the ranch' is a phrase used to link what is going on in one part of the story to what is going on in another part of the story, and it has nothing to do with cows or horses or with any people who work in rural areas where ranches are, or even with ranch dressing, which is creamy and put on salads.
>
> Lemony Snicket, *The Reptile Room*

1 Introduction

Any story must have a beginning, a middle, an end, and a number of parts in between. There have been scholarly studies of beginnings and ends in Latin epic, and even some work on middles: but how do we study and understand the division of a story into parts (scenes) and the movements between those parts?[1] "Narrative transition" is the movement between "scenes" in a longer narrative. It is a crucial part of the articulation of any narrative, and I was drawn to it by my work on the divine gaze as a transitional device in Greek and Latin epic.[2] The study of narrative structures poses particular challenges for text searching as a methodology. Word matching can only reveal a small subset of possible intertextual connections. Structures are also an important feature of intertextuality:[3] for instance, in Statius *Thebaid* 6 the order of events in the games mediates between the orders of events in Statius' main models, *Aeneid* 5 and *Iliad* 23.[4] However, particular words and formulae do mark moments of epic transition, for instance the beginnings and endings of

---

[1] On beginnings: Nuttall (1992); on endings: Roberts *et al.* (1997); on middles: De Martino/Kyriakidis (2004).
[2] On the divine gaze as a transitional motif: Lovatt (2013) 39–45.
[3] See Nelis in this volume on the importance of structures in appreciating the layered allusions of Valerius to Virgil and Apollonius.
[4] See Lovatt (2005) 12–19 on structural intertextuality in Statius' epic games.

speeches.⁵ This chapter proposes to investigate what we can learn from looking at the language of narrative transition, using as a case study Statius *Thebaid* 1 and its relationship with Virgil's *Aeneid*.⁶

Thebaid 1 is a book with a wide variety of narrative structures and transitional devices: the narrative ranges from Thebes to Argos, from the underworld to Olympus, with gods and mortals moving between them.⁷ It contains the proem, exposition, speeches, a divine council, an inset story and a hymn.⁸ The story is told from a variety of points of view, focalised by Oedipus, Eteocles, Polynices and Adrastus, not to mention Jupiter, Juno, a Fury and Mercury. Transition and journeys are important themes of the book, in a way that foreshadows the importance of liminality throughout the epic.⁹ The book sets the tone for the whole poem. Other books might fruitfully form a similar starting point: in particular, books 7 and 8 spring to mind, especially with the climactic movement of Amphiaraus from earth to the underworld at the end of book 7 and the beginning of book 8. *Thebaid* 1 has crucial intertextual relationships with, among others, *Aeneid* 1 (council of the gods, storm, arrival at hospitable location) and *Metamorphoses* 1 (council of the gods, journey of Phaethon). For reasons of space, this paper will focus on the relationship between the *Thebaid* and the *Aeneid*.

I begin by outlining the major narrative episodes of *Thebaid* 1. The poem begins with a proem (1–45) in the voice of the narrator which surveys the myth of Thebes, and praises Domitian. The first major scene is set in Thebes where Oedipus curses his sons (46–88). His prayer is heard by a Fury in Tartarus, who journeys to Thebes (88–122) and inspires Polynices and Eteocles with hatred and madness (123–141). The description of their quarrel merges into a lament on the

---

5 For formal analysis of speeches, see Highet (1972) on Virgil and Dominik (1994) on Statius. On speech presentation, see Laird (1999). On speech and silence in Apollonius and Valerius, see Finkmann (2014).
6 Intertextuality in the *Thebaid* is rich and complex, but the *Aeneid* is clearly one of the most important, if not the most important model. Ganiban (2007) covers important ground but leaves room for further investigation. On the complex and multiple intertextuality of the *Thebaid* see Smolenaars (1994) 22–23. Looking at all the intertextual relationships of the narrative transitions in *Thebaid* 1 would be a task beyond the scope of this article, which has a primarily methodological focus.
7 Heuvel (1932) does not divide his commentary into sections. There is a further commentary on *Thebaid* 1 in preparation by Hill and Gibson.
8 Bessone in this volume focusses her analysis of intertextuality mainly on *Thebaid* 1; she emphasises incest, fraternal violence and the blurring of boundaries as typically Statian modes, all of which suggest that structural intertextuality is particularly important in Statius.
9 On the epic journey see Blum/Biggs (2019). On margins and transitions in Statius, see Lovatt (2015).

part of the narrator (142–164). Thebans, including Eteocles and an anonymous critic, react to their solution: sharing rule, one year at a time, exile for Polynices (164–196). A strong scene change, of place and narrative level, takes us now up to Olympus, where Jupiter calls a divine council (197–302). This ends when he sends Mercury to fetch Laius from the underworld to help start the war between Thebes and Argos (303–311). Mercury's journey to Tartarus reverses that of the Fury, and contrasts with that of Polynices which comes next (312–377), which includes a storm both physical and psychological and ends with a simile. The next scene presents Polynices' arrival at Argos, exposition of the situation in Argos, and his quarrel with Tydeus (377–427), also ending with a simile. There is then a change of focaliser to Adrastus, and the scene of the welcome he gives to them in Argos completes the book (428–720). Within this scene we find the inset story of Coroebus (557–668) and a hymn to Apollo (696–720).

In order to examine the transitions between scenes, we need to decide what constitutes a scene. De Jong, in her narratological commentary on the *Odyssey*, offers a working definition of a scene: "A narrative unit created by a combination of events or actions taking place at the same place and involving the same characters. A scene is usually told more or less mimetically, in that the text-time matches the fabula-time."[10] By this definition not all narrative is made up of scenes: exposition and summary, for instance, operate in different ways. There are various signals of narrative transition: change of setting (time and/or place), change of perspective (which characters are involved, from whose point of view the story is told, or through whom the story is focalised). Change of mode (moving from an interchange of direct speech, to narrator summary of intervening action, for instance) could be another indicator. For instance, in *Thebaid* 1, the sequence from 123–196, when the narrator summarises the decision to alternate rule between Polynices and Eteocles, then laments, and this is followed by the reaction of Eteocles and the speech of an anonymous critic, shows several different modes.[11] Should these sections be considered part of one scene? I find it helpful to think of "scenes" and "sequences," where a "sequence" is a larger organising unit consisting of several scenes strung together, which ends with a strong break point, while a scene is a smaller unit, usually unitary in place and time, which

---

10 De Jong (2001) xvii.
11 Ahl (2015) 255 argues that 1.165–168 is a key moment for understanding *Thebaid* 1, based on the political implications of Eteocles' similarities to Domitian. This shows how even the most formal literary analyses can still be intensely political.

can end with a weak break point.¹² Narrative transitions, of course, both divide the narrative into smaller units, and link the whole into one larger unit. The tension between continuity and change is one of the factors that makes this aspect of narrative rewarding to investigate; equally this tension reflects that at the heart of epic between the totalising reach of epic and the inevitably episodic nature of long narrative.¹³

In an interesting article, Waddell examines narrative transitions in Tacitus' *Annales* in conjunction with Trajan's column and cinema.¹⁴ He uses the idea of the "quick-cut" to explore the abrupt transitions in Tacitus ("the juxtaposition of two scenes that have little or no inherent connection") and suggests various emotional and intellectual effects that this can have. I argue that the analogy with cinema is interesting and productive, but imperfect; we need to investigate transitional techniques on their own terms. Further, different genres habitually employ different narrative techniques, and even different poets use narrative transitions in their own ways. One goal of this paper, then, is to see what is Statian about Statius' narrative transitions, and whether he straightforwardly follows Virgil or produces his own version of epic narrative.

In *Thebaid* 1, the first sequence after the proem involves Oedipus' prayer going down to Tartarus, from where the Fury returns to Thebes, her actions cause various responses, the most important of which is that of Jupiter, arguably ending this sequence with the strong scene change to Olympus. However, the thematically related and contiguous journeys of the Fury, Mercury and Polynices create a sense of continuity between the events at Thebes and those in Argos and Olympus. The cosmology of epic, with its strong emphasis on divine action, also requires different narrative levels: Olympus, earth, Tartarus. But in Statius, there are strong connections between the two non-mortal spheres, so that Olympus and

---

12 A strong break point usually features changes in more than one of the indicators mentioned: time, space, focalisation/point of view, mode, characters involved. A weak break point involves more continuity: so for instance, the prayer from Oedipus goes down to the underworld, and the Fury returns to Thebes. A good example of a very weak transition occurs in *Aen.* 1 during the preparations for Dido's banquet, when Dido leads Aeneas into the palace at 1.631–632 which provides a change of scene, but continues with the same characters. This is so weak, that one might argue whether it constitutes a scene change. The transitional word *interea* is used at 1.633 to link her kindness to Aeneas with her kindness to his men, not really a transitional use. At 637 the focus moves from the actions of Dido to the preparations within the palace with the phrase *at domus*. This is a slightly stronger transition, but still quite weak and clearly part of the longer sequence leading up to the banquet.
13 On the tension between openness and closure in epic see Hardie (1993) 1–19.
14 Waddell (2013).

Tartarus offer an alternative polarity to Thebes and Argos. We can see, then, either one or two main sequences of events in *Thebaid* 1, depending on how strongly we read the move from Thebes to Olympus. The fact that the narrative returns with Mercury to Tartarus at 303–311, in a movement that will be continued in book 2, suggests that the sequence surrounding Polynices should be read as a separate one. This sequence begins with *interea* ("meanwhile," 312), which is a key transitional word. Throughout the poem there will be a strong dualistic structure, as the narrative moves between Theban and Argive perspectives, the divine and mortal spheres, Olympus and Tartarus. At the same time this dualism is continually under pressure: the war fluctuates between civil and foreign, mortals threaten to break the bounds between narrative levels, and the divine and infernal action can be viewed as two sides of the same coin.[15]

A comparison between *Thebaid* 1 and *Aeneid* 1 is useful for seeing the similarities and differences in the way they each use narrative transition. After the proem in *Aeneid* 1 the first sequence focuses on Juno, introduced by the ekphrastic formula *urbs antiqua fuit* ("There was an ancient city," 1.12). The end of Aeolus' speech to the winds (*haec ubi dicta*, "When these words had been spoken," 1.81) signals the beginning of the storm. The sequence continues when Neptune notices the disturbance, marked with *interea* (*interea magno misceri murmure pontum / emissamque hiemem sensit Neptunus*, "meanwhile Neptune notices the sea stirred up with significant sound and the storm sent out," 1.124–125) and draws to a close with the famous statesman simile at 147–156. The use of a simile to bring the sequence and the storm to a close is typical of Homeric epic.[16] The next scene begins with a different location and perspective: *defessi Aeneadae* "the exhausted followers of Aeneas" (157) arriving at the nearest shore. In this scene, Virgil uses *interea* for another weak change: from his men busy with their tasks, to Aeneas himself (*Aeneas scopulum interea conscendit*, "Aeneas meanwhile climbed the cliff," 180), from shore to cliff-top. Physical movement from one location to another marks both change and continuity. The storm sequence as a whole comes to an end at 223, with a strong break: the grieving of the Trojans ceases and we move to Olympus where Jupiter is watching them. The phrase *et iam finis erat, cum Iuppiter ...* ("and now there was an end, when Jupiter ...," 223) refers both to the particular scene of communal eating and lamentation and to the end of the whole sequence. While Venus' complaint to Jupiter will reflect on

---

15 On the relationship between the gods and the underworld in Statius, see Ganiban (2007) 117–151; on infernal dominance, see Parkes (2012) 166; on Furies as Muses, see Bessone (2011) 95–101.

16 See for instance Martin (1997) 144.

what has happened, she will focus as much on what is about to happen next, and Jupiter's speech famously presents the overarching narrative goal of *imperium sine fine* (279) to come for Rome.

The excursus onto the divine level ends when Jupiter sends Mercury to Carthage, and we return to the perspective of Aeneas with a strong break: *At pius Aeneas* ("But dutiful Aeneas," 305), and a reference to the time that has passed (night and dawn). This scene, in which Venus meets Aeneas and gives him information about Dido and Carthage, ends with Venus withdrawing to Paphos (415–417), while Aeneas continues (*corripuere viam interea*, "They seize the path meanwhile," 418). One character moves on to a new place, in a clear example of a scene ending but a sequence continuing. The rest of the book consists of the sequence in Carthage, in which Aeneas first enters the city, views the pictures in the temple of Juno, sees Ilioneus address Dido, reveals himself and is then welcomed into the palace. There is a brief excursus onto the divine level at 657 (*at Cytherea* ... "But Venus") to explain Venus' plan to swap Ascanius for Cupid; the narrative then follows Cupid's journey to Dido's palace (695). The banquet is divided into eating and entertainment by *postquam prima quies* ("after the first rest," 723) and the book ends with Dido's request to Aeneas to tell his story (753–756), so that books 2 and 3 are still technically part of this sequence.

We can make a number of observations from this analysis. In this book at least, Virgil tends to use *interea* in the context of weak transitions, and *at* in the context of strong ones. Jupiter's power breaks up the narrative more radically than that of Juno, Neptune or Venus. There are key words of transition, and motifs of physical movement, the passing of time and the responses of characters to events. It is useful to think of "zones of transition" and intertextuality within those: for instance, *Aen.* 1.297–309 from the end of Jupiter's speech to the decision of Aeneas to explore, contains several transitional motifs and key words, and is the code model for the similar transitional zone at *Theb.* 1.298–313. Before I examine these two passages in more detail, let us look at the structural similarities between the two books.

Each book consists of two main sequences, divided by a scene on Olympus in which Jupiter takes control: the anger of Juno and storm sequence, in *Aen.*1, followed by arrival in North Africa and the hospitality sequence. In *Thebaid* 1, the anger of Oedipus leads to the intervention of the Fury in Thebes, followed by the council of the gods, then Polynices' exile, journey, and the arrival in Argos and welcome from Adrastus. The most obvious differences are the displacement of the storm until after Jupiter's intervention, and the bringing forward of the inset story from books 2 and 3 into the latter stage of book 1. This is partly because the beginning of the *Thebaid* also draws on the second half of the *Aeneid*: Adrastus is both Dido and Evander (the story is told by host not guest, and Adrastus' story matches Evander's tale of Hercules and Cacus much more closely); the action involves the starting of a war by a Fury. It is not Juno, but Jupiter who is angry: the war is the central point of the poem rather than forming one of a series of obstacles in the way of the epic's goal.

While Aeneas' stay in Carthage will lead eventually both to the Punic wars and Roman empire, Polynices' relocation to Argos will lead back to war at Thebes and the destruction of both cities in a war that is its own end. The *Thebaid*'s storm, then, gives momentum to the build-up of resentment and violence in Polynices and in the epic as a whole, and it is appropriate that it should be placed after the supreme god has given his seal of approval to events.

Let us look in more detail at the hinge passage of *Thebaid* 1, at the end of the divine council, when Jupiter sends Mercury to Thebes:

'... ferat hic diro mea iussa nepoti:
germanum exsilio fretum Argolicisque tumentem
hospitiis, quod sponte cupit, procul impius aula   300
arceat, alternum regni infitiatus honorem.
hinc causae irarum, certo reliqua ordine ducam.'
paret Atlantiades dictis genitoris et inde
summa pedum propere plantaribus illigat alis
obnubitque comas et temperat astra galero.   305
tum dextrae virgam inseruit, qua pellere dulces
aut suadere iterum somnos, qua nigra subire
Tartara et exsangues animare assueverat umbras.
desiluit, tenuique exceptus inhorruit aura.
nec mora, sublimes raptim per inane volatus   310
carpit et ingenti designat nubila gyro.
interea patriis olim vagus exsul ab oris
Oedipodionides furto deserta pererrat Aoniae.

(*Theb.* 1.298–313)

Let him carry my orders to his grim grandson
his brother is confident in exile and swelling with Argive
hospitality; what he desires of his own accord, let him keep that brother
impiously far from the halls, let him withhold the alternate honour of reign.
From this the causes of anger; the rest in sure rank I shall lead.'
The offspring of Atlas obeys the words of his father and then
hurriedly binds the tops of his feet with winged sandals
and clouds over his hair and controls the starlight with a hat.
Then he inserts a staff in his right hand, by which he was accustomed
to push away sweet sleep and call it back again, to steal into
black Tartarus and bring bloodless shades to life.
He jumped down and shuddered as the thin air received him.

> No delay: he seized high flight swiftly
> through the void and traced a huge circle on the clouds.
> Meanwhile, before all this, a wandering exile from his father's shores,
> the son of Oedipus meandered in stealth through the wild places of Aonia.

This passage has many transitional features: the end of Jupiter's speech, and the response of Mercury; Mercury's journey and his preparations for it; the temporal and spatial transition back to Polynices' departure from Thebes, signalled by the key transitional word *interea*, along with other transitional phrases (*paret dictis, nec mora*). Jupiter's speech ends as if it is a proem: his instructions sum up what will happen as well as ordering the events. The final line contains some particularly telling echoes. When he uses the phrase *causae irarum* he is explaining how Mercury's visit to Eteocles will stimulate the hatred that causes the war. But he is also echoing the narrator of the *Aeneid* at 1.25 when he describes the enduring anger of Juno against the Trojans:[17]

> id metuens, veterisque memor Saturnia belli,
> prima quod ad Troiam pro caris gesserat Argis
> necdum etiam causae irarum saevique dolores
> exciderant animo ...
>
> (*Aen.* 1.23–26)

> Fearing that, the daughter of Saturn was mindful of ancient war,
> which she had first waged at Troy for her dear Argives,
> and not yet had the causes of anger and the savage griefs
> fallen out from her mind.

While the narrator of the *Aeneid* distances himself from Juno's obsession with the past, Statius' Jupiter enmeshes himself with the anger of Oedipus and his sons. His actions are not fully necessary but over-determine the causality of the poem. While Virgil's Jupiter retains at least the appearance of impartiality and aloofness, Statius' Jupiter repeats the irrational anger of Virgil's Juno. Further his *ordine ducam* emphasises his control of the narrative and of events. In *Aen.* 8 when the god Tiber promises to lead Aeneas to Evander's city, he uses the phrase *flumine ducam* (same metrical position at the end of the line):

---

[17] The phrase is not particularly common: it is also used by Tacitus at *Histories* 4.13.6, about the fate of Julius Civilis, where it may also be an allusion to Virgil.

> ipse ego te ripis et recto flumine ducam,
> adversum remis superes subvectus ut amnem.
>
> *(Aen.* 8.57–58)*

> I myself will lead you by the banks and straight along the river,
> so that you will overcome the river against you, born upstream by your oars.

This reconfigures the positive journey of Aeneas to seek an alliance in his new land as a journey leading to destruction and death in Statius. This ambivalence between constructive and destructive war is of course already present in the *Aeneid* since there is an internal echo back to this passage in book 9, the simultaneous narrative, when Nisus promises to guide Euryalus through the enemy camp as they leave the safety of the Trojan walls, heading into destruction:

> 'Euryale, audendum dextra: nunc ipsa vocat res.
> hac iter est. tu, ne qua manus se attollere nobis
> a tergo possit, custodi et consule longe;
> haec ego vasta dabo et lato te <u>limite ducam</u>.'
>
> *(Aen.* 9.321–323)*

> 'Euryalus, time to dare, to use your right hand: now the event itself calls.
> This is the way. You, keep guard so that no hand can raise itself against
> us from the rear, and keep watch all round;
> I will give you these enormities and I will lead you on a broad path.'

Here Nisus both promises epic glory along with devastation and a clear way out: but the latter is illusory and Euryalus' overambitious carnage will instead lead to their own deaths. Jupiter, then, promises divine guidance and destruction, both for the Thebans and Argives, and his own state of world order. He will not in fact be able to keep the narrative under control and will abandon the ship of epic in book 11.[18]

Mercury responds by obeying Jupiter's words, and the expression Statius uses to describe this is *paret Atlantiades dictis genitoris* ("The offspring of Atlas obeys the words of his father"). This phrase echoes the moment in *Aeneid* 1 when Cupid obeys Venus' instructions to make Dido fall in love with Aeneas:

---

18 Bernstein (2004) discusses the power vacuum created by the withdrawal of the gods in *Thebaid* 11.

> paret Amor dictis carae genetricis, et alas
> exuit et gressu gaudens incedit Iuli.
>
> (*Aen.* 1.689–690)
>
> Love obeys the words of his dear mother, and takes off
> his wings and proceeds rejoicing with the step of Iulus.

The strong similarity of wording and structure brings out the similarity of situation: a powerful god sends an assistant to carry out a devious plan that will initially lead to hospitality and love, but in the longer term to war and destruction.[19] This intertextual link also serves to de-emphasise the power of Statius' Jupiter, putting him on the level with Venus.[20] While Amor then removes his traditional iconography to disguise himself, Mercury in contrast decks himself out in his customary accoutrements, first of all his wings. Here *alis* at the end of the subsequent line (304) further reinforces the connection through *alas* at the end of *Aen.* 1.689.[21]

Arguably the use of the word *desiluit* to describe the beginning of Mercury's journey is also transitional here; the combination of *desiluit ... per inane* also occurs later in *Thebaid* 9. In Virgil the verb is used only to describe characters jumping down from chariots or horses (*Aen.* 10.453, 11.500, 12.355). In Statius it is used in a variety of situations, some of which are similar to Virgil, but others, as here, show gods moving from one scene to another.[22] At *Theb.* 9.831 Mars responds to

---

[19] Although this combination of words does not seem particularly marked, these are the only occurrences of *paret dictis genitor/tricis* in Latin epic.

[20] Ovid often plays with the relative power hierarchy between Amor and other gods: Apollo and Cupido (*Met.* 1.452–465); Venus and Dis (*Met.* 5.362–384).

[21] There may be a further slight connection with the Dido episode in the phrase *inhorruit aura* in which Mercury shudders presumably at the coldness of the air which is thin at the top of Mount Olympus. This vivid evocation of the otherness of the divine realm has some verbal similarity with Aeneas' description to Dido of Mercury's orders to him at 4.377–378: *nunc et Iove missus ab ipso / interpres divum fert horrida iussa per auras*. ("Now the messenger of the gods, sent from Jupiter himself, brings awe-inspiring orders through the breezes.") The similarity of the situations described perhaps suggests a tentative intertextual connection. But in Statius Mercury is reluctant, rather than Aeneas, or perhaps the text foreshadows the disastrous results of Jupiter's intervention in this case.

[22] The Virgilian uses include *Theb.* 7.789 of Apollo jumping down from Amphiaraus' chariot, 8.599 of Menoeceus jumping out of his chariot on hearing of the death of Atys and 9.272 of Agenor jumping down from the river bank to protect his brother. More complex are the two examples from similes: *Theb.* 7.746, of the landscape in a landslide, describing the chariot weighed down by Amphiaraus, on the battlefield, anticipating the earthquake in which he will subside to the underworld; similarly at 9.221, Hippomedon on Tydeus' horse is described as a centaur jumping down from the mountain into the valleys. I have examined the liminality of Hippomedon elsewhere in Lovatt 2015, and it is here combined with the hybridity of the centaur. At 3.293 *desiluit*

Venus' speech on behalf of the Thebans by jumping down to intervene against Artemis and precipitate the death of Parthenopaeus:

> desiluit iustis commotus in arma querelis
> Bellipotens, cui sola vagum per inane ruenti
> Ira comes, reliqui sudant ad bella Furores.
>
> (*Theb.* 9.831–833)

> The Lord of War jumped down, moved to weapons by the just
> complaints, as he rushed down through the void
> Anger alone is his companion, and the remaining Rages sweat at war.

This moment is moderately transitional, with a change of place, but continuity of time, character and narrative level (he now interacts with Diana, still on the divine level). It ends the scene, but is still tightly bound into the larger sequence. At 10.636 *desiluit* describes the journey of Virtus from beside the throne of Jupiter to inspire Menoeceus' suicide in Thebes. This is a more transitional moment, coming after a new invocation at 10.628–631, and showing a change of character as well as place and narrative level. Creon and the prophecy were the focus before the transition, although very much part of the same sequence. Similarly, the personification Pietas jumps down at 11.472 after lamenting the situation, to try and stop the fratricide. It is interesting that all these usages push against the boundary between god as character and god as personification, from the interaction of Love and War, to the interventions of Courage and Duty/Love.[23] Gods are particularly important in the narrative transitions of epic, because narrative control often resides on the divine level, and the narrator claims a special relationship with the divine through the Muses.[24] The contrast between Statius and Virgil in the use of *desiluit* is also interesting. It does not just reflect the more metaphorical, looser use of language in Statius, but also reflects a different narrative dynamic. The slow inevitable drive towards the moment of fratricide, marked by a self-conscious desire for delay, also plays out on the divine level. Each time what feels like it should be a turning point just brings us closer to what was always going to happen. Epic devices of narrative transition, therefore, are blurred into a greater degree of continuity. The gods themselves are caught up in human destruction.

---

is used of a god, in this case Mars, but jumping down from his chariot to respond to Venus' persuasive intervention, in the middle of the scene.

23 As Feeney (1991) pointed out, Statius changes the dynamics of divine representation.
24 On Zeus/Jupiter and the narrator in epic, Lovatt (2013) 33–39; see Richardson (1990) 119–123, Clay (1997) 9–25 on the closeness of the Homeric narrator to the gods.

The phrase *nec mora* (or its equivalent *haud mora*), which here in *Aeneid* 1 describes Mercury as he jumps down to the underworld, is also sometimes used in transitional contexts, and generates some interesting intratextual links, strengthening the connection between Mercury and Mars. Across the *Aeneid* and the *Thebaid* it is mainly used in four contexts: obeying orders, setting sail, dramatic action and summary.[25] I would characterise this phrase as a "quick-cut" device, to move swiftly from one point of view to another, or one action to another, which also emphasises the power of those giving orders by the speed of the response (and the energy of those carrying out the orders), and the speed and intensity of the action.[26] In a summary, it acts as a *praeteritio*, passing over smaller events as unimportant. The number of occurrences in both sets of games is striking: games feature high intensity, high speed action.[27] The one interesting difference between Statius and Virgil applies particularly to our passage: in Virgil it is not used of gods, only mortals obeying the orders of other mortals. This could be an indication that Statius has further polarised the divine hierarchy.[28]

The last two lines of our transitional zone move the focus onto Polynices as exile:

---

[25] Obeying orders: *Aen.* 5.749: Acestes accepts the rule of the new city and they get on with setting it up; 6.177: The Trojans carry out the orders of the Sibyl to bury Misenus; 7.156: The Trojans obey the orders of Aeneas to carry gifts to Latinus; *Theb.* 1.310: Mercury obeys Jupiter; 1.533: daughters of Adrastus obey his instructions to join the banquet; 6.813: Tydeus rescues Alcidamas from Capaneus in the boxing match at the orders of Adrastus. Setting sail/starting out: *Aen.* 3.207: setting sail after the storm, just before the Strophades; 3.548: setting sail after offerings at the Castrum Minervae in Italy; 5.140: start of the boat race. Dramatic action: *Aen.* 5.140: start of the boat race; 5.368: boxing match; 458: boxing match again; 11.713: Camilla's opponent tries to trick her by taunting her off her horse and riding away without delay; *Theb.* 6.887: Tydeus escapes Agylleus' grip during the wrestling match; 9.834: immediately after Mars jumps down to remove Artemis from the battlefield. Arguably *Theb.* 2.513 (in the middle of the description of the Sphinx) comes into this category too. Summary: *Aen.* 12.553: summing up battle in final line of scene before Venus intervenes to direct Aeneas' mind to attacking the Latin city. *Theb.* 8.277: dawn, council of Argives, agreement for Thiodamas to replace Amphiaraus (summary mode). Characterising Mars as impetuous: *Theb.* 3.293: Mars jumps down to respond to Venus.
[26] Delay is a major theme in Statius' narrative, as Ash (2015) 208–209 observes.
[27] It may be that Statius deliberately includes two instances of *nec mora* in the boxing match and wrestling match to equal the two instances in Virgil's boxing match.
[28] Although the fact that this scene features Mars and Venus acts to complicate any argument from divine hierarchies, since her desirability to him is set against his greater physical strength, as with Vulcan and Venus in *Aeneid* 8.

> Interea patriis olim vagus <u>exsul ab oris</u>
> Oedipodionides furto <u>deserta pererrat</u> Aoniae.
>
> (*Theb.* 1.312–313)

> Meanwhile then the son of Oedipus wandering as an exile
> from his father's shores ranges stealthily through the empty places of Aonia.

Polynices here clearly evokes Aeneas in the opening lines of Virgil's proem:

> Arma virumque cano, Troiae qui <u>primus ab oris</u>
> Italiam fato <u>profugus</u> Laviniaque venit
> litora ...
>
> (*Aen.* 1.1–2)

> I sing of arms and the man, who first from the Trojan shores
> refugee from fate came to Italy and the Lavinian
> coasts.

These lines are so famous that it does not take much to call them up, especially in the first two lines of a new section. The notion of exile and the phrase *ab oris* in the same metrical *sedes* make the link. This is strengthened by further reminiscence of the beginning of *Aen.* 3:

> Postquam res Asiae Priamique evertere gentem
> immeritam visum superis, ceciditque superbum
> Ilium et omnis humo fumat Neptunia Troia,
> diversa <u>exsilia</u> et <u>desertas</u> quaerere <u>terras</u>
> auguriis agimur divum.
>
> (*Aen.* 3.1–5)

> After the state of Asia and the undeserving race of Priam
> was seen to be overturned by the gods, and proud Ilium
> fell and the whole of Neptunian Tory smoked from ground up,
> we were driven to seek far-off exile and deserted lands
> by the auguries of the gods.

The idea of exile combined with the word *deserta* and the assonance of *errat* and *terras*, as well as the position at the beginning of a sequence, seems to me just sufficient to activate a connection.[29] If we do see this link, it has various implications. The Theban landscape becomes a wilderness when Polynices is forced out of his own society. Note, though, that Polynices is defined by his father not his

---

[29] On the importance of interpretation in deciding which verbal similarities are meaningful, see Bernstein in this volume.

city, and is already an exile within his country, alienated in the wild places. In this respect, he is more like Dido than Aeneas. For Dido too wanders through the deserted places:

> ... agit ipse furentem 465
> in somnis ferus Aeneas, semperque relinqui
> sola sibi, semper longam incomitata videtur
> ire viam et Tyrios deserta quaerere terra,
> Eumenidum veluti demens videt agmina Pentheus
> et solem geminum et duplices se ostendere Thebas.
>
> (*Aen.* 4.465–470)

> Wild Aeneas himself drives her raging in her dreams
> and always she is left alone abandoned by him, always she seems
> to go unaccompanied on a long road and to seek lands deserted of Tyrians,
> just as when mad Pentheus sees the column of the Furies
> and a twin sun and double Thebes show themselves to him.

The fact that Virgil evokes Thebes in imagining Dido's madness makes it all the more appropriate that Statius should highlight Polynices' mental instability along with his heritage from Oedipus by focalising the description of his wanderings through him. He is still at home but feels he is in a threatening wild place. Unlike Aeneas he has nowhere to go, only somewhere from which to be driven.[30]

2 *Interea*

The major new sequence that forms the second half of *Thebaid* 1 begins with the word *interea*, which has a clear transitional function, indicating that two sections of narrative have been happening at the same time, in this case the divine council and Polynices' departure. There has been some discussion of the word *interea* in Virgil's *Aeneid*: does it always signify "meanwhile" or can it also be used in a weak sense simply to signify transition to the next thing (translated "and now")? Reinmuth argues that there are several good examples of the latter, while Kinsey maintains that it can always be translated "meanwhile."[31] The question here, it seems to me, turns precisely on whether a key transitional word occasionally

---

[30] Polynices as a character is similar in his multiplicity to Silius' Hannibal: he includes both Dido and Aeneas, Pompey and Caesar, uniting opposites in a complex and unstable whole: see Fucecchi in this volume.

[31] See Reinmuth (1933) and Kinsey (1979).

loses (or weakens) its specific temporal meaning and simply implies narrative transition itself. At other times the weak nature of the transition (the fundamental continuity in the scene) makes the word hard to interpret. At *Aen.* 1.180–181, when Aeneas climbs up the cliff to look for ships and hunt stags, for instance, the description of the process of drying and milling grain before preparing bread at 174–179 allows for a temporal pause created both by the domestic preparations of the characters and by the description of the narrator, while Aeneas takes control and moves the action on by adopting a vertical perspective. The English "meanwhile" effectively portrays the adversative sense of the Latin here, but the transition is very weak.

In order to judge how much *interea* is a transitional word, I have rated each occurrence in the *Aeneid* and *Thebaid* for its associations with other transitional features (change of space, time, character, narrative mode, scene, sequence). There are 55 occurrences of the word *interea* in the *Aeneid*, but only 22 in the *Thebaid*. Table 1 shows how I rated each occurrence for transitionality, from 0 (no transitional force at all), to 5 (very strong transition).

Tab. 1: Analysis of occurrences of *interea* in the *Aeneid* and the *Thebaid*

Rating	Aeneid	Thebaid
0	1	0
1	10	3
2	7	3
3	14	4
4	16	4
5	7	8

We can see that *interea* clearly has a strong transitional force in most cases (37 out of 55 rated moderate to very strong in the *Aeneid*; 16 out of 22 in the *Thebaid*).[32] Virgil clearly uses *interea* much more than Statius does, and uses it more often without much transitional force. Proportionally, Statius uses it more often for a

---

[32] It was sometimes difficult to decide between individual cases rated 3 and 4, or 4 and 5: I did not apply criteria mechanically, but took into account how important the break between scenes was, as well as what sort of change was involved. These ratings inevitably have a degree of subjectivity, and in a larger project it would be worth discussing a number of cases in detail to explain the choices made.

strong transition. This also reveals that the *Aeneid* has many more mid-ranking transitions. A break-down of the occurrences by book (Table 2) is also revealing.

Tab. 2: Break-down of occurrences of *interea* by book

Bks	Aen.	5	4	3	2	1	0	Theb.	5	4	3	2	1
1	5				1	2	2	1	1				
2	4	1		3				1	1				
3	4		1	1	1	1		2			1		1
4	4	1		1		2		1			1		
5	3	2				1		1		1			
6	3		1			2		2		1	1		
7	1		1					1	1				
8	3			1	1	1		2		1	1		
9	5		1	1	1	1	1	2		1			1
10	11	2	3	5	1			4		1	1	1	1
11	6	1		3		1		2		1		1	
12	6			2	4			3		1		1	

As the narrative increases in pace and intensity, in both epics notably in the second halves, there are more movements between contemporaneous narratives. *Aeneid* 10 is particularly conspicuous for the large number of mostly moderate transitions from one part of the battlefield to another, or from one side of the combatants to the other. More research is needed, since *interea* is only one of many possible features of transition. *At* in particular is another important word. But *prima facie* the *Thebaid* does come out of this comparison seeming more episodic than the *Aeneid*, or with narratives less intricately intertwined. These results will need to be put in context with the other epics in the corpus, especially Lucan and the other Flavian epics. The radical influence of Ovid's narrative fluidity cannot be underestimated either.

Important for our understanding of the force of *interea* in *Thebaid* 1 is the use of *interea* in pairs. Reinmuth's complaint that Virgil often uses it not as "meanwhile" but rather "and now" can partly be addressed by exploring the various paired occurrences, where the first instance moves the narrative from one scene to another, and the second moves it back. The two narrative threads may not have action happening at the same time that directly maps onto the action in the other thread: the word can also signal movement between two narrative threads. Our passage in *Theb.* 1 moves from the divine narrative of the causes of the war to the journey of Polynices and his arrival in Argos. The divine narrative resumes at *Thebaid* 2.1:

> interea gelidis Maia satus aliger umbris
> iussa gerens magni remeat Iovis; undique pigrae
> ire vetant nubes et turbidus implicat aer,
> nec Zephyri rapuere gradum, sed foeda silentis
> aura poli.
>
> (*Theb.* 2.1–5)

> Meanwhile the winged offspring of Maia bearing the orders
> of great Jove returns through the cold shades; everywhere the sluggish
> clouds forbid him to go and the swollen air winds about him,
> nor do Zephyrs push on his step, but the foul breeze
> of the silent pole.

The words of the reconnection echo back in various ways: the cold shades recall his shiver in the cold air; *aliger* varies *alis*; Maia replaces the evocation of Atlas and his father, who now comes last in the phrase, as the ultimate destination of his return. The emphasis on his difficult flight recapitulates the difficulties of Polynices' journey through the storm. Laius' limping shade further slows him down: in all Statius' narrative thematises its own sluggishness and reluctance. It is notable that Mercury is on his way back: the first *interea* implies that Polynices' journey covered the way down; plenty of time has passed, and now this *interea* shows that both stories have moved on. At the same time the two narratives function on different levels and in different modes: there is no reason why divine actions have to conform to mortal notions of time.

Virgil uses pairings of *interea* several times: a good example is at the beginning and end of the divine council in book 10 (10.1 *panditur interea domus omnipotentis Olympi*, "meanwhile the house of all-powerful Olympus is opened," and 10.118 *interea Rutuli*, "meanwhile Rutulians …"). The first has a low level of contemporaneity since it would seem odd to have a council of the gods while Turnus is fighting his *aristeia*, but quite appropriate to do so afterwards. This Virgilian *interea* anticipates the later one, rather than overlapping in time at both ends. A different pairing effect operates at the beginning of book 11 (11.1 *Oceanum interea surgens Aurora reliquit*, "Aurora rising meanwhile left behind the Ocean") describes the move from battle to lament, from the ongoing processes of time and nature in contrast to the cutting off of human life (Mezentius) with the use of *interea* in combination with Dawn. This combination is recapitulated at the end of the lament of Evander:

> Aurora interea miseris mortalibus almam
> extulerat lucem referens opera atque labores.
>
> (*Aen.* 11.182–183)
>
> Meanwhile Aurora raised up the gentle light
> for wretched mortals, bringing back work and toil.

But instead of bracketing a particular episode, this pairing moves back to the same character again, in both cases returning to Aeneas and his mourning for Pallas. This examination of *interea* in the *Aeneid* and the *Thebaid* shows that the articulation of narrative time using words and phrases of transition in both poems is complex and subtle, and participates in rich intertextual and intratextual relationships.

3 Methodological Difficulties in Searching

Quantitative analysis of structural intertextuality is beset by a number of problems. Relatively common words such as *at* ("but"), *iam* ("now"), *postquam* ("after"), *ubi* ("where") and *talia* ("such things") form the key parts of transitional formulae.[33] These words only become significant when combined with another element, which need not always be the same: so the verb *sum* is a crucial part of the introduction to ekphrastic descriptions of places (*urbs antiqua fuit*, "there was an ancient city," or *lucus est*, "there is a grove"). The verb is in the third person singular and combined with a nominative indicator of place. It is easily spotted when reading, but quite hard to search for, because it has many variations. Similarly, the conjunction *at* is fairly common, but generally functions as a transitional formula in combination with a name or noun indicating a character (*at regina*, "but the queen," *Aen.* 4.1), or location (*at domus*, "but the house," *Aen.* 1.637). However, working through texts by reading them, and working through

---

[33] Coffee and Gawley in this volume argue that intertextual resonances are often formed from relatively rare words; however Nelis in this volume argues that structure is just as important as verbal echoes in determining whether or not an ancient audience might see a relationship between two texts. Words and phrases at the beginnings and ends of crucial passages are particularly resonant and memorable: for instance, see Landrey (2014) on the frequent use of the Virgilian tag *arma uirumque* ("arms and the man") in Silius. To Leo I owe this joke seen on Facebook: "What is Dido's twitter handle? Answer: @regina." This too relies on the recognition of two relatively common words (*at regina*, "but the queen") which form a key moment of transition in the *Aeneid*.

large numbers of results from different searches are both fruitful ways to anatomise the practice of narrative transition. It is helpful to know how common a transitional formula is, and useful to look at verbal connections as well as structural and thematic resonances.[34]

The zone of transition at *Thebaid* 1.298–313 offers a different sort of intertextuality to that of say, the parade of ancestors at 6.531–547, which I have examined in detail elsewhere.[35] Instead of detailed intertextual relationships to small and particular models, it connects to a number of different transitional zones, evoking broader thematic and structural connections: Jupiter and Juno; Mercury and Mars; Polynices and Aeneas; Polynices and Dido. The comparable passage in *Aeneid* 1 is defined more by difference than similarity:

> haec ait et Maia genitum demittit ab alto,
> ut terrae utque novae pateant Karthaginis arces
> hospitio Teucris, ne fati nescia Dido
> finibus arceret. volat ille per aëra magnum   300
> remigio alarum ac Libyae citus astitit oris.
> et iam iussa facit, ponuntque ferocia Poeni
> corda volente deo; in primis regina quietum
> accipit in Teucros animum mentemque benignam.
> at pius Aeneas per noctem plurima volvens,   305
> ut primum lux alma data est, exire locosque
> explorare novos, quas vento accesserit oras,
> qui teneant (nam inculta videt), hominesne feraene,
> quaerere constituit sociisque exacta referre.
>
> (*Aen.* 1.297–309)

> He said these things and sent down the god born from Maia from on high
> so that the lands and citadels of new Carthage should lie open
> in hospitality to the Trojans, so that Dido ignorant of fate
> should not keep them from her borders. He flies through the great heaven
> on the oars of his wings, and swift he stands on the shores of Libya.
> And now he carries out the orders, and the Phoenicians set aside their fierce
> hearts at the will of a god. From the first the queen conceived calm
> for the Trojans wishing them well in spirit and mind.
> But pious Aeneas turning over many things through the night
> when first gentle light was given, decided to go out and explore
> new places, to seek out what shores he had reached through the wind,

---

34 Bernstein in this volume argues that the existence of *Tesserae* and other quantitative software shifts the critics' task from discovery of verbal similarities onto interpretation.
35 Lovatt (2002).

who held them (for he sees uncultivated places), whether men or beasts,
and to bring back information for his allies.

While Virgil's Mercury, named by his connection to Maia, as in *Thebaid* 2, moves immediately and achieves the orders simply by arriving, Statius emphasises the difficulty and reluctance that Jupiter faces from his own narrative. The deceptively peaceful reception of Dido is like the peaceful calm of Adrastus' kingdom which Polynices will infect with his love of war. But while Polynices is defined by his relationship to Oedipus, Aeneas is defined by his *pietas* and his resilience in the face of disaster. He is active and determined, while Polynices is passive, undirected and deceptive even in his own land.

4 Conclusion

This chapter has shown the importance and interest of narrative transition, what Lemony Snicket calls the ways that authors "link what is going on in one part of the story to what is going on in another part of the story." Narrative transition gives new insights into both the workings of epic narrative in general and those of the *Aeneid* and the *Thebaid* in particular. Text-searching technologies provide some interesting starting points, leads and comparative evidence for investigating structural intertextuality. They cannot replace the act of reading (and in fact assessing the relevance and usefulness of any match involves reading and understanding the context) but verbal connections can produce links that would not otherwise have sprung to notice. There are certainly transitional words and formulae, and *interea* is a particularly interesting one. It does not always suggest contemporaneity, but sometimes acts as a short-hand for the process of narrative transition itself. Exploring the different ways that Virgil and Statius use this word in their poems already suggests some significant and interesting differences between their narrative techniques. This is a fruitful area for further study.

Bibliography

Ahl, Frederick (2015), "Transgressing boundaries of the unthinkable: Sophocles, Ovid, Vergil, Seneca and Homer refracted in Statius' *Thebaid*", in: Dominik *et al.* (2015) 240–265.
Ash, Rhiannon (2015), "'War came in disarray …' (*Theb.* 7.616): Statius and the depiction of battle", in: Dominik *et al.* (2015) 207–220.
Augoustakis, Antony (ed.) (2012), *Ritual and Religion in Flavian Epic*, Oxford.
Augoustakis, Antony (ed.) (2014), *Flavian Poetry and its Greek Past*, Leiden.

Bakker, Egbert J./Kahane, Ahuvia (eds.) (1997), *Written Voices, Spoken Signs*, Cambridge, MA.
Bakogianni, Anastasia/Hope, Valerie M. (eds.) (2015), *War as Spectacle: Ancient and Modern Perspectives on the Display of Armed Conflict*, London.
Bernstein, Neil (2004), "*Auferte oculos*: Modes of spectatorship in Statius' *Thebaid* 11", in: *Phoenix* 58, 62–85.
Bessone, Federica (2011), *La* Tebaide *di Stazio. Epica e potere*, Pisa.
Blum, Jessica/Biggs, Thomas (eds.) (2019), *Home and Away: The Epic Journey in Greek and Roman Literature*, Cambridge.
Clay, Jenny (1997), *The Wrath of Athena: Gods and Men in the* Odyssey, Lanham, MD.
De Jong, Irene (2001), *A Narratological Commentary on the* Odyssey, Cambridge.
De Martino, Francesco/Kyriakidis, Stratis (eds.) (2004), *Middles in Latin Poetry*, Bari.
Dominik, William (1994), *Speech and Rhetoric in Statius'* Thebaid, Hildesheim.
Dominik, William/Newlands, Carole/Gervais, Kyle (eds.) (2015), *Brill's Companion to Statius*, Leiden.
Feeney, Denis (1991), *The Gods in Epic*, Oxford.
Finkmann, Simone (2014), "Collective Speech and Silence in the *Argonautica* of Apollonius and Valerius", in: Augoustakis (2014) 73–94.
Ganiban, Randall (2007), *Statius and Virgil: The* Thebaid *and the Reinterpretation of the* Aeneid, Cambridge.
Hardie, Philip (1993), *The Epic Successors of Virgil*, Cambridge.
Heuvel, Herman (ed.) (1932), *Publii Papinii Statii Thebaidos Liber Primus*, Zutphen.
Highet, Gilbert (1972), *The Speeches in Virgil's* Aeneid, Princeton.
Kinsey, Thomas (1979), "The Meaning of *interea* in Virgil's *Aeneid*", in: *Glotta* 57, 259–265.
Laird, Andrew (1999), *Powers of Expression, Expressions of Power: Speech Presentation and Latin Literature*, Oxford.
Landrey, Leo (2014), "Skeletons in Armor: The *Aeneid's* proem and Silius Italicus' *Punica*", in: *AJPh* 135, 599–633.
Lovatt, Helen (2002), "Statius' ekphrastic games", in: *Ramus* 31, 73–90.
Lovatt, Helen (2005), *Statius and epic games: Sport, politics and poetics in the* Thebaid, Cambridge.
Lovatt, Helen (2013), *The Epic Gaze: Vision, Gender and Narrative in Ancient Epic*, Cambridge.
Lovatt, Helen (2015), "Death on the Margins: Statius and the Spectacle of the Dying Epic Hero", in: Bakogianni/Hope (2015) 73–92.
Martin, Richard (1997), "Similes and Performance", in: Bakker/Kahane (1997) 138–166.
Nuttall, Anthony (1992), *Openings: Narrative beginnings from the epic to the novel*, Oxford.
Parkes, Ruth (2012), "Chthonic ingredients and thematic concerns: The Shaping of the Necromancy in the *Thebaid*", in: Augoustakis (2012) 165–180.
Reinmuth, Oscar (1933), "Vergil's use of *interea*: A study of the treatment of contemporaneous events in Roman epic", in: *AJPh* 54, 323–339.
Richardson, Scott (1990), *The Homeric Narrator*, Nashville, TN.
Roberts, Deborah H./Dunn, Francis M./Fowler, Don (eds.) (1997), *Classical Closure: Reading the End in Greek and Latin Literature*, Princeton.
Smolenaars, Johannes J.L. (1994), *Statius* Thebaid VII: *A Commentary*, Leiden.
Waddell, Philip (2013), "Eloquent Collisions: The *Annales* of Tacitus, the Column of Trajan and the Cinematic Quick-cut", in: *Arethusa* 46, 471–497.

Tim Stover
Valerius Flaccus' *Argonautica* 3.598–725: Epic, History, and Intertextuality

1 Introduction

This paper has three primary aims: 1) to analyze the intricate intertextuality of Val. Fl. *Arg.* 3.598–725 where Meleager and Telamon argue about what to do in light of Hercules' sudden disappearance; 2) to offer a historicizing reading of this passage; and 3) to use my historicizing reading to shed light on the complications that arise from trying to use history as intertext. After probing the manner in which Valerius uses a dense network of allusion to depict Meleager as a rival of Hercules, I suggest that this narrative sequence is evocative of the shifting loyalties that characterized the civil war of AD 68–69 and more specifically that Valerius' depiction of Meleager bears striking similarities to one of the war's principal players, Antonius Primus, as portrayed by Tacitus in the *Histories*. As we shall see there may well be specific reasons for Meleager's resemblance to Tacitus' Primus, and this reason creates some complications for the historicizing reading offered here.

But before I begin, I should explain briefly why I chose to analyze this particular passage. First and foremost, although *Argonautica* 3.598–725 has not been wholly neglected, the passage's complex intertextuality has not been subjected to sustained examination in previous studies.[1] I hope my essay can begin the process of addressing this critical desideratum. Moreover, Valerius' many divergences from his primary model, Apollonius of Rhodes, and especially his focus on "loyalty" (*fides*) makes this narrative sequence conducive to historicizing Valerius' innovations and thus to analyzing the uniquely *Flavian* aspects of the passage's intertextuality, which is an abiding interest of mine and a primary focus of this volume.

---

[1] For good discussions of this portion of Valerius' epic, see Garson (1963) 265–266, Adamietz (1976) 51, Schenk (1986), Kleywegt (1991) 232–235, and Lovatt (2014) 218–221.

2 Hercules and Meleager

To begin with, it is important to recognize how different Valerius' account of the desertion of Hercules is from that of his primary model, Apollonius of Rhodes. This will allow the uniquely Valerian material to stand out in high relief, which will set things up for consideration of how Valerius' formal divergences from Apollonius evoke the socio-political landscape of the late 60s.

As is often the case with Valerius, the differences between his version of Hercules' departure and that found in Apollonius' poem outweigh the similarities. Among the differences between the two epics, there are three that stand out. Firstly, in Apollonius the Argonauts *accidentally* depart from Mysia without realizing that Heracles has gone missing. In Valerius, by contrast, the men are fully aware that he is not present as they prepare to set sail. As Lovatt has observed, this change puts a "greater emphasis on dissension and debate."[2] Indeed the most salient feature of the Valerian episode is the introduction of a bona fide debate between Telamon, who argues that the Argonauts should stay and look for Hercules (3.637–645, 697–714), and Meleager, who advises the men to move on without him (3.645–689).[3]

And this brings us to the second major difference between the two accounts. Whereas Telamon's unwavering devotion to Heracles is a feature of Apollonius' narrative (*Argon.* 1.1289–1295), Meleager's involvement at this stage is a Valerian innovation found in no other extant accounts of the episode.[4] Thus Meleager plays absolutely no role at this point in Apollonius' narrative.[5] In fact, there is no debate at all in the Hellenistic version. Although we are told that a quarrel broke out when the Argonauts realized that Heracles was absent (1.1284–1286), only Telamon is given a speaking part: he rebukes Jason, accusing him of orchestrating the desertion of Heracles out of jealousy (1289–1295). For his part, the Apollonian Jason does what he often does when the quarrel erupts, i.e. he sits there in stunned and silent helplessness (1286–1289). In contrast to Apollonius' reticent Jason, the Valerian Jason calls for discussion of how best to proceed (3.615–627).[6]

---

[2] See Lovatt (2014) 218.
[3] Citations of Valerius come from the editions of Liberman (1997) and Liberman (2002). Translations are taken from Mozley (1934), occasionally with slight alterations to modernize his diction.
[4] See Spaltenstein (2004) 183 and Manuwald (2015) 240.
[5] See Adamietz (1976) 51, Schenk (1986) 20, and Kleywegt (1991) 232.
[6] In terms of leadership, Valerius' Jason fares better here than Apollonius', as noted by Castelletti (2014) 179.

This initiates a debate between Telamon and Meleager, who voices the view that the Argonauts should depart posthaste. It is *his* role—and the influence his *suasoria* has on the men—that in my view merits further consideration and thus is the aspect of the episode that I concentrate on here. For in the contentious atmosphere of a fully-fledged debate over what to do in the face of a leader's abrupt disappearance Valerius' text evokes the shifting loyalties of men whose leaders experienced sudden changes of fortune during the 'Year of the Four Emperors.'

But before I turn to Meleager's un-Apollonian performance, I want to draw attention to the third principal difference between the versions of Apollonius and Valerius. In Apollonius, after Telamon reproaches Jason, he rushes at Tiphys to try to have him turn the ship around and head back to Mysia. However, Telamon is blocked by the sons of Boreas, who restrain him (1.1296–1301). At this point, the sea god Glaucus swims up and explains to the Argonauts that it is Zeus' will that Heracles go his own way (1310–1320). At this news the men rejoice, while Telamon takes Jason aside to apologize to him, an apology which Jason happily accepts. There is thus a strong sense of propriety about the Argonauts' actions in the Apollonian episode, since it is revealed to them by a god that leaving Heracles behind is the right thing to do.[7]

There is nothing like this sense of rectitude in Valerius' narrative of the same events. For although Jason had apparently been advised by an oracle that Hercules was destined to leave before the mission was complete (3.617–622), there is nothing in Valerius analogous to the divinely sanctioned closure provided by the Apollonian Glaucus. On the one hand, the oracle that Jason recalls is shadowy to say the least, since it is nowhere else mentioned in the poem.[8] On the other hand, Jason clearly does not want to leave Hercules behind and, like the other members of the crew, is saddened by their continuing on without him (717–718). And this despite the reassurance he might have gotten from the oracle![9] Consequently it is hard to tell if Valerius' Argonauts have made the right decision. The narrative in essence requires that they move on without Hercules, but the lack of divine guidance coupled with the sense of grief that attends their departure from Mysia (715–725) creates the impression that they have made a *bad* decision, raising the possibility that they have acted *disloyally*. Nor does it help that Valerius' Argonauts

---

7 See Levin (1971) 112 and Clauss (1993) 202.
8 See Spaltenstein (2004) 177 and Manuwald (2015) 235.
9 See Manuwald (2015) 47.

are persuaded to leave Hercules behind by Meleager, a fascinatingly shady character whose involvement brings the concept of *fides*, and its evil twin *perfidia*, to the fore.[10]

Meleager's perfidious character is made explicit in the words that introduce his *suasoria*, a rhetorical tour de force that runs on for forty lines (3.645–689).[11] I cite the passage in full to provide context for the discussion of specific points that follows:

> Rursum instimulat ducitque fauentes   645
> magnanimus Calydone satus, potioribus ille
> deteriora fouens semperque inuersa tueri
> durus et haud ullis umquam superabilis aequis
> rectorumue memor. 'Non Herculis' inquit 'adempti,
> sed tuus in seros haec nostra silentia questus   650
> traxit honor, dum iura dares, dum tempora fandi.
> Septimus hic celsis descendit montibus Auster
> iamque ratem Scythicis forsan statuisset in oris;
> nos patriae immemores, maneant ceu nulla reuectos
> gaudia sed duro saeuae sub rege Mycenae,   655
> ad medium cunctamur iter. Si finibus ullis
> has tolerare moras et inania tempora possem,
> regna hodie et dulcem sceptris Calydona tenerem
> laetus opum pacisque meae tutusque manerem
> quis genitor materque locis. Quid deside terra   660
> haeremus? Vacuos cur lassant aequora uisus?
> Tu comitem Alciden ad Phasidis amplius arua
> adfore, tu socias ultra tibi rere pharetras?
> Non ea pax odiis oblitaue numine fesso
> Iuno sui. Noua Tartareo fors semine monstra   665
> atque iterum Inachiis iam nuntius urget ab Argis.
> Non datur haec magni proles Iouis; at tibi Pollux
> stirpe pares Castorque manent, at cetera diuum
> progenies nec parua mihi fiducia gentis.
> En egomet quocumque uocas sequar agmina ferro   670
> plura metam; tibi dicta manus, tibi quicquid in ipso
> sanguine erit, iamque hinc operum quae maxima posco.
> Scilicet in solis profugi stetit Herculis armis
> nostra salus. nempe ora aeque mortalia cuncti
> ecce gerunt, ibant aequo nempe ordine remi   675
> Ille uel insano iamdudum turbidus aestu
> uel parta iam laude tumens consortia famae

---

10 On the relations between *fides* and *perfidia*, see Freyburger (1986) 84–86.
11 For an appreciation of the rhetorical skill on display here, see Garson (1963) 265–266.

despicit ac nostris ferri comes abnuit actis.
Vos, quibus et uirtus et spes in limine primo,
tendite, dum rerum patiens calor et rude membris   680
robur inest; nec enim solis dare funera Colchis
sit satis et tota pelagus lustrasse iuuenta.
Spes mihi quae tali potuit longissima casu
esse fuit, quiscumque virum perquirere siluis
egit amor: loca uociferans non ulla reliqui.   685
Nunc quoque, dum uario nutat sententia motu,
cernere deuexis redeuntem montibus opto.
Sat lacrimis comitique datum quem sortibus aeui
crede uel in mediae raptum tibi sanguine pugnae!'.

On the other hand, Calydon's greathearted son goads and draws on those who are for the venture, a fosterer he of worse counsel by better argument, ever persistent in aiding a perverted course, never yielding to his equals or having a thought for his leaders. 'Respect, not for lost Hercules but for you, has prolonged our silence unto these late complaints, till you should give us right and opportunity of speech. Now for the seventh day is the south wind blowing from the hills, and would perhaps have already beached our ship on the Scythian shores; but we, forgetting our home, as though no joys awaited our return but a cruel king in pitiless Mycenae, are halting in midcourse. If I could endure these barren days of waiting anywhere, I should be ruling my realm of pleasant Calydon, happy in its peace and plenty, abiding in the home where my sire and mother dwell. Why linger we in a slothful land? Why does the sea weary our unrewarded vision? Do you think that our comrade Alcides will yet join us in the land of Phasis, that his quiver will any more be allied to yours? Hatred knows no such truce, nor is Juno, though her godhead be weary, forgetful of herself. Perhaps new portents of Tartarean seed and another message from Inachian Argos is vexing him. This scion of mighty Jove we may not have, but Pollux and Castor, in birth no less, are with you still, and all the other progeny of gods, nor is my boast of lineage small. Lo! I will follow you wherever you call me; I will mow down with my sword many lines of warriors; to you is dedicated my hand, to you all my very life-blood can give, and from this moment I beg for myself the hardest tasks. Our safety, indeed, rested on the arms of truant Hercules alone: all men for sure are, look you, in aspect equally mortal, and for sure all our oars moved to an equal beat. As for him, whether a surge of madness has long since confused his mind, or he is swollen with glory already won, he scorns partnership in our renown, and refuses to sail on and share the exploits of our arms. But you who have valor and fresh-budding hope, go onward, while you have a spirit to bear what may befall and vigor is fresh within your limbs; for let it not suffice only to deal destruction to the Colchians, and to have spent all your prime in traversing the sea.'

The description of Meleager before he begins to speak, as well as the content of his speech itself, brands him as a cunning manipulator, the type of individual who knows how to exploit the uncertainty caused by a sudden change of fortune;

which is to say, Meleager is a demagogue.¹² It does not reflect well on the Argonauts that they adopt the course of action suggested by this "fosterer of worse counsel by better argument" (*potioribus ille / deteriora fouens*, 646–647). Moreover, in addition to having little concern for the best course of action, it is clear that Meleager's words are inspired largely by his jealousy of Hercules' exalted position among the Argonauts. From his first entry into the poem, Valerius depicts Meleager as a "jealous rival to Hercules."¹³ Thus Meleager's desire to set sail and to forget about Hercules, whom he portrays as a shameful deserter, has an air of self-promotion about it (676–678). Now that Hercules is gone, Meleager demands to be given what in the past would have been literally Herculean tasks (672). For him, this is an opportunity to improve his standing within the group. Or better, Meleager sees a chance to *replace* Hercules. But as with other episodes of substitution in Flavian epic, such as Thiodamas' replacement of Amphiaraus in Statius' *Thebaid*, here too the new guy is a sorry substitute for the original hero, a theme that has interesting implications as a reflection of the civil war of AD 68–69, but which is a topic for another time.

In fact, Valerius goes to some lengths to set us up for this replacement by creating the impression that Meleager is an unscrupulous *Doppelgänger* of Hercules. For example, the epic periphrasis by which Valerius introduces Meleager at 3.646—*magnanimus Calydone satus*—echoes the first usage of the term *magnanimus* in the epic, where in the same metrical position it refers to Hercules (1.634–635): *Magnanimus spectat pharetras et inutile robur / Amphitryoniades*, "Amphitryon's great-hearted son gazes on his quiver and oak club, which are useless now." It is worth pausing over this point: it seems that Valerius is here picking up on Bacchylides' depiction of the two heroes in *Ode* 5, which is not a poem often cited in discussions of the bewildering intertextuality of Valerius' epic.

By using the term *magnanimus* of both Hercules and Meleager, Valerius appears to be alluding to the moment in Bacchyl. 5 when Heracles sees the soul of Meleager in the Underworld (68–70). The first adjective that Bacchylides uses to describe Meleager's ghost is θρασυμέμνων ("brave-spirited," 69), for which term the Latin *magnanimus* is a close equivalent. What is interesting about Bacchylides' usage of this word in reference to Meleager as he meets Heracles in the Underworld is that in Homer this term is used to describe Heracles, and no one else (*Il.* 5.639 and *Od.* 11.267).¹⁴ In fact, Cairns notes that the use of θρασυμέμνων

---

12 See Spaltenstein (2004) 183.
13 See Zissos (2008) 278. See also Schenk (1986) 20.
14 See Campbell (1982) 428 and Cairns (2010) 229.

at this moment in Bacchylides' poem "may suggest an affinity between Heracles and Meleager and/or their fates."[15] It thus seems that Valerius' pointed usage of *magnanimus* to describe Meleager just before he begins to speak about Hercules in *Argonautica* 3 has an interesting poetic lineage.

As for Meleager's rivalry with Hercules in Valerius' *Argonautica*, this too is subtly prefigured in Bacchyl. 5. For example, Bacchylides' use of the rare phrase "gleaming in his armor" (τεύχεσι λαμπόμενον, 71) to describe Meleager indirectly depicts him as a potential enemy of Heracles. For as Cairns notes, elsewhere this phrase is used in reference to "significant opponents of Heracles" (i.e. Cycnus and Ares and the Giants).[16] Thus there appears to be a tradition, stemming at least from Bacchyl. 5, of allusively depicting Meleager not only as a sort of double of Hercules, but also as Hercules' rival and perhaps even his enemy, a tradition that is picked up and carried forward by Valerius.[17]

Another thing that emerges from Bacchyl. 5 that is reflected in Valerius' depiction of Meleager is that the hero is a man prone to violent actions. For example, when Heracles refers to Meleager's home, he speaks of "the palace of Oeneus, dear to Ares" (165–166). The collocation of Oeneus and Ares is interesting, given that Ovid makes Meleager a son not of Oeneus, but of Mars, a reference that comes just before he kills his uncles in a rage (*tumida frendens Mauortius ira*, "the son of Mars, gnashing his teeth in an enraged frenzy …", *Met.* 8.437).[18] The fact that he is a kin-killer is mentioned by Bacchylides' Meleager (5.127–129), although he claims to have killed his uncles accidentally (129–135), whereas in Ovid's *Metamorphoses* and Apollodorus (1.8.3) he kills them deliberately.[19] As a killer of his own kin Meleager is thus a character associated with civil war, on which more below. Now although Valerius does not refer to Meleager as a son of Mars, he does depict him as a violent man. For example, during Meleager's speech in Book 3 he asserts that he is ready and willing to "mow down with a sword many lines of warriors" (*agmina ferro / plura metam*, 3.670–671), a phrase

---

15 See Cairns (2010) 229. See also Lefkowitz (1969) 66: "Does the switch [in using θρασυμέμνων of Meleager rather than Heracles] imply that Heracles is meant to see in Meleager some resemblance to himself?"
16 See Cairns (2010) 229–230.
17 On depictions of Meleager in Greek and Roman literature generally, see the wide-ranging discussion of Grossardt (2001).
18 See Hollis (1970) 88, who in discussing the various patronymics applied by Ovid to Meleager notes that "when Meleager oversteps the mark in blind fury, 'Mavortius' is obviously the more appropriate."
19 On the variants within the tradition of Meleager's killing of his uncles, see Gantz (1993) 329–331.

that refers to his desire to engage in "utter and widespread destruction."[20] Moreover, Valerius' reference in Book 1 to Meleager's bulging muscles (1.434–435) obliquely likens him to the monstrously violent Amycus, who is described similarly at 4.244–245.[21] Valerius' Meleager, like Bacchylides' (and Ovid's) before him, is a violent individual, one whose desire to unleash mayhem seeks to rival Hercules, the agent of mass destruction *par excellence* in the mythographic tradition. Also of note is the fact that Deianira – the woman who, albeit indirectly, ultimately kills Hercules – is Meleager's sister, and that as such she is depicted by Ovid as naturally inclined to plan a violent crime, i.e. killing her rival Iole (*Met.* 9.149–151).[22] Meleager does not kill his rival Hercules, but he does jump at the chance to convince the other Argonauts that Hercules' services are no longer needed because he can be replaced by none other than Meleager himself.

But let us return to Meleager's first entry into the poem and to Valerius' reference to his bulging muscles (1.433–435):

> at tibi collectas soluit iam fibula uestes
> ostenditque umeros fortes spatiumque superbi
> pectoris Herculeis aequum, Meleagre, lacertis.

> But you, Meleager, see, the clasp is loosening your gathered raiment, and lays bare your strong shoulders and your broad breast that proudly vies with Hercules in strength of muscle.

Not only are we alerted here to Meleager's rivalry with Hercules, as noted above, but the phraseology echoes a passage at 2.544–545, where Hercules "girds his armor on his vaunting shoulders" (*aptatque superbis / arma umeris*).[23] Moreover, Meleager's impassioned plea against idleness and his fervent desire to move on ironically recalls Hercules' own criticism of inactivity during his call to action on Lemnos in Book 2.[24]

Thus it is clear that Valerius goes to some lengths to assimilate Meleager to Hercules. It is therefore unsurprising that it is Meleager who makes the case that each of the Argonauts can be his own Hercules, as it were, saying: "But you, who have valor and fresh-budding hope, go onward, while you have a spirit to bear what may befall and vigor (*robur*) is fresh within your limbs" (3.679–681). Meleager's use of the term *robur* is pointed: it subtly reinforces his argument that the

---

20 See Manuwald (2015) 247.
21 See Zissos (2008) 279.
22 On Deianira's violent 'Meleager-like' nature here, see Anderson (1972) 427 and Kenney/Chiarini (2011) 411.
23 See Kleywegt (2005) 253 and Galli (2007) 240.
24 See Shelton (1971) 160–161, 163–164.

Argonauts are Hercules' equals and that their collective *robur* is sufficient, since *robur* is a term frequently used in reference to Hercules' favorite weapon, i.e. his oaken club.²⁵ Meleager certainly sees himself as a Herculean character, and this identification is fostered and enhanced by Valerius in various ways throughout the narrative, as we have seen. It is thus ironically fitting that Meleager is brought on to speak immediately following Telamon's claim that there is "no second Hercules" among the Argonauts (*non alium ... Alciden*, 3.644). Unfortunately for Meleager, he fails to live up to his preferred model, emerging instead as a Hercules manqué. But if Hercules as a model does not quite fit Meleager, are there models that do fit the bill for this Valerian villain?

3 Epic Intertextuality: Vergil and Ovid

One figure that critics have often pointed to as a model for Valerius' Meleager is Vergil's Drances, the elderly demagogue who in *Aeneid* 11 uses his rhetorical skills to oppose Turnus and his war with the Trojans.²⁶ Certainly there are similarities: particularly significant is the fact that Drances' political position arises largely from his envy of Turnus' exalted status (*Aen.* 11.336–337). As we have seen, what motivates Valerius' Meleager to speak out is not fidelity to lofty ideals, but rather his personal rivalry with Hercules. But beyond this similarity, the Vergilian character is not a very good fit as a model for Valerius' Meleager. Most obviously, Drances is old, whereas Meleager is in his prime and Drances opposes war, whereas Meleager champions swift action.

I suggest that there is another Vergilian intertext for this Valerian sequence, one that in my view is far closer than the parallels with the scene in *Aeneid* 11 but that to my knowledge has not been examined in any detail, namely the Aeneas-Dido episode in *Aeneid* 4.²⁷ This Vergilian model is activated by way of verbal echo and has the effect of portraying Telamon as Dido while Meleager assumes the role of Aeneas. For example, the words used to describe Telamon's anger at the Argonauts' desire to depart without Hercules (*at pius ingenti Telamon iam fluctuat ira*, "but devoted Telamon is tossed on the tides of mighty wrath," *Arg.* 3.637) recalls Dido's anger at the impending departure of Aeneas at *Aen.* 4.532: *magnoque*

---

25 See Stover (2012) 184–185.
26 See Schenk (1986) 19–23, Kleywegt (1991) 235, Spaltenstein (2004) 183, Lovatt (2014) 218, and Manuwald (2015) 240; on Drances as demagogue, see Gransden (1991) 14–15.
27 On possible parallels for Meleager in Silius' *Punica*, see Manuwald (2015) 240.

irarum fluctuat aestu, "and she is tossed on a mighty wave of anger."[28] The fact that Telamon is allusively cast as a Dido-like character ironizes Valerius' use of *pius* to describe Telamon's devotion to his friend Hercules, since of course this is an epithet frequently applied to Vergil's Aeneas, not to Dido. The contentious relationship between Aeneas and Dido is evoked by Valerius again at 3.651. There Meleager tells Jason that he had not voiced his opinion about Hercules before because he was waiting for the right "opportunity to speak up" (*tempora fandi*). This phrase echoes *Aen.* 4.293–294 (*mollissima fandi / tempora*, "the most favorable opportunity for speaking"), a phrase that refers to Aeneas' desire to find the best time to speak to Dido and break the news of his departure to her.[29] Here again, then, Valerius' allusion to the *Aeneid* has the effect of depicting Meleager as an Aeneas-like character, one who is on the side of departure while the Dido-like Telamon is in favor of delaying the voyage. As a final example of this intertextual web, consider *Arg.* 3.656–660, where Meleager argues that if being idle were appealing to him, he would have stayed in Calydon. This reasoning recalls Aeneas' argument at *Aen.* 4.340–344, where Aeneas says that if he had been able to arrange things his way, he would have stayed in Troy, although Manuwald is right to note the importance of fate in the Vergilian passage, which is not at issue in the Valerian text.[30]

The network of allusions to *Aeneid* 4 that portray Telamon as a Dido-like character in favor of delaying the voyage and Meleager as an Aeneas-like character who favors sailing on is enriched by a subtle intertext early in *Argonautica* 4. There Hercules has a vision of Hylas, the boy whose disappearance caused Hercules to become separated from the rest of the crew, thus triggering the sequence that leads to the debate over what to do about Hercules that I have been discussing. In this vision, Hylas refers to Meleager as "a man of evil tongue, encourager of frenzied appeals" (*hortator ... furiis et uoce nefanda*, 4.32). Valerius' use of *hortator* evokes the passage in Ovid's *Metamorphoses* in which Ulysses and Ajax argue over which one of them deserves to be awarded the arms of Achilles. There Ajax calls Ulysses a *hortator scelerum* ("encourager of crimes," *Met.* 13.45), with the word *hortator* as the first word in the line and thus occupying the same metrical position in each text.[31]

---

28 See Langen (1896–1897) 265, Spaltenstein (2004) 181, and Manuwald (2015) 240.
29 See Manuwald (2015) 243.
30 See Manuwald (2015) 244.
31 The phrase *hortator scelerum*, in fact, is doubly associated with Ulysses in Augustan epic, since the Ovidian passage is a quotation of *Aeneid* 6.529 where Deiphobus calls Ulysses "an encourager of crimes." See Hopkinson (2000) 88 and Hardie/Chiarini (2015) 225.

Hortator is not a common word in epic. Ovid uses it twice, in the passage under discussion and at *Met.* 3.619, but there the context is far different and the word is not used in the same metrical position.[32] Vergil uses it only once (*Aen.* 6.529), the passage that is Ovid's model at *Met.* 13.45 (see note 31). Lucan also uses *hortator* once, but not as the first word in a line: at *BC* 9.549 Labienus is called *hortator* as he urges Cato to visit the temple of Ammon in Africa. Statius uses the term once as well, and also as the first word of a line. A fellow named Enyeus, an Argive trumpeter, is depicted "encouraging" his side to retreat (*Theb.* 11.51). Silius likewise has only one usage of the word but not in the initial position. At *Pun.* 15.571 the term is applied to a group of soldiers marching with Claudius as "each man urges himself" onward (*hortator sibi quisque*). Valerius, in addition to the passage at *Arg.* 4.32, uses *hortator* only one other time, of Cupid as an "encourager" of love during the wedding of Jason and Medea at 8.232; but there the word is not the first word in the line. And finally, Ennius (*Ann.* 467 Sk.) has the term *hortatore* as the first word of a line, but the context is unclear.

So to summarize, the term *hortator* is used only nine times in extant Latin epic, but only five times as the first word of a hexameter, only four of which are found in the nominative case. Two of these four uses refer to Ulysses (*Aen.* 6.529 and *Met.* 13.45); the other two refer to Valerius' Meleager (*Arg.* 4.32) and Statius' Argive trumpeter Enyeus (*Theb.* 11.51). Moreover, the Vergilian and Ovidian passages represent the only usages of *hortator* in the nominative and as the first word of a line that predate Valerius' *Argonautica*, which in my view was written but never finished between the years AD 70 and 79.[33] Consequently Statius' *Thebaid* postdates Valerius' epic, since its period of composition was most likely AD 80–92. As a result, when we encounter Hylas' use of *hortator* at *Arg.* 4.32, we are prompted to recognize behind his terminology the unsavory character of Ovid's and Vergil's Ulysses, a dubious character and something of a demagogue in his own right.[34] Valerius' evocation of the Ovidian passage is especially intriguing, not only because it retrospectively conjures up a famous debate from previous Latin epic as a way to comment on Meleager's verbal duel with Telamon, but also

---

32 At *Met.* 3.619 Epopeus is called *animorum hortator* ("encourager of spirits") because he keeps time with his voice for the rowers on Acoetes' ship.
33 My views on the date of Valerius' poem are put forth in Stover (2012) 7–26.
34 Vergil's Ulysses is consistently described by various characters in the *Aeneid* as an untrustworthy, deceptive, and manipulative schemer (see, e.g., *Aen.* 2.90, 97–99, 125, 164; 6.529; 9.602). It is also worth noting that in the Epic Cycle and Greek tragedy Odysseus is more than just a smooth-talking manipulator; he is also treacherous and violent. He is thus a far less admirable character than he is in Homeric epic. On this, see Hopkinson (2000) 14. As we have seen, treachery and a capacity for violence are traits that Valerius' Meleager has as well.

because it has the effect of casting Telamon in the role of Ovid's Ajax as he attempts to counter the slippery rhetoric of the Ulysses-like Meleager. After all, Ajax is Telamon's son, so the Ovidian intertext is particularly appropriate as a subtext for this Valerian sequence.

But how does Valerius' intertextual evocation of Ovid's Ulysses enrich the echoes of *Aeneid* 4, and what is the purpose of depicting Meleager's dispute with Telamon in terms that recall Aeneas and Dido? In regard to the first question, I suggest that by portraying Telamon as a Dido-like character by way of allusion to *Aeneid* 4 while also evoking Ulysses' debate with Ajax in *Metamorphoses* 13, Valerius subtly acknowledges that Vergil's Dido is, among other things, a reprise of Ajax, especially as he appears in Homer and Greek tragedy. Dido's madness and suicide in *Aeneid* 4 and her continued anger at Aeneas in the Underworld in *Aeneid* 6 have long been recognized as evocative of the madness and suicide of Ajax following his dispute with Odysseus over the arms of Achilles, and already in Servius Dido's appearance in Book 6 was tied directly to Homer's portrait of the angry shade of Ajax in *Odyssey* 11.[35] Thus Valerius' allusive gestures evoke not only Vergil's depiction of Aeneas and Dido, but also one of Vergil's primary models for their doomed and tragic relationship, thereby adding depth, nuance, and complexity to his portrait of Meleager's dispute with Telamon in *Argonautica* 3.

As to why Valerius would wish to model the debate between Meleager and Telamon on Aeneas and Dido, I suggest that the effects of this intertextual nexus are twofold. On the one hand, Valerius' allusive program infuses his scene with hints of tragedy. For when the Argonauts abandon Hercules, they set in motion a chain of events that will require Jason, who now lacks recourse to Hercules' extraordinary powers, to employ the assistance of Medea in order to carry out the labors set for him by Aeetes in Colchis. This relationship will of course lead to personal tragedy for Jason in Corinth. As is well known, Vergil's Dido is a Medea-like character, so Dido's intertextual presence during the debate in *Argonautica* 3 subtly foreshadows the horror that awaits Jason as a result of the abandonment of Hercules. On the other hand, and closely tied to the preceding points, by evoking Vergil's Aeneas-Dido episode Valerius tinges the debate between Meleager and Telamon with world-historical implications. Just as the personal strife between Aeneas and Dido will lead to war between Rome and Carthage, so too the seemingly 'local' and personal rivalry between Meleager and Telamon will trigger a change in the geopolitical landscape of the whole world. This is so because Me-

---

[35] See Austin (1977) 163 and Horsfall (2013) 342. On the Dido-Ajax connection generally, see Tatum (1984).

dea's departure from Colchis, triggered as we have seen by Hercules' abandonment, will lead to large-scale clashes between Asia and Greece, as Jupiter reveals in Book 1 (537–554).[36] Telamon's exclamatory *pro Iuppiter* ("oh Jupiter!") as he refers to the trouble that awaits *all* the "Greek lands" (*terris … Achaeis*, 3.697) as a result of abandoning Hercules thus recalls Jupiter's *Weltenplan* in Book 1 and the crucial role played by Medea therein. Indeed, just as Vergil's Aeneas-Dido episode is etiological for the rise of Rome at the expense of Carthage, so too is the abduction of Medea etiological for the rise of Rome to world dominance, as Jupiter makes clear at 1.555–560: Asia will yield to Greece and Greece in turn will yield to Rome. This of course includes the establishment of the Flavian dynasty, which is lauded by Valerius in the poem's dedicatory proem (1.7–21). We thus have here a blurring of myth and history, as the debate over Hercules is tied to a series of events that have far-reaching global consequences, the ultimate result of which is the rise to prominence of the current ruling family in Rome. It is to some of the episode's other historical dimensions that I want to turn now.

4 History as Intertext

In what follows I hope to show that another close parallel for Valerius' Meleager is to be found not in the pages of previous Latin epic, but rather in the pages of Tacitus' *Histories*, and I want to use my historicizing reading to point up some of the interesting complexities that arise from trying to use history as intertext.[37]

Given the aims of this section, some preliminary remarks about historicizing Valerius' *Argonautica* are in order. Luckily for those who wish to historicize the poem, there seems to be a general consensus that Valerius' *Argonautica* "takes on aspects of a cultural commentary"[38] and that it "uses traditional myth to comment on recent history."[39] It is thus apparent that Valerius adopted a longstanding practice whereby Roman poets employed Greek mythological material to comment on Roman history.[40] Moreover, within the vast corpus of Greek myth the Argonautic legend is particularly well suited to use as commentary on historical

---

36 See Manuwald (2015) 251.
37 For good discussions of history/historiography and intertextuality, see O'Gorman (2009) and Damon (2010).
38 Zissos (2003) 660.
39 Bernstein (2014) 156.
40 See McNelis (2007) 2–5.

developments.⁴¹ We are thus on solid ground when attempting to situate Valerius' text within its socio-political context.⁴²

I suggest that Valerius' Meleager is strikingly similar to a figure of great prominence in Tacitus' account of the civil war of AD 68–69, i.e. the notorious general Antonius Primus. Primus is a fascinating character: he is depicted by Tacitus as a self-aggrandizing demagogue, whose loyalty during the civil war changed to suit whichever path brought him greater influence and whose rhetorical skills were used largely for self-promotion.⁴³ Primus, who originally sided with Galba, eventually supported Vespasian but only after failing to ingratiate himself with Otho and after seeing Vitellius' fortunes decline. He is accordingly introduced by Tacitus as a perfidious demagogue, but one very useful to Vespasian, at least while the war was raging (*Hist.* 2.86.2): *strenuus manu, sermone promptus, serendae in alios inuidiae artifex, discordiis et seditionibus potens, raptor, largitor, pace pessimus, bello non spernendus*, "He was vigorous in action, ready of speech, skillful in sowing differences among his enemies, powerful in stirring up discord and strife, ever ready to rob or bribe—in short he was the worst of mortals in peace, but in war a man not to be despised."⁴⁴ Primus' allegiance was so mercurial that Ash has suggested Tacitus uses him to symbolize "the shifting political situation" of the war.⁴⁵

Primus' ever-changing *fides* ("loyalty") is similar to what we see in Valerius' Meleager. This is so because in addition to denigrating Hercules, Meleager's strategy entails proclaiming his allegiance to Jason, as we have seen (3.670–672): "I will follow you to wherever you call me; I will mow down with my sword many lines of warriors; to you is dedicated my hand, to you all my very life-blood can give, and from this moment I beg for myself the hardest tasks." Not quite as gung ho as Lucan's Laelius, who vows to stab his pregnant wife if Caesar should order

---

41 See Braund (1993) and Nelis (2012) 16–19.
42 Historicizing readings of Argonautic material are quite common. On Valerius' epic see, e.g., Davis (1990), Toohey (1993), Taylor (1994), Zissos (2003), Bernstein (2008) 30–63, Zissos (2009), Buckley (2010), Stover (2012), Bernstein (2014), Tatum (2016), and Stover (2016). For historicizing readings of Apollonius' poem, see Hunter (1993) 152–169, Stephens (2000), and Mori (2008). In addition Braund (1993) discusses the historical dimensions of Varro Atacinus' poem, while Nelis (2012) offers a historicizing reading of the Argonautic dimensions of Catullus 64. Zissos (2009) provides a very useful synopsis of earlier political readings of Valerius' epic. Newman (2001) contains a fascinating discussion of the political uses to which the Argonautic legend was put throughout the course of European history. For historicizing readings of all three Flavian epics, see Bernstein (2016).
43 See Ash (1999) 147–165 and Morgan (2006) 167–169.
44 Translations of Tacitus come from Moore (1925).
45 See Ash (1999) 165.

it (*BC* 1.356–386), but a strong endorsement nonetheless. In fact, his words recall the oaths of loyalty sworn by soldiers to their commanders, a practice that gets a lot of press in Tacitus' *Histories*. Tacitus reveals that an oath of loyalty was sworn anew each time a new ruler emerged.⁴⁶ But does this apply to Meleager? I think so. In his response to Meleager's speech, Telamon recalls an episode that took place before Argo set sail from Greece in which *all* the Argonauts—Meleager included—chose Hercules as their leader (3.699–701):

> Non hi tum flatus, non ista superbia dictis,
> litore cum patrio, iam uela petentibus austris,
> cunctus ad Alciden uersus fauor.

> Not such boasting was there then, no words so arrogant when on our country's shore, when the south winds already wooed the sails, the favor of all was turned toward Alcides.

Valerius' Telamon here refers to an episode that is narrated in Book 1 of Apollonius' *Argonautica* (1.332–362), in which the Argonauts initially vote for Heracles to be leader of the expedition, an honor which he declines and which he instead grants to Jason. As is well known this event is omitted from the pre-launch activities narrated in Valerius' *Argonautica*. However, I am in favor of following Lovatt, who suggests that this leadership vote did in fact take place, but 'off camera,' as it were.⁴⁷ Consequently, since Meleager had previously proclaimed Hercules to be his favorite, despite his personal animosity toward the man, his vow of allegiance to Jason as soon as Hercules is gone is evocative of the insincerity and swift mutability of *fides* during the recent civil war. As Tacitus puts it, the civil war was a time when "Nowhere was there any loyalty or affection. Fear and necessity made men shift now to one side, now to the other" (*nusquam fides aut amor; metu ac necessitate huc illuc mutabantur*, *Hist.* 1.76.1).

There are several other points of contact between Valerius' Meleager and Tacitus' Primus. For instance, one of the ways that Primus tried to ingratiate himself with the troops was to offer them higher positions, positions that were once held by men who had either deserted or died. A good example of this is found at *Hist.* 3.49.2: "To inspire the soldiers with a spirit of license, he offered to the rank and file the places of the centurions who had fallen" (*utque licentia militem imbueret interfectorum centurionum ordines legionibus offerebat*). This is similar to what Valerius' Meleager does: sandwiched between the suggestion that Hercules has

---

46 See Campbell (1984) 25–32.
47 See Lovatt (2014) 220. See also Manuwald (2015) 252.

either deserted (3.677–678) or died (688–689), is a call by Meleager for the Argonauts to replace their lost comrade by becoming a kind of 'collective Hercules' (679–681). Those who once openly recognized their inferiority to Hercules by unanimously voting him their captain are now prodded by Meleager to believe that they are his equals. In fact Meleager, like a good demagogue, is here telling the Argonauts exactly what they want to hear. For before Meleager's speech, we learn that the men are now inclined to believe that they are *not* inferior to Hercules (3.629–631): "They say that their large company would lack only one, that their blood is as noble, and that their right hands are as strong" (*unum tanto afore coetu / nec minus in sese generis dextrasque potentes / esse ferunt*).

Other resemblances between the Valerian Meleager and the Tacitean Primus I mention only in passing in the interest of brevity: for instance, Meleager's rivalry with Hercules is similar to Primus' rivalry with Mucianus (see *Hist*. 3.53, 4.11, 4.39, 4.68, 4.80).[48] Moreover, both Primus and Meleager are depicted as men of action who champion *festinatio* ("haste"; on Primus, see *Hist*. 3.1–3 and 3.52–53; on Meleager, see *Arg*. 3.649–689). And finally both men are marked by *superbia* ("arrogance"; on Primus, see *Hist*. 3.49 and 4.80; on Meleager, see *Arg*. 1.434–435, with Shelton (1971) 26–27).

Of course, Meleager's arguments win the day, as he manages to persuade the Argonauts that they should set sail without further ado. The behavior of the Argonauts as a group throughout the episode is also interesting. Although they initially miss Hercules terribly (3.601–603), after hearing Meleager's words they are incited to depart without him (690–691). And yet, after Telamon makes one final plea for delay, the men are again reduced to grief and tears, even as they leave without Hercules (715–725). Thus I suggest that the Argonauts are depicted as a 'fickle mob'—a staple of Roman political discourse—primed for manipulation by an ambitious and opportunistic demagogue like Meleager. Valerius is certainly not opposed to such anachronistic Romanizing tendencies: for example, he depicts the populace of Iolcus as a "fickle mob" (*populum ... leuem*) at 1.71, a passage whose Roman coloring is noted by Zissos.[49] The Argonauts thus possess the protean loyalties characteristic of the *uulgus* ("crowd") in Roman political discourse, as they waver back and forth in response to the speeches of Meleager and Telamon.

So it appears that recent history provides a productive intertext for some of the formal aspects of *Arg*. 3.598–725. But there are some interesting complica-

---

48 On Primus and Mucianus, see also Ash (1999) 162–163.
49 See Zissos (2008) 123.

tions, even beyond the question of how precise one ought to be when historicizing Valerius' poem.⁵⁰ For example, as noted previously Valerius' Meleager is partially modeled on Vergil's Drances in *Aeneid* 11. This same Vergilian character has also been seen as an important model for Tacitus' Primus.⁵¹ This raises the possibility that Valerius' Meleager and Tacitus' Primus are similar at least partly because they both descend from Vergil's Drances.

Moreover, is it possible that Tacitus, in an act of combinatorial imitation, also used Valerius' Meleager as a model for his Primus? After all, combinatorial imitation is a hallmark of Vergil's epic successors, as Hardie has shown, and Joseph demonstrates that Tacitus too is an 'epic successor' of sorts.⁵² Unsurprisingly, Tacitus' usage of Valerius' *Argonautica* is largely uncharted territory, but at least a few critics have attempted to navigate these waters.⁵³ For example, Ash has suggested that Tacitus made use of Valerius' description of the Sarmatians' fighting style.⁵⁴ Indeed, at times the texts are strikingly similar. A fairly well-known case of this can be seen at *Hist.* 3.74.1, where Tacitus' *aramque posuit casus suos in marmore expressam* ("and [Domitian] built an altar on which his escape was represented in marble") appears to be modelled on *Arg.* 1.398–399, where of Phalerus it is said *casusque tuos expressa, Phalere, / arma geris* ("and on your arms, Phalerus, is stamped the picture of your fortune"). The proximity of these two passages, especially the remarkable usage of *casus* in each text, was enough to prompt both Courtney and Woodman to see here direct usage of Valerius by Tacitus, and I am inclined to agree with them.⁵⁵ In fact, I think their view can be strengthened by considering the *contexts* of each passage. In Valerius, we hear of objects—weapons—decorated with a scene of the salvation of Phalerus, whose father saved him from death by snake strangulation when he was younger (1.399–401).⁵⁶ The Tacitean passage likewise describes an object—an altar—that is decorated with a scene of salvation, namely Domitian's escape from near death on the Capitoline during the fighting in Rome in AD 69 (*Hist.* 3.74). So thankful was he

---

50 On this issue, see Bernstein (2014) 154–155.
51 See Ash (2007) 337 and Joseph (2012) 129, n. 28.
52 See Hardie (1989) and Joseph (2012).
53 On Tacitus' use of Silius' *Punica*, see Woodman (2009b) 37 and Manolaraki/Augoustakis (2012). On Tacitus' use of Statius' epics, see Woodman (2009b) 36–37.
54 See Ash (2010) 148.
55 See Courtney (2004) 428 and Woodman (2009b) 37. On the use of *casus* in the Valerian passage, see also Kleywegt (2005) 233, Galli (2007) 224, and Zissos (2008) 268, each of whom notes the parallel in Tacitus. For a similar use of *casus* at *Arg.* 2.654, see Poortvliet (1991) 320.
56 On this myth, see Zissos (2008) 267.

at being saved that Domitian built a *sacellum* ("small shrine") to Jupiter Conservator and later a larger temple to Jupiter Custos on the spot where he hid out.[57] Thus in both passages we are dealing with salvation from impending death and the subsequent memorialization of this salvation by way of artistic representation.

I would like to propose yet another example of Tacitus' usage of Valerius' epic, one that takes us back to the latter's depiction of Meleager. Of Primus' haughtiness Tacitus refers to *superbia uiri aequalium quoque, adeo superiorum intolerantis*, "the arrogance of a man who could not endure even his equals, to say nothing of his superiors" (*Hist.* 4.80.1). Compare Valerius' description of Meleager at *Arg.* 3.648–649 as someone who is "never yielding to his equals or having a thought for his leaders" (*haud ullis umquam superabilis aequis / rectorumue memor*). In my view, this is a very close verbal echo, with Tacitus' wording being used of a character who, as we have seen, has much in common with Valerius' Meleager. However, it should be noted that this echo may be a mirage. Seeing Valerius' text as saying the same thing about Meleager that Tacitus says about Primus requires adopting Wagner's reading of the Valerian passage, whereby *aequis* equals *aequalibus* ("peers") and *rectorum* is taken as the genitive of *rector* ("leader"). Spaltenstein objects to this reading, and instead takes both *aequis* and *rectorum* as neuter plural; he thus interprets the passage as having a strong moral charge.[58] Regarding the interpretation of *rectorum*, however, it would be more natural for Valerius, if he wished to refer to Meleager's disregard for "rectitude," to have used the singular *recti*. At any rate, it may be that the closeness between Tacitus' Primus and Valerius' Meleager is due not only to recent history as intertext, but also to Tacitus' *Histories* as intertext. Such factors make historicizing Valerius' poem far from unproblematic.[59]

---

57 On these structures, see Darwall-Smith (1996) 110–112, 179. For a recent attempt to locate the sites of these sacred buildings, see Arata (2010).
58 See Spaltenstein (2004) 184. He is followed in this by Liberman (1997) 107 and Manuwald (2015) 242–243.
59 Two other examinations of Valerius and Tacitus, neither of which sees direct usage of the *Argonautica* by the historian, are worth noting here as well: on Tacitus and Valerius sharing a uniquely 'Flavian experience' of tyranny and thus depicting tyrants in similar ways, see Baier (2017). On Valerius as a 'Tacitean' author more broadly, see Buckley (2018).

5 Conclusion

I hope to have revealed the complex intertextuality of *Argonautica* 3.598–725, a sequence whose divergences from Apollonius invite careful scrutiny. Allusions to Bacchylides, Vergil, and Ovid add richness and nuance to Meleager's verbal showdown with Telamon, while also linking the episode to some of the broader themes of Valerius' epic. I hope also to have shown how the formal aspects of this sequence lend themselves to a historicizing reading in which Hercules' sudden departure and Meleager's rivalrous attempt to gain ascendency within the group caused by it evoke the unsteady climate of the 'Year of the Four Emperors' and the protean nature of *fides* that characterized it. Moreover, I used my historicizing reading to point up some of the interesting complications that can arise when trying to use history as intertext: Valerius' Meleager may resemble a figure known from the pages of history like Antonius Primus, not only because both Tacitus and Valerius used Vergil's Drances as a model for these shady characters, but also because Tacitus may have used Valerius' Meleager himself as a model for Primus. Such considerations make historicizing Valerius' *Argonautica* a tricky process, but one that I believe must be undertaken if we are to understand fully the epic's uniquely *Flavian* intertextuality.

Bibliography

Adamietz, Joachim (1976), *Zur Komposition der* Argonautica *des Valerius Flaccus*, Munich.
Anderson, William S. (1972), *Ovid's* Metamorphoses: *Books 6–10*, Norman.
Arata, Francesco P. (2010), "Osservazioni sulla topografia sacra dell' 'Arx' capitolina", in: *MEFRA* 122, 117–146.
Ash, Rhiannon (1999), *Ordering Anarchy: Armies and Leaders in Tacitus'* Histories, Ann Arbor.
Ash, Rhiannon (2007), *Tacitus,* Histories *Book II*, Cambridge.
Ash, Rhiannon (2010), "Rhoxolani Blues (Tacitus, *Histories* 1.79): Virgil's Scythian Ethnography Revisited", in: Miller/Woodman (2010) 141–154.
Austin, Roland G. (1977), *P. Vergili Maronis Aeneidos Liber Sextus*, Oxford.
Baier, Thomas (2017), "Anfang ohne Ende: Abgebrochene Kommunikation bei Valerius Flaccus", in: Schmitz et al. (2017) 199–220.
Bernstein, Neil W. (2008), *In the Image of the Ancestors: Narratives of Kinship in Flavian Epic*, Toronto.
Bernstein, Neil W. (2014), "*Romanas veluti saevissima cum legiones Tisiphone regesque movet*: Valerius Flaccus' *Argonautica* and the Flavian Era", in: Heerink/Manuwald (2014) 154–169.
Bernstein, Neil W. (2016), "Epic Poetry: Historicizing the Flavian Epics", in: Zissos (2016) 395–411.

Boyle, Anthony J. (ed.) (1990), *The Imperial Muse: Ramus Essays on Roman Literature of the Empire. II, Flavian Epicist to Claudian*, Bendigo.
Boyle, Anthony J./Dominik, William J. (eds.) (2003), *Flavian Rome: Culture, Image, Text*, Leiden.
Braund, David (1993), "Writing a Roman *Argonautica*: the historical dynamic", in: *Hermathena* 154, 11–17.
Buckley, Emma (2010), "War-epic for a New Era: Valerius Flaccus' *Argonautica*", in: Kramer/Reitz (2010) 431–455.
Buckley, Emma (2018), "Flavian Epic and Trajanic Historiography: Speaking into the Silence", in: König/Whitton (2018) 86–107.
Cairns, Douglas L. (2010), *Bacchylides, Five* Epinician Odes *(3, 5, 9, 11, 13)*, Cambridge.
Campbell, David A. (1982), *Greek Lyric Poetry*, Bristol.
Campbell, Brian J. (1984), *The Emperor and the Roman Army, 31 BC–AD 235*, Oxford.
Castelletti, Cristiano (2014), "A Hero with a Sandal and a Buskin: The Figure of Jason in Valerius Flaccus' *Argonautica*", in: Heerink/Manuwald (2014) 173–191.
Clauss, James J. (1993), *The Best of the Argonauts*, Berkeley, CA.
Courtney, Edward (2004), "The 'Greek' Accusative", in: *CJ* 99, 425–431.
Damon, Cynthia (2010), "Déjà vu or déjà lu? History as Intertext", in: *PLLS* 14, 375–388.
Darwall-Smith, Robin H. (1996), *Emperors and Architecture: A Study of Flavian Rome*, Brussels.
Davis, Martha (1990), "*Ratis Audax*: Valerius Flaccus' Bold Ship", in: Boyle (1990) 46–73.
Dominik, William J./Garthwaite, John/Roche, Paul A. (eds.) (2009), *Writing Politics in Imperial Rome*, Leiden.
DuQuesnay, Ian M. Le M./Woodman, Anthony J. (eds.) (2012), *Catullus: Poems, Books, Readers*, Cambridge.
Feldherr, Andrew (ed.) (2009), *The Cambridge Companion to the Roman Historians*, Cambridge.
Freyburger, Gérard (1986), *Fides: étude sémantique et religieuse depuis les origines jusqu'à l'époque augustéenne*, Paris.
Galli, Daniela (2007), *Valerii Flacci* Argonautica *I: Commento*, Berlin.
Gantz, Timothy (1993), *Early Greek Myth*, Baltimore.
Garson, Ronald W. (1963), "The Hylas Episode in Valerius Flaccus' *Argonautica*", in: *CQ* 13, 260–267.
Gransden, Kenneth W. (1991), *Virgil*, Aeneid *Book XI*, Cambridge.
Grossardt, Peter (2001), *Die Erzählung von Meleagros*, Leiden.
Harder, Annette/Regtuit, Remco F./Wakker, Gerry C. (eds.) (2000), *Apollonius Rhodius*, Leuven.
Hardie, Philip (1989), "Flavian Epicists on Virgil's Epic Technique", in: *Ramus* 18, 3–20.
Hardie, Philip/Chiarini, Gioachino (2015), *Ovidio: Metamorfosi Volume VI (Libri XIII–XV)*, Milan.
Heerink, Mark/Manuwald, Gesine (eds.) (2014), *Brill's Companion to Valerius Flaccus*, Leiden.
Hollis, Adrian S. (1970), *Ovid*, Metamorphoses *Book VIII*, Oxford.
Hopkinson, Neil (2000), *Ovid*, Metamorphoses *Book XIII*, Cambridge.
Horsfall, Nicholas (2013), *Virgil*, Aeneid 6: *A Commentary*, Berlin.
Hunter, Richard (1993), *The Argonautica of Apollonius: Literary Studies*, Cambridge.
Joseph, Timothy A. (2012), *Tacitus the Epic Successor: Virgil, Lucan, and the Narrative of Civil War in the* Histories, Leiden.
Kenney, Edward J./Chiarini, Gioachino (2011), *Ovidio*, Metamorfosi. *Volume IV (Libri VII–IX)*, Milan.
Kleywegt, Adrianus J. (1991), "Die 'Anderen' Argonauten", in: Korn/Tschiedel (1991) 225–237.
Kleywegt, Adrianus J. (2005), *Valerius Flaccus*, Argonautica, *Book 1: A Commentary*, Leiden.

König, Alice/Whitton, Christopher (eds.) (2018), *Roman Literature under Nerva, Trajan and Hadrian: Literary Interactions, AD 96–138*, Cambridge.
Korn, Matthias/Tschiedel, Hans J. (eds.) (1991), *Ratis omnia vincet*, Hildesheim.
Kramer, Norbert/Reitz, Christiane (eds.) (2010), *Tradition und Erneuerung: Mediale Strategien in der Zeit der Flavier*, Berlin.
Langen, Peter (1896–1897), *C. Valerii Flacci Setini Balbi Argonauticon Libri Octo*, Berlin.
Lefkowitz, Mary R. (1969), "Bacchylides' Ode 5: Imitation and Originality", in: *HSCP* 73, 45–96.
Levin, Donald N. (1971), *Apollonius'* Argonautica *Re-examined: The Neglected First and Second Books*, Leiden.
Liberman, Gauthier (ed.) (1997), *Valerius Flaccus*, Argonautiques, Chants I–IV, Paris.
Liberman, Gauthier (ed.) (2002), *Valerius Flaccus*, Argonautiques, Chants V–VIII, Paris.
Lovatt, Helen (2014), "Teamwork, Leadership and Group Dynamics in Valerius Flaccus' *Argonautica*", in: Heerink/Manuwald (2014) 211–228.
McNelis, Charles (2007), *Statius' Thebaid and the Poetics of Civil War*, Cambridge.
Manioti, Nikoletta (ed.) (2016), *Family in Flavian Epic*, Leiden.
Manolaraki, Eleni / Augoustakis, Antony (2012), "Silius Italicus and Tacitus on the Tragic Hero: The Case of Germanicus," in: Pagán (2012) 386–402.
Manuwald Gesine (2015), *Valerius Flaccus*, Argonautica Book III, Cambridge.
Miller, John F./Woodman, Anthony J. (eds.) (2010), *Latin Historiography and Poetry in the Early Empire*, Leiden.
Moore, Clifford H. (1925), *Tacitus*, The Histories, Books I–III, Cambridge, MA.
Morgan, Gwyn (2006), *69 A.D.: The Year of Four Emperors*, Oxford.
Mori, Anatole (2008), *The Politics of Apollonius Rhodius'* Argonautica, Cambridge.
Mozley, John H. (1934), *Valerius Flaccus*, Argonautica, Cambridge, MA.
Nelis, Damien P. (2012), "Callimachus in Verona: Catullus and Alexandrian Poetry", in: DuQuesnay/Woodman (2012) 1–28.
Newman, John K. (2001), "The Golden Fleece. Imperial Dream", in: Papanghelis/Rengakos (2001) 309–340.
O'Gorman, Ellen (2009), "Intertextuality and Historiography", in: Feldherr (2009) 231–242.
Pagán, Victoria E. (ed.) (2012), *A Companion to Tacitus*, Malden, MA.
Papanghelis, Theodore D./Rengakos, Antonios (eds.) (2001), *A Companion to Apollonius Rhodius*, Leiden.
Poortvliet, Harm M. (1991), *C. Valerius Flaccus*, Argonautica, Book II: A Commentary, Amsterdam.
Schenk, Peter (1986), *Die Zurücklassung des Herakles: Ein Beispiel der epischen Kunst des Valerius Flaccus (Argonautica III.598–725)*, Mainz.
Schmitz, Christine/Telg, Jan genannt Kortmann/Jöne, Angela (eds.) (2017), *Anfänge und Enden: narrative Potentiale des antiken und nachantiken Epos*, Heidelberg.
Shelton, James E. (1971), *A Narrative Commentary on the* Argonautica *of Valerius Flaccus*, PhD Dissertation, Vanderbilt University.
Spaltenstein, Francois (2004), *Commentaire des* Argonautiques *de Valérius Flaccus (livres 3, 4, et 5)*, Brussels.
Stephens, Susan A. (2000), "Writing Epic for the Ptolemaic Court", in: Harder *et al.* (2000) 195–215.
Stover, Tim (2012), *Epic and Empire in Vespasianic Rome: A New Reading of Valerius Flaccus'* Argonautica, Oxford.
Stover, Tim (2016), "*Opibusque ultra ne crede paternis*: Fathers and Sons on the Wrong Side of History in Valerius' *Argonautica*", in: Nikoletta Manioti (2016) 14–40.

Tatum, James (1984), "Allusion and Interpretation in *Aeneid* 6.440–76", in: *AJPh* 105, 434–452.
Tatum, Jeffrey W. (2016), "Why is Valerius Flaccus a Quindecimvir?" in: *CQ* 66, 239–244.
Taylor, Ruth P. (1994), "Valerius' Flavian *Argonautica*", in: *CQ* 44, 212–235.
Toohey, Peter (1993), "Jason, Pallas and Domitian in Valerius Flaccus' *Argonautica*", in: *ICS* 18, 191–201.
Woodman, Anthony J. (ed.) (2009a), *The Cambridge Companion to Tacitus*, Cambridge.
Woodman, Anthony (2009b), "Tacitus and the Contemporary Scene", in: Woodman (2009a) 31–43.
Zissos, Andrew (2003), "Spectacle and Elite in the *Argonautica* of Valerius Flaccus", in: Boyle/Dominik (2003) 659–684.
Zissos, Andrew (2008), *Valerius Flaccus'* Argonautica: *Book 1*, Oxford.
Zissos, Andrew (2009), "Navigating Power: Valerius Flaccus' *Argonautica*", in: Dominik et al. (2009) 351–366.
Zissos, Andrew (ed.) (2016), *A Companion to the Flavian Age of Imperial Rome*, Malden, MA.

Damien Nelis
Allusive Technique in the *Argonautica* of Valerius Flaccus

It is generally accepted by scholars working on Valerius Flaccus that his two main models are Apollonius Rhodius and Vergil.[1] There also seems to be a consensus that Apollonius Rhodius was a key model for Vergil when he was composing the *Aeneid*.[2] Assuming widespread agreement on these two points, my aim in this paper is a straightforward one: to offer an example of the kind of analysis that is necessary if we are to deepen our understanding and appreciation of one crucial aspect of the intertextual strategies at work in Valerius' *Argonautica*. When reading this text, we must keep constantly in mind the profound and pervasive influence of the *Argonautica* of Apollonius Rhodius on Vergil's *Aeneid*. When we do so, it becomes clear that Valerius' narrative is based on a continuous process of double or two-tier allusion to both Apollonian and Vergilian models. Valerius read the *Aeneid* with a sharp eye for reference to Apollonius and he also read Apollonius in full awareness of the importance of that poem as a key model for the *Aeneid*.[3] In what follows, I offer a study of one section of Valerius' poem as an example of how to go about reading it as a reaction to Vergil's heavily Argonautic *Aeneid*. The presence of constant, simultaneous reference to both Vergil and Apollonius will be demonstrated in terms of scenic structure and verbal parallels.[4] As a result, a key aspect of Valerius' epic technique will be illustrated.[5]

---

[1] See, for example, Hershkowitz (1998) 35–37, Hutchinson (2013) 170–176, Deremetz (2014) 53–55, van der Schuur (2014). For a salutary reminder that Homer must also remain in the picture see Zissos (2002); see also Schenk (1999) 135–138. Feeney (1991) 315–337 is an excellent demonstration of the sophistication of Valerius' intertextual and generic poetics.
[2] See, for example, Hunter (1993) chapter 7, Nelis (2001) *passim*.
[3] For this methodology in relation to the interpretation of Flavian poetry see the important paper by Cowan (2014). Hardie (1989) and (1993), Dewar (1991), and Smolenaars (1994) are landmark studies of the intensity and sophistication of Flavian intertextuality.
[4] I am fully aware that Valerius also uses many other predecessors as sources and models, as discussed recently, for example, in Heerink/Manuwald (2014) chapters 15–17 and by Manuwald (2015) 16–19. But I will focus on Apollonius and Vergil in the firm belief that in the scenes I will be looking at it is the imitation of these two texts that provides the fundamental narrative structure within which verbal allusion to other authors must be situated and interpreted.
[5] This chapter reworks and builds on material from a forthcoming paper in which I offer a detailed analysis of the opening of *Argonautica* 5 in terms of both narrative structure and verbal allusion. Hardie (1989) 3–9 and (1993) 83–87 are two short but fundamental contributions to our understanding of Valerius' use of the *Aeneid*. Nordera (1969) = Nordera (2016) is an excellent

This rather obvious, mechanical and monotonous approach seems worth adopting for two reasons. First, I have not found anywhere in the bibliography on Valerius Flaccus an analysis that takes into account consistently his elaboration of a cohesive system of allusion both to Apollonius and to the *Aeneid*'s reworking of Apollonius' *Argonautica*. Second, despite the many excellent commentaries that we now have on Valerius' poem, I believe that the intrinsic selectivity of that scholarly genre has not allowed commentators to do full justice to the intertextual complexities of his poem. These works have taught us much and contain a great deal of accurate and useful information. They have laid the foundations for the new generation of commentaries with a focus limited to intertextuality that is now a major scholarly requirement, if our understanding of this fascinating poem is to progress in the years to come.

At the start the fifth book of the *Argonautica* two members of the crew, Idmon and Tiphys, die, during the stay with Lycus in the land of the Mariandyni. After their burial, the Argonauts move on along the southern Black Sea towards the River Phasis, the goal of their voyage. Once arrived there, the series of events that will lead to the climactic meeting with Colchian king Aietes and the request for the Golden Fleece begins to unfold. The basic content and order of events in this section of Valerius' poem may be summarized as follows:

Valerius Flaccus, *Arg.* 5.1–328
START OF A NEW BOOK
- 5.1–72: death and burial of Idmon and of Tiphys; Erginus chosen as helmsman; departure.
- 5.73–176: voyage along the southern coast of the Black Sea; the Argonauts sail past the Chalybes and Prometheus.
- 5.177–216: evening and arrival in the Phasis; prayer of Jason; Argonauts disembark.
- 5.217–277: invocation of a Muse; the situation in Colchis.
- 5.278–295: divine intervention: Juno and Minerva.
- 5.296–328: Argonauts make their way to the city and palace of Aietes.

This whole section of narrative names many of the same places and recounts most of the same events that occur in the corresponding sections of Apollonius Rhodius'

---

study of the subtlety of Valerius' allusive art on the purely verbal level; see also, from a large bibliography, Galli (2007) 19–23, Zissos (2008) xxxiv–xxxvi, Ganiban (2014), all with bibliography. On the structure of the *Argonautica* see Venini (1971), Adamietz (1976).

Argonautica 2. In that poem, we also learn of the stay in the land of the Mariandyni and the deaths of Idmon and Tiphys, the journey along the southern coast of the Black Sea, the arrival in the Phasis and the events leading up to the encounter with Aietes. Apollonius' version of these events may be summarized as follows:

Apollonius Rhodius, *Argon.* 2.720–3.212
- 2.720–900: arrival in the land of the Mariandyni; death and burial of Idmon and of Tiphys; Ancaeus chosen as helmsman; departure.
- 2.901–1259: voyage along southern coast of Black Sea; Argonauts sail past Prometheus.
- 2.1260–1285: night and arrival in the Phasis; prayer of Jason; speech of Ancaeus; Argo at anchor.

START OF A NEW BOOK
- 3.1–5: invocation of the Muse Erato.
- 3.6–166: divine intervention: Hera, Athena, Aphrodite and Eros.
- 3.167–212: Argonauts make their way to the city and palace of Aietes.

The similarities between the two narratives are obvious, and they have long been appreciated by scholars working on Valerius Flaccus' poem.[6] What has been less well understood is that this same section of the *Argonautica* of Apollonius Rhodius had already been systematically reworked by Vergil at the opening of *Aeneid* 7, where we have the death of Caieta, the voyage past Circe's island, the arrival in the Tiber, the invocation of Erato and the account of recent events in Latium. Subsequently, comparison with the summary of *both* the Valerian and Apollonian narrative presented above reveals the main similarities with *Aeneid* 7.[7] These are, in order of appearance in Vergil: the presence of a book division, the death and burial of a comrade, the motifs of departure and of arrival in a river

---

[6] See, for example, Harmand (1898) 5, Langen (1896) on 5.73; the presentation of the main scenic parallels between the two narratives by Soubiran (2002) 23–27 is particularly useful.
[7] Mehmel (1934) 56 is fully aware of the links between the opening of *Argonautica* 5 and *Aeneid* 7, but does not bring Apollonius into the picture. Schetter (1959) comes closest to grasping the interrelations between the three texts, but focuses only on a couple of details and does not develop a broader argument; he is followed by Adamietz (1976) 66–68, but he studies only scenic parallels and does not discuss verbal connections. Schenk (1999) 135–136 is aware of the importance for Valerius of linked passages in Apollonius and Vergil, but, like Schetter and Adamietz, does not develop the point. van der Schuur (2014) is an insightful and important discussion of the opening scene of *Argonautica* 5; see also Barich (2014) 35–47. See Nelis (2001) 255–282 for the full details of Vergil's use of Apollonius in the opening scenes of *Aeneid* 7.

mouth, and the invocation of a Muse at a key juncture in the narrative, all of which may be summarized thus:

Vergil, *Aen.* 7.1–285
START OF NEW BOOK
- 7.1–7: death and burial of Caieta; departure.
- 7.8–24: voyage along the coast; Trojans pass Circe.
- 7.25–36: dawn and arrival in Tiber.
- 7.37–106: invocation of the Muse Erato and the situation in Latium.
- 7.107–147: the Trojans disembark; prayer of Aeneas; sacrifices.
- 7.148–285: Trojans make their way to the city and palace of Latinus.

This broad-brush presentation of the basic narrative parallels between the three poems will now be used as the basis for a more detailed scene-by-scene analysis. Obviously, within the scope of a single chapter, it will not be able to provide a fully detailed study of every aspect of every section. But even a selective approach will, I hope, reveal the essential aspects of Valerian technique. Having already examined elsewhere the first episode of book 5 and the connections between Valerius' version of the death and burial of both Idmon and Tiphys and the death and burial of Caieta in Vergil, I will begin my analysis in this chapter from *Argonautica* 5.63.[8]

1 *Argonautica* 5.63–72: Erginus Chosen as Helmsman; Departure

The events recounted in this passage correspond to Apollonius *Argonautica* 2.858–900, which is thus obviously contracted in the process. In Apollonius' version the Argonauts fall into profound despair after the deaths of Idmon and Tiphys (κατήμυσαν δ' ἀχέεσσιν / θυμόν, *Argon*. 2.862–863; their hearts were downcast in distress), and in preference to Erginus, Nauplius and Euphemus it is Ancaeus who is chosen to replace Tiphys, following the intervention of Hera and a conversation between Peleus and Jason. Valerius omits almost all of this detail. He retains only the despair of the whole crew after the deaths of their two comrades (*maesti omnes*, "downcast were all", Val. Fl. 5.63), and he then has Argo's

---

[8] See Nelis (forthcoming). The diagram at the end of this paper attempts to present the main interrelations between the three texts as clearly as possible.

prophetic oak chose Erginus as the new pilot, in preference to the volunteers Ancaeus and Nauplius. The use here of the motif of Argo's talkative beam and the variation in the choice of Erginus rather than the Apollonian Ancaeus as the new pilot probably reflect the fact Valerius is following an alternative version of the story at this point.[9] Already, therefore, as examples of imitative strategies, we can see in operation in these few verses similarity of epic action giving rise to verbal parallels, narrative contraction, and variation on the Apollonian version of events because of probable use of an alternative version of the Argo's voyage.

As far as Vergil is concerned, it is the death of the Trojan pilot Palinurus that corresponds most closely to the Argonauts' loss of Tiphys.[10] But Vergil links this death, which he places at the end of his fifth book, to the demise of two other characters, Misenus (at *Aen.* 6.149–152, 162–235) and Caieta (at *Aen.* 7.1–4).[11] It is the death of the latter, by its position as the opening scene of *Aeneid* 7, that in terms of narrative structure provides the model for the deaths of the two Argonauts Idmon and Tiphys at the opening of *Argonautica* 5.[12] On one level, Valerius has replaced Vergil's three dead comrades with two of his own, following Apollonius closely. On another level, he has combined both Palinurus (death of pilot) and Caieta (death and burial at book opening) in his Tiphys (death and burial of pilot at book opening), also following Vergil closely. As we shall see throughout this paper, Valerius' narrative is inextricably connected to both models in this way.

When the Argonauts leave Lycus and sail away after burying Idmon and Tiphys and choosing their new pilot (Val. Fl. 5.69–72), Valerius carefully shows that this departure scene corresponds to the departure at *Aeneid* 7.7b–9, immediately following the burial of Caieta, as well as to the Argonauts' departure from the Mariandyni in Apollonius (*Argon.* 2.899–900). Valerius' Argo sails away into a clear night under the guidance of its new pilot (Val. Fl. 5.69b–71):

> ... primo laetus sic tempore rector
> ingreditur cursus. etenim dat candida certam
> nox Helicen.

---

9 See Spaltenstein (2004) 402–403; more generally, see also Zissos (1999).
10 See Nelis (2001) 221–223.
11 On the connections between Palinurus, Misenus and Caieta and on these three Vergilian figures as a three-way distribution of the single figure of Elpenor see Knauer (1979[2]) 135–139, Knauer (1964) 66. See also Kyriakidis (1998).
12 See Mehmel (1934) 56, Spaltenstein (2004) 389, Nelis (forthcoming).

> ... so joyfully does the steersman start on his first voyage; for a bright night shows Helice clear and true.
>
> (Mozley)

There is nothing similar in Apollonius at the moment of departure after the deaths of Idmon and Tiphys. Instead, these words recall *Aeneid* 7.7–9:

> ..., tendit iter velis portumque relinquit.
> aspirant aurae in <u>noctem</u> nec <u>candida</u> <u>cu</u>rsus
> <u>luna</u> negat.
>
> ..., sails forth on his way, and leaves the haven. Breeze blow into the night, and the Moon, shining bright, smiles on their voyage.
>
> (Fairclough/Goold)

Both poets describe a burial followed by departure and sailing in a brightly moonlit sea. Vergil's *candida ... luna* ("bright moon") becomes Valerius' *candida ... nox* ("bright night"), with *candida* in precisely the same metrical position and both the related nouns *nox* and *luna* also in first position in the following hexameter.[13] Vergil's *nec ... negat* becomes simply *dat*. Also, as well as repeating the noun *cursus*, Valerius uses a clausula <u>*candida*</u> <u>*ce*</u>*rtam* that echoes Vergil's <u>*candida*</u> <u>*cu*</u>*rsus*.[14]

In addition to these verbal similarities, it is essential to consider whether on the structural level Valerius' debt to Vergil is even more obvious. Events that occur just after the middle of the second book of Apollonius' *Argonautica* are used by Vergil for the opening of *Aeneid* 7. Valerius then recounts the same Argonautic events but follows Vergil in placing them at the opening of *Argonautica* 5.[15] Structural and verbal similarities obviously go hand in hand, but this may well be a case when the former are more easily visible than the latter.

---

13 Vergil is the first to combine *luna* and *candida* in surviving Latin. Subsequently, Propertius (2.15.1) and Ovid (*Her.* 16.320) use them together in the erotic context of a memorable night of love-making. Langen (1896) on 5.70 notes the originality and audacity of Valerius' combination of *candida* and *nox* to describe sailing in a night brightened by moonlight; it should be appreciated as an elegant variation on a marked Vergilian original.
14 If Valerius by any chance read *cursum* at 7.8 (this is the reading of R, for example) then the similarity is slightly increased to <u>*cu*</u>*rsum* / <u>*ce*</u>*rtam*.
15 This was the essential insight of Schetter 1959, who used it to propose that *Argonautica* 5 must therefore be the first book of the second half of the epic and that Valerius therefore planned his poem in 8 books. See also Nelis (forthcoming), developing Schetter's basic point. That Valerius did indeed plan his book in eight books rather then in ten or twelve now seems to be generally accepted: see, for example, Stover (2012) 25, Manuwald (2015) 6.

2 *Argonautica* 5.73–176: Voyage along Southern Coast of Black Sea; The Argonauts Sail Past the Chalybes and Prometheus

When Valerius describes the next leg of the voyage of the Argo along the southern coastline of the Black Sea, he follows very closely Apollonius' account of the journey through exactly the same waters at *Argon.* 2.901–1259. Valerius has the Argonauts sail past the Acherusian headland and pass by the mouth of the River Callichorus, describing its Bacchic associations (Val. Fl. 5.973–981). He does so in close imitation of Apollonius, who mentions in order the River Acheron and then the River Callichorus and its connection with Dionysiac rituals (*Argon.* 2.901–910).[16] Valerius then mentions in order the tomb of Sthenelus, Crobialus, the river Parthenium, Cromna, Cytorus, Erythia, Carambis and Sinope, where the Argonauts pick up Autolycus, Phlogius and Deilion, stranded comrades of Hercules (Val. Fl. 5.82–119).[17] All of this resembles Apollonius' account, which mentions the tomb of Sthenelus, the river Parthenius, Sesamus, Erythini, Crobialus, Cromna, Carambis and Sinope, where Deilion, Autolycus and Phlogius are rescued (*Argon.* 2.911–961). Both poets next mention the rivers Halys, Iris, Thermodon and the land of the Amazons (Val. Fl. 5.120–139 and *Argon.* 2.962–1000a). Next in both voyages comes the land of the Chalybes (Val. Fl. 5.140–146 and *Argon.* 2.1000b–1008), and it is at this point that Vergil again comes into the picture.

In his version Apollonius devotes seven verses to describing the Chalybes, workers of iron who live in perpetual smoky darkness. Then, after mentioning the journey past the rock of Jupiter Genetaeus, the Tibarenes, the Mossynians, the stopover on the island of Ares, the island of Philyra, the Macrones, the Becheirians, the Sapeires and Byzeres and (*Argon.* 2.1009–1245), he describes how the Argonauts hear the cries of Prometheus, as his liver is eaten by the eagle (*Argon.* 2.1256–1257):

---

16 On the connection between the Acherusian headland and the River Acheron see Wijsman (1996) on 73.
17 At Val. Fl. 5.107–108, *alta Ca̲rambis / ra̲ditur* ("closely skim they high Carambis") refers to Aen. 7.10, *proxima Ci̲rcaeae ra̲duntur litora terrae* ("the next shores thy skirt are those of Circe's realm"). Where Apollonius and Valerius mention many places passed by after leaving behind the burial place of Idmon and Tiphys, Vergil contracts drastically and names only one after the departure from Caieta, that is the abode of Circe.

δηρὸν δ' οὐ μετέπειτα πολύστονον ἄιον αὐδὴν
ἧπαρ ἀνελκομένοιο Προμηθέος ...

Not long thereafter, they heard the tormented cry of Prometheus as his liver was being torn out.

(Race)

Next comes the arrival in the Phasis and the end of the book (*Argon.* 2.1260–1278). This whole passage is the model for Vergil's description of how the Trojans, after leaving Caieta, sail along the coast of Italy towards the Tiber and in doing so pass Circe's island, whence they too hear noises coming from the nearby coastline, in the form of roaring animals (*Aen.* 7.15):[18]

hinc <u>exaudiri gemitus</u> iraeque leonum.

From these shores could be heard the angry growls of lions.

(Fairclough/Goold)

Valerius clearly spotted this particular Vergilian reference of Apollonius. On two occasions he works the detail of sounds coming from the shore into his narrative of the closing stages of the Argo's voyage (cf. also Valerius at 2.579–583). First, he describes the way in which the Argonauts hear the labours of the Chalybes as they skirt their coastline during the night (Val. Fl. 5.140–141):

nocte sub extrema clausis telluris ab antris
pervigil <u>auditur</u> Chalybum labor.

At the dead of night they hear from the closed caverns of the earth the unresting labour of the Chalybes.

(Mozley)

Then, after rapidly mentioning the journey past the rock of Genetaean Jupiter, the Tibarenes, the Mossynians, the Macrones, the Byzeres and the island of Philyra (Val. Fl. 5.147–153), he too describes how the Argonauts hear the roars of Prometheus as his liver is eaten (Val. Fl. 5.168–170):

tum <u>gemitu</u> propiore chalybs densusque revulsis
rupibus <u>audiri</u> montis labor et grave Titan
vociferans ...

---

18 See Schetter (1959) 301, n.1, Blänsdorf (1982) 88–89, Nelis (2001) 261–262.

> Then as the noise grew nearer the sound of the iron and the rending of the crags, and the manifold travail of the mountain is heard, and the loud clamour of Prometheus ...
>
> (Mozley)

Pointing out the double reuse of Vergil's *exaudiri* in Valerius' *auditur* and *audiri* may give rise to a number of possible reactions. Among the polite ones is the objection that the very banality of the verb means that a recognizable verbal echo here is impossible. A second objection involves agreement that there is here a verbal parallel worth recording but certainty that it can have no interpretable literary significance. But it may be that these responses are based on false assumptions about the ways in which Valerius' audience made sense of his narrative. Much of the excellent work that has been done on verbal allusion in Latin poetry has been based on distinguishing verbal parallels created almost inevitably by generic conventions from deliberately referential allusions, and on proceeding to tease out the implications of the latter. Post-Vergilian epics have been one of the major beneficiaries of this scholarly trend, as what was long seen as slavish adherence to classical models has come to be appreciated as sophisticated manipulation of the dynamics of literary histories.[19] But it is also useful to look at the same question from a different perspective. To put it simply, what modern readers tend to do is to fix on a verbal parallel and then work upwards and outwards to establish a context for it. But ancient readers will also have done the opposite, first appreciating allusive connections with earlier epic poems on the scenic level and in terms of overarching narrative structures covering hundreds of verses and even whole books, and only then moving on to an appreciation of more detailed verbal connections.[20] For the passages in discussion here, we must imagine readers fully aware of the fact that on the scenic level the whole final section of the journey of Apollonius' Argonauts towards the Phasis in the second half of *Argonautica* 2 was reworked by Vergil for his version of the last leg of the Trojans' voyage towards the Tiber at the start of *Aeneid* 7 and that Valerius Flaccus is drawing in relatively obvious ways on both models simultaneously for his own description of the concluding section of the journey of his Argonauts towards the Phasis at the start of *Argonautica* 5. When allied to this knowledge of the allusive force of individual scenes and wider narrative structures, the verbal similarities fall neatly into place. And as Valerius' narrative continues, we can trace exactly

---

19 For insightful discussion of these matters, from a huge bibliography, see Hinds (1998) chapter 2. See also Gervais (2017) 305 on the way in which study of allusion has dominated recent work on Flavian epic.
20 See Knauer (1964) 67, Knauer (1979²) 145–147; also Hinds (1998) 100–104.

the same process of double allusion linked to both scenic and verbal similarities consistently at work.

3 *Argonautica* 5.177–216: Evening and Arrival in the Phasis. Prayer of Jason

The Argonauts finally arrive in the Phasis as the sun sets (Val. Fl. 5.177–180a). Jason orders his comrades to stop rowing, and as they come to a halt near the tomb of Phrixus he prays (Val. Fl. 5.184–209) and the crew disembarks (Val. Fl. 5.210b–216). At this climactic point, the conclusion of the first half of the epic narrative, the narrator stops to invoke a Muse (Val. Fl. 5.217–221). This whole scene repeats with some significant variations Apollonius' account of the same events: there, the Argonauts arrive at the Phasis during the night (*Argon.* 2. 1260–1270). The narrator then tells how Jason offers libations and prayers to the local divinities for support (*Argon.* 2.1271–1275). It is Ancaeus whose words are recorded in direct speech, as he ponders how the Argonauts are going to go about winning the Golden Fleece (*Argon.* 2.1277–1280). The Argonauts do not disembark immediately, but stay at anchor in a shady backwater, and then dawn arrives in the very last line of the book (*Argon.* 2.1285). Then comes in the first lines of book three the invocation of Erato, asking her to help tell the story of Jason and Medea and the winning of the Fleece (*Argon.* 3.1–5).

It is this Apollonian passage, as has long been recognized, that provides the crucial model for the scene that follows Vergil's Caieta and Circe episodes at the opening of *Aeneid* 7. There, sailing on along the coast (*Aen.* 7.23–24), the Trojans finally arrive at the mouth of the Tiber at dawn, and Aeneas orders the fleet to enter the shady river (*Aen.* 7.25–36). And so, exactly as before, Valerius in turn draws on this Vergilian imitation of Apollonius as well as on the Apollonian original. And as before also, while similarity of action at the scenic level is obvious, precise verbal reference is slight and relatively unobtrusive. By following the order of events in Valerius' version it is easy to trace the influence of both predecessors. First of all, the actual moment of arrival (Val. Fl. 5.177–182):

> Sol propius flammabat aquas extremaque fessis
> coeperat optatos iam lux ostendere Colchos,
> magnus ubi adversum spumanti Phasis in aequor
> ore ruit. cuncti pariter loca debita noscunt   180
> signaque commemorant emensasque ordine gentes
> dantque ratem fluvio.

The sun was kindling the waters with nearer ray, and the last light began to show the longed-for Colchis to the weary crew, where mighty Phasis with foaming mouth rushes to meet the ocean. Together all recognise their destined goal, and mark the signs and tell the tale of peoples they have passed, as they set their vessel for the river.

(Mozley)

These lines correspond to *Aeneid* 7.25–36, the Trojans' dawn arrival at the mouth of the Tiber and their entry into the river. Vergil's dawn (*Iamque rubescebat radiis mare et aethere ab alto / Aurora in roseis fulgebat lutea bigis*, "Now the sea was reddening with the rays of dawn, and from heaven's height the goddess of Dawn on her rosy chariot shone in saffron light", 7.25–26) becomes Valerius' evening (*Sol propius flammabat aquas extremaque fessis / coeperat optatos iam lux ostendere Colchos*, "The sun was kindling the waters with nearer ray, and the last night began to show the longed-for Colchians to the weary crew"), which thus recalls more closely Apollonius' arrival at night (ἐννύχιοι, *Argon.* 2.1260, "during the night"). When the Phasis is described as bursting into the sea (*magnus ubi adversum spumanti Phasis in aequor / ore ruit*, "where mighty Phasis with foaming mouth rushes to meet the ocean") Valerius recalls the mighty flow of Apollonius' Phasis at *Argonautica* 2.1265, ποταμοῖο μέγαν ῥόον ("the mighty current of the river").[21] But he also recalls the description of the Tiber at *Aeneid* 7.30–32a:[22]

> hunc inter fluvio Tiberinus amoeno
> verticibus rapidis et multa flauus harena
> in mare prorumpit.
>
> Through its midst the Tiber's lovely stream leaps forth to see in swirling eddies with his burden of golden sand.
>
> (Fairclough/Goold)

The only verbal resemblance occurs when Valerius' *in aequor ... ruit* seems to echo Vergil's *in mare prorumpit*. And when the Argo actually enters the river, Valerius' *dantque ratem fluvio* recalls Vergil's *fluvio succedit opaco* at *Aeneid* 7.36. Next, when Valerius says that the Argo is propulsed into the river by hard rowing (*dum prima gravi ductor subit ostia pulsu*, 184, "with heavy beat of oar") he again must have in mind Apollonius, *Argonautica* 2.1264–1265, where the Argonauts row (ἐρετμοῖς / εἰσέλασαν, "they quickly rowed into the mighty stream") into the strong current of the Phasis. Vergil has the Trojans rowing hard in very calm water *before* Aeneas sees the river mouth (*in lento luctantur marmore tonsae*, *Aen.* 7.28,

---

21 See Wijsman (1996) on 179.
22 See Spaltenstein (2004) 432.

"the oars toil slowly against the marble smoothness of the water"). Then, when Valerius describes how Jason sees on the shore some trees and the tomb of Phrixus (*populeos flexus tumulumque virentia supra / flumina cognati medio videt aggere Phrixi*, "he sees a ring of poplars and a mound that rises above the green river, the tomb of his kinsman Phrixus", Val. Fl. 5.185–186) he seems to be recalling a detail at *Aeneid* 7.29–30, where Aeneas spots on the shore a grove, *atque hic Aeneas ingentem ex aequore lucum / prospicit* ("At this moment Aeneas, looking from the sea, beholds a might forest"). Finally, when Jason orders (*iubet*, Val. Fl. 5.190) his comrades to stop the ship, it recalls both the moment when Apollonius' Jason orders (ἐκέλευσεν, *Argon*. 2.1282) his crew to rest at anchor in a shady backwater and when Aeneas orders (*imperat*, *Aen*. 7.36) the Trojans to turn into the shady river.[23] These detailed points of contact show how the three texts are almost inextricably linked. But they also help point up the moments when Valerius departs from his models. In order to appreciate this aspect, it will be useful to revisit briefly the overall structure of the three narratives in which this long-awaited moment of arrival at the end of a long voyage takes place.[24]

When Apollonius' Argonauts row into the stream of the Phasis, Jason pours libations in honour of Earth, local deities and the souls of the dead and prays for their support and a kindly reception (*Argon*. 2.1271–1275). Immediately, Ancaeus speaks to announce that they have indeed arrived at their goal and advise that it is time to plan how to go about winning the Golden Fleece (*Argon*. 2.1276–1280). Finally, following the advice of Argus, Jason orders the ship to be anchored in a shady backwater. There they spend the night and eventually dawn appears (*Argon*. 2.1281–1285). Vergil omits at this point in his narrative the libations, the

---

23 Two further references are worth mentioning here, because they involve use of *Aeneid* 7 and so help illustrate that this book in particular is very relevant to the appreciation of *Argonautica* 5. When at Val. Fl. 5.180 the Argonauts realize that they have reached their destination, Valerius expresses the idea thus: *cuncti pariter loca debita noscunt* ... ("together all recognize their destined goal"); commentators (e.g. Wijsman (1996) *ad loc.*) note the parallel with *Aen*. 7.120, *salve fatis mihi debita tellus* ("Hail land destined as my due"); cf. also the *debita moenia* ("destined walls") of *Aen*. 7.145. The verbal reuse plays a small part in the larger series of similarities that consistently links Valerius' depiction of Colchis to Vergil's Latium, the latter being already very systematically modelled on Apollonius' Colchis (on which see Nelis (2001) chapter 7) Next, when Valerius has Jason pray to Helle at Val. Fl. 5.198, for the reader who is aware of his use of the opening of *Aeneid* 7 at this point, the words *tu quoque nunc, tumulo nequiquam condita inani* ("Do you too now, vainly laid in an empty tomb") cannot fail to recall *Aen*. 7.1–6 *Tu quoque, ... aggere composito tumuli* ... ("You too, Caieta ... and the funeral mound was raised"); Valerius has transferred a detail from Caieta's tomb to that of Helle.
24 The diagram at the end of this paper attempts to present all the various links as clearly as possible.

prayer, a speech by the pilot and the anchoring of the ship. In a trimmed-down narrative he has the Trojans enter into and sail up the Tiber at dawn (*Aen.* 7.25–36). It is only later at *Aeneid* 7.102–106 that, after invoking the Muse Erato and describing the situation in Latium at the moment of the Trojans' arrival (*Aen.* 7.37–105a), he brings this excursus to a close and returns the attention to the arriving Trojans and describes their actual landing (*Aen.* 7.102–106):

> haec responsa patris Fauni monitusque silenti
> nocte datos non ipse suo premit ore Latinus,
> sed circum late volitans iam Fama per urbes
> Ausonias tulerat, cum Laomedontia pubes   105
> gramineo ripae religavit ab aggere classem.

> This answer of his father Faunus, and the warning he gave in the silent night, Latinus keeps not shut within his own lips; but Rumour, flitting far and wide, had already borne the tidings through the Ausonian cities when the sons of Laomedon moored their ships to the river's grassy bank.
>
> (Fairclough/Goold)

After this, at *Aeneid* 7.107–147 the Trojans disembark, prepare a meal (during which the incident of the 'eating of the tables' takes place) and then Aeneas prays to various gods, including the *genius loci* and Earth (*genium loci primamque deorum / Tellurem*, *Aen.* 7.136–137; cf. Γαίῃ τ' ἐνναέταις τε θεοῖς, "in honour of Earth, the indigenous gods", at *Argon.* 2.1273). This prayer is immediately greeted by an omen involving a triple peal of thunder and a bright light in the sky, signs that the Trojans take as favourable, before setting to feasting more heartily (*Aen.* 7.141–147). It is obvious that Vergil has here distributed Apollonian detail over two separate scenes. Where Apollonius has arrival at night, prayers, anchorage and dawn all together, Vergil has dawn and arrival first and then, only after the innovation of Erato and a lengthy excursus about recent events in Latium, the landing and the prayers. And so the obvious question arises, how does Valerius react to this Vergilian variation on Apollonius? As we shall see, he draws on both models in constructing his own narrative.

In order, Valerius describes the setting of the sun, the entry into the river, libations and a prayer by Jason, an omen, and a meal. Then he breaks off to invoke a Muse, whom he addresses only as *dea* (Val. Fl. 5.217). In all of this he follows more closely the order of events in Apollonius. When we turn attention to the verbal parallels, we find, exactly as before, that the level of verbal similarity is relatively slight. When Valerius's Jason orders his crew to tie up the ship's cable (*sistere tum socios iubet atque hinc prima ligari / vincula*, "Then he bids the rowers stop and here first make fast the cables", Val. Fl. 5.190–191) he recalls mainly

Apollonius, both in terms of action but also in terms of narrative placing, i.e. at the moment of arrival (Ἄργου δ' αὖτε παρηγορίῃσιν Ἰήσων / ὑψόθι νῆ' ἐκέλευσεν ἐπ' εὐναίῃσιν ἐρύσσαι / δάσκιον εἰσελάσαντας ἕλος, "but on the advice of Argus, Jason ordered them to hold the ship afloat with anchors after rowing it into an overgrown backwater", *Argon.* 2.1281–1283a). But also seems to nod lightly to Vergil (*cum Laomedonteae pubes / gramineo ripae religavit ab aggere classem*, "when the sons of Laomedon moored their ships to the river's grassy banks", *Aen.* 7.105–106), whose landing is, of course, narrated only after the excursus about Latium. When Valerius' Jason prays (*ipse gravi patera sacri libamina Bacchi*, "Himself duly bearing in a heavy bowl the sacred offering of wine", Val. Fl. 5.192;), we recall Apollonius's Jason doing the same thing (αὐτὸς δ' Αἰσονίδης χρυσέῳ ποταμόνδε κυπέλλῳ / οἴνου ἀκηρασίοιο μελισταγέας χέε λοιβάς, "Jason himself from a golden goblet poured libations of sweet honey and unmixed wine", *Argon.* 2.1271–1272), but there also be here a faint reminiscence of *Aeneid* 7.133, where Aeneas orders his men to prepare libations (*nunc pateras libate Iovi*, "now pour your cups to Jove") with, again, the placing corresponding closely to that of Apollonius. Jason's prayer follows at *Argonautica* 5.194–209, corresponding, as we have seen, to that of Jason at *Argonautica* 2.1273–1275, with direct speech replacing narration, and to that of Aeneas at *Aeneid* 7.135–140, with Valerius' placing again being Apollonian rather than Vergilian. But Vergil had then added to his Apollonian model the detail of an omen in response to the prayer, and in this Valerius follows the *Aeneid*. In answer to Aeneas, Jupiter thunders (*Aen.* 7.141–147); in answer to Jason, the Argo spins around and points its bow towards the open sea, as of ready for departure (Val. Fl. 5.210–212a). Feasting follows at once in both texts (*Aen.* 7.146–147, prolonging that begun at 7.107–115, and Val. Fl. 5.215–216; cf. *Cererem* at *Aen.* 7.113 and *Ceres* at Val. Fl. 5.216).

What these various similarities add up to is the realization that it was obviously not only by means of identifying specific verbal allusions that readers were able to pick up the connections between Valerius' narrative of events and those of his two main models. What we have instead is a reading process involving recognition of similarities between broad narrative structures involving individual type scenes allied to awareness of the presence of a relatively thin tissue of verbal parallels. It is armed with this combined approach to intertextuality that the ideal reader is able to appreciate both Valerius' debt to his sources and his originality. The next scene offers further illustration.

4 *Argonautica* 5.217–277: Invocation of a Muse and the Situation in Colchis

Immediately following the Argonauts' safe arrival in the Phasis and the appearance of dawn at the end of *Argonautica* 2, Apollonius opens the third book of his four-book poem with the invocation of the Muse Erato, thus precisely dividing his poem into two two-book halves:

> Εἰ δ' ἄγε νῦν, Ἐρατώ, παρά θ' ἵστασο, καί μοι ἔνισπε,
> ἔνθεν ὅπως ἐς Ἰωλκὸν ἀνήγαγε κῶας Ἰήσων
> Μηδείης ὑπ' ἔρωτι. σὺ γὰρ καὶ Κύπριδος αἶσαν
> ἔμμορες, ἀδμῆτας δὲ τεοῖς μελεδήμασι θέλγεις
> παρθενικάς· τῶ καί τοι ἐπήρατον οὔνομ' ἀνῆπται.
>
> Come now, Erato, stand by my side and tell me how from here Jason brought the fleece back to Iolcus with the aid of Medea's love, for you have a share also of Cypris' power and enchant unwed girls with your anxieties; and that is why your lovely name has been attached to you.
>
> (Race)

Vergil also has a narrative involving dawn, arrival and Erato, but he famously avoids placing the invocation of the Muse at the beginning of first book of the second half of his twelve-book epic. The reader has to wait until lines 7.37–45a before encountering Erato:

> Nunc age, qui reges, Erato, quae tempora, rerum
> quis Latio antiquo fuerit status, advena classem
> cum primum Ausoniis exercitus appulit oris,
> expediam, et primae revocabo exordia pugnae.   40
> tu vatem, tu, diva, mone. dicam horrida bella,
> dicam acies actosque animis in funera reges,
> Tyrrhenamque manum totamque sub arma coactam
> Hesperiam. maior rerum mihi nascitur ordo,
> maius opus moveo.   45
>
> Awake now, Erato! Who were the kings, what were the times, what the state of affairs in ancient Latium, when first that foreign army landed on Ausonia's shore—this will I unfold; and the prelude of the opening strife will I recall. And you, goddess, prompt your bard! I will tell of grim wars, will tell of battle array, and princes in their valour rushing upon death—of Tyrrhenian bands, and all Hesperia mustered in arms. Greater is the story that opens before me; greater is the task that I attempt.
>
> (Fairclough/Goold)

When we turn to Valerius, we find that the invocation that follows the moment of arrival occurs even farther into the book, coming at *Argonautica* 5.217–221:

> Incipe nunc cantus alios, dea, visaque vobis
> Thessalici da bella ducis. non mens mihi, non haec
> ora satis. ventum ad furias infandaque natae
> foedera et horrenda trepidam sub virgine puppem;   220
> impia monstriferis surgunt iam proelia campis.

> Begin now, goddess, another strain, and relate the wars of the Thessalian chief which ye yourselves beheld; no power have I, no utterance meet. We are come to the madness and unholy compact of the princess, and how the vessel shuddered beneath the terrible maid; the accursed contests on the portent-bearing fields arise before me.
>
> (Mozley)

There can be no doubt that Valerius' invocation here is indebted to both that of Apollonius and to Vergil's strikingly obvious imitation of Apollonius. The actual verbal similarities between the three passages are again slight (between Valerius and Vergil the only words in common are *nunc* at Val. Fl. 5.217 and *Aen.* 7.37, *bella* at Val. Fl. 5.218 and *Aen.* 7.41, and *mihi* at Val. Fl. 5.218 and *Aen.* 7.44), but in structural terms these lines represent a linchpin in the whole structure of Valerius' narrative patterning. And once the structural importance of the invocation within the whole section of narrative in which it occurs is fully appreciated, more aspects of Valerius' consistent reuse of Vergil's reuse of Apollonius come to light. As before, readers of the whole opening sequence of *Argonautica* 5 must continue to engage with a continuous process of double allusion to both an Apollonian model (long recognized) and a Vergilian reworking of that Apollonian model (the presence of which has not been sufficiently appreciated by scholars working on Valerius) in the opening scenes of the seventh book of the *Aeneid*.

Immediately following the invocation of the Muse, Valerius turns to explain the situation in Colchis. He recounts the death of Phrixus and how he left the Golden Fleece in the grove of Mars, and how he appeared to Aeetes in a dream and how war broke out between Aeetes and his brother Perses (Val. Fl. 5.222–277). Then comes the divine intervention of Juno and Minerva (Val. Fl. 5.278–296). Finally, at *Argonautica* 5.297, attention returns to the Argonauts camped by their ship. In structuring his narrative in this way Valerius varies significantly Apollonius' version of events in his third book and in doing so follows more closely Vergil's reworking of the same section of *Argonautica* 3. Following the invocation (*Argon.* 3.1–5), after a short reference to the Argonauts waiting in the Phasis (*Argon.* 3.6–7a) Apollonius turns immediately to the divine intervention of Hera and

Athena, which leads to Aphrodite's sending of Eros from Olympus towards Colchis (*Argon.* 3.7b–166). Then, at *Argonautica* 3.167, attention returns to the Argonauts on board their ship. Vergil's adaptation of this Apollonian narrative for his own purposes in *Aeneid* 7 is marked by both close imitation and significant variation. Immediately after the invocation of Erato in line 37, an allusion that so strikingly confirms the Apollonius as Vergil's key model here, Vergil turns to describing the situation in Latium and recent events involving Latinus (*Aen.* 7.45b–101). Then he brings attention to the Trojans at the moment of their landing on the bank of the Tiber (*Aen.* 7.102–106). Further events follow (*Aen.* 7.107–285, including the first encounter between the Trojans and Latinus), before we eventually come to the divine intervention of Juno beginning at *Aeneid* 7.286.

It thus becomes obvious that Valerius' description of events in Colchis leading up to the moment of the Argonauts' arrival, a passage that has no Apollonian model, is in fact a reworking of Vergil's description of recent events in Latium and the situation there at the moment of the Trojans' arrival, with the role of Aeetes corresponding to that of Latinus, who is himself modelled on the Apollonian Aeetes.[25] As before, Valerius' basic technique is to describe similar epic action with only a light dusting of verbal reference. The fundamental links are as follows. When Valerius has Phrixus appear to Aeetes in a dream vision, Valerius has in mind *Aeneid* 7.58–101. There, the settling of bees on a laurel tree in Latinus' palace is interpreted as a sign of the arrival of strangers (*Aen.* 7.59–70). Then, when Lavinia's hair appears to catch fire the event is interpreted as a sign of future renown but also of imminent war (*Aen.* 7.71–80). Worried by all this, Latinus consults the oracle of Faunus, only to be told that Lavinia must be given in marriage to a foreigner who will arrive in Latium (*Aen.* 7.81–103). Valerius combines all three stages of portents that touch Latinus with the single dream in which Phrixus warns Aeetes that loss of the Golden Fleece will mean destruction for his city. Secondly, his warning that Medea must marry anyone but not a Colchian corresponds to Faunus' declaration that Lavinia must wed the foreigner who is soon to arrive. On the purely verbal level, there are several parallels, individually slight but collectively rather more obvious. Phrixus' appearance to Aeetes occurs in the middle of the night, when he talks about the marriage of the king's daughter (Val. Fl. 5.231–40):

> quondam etiam <u>tacitae</u> visus per tempora <u>noctis</u>
> effigie vasta socerumque exterruit ingens
> <u>prodita vox</u>: '<o> qui patria tellure fugatum

---

[25] See especially Adamietz (1976) 69–71 on these similarities.

> quaerentemque domos his me considere passus
> sedibus, oblata generum mox prole petisti, 235
> tunc tibi regnorum labes luctusque supersunt
> rapta soporato fuerint cum vellera luco.
> praeterea infernae quae nunc sacrata Dianae
> fert castos Medea choros, quemcumque procorum
> pacta <u>petat</u>, maneat regnis ne <u>virgo</u> paternis.' 240

Once too did he appear, a vast phantom, in the silent hours of night, and a great voice spoke forth and struck terror into the father of his bride: 'O thou who didst suffer me, a fugitive from my native land in search of a home, to settle in these abodes, and soon offering thy daughter invited me to be thy son-in-law, dolour and ruin of thy realm shall abound for thee what time the fleece is stolen from the sleep-drugged grove. Moreover, Medea, who now is consecrated to Diana of the underworld and leads the holy dance—let her look for betrothal to any suitor, suffer her not to abide in her father's kingdom.'

(Mozley)

As a result, the young Medea is promised to an Albanian prince, i.e. Styrus (Val. Fl. 5.257–258):

> <u>plena</u> necdum Medea iuventa
> adnuitur <u>thalamis</u> Albani <u>virgo</u> tyranni.

and Medea, though her girlhood be not yet mature, is plighted to to the Albanian prince's marriage chamber.

(Mozley)

These lines pick up details from *Aeneid* 7.87, where Latinus goes to consult the oracle of Faunus at dead of night, *sub nocte silenti*, and also lines 7.53 and 95–98, where concerning the marriage of his young daughter Lavinia the prophetic voice of Faunus tells Latinus to seek a foreign husband:[26]

> iam matura <u>virgo</u>, iam <u>plenis</u> nubilis annis 53
>   [...]
>   ... ex alto <u>vox</u> <u>red</u>dita luco est: 95
> 'ne <u>pete</u> conubiis natam sociare Latinis,
> o mea progenies, <u>thalamis</u> neu crede paratis;
> externi venient generi, ...

---

26 See Spaltenstein (2004) 449; cf. also *praeterea* at Val. Fl. 5.238 and *Aen.* 7.71 and Spaltenstein (2004) 450.

now ripe for a husband, now of full age to be a bride ... Suddenly a voice came from the deep grove: 'Seek not, my son, to ally your daughter in Latin wedlock, and put no faith in the bridal chamber that is ready at hand. Strangers will come, ...

(Fairclough/Goold)

Valerius thus models his Medea and Aeetes on Vergil's Lavinia and Latinus as well as on the Apollonian Medea and Aeetes, on whom the Vergilian characters were already modelled.[27]

Enough has been said both to clarify the main point I want to make in this paper. What we now need is a full-scale study of Valerius' *Argonautica* that takes into account, as I have tried to do here, Valerius' knowledge of Vergil's profound debt to Apollonius Rhodius throughout the *Aeneid*. This is a project on which I have begun working for some time, but much remains to be done. In addition to working out the basic narrative structure based on both Apollonius' *Argonautica* and Vergil's *Aeneid*, it is also necessary to factor in Valerius' debt to other authors, especially Homer, but also including Greek and Roman tragedy, Ovid, Lucan, Seneca, other versions of the Argonautic saga, and so on. The size and the complexity of the task are daunting. Subsequently, the interpretive challenge will have to be faced. Scholars have warned for a long time that it will not do to cite endless literary parallels without going to offer some interpretation of what they may mean. In this paper I have not attempted to come up with any overall interpretive reading of Valerius' reworking of both Apollonius Rhodius and Vergil in the opening scenes of *Argonautica* 5. If challenged on this matter, I would have to reply that for the moment I do not know what it all means. I would add that it would probably be rash to assume that one can attempt to make a claim about any overall meaning on the basis of such a small selection of text. Before basing arguments on individual allusions, one is best advised to contextualize that allusion as carefully as possible. And that means attempting to come to grips with the grand allusive strategy that underpins the composition of Valerius' whole poem, which I take to be based on his reading of the *Argonautica* of Apollonius through the lens of the whole of Vergil's *Aeneid*. Once that has been achieved, numerous questions will, of course, remain to be asked and answered. But at least the business of literary interpretation will be based on a more complete knowledge of Valerius' intertextual strategies than is available today.

---

27 Cf. also Val. Fl. 5.276–277 <u>cum</u> *Marte remisso / debitus Aeaeis dux Thessalus appulit oris* recalling *Aen.* 7.105–106 <u>cum</u> *Laomedontia pubes / gramineo ripae religavit ab aggere classem*, in each case bringing the outline of background events to a close; for this point see Adamietz (1976) 70, n. 6.

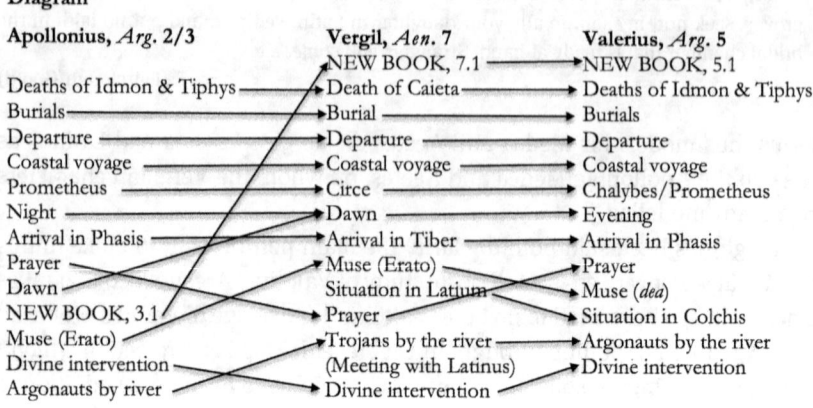

Fig. 1: Synoptic diagram of scenic similarities in Apollonius, Vergil's *Aeneid* and Valerius Flaccus.

Bibliography

Adamietz, Joachim (1976), *Zur Komposition der Argonautica des Valerius Flaccus*, Munich.
Augoustakis, Antony (ed.) (2014), *Flavian Poetry and its Greek Past*, Leiden.
Augoustakis, Antony (ed.) (2016), *Flavian Epic*, Oxford.
Barich, Michael (2014), "Poets and Readers: Reflections on the Verbal and Narrative Art of Valerius Flaccus *Argonautica*", in: Heerink/Manuwald (2014) 29–48.
Blänsdord, Jurgen (1982), "Unepische Szenenfolge in der *Aeneis*", in: *WJA* 8, 83–104.
Cowan, Robert (2014), "Fingering Cestos: Martial's Catullus' Callimachus", in: Augoustakis (2014) 345–371.
Deremetz, Alain (2014), "Authorial Poetics in Valerius Flaccus' *Argonautica*", in: Heerink/Manuwald (2014) 49–71.
Dewar, Michael (1991), *Statius, Thebaid IX. Edited with an English Translation and Commentary*, Oxford.
Feeney, Denis (1991), *The Gods in Epic. Poets and Critics of the Classical Tradition*, Oxford.
Fratantuono, Lee/Stark, Caroline (eds.) (forthcoming), *A Companion to Latin Epic, 14–96 C.E.*, Malden, MA.
Galli, Daniela (2007), *Valerii Flacci* Argonautica *I*, Berlin.
Gervais, Kyle (2017), "*Odi(tque moras):* Abridging allusions to Vergil, *Aeneid* 12 in Statius, *Thebaid* 12", in: *AJPh* 138, 305–329.
Hardie, Philip (1989), "Flavian Epicists on Virgil's Epic Technique", in: *Ramus* 18, 3–20.
Heerink, Mark/Manuwald, Gesine (eds.) (2014), *Brill's Companion to Valerius Flaccus*, Leiden.
Hershkowitz, Debra (1998), *Valerius Flaccus' Argonautica. Abbreviated Voyages in Silver Latin Epic*, Oxford.
Hunter, Richard (1993), *The* Argonautica *of Apollonius. Literary Studies*, Cambridge.

Hutchinson, Gregory (2013), *Greek to Latin: Frameworks and Contexts for Intertextuality*, Oxford.
Kyriakidis, Stratis (1998), *Narrative Structure and Poetics in the* Aeneid: *The Frame of Book 6*, Bari.
Knauer, Georg Nicolaus (1964), "Vergil's *Aeneid* and Homer", in: *GRBS* 5, 61–84.
Knauer, Georg Nicolaus (1979²), *Die* Aeneis *und Homer. Studien zur poetischen Technik Vergils mit Listen der Homerzitate in der* Aeneis, Göttingen.
Langen, Peter (1896), *C. Valeri Flacci Setini Balbi* Argonauticon *libri octo*, Berlin.
Manuwald, Gesine (2015), *Valerius Flaccus,* Argonautica *Book III*, Cambridge.
Mehmel, Friedrich (1934), *Valerius Flaccus*, Hamburg.
Nelis, Damien P. (2001), *Vergil's* Aeneid *and the* Argonautica *of Apollonius Rhodius*, Leeds.
Nelis, Damien P. (forthcoming), "Valerius Flaccus, Vergil and Apollonius Rhodius: the intertextual strategies of a Flavian poet", in: Fratantuono/Stark (forthcoming).
Nordera, Roberta (1969), "I virgilianismi in Valerio Flacco", in: Nordera *et al.* (1969) 1–92.
Nordera, Roberta/Bertotti, Tullio/Bezzi, L./Pianezzola, Emilio/Lunelli, Aldo (eds.) (1969), *Contributi a tre poeti latini*, Bologna.
Nordera, Roberta (2016), "Virgilianisms in Valerius Flaccus", in: Augoustakis (2016) 45–79.
Schenk, Peter (1999), *Studien zur poetischen Kunst des Valerius Flaccus. Beobachtungen zur Ausgestaltung des Kriegsthemas in den* Argonautica, Munich.
Schetter, Willy (1959), "Die Buchzahl der *Argonautica* des Valerius Flaccus", in: *Philologus* 103, 297–308.
Smolenaars, Johannes J.L (1994), *Statius*, Thebaid *VII*, Leiden.
Soubiran, Jean (2002), *Valerius Flaccus,* Argonautiques, Leuven.
Spaltenstein, François (2004), *Commentaire des* Argonautiques *de Valerius Flaccus (livres 3, 4 et 5)*, Brussels.
Stover, Timothy (2012), *Epic and Empire in Vespasianic Rome: A New Reading of Valerius Flaccus'* Argonautica, Oxford.
van der Schuur, Marco (2014), "Conflating Funerals. The deaths of Idmon and Tiphys in Valerius' *Argonautica*", in: Augoustakis (2014) 95–112.
Venini, Paola (1971), "Sulla struttura delle *Argonautiche* di Valerio Flacco", in: *RIL* 105, 597–620.
Wijsman, Henri J.W. (1996), *Valerius Flaccus* Argonautica, *Book V: A commentary*, Leiden.
Zissos, Andrew (1999), "Allusion and narrative possibility in the *Argonautica* of Valerius Flaccus", in: *CPh* 94, 289–301.
Zissos, Andrew (2002), "Reading Models and the Homeric Program in the *Argonautica* of Valerius Flaccus", in: *Helios* 29, 69–96.
Zissos, Andrew (2008), *Valerius Flaccus,* Argonautica *1. Edited with Introduction, Text, Translation and Commentary*, Oxford.

Raymond Marks
Searching for Ovid at Cannae: A Contribution to the Reception of Ovid in Silius Italicus' *Punica*

Silius Italicus does not shy away from acknowledging literary figures in the *Punica*. In the catalogue of book 8 he gives the forces from Arpinum a leader named Tullius, which occasions a brief homage to Cicero (8.404–411), and later, when describing cohorts from Mantua, praises Virgil (8.591–595). In Sardinia we run into the poet Ennius (12.387–419), and in the underworld the shade of Homer (13.779–791). Asconius Pedianus is commemorated in a poet-warrior from Patavium named Pedianus, who fights at Nola (12.212–222), and even the literary pursuits of the emperor Domitian are noted (3.618–621).[1] Different factors motivate these acknowledgments, but Homer, Ennius, and Virgil are surely recognized for their contributions to epic, the genre of the *Punica* itself, and in Virgil's case, additionally, because he is Silius' most important poetic model.[2] And yet, other literary figures whose influence is considerable have not been shown to enjoy such a distinction; the historian Livy and the poets Ovid and Lucan come to mind.[3]

As I shall argue in this chapter, Ovid is given such special recognition, however, and, in fact, his presence in the text, though signaled less directly than that of the aforementioned, is, nevertheless, quite extensive and organically integrated into the narrative. Silius accomplishes this through verbal allusions and thematic parallels that evoke Ovid's biography as constructed by the poet himself in his own poetry, and these allusions and parallels appear with notable frequency in the Cannae books (8–10), especially in the narrative leading up to the battle; the catalogue of Rome's forces in book 8 and the events on the day before and the eve of the battle early in book 9 will prove to be key moments. The context of Cannae is not inconsequential for our understanding of this Ovidian program. It is important to note that Rome is not only soundly defeated by Hannibal in that battle,

---

[1] For these and other literary figures in the *Punica*, see Casali (2006), Manuwald (2007), Marks (2010a), and Schaffenrath (2010b).
[2] For Virgil's influence on the *Punica*, see the bibliography given in Stocks (2014) 61, n. 21. Silius' personal admiration of Virgil was well known (Mart. 11.48, 50[49]; Plin. *Ep.* 3.7.8). Silius was also a great admirer of Cicero; see Mart. 7.63 and 11.48 with Ripoll (2000).
[3] For Livy's influence, see Nesselrath (1986), Lucarini (2004), and Pomeroy (2010). On Lucan and Silius, see Brouwers (1982) and Marks (2010b). On Ovid and Silius, see Bruère (1958) and Bruère (1959), Wilson (2004), and n. 5 below.

but, as it were, defeats herself, a point conveyed by the reckless behavior of the consul Varro, who instigates the conflict, and by numerous references and allusions to Rome's history of civil strife throughout the narrative.[4] This self-destructive aspect of the battle ties in nicely with the biographical Ovid whom Silius invites us to reflect on; for that Ovid is, above all, the exiled Ovid, the poet who, while punished by Augustus, accepts blame for his own ruin, attributing it, as he famously puts it, to his own poetry and a mistake, *carmen et error* (*Tr.* 2.207). The defeat at Cannae thus reflects the self-inflicted demise of Ovid himself.

1 Ovid in the Catalogue of Book 8

The narrative leading up to the battle of Cannae is set in motion by a character with Ovidian ties: Anna Perenna. After Fabius Maximus slows down Hannibal's progress in book 7—the Carthaginian had previously won victories against the Romans at the Ticinus and the Trebia in book 4 and at Lake Trasimene in book 5—Juno instructs Anna to tell Hannibal to go to Cannae (8.25–43). This occasions an excursus in which Silius explains how Anna came to Italy and was transformed into a river nymph there (8.44–201); the excursus shows signs of Virgilian influence, but is especially indebted to Ovid's treatment of the festival of Anna Perenna in *Fast.* 3.523–710.[5] Thereafter, we follow Anna as she appears to Hannibal and encourages him to march to Cannae (8.202–241). The scene then shifts to Rome, where Varro, who rejects Fabius' tactics, is elected consul and pushes for open battle with the Carthaginian (8.242–283). Paulus, who is also elected consul, and Fabius oppose Varro's plan (8.284–348), but the Romans march to Cannae anyway (8.349–355). A catalogue of Rome's forces at Cannae comes next (8.356–621).

It is here that Silius first hints at the biographical Ovid, specifically in the section of the catalogue where he describes the Marsian contingent and their allies (8.495–510). Silius begins by emphasizing the Marsi's prowess in war and

---

[4] Of particular note are those combatants who anachronistically evoke civil war namesakes (McGuire (1997) 61–63, 85, 136–144) and the many allusions to Lucan (Marks (2010b) 135–139). For more on the self-destructive nature of the Cannae battle, see Marks (2005) 133–134. Also, see n. 12 below.

[5] See Marks (2013). For a recent discussion of the Virgilian material in Anna's story, see Stocks (2014) 91–96. The *Fasti* is a work on which Silius draws heavily elsewhere in the *Punica* too, such as in Cilnius' account of the defeat of the 300 Fabii (7.38–65; cf. *Fast.* 2.195–242 with Marks 2014) and the advent of the Magna Mater at Rome (17.1–47; cf. *Fast.* 4.247–348 with von Albrecht 1968).

their ability to charm snakes and treat venomous bites (8.495–497) and attributes their knowledge of magic to one Angitia, who taught them not only how to handle snakes, but to control nature in other ways, such as drawing down the moon or arresting the flow of rivers (8.498–501). He next derives the Marsian name from Marsyas, who fled to Italy from Phrygia (8.502–504), and takes note of two of their more famous cities, Marruvium and Alba (8.505–509). In conclusion, he says that Paelignians from Sulmo joined their ranks (8.509–510).

By a combination of allusions and biographical details Silius invites us to think about Ovid in this passage. Consider, first, the reference to troops from Sulmo at its end: *coniungitur acer / Paelignus gelidoque rapit Sulmone cohortes* ("The eager Paelignian joins their ranks, hastily bringing troops from cool Sulmo," 8.509–510). As Sulmo is Ovid's birthplace (*Am.* 2.16.1, 3.15.11; *Fast.* 4.81; *Tr.* 4.10.3; *Pont.* 4.14.49), this detail alone might remind us of the poet. *Gelido* (510), though, clinches the link, as this adjective is twice used in reference to Sulmo in Latin literature, both times in Ovid: *Sulmonis gelidi* ("of cool Sulmo," *Fast.* 4.81); *Sulmo ... gelidis uberrimus undis* ("Sulmo ... most abundant in cool waters," *Tr.* 4.10.3). Another telling moment is Silius' derivation of the Marsian name:

> sed populis nomen posuit metuentior hospes,
> cum fugeret Phrygias trans aequora Marsya Crenas,
> Mygdoniam Phoebi superatus pectine loton.
>
> (8.502–504)

> But a rather anxious visitor gave his name to these people when Marsyas fled Phrygian Crenae across the sea after his Mygdonian flute was defeated by Phoebus' lyre.

Our earliest attestation of direct contact between the Marsi and a Marsyas is provided by Pliny (*HN* 3.108), who says that Archippe, a Marsian town, was founded by a leader of the Lydians named Marsyas.[6] Otherwise, we hear of men who were sent from Phrygia by a king Marsyas to teach the Italians divination (Serv. *ad Aen.* 3.359) and of Cacus and a Phrygian named Megales who were sent by king Marsyas to the Etruscan Tarchon (Solin. 1.8). Silius, as we can see, deviates from these versions in that he identifies Marsyas with the satyr of the same name who had challenged Apollo and was defeated by the god in a music contest, and he is the only one to do so.[7]

---

[6] Solinus 2.6 reports essentially the same.
[7] So, Spaltenstein (1986) 540.

Given the reference to Sulmo only six lines later, we might ask ourselves whether this aetiology has anything to do with Ovid or is meant to evoke him. Marsyas' being a musician is itself suggestive of a connection with the poet, and one might be reminded that Ovid tells Marsyas' story in the *Metamorphoses* (6.382–400) and the *Fasti* (6.693–710). In fact, Silius' aetiology contains verbal parallels with these moments in the Ovidian corpus: the name *Marsyas* and the adjective *Phrygius* (8.503) appear together in *Met.* 6.400 (*Marsya nomen habet, Phrygiae liquidissimus amnis*; "it has the name 'Marsyas', the clearest river in Phrygia"), and the collocation *Phoebi superatus* (8.504) echoes *Phoebo superante* ("Phoebus prevailing," *Fast.* 6.707). There are two other Ovidian details in these lines as well: the comparative form of the participle *metuens* (*metuentior*, 8.502) is rare, appearing only three times in pre-Silian Latin, each time in Ovid (*Her.* 19.83; *Met.* 1.323; *Fast.* 6.259), and the synecdoche of *lotos* to refer to a flute (*loton*, 8.504) is well attested in Greek literature, but is not found in Rome until Ovid, who supplies, in fact, two of the three pre-Silian instances of its usage in Latin (*Rem.* 753; *Fast.* 4.190).[8]

As to why Ovid is evoked here in the catalogue and in such close connection with Marsyas, my hunch is that it has something to do with the punishment of exile Augustus imposed on him, a punishment Ovid claims to have brought upon himself in part because of his own poetry.[9] This hunch is informed by the wider context in which the catalogue appears, the "run-up" to Rome's self-destructive defeat at Cannae, and looks ahead to a specific instance of self-destruction there, the deaths of Satricus and Solymus on the eve of battle, in which Ovid will be evoked several times, as we shall see. Marsyas figures into this reading as well. For while Silius only refers to his defeat in the music competition with Apollo (8.504), one might easily recall that he was subsequently punished by the god— he was flayed alive—and compare him with Ovid, who was punished by Augustus. One might also read the detail of Marsyas' flight from Phrygia across the sea (*fugeret ... trans aequora*, 8.503) as a hint at Ovid's exile from Rome.[10] It should be noted, furthermore, that Ovid supplies the precedent for his identification with Marsyas; more than one reader has seen in his treatments of Marsyas' punish-

---

8 The third is Pliny, *HN* 16.172. It is also attested in Silius' contemporary Martial (8.50[51].14).
9 Ovid makes this claim several times in his exilic poetry: e.g., *Tr.* 1.1.56; 2.2, 207 (*carmen et error*); 3.3.74; 3.14.6; *Ib.* 5–6.
10 In retrospect, Anna's story, recounted earlier in the book, would appear to be all the more relevantly Ovidian; for she is an exile too (cf. 8.54–70, 158–159).

ment a way of touching on his own artistic career, and at one point in the *Epistulae ex Ponto*, when discussing how his poetry has harmed him, Ovid compares himself to Marsyas (*Pont.* 3.3.42).[11]

2 Ovid in the Satricus-Solymus Episode

After the catalogue, Silius describes ill omens that appeared to the Romans upon their arrival at Cannae and has a soldier prophesy defeat for them in the coming battle (8.622–767). Our attention then turns to the Roman consuls Varro and Paulus: Varro, who is anxious to engage Hannibal in battle, rebukes Paulus, who is in charge of the army that day, for holding back, and Paulus pleads with Varro not to attack when it is his turn to command the next day (9.1–65). Hereafter, Silius recounts the story of Satricus and Solymus (9.66–177). On the eve of battle Satricus, who had been captured by the Carthaginians in the First Punic War, escapes from the Carthaginian camp and puts on the arms of someone slain in a prior skirmish; this turns out to be his own son Mancinus (cf. 9.9–14), whom he does not recognize. Solymus, who is on night-watch, sees someone wearing his brother's armor, attacks him and mortally wounds him; this is his father, of course. The father and son recognize each other, and after the father dies, Solymus kills himself, writing in blood a warning to Varro on his shield (*fuge proelia Varro*, "Avoid battle, Varro," 9.175). As the next day dawns, we witness Hannibal addressing his men before battle and are informed of the disposition of his troops (9.178–243). Varro, in turn, sends his troops forth from camp, who are alarmed by the discovery of the double deaths and the warning on the shield, but the consul dismisses the omen (9.244–266); the disposition of Rome's forces is next described (9.267–277). Thereafter, the two armies close in on each other, and the battle begins (9.278–286).

There are several details that evoke Ovid between the catalogue in book 8 and the beginning of the battle in book 9, but I will begin with the story of Satricus and Solymus as it contains an especially strong allusion to Ovid. Its themes of familial slaughter and suicide shape our reading of the subsequent battle as an instance of Rome's self-destruction, an interpretation supported by numerous references to civil war events and persons and by allusions to Lucan in the battle

---

11 See, e.g., Lundström (1980) 25–26, Newlands (1995) 198–202, and Feldherr (2004) 84–85.

itself and in the narrative leading up to it.¹² Ovid, though, is key to our reading of the episode too, and it is, again, the poet's birthplace, Sulmo, that signals his presence here; for Satricus and his sons come from Sulmo, and one of his sons, the one who kills the father and then commits suicide, Solymus, even evokes the town's name in his own. But Silius is not content to suggest an Ovidian connection merely on these grounds. When reporting their Sulmonian origins, he alludes to Ovid's treatment of Sulmo's foundation legend in *Fasti* 4:¹³

> huic domus et gemini fuerant Sulmone relicti 70
> matris in uberibus nati, Mancinus et una
> nomine *Rhoeteo* Solymus. nam *Dardana* origo
> et Phrygio genus a proauo, qui sceptra secutus
> Aeneae claram *muris* fundauerat urbem
> ex sese dictam Solymon. celebrata colonis 75
> mox Italis paulatim attrito nomine Sulmo.
>
> (9.70–76)

He [Satricus] had a home in Sulmo and had left behind there two sons when they were still suckling babes, Mancinus and Solymus, who has a Rhoetean name. For their ancestry is Trojan, and their line descends from a Phrygian forefather, who had been a follower of Aeneas and had founded a famous city, which he named after himself, Solymus. But, afterwards, when Italian settlers flocked to it, its name was gradually shortened to Sulmo.

> serus ab *Iliacis*, et post Antenora, flammis
>   attulit Aeneas in loca nostra deos.
> huius erat Solimus Phrygia comes unus ab Ida
>   a quo Sulmonis *moenia* nomen habent, 80
> Sulmonis gelidi, patriae, Germanice, nostrae.
>   me miserum, Scythico quam procul illa solo est!
>
> (*Fast.* 4.77–82)

After Antenor, Aeneas eventually brought from the flames of Troy his gods to our lands. One of his companions from Phrygian Ida was Solimus, from whom the walls of Sulmo take their name, cool Sulmo, our homeland, Germanicus. Poor me! How far is it from this Scythian land!

Satricus and his sons, as we can see, are not only Ovid's ancestors in virtue of being from Sulmo, but are themselves the product of Ovid's literary imagination,

---

12 The Satricus-Solymus story is itself based on" double death" tales associated with Rome's history of civil strife; see Fucecchi (1999) 315–322, 332–336. For other allusions and references to civil war at Cannae, see n. 4 above.
13 The parallel is noted by Bruère (1959) 230, Spaltenstein (1990) 12, and Wilson (2004) 243–246.

their ancestry being shaped, as we can see, by *Fasti* 4. Satricus and Ovid, specifically, are similar in that they both experience exile: as I mentioned above, when we run into Satricus, he has already been away from home for many years and is trying to return there (cf. 9.66–69, 77–82), and as line 82 in the *Fasti* passage indicates, Ovid is presently in exile and wishes he could return home.[14] Another hint at Ovid comes when Satricus, as he is dying, instructs his son to advise Paulus not to engage in battle and not to let Varro do so as well:

> 'curarum tibi prima tamen sit, nate, referre
> ductori monitus Paulo: producere bellum   135
> nitatur Poenoque neget certamina Martis.
> augurio exsultat diuum immensamque propinqua
> stragem acie sperat. quaeso, cohibete furentem
> Varronem; namque hunc fama est impellere signa.
> sat magnum hoc miserae fuerit mihi cardine uitae   140
> solamen, cauisse meis.'
>
> (9.134–141)

'Nevertheless, son, let your first concern be to relate to the leader Paulus a warning: he should try to delay the war and deny the Carthaginian an opportunity to engage. He [i.e. Hannibal] is elated by a divine omen and expects great slaughter, should battle be joined. Please, check Varro in his madness; for rumor has it that he is urging the standards on. Let this be for me a great enough solace at the end of my sad life: to have forewarned my own.'

Note how the initial letters in lines 136–140 spell the word *nasus*, "nose", and thus form an acrostic pun on Ovid's cognomen, *Naso*.[15] That this constitutes a reference to Silius' literary predecessor is further suggested here by words and phrases that often signal allusive annotation, as in 'Alexandrian footnotes' (*referre*, 9.134; *fama est*, 139) or as language relating to memory (*monitus*, 9.135).[16]

3 The *Ibis* at Cannae

There are other Ovidian details in the Satricus-Solymus episode, and we shall take note of them shortly. But for the moment I would like to turn my attention to the quarrel between Paulus and Varro, with which book 9 begins, as it shows the

---

14 And note that, like Solymus/Solimus, Sulmo's founder, Marsyas, who was discussed above in connection with Sulmo in the catalogue of book 8, is an exile from Phrygia (8.503).
15 Hilberg (1899) 300 notes the acrostic.
16 On these annotative strategies, see Hinds (1998) 1–16.

influence of an Ovidian work that will prove critical for our understanding of Ovid's place at Cannae, the *Ibis*. The relevant portion of Silius' text is the end of Paulus' response to his consular colleague:

> 'sin nostris animus monitis precibusque repugnat,
> aures pande deo. cecinit Cymaea per orbem
> haec olim uates et te praesaga tuosque
> uulgauit terris proauorum aetate furores,
> iamque alter tibi, nec perplexo carmine, coram   60
> fata cano uates: sistis ni crastina signa,
> firmabis nostro Phoebeae dicta Sibyllae
> sanguine. nec Graio posthac Diomede ferentur,
> sed te, si perstas, insignes consule campi.'
> haec Paulus, lacrimaeque oculis ardentibus ortae.   65
>
> (9.56–65)

'But if your heart refuses to heed our warnings and entreaties, listen to god. Long ago the Cumaean prophetess sang these things far and wide and in the time of our forefathers foretold you and your madness to the world, and now I, another prophet, sing your fate to you plainly and not in ambiguous language: unless you hold in check the standards tomorrow, you will ensure by our blood that the words of the Phoebean Sibyl come to pass. And, afterwards, these fields will be known not for Greek Diomedes, but, if you persist, for you, a consul.' Thus Paulus spoke, and tears welled up in his burning eyes.

This passage echoes the conclusion to Ovid's description of Ibis' ill-omened birth (*Ib.* 209–250). While the Furies are attending to the newborn, they place a smoking torch close to his face to make him weep, thus eliciting tears that will fall for many years to come, as one Fury explains (*Ib.* 237–242). Next, the Fate Clotho offers a brief prophecy, whose meaning Ovid goes on to clarify:

> dixerat; at Clotho iussit promissa ualere,
>   neuit et infesta stamina pulla manu;
> et, ne longa suo praesagia diceret ore,   245
>   'fata canet uates qui tua' dixit 'erit.'
> ille ego sum uates: ex me tua uulnera disces,
>   dent modo di uires in mea uerba suas.
>
> (*Ib.* 243–248)

She [i.e. one of the Furies] had spoken. But Clotho ordained that her promises come to pass and wove black threads with a hateful hand. And so as not to give a lengthy prophecy, she said: 'There will be a prophet who will sing your fate.' I am that prophet; from me you will learn your sufferings so long as the gods lend their strength to my words.

Both passages are thematically similar in that each refers to a prophecy, delivered in the past, that anticipates a cursed future for the addressee and then contains a statement, delivered by the passage's speaker to the addressee, that confirms and elucidates that prophecy. Accordingly, Silius' Sibyl (*Cymaea uates*, 57–58) corresponds to Ovid's Clotho (*Clotho*, *Ib.* 243), and Silius' Paulus to Ovid himself. Paulus and Ovid, though, are comparable on still other grounds. First, Paulus' identification of himself as *uates* echoes Clotho's foretelling of a subsequent *uates*, who turns out to be Ovid: *fata cano uates* (9.61) = *fata canet uates* (*Ibis* 246).[17] Second, each stands in hostile relation to and is even harmed by his addressee: Paulus meets his death in the battle at Cannae, which, despite his objections, Varro precipitates – note the hint at Paulus' eventual death in *nostro sanguine* (9.62–63) – and Ovid, while in exile, has been the subject of Ibis' attacks back in Rome, which is what motivates his composition of the *Ibis* in the first place. There are other details that invite us to read the two passages in relation to one another as well: Silius' *praesaga* (9.58) recalls Ovid's *praesagia* (*Ib.* 245); Paulus' reference to the Sibyl's prophecy as *perplexo* (9.60) picks up on the detail of Clotho's weaving (*neuit*, *Ib.* 244); and the tears that Paulus sheds from his "burning eyes" after his speech (*lacrimaeque oculis ardentibus ortae*, 9.65) remind us of the tears Ibis shed when the Furies "placed a torch close to his eyes" (cf. *admorunt oculos usque sub ora faces*, *Ib.* 238; *flebat*, 239; *lacrimas*, 241).[18]

But this is not Silius' only engagement with the *Ibis* at Cannae; he draws on it elsewhere and in doing so not only underlines Paulus' relation to Ovid, but identifies their rivals with one another, Varro and Ibis, respectively, and even brings Satricus and Solymus into consideration. All three of these pairs, for one, are similar in that they represent relationships that should otherwise not be hostile: Satricus and Solymus are father and son; Varro and Paulus are both Roman and fellow consuls; and Ibis and Ovid are former friends.[19] But these relationships become hostile when one in each pair antagonizes the other in some fashion:

---

17 The collocation *fata can-* is found elsewhere at the beginning of a line (Verg. *Aen.* 3.444, 8.499, 10.417; Val. Fl. 5.43; Sil. 9.548), at other positions in a line of verse (Tib. 2.5.16; [Tib.] 3.7.203; Ov. *Her.* 1.28, 21.232; *Met.* 14.381), and once in prose (Cic. *Div.* 2.98), but it is only followed by a form of *uates* in these two instances. Darcy Krasne has called my attention to the possibility that the phrase *alter uates* (9.60–61) may be another Ovidian, intertextual "cue"; for while the phrase, within the context of Paulus' speech, identifies him as a "second *uates*," following the Sibyl, by allusion it suggests that Paulus is also a "second Ovid," as it were.
18 The phrase *oculis ardentibus* also appears in Lucan's *Bellum Civile* (6.179), where Scaeva, having shoved a torch into someone's face, sets the eyes on fire. The Lucanian echo cleverly complements and reinforces the allusion to Ovid's *Ibis* because it activates our recollection of what led Ibis to shed tears, namely, the Furies similarly shoving a torch in his face.
19 That Ovid and Ibis used to be friends seems to be the implication of *Ib.* 39–40.

Varro pushes for the battle at Cannae, which sets him at odds with Paulus; Satricus, when fleeing the Carthaginian camp, wears his son Mancinus' armor, which leads, albeit unintentionally, to his being attacked by his other son Satricus; and Ibis casts aspersions on Ovid, which prompts the poet to inveigh against him. Silius also underlines the up-ending of these normal relations in a similar way, by figuring the antagonists in each case as African "others". Fabius, in his conversation with Paulus about Varro's command in book 8, suggests this when he describes Varro as an enemy in the Roman camp (*teque hostis castris grauior manet*; "And a more formidable enemy awaits you in the camp," 8.301) while Paulus in his response is more direct, calling himself Rome's consul and Varro Carthage's (*consul datus alter, opinor, / Ausoniae est, alter Poenis* ("One consul, I think, has been given to Ausonia, the other to the Carthaginians," 8.332–333).[20] Satricus tells Solymus he is blameless for attacking his father because he did not know who he was and took him to be Carthaginian, or, as the father puts it, he was Carthaginian at the time: *haud tua, nate, / fraus ulla est. iaceres in me cum feruidus hastam, / Poenus eram* (9.128–130: "Son, it is no fault of yours. When in anger you threw the spear at me, I was Carthaginian"). As for Ovid's Ibis, he has a connection to Africa too: he was born there: *qui simul impura matris prolapsus ab aluo / Cinyphiam foedo corpore pressit humum* (*Ib*. 221–222: "As soon as he slipped out of his mother's filthy womb and touched the Cinyphian ground with his ugly body").

Another point of comparison between Varro and Ibis is that both are described as barking. In the section on Ibis' birth, to part of which Silius alludes in 9.56–65, as we have seen, Ovid says that the Furies, when attending to the newborn Ibis, made him drink dog's milk (*Ib*. 229–231), which resulted in the child barking in the forum: *latrat et in toto uerba canina foro* ("And he barks dog-like words all over the forum," *Ib*. 232); this anticipates the adult Ibis hurling invectives at Ovid, as a similarly phrased line at the beginning of the poem shows: *iactat et in toto nomina nostra foro* ("And he tosses my name about all over the forum," *Ib*. 14). Varro, once elected consul, is also described as barking when he criticizes the senate (*oblatratque senatum*, "And he barks at the senate," 8.249) and, a few lines before and after, is said to have been speaking from the *rostra*, which places him in the forum (*saeuit iam rostris Varro*, "Now Varro rages from the rostra," 8.244; *e rostris bella ciebat*, "He was calling for war from the rostra," 8.262). Shortly hereafter, when Silius introduces Varro's consular colleague Paulus, we learn that he too has been barked at, though not by Varro; this happened

---

20 Also, cf. 9.637–639, where Paulus asks whose birth was more cursed, Varro's or Hannibal's.

some years before when his victories in Illyricum provoked envy among his political opponents: *nigro allatrauerat ore / uictorem inuidia* ("Envy with its black mouth had barked at the victor," 8.290–291).[21]

As for Ovid and Paulus, they are comparable not only for being victimized by their enemies, but for being *uates* who sing of their rivals' *fata* too; this was established, as we saw above, through parallels with *Ib.* 243–250 in 9.56–65. But that section of the *Ibis* and, in fact, the very lines in which Ovid is identified as *uates* resonate still more widely in Silius' text, furthering the association between Paulus and Ovid and inviting us to reflect on their relation to Satricus and Solymus as well. Here again is *Ib.* 246–247: *'fata canet uates qui tua' dixit 'erit.' / ille ego sum uates*. As was noted above, the first words of Clotho's prophecy, which refers to Ovid (*fata canet uates*, *Ib.* 246), are echoed in Paulus' identification of himself as *uates* to Varro (*fata cano uates*, 9.61). What grounds their likeness to one another, as we also noted, is that each *uates* is anticipated as such by an earlier prophecy, Ovid by that of Clotho (*Ib.* 243), Paulus by that of the Cumaean Sibyl (9.57–58). But Satricus and Solymus might be compared here as well. There is, for one, a similarly two-staged prophetic or admonitory sequence in their story: Satricus, first, advises Solymus to tell Paulus to avoid battle and to stop Varro (9.134–141)—this, incidentally, is the passage in which the acrostic *NASVS* appears—and, then, Solymus, after stabbing himself, relays his father's warning by writing a message for Varro in blood on his shield: *mananti sanguine signat / in clipeo mandata patris FVGE PROELIA VARRO* ("In his blood, still flowing, he writes on the shield his father's command: avoid battle, Varro," 9.174–175). Second, when Varro later dismisses this message, he refers to it as a *carmen* (9.266); the term is appropriate enough given the warning's prophetic content, but it also hints at Solymus' role as a poet and thus invites comparison with those *uates* who "sing" of coming misfortunes, Ovid (*canet*, *Ib.* 246) and Paulus (*cano*, 9.61).[22]

Ovid's identification of himself as the *uates* foretold by Clotho (*ille ego sum uates*, *Ib.* 247) also finds resonance in these Silian characters. When Satricus reveals to his son who he is, he uses the same formula, *ille ego sum*, and it likewise begins its hexameter: *ille ego sum Satricus* ("It is I, Satricus," 9.128). The other parallels with the *Ibis* in the events leading up to the Cannae battle recommend this case of allusion. But even if one does not take them into account, one might recognize the formula as Ovidian; for in pre-Silian Latin there are twenty-eight

---

21 For more on Ibis' canine character, see Williams (1996) 20–21, who cites, in fact, 8.290–291 as a *comparandum*.
22 For *carmen* in these senses (i.e. "prophecy" and "song" or "poetry"), see *OLD*, s.v. *carmen* 1c, 2, and 3.

instances of the collocation *ille ego* (including *Ib.* 247), twenty-two of which are in Ovid, and of the twelve instances in which it is followed by the verb *sum* (again including the *Ibis* instance) nine appear in Ovid.[23] What is also notable is that in all but five instances of *ille ego* in the Ovidian corpus (those in the *Heroides* and *Metamorphoses* and the one in *Tristia* 4.5.12) Ovid is speaking of himself; the collocation serves, in other words, as an autobiographical cue, flagging his presence as a "flesh-and-blood" (literary) historical figure.[24] In light of this, it may not surprise that the other occurrence of *ille ego* at Cannae involves Paulus. In book 10, when the battle is lost and Lentulus, who is wounded and preparing to flee, runs into Paulus, he tries to convince him to flee with him (260–275); the consul, however, refuses and tells Lentulus to leave without him (276–291). Here is the conclusion of Paulus' speech to Lentulus, his last words before he is overwhelmed by the enemy and slain moments later (cf. 10.303–305):

> 'nec talia Paulo
> pectora, nec manes tam parua intramus imago.
> ille ego – sed uano quid enim te demoror aeger,
> Lentule, conquestu? perge atque hinc cuspide fessum   290
> erige quadrupedem propere.'
>
> (10.287–291)

'Neither is Paulus' heart of such a sort nor do we cut such a small figure in death. I am that one—but why do I in my weakened condition delay you, Lentulus, with a worthless complaint? Go on and hasten from here, prodding your weary horse on with your spear-tip.'

There are several ways to interpret the aposiopesis in line 289 (*ille ego –*); it may reflect, for example, Paulus' inability to continue speaking because of exhaustion

---

23 Ovid: *Am.* 2.1.2, 3.8.23; *Ars* 2.451, 452; *Her.* 16.246; *Met.* 1.757, 4.226 (*sum*), 15.500 (*sum*); *Tr.* 4.5.12 (*sum*), 4.10.1, 5.7b.55; *Pont.* 1.2.33 (*sum*), 34 (*sum*), 129 (*sum*), 131, 136, 4.3.11 (*sum*), 13, 15, 16, 17 (*sum*). Others: Plaut. *Amph.* 601; Tib. 1.5.9, 6.31 (*sum*); [Tib.] 3.4.72; Prop. 4.9.38 (*sum*); Calp. *Ecl.* 3.55 (*sum*). Elsewhere in Silius and in his contemporaries: Sil. 10.289 (discussed next), 11.177, 180; Stat. *Theb.* 8.666, 9.434, 11.165 (*sum*); *Silv.* 4.3.76, 5.5.38 and 40; *Ach.* 1.650; Mart. 9 pr. 11 (*sum*), 9.28.2 (*sum*), 10.53.1 (*sum*). The collocation *illa ego* is also found in pre-Silian Latin five times, twice in Ovid (*Her.* 12.105; *Fast.* 3.505) and three times in the *Ciris* (409, 411, 414); it also appears in Silius twice (15.59, 61) and Statius' *Thebaid* once (5.34).
24 See Farrell (2004), who argues that Ovid uses the phrase *ille ego (qui)* to set his literary career in relation to Virgil's. While it is not clear that the phrase should be read as Virgilian or quasi-Virgilian—its Virgilian attribution is due to the fact that it begins the famous four-line prepromium that, according to Servius, was removed from the beginning of the *Aeneid* after the poet's death (see Farrell (2004) 47–48)—Ovid's use of it to reflect on his poetic career and self-fashioned literary biography is quite certain.

or the wounds he has received or it may indicate his unwillingness to delay Lentulus' flight any longer.[25] But whatever Paulus' reason for discontinuing his thought, his likeness to Ovid, established before the battle, and the Ovidian resonance of *ille ego* invite us to identify him with Ovid. In the final moments of his life, therefore, Paulus is an Ovidian figure, just as Satricus was when he was about to die.

These Silian characters evoke Ovid and Ibis in two other ways. One is through shipwreck imagery. In *Ib.* 17–18 Ovid describes the disgrace of his exile as if it were a shipwreck and Ibis as if he were fighting him for the ship's planks: *cumque ego quassa meae complectar membra carinae, / naufragii tabulas pugnat habere mei*, "And as I embrace the smashed pieces of my ship, he fights to comandeer the planks of my wreck." The image recurs later when Ovid imagines his death one day by shipwreck (*Ib.* 147–148) and when he hopes that Ibis meets a similar fate (*Ib.* 593–594).[26] Compare Varro and Paulus, who are likewise tied together through their shared experience of a figurative shipwreck, the defeat at Cannae. When Lentulus tries to convince Paulus to flee from the battlefield, he compares the defeat to a storm and pleads with the consul not to abandon the ship, namely, Rome, which needs him to stay alive to guide her affairs (10.267–273);[27] Paulus, as we have seen, declines and is subsequently killed. And, shortly thereafter, once the battle is over, Silius compares bodies strewn along the banks of the Aufidus to a ship's crew and its wreckage strewn about the surface of the sea (10.318–325). As for Varro, when his return to Rome after the defeat is anticipated later in the book, he is compared to a disgraced captain who abandoned his ship and is its sole survivor (10.608–612).[28]

Another theme by which Ovid and Ibis are evoked in Silius' Cannae pairs is that of self-destruction. In the story of Satricus and Solymus this is conveyed not only by the death of the father, a case of familial violence of course, but by the death of the son, who commits suicide (9.173–177). Varro is self-destructive in that he pushes for the ill-fated conflict with Hannibal and thus brings defeat on himself and his own city, Rome, and, in fact, before fleeing the battlefield, he

---

25 Spaltenstein (1990) 76 considers the latter possibility.
26 For more on shipwrecks and the *Ibis*, see Hawkins (2014) 63–69. Note, incidentally, that Silius' Ovidian Anna was the victim of a shipwreck too (*naufraga*, 8.70).
27 *Deseris in tantis puppim si, Paule, procellis* ("If, Paulus, you abandon your ship in such a great squall," 10.269); *gubernas* ("You steer," 10.270); *uiuisque in turbine tanto* ("And you live through such a great storm," 10.271).
28 While there is no use of such imagery at the corresponding moments in Livy, Varro's letter to the senate, in which he compares the Cannae defeat to a shipwreck (22.56.2), may have inspired Silius, as Spaltenstein (1990) 99 points out.

considers killing himself (9.649–655). This point is made by the death of Paulus too, not only because it is in no small part due to the actions of his fellow consul Varro, but because Paulus is himself ready and willing to die; here we may advert to his refusal to leave the battlefield or how he resembles at Cannae a *devotus* in several respects.²⁹ As for Ibis and Ovid, they are engaged in a form of mutually assured destruction: Ibis attacks Ovid, Ovid attacks Ibis, and they both end up, at least figuratively, together, fighting over planks in the same shipwreck (cf. *Ib.* 17–18, discussed above). Ovid, moreover, hopes that Ibis will destroy himself by various means, including suicide (e.g., *Ib.* 493–494, 611–614), and elsewhere in his exile poetry tells us several times that he considered suicide too (e.g., *Tr.* 1.5.5; *Pont.* 1.6.41–44; 1.9.21–22). Of course, Ovid also blames himself for his exile, famously attributing his downfall to "a mistake and a poem" (*carmen et error*, *Tr.* 2.207).³⁰

4 *Carmen*: Poetry and Self-Destruction

Thus far I hope to have shown that there are sufficient grounds for placing Ovid as a (literary) historical figure at Cannae, both in the events leading up to the battle and, in some cases, during and shortly after it. I would now like to follow up on my hunch that Ovid's presence at Cannae has something to do with his claim to have been punished for and by his own poetry. The detail of Marsyas in the catalogue of book 8 already points us in that direction, as does the theme of self-destruction at Cannae, whether as seen, more broadly, in the battle itself or as seen in the Ovidian figures of Satricus, Solymus, Varro, and Paulus. But there are two other pieces of evidence to take into account.

The first is Varro's reaction to the news of Satricus and Solymus' deaths and to the warning written by Solymus on the shield:

> ille ardens animi 'ferte haec' ait 'omina Paulo.
> namque illum, cui femineo stant corde timores,
> mouerit ista manus, quae caede imbuta nefanda,
> cum Furiae expeterent poenas, fortasse paterno   265
> signauit moriens sceleratum sanguine carmen.'
>
>   (9.262–266)

---

29 On Paulus as *deuotus*, see Marks (2005) 135–143.
30 For other instances in which he claims his poetry harmed him, see n. 9 above.

> He, seething, says: 'Take these omens to Paulus. For he, who is susceptible to such fears in his womanish heart, might be stirred by that hand, which, when the Furies sought retribution, was stained with unspeakable murder and, while dying, wrote that abominable message perhaps in his father's own blood.'

By an allusion in these lines Silius invites us to reflect on the story of the Thracian king Pyreneus. During a storm he offered the Muses shelter in his palace; once inside, he locked the doors, intending to rape them, but the Muses flew away; he tried to pursue them by jumping off a tower, but fell to his death. We only know this story from Ovid, who has one of the Muses recount it to Minerva in *Met.* 5.268–293. The end of the story is given there as follows:

> ipse secuturo similis stetit arduus arce
> 'qua'que 'uia est uobis, erit et mihi' dixit 'eadem'   290
> seque iacit uecors e summo culmine turris
> et cadit in uultus discussisque ossibus oris
> tundit humum moriens scelerato sanguine tinctum.
>
> (*Met.* 5.289–293)

> He himself [i.e. Pyreneus] stood high up on a tower as if to follow them and said: 'Whichever path is yours is mine as well.' And in his madness he throws himself from the very top of the tower, falls headlong, and, shattering the bones in his face, strikes the ground, staining it with his abominable blood as he dies.

As we can see, the last line in the Silian passage is modeled after the last line in the Ovidian one: *signau<u>it moriens sceleratum sanguine</u>* carmen (9.266) = *tund<u>it humum moriens scelerato sanguine</u> tinctum* (*Met.* 5.293). But there are other details that support this case of allusion. When Varro refers to Paulus' womanly fears (*cui femineo stant corde timores*, 9.263), we are reminded of a remark made by the Muse immediately before she recounts the Pyreneus story. After Minerva, who is visiting Helicon, calls the Muses fortunate for living where they do (*Met.* 5.264–268), the Muse acknowledges that fact, but remarks that they do not always feel safe (*Met.* 5.268–272) because, she says, all things terrify the minds of maidens (*omnia terrent / uirgineas mentes*, *Met.* 5.273–274); she then recounts a previous instance in which their safety had been threatened, namely, when Pyreneus tried to do them harm (*Met.* 5.274–293). Another suggestive detail is the reference to the warning written on the shield as a *carmen* (9.266). I noted above how this word invites comparison between Ovid and Solymus as singers or poets. Now, we may note how it does so in combination with the echo of *Met.* 5.293 in the same line: Ovid, the poet from Sulmo, is alluded to in reference to a "song" (*carmen*) written by someone from Sulmo (Solymus).

The death of Pyreneus, so recalled, fittingly underlines the self-destructive madness of Varro at Cannae: just as the Thracian king in foolish pursuit of the Muses brings about his own demise, so Varro in foolish pursuit of victory leads Rome to her greatest defeat in the Second Punic War. And yet, Silius, I propose, is inviting us to reflect on a detail of Ovid's biography as well: that his own poetry was partly to blame for his punishment of exile. To be sure, Pyreneus' fate has something to do with his attempted violation of the Muses and may be read as deserved comeuppance for that. But the fact that his pursuit of them precipitates his death also hints at the idea of self-inflicted artistic failure, a theme that might remind us of Ovid's own downfall.[31] Of course, what invites specific consideration of Ovid's biography at this point is that the allusion in 9.266 is made in connection with the "song" of the Ovidian Solymus, as was just noted. Another suggestive detail in this regard is the verb *signauit* (9.266), which Silius also used to describe Solymus when he originally composed the warning on the shield (*signat*, 9.174). In both cases the verb indicates that Solymus "marked" or "stained" the shield with his blood. But in light of the many allusions to Ovid's poetry at Cannae and considering the fact that so many of them hint at the poet's biography, we might also consider the verb in the sense of "to seal" and be reminded of the poetic convention of the *sphragis*, "seal," whereby a poet presents himself in his own text as a "flesh-and-blood" individual; to that end he may name himself or identify himself by other biographical details, such as his birthplace or literary accomplishments, and often, but not always, does so at the end of a work or a part thereof or at some retrospective moment or moments in his literary career.[32] Such an understanding of the verb, in fact, suits well the timing of its occurrence in 9.174 (*signat*), where, Solymus, after all, is dying and is thus composing his last "poem" (*carmen*), as it were. Its use in 9.266 in reference to that event (*signauit*) also marks or "seals off" an end; for that line stands as the last mention of Solymus' warning and is the last reference to the Satricus-Solymus story in the epic. But as the latter instance, additionally, coincides with an allusion to Ovid's *Metamorphoses*, its evocation of the self-reflective poetic convention of the *sphragis* would not only annotate that allusion nicely, but in combination with it invites us

---

31 The interpretation of Leach (1974) 113, who similarly reads Pyreneus as a figure "seeking poetic inspiration," has not won many adherents, as far as I have been able to ascertain, but, perhaps, Silius' allusion to the tale lends support to her reading. For a different way of reading Ovid's biography in connection with the story, see Schmitzer (1990) 188–201, who views Pyreneus as an Augustus-figure who both rivals and oppresses the Muses of Ovidian song.
32 For the verb in the sense of "to seal," see *OLD*, s.v. *signo*, 8. For the literary *sphragis*, see Kranz (1961).

to think about the self-destructive end of Ovid's life and literary career in comparison with that of his fellow Sulmonian. And so, as we linger on their self-inflicted downfalls, Solymus' death by his own sword, Ovid's punishment for his poetry, we come to see Solymus' *sphragis* or, rather, the *sphragis* Silius composes for him as a *sphragis* for Ovid himself.

But there is another remarkable detail to consider: the last reference to the Satricus-Solymus story in 9.266 (*signauit moriens sceleratum sanguine carmen*) takes us back to line 9.66, with which Silius begins his account of their tale: *necnon et noctem sceleratus polluit error*, "Also, an abominable mistake defiled the night". Note how the adjective *sceleratus* appears here in the same metrical *sedes* as in 9.266, but also note what stands in place of *carmen* at the end of the line: *error*. The *error* or "mistake" to which Silius refers is the misunderstanding that leads Solymus to kill his father Satricus, a fact confirmed by Satricus' use of the word when he later addresses his son: *non nox errorem nigranti condidit umbra?* (9.148: "Did the night not conceal your mistake in its black darkness?"). Could Silius between *error* in 9.66 and *carmen* in 9.266 be recalling Ovid's claim that he was ruined by *carmen et error* (*Tr.* 2.207)? Given the many hints at Ovid's biography in the episode and at Cannae more widely, this appears to me likely. In fact, the two are juxtaposed when the Roman troops report to Varro the discovery of the dead father and son: *ocius erroris culpam deflendaque facta / ductori pandunt atque arma uetantia pugnam* (9.260–261: "They quickly disclosed to their leader the crime brought on by a mistake, the deplorable deeds, and the arms forbidding battle."). Note *erroris* (260) and the phrase *arma uetantia pugnam* (261), which refers to the warning Solymus writes on his shield, a warning that five lines later is called *carmen* (9.266).[33]

Silius repeatedly evokes the biographical Ovid in the Cannae books, especially in the narrative leading up to the battle. The context of this Ovidian program, as I suggested at the outset, is fitting in that the Cannae defeat represents, to a good extent, Rome's self-destruction; in the portions we have looked at this is impressed upon us by the conflict between the consuls Paulus and Varro and by the fates of Satricus and Solymus. This point is further conveyed, as I noted earlier, by numerous allusions and references to civil war in the Cannae books

---

33 *Culpam* and *facta* (9.260) seem to hint at *Tr.* 2.208 too: *alterius facti culpa silenda mihi*, "I must remain silent about the fault of the other deed." It may also be significant that Silius has Solymus write his message on a weapon, a shield (*in clipeo*, 9.175), later called *arma* (9.261), as we have just seen. As allusions to the *Ibis* have played such an important role in placing Ovid at Cannae, it would be fitting that a weapon provides the means by which Solymus conveys his warning (curse?) to Varro; for it is a commonplace in invective poetry to speak of one's words as weapons, and in the *Ibis* Ovid does just that (e.g., 1–2, 9–10, 39–40, 45–54, 135–140).

and, as we now see, by the presence of the exiled Ovid, the Ovid who brought ruin upon himself because of a mistake and a poem. Along these lines, we might observe that Ovid's connection with such strife is closer than even references to his downfall in his late works indicate. In the last poem of the *Amores* he offers a *sphragis* in which he notes that he comes from a place that had taken up arms against Rome in the Social Wars:

> Paelignae dicar gloria gentis ego,
> quam sua libertas ad honesta coegerat arma,
> cum tonuit socias anxia Roma manus.
>
> (*Am.* 3.15.8–10)

I will be spoken of as the glory of the Paelignian people, whom the cause of freedom had compelled to take up noble arms when worried Rome thundered against allied forces.

One detail of Ovid's biography that Silius is particularly interested in, however, is the poet's conflicted relationship with his own poetry, that it contributed to his eventual demise; we see this in the detail of Marsyas in the catalogue, the parallelism between Paulus and Ovid as singing *uates*, the allusion to Pyreneus' death, and the reference to Solymus' warning as *carmen*. By way of conclusion, I would propose that this emphasis suggests a specific way in which Silius read Ovid's *Ibis*, a work whose influence, as we have seen, is quite considerable in the Cannae books. It has long been debated who Ibis is in that poem, with interpreters identifying him with any number of historical figures. But Darcy Krasne has recently proposed that the *Ibis* is directed against Ovid himself or, rather, against his poetry or the Muses, who inspired his poetry and thus contributed to his punishment of exile.[34] Granted, Silius' use of the *Ibis* at Cannae may suggest that our poet took Ovid to be at odds with a real person, someone close to him or someone with whom he was previously on good terms; if so, the "conflicts" between father and son (Satricus and Solymus) and between fellow consuls (Paulus and Varro) would seem to mirror that detail in Ovid's life as presented in the *Ibis*. But Silius' emphasis on the theme of self-inflicted artistic failure in combination with the many biographical details we have observed might also suggest that our poet took Ibis to be Ovid himself or his own poetry. If so, Rome's defeat at Cannae and Ovid's downfall stand in a still tidier relation to each another, each being an instance of self-destruction.

---

[34] Krasne (2012) 84–95.

Bibliography

von Albrecht, Michael (1968), "Claudia Quinta bei Silius Italicus und bei Ovid", in: *Der altsprachliche Unterricht* 11, 76–95.
Augoustakis, Antony (ed.) (2010), *Brill's Companion to Silius Italicus*, Leiden.
Augoustakis, Antony (ed.) (2013), *Ritual and Religion in Flavian Epic*, Oxford.
den Boeft, Jan/Kessels, Antonius H.M. (eds.) (1982), *Actus: Studies in honour of H.L.W. Nelson*, Utrecht.
Brouwers, Johannes H. (1982), "Zur Lucan-Imitation bei Silius Italicus", in: den Boeft/Kessels (1982) 73–87.
Bruère, Richard T. (1958), "*Color Ovidianus* in Silius' *Punica* 1–7", in: Herescu (1958) 475–499.
Bruère, Richard T. (1959), "*Color Ovidianus* in Silius *Punica* 8–17", in: *CPh* 54, 228–245.
Casali, Sergio (2006), "The Poet at War: Ennius on the Field in Silius' *Punica*", in: *Arethusa* 39, 569–593.
Esposito, Paolo/Nicastri, Luciano (eds.) (1999), *Interpretare Lucano. Miscellanea di studi*, Naples.
Farrell, Joseph (2004), "Ovid's Virgilian Career", in: *MD* 52, 41–53.
Feldherr, Andrew (2004), "Flaying the Other", in: *Arethusa* 37, 77–87.
Fucecchi, Marco (1999), "La vigilia di Canne nei *Punica* e un contributo alla storia dei rapporti fra Silio Italico e Lucano", in: Esposito/Nicastri (1999) 305–342.
Hawkins, Tom (2014), *Iambic Poetics in the Roman Empire*, Cambridge.
Herescu, Niculae I. (ed.) (1958), *Ovidiana. Recherches sur Ovide*, Paris.
Hilberg, Isidor (1899), "Ist die *Ilias Latina* von einem Italicus verfaßt oder einem Italicus gewidmet?", in: *Wiener Studien* 21, 264–305.
Hinds, Stephen (1998), *Allusion and Intertext. Dynamics of Appropriation in Roman Poetry*, Cambridge.
Konstan, David/Raaflaub, Kurt A. (eds.) (2010), *Epic and History*, Oxford.
Kranz, Walther (1961), "*Sphragis*. Ichform und Namensiegel als Eingangs- und Schlußmotiv antiker Dichtung", in: *RhM* 104, 3–46, 97–124.
Krasne, Darcy (2012), "The Pedant's Curse: Obscurity and Identity in Ovid's *Ibis*", in: *Dictynna* 9 (http://dictynna.revues.org/912).
Leach, Eleanor W. (1974), "Ekphrasis and the Theme of Artistic Failure in Ovid's *Metamorphoses*", in: *Ramus* 3, 102–142.
Lucarini, Carlo M. (2004), "Le fonti storiche di Silio Italico", in: *Athenaeum* 92, 103–126.
Lundström, Sven (1980), *Ovids Metamorphosen und die Politik des Kaisers*, Uppsala.
Manuwald, Gesine (2007), "Epic Poets as Characters: On Poetics and Multiple Intertextuality in Silius Italicus' *Punica*" in: *RFIC* 135, 71–90.
Marks, Raymond (2005), "*Per Vulnera Regnum*: Self-Destruction, Self-Sacrifice, and *Devotio* in *Punica* 4–10", in: *Ramus* 34, 127–151.
Marks, Raymond (2010a), "The Song and the Sword: Silius' *Punica* and the Crisis of Early Imperial Epic", in: Konstan/Raaflaub (2010) 185–211.
Marks, Raymond (2010b), "Silius and Lucan", in: Augoustakis (2010) 127–153.
Marks, Raymond (2013), "Reconcilable Differences: Anna Perenna and the Battle of Cannae in the *Punica*", in: Augoustakis (2013) 287–301.
Marks, Raymond (2014), "*Nosces Fabios certamine ab uno*: The Tale of the Three Hundred Fabii in *Punica* 7", in: *Illinois Classical Studies* 39, 139–169.

McGuire, Donald T. (1997), *Acts of Silence: Civil War, Tyranny, and Suicide in the Flavian Epics*, Hildesheim.

Nesselrath, Heinz-Günther (1986), "Zu den Quellen des Silius Italicus", in: *Hermes* 114, 203–230.

Newlands, Carole E. (1995), *Playing with Time: Ovid and the* Fasti, Ithaca.

Pomeroy, Arthur J. (2010), "To Silius Through Livy and his Predecessors", in: Augoustakis (2010) 27–45.

Ripoll, François (2000), "Silius Italicus et Cicéron", in: *LEC* 68, 147–173.

Schaffenrath, Florian (ed.) (2010a), *Silius Italicus. Akten der Innsbrucker Tagung vom 19.–21. Juni 2008*, Frankfurt am Main.

Schaffenrath, Florian (2010b), "Epische Erzähler in den *Punica*", in: Schaffenrath (2010a) 111–126.

Schmitzer, Ulrich (1990), *Zeitgeschichte in Ovids Metamorphosen. Mythologische Dichtung unter politischem Anspruch*, Stuttgart.

Spaltenstein, François (1986), *Commentaire des* Punica *de Silius Italicus (livres 1 à 8)*, Geneva.

Spaltenstein, François (1990), *Commentaire des* Punica *de Silius Italicus (livres 9 à 17)*, Geneva.

Stocks, Claire (2014), *The Roman Hannibal: Remembering the Enemy in Silius Italicus'* Punica, Liverpool.

Williams, Gareth D. (1996), *The Curse of Exile: A Study of Ovid's* Ibis, Cambridge.

Wilson, Marcus (2004), "Ovidian Silius", in: *Arethusa* 37, 225–249.

Michael Dewar
The Flavian Epics and the Neoterics

The poets of the Augustan age bear abundant witness to the powerful effects of the neoteric revolution that preceded them, and also to their own awareness of how that revolution had greatly extended the range of styles in which they themselves could now choose to write.[1] The most joyous evidence for a poet's delight in this new-found abundance is provided by the sixth *Eclogue* of Virgil, in which the master-poet begins the song of Silenus by ventriloquizing the solemn grandeur of Lucretian didactic, only then to turn, with dizzying speed, to the voluptuous sentimentality of Calvus, of whose lost epyllion *Io* the melodious old drunken satyr even preserves a phrase for us.[2] It was a time of change and excitement, in which Latin poetry came of age, and the best-read poets of the day knew it. In *Amores* 1.15, Ovid seeks to establish a canon of Latin poets whose works will match the glories of the Greeks and live for ever. Prophecy makes fools of us all, and though his list includes Varro of Atax (1.15.21–22) and Gallus (1.15.29–30), whose poetry now lies in utter ruin, it makes no space for Catullus, whose "trifles" (*nugas*, 1. 4) have outlived not only Varro and Gallus but also Calvus, Catullus' own close friend and colleague in the confraternity of irreverent modernists. The wrong calls matter less, for the moment, than the reminder that in any generation some poets make it on to the reading lists, be they standard or merely ideal, while others are read only by the true enthusiasts and the specialists.

Virgil and Horace became canonical soon after their deaths, and their consequent centrality to the Roman educational system no doubt further displaced the neoterics to the margins, while few poets, even those we think of as "full-time" or as "professionals", can ever have read as widely as Ovid. Even so, "everybody does not disappear at once: people straddle the generations who represent a former way of looking at things"[3]—and, we could add, of writing about them. The survivors last long enough to leave a mark on the memory of those who themselves live for several decades more. It is correspondingly less surprising, then,

---

1 Courtney (1993) 189 firmly declares that "neoterics", a term we borrow from Cic. *Att.* 7.2.1, is "a word we should cease to use, since no ancient author employs it" in the sense in which it is understood in modern criticism. It is also true that Cicero was not referring to any kind of organized "school" of poets. Yet the term remains in common use more than twenty years later, for the good reason that, in the absence of any clearly legitimate alternative, it continues to serve as a useful and familiar designation for a recognizable literary-historical phenomenon.
2 Verg. *Ecl.* 6.47 *a, uirgo infelix* ("Ah, unhappy girl!"). See further Hollis (2007) 64–65.
3 Nisbet (1995) 390.

that subsequent generations in the early imperial period can be shown to have had a continuing interest in some quite recherché material from the last days of the Republic, material that is, for us, now fragmentary. Ovid's prediction of eternal fame for Varro of Atax and his *Argonautae* looks rather less rash when we note that Seneca the Elder seems to have been familiar with the poem. He at any rate records with apparent approval the argument made by Julius Montanus to the effect that, in his description of the deep silence of the night, Virgil (*Aen.* 8.26–27) was adapting a line or two from Varro's earlier epic:

> at Vergilio imitationem bene cessisse, qui illos optimos uersus Varronis expressisset in melius:
>
> 'desierant latrare canes urbesque silebant;
> omnia noctis erant placida composta quiete.'
>
> (Sen. *Controv.* 7.1.27; 10.1–2 Courtney = 129.1–2 Hollis)

But [Julius Montanus said] Virgil had carried off his imitation successfully, because he had improved the wording of those excellent lines of Varro:

'The dogs had ceased to bark and the cities were silent;
Everything had been laid to rest in the peaceful quiet of night.'

His son, Seneca the Younger, also quotes the second of those two lines, in a discussion of the importance of silence for the concentration required for the serious study of philosophy:

> animum enim cogo sibi intentum esse nec auocari ad externa; omnia licet foris resonent, dum intus nihil tumultus sit, dum inter se non rixentur cupiditas et timor, dum avaritia luxuriaque non dissideant nec altera alteram uexet. nam quid prodest totius regionis silentium, si adfectus fremunt?
> 'omnia noctis erant placida composta quiete.'
>
> (Sen. *Ep.* 56.5–6; Courtney 10.2 = Hollis 129.2)[4]

---

4 Not that the philosopher could leave without comment and rebuke what he considered the woolly-minded thinking of the poet, for he continues: *falsum est: nulla placida est quies nisi quam ratio composuit; nox exhibet molestiam, non tollit, et sollicitudines mutat*, "This is not true: no quiet is peaceful unless reason has laid it to rest; night puts our troubles on display, it does not remove them, and it changes our worries for others."

> For I compel my mind to be intent upon itself and not to be distracted by things outside; everything outdoors may be in uproar, so long as there is no element of agitation within, so long as desire and fear are not engaged in quarrels among themselves, and so long as miserliness and extravagance are not at loggerheads and neither plagues the other. For what good is silence all around us, if our emotions are roaring?
> 'Everything had been laid to rest in the peaceful quiet of night.'

It could of course be objected that Seneca the Younger's knowledge of the line may have come, not directly from his own reading of Varro, but second hand, from his having read his father. Against this objection, however, we should weigh the striking fact that, unlike his father, he quotes Varro without naming him, apparently in the expectation that his readers will have no difficulty in recognizing the line. In the Flavian age, Statius also seems to refer to Varro without thinking it necessary to name him, in a catalogue of epic poets (*Silv.* 2.7.77 *et qui per freta duxit Argonautas*, "and he who led the Argonauts through the narrows"), while Quintilian declares him, though a translator rather than an original poet, "not to be scorned" (*non spernendus*), albeit with reservations, as a model for the style of those who aspire to become orators (*Inst.* 10.1.87). In all truth, though, it is hard indeed to see, from the surviving fragments, precisely what influence he may have had on either any Roman orator or on Valerius Flaccus, the Flavian poet who sang, as he had sung, of the voyage of the Argo.[5]

Although Varro translated Apollonius, and followed him closely, and though his poetry shows traces of what might be called neoteric techniques, perhaps he would not count in everyone's eyes as a true "neoteric."[6] Consider instead the still more suggestive case of Aemilius Macer, author of *Ornithogonia* and *Theriaca*, self-consciously learned poems in that most beloved of genres among the Hellenistic poets, didactic. He hailed, like Catullus, from Verona, though he was probably a decade or so younger,[7] and he lived long enough for the youthful Ovid to have been able to attend his recitations when Macer himself was already "quite advanced in years" (*grandior aeuo*, *Tr.* 4.10.43–44). Some eighty years or so after that encounter between the generations, another young prodigy of a poet seems

---

5 For Varro's place in the Latin literary tradition see the comments of Zissos (2008) xxii and Manuwald (2015) 3. Feletti (1998) offers the most thorough and ambitious attempt in recent scholarship to establish the relations between his poem and that of Valerius. Her conclusion is not encouraging (p. 121): "Der Vergleich zwischen Valerius Flaccus' Gedicht und den wenigen erhaltenen Fragmenten der *Argonautae* scheint zu beweisen, daß diese für Valerius kein akzeptables poetisches Modell waren."
6 Hollis (2007) 177–178.
7 Hollis (2007) 100.

to have found Macer worthy of his attention; the scholiast on Lucan 9.701 suggests that the infamous catalogue of African serpents owes much to the *Theriaca*.[8] A generation later still, the younger contemporaries of our Flavian epicists were being advised by Quintilian that Macer, whom he mentions in the same breath as Lucretius, was worth their attention, even if, like Varro, not quite ideal as a model for oratory.[9]

Not that we should imagine that the Flavian poets necessarily cared very much for Quintilian's judgements on other poets as exemplars for orators. They will surely have had their own motives for reading any poets he had read, and others besides. All the same, it is worth our while to remind ourselves how easily we can trace, even with such fragmentary poets, chains of continuity in reading that extend from the time of the second triumvirate to the time of the second dynasty of the principate. All this gives strength to, for example, Hollis's tentative suggestion that the line of Cinna quoted by the scholiast on Juv. 6.155, *atque imitata niues lucens legitur crystallus*, "and shining crystal that looks like snow is gathered" (5 Courtney = 17 Hollis), has left a trace in that most prosaic of works, the encyclopedia of Pliny the Elder (*HN* 37.118 *iasponyx ... niues imitata*, "jasper onyx ... which looks like snow").[10] And if Pliny could read Cinna, it is all the less surprising that his nephew should quote a few polemical lines of Catullus in defence of his own dalliance with frivolous hendecasyllables (Plin. *Ep*. 4.14.5, citing Catull. 16.5–8), or that he should have a friend, Pompeius Saturninus, who liked to compose verse that imitated both Catullus and his inseparable companion Calvus, and who even sought to infuse authenticity into his poems by adding in elements that seemed to their own age a little unrefined:

---

8 For details, see Courtney (1993) 295 on fragment 6 in his numeration (= 54 Hollis): Schol. Bern. Lucan. 9.701 *'aspida somniferam tumida ceruice levavit'*: *serpentum nomina aut a Macro sumpsit de libris Theriacon (nam duos edidit) aut ...*, "'raised up the asp, which with its swollen neck brings sleep': The names of the snakes he either took from Macer, from his books of *Theriaca* (for he produced two of them) or else ..." Courtney (*ibid*.) argues that the dependence will have extended far beyond that one line: "Lucan must have derived much from Macer in 700–937." Hollis (2007) 108–109 takes this insight considerably further, arguing that Lucan is "deliberately writing in the older poet's manner" and that this influence can be seen both in numerous stylistic features and also in his decision to provide a learned origin-myth for Africa's many dangerous serpents.
9 Quint. *Inst*. 10.1.87: *nam Macer et Lucretius legendi quidem, sed non ut phrasin, id est, corpus eloquentiae faciant, elegantes in sua quisque materia sed alter humilis, alter difficilis*, "For Macer and Lucretius should be read, to be sure, but not so as to form style, that is, the body of eloquence, each being elegant in his own subject-matter, but one unelevated and the other obscure."
10 Hollis (2007) 48.

praeterea facit uersus, quales Catullus meus aut Caluus, re uera quales Catullus aut Caluus. quantum illis leporis dulcedinis amaritudinis amoris! inserit sane, sed data opera, mollibus leuibusque duriusculos quosdam; et hoc quasi Catullus aut Caluus.

(Plin. *Ep.* 1.16.5)

In addition, he writes such poetry as my beloved Catullus or Calvus did, truly such poetry as Catullus or Calvus wrote. How much of the charm and sweetness and bitterness of love they have! In fact, he puts in among the soft and smooth lines, on purpose, a few that are a little on the harsh side; and that too is just like Catullus or Calvus.

We should add that at least one of Calvus' speeches was also still being widely read in the Flavian age, as Tacitus informs us:

ipse mihi Caluus, cum unum et uiginti, ut puto, libros reliquerit, uix in una aut altera oratiuncula satis facit. nec dissentire ceteros ab hoc meo iudicio uideo: quotus enim quisque Calui in Asicium aut in Drusum legit? at hercule in omnium studiosorum manibus uersantur accusationes quae in Vatinium inscribuntur, ac praecipue secunda ex his oratio; est enim uerbis ornata et sententiis, auribus iudicum accommodata, ut scias ipsum quoque Caluum intellexisse quid melius esset, nec uoluntatem ei quo <minus> sublimius et cultius diceret sed ingenium ac uires defuisse.

(Tac. *Dial.* 21.1–2)

Calvus himself, if you ask me, for all that he has left behind, I believe, twenty-one books, only just comes up to scratch in one or two of his little speeches. And I can see that none of the other critics dissents from this judgement of mine: how many people are there, after all, who have read Calvus' attacks on Asicius or Drusus? And yet, goodness me, the speeches for the prosecution entitled "Against Vatinius" can be found in the hands of all the scholars, and in particular the second of them. For it is rich in diction and argument, and well suited to the ears of those who were sitting in judgement, so that you can be sure that Calvus himself also understood what was more effective, and that what he lacked was not the will to speak in a more sublime and refined manner but the natural talent and the force.

All this is perhaps a little tendentious, as the speaker is making a particular point, and even if Calvus' oratory was still being read and admired, that would not of itself absolutely guarantee that his verse was being read too. Even so, if his prose was still on the reading-lists of the *studiosi*, no doubt at least some of them are likely to have taken the time to hunt down his naughty verse to amuse themselves when the courts were closed.

So far we have been concerned with establishing a chain of continuity and with the reading practices of the first century. The names of individual readers have therefore been of largely incidental and documentary importance. But what of our Flavian epic poets? Certainly, it seems plausible in principle that any of the three of them could appear in the category imagined above, of poets who read more widely in earlier poetry than what appears in Quintilian's list of recommended reading. Before we consider the surviving Flavian epics, we should remind ourselves that there is clear evidence that at least one of the neoterics was indeed being read and imitated in the Flavian Age. Except for Catullus, all of the neoteric poets are now fragmentary, but even if the *codex Veronensis* had never seen the light of day, we would still know that three Flavian poets, including two of those who are still extant, were familiar with the Catullan corpus. Both Statius and Martial write in celebration of the merits of their rich aristocratic friend Arruntius Stella, whom they praise for the fine poetry he wrote in honour of his poetic mistress and, later, wife Violentilla. Martial (1.7, 7.14.3–6) makes it clear that Stella's poems drew on the "sparrow poems" of Catullus, with his "Ianthis" or "Asteris" taking the role of Lesbia and with a pet dove replacing Catullus' no doubt much drabber bird. It may be more complex even than that. When Statius expresses the depth of Stella's love for Violentilla-Asteris, and hints at its contemporary fame, he tells how the poet sang her name all through the city from dawn to dusk:

> Asteris et uatis totam cantata per Vrbem,
> Asteris ante dapes, nocte Asteris, Asteris ortu.
>
> (Stat. *Silv*. 1.2.197–198)

> And the poet's Asteris, of whom he sang throughout the city,
> Asteris before the banquet, by night Asteris, and Asteris at daybreak.

Both the conceit and the reliance on anaphora to articulate it dimly recall what is perhaps the loveliest of the surviving fragments of Cinna, from his epyllion *Smyrna*:

> te matutinus flentem conspexit Eous,
> te flentem paulo uidit post Hesperus idem.[11]
>
> (6 Courtney = 10 Hollis)

> You in the morning, as you were weeping, the Eastern Star espied,
> You, as you were weeping, the same star a little later, now Western, saw.

As we can see from Hollis's discussion, however, there are numerous possible intermediaries between Cinna and Statius.[12] All the same, it remains possible that Statius is either alluding to Cinna directly or even cleverly adapting into his own

---

[11] Hollis's emendation of the transmitted *et* to *te* in the second line (2007, 40) is convincing.
[12] Hollis (2007) 40.

hexameters what had earlier been adapted by Stella himself, in his elegiacs, from the original hexameters of the neoteric poet.[13]

We know, then, from Pliny the Younger, Statius, and Martial, that, among the neoterics, Catullus and Calvus were certainly being read in the Flavian period, and we learn from *Silvae* 1.2 that at least one of our three Flavian epicists was familiar with at least some of the poems of Catullus. It could be argued that we have taken a very circuitous route, only to find ourselves in much the same place as Dilke was more than sixty years ago, when he noted that Catullus' epyllion, *Carmen* 64, his account of the wedding of Peleus and Thetis, has left some traces in the phrases used by Statius in the *Achilleid*, his own unfinished account of the life-story of the son whose birth and glory the Parcae predict in Catullus' poem.[14] It is to be hoped, however, that the circuitous route was still worth taking,

---

13 Lady Macbeth comes importunately to mind: "These deeds must not be thought / After these ways; so, it will make us mad" (*Macbeth*, 2.2.44–45). For Statius' own allusions to Catullus in the *Silvae*, albeit combined with allusion to Virgil, see Newlands (2011) 166 (on *Silv.* 2.3.22) and 207 (on *Silv.* 2.6.24–25).

14 See Dilke (1954) 12. We can add two observations. First, Statius ends the first book of his epic with a very close and provocative imitation, since the fruitless promises of Theseus to the abandoned Ariadne (Catull. 64.59: *irrita uentosae linquens promissa procellae*, "leaving fruitless promises to the gusting gale") add a grim, ironic tone to the poet's own judgement on the similarly worthless promises that the naïve young Achilles makes to his beloved (*Ach.* 1.960: *irrita uentosae rapiebant uerba procellae*, "the gusting gales snatched his fruitless words away"). In truth, he will not live to see the fall of Troy or to bring her back the gifts of victory: but then, all readers of Catullus 64, as all readers of Homer, already knew that. Secondly, the prediction of Achilles' speed on foot made by the Parcae at Catull. 64.341 *flammea praeuertet celeris uestigia ceruae*, "will outstrip the fiery prints of the swift hind" has indeed, as Dilke observes, shaped *Ach.* 2.111–112 *uolucris cum iam praeuertere ceruos / ... cogebat*, "when now he compelled me to outstrip the wing-footed stags", also of Achilles' speed, but the Catullan line seems to have left a particularly strong impression on Statius. It is also recycled to describe the speed of Parthenopaeus' horse at *Theb.* 4.271 (*cornipedem trepidos suetum praeuertere ceruos*, "horse accustomed to outstrip the trembling stags") and that of a hind hunted by Diana on the ancient Aventine at *Silv.* 2.3.22 (*Auentinaeque legit uestigia ceruae*, "and tracks the prints of the Aventine hind"). See further Hinds (1998) 124–129 and the observations of Davis (2015) 167–168, Ganiban (2015) 85–86 and Micozzi (2015) 331. A full catalogue of the Flavian epicists' allusions to Catullus cannot be offered in the space available here. For some further traces of Catullus 64 in the *Thebaid*, however, see Gervais (2017) 146 (note on 2.214–215), and for Valerius Flaccus' intertextual relationship with the same poem see e.g. Zissos (2008) 155, 159. Note also how Silius 7.413–414 *cum trepidae fremitu uitreis e sedibus antri / aequoreae pelago simul emersere sorores*, "when, trembling at the uproar, the sea-born sisters from the glassy seats in their grotto rose up together from the deep" ingeniously combines the nymphs of Virgil (*G.* 4.350–351 *uitreisque sedilibus omnes / obstipuere*, "and all upon their glassy seats were startled") with their Catullan predecessors (Catull. 64.14–15 *emersere freti candenti e gurgite uultus / aequoreae monstrum Nereides admirantes*,

as it helps bring out two important points. First, Catullus was not the only neoteric poet whose work was demonstrably still being read in the late first century. Secondly, if Catullus looms larger in the existing scholarly discussions than any of his neoteric contemporaries, then that is mainly for the simple reason that Catullus is preserved, if not entirely intact, then almost so.

What, however, can we say, for sure or even tentatively, about the presence in the *Argonautica*, the *Punica*, the *Thebaid*, and the *Achilleid* of those neoteric poets whose works are now preserved for us only in scattered fragments? A wholly comprehensive review of the evidence cannot be offered in the space available to us here, especially since some attention must of necessity be given to reviewing what has already been gleaned by those who have considered the question before. Yet we can perhaps add something of our own: *hoc opus, hic labor est*. In what follows, let us consider, as test cases, three once-famous poems that for us now exist only in a ruinous state.

1 Cinna, *Propempticon Pollionis*

"The first poet whom we definitely know to have used the title *Propempticon* ... was Parthenius ... It would not be surprising if Parthenius' poem exercised considerable influence on Cinna's, and that of Cinna on all Latin poems in the same genre down to Statius (*Silvae* 3.2)."[15] It follows, then, that the loss of Cinna's *Propempticon* is to be regretted by literary historians as much as by anyone who would have taken pleasure in its undoubted elegance or in the geographical and historical learning that inspired Julius Hyginus to equip the poem with a scholarly commentary.[16] The most substantial surviving fragment is of particular interest:

> nec tam donorum ingenteis mirabere aceruos
> innumerabilibus congestos undique saeclis

"from the sea's shining waters the sea-born Nereids raised their faces, gazing in wonder at the portentous sight"), and see Littlewood (2011) 169–170 for an interpretation of the significance of the allusion.
15 Hollis (2007) 22.
16 Hollis (2007) 22–23.

> iam inde a Belidis natalique urbis ab anno
> Cecropis atque alta Tyrii iam ab origine Cadmi.[17]
>
> (1 Courtney = 6 Hollis)

> Nor will you gaze so much in wonder at the vast piles of gifts, heaped up from every quarter through centuries beyond counting, all the way from the sons of Beleus and from the birth-year of Cecrops' city, and all the way from the deep-buried origins of Cadmus in Tyre.

Cinna seems to be describing the treasures offered by the Greek cities to Apollo at Delphi. The larger context is unclear, but perhaps he was saying that Pollio would admire some other prominent tourist attraction—a site in Athens, say, associated with philosophy and wisdom, such as the Academy—with greater pleasure (*nec tam ... mirabere*) than any earthly treasure-house.[18] What is clear is that, while the poet refers to three of the most important cities of the Greeks, such is his *doctrina* that he will resort to nothing so jejune and workaday as their actual names. He chooses instead to identify them through allusions to the ancestors of their royal lines: the descendants of Beleus ruled over Argos, Cecrops was the first king of Athens, and Cadmus, prince of Tyre, founded the city of Thebes. It has been pointed out that there is a remarkably sustained imitation of these four lines of Cinna in a poet whose devotion to Virgil should not mislead us into thinking he read Virgil and Virgil alone among the poets, namely Silius Italicus:

> fama est intactas longaeui <u>ab origine</u> fani
> <u>creuisse</u> in medium <u>congestis undique donis</u>
> <u>immensum</u> per <u>tempus</u> opes <u>lustrisque</u> relictum
> <u>innumeris</u> aurum solo seruante pauore.
>
> (Sil. 13.86–89)

> The story goes that the treasure, never touched, had grown from the origin of the ancient shrine through gifts from every quarter, heaped up in common through time beyond measure, and that the gold had been left there through uncounted years, with fear alone to keep guard upon it.

Hollis, whose underlining is reproduced above for the reader's convenience, is in no doubt about it: "This fragment is closely and extensively imitated by Silius

---

17 So Courtney (1993) 214, accepting Müller's conjecture (*Tyrii iam*) in the fourth line. Hollis (2007) 29 reads *Tyriorum* with Keil and emends *Cadmi* to *Cadmo*.
18 In his own propempticon (1.6.13–14) Propertius gives us an insight into what he expected his friend Tullus to visit in the striking combination *doctas cognoscere Athenas / atque Asiae ueteres cernere diuitias*, "to come to know learned Athens and to see the ancient riches of Asia."

Italicus, in the same number of lines … Silius describes the grove of Feronia, whose treasures had been preserved inviolate through many centuries simply by the religious awe which the place inspired."[19] The same fragment of Cinna's poem may also have left some faint traces in the epic poetry of Statius. To line 4 *Tyriii … ab origine Cadmi* Courtney compares Stat. *Theb.* 2.613 *ecce Chromis Tyrii demissus origine Cadmi*, "and here is Chromis, descended of a line that began with Tyrian Cadmus."[20] A sceptic might object that, in a poem about Thebes, that is a very obvious hexameter line-ending, one that any dactylic poet could have found for himself. Note, then, the use of a similar phrase at *Theb.* 8.228 *ueteresque canunt ab origine Thebas*, "and they sing of ancient Thebes from its beginnings", which could perhaps be used as corroborating evidence either for the presence of Cinna at 2.613, or, by the doubters, as evidence against it, given that *origine* appears many times in Latin hexameters, and pretty much always in the same metrical *sedes*, i.e. occupying the fifth foot (e.g. Ov. *Met.* 4.213 *a prisco … origine Belo*, Stat. *Theb.* 9.333 (the shield of Crenaeus) *lucidus Aoniae caelatur origine gentis*).[21] We find ourselves on rather firmer ground, however, when we press upon the learned patronymic *Belidis* (1.3 Courtney = 6.3 Hollis). Cinna employs a form of the patronymic with a long *i* that assumes, for the name of the progenitor, the nominative form *Beleus* rather than the commoner *Belus*, and Virgil follows suit at *Aen.* 2.82 *Belidae … Palamedis*. The form was rare enough to confuse the grammarian Charisius, who mistook Cinna's ablative plural *Belidis* for a genitive singular.[22] Those who are familiar with Statius' deep learning, however, will not be surprised to find out that he made no such error, and Hollis[23] points us in the direction of *Theb.* 6.290–293, part of the description of the procession of images of the ancestors of the Argives that precedes the funeral games for Archemorus:

---

19 Hollis (2007) 26.
20 Courtney (1993) 215. To this we might add Claud. *Stil.* 1.318 *Tyrii sed uomere Cadmi*, though it seems far more likely that the collocation came to Claudian through Statius than directly from Cinna. See further Gervais (2017) 285–286.
21 An excellent argument in favour of seeing Cinna as a model for Statius at *Theb.* 8.228 has been pointed out to me by my friend and colleague Dr Lorenza Bennardo, who suggests that Statius may in fact be deliberately reproducing the earlier poet's emphasis on the antiquity of Thebes (*alta … origine*) while consciously varying his diction (*ueteres … Thebas*), and that Silius does much the same thing at *Pun.* 13.86 (*longaeui … fani*). As she also observes, we should note that elsewhere Statius is apt to insist not on the antiquity of Thebes but on its guilt, most notably in the proem (*sontesque euoluere Thebas*, 1.2). In truth, however, the antiquity and the guilt are deeply entwined (*longa retro series*, 1.7).
22 Hollis (2007) 29 thinks Charisius' error is "grotesque" and suggests it would be "astonishing" if the "blunder" had been found in Julius Hyginus' commentary on the poem.
23 Hollis (2007) 29.

iungunt discordes inimica in foedera dextras
<u>Belidae fratres</u>, sed uultu mitior astat
Aegyptus; Danai manifestum agnoscere ficto
ore notas pacisque malae noctisque futurae.

(Stat. *Theb*. 6.290–293)

The brothers, sons of Beleus, join right hands full of strife in a treaty full of enmity, but it is as the gentler in expression that Aegyptus stands there; as for Danaus, plain it is to recognize upon his dissembling face the marks both of an evil peace and of the night that will come to pass.

For our present purposes, however, the Statian passage deserves yet closer examination. As if he knew that his learned periphrasis might baffle his readers just as Cinna baffled Charisius, Statius expands on the phrase *Belidae fratres* so that the full context makes it clear that we are dealing with Aegyptus and Danaus, sons of Belus—or, as the better-educated poets call him, Beleus. As Hollis notes,[24] Cinna was referring to the same pair of brothers, ancestors of the royal house of Argos. If so, then Statius is quite possibly adapting the phrase directly from Cinna, and not from an intermediary such as Virgil. In short, there is clear evidence that Silius was familiar with Cinna's *Propempticon Pollionis*, and good evidence in the *Thebaid* that Statius was too. That possibility will be strengthened further when we come to consider the marks left by Cinna's poem on Statius' non-epic poetry. Here, though, we are primarily concerned with Statius the Flavian epicist, and it should be made clear that there is, at any rate, no good reason to doubt that Cinna was a poet whom Statius knew and admired, as a highly prominent allusion elsewhere in the *Thebaid* demonstrates. That is, Statius also seems to have known the charming little epigram of Cinna on a volume of Aratus that he brought back from Bithynia for a friend:

haec tibi Arateis <u>multum uigilata</u> lucernis
   carmina, quis ignes nouimus aerios,
leuis in aridulo maluae descripta libello
   Prusiaca uexi munera nauicula.

(11 Courtney = 13 Hollis)

These songs, by means of which we know the fires of the skies, and over which many a sleepless night was passed by Aratean lamp-light, I have brought as a gift for you on a little ship from the kingdom of Prusias, written out upon the wee dry teeny bark of a smooth mallow.

---

24 Hollis (2007) 29.

It must be noted that *uigilata* in the first line is in fact a correction from the pen of Scaliger: the manuscripts have *inuigilata*. It is an imitation in *Ciris* and two more in Statius, one of which is especially significant, that help us restore Cinna's text:

> accipe dona meo <u>multum uigilata</u> labore
>
> (*Ciris* 46)
>
> Accept gifts over which many a sleepless night was passed while I laboured.
>
> ... docto <u>multum uigilata</u> Myroni
> aera.
>
> (*Silv*. 4.6.25–26)
>
> Bronzes over which skilled Myron worked on many a sleepless night.
>
> durabisne procul dominoque legere superstes,
> o mihi bissenos <u>multum uigilata</u> per annos
> Thebai?
>
> (*Theb*. 12.810–812)
>
> Will you endure till far-off times, and be read when your master is no more, O my *Thebaid*, over whom I passed many a sleepless night through twice six years?

One could argue that, by the Flavian age, it had almost become routine for the careful poet to present his work as something over which he had laboured deep into the small hours with the aid of lamp-light. It is nonetheless striking that, as he brings his great epic, on which his fame is to rest, to its conclusion, and as, with true humility or false modesty, he declares its inferiority to the *Aeneid* (*Theb*. 12.816–817), Statius makes use of this particular phrase, taken from Cinna, to draw attention to his meticulous craftsmanship and therefore to his acceptance of the principles of the neoteric revolution. We are left to consider for ourselves what an achievement it is that he has sustained his loyalty to those principles, not over the length of a short graceful epigram, or even the single *libellus* in which Cinna has transported Aratus' *Phaenomena* to Rome, but over twelve magnificent books of epic hexameters.[25]

---

[25] Statius' programmatic allusion to Cinna, by means of which he emphatically "situates his poetry in the tradition of Roman Callimacheanism", is discussed at McNelis (2007) 23.

2 Calvus, *Io*

Of all the fragmentary neoteric epyllia, it is the *Io* of Calvus that has left the clearest marks on later Latin poetry, particularly, of course, in the sixth *Eclogue* of Virgil and in Ovid's own reworking of the tale of how the unfortunate daughter of Inachus was transformed into a cow (*Met.* 1.583–746). So it is that Hollis rightly observes, "[i]f … we possessed a complete text of Calvus' epyllion, we might find that it exercised as strong an influence as Catullus 64 on later Latin poetry at least until the death of Ovid."[26] Note the caution that infuses that last phrase, a caution which is echoed a little later when Hollis adds that it is "uncertain to what extent Calvus' epyllion would still have been in the literary consciousness of Valerius' contemporaries."[27] And yet it should not be in the slightest surprising that poets who read Cinna and Catullus should also read the *Io*, all the more so given that we already know that Calvus' other poetry was still providing material for Pliny's friend to imitate and that one of his speeches was still read widely enough to make him a familiar name to educated people. The obvious place to look is in the re-telling of the story of Io that Valerius Flaccus puts into the mouth of Orpheus in the fourth book of his *Argonautica* (4.344–421), but anyone attempting to establish a connection soon faces an apparently insurmountable obstacle: there simply seems not to be a single clear verbal echo in Valerius of any of the surviving fragments of Calvus' poem. Consequently, the best that Hollis can offer as evidence of Valerius' possible imitation of *Io* is to include him twice in his catalogue of motifs and themes—Io's seeing her horns reflected in water, her trying to speak but not being able to do anything other than moo, her eating food appropriate to cattle, and so on—that he lists from later authors who may have drawn on Calvus as a common source.[28] Valerius does make a couple of appearances in that catalogue, under entries "(iii) She tries vainly to speak" (4.372) and "(v) She eats bovine fodder" (4.379). We can even add slightly to this list if we broaden (v) out a little, to include Io's having been compelled to drink foul or muddy waters: Ov. *Met.* 1.634 *limosaque flumina potat*, "and drinks muddy river-water" and Val. Fl. 4.378–379 *heu quotiens saxo posuit latus aut, ubi longa / aegra siti, quos ore lacus, quae pabula carpsit!*, "Alas, how many times did she lay down her side upon a bed of stone or, when fainting with long-lasting thirst, what wa-

---

[26] Hollis (2007) 60.
[27] Hollis (2007) 62.
[28] Hollis (2007) 63.

ters did she drink, what fodder did she taste upon her lips!" This, it must be admitted, is a truly trivial addition to our evidence for Valerius' familiarity with Calvus, but we shall come back to the matter of Calvus' influence on Flavian epic below, with some possible verbal evidence that may seem more persuasive.[29]

3 Cornificius, *Glaucus*

The unusual myth of metamorphosis that provided the subject-matter of the lost *Glaucus* of Cornificius can be shown to have exercised great influence upon the imagination of the Hellenistic and neoteric poets.[30] Glaucus was a Boeotian fisherman who noticed that some fish he had caught were marvellously reanimated by contact with plants growing on the spot where he had placed them on the shore. Rather daringly, he ate some of them himself, with the result that he was magically transformed into a sea-god, taking on the form of a hybrid, man above the waist and fish below. The poets who wrote about him include Callimachus and Nicander, and as a divinity of the sea he features in prayers, or else appears in person to deliver oracles or advice, in Apollonius of Rhodes, Parthenius, Virgil, Statius, and Valerius Flaccus. The fullest and richest surviving treatment of the Glaucus myth, however, in either Greek or Latin, is the extended account spanning the thirteenth and fourteenth books of the *Metamorphoses* of Ovid (13.904–14.69), in which the half-fish half-god courts Scylla and in which he himself explains how he was transformed. Scylla remains unimpressed, and though Ovid is not explicit, this seems to be not least because, being all fish below the waist, he has nothing to offer a human bride. When Glaucus appeals to the witch Circe for help in his erotic quest, she adds a new twist to the story by revealing her own love for him. She, however, is rejected in her turn, and then, in her spite and fury, exacts revenge by poisoning with another set of magic plants a pool in which her hated rival Scylla delighted to bathe, with the result that Scylla undergoes her own, in this case truly monstrous, transformation.

Cornificius' epyllion has suffered particularly badly at the hands of time and decay. Indeed, of the three surviving fragments of his poetry, only one—not even a complete line—can be assigned with certainty to the *Glaucus*: *Centauros foedare bimembris* (2 Courtney = 96 Hollis). It is preserved for us by Macrobius (*Sat.*

---

[29] Certainly, it is impossible to attempt, in the case of Valerius and Calvus, the kind of rich and fascinating examination that Davis (2009) offers of the intertextual relations between Valerius and Ovid.
[30] Dewar (1991) 121–122, Hollis (2007) 152.

6.5.13), as part of his general argument that many epithets attributed to Virgil were in truth borrowings from earlier poets. Thanks to Macrobius, who identifies the fragment's origin very clearly ("*Cornificius in Glauco*"), and to the textual traditions of Virgil and of the surviving Flavian epicists, we can construct the following sequence:

Centauros foedare bimembris

(2 Courtney = 96 Hollis)

"To befoul [sc. with blood] the biformed Centaurs."

tu nubigenas, inuicte, bimembris
Hylaeumque Pholumque manu, tu Cresia mactas
prodigia et uastum Nemeae sub rupe leonem.

(Verg. *Aen.* 8.293–295)

You slay, unconquered hero, with your hand the cloud-born biformed ones, both Hylaeus and Pholus, you slay the monsters of Crete and the huge lion beneath Nemea's crag.

pariter stabulare bimembres
Centauros unaque ferunt Cyclopas in Aetna
compositos.

(Stat. *Theb.* 1.457–459)

They say that the biformed Centaurs are stabled together and that the Cyclopes lie down on Etna with one another.

nec leuior uinci Libycae telluris alumnus
matre super stratique genus deforme bimembres
Centauri frontemque minor nunc amnis Acarnan.

(Sil. *Pun.* 3.40–42)

And laid low too was the nursling of the Libyan land, no easier to slay when standing upon his mother, and the shapeless race, the biformed Centaurs, and Acarnania's river, his brow now stolen half away.

It looks as if Statius and Silius may be playing with the demands they make of their learned readers' own familiarity with the Roman literary heritage. Certainly, Statius in particular seems at first glance to be removing Virgil's highly mannered substitution of *nubigenas* for *Centauros* and deliberately restoring the original phrase, while *ferunt*—an "Alexandrian footnote", perhaps,[31]—may hint that he is alluding more widely to the original context in Cornificius. Then again, a sceptic could object that it would be easy enough for either poet, as it were, to "gloss" Virgil's *nubigenas* without knowing Cornificius.

Such scepticism, however, would probably be overdone, given that Statius does allude to the strange myth of Glaucus in two particularly learned and highly coloured parts of his epic poetry. True, he will of course have been familiar with Ovid's extended treatment of that myth in an erotico-comic style in the *Metamorphoses*. Statius' own references to Glaucus, however, are not remotely comic in tone, and full citation will bring out the poet's horrified and melancholy fascination with the bizarre details of the transformation that the fisherman undergoes:

> refluumque meatu
> Euripum, qua noster, habent teque, ultima tractu
> Anthedon, ubi gramineo de litore Glaucus   335
> poscentes inrupit aquas, iam crine genisque
> caerulus, et mixtos expauit ab inguine pisces.
>
> (*Theb.* 7.333–337)

And they who hold Euripus, where it is ours, flowing backwards as it wanders, and you, Anthedon, last of these lands, where from the grassy shore Glaucus burst into the waters that summoned him, already sea-green in hair and face, and gazed in horror at the fish confounded with his loins.

> non Anthedonii tegit hospitis inguina pontus
> blandior, aestiuo nec se magis aequore Triton
> exerit, aut carae festinus ad oscula matris
> cum remeat tardumque ferit delphina Palaemon.
>
> (*Theb.* 9.328–331)

Not more gentle is the sea that covers the loins of the Anthedonian guest, nor does Triton rise higher from the summer sea, nor Palaemon, when he returns in haste to his dear mother's embraces and strikes his laggard dolphin.

The second of these passages in fact precedes the description of Crenaeus' shield, in which, as we briefly saw above, there may be an echo, albeit very faint indeed, of Cinna's propempticon for Pollio.[32] That is all the more intriguing when we note two additional facts. First, Glaucus is paired in the second passage with two other

---

[31] Ross (1975) 78, Hinds (1998) 1–2. As with "neoteric", the accuracy of the term "Alexandrian" is sometimes called into question, but for many of us it serves as useful shorthand and so remains in general currency.

[32] See page 116 above.

sea-divinities, Triton and Palaemon. Secondly, all three appear together again in Statius' own propempticon for the young Maecius Celer:

> hinc multo Proteus geminoque hinc corpore Triton   35
> praenatet et subitis qui perdidit inguina monstris
> Glaucus, adhuc patriis quotiens adlabitur oris
> litoream blanda feriens Anthedona cauda.
> tu tamen ante omnes diua cum matre, Palaemon,
> adnue, si uestras amor est mihi pandere Thebas   40
> nec cano degeneri Phoebeum Amphiona plectro.
>
> (*Silv.* 3.2.35–41)
>
> Let Proteus of the many bodies, and Triton who has two, swim ahead of you on this side, and also he who lost his loins in a sudden monstrous change, Glaucus, whenever he glides to the shores that are still his fathers', striking Anthedon, famous for her beach, with his gentle tail. But do you, above all others, grant your assent, along with your goddess mother, Palaemon, if it is my delight to tell of your Thebes and I do not sing with unworthy lyre of Phoebus' beloved Amphion.

Since Palaemon was a member of the royal house of Cadmus, and Glaucus of Anthedon a Boeotian, Statius, author of a poem on Boeotian Thebes, lays claim to their aid by reminding them that he had composed a Theban epic. And, like Glaucus, Palaemon was a human who had been transformed, along with his mother Leucothea, into a divinity of the sea.[33] In both *Theb.* 9 and *Silv.* 3.2, then, there is a whole nexus of learned references to Boeotians who became sea-gods that may plausibly be said to hint at both Cinna and Cornificius. We should also now note the significance of Hollis's observation on another fragment of the *Propempticon Pollionis* of Cinna, one which we have not yet considered: *lucida quom fulgent alti carchesia mali* (2 Courtney = 2 Hollis, "when the maintop of the lofty mast glows bright", tr. Hollis). Hollis argues that the line "undoubtedly refers to the electrical discharge known as St Elmo's fire, which appears on the mast and rigging of ships and was thought to indicate the presence and protection of the Dioscuri, Castor and Pollux." He then goes on to suggest that, following the example of Cinna, it perhaps became a regular topos in a propempticon to invoke St Elmo's fire as protection for the voyager.[34] In support of this suggestion, he cites lines from a poem with which we are now becoming familiar, Statius' propempticon for Maecius Celer:

---

[33] Their names when still human had been Melicertes and Ino. See Dewar (1991) 122.
[34] Hollis (2007) 23, citing Nisbet and Hubbard (1970) 46, on Hor. *Carm.* 1.3.2 *fratres Helenae, lucida sidera*. The Horatian poem, of course, is yet another propempticon, in this case for Virgil.

> proferte benigna
> sidera et antemnae gemino considite cornu,
> Oebalii fratres; uobis pontusque polusque
> luceat.
>
> (Stat. *Silv*. 3.2.8–11)

> Bring forth your kindly stars, brothers born of Oebalus, and take your seat upon the yard-arm's twin horns; for you may sea and sky shine bright.

Let us return, however, to Cornificius and to Glaucus. As we have seen, in Statius the tone is not, as in Ovid, comic, but rather it is pathetic. The emphasis is placed on a mixture of wonder and horror, as we deal not only with the transformation but also with what it entails, the loss of Glaucus' human manhood. Statius' treatment of the myth is also self-consciously learned, and all this, of course, is very much in the neoteric style. Especially noteworthy is the fact that, in all three of the passages quoted above in which Glaucus appears, Statius takes care to make it clear that the god comes from the city of Anthedon in Boeotia. There is a similar concern for his home town in Ovid, who relates his arrival with these words:

> ecce fretum scindens alti nouus incola ponti
> nuper in Euboica uersis Anthedone membris
> Glaucus adest.
>
> (*Met*. 13.904–906)

> Behold, cleaving the strait, new-made denizen of the deep sea, with his limbs but recently transformed in Euboean Anthedon, Glaucus is there.

What underlies all this may be a very Alexandrian preoccupation with the varieties of myth and the scholarly need not to confuse individuals from different mythical traditions who happened to have the same name. That is, it may be that both Ovid and Statius wish to encourage their readers not to confuse Glaucus the sea-god with another, much less salubrious character, Glaucus of Potniae, son of Sisyphus and king of Corinth, who fed his mares on human flesh but was himself eaten by them in his turn. Each of the two was the subject of a play by Aeschylus of which a few lines remain, and the learned Hellenistic poets and their imitators no doubt addressed the myths associated with each as their own taste and poetic agenda dictated.[35]

---

[35] For details see Courtney (1993) 152. Like any other Roman poet of his generation, however, Statius may have been more familiar with the myth of Glaucus of Potniae from its brief appearance in Virgil: *G*. 3.267–268 *quo tempore Glauci / Potniades malis membra absumpsere quadrigae*, "at the time when Glaucus' team of four Potnian steeds with their jaws consumed his limbs."

The learned poets like to set us tests of our own learning. At *Theb.* 9.328 Glaucus is not even named, but instead he is referred to in a learned periphrasis as the *Anthedonius hospes*. The majestic place-name adjective is not attested in surviving Latin poetry before Statius, although three centuries later, in his *Mosella*, Ausonius parades his own familiarity with the myth of Glaucus' transformation:

> sic Anthedonius Boeotia per freta Glaucus,
> gramina gustatu postquam exitialia Circes
> expertus carptas moribundis piscibus herbas
> sumpsit, Carpathium subiit nouus accola pontum.
>
> (Auson. *Mos.* 276–279)

> Just so Anthedonian Glaucus through the Boeotian straits, after he learned by tasting them the destructive power of Circe's plants, took up the herbs plucked by the dying fish, and went, a new denizen, under the Carpathian sea.

Ausonius, however, takes pity on his reader and supplies the missing name to go with the epithet. His display of his own learning does not end there, and we observe how he combines Statius' wording with a slight adaptation of half a line from Ovid's account: to *nouus accola pontum* compare *Met.* 13.904 *nouus incola ponti*.

Of course, like most modern readers, Statius may have known the story of Glaucus through Ovid. Nothing proves that the learned place-name adjective *Anthedonius* once appeared in Cornificius. And we should bear in mind that so scholarly an epithet may possibly have appeared—instead or as well—in, to name just one obvious candidate, the lost *Glaucus* of Callimachus.

4 Calvus, *Io*: Reprise

All the same, it is tempting to imagine that Statius did indeed find that learned epithet in Cornificius' lost poem, and, in the absence of more substantial portions of the neoteric poets, learned epithets may occasionally be among the most important pieces of evidence for such connections. One particularly intriguing case is the extremely rare adjective *Phorōnēus*, "belonging to, or associated with, Phoroneus." Phoroneus, son of Inachus and brother of Io, is a character about whom our surviving literary sources say very little. It is all the more striking, then, that he is mentioned four times in the *Thebaid*, as one of the ancestors of the Argives and a founder of Argos, and in particular in connection with treasured artifacts that form part of the inheritance of King Adrastus. The first appearance of his name comes in the great scene of the Council of the Gods in the first book of the poem. Juno, reminding her husband of her long-standing love for Argos and its ruling family, reacts angrily to his declared intent to bring destruction down upon the Argives:

> talia Iuno refert: 'mene, o iustissime diuum,
> me bello certare iubes? scis, semper ut arces
> Cyclopum magnique Phoroneos incluta fama
> sceptra uiris opibusque iuuem, licet improbus illic
> custodem Phariae somno letoque iuuencae
> extinguas, saeptis et turribus aureus intres.'

(Stat. *Theb.* 1.250–255)

> Thus Juno said in answer: 'Is it I, O most just of the gods, is it I whom you bid make war? You know how I always aid, with men and riches, the citadels of the Cyclopes and the sceptre of great Phoroneus, glorious in fame, even though there in your shamelessness you snuff out with sleep and death the keeper of the Pharian heifer, and in form of gold enter the guarded towers.'

We remember here how Juno's capacity for holding a grudge drives the whole plot of the *Aeneid*; its hero suffered so much and for so long *saeuae memorem Iunonis ob iram*, "for the unforgetting anger of savage Juno", *Aen.* 1. 4. The "unforgetting anger" of the goddess, however, as she appears in that poem is bolstered by her deep familiarity with earlier poetry, above all, Homer and the *Annales* of Ennius.[36] When Statius' Juno now reminds Jupiter of her loyalty to Argos, she assumes that he already knows full well what she has to tell him (*scis*, *Theb.* 1.251), and when she names "mighty Phoroneus", for all that he may be obscure to us, she takes his fame for granted (*incluta fama*, *Theb.* 1.252). All that has the look of another "Alexandrian footnote."[37] If so, we should probably be asking ourselves what poem she and Jupiter have been reading that we ourselves are also expected to have read.

The other mentions of Phoroneus in the *Thebaid* are brief, but confirm the impression that he is someone with an established literary persona, someone with acknowledged attributes. When King Adrastus, one of Phoroneus' successors on the throne of Argos, has found his future sons-in-law fighting at his hearth and has broken up their dangerous scuffle, he drinks their health from a cup, a royal heirloom *qua Danaus libare deis seniorque Phoroneus / adsueti*, "from which

---

[36] Feeney (1991) 130–131.
[37] See n. 31 p. 122 above. Note also Verg. *Aen.* 2.82, Stat. *Theb.* 12.331–332 *ubi mater, ubi incluta fama / Antigone?* "Where is your mother, where Antigone, renowned in fame?"

Danaus and old Phoroneus were accustomed to make libation to the gods" (*Theb.* 1.542–543); among the images adorning the hall in which the marriages of Adrastus' daughters are celebrated we find *placidus ... Phoroneus*, "peaceful Phoroneus" (*Theb.* 2.219); and the spirit of *mitis ... Phoroneus*, "gentle Phoroneus" (*Theb.* 4.589) features among the Argive ghosts who appear to Tiresias and his daughter Manto in the necromancy at Thebes. It looks as if some earlier poetic tradition may have taught Statius that Phoroneus was *placidus* and *mitis* in character and that he lived to a great age. This characterization, we should also note, closely aligns him with King Adrastus himself (*Theb.* 1.448, 1.467, 7.537, 11.110).

Those are the four appearances of his proper name, but Statius also twice uses the epithet *Phorōnēus* mentioned above, one formed from the personal name, and this is an epithet that cannot be shown to have been employed by any other extant Roman poet. One of the appearances of the epithet comes in the *Thebaid* and looks—though looks in so learned a poet can be deceiving—largely ornamental: *Iuno Phoroneas inducit praeuia matres*, "Juno, leading the way, brings in the Phoronean matrons" (*Theb.* 12.465). The other, however, is more intriguing, as it is found in a poem that we have already had reason to connect with a famous poem by Cinna but also with the story of Glaucus and so, just possibly, with Cornificius' poem on the subject of his transformation. The poem in question is, once more, Statius' propempticon for Maecius Celer, for it happens to be the case that Celer is on his way to Alexandria, and Statius therefore entrusts the safety of his young friend above all to Isis, the Egyptian goddess whom Io became at the end of her troubled wanderings:

> Isi, Phoroneis olim stabulata sub antris,
> nunc regina Phari numenque Orientis anheli,
> excipe multisono puppem Mareotida sistro.
>
> (*Silv.* 3.2.101–103)
>
> Isis, who once were stabled beneath the shelter of the Phoronean caves, now queen of Pharos and divinity of the panting East, welcome with your much-sounding rattle a Mareotic ship.

This is heady stuff indeed, and very much in the highly learned Hellenistic-neoteric style. To understand the address, the reader must be familiar with the myth, and so able to supply from memory the name and story of the human princess, sister of Phoroneus, who once was a heifer, who wandered far and wide, and who ended up as the great goddess Isis in "the panting East" and became "Queen of Pharos." Consider again the first reference in the *Thebaid* to Io's brother:

>   scis, semper ut arces
> Cyclopum magnique Phoroneos incluta fama
> sceptra uiris opibusque iuuem, licet improbus illic
> custodem Phariae somno letoque iuuencae
> extinguas, saeptis et turribus aureus intres.
>
> (*Theb.* 1.251–255)

> You know how I always aid, with men and riches, the citadels of the Cyclopes and the sceptre of great Phoroneus, glorious in fame, even though there in your shamelessness you snuff out with sleep and death the keeper of the Pharian heifer, and in form of gold enter the guarded towers.

We may now note with heightened interest that, though Juno names Io's brother, it seems that in her "unforgetting anger" she cannot bring herself to utter the name of her odious rival for Jupiter's love. Instead, in a highly allusive and indirect fashion, she succinctly recalls the story of how Argus was set to guard "the Pharian heifer" and met his death as a result.[38] In calling Io "the Pharian heifer", the goddess speaks with more venom than chronological accuracy, since it was long after the death of Argus, and in Egypt, far from her native Argos, that Io was in fact set free from her transformation and in time became, as the poet said in the propempticon to Maecius Celer, *regina Phari*, the queen of Pharos. Here we perhaps receive an inkling of which poet Juno was recalling in her speech to Jupiter, because the phrase *Phariae ... iuuencae* looks like a contentious recasting of the well-known *Inachiae ... iuuencae* used of Io by Virgil (*G.* 3.153 *Inachiae Iuno pestem meditata iuuencae*, "Juno, devising the Inachian heifer's pest"), and then used in the Flavian period by Valerius Flaccus, in his own account of the story of Io (4.357 *tum trepida Inachiae paelex subit ora iuuencae*, "then the trembling mistress takes on the features of an Inachian heifer"), and also by Silius Italicus, with reference, as in Juno's speech to Jupiter, to the death of Argus (10.346–347 *custos / Inachiae multa superandus nocte iuuencae*, "the guardian of the Inachian heifer, who must be overcome with abundant darkness"). The prominence of the phrase, its self-conscious learning, and the favourite neoteric rhyme all give weight to the suggestion, made by Richard Thomas, that *Inachiae ... iuuencae* comes ultimately from Calvus.[39] If so, then Statius would be adding a clever twist, by reminding us that the Inachian heifer will one day be worshipped in Egypt in connection with her son by Jupiter, namely Epaphus, the Apis Bull, an identifi-

---

[38] This is, of course, the story best known to us from Ov. *Met.* 1.622–721.
[39] Thomas (1982) 85, n. 17. Hollis (2007) 64, adds that, if true, this would mean that Calvus probably had in mind Moschus, *Europa* 51.

cation which, as Hollis argues, is likely to have featured prominently in Callimachus' lost *De Aduentu Isidis*.⁴⁰ To all this we can now, if only tentatively, add the possibility that the very abstruse epithet *Phorōnēus*, and the "Phoronean caves" in which the princess Io took shelter, long before she became Isis and when she was still in her bovine form, may also have appeared in Calvus' *Io*.⁴¹

It must be acknowledged that, even if Calvus did use the epithet in his epyllion, he may well have been following the example of a learned Greek predecessor, Callimachus being here, as so often, the most likely candidate. Even so, if we allow for the moment the possibility that Statius, in his propempticon to Maecius Celer, connects Isis-Io with "Phoronean caves" because he knew of them from Calvus, we find ourselves in possession of a considerable collection of suggestive data: Silius was clearly familiar with Cinna's *Propempticon Pollionis*, which seems also to have left its mark on Statius' propempticon for Maecius Celer, while Statius' propempticon in its turn may also have preserved a learned trace or two of the *Io* of Calvus. In addition, Glaucus features prominently, and with self-conscious *doctrina*, in both Statius' propempticon and his *Thebaid*, while the *Thebaid* provides us with a direct verbal reproduction of the collocation *Centauros bimembris* preserved in the one and only securely attested surviving fragment of Cornificius' *Glaucus*.

We can now sum up. That the fragmentary epyllia of the neoteric Latin poets have left some mark on Flavian epic is *prima facie* likely, even if the scantness of the fragments sometimes makes demonstrating this difficult in the extreme. It is also clear that the neoterics were indeed known to the Flavians: the lyric and non-narrative poetry of Catullus and Cinna has left identifiable marks on Statius' *Silvae* and Silius' *Punica*, as well as on Martial. None of this should be considered at all surprising, particularly in the case of Statius, who is, surely, the most learned

---

40 Hollis (2007) 64. For the substitution of the one epithet by the other Statius had precedent in Ovid's reference to female devotion to Isis in contemporary Rome in the phrase *Phariae sistris operata iuuencae*, "in service with her rattle to the Pharian heifer" (*Ars* 3.635), as did his contemporary Martial (10.48.1 *nuntiat octauam Phariae sua turba iuuencae*, "her own crowd of votaries announces the eighth hour to the Pharian heifer": cf. also *Niliacae per bouem iuuencae*, "by the bull of Nile's heifer", of Apis, at 8.81.2). In Ovid and Martial the epithet is no doubt intended to draw attention to the foreign nature of the cult, but the reference in Statius is much more strongly marked: Juno, never forgetting her husband's offences towards her, still resents both the beginning of Jupiter's love-affair with Io in Greece and the, for her, outrageous reward of divinity that Io received in Egypt at the end of her wanderings.

41 Ovid, whose account of Io is generally accepted to have drawn on Calvus, does not use the learned epithet, but he does refer to Io's sufferings as *mala tanta Phoronidos*, "the terrible sufferings of Phoroneus' sister" (*Met.* 1.668) and to Io herself as *Argolica ... Phoronide*, "the Argive sister of Phoroneus" (*Met.* 2.524).

of the three epic poets of the Flavian period, and who is probably more familiar with recherché poetry of all kinds, Greek and Latin, than almost any Roman poet except Ovid. No doubt we shall never know for sure, but, to take once more as our example the most ruinous of the neoteric epyllia, the *Glaucus* of Cornificius, it is at least well within the realms of possibility that our best guide to its likely tone and colouring lies not in the two words preserved by Macrobius nor in Ovid's comically salacious retelling. Our best guide may be Statius' richly ornamented neoteric-style blend of pathos and horror:

> refluumque meatu
> Euripum, qua noster, habent teque, ultima tractu
> Anthedon, ubi gramineo de litore Glaucus
> poscentes inrupit aquas, iam crine genisque
> caerulus, et mixtos expauit ab inguine pisces.

(*Theb.* 7.333–337)

And they who hold Euripus, where it is ours, flowing backwards as it wanders, and you, Anthedon, last of these lands, where from the grassy shore Glaucus burst into the waters that summoned him, already sea-green in hair and face, and gazed in horror at the fish confounded with his loins.

Bibliography

Courtney, Edward (1993), *The Fragmentary Latin Poets. Edited with Commentary*, Oxford.
Davis, Peter J. (2009), "Remembering Ovid: The Io Episode in Valerius Flaccus' *Argonautica*", in: *Antichthon* 43 [*Roman Byways. Papers from a Conference in Memory of Charles Tesoriero*], 1–11.
Davis, Peter J. (2015), "Statius' *Achilleid*: The Paradoxical Epic", in: Dominik *et al.* (2015), 157–172.
Dewar, Michael (1991), *Statius*, Thebaid *IX. Edited with an English Translation and Commentary*, Oxford.
Dilke, Oswald A.W. (1954, reprinted 1979), *Statius*, Achilleid. *Edited with Introduction, Apparatus Criticus and Notes*, Cambridge.
Dominik, William/Newlands, Carole/Gervais, Kyle (eds.) (2015), *Brill's Companion to Statius*, Leiden.
Eigler, Ulrich/Lefèvre, Eckard/Manuwald, Gesine (eds.) (1998), *Ratis omnia vincet. Neue Untersuchungen zu den* Argonautica *des Valerius Flaccus*, Munich.
Feeney, Denis C. (1991), *The Gods in Epic. Poets and Critics of the Classical Tradition*, Oxford.
Feletti, Daniela (1998), "Valerius Flaccus und die *Argonautae* des Varro Atacinus", in: Eigler *et al.* (1998) 109–121.
Ganiban, Randall T. (2015), "The Beginnings of the *Achilleid*", in: Dominik *et al.* (2015) 73–87.
Gervais, Kyle (2017), *Statius*, Thebaid 2. *Edited with an Introduction, Translation, and Commentary*, Oxford.

Harrison, Stephen J. (ed.) (1995), *Collected Papers on Latin Literature*, Oxford.
Hinds, Stephen (1998), *Allusion and Intertext. Dynamics of Appropriation in Roman Poetry*, Cambridge.
Hollis, Adrian S. (2007), *Fragments of Latin Poetry c. 60 BC–AD 20. Edited with Introduction, Translation, and Commentary*, Oxford.
Littlewood, R. Joy (2011), *A Commentary on Silius Italicus'* Punica *7*, Oxford.
Manuwald, Gesine (2015), *Valerius Flaccus*, Argonautica *Book III*, Cambridge.
McNelis, Charles (2007), *Statius'* Thebaid *and the Poetics of Civil War*, Cambridge.
Micozzi, Laura (2015), "Statius' Epic Poetry: A Challenge to the Literary Past", in: Dominik *et al.* (2015) 325–342.
Newlands, Carole E. (2011), *Statius*, Silvae, *Book II*, Cambridge.
Nisbet, R.G.M. (1995), "The Survivors: Old-Style Literary Men in the Triumviral Period", in: Harrison (1995) 390–413.
Nisbet, R.G.M./Hubbard, Margaret (1970), *A Commentary on Horace:* Odes *Book 1*, Oxford.
Ross, David O. Jr (1975), *Backgrounds to Augustan Poetry: Gallus, Elegy and Rome*, Cambridge.
Thomas, Richard F. (1982), "Gadflies (Virg. *Geo.* 3.146–148)", in: *HSPh* 86, 81–85.
Zissos, Andrew (2008), *Valerius Flaccus'* Argonautica, *Book I: A Commentary*, Oxford.

Federica Bessone
Allusive (Im-)Pertinence in Statius' Epic

My title alludes to an essay by Mario Labate, *La memoria impertinente e altra intertestualità ovidiana*, dedicated to quasi-citations in the *Amores* and the *Ars*: exhibited borrowings from illustrious models, that, with their non-pertinence, create parodic effects. Parody is here intended as the self-ironic denunciation of the disproportion to a 'serious' paradigm, bent to an incongruous use in a frivolous context: it is the line traced by Eduard Kenney in *Nequitiae poeta*.[1] I will deal with quasi-citations as well. The approach of the research project related to this colloquium has orientated me towards the concrete component of allusivity, the verbal material of poetic memory, detectable also with digital tools, and which, together with more immaterial elements, constitutes that complex of relations that we call intertextuality. An intertextual microanalysis, then (with all the associated risks): I will study rhythmic-verbal matrices, hemistichs, incipits, clausulae, hexameter frames, junctures or even single terms that function as precise evocations of well known models, in the first place Latin ones. My interest in Statius has recently turned to stylistic research: I think it is time to outline also for this successor of Vergil an "anatomy of style".[2] That of Statius is a 'style of paradox', informing the text at all levels; one of the hypotheses I would like to test here is that even verbal allusiveness contributes to the construction of this paradoxical style.

In line with Labate, I will examine allusions that have almost the status of a quotation ("... una memoria che tende a riprodurre la forma del testo evocato con l'aderenza di una citazione"), that evoke "textual segments ... provided with particular memorability" and involve "the unmotivated transfer of a well recognizable 'author phrase' into a decidedly dishomogeneous context".[3] Here, however, my path begins to diverge. I intend to deal also with the 'impertinent' transfer into a *non* dishomogeneous context: for instance, the reuse of formulas from Vergil's epic in a context not different in genre, elevation of tone and stylistic register, and yet radically extraneous, where the Vergilian word clashes with a world of values it does not belong to, resulting in unrecognizable meaning, 'unmoti-

---

1 Labate (1991); Kenney (1958).
2 Cf. Conte (2007²) 5–63, quoting Flaubert's definition in exergue.
3 Labate (1991) 44 (translation mine). Cf. Conte (1985²) 65 on the "allusione ironica", opposed to the "allusione metaforica".

https://doi.org/10.1515/9783110602203-007

vated', not integrated, or violently twisted—it would be useful to refer to an analysis on this kind of 'impertinent' memory in the *Metamorphoses* or the *Pharsalia*, but an overall study of this kind has not yet been written.[4]

Here, then, I take the term 'impertinence' in a broader meaning than Labate, comprising, not only the playful shamelessness of the reuse in an incongruous ambit, and at a lower level, but, more generally, the procedures of blatant forcing, of sense or form, that bend celebrated formulations into an unexpected, provoking, and surprising use.

For Statius it will not always, or mainly, be a matter of parody—in the sense hinted at above for the erotic Ovid. Effects of quasi-parodic intertextuality are there, I believe, in the half-serious style of the *Achilleid*, and I will try to give some examples of it. In the *Thebaid* there is less fun for the reader. And yet, here also the 'ironic' gap acts in similar ways—only, in a gloomy version—, in the effects of *tragic* parody, perverse and almost grotesque deformation, disfigurement or even provocative reversal of canonical models, Vergil in particular: a 'strain' that, still, recognizes the canonicity of the model.

After all, allusive impertinence is only the extreme attitude of a poetry that almost cannot help speaking in Vergilian language; at the opposite extreme stand the reuses that, by displaying their pertinence, claim an assimilation to the model, instead of a misappropriation of it: it ranges from reverence to violence, to resume distinctions by Philip Hardie.[5] Schematizing broadly, here I will attempt to form a discourse focused on the extreme attitudes. In general, I am interested in the consciousness with which the Flavian poet uses allusive art to signal continuity or discontinuity with models, genres, literary and stylistic traditions. An epic which is at the same time traditional and experimental, secondary and self-conscious, as Statius' is, invites reflection on both allusive pertinence and impertinence, on signs of reverence and gestures of rupture towards tradition.

Not only the extended citation, but even the minimal verbal borrowing—if it is not isolated, but included in a series (or an allusive context), or if it is truly 'unique', recognizable and evocative —can contain in itself a program, send a

---

[4] On Lucan cf. Conte (1988) 38–39: "... caricatura a scopo di parodia ... Scrivere con appassionata serietà di una cosa terribilmente seria, usando strumenti non lontani dalla parodia ..."; examples of antiphrastic allusivity in Narducci (2002) 211–214 ("imitazione 'blasfema"); 223–224; a more complex perspective (Lucan's revealing the anti-Vergil in Vergil) in Casali (2011), cf. 89: "an outcome that borders on parody"; Sklenár (2011) is limited by a formalistic point of view. On the *Metamorphoses* see e.g. Baldo (1995) 253–265, with bibliography.
[5] Hardie (2007) 171.

signal of literary affiliation or extraneity, express ideological alignment or dissent, imprint on an expressive tradition its own brand of style. The risk of overinterpreting is there, and must be calculated.[6] Verbal contacts are not always so loaded with meaning: reuses of Vergilian formulas are often facts of poetic *langue*, and an instrument like Tesserae now allows to quantify at a glance the pervasive Vergilianness of Flavian epic language; and yet, even in two parallel columns of stereotyped and nearly identical clausulae there may be hidden a single fulminating contact.

Just one example. *Audiit et* at the beginning of the hexameter appears four times in the *Aeneid* and four in the *Thebaid*,[7] but that does not prevent the replica of the incipit in Tisiphone's appearance in book 1 from being a pertinent citation of Allecto's appearance in *Aeneid* 7 —a structural model of the episode—, as other splinters of Vergilian language from the same scene confirm.[8] On the other hand, a minimal verbal segment, but unique in *Aeneid* and *Thebaid*, though seemingly meaningless, can be an invitation to a comparison that lets the difference between two worlds be perceived. '*Spectent*', said by Polynices to Adrastus before the fraternal duel, was already in Turnus' words to Latinus at the beginning of *Aeneid* 12. But Turnus invited the Latins to admire the prowess that would send Aeneas to Hades and secure victory; Polynices instead invites mothers and fathers of the decimated warriors of the two sides to relish the spectacle of revenge and cheer for his opponent, while he expiates his sins by confronting his brother. We move from the spectacle of epic heroism to morbid satisfaction in a disturbed epic world; further resonances from Turnus' speeches in the same book confirm the paradoxically 'systematic' character of this 'local' allusion.[9]

Again, a rare term, accompanied by a negation, can function as ironic distancing from a model. At the beginning of the *Achilleid*, the failed tempest is founded on the dialogue with the *Aeneid*. Thetis' prayer to Neptune to wreck Paris' ship quotes Juno's entreaty to Aeolus, in a clausula complete with the enjambement ('*obrue puppes, / aut*').[10] Here also the demanding compound *in-*

---

6 For a discussion of related problems see Farrell (2005).
7 Verg. *Aen.* 7.225, 516; 9.630; 11.794; Stat. *Theb.* 1.118; 6.165; 9.820; 11.425.
8 Cf. *Theb.* 1.118–122 (and 116 *signum terris*) with *Aen.* 7.516–518 (and 513 *pastorale canit signum*).
9 Cf. Stat. *Theb.* 7.185–186 '*fratri concurro, quid ultra est? / spectent et votis victorem Eteoclea poscant*' with Verg. *Aen.* 12.14–15 '*aut hac Dardanium dextra sub Tartara mittam / desertorem Asiae (sedeant spectentque Latini)*'. The distinction between 'local' and 'systematic allusion' is that by Hinds (1998).
10 Stat. *Ach.* 1.71–74 '*has saltem – num semideos nostrumque reportant / Thesea? – siquis adhuc undis honor, obrue puppes, / aut permitte fretum! nulla inclementia: fas sit / pro nato timuisse*

clementia is an allusive gesture: Thetis distances herself from the '*divum inclementia, divum*', of Neptune in the first place, represented in Venus' revelation in *Aeneid* 2, a theological 'scandal' (Verg. *Aen.* 2.602).[11] With *nulla inclementia* (sc. *mihi est*) at *Ach.* 1.73, Thetis 'reminds' Neptune of the qualification that he (together with Juno) will get for destroying the *Neptunia Troia*, and opposes to it her own preventive plan *to avoid war*; the goddess concerned for Achilles thus descends from the problematic sublime of the *Aeneid* to a 'minor' epic level, dominated by maternal fear and suspended between pathos and humour. An epic that, once the project of *poetica tempestas* has come to nothing, will shift into the comedy of deception on Scyros.[12]

On the other hand, an extended and precise verbal contact can appear as little more than a coincidence. If a search is launched on Tesserae with the *Achilleid* as "target" and the *Aeneid* as "source", one of the richest "score 10" that comes out from it is the almost perfect identity of a segment longer than the hemistich: *Ach.* 1.493 *magno vatem Calchanta tumultu* ≈ *Aen.* 2.122 *vatem magno Calchanta tumultu*.[13] At first glance, the contact does not much more than signal a typical epic scene —'Seer reproached by impetuous warrior'—, thereby restating a generic belonging. This might look like one of the many facts of poetic *langue*. And yet, Ripoll and Soubiran are right when they take time to observe the substitution of the presumed fraudulent gesture by Ulysses, narrated by the fraudulent Sinon, with the passionate gesture of the heroic Protesilaus. Here the topos is returned to its 'authentic' matrix, while the role of cold plotter of a different deceit, lighter and funnier, is reserved for Ulysses.[14] This, then, proves to be an allusion that comments on Vergil, stripping Ulysses of a fictive attitude that does not belong to him—and foreshadowing the tragic destiny of the eager Protesilaus.

In sum, the continual reproposition of the Vergilian text in the form of fragments in Statius' language —fragments pulverized or conspicuous, isolated or in

---

mihi' recalls Verg. *Aen.* 1.69–70 '*incute vim ventis submersasque obrue puppes, / aut age diversos et dissice corpora ponto*' (cf. Uccellini (2012) *ad loc.*). What Statius substitutes after *aut* connotes Thetis as a mother-goddess and minor divinity, far from the persecuting power of Juno, subject to Neptune, and moved, not by rancour against a Trojan, but by maternal fear.

11 Cf. Verg. *Aen.* 2.601–625, with Horsfall (2008). Thetis also opposes the cruelty of Juno, which is stigmatized by Venus in her prayer to Neptune in *Aeneid* 5, another model for this scene (*Aen.* 5.778–796; the formula of l.796 *quod superest* is repeated in the preceding monologue by Thetis, *Ach.* 1.49).

12 See Bessone (forthcoming). For another example of a single term that, accompanied by a negation, signals the overturning of a model see *infra*, n. 78.

13 Stat. *Ach.* 1.493–496; Verg. *Aen.* 2.122–144 (Sinon).

14 See Ripoll/Soubiran (2008) 221, on 491–513.

a sequence—poses problems not so distant from those posed by the technique, and poetics, of the cento, analyzed by Philip Hardie: "... but in an age when the Vergilian texts were imprinted on the elite cultural memory, the fragments that make up a Vergilian cento are supersaturated with memory traces of their original contexts".[15] Even in an extreme case such as Hosidius Geta's *Medea*, there is not always a degree zero of interpretability of the borrowings (or "microtextual allusions", McGill (2005) 27), and it is not always possible to think that the original contexts are neutralized in the reader's memory: "Can we maintain a distinction between, let us call it, the formulaic use of fragments as markers of typical scenes or Proppian narrative functions, on the one hand, and, on the other, allusion to specific characters, actions, and contexts?". This question is often valid for the interpreter of Statius as well.

Let us come back now to pertinence and impertinence. We know that a quasi-citation can comment, like a "self-reflexive annotation", on the whole procedure of rewriting of a poetic paradigm, and that a poet can thus reconstruct by himself his own tradition ("do-it-yourself literary tradition"). Hinds has shown this with regard to the *Achilleid*, where pointed reuses redesign an epic tradition that has at its centre Catullus 64 and Ovid's *Metamorphoses*.[16] The exhibited verbal allusion functions in this case as a generic label, or a style brand, an explicit mark of belonging. This kind of grafting constructs a sort of natural continuity with the source text.

But quoting, or nearly so, an all too well known text can produce, on the contrary, an almost violent estrangement. The transplanted words can be made to clash with the receiving context, triggering a rejection crisis, and thereby signalling the incompatibility between different poetic tissues; or, again, they can be 'genetically modified'—perverted in form, inverted in sign, varied in a subtle and disruptive way, so that the new sense collides with the original formulation. Here we are, then, in the sphere of 'impertinence', in which I include the impropriety of the matching and the impudence of the operation, a sphere which is contiguous to parody, intended as "repetition with ironic critical difference" (they are different degrees of irony).[17] In this case, the artificial character peculiar to any reuse is extolled, through an intolerance reaction artfully provoked, or an invasive manipulation.

---

15 Hardie (2007) 172, for this quotation and the following one.
16 Hinds (1998) chapter 5.
17 Hutcheon (1985).

Before going on, I want to specify that the dichotomy 'pertinence'/'impertinence' can be useful on the empirical level for a discourse on the extremes of allusive possibilities, but at a theoretical level, if absolutized, risks being misleading. We know well that, in allusion, pertinence and impertinence always coexist in various degrees, and stand in a dialectical relation to each other, in the same way as, in metaphor, proper and figurative senses stand in reciprocal tension, to quote *Memoria dei poeti e sistema letterario*; a certain degree of impertinence is constitutive of every allusive act: to quote *Dell'imitazione. Furto e originalità*, the appropriation of the other's words is always a 'sleight-of-hand theft', be it exhibited or camouflaged.[18]

Statius, then, explores widely the potential of allusive art, with a range of sophisticated solutions that it would be vain to try to classify. Some trends can however be indicated. In this context, my analysis will move mostly around one of the two extremes of the spectrum, the boldest impertinence. My case studies will illustrate the effects of paradox, perversion and ironic provocation realized through poetic memory. I will draw from the *Thebaid* examples of paradoxical and oxymoronic intertextuality, with implications of style or heroic-epic ideology; from the *Achilleid* examples of ironical provocation, bordering on parody.

In both cases, the visibility of the quasi-citation grants Statius' allusive perversions the programmatic force of a manifesto—literary, ideologic or stylistic. The models involved are Catullus and the Augustans, and above all the school classic is at stake, the poet of the *Aeneid*. In the Theban poem, Vergil is the constant reference of an anti-*Aeneid* that could not be more Vergilian: the wrong-footing citation is here the verbal sign of the re-founding of a genre (the epic of *nefas*) and formal perversion is the mark of a perverted world of values—a technique that, on the theme of civil war, has its precedent in Lucan. Once Vergil has been consecrated in the envoi of the *Thebaid*, in his second epic, Statius allows himself to joke with the saints—in Ovidian spirit—and repeatedly cites fragments of Vergil's epic discourse in a context that is at the same time both akin and "mischievously dishomogeneous" to the *Aeneid* (the stop in Scyros as a half-serious version of the *mora* in Carthage; the disguised Achilles and Deidamia as a degradation of Aeneas and Dido; Ulysses' deceits in a comedy plot, and so on). What emerges is the versatility and consciousness with which Statius exploits the potentialities of allusive art, so as to construct an original poetic discourse—in the grave and sublime register, as in the playful and brilliant one.

---

18 Conte (1985²) ch. 1, 17–35; Conte (2014) ch. 1.

1 Paradox and Allusive Perversion in the *Thebaid*

1.1 Paradoxical Allusivity

After the proem, the *Thebaid* opens with Oedipus, a paradox made into a person:

> impia iam merita scrutatus lumina dextra
> merserat aeterna damnatum nocte pudorem
> Oedipodes longaque animam sub morte trahebat.
> illum indulgentem tenebris imaeque recessu
> sedis inaspectos caelo radiisque penates   50
> servantem <u>tamen adsiduis *circumvolat alis*</u>
> <u>saeva dies animi, scelerumque in pectore Dirae.</u>
>
> (Stat. *Theb.* 1.46–52)

> Oedipus had already probed his impious eyes with guilty hand and sunk deep his shame condemned to everlasting night; he dragged out his life in a long-drawn death. He devotes himself to darkness, and in the lowest recess of his abode he keeps his home on which the rays of heaven never look; and yet the fierce daylight of his soul flits around him with unflagging wings and the Avengers of his crimes are in his heart.
>
> (transl. Shackleton Bailey (2003)).

Three verses offer a summary of past episodes (*iam*) and a review of models (Seneca, the 'Theban' Ovid, the Euripides of the *Phoenician women* translated in Senecan language, besides Sophocles); four more verses bring to the fore the 'new' Oedipus of Statius. Everything, here, is paradoxical: the hand that is at the same time an executioner and guilty (cf. *impiă ... meritā*: for the ambiguity of *merita*, an antithetical and synonymical pairing at the same time); the attempt to sink in an eternal night, with the sense of sight, also the sense of shame (*merserat ... pudorem*); dragging life in a long death (*longaque animam sub morte trahebat*); a self-punishment (*merita, damnatum*) that is also self-protection (*indulgentem tenebris*) and almost a morbid attachment to a cursed house (*penates / servantem*), a prelude to the reiteration of familial crimes.

Literal poetic memory emphasizes an exercise in the 'style of paradox': *scrutatus lumina*, from Seneca's *Oedipus*, thanks to the adjectives becomes the gesture of a criminal executioner; *aeterna damnatum nocte*, a formula for the blinding of Tiresias in the *Metamorphoses*, here underlines the *self*-punishment of the hero, now turned into a clairvoyant blind on a par with the seer, as the latter had foretold to him in the *Oedipus rex*.[19] At the same time, the abstract *pudorem*, substituted to *lumina*, says the impossible blinding of conscience; *longa ... morte*, again from the *Oedipus*, adds a paradox to Euripides' expression ὅς ἔτι ... ἕλκεις μακρόπνουν ζόαν, "you that still ... draw out a long-breathed life" (*Phoen.* 1533–1535),[20] displacing the adjective from life to death (*longaque animam sub morte trahebat*);[21] more than that, the translation of ζόαν by the polysemic *anima* suggests the image of Oedipus as a shadow on earth, evoked a little later in the *Phoenician women* (πολιὸν αἰθέρος ἀφανὲς εἴδωλον ἤ / νέκυν ἔνερθεν ἤ / πτανὸν ὄνειρον, "a grey and obscure image formed of ether, a dead man from the nether world, or a winged dream?", *Phoen.* 1543–1545).

In lines 49–52, the syntax is strained towards the *aprosdoketon*. The appearance of the subject, delayed in *enjambement*, is redoubled and dilated so as to invade a whole line. The contrast between darkness and light, which gives form to Oedipus' story since Sophocles, here has an unprecedented development. The darkness of blindness by which the culprit has punished himself is at the same time a refuge and an irrational escape from knowledge, as already in the *Oedipus rex*. Here, more than in Seneca, it is also an object of desire, and turbid complacency (*indulgentem tenebris*, v. 49; cf. Sen. *Oed.* 999 *iuvant tenebrae*; 1012 *quis frui tenebris vetat?*), in which there hides the obscure urge of repetition compulsion (darkness does not shelter Oedipus from guilt, since he was in his mother's womb, and from darkness he is going to cast his curse and listen to the fight between his sons).[22]

Oedipus has escaped daylight (φῶς, *dies*), has refused to see (his crimes) and to be seen (as a criminal): thus far, we are in line with Sophocles and Seneca.[23] But Statius goes beyond them. In the *Oedipus rex*, tragic irony identifies the contradiction in Oedipus' gesture: blinding the sight does not annul the memory, nor

---

[19] Cf. also Keith (2004–2005) 185.
[20] For the text of Eur. *Phoen.* I follow Mastronarde (1988), for the translation Kovacs (2002), modified according to Mastronarde's edition, or substituted with the translation of some lines in his commentary (Mastronarde 1994).
[21] For *traho* and *longus*, though without this meaningfulness, cf. also Sen. *Phoen.* 46–48 *omitte poenas languidas longae morae / mortemque totam recipe; quid segnis traho / quod vivo?*
[22] The hero was guilty when he "had not yet seen the daylight", closed in the maternal womb (Sen. *Phoen.* 245–253); and so he hides in the woods of the Cythaeron—almost a prenatal regression—to hear his sons' fight (Sen. *Phoen.* 358–362, with Petrone (1997) 69, n. 70).
[23] Ὦ φῶς, τελευταῖόν σε προσβλέψαιμι νῦν, "Oh, light, may I now look on you for the last time", Soph. *OT* 1183 (transl. Lloyd-Jones 1994); 1271–1274; 1334–1338; 1371–1390; 1409–1412, to which Creon adds himself in 1424–1431; Sen. *Oed.* 971 *tantum est periclum lucis*; 1001 *conscium evasi diem*; *Phoen.* 9–10 *non video noxae conscium nostrae diem / sed videor*.

the thought, of evils: "Alas, alas once more! How the sting of these goads has sunk into me together with the remembrance of my troubles!"[24] (οἴμοι, / οἴμοι μάλ' αὖθις· οἷον εἰσέδυ μ' ἅμα / κέντρων τε τῶνδ' οἴστρημα καὶ μνήμη κακῶν, Soph. *OT* 1316–1318, with the later comment by the coryphaeus, "Wretched in your mind and wretched in your fortune ...!", δείλαιε τοῦ νοῦ τῆς τε συμφορᾶς ἴσον, 1347); "It is a joy to live with one's thoughts beyond the reach of sorrow" (τὸ γὰρ / τὴν φροντίδ' ἔξω τῶν κακῶν οἰκεῖν γλυκύ, 1389–1390).

In Statius the contradiction becomes an explicit antithesis, and a paradoxical compresence. Darkness does not dispel light (*tenebris ... inaspectos radiis caeloque ... tamen ... dies*) and here daylight, by an unheard-of interiorization, has become "the day of the soul", "the light of conscience". *Dies animi* is the negative of *nox animi*, another singular juncture, coined by Ovid for Tereus' metaphorical blinding: *tantaque nox animi est* ("so dark the night that blinds him", *Met.* 6.652; tragic human blindness is a Leitmotiv of the episode: 472–473 *pro superi, quantum mortalia pectora caecae / noctis habent!*, "ye Gods above, how black the night that blinds our human hearts!").[25]

Ovid presupposes a formula by Lucretius: *hunc ... terrorem animi tenebrasque* ("this terror of mind ... and this gloom", Lucr. 1.146).[26] In the *DRN* the *animi tenebrae* are the darkness of ignorance, engendering irrational fears. *Nox animi*, in Ovid, is the cognitive blindness, which corresponds to tragic ἄτη. Statius reverses the image, and goes deeper: *dies animi* defines, in antithesis with the exterior dark, and that of the senses, the interior light of conscience, and the torment that comes from the knowledge of evil.[27] After the revelation, Oedipus is 'blind in *his* eyes' but no more 'blind in *his* mind', to use Sophocles' language (*OT* 371), and he does not live in 'one unbroken' or 'endless night' (*OT* 374), but in a perpetual darkness torn by light.[28]

---

24 The parallelism may suggest that even the memory of evils is a "sting", an οἴστρημα: for interpretive cues in this direction see the discussion by Bollack (1990) 909–910 *ad loc*.
25 See Rosati (2009) *ad loc.*, on 652 and 587–600.
26 Cf. Lucr. 1.146–148 (= 2.59–61; 3.91–93; 6.39–41).
27 On a different, concrete, level, Sen. *Ep.* 122.14 (cit. by Delarue (2000), 257) *et gravis malae conscientiae lux est*.
28 In Sophocles such images, used by Oedipus for Tiresias, by tragic irony are retorted against him: Soph. *OT* 371–374 "OED. you are blind in your ears, in your mind, and in your eyes. TIR. It is sad that you utter these reproaches, which all men shall soon utter against you. OED. You are *cherished by one unbroken night* (μιᾶς τρέφῃ πρὸς νυκτὸς: transl. Lloyd-Jones (1994), modified along a suggestion by Jebb 1902).

There is more. Oedipus' inner light is a "savage" light, *saeva*;[29] it is one and the same thing with "the avenging goddesses inside the mind";[30] and, with them, it "flies around unceasingly with its wings" (*adsiduis circumvolat alis*).[31] The hendiadys *saeva dies animi scelerumque in pectore Dirae*, exalted by the alliteration, combines in a paradoxical language of interiority the daylight and the *Dirae*, daughters of the Night: by a learned superimposition, the latter are here avenging goddesses, akin to the Furies (like those incumbent on Orestes or invoked by Dido in *Aeneid* 4)[32] and, at the same time, ominous winged goddesses, like that which, in the form of a nocturnal bird, announces death to Turnus in *Aeneid* 12.[33]

The image of Oedipus persecuted by his crimes may have been suggested by the chorus of the *Oedipus rex* that portrays the culprit as a runaway: "after him come dread spirits of death that never miss their mark", and "he travels ... like a bull ... trying to leave far behind the prophecies coming from earth's centre; but they hover about him, ever alive" (Soph. *OT* 471–472 δειναὶ δ'ἅμ'ἕπονται / Κῆρες ἀναπλάκητοι; 477–482 φοιτᾷ ... ὁ ταῦρος ... τὰ μεσόμφαλα γᾶς ἀπονοσφίζων / μαντεῖα· τὰ δ'ἀεὶ / ζῶντα περιποτᾶται). Sophocles shows in a sequence the images of a man hunted by Apollo, by the Cherae, and by the "ever alive" oracle, that "flies around him" as a bird of prey—or a horsefly—around a bull; Statius turns those images into the complex vision of an interior torment. The psychonyms (*animi, in pectore*) change *dies* and *Dirae* into metaphor and symbol, figurative language and rationalization of myth.[34] In this picture of psychic distress, something of the degrading and animalistic portrait in the tragedy remains: the goddesses of destiny (Cherae, or *Dirae*), the idea of persistence (*adsiduis* is the equivalent of ἀεὶ ζῶντα) and a verbal trace: *circumvolat* corresponds to Sophocles' περιποτᾶται (as in Horace *circum volat* translated Sappho's ἀμφιπόταται).[35]

But *circumvolat* has also a history of its own in Latin poetry: Statius knows it well, and reminds his readers of it. Here is the quasi-citation that interests us. The

---

29 *Saeva dies* is in *Theb.* 10.381–382 the dawn that will betray Hopleus and Dymas; the juncture recurs in Latin in two late passages.
30 Caviglia (1973) *ad loc.* compares Luc. 2.79–80.
31 For an analogous concrete image of an internal torment cf. Hor. *Carm.* 2.16.10–12 *miseros tumultus / mentis et* curas *laqueata* circum / *tecta* volantis, with Nisbet/Hubbard (1978) *ad loc.*
32 Verg. *Aen.* 4.610 *Dirae ultrices*; cf. 4.473 *ultricesque ... Dirae.*
33 Cf. Tarrant (2012) on *Aen.* 12.845–852. An analogous image of persecution in *Theb.* 3.74–77 (see Snijder (1968) *ad loc.*).
34 Delarue (2000) 256–260 compares Cicero's rationalization of the Furies acting *in fabulis* or *in scaena*: Cic. *Rosc. Am.* 67; *Pis.* 46 (see Nisbet (1987) *ad loc.*); *Leg.* 1.40.
35 Hor. *Carm.* 1.2.34; Sapph. fr. 22 V., 11–12; cf. also Catull. 68.133, cit. by Nisbet/Hubbard (1970) *ad loc.*

clausula *circumvolat alis* appears for the first time in Horace's *Satires*, in a sudden heightening of style that evokes the impending of death: Hor. *S.* 2.1.58 *seu mors atris circumvolat alis* ("whether ... or Death hovers round with sable wings").[36] It is a hypothesis by Norden that here Horace presupposes Ennius: this is suggested by the affinity with Vergilian clausulae, like that which describes the "night" around Marcellus' head in *Aeneid* 6, '*sed nox atra caput tristi circumvolat umbra*' ("yet the night flutters menacing shadows around him, darkens his head", Verg. *Aen.* 6.866).[37] The ominous darkness (*atra*, like the wings of death in Horace) is a figure of the premature destiny that awaits the young; even before ascending to life, Marcellus is surrounded by a shadow of death.

Statius shares with Horace the exact form of the clausula, *circumvolat alis*, and its surroundings (the adjective agreeing with *alis*: here *adsiduis*, in Horace *atris*); at the same time, he exhibits a contrast between light and dark, and a conceptual paradox, that are a mirror-image of those in Vergil.[38] In the *Aeneid*, the 'night' that obscures Marcellus contrasts with the splendor of the arms that illuminates him, and a soul of Hades, destined to life, appears marked by future death; in the *Thebaid*, a living dead, who serves his time on earth in the dark of a hell-house, is illuminated as if by daylight by the consciousness of his past life. In both texts an adversative move, entrusted to a character's voice (*sed ... sed ...*, said by Aeneas) or to the voice of the narrator (*tamen*), signals the effect of contrast.

An image of a sublime stamp—the rapacious flight of night or death, the one a figure of the other—is associated to a clausula, perhaps already Ennian, with an illustrious history. Statius evokes the traditional image by citing its metrical-verbal matrix, but then reverses it by surprise, defers the subject and overturns

---

[36] The clausula elsewhere indicates birds' flight properly (Ov. *Met.* 14.507; rapacious in 2.719). An interesting figurative use, that however presupposes the iconography of winged Victory, is in a solemn and 'imperial' line by Ovid, *Tr.* 2.171 *Ausoniumque ducem solitis circumvolet alis* (sc. *Victoria*).

[37] Verg. *Aen.* 6.860–866 *atque hic Aeneas (una namque ire videbat / egregium forma iuvenem et fulgentibus armis, / sed frons laeta parum et deiecto lumina vultu) / 'quis, pater, ille, virum qui sic comitatur euntem? / filius, anne aliquis magna de stirpe nepotum? / qui strepitus circa comitum! quantum instar in ipso! / sed nox atra caput tristi circumvolat umbra'*. Cf. *Aen.* 2.360 *nox atra cava circumvolat umbra*, with Austin (1964) and Horsfall (2008) *ad loc.* This Vergilian form of the clausula is repeated in an equivocal way in *Theb.* 5.163 (here *umbra* is the subject).

[38] The wings of the Night, an iconographic detail presupposed by Vergil's image (as already by Enn. *Ann.* 414 Sk.), are attributed by Statius to the day through the hendyadys with the winged *Dirae*.

it: from "night" to "day", from "death" to "light". In the poem's ouverture, a literal poetic memory, solicited by a memorable clausula, exalts an oxymoron (blindness, in the dark, illuminated as by daylight) that is also a striking allusive opposition. In this violent contrast, contextual and intertextual, the two levels strengthen each other; the rhetorical antithesis between light and dark, that gives form to a conceptual paradox, is potentiated by a blatant gesture of allusive perversion.

1.2 *Perversa vota*: Prayer Formulas and Allusive Perversion

A little later, Oedipus' prayer to the Fury offers another example of allusive perversion:

> ' ... multumque mihi consueta vocari
> adnue, Tisiphone, perversaque vota secunda:
> *si bene quid merui,* si me de matre cadentem   60
> fovisti gremio et traiectum vulnere plantas
> firmasti
>   [...]
>   si Sphingos iniquae
> callidus ambages te praemonstrante resolvi,
> si dulces furias et lamentabile matris
> conubium gavisus ini noctemque nefandam
> saepe tuli natosque tibi, scis ipsa, paravi,   70
> mox
>   [...]
> exaudi, si digna precor quaeque ipsa furenti
> subiceres ...'
>
> (*Theb.* 1.58–62, 66–71, 73–74)

'... and Tisiphone, on whom I so often call: give me your nod and favour my warped desire. If I have done aught of service, if you cherished me in your lap when I dropped from my mother and strengthened me when they pierced my feet [...] if under your tutelage I had cunning to solve the riddle of the cruel Sphinx; if I joyfully entered sweet madness and my mother's lamentable wedlock, enduring many a night of evil and making children for *you*, as well you know; if thereafter [...] hear oh hear, if my prayer be worthy and such as you yourself might whisper to my frenzy ...'.

The first speech of the poem—almost a tragic prologue in the Senecan manner—[39] is a prayer to the infernal gods (55–56), uttered "with cruel voice" (54), beating

---

[39] Briguglio (2014).

the ground "with bloody hands" (53–54). Tisiphone is selected in the name of the long reciprocal fidelity that binds her to Oedipus. The recapitulation of one's 'merits', that here also has the function of summarizing the backstory, is part of the traditional repertoire of prayer (it is the '*da, quia dedi*' motif).

But here there is a double strain. He who vaunts his merits is a guilty man who has punished himself for his faults. What is more, he begins with a well recognizable Vergilian formula: '*si bene quid merui*' (60), almost the same words as Dido's in her supplication to Aeneas: Verg. *Aen.* 4.317–318 '*si bene quid de te merui, fuit aut tibi quicquam / dulce meum*', "'If I have ever earned your thanks with services rendered, or given you any pleasure'". It is a quasi-citation, barely avoiding the cento-effect or the parody-risk. The Vergilian segment (extended up to the hephthemimeral caesura) is here reduced to a hemistich: "*de te*" is suppressed, which gave the most personal and pathetic tone to the words of the abandoned lover.

In spite of the topical character of the motif (*si merui* recurs in other Statian prayers),[40] the almost exact replica of a famous opening does not seem accidental here, and is certainly not flat. Ovid had already let Dido's expression be 'quoted' by Procris, dying in Cephalus' arms: Ov. *Met.* 7.854 "*per si quid merui de te bene*"; a more than 'pertinent' quasi-citation, that evokes a fundamental model of the love story in the *Metamorphoses*.

Entirely different is the climate in the *Thebaid*—and even the meaning of the words, here, takes a turn for the worse. Oedipus has just said: "favour my warped desire" (59); *perversa vota* announces, not only a perverse prayer, but a poetics of perversion. In the mouth of Oedipus invoking the Fury, a traditional phrase, made even more evident by the Vergilian stamp, sounds jarring: *si bene quid merui* becomes a vindication of *crimes*, that are—by a paradox—as many merits with the infernal goddess who inspired them.[41]

I could stop here, but I would like to pose some questions. It is difficult to say if secondary implications may have been calculated by Statius. Why choose as a model the prayer of a lover to a beloved? Is it only the confidential tone at stake— that "soft and familiar" tone Seneca recognizes in Dido's words (*Ben.* 7.25.2 *satis abundeque est submissis et familiaribus verbis memoriam revocare: 'si bene quid de te merui, fuit aut tibi quicquam / dulce meum*', "It would be enough, and more than enough, to refresh his memory with the gentle and friendly words: '...'")—, or is there a suggestion of the intimate nature of the relation between Oedipus and the

---

40 *Theb.* 12.267; *Silv.* 2.1.29; 3.4.101.
41 Cf. the ambiguity of the part.-adj. *merita* at l. 46 (see *supra*, § 1.1, p. 139); for plays of ambiguity on *mereo* and derived words see Bessone (1997) 93 on Ov. *Her.* 12.21.

Fury? Some details seem to hint at an almost incestuous intimacy, a replica of the perverse familial relation with the female figure, in which Tisiphone almost appears a surrogate mother of Oedipus, and then a surrogate mother of his sons (60–61; 70). Has there been "something sweet" going on between them, as between Dido and Aeneas? Do the *dulces furias* that Oedipus has "entered" in sleeping with his mother (68–69)[42] perhaps adumbrate a sort of erotic thrust towards the Fury, and almost a symbolic superimposition between Tisiphone and Jocasta? Is this analogy suggested also by *i media in fratres*, which is the traditional gesture of Jocasta—the mediation—, but is here inverted in sign? Thus, when in book 7 Jocasta will try in vain to mediate between the brothers, getting the opposite result, she will be compared to the most important of the Furies.[43] Again, is the phrase *natos ... tibi ... paravi* (70) to be taken in the more generic sense of "I have provided you with, I have prepared sons for you" (with a dative of advantage that does not imply familial relations), or is the proper sense of "generating sons" to someone (almost as if it were also *with* someone) to be heard in the background?[44] Is it perhaps insinuated that, metaphorically, for the Fury as for Jocasta, Oedipus is at the same time son, bridegroom, and father? We have gone too far, perhaps: here is the calculated risk of overinterpreting; there remains, however, something that interests us more.

Here also we see a gesture of intertextual perversion: an inversion in meaning of the 'famous words' quoted, achieved this time without varying their form, but through the forced insertion into a clashing context—an 'impertinent' as much as an impeccable quotation, almost exact. Here also, the paradoxical use of allusivity gives form to a conceptual paradox—the crimes as merits—, and impresses on this perverse epic the stylistic stamp of formal perversion.

1.3 Heroic Programme and Perverse Epic

The programmatic perversion of a Vergilian formula connotes also Polynices' portrait:

> tenet una dies noctesque recursans
> cura virum, si quando humilem decedere regno

---

[42] The ambiguous use of *ineo* can suggest also the sexual meaning (*OLD* s.v. 3; *ThlL* VII.1, 1296, 36–62; Pinotti (1988) on Ov. *Rem. am.* 402).
[43] Cf. Theb. 7.477 *Eumenidum velut antiquissima*, with Smolenaars (1994) *ad loc.*
[44] Cf. *OLD* s.v. *paro*, 2 (Varro *Sat. Men.* fr. 552.1; Lucr. 1.199); Gell. *NA* 13.23.14 (Ersilia's prayer to Tatius in Gnaeus Gellius' *Annales*).

> germanum et semet Thebis opibusque potitum
> cerneret; <u>hac aevum cupiat pro luce pacisci</u>.
>
> (*Theb.* 1.316–319)

> One thought obsesses him day and night, ever recurring: would he one day see his brother humbly leave the throne and himself in possession of Thebes and power? For that day he would willingly barter a lifetime.

The phrase *hac aevum cupiat pro luce pacisci* (1.319) distorts a banner of the heroic code. In the regatta of *Aeneid* 5, the narrator extols the rush of the competitors with a hyperbole, "for glory, they'd eagerly trade life", <u>*vitamque volunt pro laude pacisci*</u> (Verg. *Aen.* 5.230, transl. by Ahl 2007). With an intensification of the pathos, and the substitution of *letum* for *vitam*, the formula recurs at the beginning of book 12. Here Turnus, having now gained an 'awareness of death', before Latinus states his programme: '<u>*letumque sinas pro laude pacisci*</u>' ("'permit me to wager my death against glory'", *Aen.* 12.49).[45] Everything in the form of this sentence, in its two variants, contributes to impress it on the readers' memory, like a slogan.[46] A proof of this is Ovid's parody: in *Amores* 1.10 the interdiction to the fair ones to "agree on a price for the night" (*Am.* 1.10.47 *parcite, formosae, pretium pro nocte pacisci*) brings back the commercial metaphor to the crude letter.[47]

Statius exploits the memorability of the matrix to alter its nature, manipulating its form to empty its meaning.[48] The nearly identical clausula, *pro luce pacisci* for *pro laude pacisci*, exhibits the paronomastic substitution of *laude* with *luce*, that is qualified by *hac* in the first hemistich. All the rest remains almost unchanged. *Cupiat* replaces *volunt*, in tune with the erotic stylization of Polynices' lust for power; the segment between trithemimeral and hepthemimeral caesura keeps its structure intact (*vitamque volunt*; *letumque sinas*; *aevum cupiat*); *aevum* is substituted for *vitam*, and is contrasted to the term substituted in the clausula, and its adjective (*hac ... luce*).

The key of the variation is just *hac ... luce*, in place of *laude*: here there is no longer the exchange between two absolute goods—life and glory—, where eternity wins over the brief duration; on the contrary, with an inversion that produces

---

[45] See Traina (1997) *ad loc.* for the choice of the 'archaic and poetic' "*letum* instead of the isoprosodic *mortem* for the alliteration that links it to the antithetical *laudem*".
[46] Tarrant (2012) on 12.49: "'to barter death for glory' (Mandelbaum): an encapsulation of the heroic outlook that sees death as the worthwhile cost of lasting fame".
[47] Cf. McKeown (1989) *ad loc.*
[48] That the Vergilian matrix remains productive can be seen from Tertullian (*Apol.* 50.7, cit. by Tarrant (2012) *ad loc.*), who applies *de laude pacisci* to suicide as a means of gaining glory. For the "commercial colloquialism" *pacisci* see Hardie (1994) on *Aen.* 9.206.

bathos, there is the longed-for exchange between a whole life and a single day, between what is brief and what is even—literally—ephemeral: an existence consumed in a long restless hope is the price that Polynices would pay for the *day* of joy in which to see himself king, and his brother dethroned. Towards the end of the poem, that hoped-for goal will be *not even* the joy of a day, but the illusion of a moment: in the duel, Polynices dies an instant after deluding himself that he has wounded Eteocles to death and that he is still in time to wear the crown in front of his eyes (*Theb.* 11.557–560).

A gesture of allusive perversion here makes plastically visible the perversion of the heroic ideal: the horizon of glory has disappeared, expunged from the *Thebaid*'s text; and the perversion of the programme of Vergil's heroes is the mark of an epic that, in style as well as in ethics, practices perversion as a programme.

This kind of allusive relation between Statius and Vergil is akin to Lucan's attitudes. We can place side by side with it an example from the first book of the *Pharsalia*. Confronted with Caesar's hesitation at the Rubicon, Laelius draws out, as a paraenesis, a heroic move by Vergil: '*usque adeo miserum est civili vincere bello?*' (Luc. 1.366). The rhetorical question is an 'impertinent'—and spine-chilling—echo of Turnus' self-exhortation to confront death: '*usque adeone mori miserum est?*' ("'Is dying really so bad?'", Verg. *Aen.* 12.646).[49] With a simple retouch, a famous Vergilian tag, having become a proverb, is effectively perverted into the new ethical manifesto of the civil war.[50]

---

[49] Cf. Tarrant (2012) *ad loc.*

[50] A case that involves Vergil, Ovid and Lucan is *Theb.* 7.546–547 (Tydeus to Polynices) tu *porro sequeris,* / heu NIMIUM *mitis* NIMIUMque oblite tuorum? Of a common matrix, constructed around the clausula *oblite tuarum/tuorum* and used as a call to the 'duties' of a hero, Statius takes: from Ovid (*Her.* 1.41 *ausus es –* o NIMIUM NIMIUMque oblite tuorum*!*, Penelope to Ulysses) the syntax, with a reversal of the sense ("non: «dimentico dei tuoi cari», ma: «dimentico di quanto siano malvagi i tuoi familiari»", Casali (1999) 233–234, n. 18, with further discussion and examples on pp. 232–234; cf. Smolenaars 1994 *ad loc.*); from Vergil (*Aen.* 4.265–267 '*tu nunc Karthaginis altae / fundamenta locas pulchramque uxorius urbem / exstruis?* heu regni rerumque oblite tuarum*!*', Mercurius to Aeneas) the rebuke for giving up the aspiration to a reign, a moral imperative perverted in the *Thebaid* into an impious design (cf. *Theb.* 7.537 *exciderat regnum*); from Lucan (4.212–213 '*immemor o patriae, signorum oblite tuorum,* / ... *miles*', Petreius to the Pompeians) the inhibition of a fraternization that would put an end to a civil conflict (for the link between the two scenes see Micozzi (1999) 354–355). The perversion of Vergil's heroic imperative by Statius presupposes the exploration of the tragic paradoxes of civil war in Lucan's anti-*Aeneid*.

1.4 Civil war: Intertextual Inversions and Formulas from Roman Tradition

Inversion is a gesture typical of Statius, as of Lucan. In the *Thebaid*, paradox informs all levels of the text: even the 'paradoxical' use of intertextuality is the stylistic correlative of a distorted reality. Conventional epic language is subjected to a deforming twist. I have shown elsewhere some examples of this from the brothers' duel, where Statius perverts Vergil's language into the style of an impious epic, creating disturbing *iuncturae* by the substitution of an element, e.g. constraining into a sacrilegious union a verb that has a ritual import with a synonym of fratricidal impiety.[51] Even intertextual inversions express the character of an 'unnatural' epic, which reverses traditional paradigms to represent a subverted world of values.

Intertextual inversion operates at the level of compositional structures as well as in the form of expression. The first extended simile in the poem likens the discordant brothers to two oxen intolerant of the yoke, that "pull opposite ways":

> sic ubi delectos per torva armenta iuvencos
> agricola imposito sociare adfectat aratro,
> illi indignantes, quis nondum vomere multo
> ardua nodosos cervix descendit in armos,
> in diversa trahunt atque aequis vincula laxant   135
> viribus et vario confundunt limite sulcos:
> haud secus indomitos praeceps discordia fratres
> asperat.
>
> (*Theb.* 1.131–138)

> So when a farmer essays to yoke two bullocks chosen from the fierce herd at one plough, they rebel; not yet has many a ploughshare bowed their lofty necks into their brawny shoulders. They pull opposite ways and with equal strength loosen their bonds, perplexing the furrows with motley track. Not otherwise does headlong strife enrage the tameless brethren.

Statius inverts the Homeric simile that compares the concordant work of two Ajaxes to that of a pair of oxen (Hom. *Il.* 13.701–708), and thus announces in a programmatic way, through the intertextual antiphrasis, his inversion of the epic of κλέα ἀνδρῶν—from heroic friendship to fraternal enmity. Almost at the other end of the poem, the apostrophe to the brothers reverses that of Vergil to Euryalus

---

51 See Bessone (2018a).

and Nisus: the promise of poetic memory is overturned into a paradoxical promise of oblivion.[52] Framing the story of Eteocles and Polynices, a blatant antiphrastic gesture indicates Homer and Vergil as destituted authorities. The writing of civil war is also an internal war inside the epic code.[53]

The inversion of Homer is more precise than has been observed:

Αἴας δ' οὐκέτι πάμπαν, Ὀϊλῆος ταχὺς υἱός,
ἵστατ' ἀπ' Αἴαντος Τελαμωνίου οὐδ' ἠβαιόν,
ἀλλ' ὥς τ' ἐν νειῷ βόε οἴνοπε πηκτὸν ἄροτρον
ἶσον θυμὸν ἔχοντε τιταίνετον· ἀμφὶ δ' ἄρα σφι
πρυμνοῖσιν κεράεσσι πολὺς ἀνακηκίει ἱδρώς·   705
τὼ μέν τε ζυγὸν οἶον ἐΰξοον ἀμφὶς ἐέργει
ἱεμένω κατὰ ὦλκα· τέμει δέ τε τέλσον ἀρούρης·
ὣς τὼ παρβεβαῶτε μάλ' ἔστασαν ἀλλήλοιιν.

(Hom. *Il.* 13.701–708)

And Aias, the swift son of Oïleus, would no longer by any means stand apart from Aias, son of Telamon, not even a little; but just as in fallow land two wine-dark oxen with one accord strain at the joined plough, and about the roots of their horns wells up the sweat in streams—the polished yoke alone holds the two apart as they labor through the furrow, till the plough cuts to the limit of the field—just so these two came together and stood close by each other's side.

(transl. Murray/Wyatt 1999)

Homer's oxen, and warriors, proceed "close by each other's side" (παρβεβαῶτε ... ἀλλήλοιιν, 708), are separated only by the yoke (706) and "draw at full stretch" the "compacted" plough (703–704 πηκτὸν ἄροτρον ... τιταίνετον); Statius' oxen (and brothers) "pull opposite ways" (*in diversa trahunt*) and "loosen" the bond of the yoke (*vincula laxant*), while the "equal strengths" tending in opposite directions (*aequis ... viribus*) substitute the sweat of the common work (*Il.* 13.704–705); those oxen do an exemplary job, follow the "furrow" (ἱεμένω κατὰ ὦλκα) going along the field up to the "limit", the "borderline" (τέλσον ἀρούρης); these oxen trace an irregular "line" (*limes* is also "limit", like τέλσον) and muddle the "furrows" (*vario confundunt limite sulcos*).

There is something more than an inversion here. Between Homer and Statius, the imagery of tragedy has opened a new metaphorical world, and Statius explores it. In a figurative exchange between generation and agriculture, which is

---

52 Cf. Bessone (2011) 80–89.
53 See Bessone (2018a), § 2.

traditional in the myth of Oedipus, here the brothers(-oxen) replicate the confusion of the (maternal) furrows they are born from.⁵⁴ The oxymoron of the 'confused boundary' (*vario confundunt limite*) recalls the proem, 1.16–17 *limes mihi carminis esto / Oedipodae confusa domus*. Even the 'line' of song, when the subject of the epos is the house of Thebes, becomes a place of confusion, a deviated track.

Homer overturned, then, and rethought through tragedy, to give form to the new epic of *nefas*. But the gesture of inversion, which is a gesture of programmatic impertinence, coexists with the 'pertinent' citation of formulas that have already become traditional at Rome, in the poetic writing of civil wars. Just in this anti-Iliadic simile, allusive art traces a line of Latin tradition in which Statius aspires to insert himself.

In a bilingual wordplay, the "equal mind" of Homer's oxen and warriors (ἶσον θυμὸν ἔχοντε, *Il*. 13.704) is here turned into its opposite, the Latin compound that means having a "different heart", *dis-cordia* (from *dis+cor*). The term has almost become a synonym of civil war (and, in epic, the Ennian role of *Discordia* has passed over to the Vergilian Fury Allecto, who starts in Latium a quasi-civil war).⁵⁵

But here there is not only the noun *discordia*, repeated (1.130, 137). There is a clausula that is like a seal: *discordia fratres* (1.137). In the start of his poem, Statius lets a well known cadency resound, that was inaugurated in the *Georgics*. It is the passage of the second book that elaborates the experience of civil wars into a cultural-historical reflection, and opposes political ambition to the ideal of country life: *illum non populi fasces, non purpura regum / flexit et infidos agitans discordia fratres, / aut coniurato descendens Dacus ab Histro, / non res Romanae perituraque regna*, "Him no honours that people give can move, no purple worn by despots, no strife which leads brother to betray brother; untroubled is he by Dacian incursion swooping down from a Danube leagued in war, untroubled by Rome's policies spelling doom to kingdoms", Verg. *G*. 2.495–498 (transl. Fairclough 1916).⁵⁶

---

54 Cf. Aesch. *Sept*. 752–756; Soph. *OT* 260, 459–460, 1256–1257.
55 Verg. *Aen*. 7.335–336 '*tu potes unanimos armare in proelia fratres / atque odiis versare domos*'.
56 Cf. Verg. *G*. 2.510–513 *gaudent perfusi sanguine fratrum / exilioque domos et dulcia limina mutant / atque alio patriam quaerunt sub sole iacentem. / agricola incurvo terram dimovit aratro* ... In Vergil the world of fraternal discord is contrasted to that of agricultural work, where the farmer who plows and maintains the oxen is a figure opposed to the impiety of politics—Statius breaks by a paradox this axiological opposition, introducing even in the sphere of agriculture the harshness of human society (for a similar effect see *G*. 1.493–497, as Damien Nelis suggests to me).

By Statius' time, this clausula already has a history of its own. From Vergil's meditation it has been borrowed in the representation of *chaos* at the beginning of the *Metamorphoses* (1.57–60), where the strife of the brother-winds is a cosmic projection of civil conflict:[57] (*... tanta est discordia fratrum*), "so fierce is brothers' strife", Ov. *Met.* 1.60. Ovid here recalls not only the *Georgics*, but the 'cosmic' opening of the *Aeneid*, where the fight of the winds, unleashed in the tempest, is a figure of the natural and political chaos desired by Juno (Verg. *Aen.* 1.52–57).

In the *Thebaid*, Statius recalls at the same time the clausula of the *Georgics*, its recalling in the *Metamorphoses*, and the passage of the *Aeneid* that is Ovid's other model. Inside the simile, the incipit *illi indignantes* (*Theb.* 1.133) describes the intolerance of the yoke with the Vergilian formula for the winds' insubordination, and their intolerance of divine control: Verg. *Aen.* 1.55–56 *illi indignantes magno cum murmure montis / circum claustra fremunt*, "hating restraint, they seethe all round their bolted escape routes". The plough "imposed" by the *agricola* (*imposito ... aratro*), like the mountain "imposed" by Jupiter (*Aen.* 1.60–62 *pater omnipotens ... molemque et montis insuper altos / imposuit*, "the Almighty Father ... superimposed high mountainous masses"), is a brake—here really precarious—to the fight for power. The two Vergilian quotations, one of which is Ovidian-Vergilian, connect Statius' political discourse to an acknowledged tradition of the discourse on power in Latin epic (didactic and mythological).[58]

1.5 *Regendi / saevus amor*: the Eros of Power

From Vergil, to Ovid, to Lucan: with a series of quasi-citations, Statius fits into a line of epic tradition. However, a Vergilian quasi-citation from a *non*-epic context is the means by which the Flavian poet adds a new note to the representation of

---

[57] Here in Ovid, for the first time, winds are acknowledged as "brothers"—although they have been known to be sons of Eos/Aurora and of the Titan Astraeus since Hesiod. Ovid gives a novel twist to an epic topos, the battle of the winds, exploited in war similes and storm descriptions from Homer on. Vergil is vague on this in *Aeneid* 1, where the winds may seem to strive against imprisonment rather than against each other (line 50 *luctantis ventos*), and are said to work "together" in the storm (85 *una*), in what looks like a common fight against sea and land; however, *discordes venti* fight against each other *animis et viribus aequis* in a comparison at *Aen.* 10.356–361, and their conflicting assaults illustrate a confused multiple battle in *Aen.* 2.413–419. Ovid comments on, and complements, the *Aeneid*'s text: the idea of fighting brothers revises Vergil's picture, while pursuing his reflection on power relations in the natural world.

[58] From the beginning of the poem, Statius exhibits the Roman rhetoric of civil wars deprecation, reusing strongly connoted expressive formulas: cf. Bessone (2011) 58–61; Bessone (2018a), § 1.

the lust for power. In the description of the effects produced by Tisiphone on the brothers, the phrase *regendi / <u>saevus amor</u>* stands out (1.127–128):

> atque ea Cadmeo praeceps ubi culmine primum
> constitit adsuetaque infecit nube penates,
> protinus attoniti fratrum sub pectore motus,   125
> gentilisque animos subiit furor aegraque laetis
> invidia atque parens odii metus, inde <u>regendi</u>
> <u>saevus amor</u>, ruptaeque vices iurisque secundi
> ambitus impatiens, et summo dulcius unum
> stare loco, sociisque comes discordia regnis.
>
> (*Theb.* 1.123–130)

When first she stayed her headlong course at the Cadmean citadel and tainted the dwelling with her wonted mist, shock stirred the brothers' hearts. The family madness invaded their minds, envy sick at another's good fortune and fear, parent of hate, then fierce love of rule, breach of give and take, ambition intolerant of second place, hankering to stand at the top alone, strife, the companion of shared sovereignty.

In a context dense with echoes of Lucan,[59] these words rather recall the effect of the Fury on Turnus: *<u>saevit amor ferri</u> et scelerata insania belli, / ira super* ("Love of the sword linked with criminal madness for war brutalizes: top it with anger ...", Verg. *Aen.* 7.461, already echoed by Sen. *Thy.* 84–85 *inferque tecum proelia et <u>ferri malum</u> / regibus <u>amorem</u>*, "along with yourself instil battles and the evil love of the sword in kings").[60] The war fury, however, is here substituted with a fury for power that has an even stronger erotic connotation, restated by *dulcius* (v. 129).[61] This is something similar to the *regnandi ... dira cupido* of the proem to the *Georgics*, a lust so (Lucretianly) terrible as to make even the reign of the Underworld be desired, or a ruinous passion for the title of *rex* in itself.[62]

---

[59] Cf. ll. 128–129 with Luc. 1.4 and 1.92–93, as well as 1.123–124.
[60] Cf. Horsfall (2000) on *saevit*: "Here suggestive of the peculiar cruelty of (civil) war"; on *amor ferri*: "The language is familiar [...] but the juxtaposition [...] perverse and monstrous, though neither unheroic, nor unknown in the civil wars".
[61] Cf. *Theb.* 2.339 '<u>dulcis amor regni</u> blandumque potestas', with Gervais (2017); (elsewhere *amor regni/regnandi* only in Livy 40.8.18); 11.655–656 *pro blanda potestas / et <u>sceptri</u> malesuadus <u>amor</u>!* An analogous connotation has *dulcius* in *Theb.* 5.78; cf. also 5.162 *dulce nefas* (with Rosati 2005). Lines 1.129–130 *et summo dulcius unum / stare loco* look like a response to Lucr. 2.7–13 *sed nil dulcius est, bene quam munita tenere / edita doctrina sapientum templa serena* ... (cf. 12–13 *niti ... ad summas emergere opes rerumque potiri*): an opposition between choices of life.
[62] Cf. Verg. *G.* 1.36–37 with Thomas (1988), quoting, for *regni/regnandi cupido* as "a political phrase of the utmost opprobrium", Liv. 1.6.4, 17.1; 21.10.4 (and Brutus in Cic. *ad Brut.* 24.3 *cupiditatem regni*); add Sall. *Hist.* 4.69.5 [= 4.67.5 McG.].5.17 *cupido profunda imperi et divitiarum*. For

Statius gets this effect of 'eroticization' by quoting a famous incipit of the *Eclogues*, that describes Medea's "cruel love", with its consequences—another *saevus amor*, at the origin of another intra-familial tragedy—:

> <u>saevus amor</u> docuit natorum sanguine matrem
> commaculare manus.
>
> (Verg. *Ecl.* 8.47–48)
>
> Ruthless Love taught a mother to stain her hands in her children's blood.
> (transl. Fairclough 1916).

The famous *iunctura* appeared in the prologue to Ennius' *Medea* (Enn. *Med. ex.* 216 Joc. *Medea animo aegro amore saevo saucia*, "Medea, sick at heart, smitten by savage love") and recurred in Seneca (Sen. *Med.* 849–851 *quonam cruenta Maenas / praeceps amore saevo / rapitur?*, "where is the bloodstained maenad being driven impetuously by savage love?"). But Statius derives the force of his expression from the form of Vergil's text. In the *Thebaid*, the surprise effect is the result of a calculated progression: *regendi*, in the clausula (with the suspension of the enjambement), anticipates the different, and differently perverted, nature of this "cruel love", which is a sort of 'eros of power', a motif that goes back to the theorization on the tyrant in Plato, that is central to Seneca's theatre—as Rosati has shown[63]—and that has in the *Thebaid* an important and pervasive development.[64]

2 Allusivity and Irony in the *Achilleid*

There is room only for a brief mention of allusive procedures in the *Achilleid*, almost all already known. I will dwell on some examples of ironic provocation. It is my impression that the procedures of exhibited verbal allusivity in the *Achilleid* are pervasive and crucial—almost as if the half-serious style of this epic experiment contemplated as a programme the ironical use of quotations, with nuances ranging from light humour, to provocation, to nearly overt parody. In an elusive narrative tone, continual excursions create a precarious balance between pathos

---

the erotic connotation of *dira cupido* (cf. Lucr. 4.1090 *dira cuppedine* with Brown (1987); 4.1046 *dira lubido*) see Hardie (1994) on *Aen.* 9.184–185.
63 Rosati (2006).
64 As Briguglio (2017a) 48–62 and (2017b) shows, and as I argue in Bessone (2018b).

and humour (which presupposes Ovid's *Metamorphoses*). Statius lets frequent swerves be perceived from one register to the other, also thanks to an overt and wrong-footing use of allusive art. High ambitions and caricatural falls, pretences of the sublime and the grotesque, pathos and melodrama alternate in the poem, as recent criticism has recognized,[65] in an up and down dynamic that produces effects of ironical estrangement, or even epic parody.

2.1 Catullus 64

An ironic nuance often accompanies even the most 'pertinent' citations, those 'self-reflexive annotations' that recreate a literary tradition. The relation with Catullus 64, very well studied, offers a vast range of allusive procedures, highly self-conscious. It is well known that the line that closes the first book (*inrita ventosae rapiebant verba procellae*, "The airy gusts swept his vain words away", *Ach.* 1.960), after four verses of promises by Achilles to Deidamia, barely varies an hexameter frame on the vain promises made to Ariadne (*inrita ventosae linquens promissa procellae*, "leaving his perjured vows to the gusty gales", Catull. 64.59). The stylistic seal consecrates Deidamia in the role of the *relicta*, while the lexical-syntactical variation partly absolves Achilles from Theseus' faults (thus leaving space for future deeds, both heroic and erotic).[66] Echoes of the Parcae's prophecy in the epithalamium show that, in part, it has already come true, by an exercise in "continuity of the stories and continuation of the texts" (Barchiesi 1986), commented on by metaliterary signals. Achilles' future deeds in part have "already" (*iam*) been precociously realized, in his education as an *enfant prodige* by Chiron.[67] And conversely, now, on the eve of the Trojan war, is accomplished what "already then" (*iam tunc*) had been prophesied (*Ach.* 2.55–57). Subtler effects are not missing. In the evocation of Theseus' deed, formulated like a philological *zetema* (*canit ille* ... *quanto circumdata nexu / ruperit Aegides Minoia bracchia tauri*, 'he sings ... with how strong a grip the son of Aegeus encircled and broke the limbs of Minos' bull', *Ach.* 1.189–192), the 'equivocal' citation of a clausula from the simile of poem 64, *bracchia tauri* for *bracchia Tauro* (Catul. 64.105), is a learned comment upon Catullus' text. Statius "unriddles" it, giving back the

---

65 Barchiesi (1996); see also Klodt (2009).
66 Rosati (1994) 53–54 and n. 95; Hinds (1998) 126.
67 See Hinds (1998) 125–126. Cf. *Ach.* 2.110–116 ... *volucres cum iam praevertere cervos / et Lapithas cogebat equos praemissaque cursu / tela sequi; saepe* ... with Catul. 64.340–341 *qui persaepe vago victor certamine cursus / flammea praevertet celeris vestigia cervae* (and Pind. *Nem.* 3.53–54).

"arms" from the oak to the monster, and the name of mount *Taurus* to the Minotaur.[68] More immaterial allusivity has no less weight: Achilles' song on the lyre breaks off on *maternos ... toros* (1.193), almost an alternative title of the epyllion, which arouses in Thetis a smile of acknowledgement. And the interruption of the Catullan sequence in the midst of the wedding feast seems to suggest that Achilles refrains—for now—from singing *his own* deeds (substituting himself for the Parcae). The reader smiles, and prepares for the next self-celebrations of the hero, in front of Deidamia and then of Ulysses and Diomedes.[69]

2.2 Vergil's *Aeneid*

The relation with the *Aeneid* is even richer. A series of 'systematic quotations' structures whole textual sequences on precise Vergilian models. In the scene of the failed tempest, clusters of citations from *Aeneid* 1, 5 and 7—above all incipits and clausulae—connote Thetis as a weakened Juno and a Venus without hope.[70] On their part, Achilles and Deidamia appear like Aeneas and Dido in a debased version thanks to the borrowing, not only of motifs, but of verbal-metrical structures from *Aeneid* 1 and 4.[71] In this literal memory, pertinence and impertinence are inseparable; this is a structural and impudent allusivity at the same time, which signals a fundamental model and systematically disregards it, thus connotating the *Achilleid* as an epic 'in a minor key'.[72]

---

[68] Cf. Hardie in Hinds (1998) 127, n. 2; Hunter (2006) 100 and n. 42; not much in Lauletta (1993) 89, n. 26.
[69] *Ach.* 1.577–579; 2.94–167. See Hinds (1998) 127; Heslin (2005) 88–89.
[70] Cf. e.g. *Ach.* 1.43 'non potui infelix ...?' with *Aen.* 7.308–309 (Juno) '... *nil linquere inausum / quae* potui infelix...' and 4.600 (Dido) 'non potui *abreptum divellere corpus ...?*'. See *supra*, n. 10.
[71] For the fundamental role of the *Aeneid* as model see esp. Feeney (2004).
[72] Not only the *Aeneid* is involved in this play of quotations bordering on parody. The Vergilian sound of *Ach.* 1.250 dubitatque agnoscere matrem (cf. Verg. *Ecl.* 4.60 *incipe, parve puer, risu* cognoscere matrem) has not escaped Barchiesi (2005) 53: "This is a traumatic distortion of the confident model of heroic childhood, the *puer* of *Eclogue* IV". Statius presents Achilles' awaking in Scyros as a re-birth (cf. Bessone (2016), 187) and insists on his problematic semi-divinity: here not only there is no smile of the *puer*, and, by a paradox, even no acknowledgement of the mother (an extraneous since always), but there is a disquieting estrangement—and the denial of a divine destiny for the hero.

2.2.1 Dissonances in clausula and incipit

The relation, close and conflictual, between the hero of the *Achilleid* and the protagonist of the *Aeneid* offers one of the most provoking examples of Statius' allusive art: the 'equivocal' citation of a clausula, followed in enjambement by another striking citation in incipit. Achilles' words to Deidamia after the rape, as is well known, coincide in sound with Aeneas' posthumous excuses to Dido:

> 'nec ego hos cultus aut foeda subissem
> tegmina, ni primo te visa in <u>litore: cessi</u>
> <u>te propter</u>, tibi pensa manu, tibi mollia gesto
> tympana'.
>
> (*Ach.* 1.652–655)

> 'Nor should I have donned this habit, these shameful clothes, if I had not seen you at the shore's verge; on your account I yielded, for you I handle wool and bear womanish drums'.

The clausula *litore: cessi* is a replica, 'equivocal' in syntax and sound, of '*invitus, regina, tuo de <u>litore cessi</u>*' ("It was no choice of my will, good queen, to withdraw from your country", Verg. *Aen.* 6.460)—in its turn, a famous, and intriguing, citation of Berenice's lock in Catullus (*invita, o regina, tuo de vertice <u>cessi</u>, / invita ...*, "Unwillingly, your queen, did I quit your brow, unwillingly", 66.39 (transl. Burton (1894)).[73]

We smile at this sort of self-apologetic automatism, that keeps reproducing itself in disparate, yet comparable contexts. In Statius the juncture *in litore*, in place of *de litore*, says that, on the shore where he fell in love, Achilles has remained (and willingly so), unlike Aeneas; and with *cessi* (here absolute) the hero says that he has "yielded" to love: as opposed to Aeneas, without backtracking, at least for now. The very words that Achilles cites from his model detach him

---

[73] Discussion in Barchiesi (1997) 212–217 (216: "La riconoscibilità della clausola *litore: cessi* è tanto nitida che Stazio si può permettere di incuneare una forte pausa di senso fra le due parole"; 217: "Il problema di identità sessuale posto dal nuovo contesto è ricapitolato nella genealogia dell'allusione: parole che hanno un'intera storia di genere incerto, da un ambiguo maschile callimacheo a un femminile catulliano a un preoccupato maschile virgiliano"); see also (2005), 59: "The hero [...] echoes the most (in)famous bisexual line of ancient literature, a line that was uttered by a male lock severed from a female hair (Callimachus), by a female lock (Catullus), by a male hero (Virgil)". Cf. now Knox (2015) 302–315, in a paper which discusses a set of problems not far from my concerns.

from Vergil's hero, for the moment: this Achilles is, and is not, an Aeneas; he professes himself different, even if, for the future, he profiles in fact identical.[74]

But another fact is striking. Just after citing Aeneas, Achilles seems to cite Dido, and one wonders if this surprising cento-effect is calculated by Statius.[75] The Vergilian clausula, changed in the syntax (*litore: cessi*), creates a suspension, that is filled after the enjambement by *te propter*: "(I yielded) because of you, out of love for you". In the hexameter incipit, we find again an infrequent *iunctura*, which is found in incipit, and is even iterated, in Dido's first speech to Aeneas in *Aeneid* 4: '*te propter Libycae gentes Nomadumque tyranni / odere, infensi Tyrii; te propter eundem / exstinctus pudor et, qua sola sidera adibam, / fama prior*' ("'Libyan tribesmen, nomad sheikhs all loathe me. The Tyrians hate me on your account; and on your account I have ruined my sole claim to a stellar distinction: my chastity's good name, once honoured, even by Rumour'", Verg. *Aen.* 4.320–323). The tone can be more recriminating or more persuasive, but the move is identical: to remind one's beloved up to which point one has demeaned himself, or herself, out of love for her, or him—Dido has lost "chastity" and "fame", and gained hostility; Achilles has stooped to bringing in his hand "wool" and "womanish drums".

Achilles speaks, in a sequence, like Aeneas and like Dido. In the passage from one line to the other, we see him first break free from the male role, then take on the female one, and we smile as we hear again in one and the same mouth, conflicting with each other, the two voices of the Vergilian couple—all this while the hero reveals himself as a *vir* and dissolves in front of Deidamia his sexual ambiguity. The allusive confusion seems to comment on the gender confusion.

This 'female' role—lowering oneself or enduring "because of a lover", "out of love for someone"—is not new for Achilles in Latin poetry. *Propter te*, or *propter aliquam/-em*, is a typical move of love discourse, elegiac in particular; and elegy has consecrated Achilles as a hero capable of everything "because of" a woman, Briseis. This is the romantic, post-Homeric, rereading of the relationship between the two in the *Iliad*.[76] Thus, from the mention of the slave, in Homer, as the γέρας, the "prize [...] for which I toiled so much" (Hom. *Il.* 1.161–162 γέρας ... / ᾧ ἔπι

---

74 Heslin (2005) 100–101 even strives to detect the erased *invitus* of Vergil's text in Statius' "syllabic rearrangement" (*tu vis' in*).
75 A hint in Barchiesi (1997) 217, n. 11.
76 Cf. now Fantuzzi 2012, chapter 3. Even Achilles' following question, *Ach.* 1.655–656 '*quid defles magno nurus addita ponto? / quid gemis ingentes caelo paritura nepotes?*', lets the reader hear again an incipit by Propertius that assimilates Cynthia to Briseis, crying for the abduction from Achilles: Prop. 2.20.1 *quid fles abducta gravius Briseide? quid fles ...?* (see Fedeli 2005 *ad loc.*).

πολλὰ μόγησα), and from Achilles' final condemnation of his raging "for the sake of a girl" (εἵνεκα κούρης, *Il.* 19.58), we come to the formulations of totalizing love in Propertius and Ovid: *omnia formosam propter Briseida passus* ("enduring it all for the sake of lovely Briseis", Prop. 2.8.35) and, said by Briseis, *propter me mota est, propter me desinat ira* ("For me your anger was stirred, through me let it be allayed", Ov. *Her.* 3.89).[77] In Statius' Achilles we see the Achilles of the *Iliad*, revised by Latin erotic elegy: love—for Deidamia, or Briseis—transforms the best of the Achaeans into the humblest and most feminine of lovers.[78]

2.2.2 Quasi-parodic Hemistich

The recreation of narrative situations comparable to the *Aeneid* often involves an effect of bathos, which the ironic quotations exalt. Ulysses at Scyros is like Mercurius at Carthage: the agent of a recall of the hero to his mission, from a so much more inglorious context. A hemistich of the divine rebuke to Aeneas is re-employed to rebuke Achilles: *heia, abrumpe moras!* ("Up now, no more delay!", *Ach.* 1.872) is a quasi-citation of: *heia age, rumpe moras* ("Hang the delays!", Verg. *Aen.* 4.569).[79] The removal of *age* (substituted with the preverb *ab-*) barely avoids the effect of overt parody. It is interesting that, to the contrary, the same hemistich is cited in its exact form in the parody by Martial 2.64, an epigram that dramatizes Laurus' indecision between becoming a rhetor or an advocate, and attacks the addressee with a disproportionately authoritative voice: *heia age, rumpe moras: quo te sperabimus usque? / dum quid sis dubitas, iam potes esse nihil* ("Up now, no more paltering! How long are we to wait for you? While you're dithering about

---

77 See Barchiesi 1992 *ad loc.* Cf. now Bessone (2018c), 202–203.

78 The refusal of Aeneas' model is signalled elsewhere by borrowing single terms, qualified by a negation or inverted in their function. Achilles, *non ipse inmotus*, "consoles" Deidamia in their only night as newlyweds: *Ach.* 1.956–957 *talia dicentem non ipse inmotus Achilles / solatur*. The hero does not repress, like Aeneas, the desire of "consoling" the *relicta* (*Aen.* 4.393–394 *at pius Aeneas, quamquam lenire dolentem / solando cupit ...*) and appears "not unmoved", as opposed to the "irremovable" Vergilian hero: *Aen.* 4.331–332 *dixerat. ille Iovis monitis immota tenebat / lumina* (just after Dido's 'saltem', v. 327, echoed by Deidamia at *Ach.* 1.953: see below, §2.2.3, pp. 161–162).

79 On this echo, from a different point of view, see Ripoll in this volume. The sole *abrumpe moras* recurs in *Theb.* 11.201 (the Fury, disguised as Phereclus, scolds a lingering Polynices; the hero's reaction is comparable).

what to be, you can already be nothing", Mart. 2.64.9–10 (transl. Shackleton Bailey 1993).[80]

The Vergilian segment must have been perceived as a memorable piece of an exemplary scolding, pronounced with a colloquial inflexion in a sublime context.[81] Martial exploits it jokingly to spur an irresolute to the choice of the profession, Statius, to recall Achilles to the choice of his identity. A thin line here divides the *Achilleid* from Martial, a 'parodic' epic from the parody of epic.

I wonder if Statius' reader is invited not only to consider the general parallelism between the episodes of Scyros and Carthage, but also to compare the specific contexts. Mercury's two speeches catch Aeneas, first in the role of *vir uxorius*, dressed in oriental fashion in the queen's retinue (*'tu nunc Carthaginis altae / fundamenta locas pulchramque uxorius urbem / exstruis?'*, "'*You*, laying foundations for mighty Carthage!', he said, 'Obsessed with your wife, you're now building a lovely city for her'", *Aen*. 4.265–267), then exposed to the dangers of a *femina*: the comment *'varium et mutabile semper / femina'* ("'What you face is a complex and changeable constant: woman'", 4.569–570) follows the hemistich quoted in the *Achilleid*. Between Vergil and Statius there is a comic degradation, from the submission to a woman to the feminization of the hero. The quasi-citation from the *Aeneid* would seem to aim mischievously at this point. The disguised Achilles is a sort of degradation, and almost a parody, of the *uxorius* Aeneas in oriental dress, scandalously unaware that "woman is fickle". For the hero of Scyros, the choice of the heroic identity is also a necessary choice of sexual identity.[82]

Aeneas, then, must choose between constructing Carthage or founding Rome, Laurus between becoming *rhetor* or *causidicus*, Achilles between being *Pelea virgo* or *semiferi Chironis alumnus*. The same Vergilian hemistich offers itself as a ready-made formula for inviting a choice between identity and social role; as a connoted poetic language, capable of conferring ironic depth to lower poetic contexts, different from each other, like half-serious epic and epigram;

---

[80] Cf. Mart. 2.64.1–2 *dum modo causidicum, dum te modo rhetora fingis / et non decernis, Laure, quid esse velis* ... See Williams (2004) on 2.64.9.
[81] See Austin (1955) on 4.569 *heia age*; Hardie (1994) on 9.38 *heia*. On *Aen*. 4.267 see above, §1.3, p. 148 n. 50.
[82] The *bathos* is compensated, again in a humorous key, by the instant choice with which Achilles responds to the heroic imperative, unlike the doubtful Aeneas. Amusing details complete the picture: if Aeneas' hair stands up at the appearance of the god (*Aen*. 4.280 *arrectaeque horrore comae*), Achilles' hair stands up at the sight of himself mirrored in the shield, and even "*leaves his forehead*"—by a hyperbole, but also so as to uncover the male face that it masked so far (*Ach*. 1.856 *et fronte relicta / surrexere comae*).

and, in the *Achilleid*, as the stamp of a sublime epic tradition, at the same time pursued and ironically disregarded.

2.2.3 Parodic Mini-cento

An example of quasi-citation with a parodic function, where ironic gap, comic characterization and dramatic irony are at play together, is the passage where Lycomedes, disconsolately devoid of male offspring, speaks to Ulysses almost with Dido's words to Aeneas: '*saltem si suboles, aptum quam mittere bello – / nunc ipsi viresque meas et cara videtis / pignora: quando novos dabit haec mihi turba nepotes?*', "'At least if I had offspring meet to send forth to war—but now you see for yourselves my strength and my dear children. When shall this throng give me new grandsons?'", *Ach*. 1.780–782. One of the most pathetic points of the *Aeneid* resounds in a context which is at the same time similar and deliciously incongruous. The Vergilian mini-cento reuses the pathetic regret of Dido at not having a son as Lycomedes' 'comic' regret for his lack of offspring or grandsons to send to war—a regret that will be immediately refuted.

The hemistich *saltem si suboles* combines, in order, parts of the first hemistich of two successive hexameters in the famous passage of the *Aeneid* (and welds them together in alliterative contact): '*saltem si qua mihi de te suscepta fuisset / ante fugam suboles, si quis mihi parvulus aula / luderet Aeneas, qui te tamen ore referret, / non equidem omnino capta ac deserta viderer*', "'If I'd at least, before you ran off, conceived from our closeness some child fathered by you, if there just were a baby Aeneas playing inside my halls, whose face might in some way recall you, I would not feel so wholly trapped yet wholly deserted'", Verg. *Aen*. 4.327–330.[83] Statius practices a surgical cut on the Vergilian text. He expunges the verb of 'generating', implies a dative of possession (*mihi esset*) and truncates the sentence with an aposiopesis that, as often in the *Achilleid*, is a mark of irony. The interruption at the words *mittere bello* is prophetic, and what follows is full of dramatic irony: not only is Achilles hiding among his daughters (*cara ... pignora*), but the question "When shall this throng give me new grandsons?" finds an answer in the hero's words, one hundred and twenty lines later: '*iam socer es*' – *natum ante pedes prostravit et addit* – / '*iamque avus*', "'Already you are my father in law'—he laid the babe at his feet and adds—'and already a grandfather'", 1.908–909.

---

[83] On *saltem*, only here in the first hexameter *sedes* both in Vergil and Statius, see Austin (1955) on 327.

The quasi-citation of Dido's words (already recalled by Thetis, and later by Deidamia) stresses the distance between two parallel stories of seduction and abandonment.[84] Here a son, or rather, a grandson, is there, but Lycomedes ignores that; he is already born, and the grandfather is on the point of meeting him. Different levels of amusement are here offered to the reader: the ironic gap of the descent from a context of sublime pathos to one of a comedy of deceits; the dramatic irony, potentiated by the 'impertinent' citation; the caricature of Lycomedes, a victim of every deceit, and who, moreover, speaks in an incongruously and comically pathetic tone. Here we are really near to parody.

Finally, a bilingual wordplay enhances the effect. Of the grandson, Lycomedes guesses the name that appears inscribed in these lines by etymological decomposition. The adjective *novus* (not elsewhere in Latin with *nepos, filius*, synonyms and female correspondents) seems to be chosen on purpose, after *bello*, to suggest the compound Νεο-πτόλεμος: "Neoptolemos", the name of the hero "sent *young* to the *war*".

2.2.4 'Diluted' or 'Diffused' Quotation

This is not the only example of irony exercised behind the character's back through a Vergilian quasi-citation. The narrator's exclamation at *Ach.* 1.846–847 *heu simplex nimiumque rudis, qui callida* dona / *Graiorumque* dolos *variumque ignoret* Ulixen!, "Alas, too simple and inexperienced, he knows not of cunning presents and Grecian wiles and shifty Ulysses", is a transcription in a minor tone of Laocoon's famous apostrophe in Verg. *Aen.* 2.42–44 *et procul: 'o miseri, quae tanta insania, cives? / creditis avectos hostis? aut ulla putatis /* dona *carere* dolis Danaum? sic notus Ulixes?'*, "shouting while still far off: 'Poor citizens, what utter madness seizes you? Do you believe the foe's gone, or that gifts from Danaän Donors don't involve ruses? Is that what you know of Ulysses?'"—as is known, and is recalled elsewhere in this volume.[85] Those words, highly citable, had already become a Vergilian tag, as is proved by their parodic use in Petronius. In the mouth of Trimalchio, *'sic notus Ulixes?'* (39.3) is a disproportionate eulogy of his

---

84 Thetis had already imitated Dido soon after her son's *coup de foudre*, as she wished to carry in her bosom an *alius Achilles* (*Ach.* 1.321–322 *'o si mihi iungere curas / atque alium portare sinu contingat Achillen!'*). Deidamia, in the close of the book, will repeat *saltem* as she recommends Achilles to take her son to heart (1.952–955 *'attamen hunc, quem maesta mihi solacia linquis, / hunc saltem sub corde tene ...'*): in spite of the wedding, and the accomplished dream of a son, she too, like Dido, will feel *capta ac deserta*.
85 Rosati (1994) 20–22 (with n. 32 on the formal aspect of the echo).

own 'Odyssean' wiliness in staging the surprises of the banquet. Statius' procedure is more sober: in the narrator's voice, a sort of diluted quasi-citation, a paraphrase that maintains key terms, and formal values, in a barely varied matrix (paronomasia *dona/doli*, construction with the genitive, interjection, exclamative in place of the interrogative clauses).

The comment by the omniscient narrator reduces the *pathos* and sublime of the model, re-adapting the Vergilian formula to a preceding, and much more 're-laxed', episode of Ulysses' career as a deceiver. Here there is not a passionate rebuke of one's fellow citizens' tragic *insania*, but the playful commiseration of a character *simplex* and *rudis*, who plays his ingenuous part in comedy. A characterization that sounds also like a metaliterary signal: a 'charge of ignorance' for not reading the *Aeneid*.[86]

The citation is, furthermore, an exercise in "continuity of the stories and continuation of the texts". This deceit by Ulysses, who mixes the weapons with the baskets and lets the war trumpet sound in the royal palace, to drive out the disguised Achilles, is a prelude to the hero's role in the *Aeneid*, almost a comedy version of the Trojan horse, or a rehearsal in a farcical key of elements that will recur with pathetic gravity in the impending war.

From the tragic irony on the Trojans' illusion to the dramatic irony of the comedy of deceits in which Lycomedes is a victim; here the deceit acts as prelude to a happy end: a comic resolution, a recognition for fun. The allusive exactness and the renown of the model make most overt the borrowing and most evident the playful relaxation of the tone. Statius' epic experiment is thus connoted as a divertissement in the margin of a sublime epic tradition.[87]

2.3 Ovid's *Metamorphoses*

Finally, a various typology of verbal borrowings also marks the *Achilleid*'s relationship with Ovid. Verbal allusiveness is but one aspect, though not the least

---

[86] Rosati (1994) 22.
[87] The 'diluted' or 'diffused quotation' is well represented in the *Achilleid*; also elsewhere it concerns "local" allusions that, however, signal important models, pointing to continuities (or analogies) in mythical stories. This is the case with the well known echo of Horace, *Carm.* 2.5.21–24, whose key terms return in the scene of Achilles' disguise, *Ach.* 1.335–337 (see Hinds (1998) 135–137). Statius re-inscribes Horace's words into the very myth alluded to in the *Ode* (a procedure dear to Ovid); this 'local' echo, but a thematically meaningful and verbally rich one, tracks 'Achilles at Scyros' in Latin poetry, and declares a poetics of ambiguity. See also Bessone (forthcoming), §5, n. 40 on *Ach.* 1.255–258 and *Aen.* 12.149–150 (Thetis like Juturna).

interesting, of a sustained engagement with Ovid's work, that provides Statius with the fundamentals of a poetics of appearances and deceit, and shapes an 'epic of ambiguity' challenging genre (and gender) boundaries.[88] A detailed analysis must be reserved for another venue, but here recalling a pair of examples will serve as a conclusion.

On the relationship with the 'code-model' of the *Metamorphoses*—a constitutive relation, declared as early as in the proem—it seems difficult to add much to the studies by Rosati, Hinds and Heslin.[89] And yet, I believe that precisely the irony with which Statius portrays his protagonist owes much to Ovid's demystifying attitude towards epic heroes, Achilles in particular. The greatest hero, who in the *Metamorphoses* is the greatest eulogist of himself, is on the field of battle almost a disavowal of his greatness. In book 12, Ovid presents an Achilles, first undergoing an identity crisis in the duel with Cygnus, then ready to extol with words his own victory in the banquet talks, and finally confronted with his non-Homeric image by Nestor's tale on Caenis/Caeneus, who is almost his 'double' for the parallel story of heroism and sexual ambiguity.[90] In the following book, the allusion gets direct, with Ulysses' recalling of the Scyros episode, which supplements the 'all-round', not-only-Iliadic, portrait of the hero.

I have dealt elsewhere with the self-reflexive marks that, in the second book of the *Achilleid*, comment on Achilles' tale about his education by Chiron, and are as many allusions to, or quotations of, Ovid.[91] The narrator insinuates that recounting his own deeds is not at all unpleasant to Achilles; the rhetorical question *quem pigeat sua facta loqui? tamen ille modeste / incohat, ambiguus paulum propiorque coacto* ('Whom would it irk to tell of his own deeds? Yet he begins modestly, a little hesitant, as if constrained', *Ach.* 2.94–95) alludes to an analogous ironic intervention by Ovid in his 'little *Iliad*': *quid enim loqueretur Achilles, / aut quid apud magnum potius loquerentur Achillem?* ("What else indeed should be Achilles' theme? / What else their theme with great Achilles there?", *Met.* 12.162–163).[92] Here the very form of the question signals the relation with the narrative mode, as well as the theme, of the Ovidian episode: an impalpable echo, that escapes digital tools, and yet is an index of a constitutive relationship with

---

[88] Rosati (1994) 25–30.
[89] Cf. Rosati (1994); Hinds (1998) (e.g. 137–138 on Statius' quoting Ovid's formula for metamorphic change, *falsi sub imagine* with gen., at *Ach.* 1.560); Heslin (2005).
[90] On Statius' engagement with Nestor's account of the Centauromachy in Ovid's 'little *Iliad*', from a different point of view, see Chinn (2013).
[91] Bessone (2016) 200–203.
[92] Cf. 12.163–164 *inque vices adita atque exhausta pericula saepe / commemorare iuvat*. Cf. also the opposite authorial question in *Met.* 9.4–5 '*quis enim* sua proelia victus / *commemorare velit*?'.

the poetics of the *Metamorphoses*, and the disenchanted and ironic declension of heroic epic by Ovid.

But the relationship with Ovid's epic is made also of more concrete material. Another self-reflexive sign, and a strongly ironic one, closes Achilles' tale, and the poem: '*hactenus annorum, comites, elementa meorum / et memini et meminisse iuvat: scit cetera mater*' ("'So far, comrades, I remember the training of my early years and joy in the memory. My mother knows the rest'", *Ach.* 2.166–167). Statius ironizes on Achilles' voluntary selection of memories[93] by varying some Ovidian lines from Glaucus' narrative of his own metamorphosis: '*hactenus acta tibi possum memoranda referre, / hactenus et memini; nec mens mea cetera sensit*' ("'so far I can relate what I recall, so far remember; but the rest is lost'", *Met.* 13.956–957). The matrix *hactenus ... et memini*, reproduced with a minimal metrical change, followed in the clausula by the identical antithesis with *cetera*, and varied with the peremptory *et meminisse iuvat* in place of *possum memoranda referre*, exalts a decisive difference, thus creating an ironical effect at the expenses of Achilles. In the culminating moment of his transformation from man to god, Glaucus lost consciousness. Therefore, he is not able to remember what he did not perceive. Achilles, by his disguise, has experienced a metamorphosis, but a wholly conscious and chosen one. On his way to Troy, in front of Ulysses and Diomedes, the hero now edits his past, and censors the undignified Scyros episode which was his mother's plot.

Achilles' hyper-epic *apologoi* on his education by Chiron are thus framed by two allusions to Ovid's epic, a most immaterial and a most material one, both crucial to our understanding of Statius' poetics—and its 'Ovidian' irony. Here is an emblematic example of that complex of material and immaterial relationships that we call intertextuality, and that we cannot but investigate with a synergy of traditional and technological instruments.

Bibliography

Ahl, Frederick (2007), *Virgil*, Aeneid, Oxford.
Asso, Paolo (ed.) (2011), *Brill's Companion to Lucan*, Leiden/Boston.
Austin, Roland G. (1955), *P. Vergili Maronis Aeneidos Liber Quartus, Edited with a commentary*, Oxford.

---

[93] At the same time, the hero claims for himself the authority attributed to the Muses by Vergil: *Aen.* 7.645 *et meministis enim, divae, et memorare potestis*. Even *meminisse iuvat* echoes Vergil (*Aen.* 1.203). For *scit cetera* as a *praeteritio* cf. Ov. *Am.* 1.5.25 *cetera quis nescit?*

Austin, Roland G. (1964), *Virgil*, Aeneid, *Book 2*, Oxford.
Baldo, Gianluigi (1995), *Dall'*Eneide *alle* Metamorfosi. *Il codice epico di Ovidio*, Padua.
Barchiesi, Alessandro (1986), "Problemi di interpretazione in Ovidio: continuità delle storie, continuazione dei testi", in: *MD* 16, 77–107.
Barchiesi, Alessandro (1992), *P. Ovidii Nasonis Epistulae Heroidum 1–3*, Florence.
Barchiesi, Alessandro (1996), "La guerra di Troia non avrà luogo: il proemio dell'*Achilleide* di Stazio", in: *AION*(filol) 18, 45–62.
Barchiesi, Alessandro (1997), "Otto punti su una mappa dei naufragi", in: *MD* 39, 209–226.
Barchiesi, Alessandro (2005), "Masculinity in the 90's: The Education of Achilles in Statius and Quintilian", in: Paschalis (2005) 47–75.
Bessone, Federica (ed.) (1997), *P. Ovidii Nasonis Heroidum Epistula XII. Medea Iasoni*, Florence.
Bessone, Federica (2011), *La* Tebaide *di Stazio. Epica e potere*, Pisa/Rome.
Bessone, Federica (2016), "The Hero's Extended Family. Familial and Narrative Tensions in Statius' *Achilleid*", in: Manioti (2016) 174–208.
Bessone, Federica (2018a), "Signs of Discord. Statius' Style and the Traditions on Civil War", in: Ginsberg/Krasne (2018) 89–107.
Bessone, Federica (2018b), "Stili di potere. Linguaggio politico, genere ed eros nella poesia imperiale romana", in: *Eugesta* 8, 145–183.
Bessone Federica (2018c), "Storie di eroi, scrittura di eroine. Storia e critica letteraria nelle *Heroides*", in: Fedeli/Rosati (2018) 181–213.
Bessone, Federica (forthcoming), "'*Nimis ... mater*': Mother Plot and Epic Deviation in the *Achilleid*", in: Keith/Sharrock (forthcoming).
Bollack, Jean (1990), *L'Oedipe roi de Sophocle, IV. Commentaire. Troisième partie. Index et bibliographie*, Lille.
Briguglio, Stefano (2014), "*Perversa vota*. Edipo, Tisifone e la poetica della *Tebaide*", in: *SIFC* 107, 4° ser., 12.2, 235–250.
Briguglio, Stefano (2017a), Fraternas acies. *Saggio di commento a Stazio*, Tebaide, *1, 1–389*, Alessandria.
Briguglio, Stefano (2017b), "'O voluttà del soglio': eros e potere nella *Tebaide* di Stazio", in: De Paolis/Romano (2017) 310–326, https://www.classicocontemporaneo.eu/index.php/biblioteca/vol-5-atti-del-iii-seminario-nazionale/291-o-volutta-del-soglio-eros-e-potere-nella-tebaide-di-stazio.
Brown, Robert D. (1987), *Lucretius on Love and Sex*, Leiden/New York/Copenhagen/Cologne.
Burton, Sir Richard Francis (1894), *The Carmina of Gaius Valerius Catullus*, London.
Casali, Sergio (1999), "Mercurio a Ilerda: *Pharsalia* 4 ed *Eneide* 4", in: Esposito/Nicastri (1999) 223–236.
Casali, Sergio (2011), "The *Bellum Civile* as an Anti-*Aeneid*", in: Asso (2011) 81–109.
Caviglia, Franco (1973), *P. Papinio Stazio*, La Tebaide, *Libro I*, Rome.
Chinn, Christopher (2013), "Statius' Ovidian Achilles", in: *Phoenix* 67, 320–342.
Conte, Gian Biagio (1985), *Memoria dei poeti e sistema letterario*, 2nd ed., Turin.
Conte, Gian Biagio (1988), *La 'guerra civile' di Lucano. Studi e prove di commento*, Urbino.
Conte, Gian Biagio (2007), *Virgilio. L'epica del sentimento*, 2nd ed., Turin.
Conte, Gian Biagio (2014), *Dell'imitazione. Furto e originalità*, Pisa.
Delarue, Fernand (2000), *Stace, poète épique. Originalité et cohérence*, Leuven/Paris.
De Paolis, Paolo/Romano, Elisa (eds.) (2017), *Atti del III seminario nazionale per dottorandi e dottori di ricerca in studi latini, Roma, 20 novembre 2015* (Biblioteca di Classico Contemporaneo, 5).

Esposito, Paolo/Nicastri, Luciano (1999), *Interpretare Lucano. Miscellanea di studi*, Naples.
Fairclough, H. Rushton (1916), *Virgil, Eclogues, Georgics, Aeneid 1–6*, Cambridge, MA/London.
Fantuzzi, Marco (2012), *Achilles in Love: Intertextual Studies*, Oxford.
Farrell, Joseph (2005), "Intention and Intertext", in: *Phoenix* 59, 98–111.
Fedeli, Paolo (2005), *Properzio, Elegie, Libro II. Introduzione, testo e commento*, Cambridge.
Fedeli, Paolo/Rosati, Gianpero (eds.) (2018), *Ovidio 2017. Prospettive per il terzo millennio. Atti del Convegno internazionale, (Sulmona 3/6 aprile 2017)*, Teramo.
Feeney, Denis C. (2004), "*Tenui ... latens discrimine*: Spotting the Differences in Statius' *Achilleid*", in: *MD* 52, 85–105.
Gallo, Italo/Nicastri, Luciano (eds.) (1991), *Cultura poesia ideologia nell'opera di Ovidio*, Naples.
Gervais, Kyle (2017), *Statius, Thebaid 2*, Oxford.
Ginsberg, Lauren D./Krasne, Darcy A. (eds.) (2018), *After 69 CE: Writing Civil War in Flavian Literature*, Berlin/Boston.
Glei, Reinhold F. (ed.) (2009), *Ironie: griechische und lateinische Fallstudien*, Trier.
Günther, Hans-Christian (ed.) (2015), *Virgilian Studies. A Miscellany Dedicated to the Memory of Mario Geymonat*, Nordhausen.
Hardie, Philip (1994), *Virgil, Aeneid, Book IX*, Cambridge.
Hardie, Philip (2007), "Polyphony or Babel? Hosidius Geta's *Medea* and the poetics of the cento", in: Swain et al. (2007) 168–176.
Herescu, Nicolae I. (ed.) (1959), *Ovidiana. Recherches sur Ovide*, Paris.
Heslin, Peter (2005), *The Transvestite Achilles. Gender and Genre in Statius'* Achilleid, Cambridge.
Hinds, Stephen (1998), *Allusion and Intertext. Dynamics of Appropriation in Roman Poetry*, Cambridge.
Horsfall, Nicholas (2000), *Virgil, Aeneid 7. A Commentary*, Leiden/Boston/Cologne.
Horsfall, Nicholas (2008), *Virgil, Aeneid 2. A Commentary*, Leiden/Boston.
Hunter, Richard (2006), *The Shadow of Callimachus. Studies in the reception of Hellenistic poetry at Rome*, Cambridge.
Hutcheon, Linda (1985), *A Theory of Parody. The Teachings of Twentieth-Century Art Forms*, Urbana/Chicago.
Jebb, Sir Richard C. (1893), *Sophocles, The Plays and Fragments, Part I. The* Oedipus tyrannus, 3rd ed., Cambridge [stereotyped edition 1902].
Keith, Alison (2004–2005), "Ovid's Theban narrative in Statius' *Thebaid*", in: *Hermathena* 177–178, 181–207.
Keith, Alison/Sharrock, Alison (eds.) (forthcoming), *Maternal Conceptions in Classical Literature and Philosophy* (Phoenix Supplementary Volumes), Toronto.
Kenney, Edward J. (1958), "*Nequitiae poeta*", in: Herescu (1958) 201–209.
Klodt, Claudia (2009), "Der kleine Achill: ironische Destruktion homerischen Heldentums in der *Achilleis* des Statius", in: Glei (2009) 179–227.
Knox, Peter E. (2015), "Virgil's Catullan One-Liner", in: Günther (2015) 287–319.
Kovacs, David (2002), *Euripides*, Helen, Phoenician Women, Orestes, Cambridge, MA/London.
Labate, Mario (1991), "La memoria impertinente e altra intertestualità ovidiana", in: Gallo/Nicastri (1991) 41–59.
Lauletta, Mario (1993), "L'imitazione di Catullo e l'ironia nell'*Achilleide* di Stazio", in: *Latomus* 52, 84–97.
Lloyd-Jones, Hugh (1994), *Sophocles*, Ajax, Electra, Oedipus Tyrannus, Cambridge, MA/London.

Manioti, Nikoletta (ed.) (2016), *Family in Flavian Epic*, Leiden/Boston.
Mastronarde, Donald J. (1988), *Euripides*, Phoenissae, Leipzig.
Mastronarde, Donald J. (1994), *Euripides*, Phoenissae, *with introd. and comm.*, Cambridge.
McGill, Scott (2005), *Virgil Recomposed: The Mythological and Secular Centos in Antiquity*, New York/Oxford.
McKeown, James C. (1989), *Ovid*, Amores. *Text, Prolegomena and Commentary, Vol. II. A Commentary on Book One*, Leeds.
Micozzi, Laura (1999), "Aspetti dell'influenza di Lucano nella *Tebaide*", in: Gallo/Nicastri (1991) 343–387.
Murray, Augustus T./Wyatt, William F. (1999), *Homer, Iliad, with an English translation by Murray, revised by Wyatt*, I-II, Cambridge, MA/London.
Narducci, Emanuele (2002), *Lucano. Un'epica contro l'impero*, Rome/Bari.
Nisbet, R.G.M. (1987), *Cicero*, In L. Calpurnium Pisonem Oratio, Oxford.
Nisbet, R.G.M./Hubbard, Margaret (1970), *A Commentary on Horace, Odes, Book I*, Oxford.
Nisbet, R.G.M./Hubbard, Margaret (1978), *A Commentary on Horace, Odes, Book II*, Oxford.
Paschalis, Michael (ed.) (2005), *Roman and Greek Imperial Epic*, Crete.
Petrone, Gianna (1997), *Lucio Anneo Seneca*, Le Fenicie, Milano.
Pinotti, Paola (1988), *P. Ovidio Nasone*, Remedia amoris, *introduzione, testo e commento*, Bologna.
Raffaelli, Renato/Danese, Roberto M./Falivene, Maria Rosaria/Lomiento, Liana (eds.) (2005), *Vicende di Ipsipile. Da Erodoto a Metastasio, Colloquio di Urbino, 5–6 maggio 2003*, Urbino.
Ripoll, François/Soubiran, Jean (2008), *Stace*, Achilléide, Leuven/Paris/Dudley, MA.
Rosati, Gianpiero (1994), *Stazio*, Achilleide, *introduzione, traduzione e note*, Milan.
Rosati, Gianpiero (2005), "Il 'dolce delitto' di Lemno. Lucrezio e l'amore-guerra nell'Ipsipile di Stazio", in: Raffaelli *et al.* (2005) 141–167.
Rosati, Gianpiero (2006), "*Libido amandi* e *libido regnandi*, ovvero elegia e potere nel teatro senecano", in: *Dioniso* 5, 94–105.
Rosati, Gianpiero (2009), *Ovidio, Metamorfosi, vol. III, libri V–VI, trad. di G. Chiarini*, Milan.
Shackleton Bailey, David R. (1993), *Martial*, Epigrams, *I-III*, Cambridge, MA/London.
Shackleton Bailey, David R. (2003), *Statius*, Thebaid, *Books 1–7*; Thebaid, *Books 8–12*. Achilleid, *I-II*, Cambridge, MA/London.
Sklenář, Robert (2011), "Lucan the Formalist", in: Asso (2011) 317–326.
Smolenaars, Johannes J.L. (1994), *Statius*, Thebaid VII. *A Commentary*, Leiden/New York/Cologne.
Snijder, Harry (1968), *P. Papinius Statius*, Thebaid, *A commentary on book III, with text and introduction*, Amsterdam.
Swain, Simon/Harrison, Stephen/Elsner, Jaś (eds.) (2007), *Severan Culture*, Cambridge.
Tarrant, Richard (2012), *Virgil*, Aeneid, *Book XII*, Cambridge.
Thomas, Richard F. (1988), *Virgil*, Georgics, *Vol. 1, Books I–II*, Cambridge.
Traina, Alfonso (1997), *Virgilio. L'utopia e la storia. Il libro XII dell'*Eneide *e antologia delle opere*, Turin.
Uccellini, Renée (2012), *L'arrivo di Achille a Sciro. Saggio di commento a Stazio*, Achilleide 1, 1–396, Pisa.
Williams, Craig A. (2004), *Martial*, Epigrams. *Book Two, Edited with introduction, translation, and commentary*, New York.

Antony Augoustakis
Collateral Damage? *Todeskette* in Flavian Epic

1 Definition and Function

Epic poems traditionally sing about the κλέα ἀνδρῶν, the heroic achievements of male warriors whose virtue and bravery reach their peak in death; epic poems then are about death ultimately, a celebration of heroic demise, which for the protagonists usually comes at the end of an ἀριστεία, the final display of masculinity, daring, and sacrifice. It is in such scenes of gory battle of manslaughter (ἀνδροκτασία) that we encounter *Todeskette*, "chains of the names of those slain by a great warrior."[1] A frequent device in ancient epic, these chains of names are employed to enliven the action and underscore its rapidity, as well as to highlight the glory of the victorious warrior, even when his streak of success is about to end with death.[2] At the same time, *Todeskette* give the poet the opportunity to display exemplary artistry in naming otherwise insignificant characters, distinguishing—and decorating—them with an abundance of epithets and short descriptions, and narrating in more detail the horrific death of one, usually the last mentioned. For sure, the device also helps the poet to avoid monotony and communicate pathos to a higher level, as we the readers are invited to visualise a long list of warriors who meet their death at the hands of an Achilles, Ajax, Aeneas, or Hannibal.

It is no surprise then that such list of warriors fighting and dying en masse during battle descriptions is part or rather a subsection of a catalogue, an epic ploy from Homer onwards that adds special colour to oral performances in particular and is exploited for the opportunity afforded to digress from the narrative.[3]

---

1 Dewar (1991) 83.
2 Cf. Greene (1963) 16: "It is important that every combatant who is killed in the *Iliad* have a name, for the name is an index to the victor's accomplishment. A hero wears his victims' names like scalps, and his own name is aggrandized by theirs. The epic tries to define the relation between the hero's name and his death."
3 Especially by Strasburger (1954) and Beye (1964); see Beye (1964) 345: "It has recently been observed that the *androktasiai* of the Iliad are in some way similar to the various passages in Homer which have been traditionally called catalogues. The impression that Homeric battle narrative is closely related to bare metered lists is strengthened by the presence in epics in other languages of battle scenes still more mechanical and list-like."

In fact, Charles R. Beye has identified a pattern followed by Homer and his successors in recounting *androktasiai* in battle narratives: first, the poet supplies the basic information about the person killed, followed then by an anecdote (at times associated with the slain's provenance), and finally some contextual information related to the manner of death.[4] The recurrence or rather recycling of certain names is simply attributed to metrical convenience—these names become in a way formulaic.[5] And as Richard Tarrant notes on Virgil's technique in the *Aeneid*, "predominantly dactylic lines are used to list the names of those killed in battle, probably suggesting the quick succession of their deaths."[6]

In this chapter, I would like to revisit these traditional lists as they appear in Flavian epic from a different perspective: as the Flavian poets recycle the epic tradition, they reuse *Todeskette* as miniature catalogues, a catalogue *en abyme* that highlights how the *androktasia* reflects on the wider narrative, that is, the description of the hero's *aristeia*, of which it only occupies but a few lines. If we look, for instance, at Parthenopaeus' *aristeia* in Statius' *Thebaid* 9, we can see how the poet zooms in to narrate the rapid succession of victims, especially at 758–759 and then 764–769:[7]

> quos, age, Parrhasio sternis, puer improbe, cornu?
> prima Tanagraeum turbauit harundo Coroebum   745
> extremo galeae primoque in margine parmae
> angusta transmissa uia: stat faucibus unda
> sanguinis, et sacri facies rubet igne ueneni.
> *saeuius Eurytion, cui luminis orbe sinistro*
> *callida tergeminis acies se condidit uncis.*   750
> *ille trahens oculo plenam labente sagittam*
> *ibat in auctorem: sed diuum fortia quid non*
> *tela queant? alio geminatum lumine uulnus*
> *expleuit tenebras; sequitur tamen improbus hostem,*
> *qua meminit, fusum donec prolapsus in Idan*   755
> *decidit:* hic saeui miser inter funera belli
> palpitat et mortem sociosque hostesque precatur.

---

4 Of course variation is explored in manifold ways in a catalogue of this sort: for instance, there can be two or more men killing others; cf. *ferus occupat Actor / implicitum fratri Thamyrin, Tagus haurit Echecli / terga coronati, Danaus caput amputat Hebri* (Stat. *Theb.* 10.313–315).
5 See Beye (1964) and Kühlmann (1973) 28–39.
6 Tarrant (2012) 40 (and also on Verg. *Aen.* 12.445–447, 457–458, 476, 539, 696–698).
7 I have underlined the names of the dead and italicised passages where chains of names occur in succession. On an earlier scene where Hippomedon also annihilates various victims, Hulls (2006) 141 observes that these men exist as "cannon-fodder ... only to die and bring greater glory ... to a major character."

> addit <u>Abantiadas</u>, insignem crinibus <u>Argum</u>
> et male dilectum miserae <u>Cydona</u> sorori.
> [illi perfossum telo patefecerat inguen]   760
> ....
> huic geminum obliqua traiecit harundine tempus,
> exilit hac ferrum, uelox hac penna remansit;
> fluxit utrimque cruor. *nulli tela aspera mortis
> dant ueniam, non forma <u>Lamum</u>, non infula <u>Lygdum</u>,
> non pubescentes texerunt <u>Aeolon</u> anni:*   765
> *figitur ora <u>Lamus</u>, flet saucius inguina <u>Lygdus</u>,
> perfossus telo niueam gemis, <u>Aeole</u>, frontem.
> te praeceps Euboea tulit, te candida Thisbe
> miserat, hunc uirides non excipietis † Amyclae.*
>
> (Stat. *Theb.* 9.744–769)[8]

Boy overbold, whom, pray, do you lay low with your Parrhasian bow? The first arrow confounded Coroebus of Tanagra, despatched through the narrow opening between the lowest edge of the helmet and the uppermost of the shield; in his throat stands a wave of blood and his face flushes with the fire of sacred poison. More cruelly dies Eurytion; the cunning point with triple barb buried itself in the orb of his left eye. Pulling out the arrow replete with the collapsing organ, he ran at the archer. But what cannot the strong shafts of the gods accomplish? The wound was doubled in the other eye, completing darkness. Unconscionable he still pursues his enemy by memory, until he falls tripping over prostrate Idas. Here, poor guy, he gasps among the cruel war's corpses, praying foes and comrades for death. He adds the sons of Abas, Argus, remarkable for his hair, and Cydon, loved amiss by his unhappy sister. [The groin of one he had shot and laid open with his spear] ... The other he pierced through his temples with transverse shaft; the steel sprang out on one side, on the other the swift feather remained, blood flowed on both. To none do the sharp arrows show mercy. His beauty did not protect Lamus, nor his fillet Lygdus, nor Aeolos his youthful years. Lamus is pierced in the face, Lygdus bewails a wound in the groin, and you, Aeolos, groan with your white forehead gashed deep by a dart. You steep Euboea bore, you white Thisbe had sent, him green Amyclae (?) shall not recover.

In the second *Todeskette*, the pathetic repetition of *te*, reminiscent of pastoral,[9] heightens the pathos while also emphasizing the Flavian poet's predilection for extreme stylization, "intended to dignify and render more pathetic the poem's gruesome *tueries*."[10] Statius exploits the name of Aeolos from the Greek epithet αἰόλος, "quick moving," a quality which is here tragically and ironically taken up

---

8 For Statius' *Thebaid*, I follow the Latin text of Hill (1996²) and have modified the translation from Shackleton Bailey (2003).
9 Dewar (1991) 201.
10 Dewar (1991) 200.

by the murderous dart instead. And though we can hardly disagree that the Flavian poets highly stylize such passages, I would like to explore further the function of these lists/catalogues and the place of their insertion. As has already been noted by scholars of Flavian epic, catalogues of names constitute strategy to underscore the temporary, ephemeral insignificance of these minor characters.[11] And as Karla Pollmann observes, "these catalogues help to organise the chaotic space of battle, provide proof of the narrator's precise and detailed knowledge, and they stand for the anonymous, infinite number of victims, trying to channel the uncontrollable omniscience of the author. The catalogues serve rather to dissipate and obscure the memory of the victims than to commemorate them."[12]

While I fundamentally agree with the observations and comments of critics on such scenes, I believe we can pursue a further study of the deeper function in the miniature catalogues such as *Todeskette*. This is a locus of intertextual recycling of epic names and epic deaths, but also one of originality. Recycling and originality are not mutually exclusive; by repetition, the Flavian epicists claim their own standing within the long epic tradition, while they contribute their own innovative versions of Homeric and Virgilian scenes. Beyond doubt resources such as Tesserae facilitate this locating of recycled names among the Flavian poets and allow us to follow various, new paths of interpretation.

Let us begin our investigation by looking at the epic tradition, and more precisely how the trend of recycling and innovating in *Todeskette* can already be seen in Ovid, where Ulysses repeats, recycles, and exploits his past Homeric *aristeiai*:

>   cum multo sanguine fudi
> *Coeranon Iphitiden et Alastoraque Chromiumque*
> *Alcandrumque Haliumque Noemonaque Prytaninque*
> exitioque dedi cum Chersidamante Thoona
> et Charopem fatisque inmitibus Ennomon actum   260
> quique *minus celebres* nostra sub moenibus urbis
> procubuere manu.
>
> (Ov. *Met.* 13.256–262)[13]

---

11 See Georgacopoulou (1996) 100–101: "Réservées aux aristies, ces listes de guerriers terrassés se transforment en une opération funèbre. On reconnaît ici le caractère fondamental et originel d'une liste qui est en quelque sorte rituelle. Grâce à elle, surgissent des noms qui deviennent des personnages éphémères. Dès sa fin, ceux-ci retombent vite dans l'oubli."
12 Pollmann (2004) 267–268.
13 For Ovid, I follow the text and translation of Miller/Goold (1984).

I laid low in bloody slaughter Coeranos, the son of Iphitus, Alastor and Chromius, Alcander, Halius, Noemon, Prytanis, slew Thoön and Chersidamas, Charopes, Ennomos, driven by the pitiless fates; and others less renowned fell by my hand beneath their city's walls.

ἔνθ' ὅ γε Κοίρανον εἷλεν Ἀλάστορά τε Χρομίον τε
Ἄλκανδρόν θ' Ἅλιόν τε Νοήμονά τε Πρύτανίν τε.
καί νύ κ' ἔτι *πλέονας* Λυκίων κτάνε δῖος Ὀδυσσεὺς
εἰ μὴ ἄρ' ὀξὺ νόησε μέγας κορυθαίολος Ἕκτωρ·

(Hom. *Il.* 5.677–680)[14]

Then he slew Coeranus and Alastor and Chromius and Alcandrus and Halius and Noëmon and Prytanis; and yet more of the Lycians would noble Odysseus have slain, had not great Hector of the flashing helmet been quick to notice.

ὁ δὲ πρῶτον μὲν ἀμύμονα Δηιοπίτην   420
οὔτασεν ὦμον ὕπερθεν ἐπάλμενος ὀξέι δουρί,
αὐτὰρ ἔπειτα Θόωνα καὶ Ἔννομον ἐξενάριξε.
Χερσιδάμαντα δ' ἔπειτα, καθ' ἵππων ἀΐξαντα,
δουρὶ κατὰ πρότμησιν ὑπ' ἀσπίδος ὀμφαλοέσσης
νύξεν· ὁ δ' ἐν κονίῃσι πεσὼν ἕλε γαῖαν ἀγοστῷ.   425
τοὺς μὲν ἔασ', ὁ δ' ἄρ' Ἱππασίδην Χάροπ' οὔτασε δουρί,
αὐτοκασίγνητον εὐηφενέος Σώκοιο.

(Hom. *Il.* 11.420–427)

But first he struck incomparable Deiopites from above in the shoulder, leaping on him with sharp spear; and then he slew Thoön and Ennomus, and then Chersidamas as he leapt down from his chariot he stabbed with his spear on the navel beneath his bossed shield; and he fell in the dust and clutched the earth with his hand. These then he left, but struck Charops, son of Hippasus, with a thrust of his spear, the brother of wealthy Socus.

As has been observed,[15] Ovid's Ulysses repeats almost verbatim his exploits from the Homeric epic's fifth book in 258–259: he recycles all seven names and adds a patronymic to the otherwise Asiatic but Hellenized name of Coeranos,[16] now made the son of Iphitus, itself a loan from another passage in the *Iliad* and ascribed to a charioteer; it is no coincidence that the second Coeranos in the *Iliad* is a charioteer (17.611–614).[17] Then in 260–261, Ulysseus condenses his second Homeric *aristeia* from *Iliad* 11 by rearranging the Homeric passage and omitting Deiopites. In addition, the Homeric πλέονας from *Iliad* 5 is glossed by *minus celebres*

---

14 For Homer, I follow the text and translation of Murray/Wyatt (1999). I have underlined the names of the dead and italicised the chains of names in succession.
15 Hopkinson (2000) 134–135.
16 Kirk (1990) on Hom. *Il.* 5.677–678.
17 Hopkinson (2000) 136.

in Ovid. Furthermore, in this creative imitation, Ovid's originality lies in repeating a Virgilian line from *Aeneid* 9.769 (*Alcandrumque Haliumque Noemonaque Prytanimque*), Turnus' *aristeia*: Ovid corrects Virgil and restores the line's original context.[18]

Such intertextual games are common in ancient epic, and the Flavian epicists constitute no exception. While *Todeskette* are often employed to showcase the poet's penchant for a creative exploitation of local geography and history, as they become a locus of intertextual recycling and innovation, at the same time they serve as fascinating points of contact among the Flavian poets themselves:

> Nisaeum Telamon et Ophelten uana sonantem
> per clipei cedentis opus artemque trilicem,
> qua stomachi secreta, ferit laetusque profatur: 200
> 'di, precor, hunc regem aut aeque delegerit alta
> fors mihi gente satum magnusque et *flebilis urbi*
> conciderit'. super addit Aren fratremque Melanthum
> Phoceaque Oleniden, <Le>legum qui pulsus ab oris
> regis amicitiam et famuli propioris honores   205
> (qua patiens non arte?) tulit.
>
> (Val. Fl. 3.198–206)[19]

Telamon crushed Nisaeus and Opheltes, the idle boaster, piercing his huge shield of threefold wickerwork where it covered his belly, and cried in triumph: 'I pray that heaven or chance has chosen me a king or one sprung of lineage as ancient, and that a mighty one has fallen, and a lamentation to his city!' He slew moreover Ares and his brother Melanthus, and Phoceus son of Olenus, who, exiled from the land of the Leleges, won the friendship of the king and (schooling himself to every art) the rank of a close attendant.

This is the *nyktomachia* episode in Valerius, when the confused Argonauts return to Cyzicus to slay by mistake their hosts and the eponymous king of the city. In this scene, Valerius' Telamon is given an *aristeia* and kills five opponents (as opposed to only one in Apollonius' account in 1.1043).[20] These men are drawn from a rich register of names from the epic tradition and elsewhere,[21] but one of them,

---

18 Hardie (1994) 236–237.
19 For Valerius, I follow Ehlers' (1980) Latin text and have modified the translation of Mozley (1934).
20 Manuwald (2015) 118.
21 In his commentary, Spaltenstein (2004) 37–38 observes that Valerius invents many such names: "[A]ucune tradition historique ou poétique ne pouvait les lui fournir … [L]a plupart des noms … sortent de l'imagination de Val. … Certains noms semblent banals … Val. reprend aussi quelques noms de la géographie … D'autres noms… cultivent la couleur locale, font allusion à

Opheltes, presents a good example of a future exploitation by another Flavian poet, Statius: this Opheltes the Cyzican will be *flebilis urbi* just like the Nemean baby, son of Lycurgus,[22] Opheltes or Achemorus becomes the first victim of the Seven against Thebes in Statius' *Thebaid*: *flebilis infans* ("a baby to mourn," *Theb.* 6.245). The Valerian *magnus Opheltes* appears in a miniature catalogue; Statius transforms this *magnus Opheltes* into a small baby which then becomes famous.

Valerius' wit and innovation in cataloguing the minor characters in battle is also evident in the list of Amazons participating in the civil war of the sixth book:

> ille nouas acies et uirginis arma
> ut uidet 'has etiam contra bellabimus?' inquit
> 'heu pudor!' inde Lycen ferit ad confine papillae,
> inde Thoen qua pelta uacat, iamque ibat in Harpen   375
> uixdum prima leui ducentem cornua neruo
> et labentis equi tendentem frena Menippen
> cum regina grauem nodis auroque securem
> congeminans partem capitis galeaeque ferinae
> dissipat.
>
> (Val. Fl. 6.372–380)

> He when he sees the new conflict and the maiden's weapons cries: 'Women too, then, are we to fight? ah, for shame!' Then he strikes Lyce near the breast and Thoe where her shield leaves a space; and now was he rushing against Harpe, who scarce yet had begun to draw the bow-horns with the light string, and Menippe, who was pulling up her stumbling horse, when the princess, with redoubled blows of a battle-axe heavy with knobs of gold, cleaves in sunder his head and his helm of wild beast's hide.

Gesander's brief *aristeia* includes this group of four Amazons (Lyce, Thoe, Harpe, and Menippe), before Euryale strikes the final blow and splits Gesander's head apart. As commentators show, all four names are evocative and appropriate, recycled from the epic tradition and applicable to the situation of manly women-warriors: Lyce is associated with "wolf," Harpe with "kite" (or a sickle and the verb "to snatch," ἁρπάζω), Thoe with running, and Menippe with horses.[23] And yet, despite the evocation in Greek of a specific quality in these names, all girls

---

l'histoire, à la mythologie ... ou encore paraissent chercher le calembour ... Val. présente aussi certains noms inattendus et dont la clé, s'il y en a une, nous reste mystérieuse."

22 There is also a son of the Thracian king, Lycurgus, with the same name, as well as Euryalus' father in Virgil (*Aen.* 9.201); see Spaltenstein (2004) 67.

23 See Baier (2001) 190: "Die Eigennamen hat VF wohl erfunden"; Spaltenstein (2005) 111: "noms évocateurs font calembour"; Fucecchi (2006) 327: "nomi greci di particolare spessore evocativo."

fall short of surviving Gesander's assault: Lyce dies a traditional Amazonian death, struck in the very seat of her femininity, the *papilla*;[24] Thoe cannot escape despite the quality of her name; Harpe is attacked as she is drawing the bow and is thus "snatched" in the middle of action; and finally, Menippe, who is supposed to be good in managing horses, can never really finish her job of pulling up her horse.[25]

In the civil war narrative of this book, another *Todeskette* provides the reader with explicit clues as to possible connections between the names of the killed and their meaning:

> talis in extremo proles Iouis emicat aeuo
> et nunc magnanimos Hypetaona Gessithoumque
> nunc Arinen Olbumque rotat. iam saucius Aprem
> et desertus equo Thydrum pedes excipit hasta
> Phasiaden, pecoris custos de more paterni   640
> Caucasus ad primas genuit quem Phasidis undas.
> hinc puero cognomen erat ...
>
> (Val. Fl. 6.636–642)

> So violently darts forth the son of Jove at his life's end, and now he slays the greathearted Hypetaon and Gessithous, and now Arines and Olbus; already wounded and on foot, his charger lost, he slays with his lance Apres and Thydrus Phasiades, whom Caucasus, guarding, as was his custom, his father's flock begat by the side of Phasis' waters; hence had the boy his surname ...

The son of Jupiter, Colaxes, cuts down several minor characters in his passing, again in quick succession and with no discrimination, except for the last person who receives adequate attention on the poet's part. While Hypetaon (perhaps from ὕπατος, "supreme," an epithet of Zeus), Gessithous (θοός, "fast," combined with the Latin *gaesum*, "spear"), and Olbus (from ὄλβος, "blessing") have a clear Greek derivation,[26] and while Apres may allude to an Egyptian pharaoh or the *colonia Aprensis* in Thrace or the Latin noun for "boar,"[27] Valerius indulges in an

---

[24] Cf. Verg. *Aen.* 11.803–804.
[25] On Menippe's name, see the Baier (2001) 190–191, Fucecchi (2006) 329 (also on the textual *crux* of the phrase *et labentis*).
[26] Liberman (2002) 267–268, with a speculation of Arines being associated with Africa (Carthage, Mauritania) or a Dacian river.
[27] Liberman (2002) 268.

etymological explanation of Thydrus' name from the waters of Phasis, glossing the Greek ὑδρ- with the Latin *unda* at the end.²⁸

But one wonders whether the pentasyllabic and unique Valerian innovation *Hypetaona* does not resurface changed in Statius in the same context of an *androktasia*:

> iaculo <u>Phlegyan</u> iaculoque superbum
> <u>Phylea</u>, falcato <u>Clonin</u> et <u>Chremetaona</u> curru
> comminus hunc stantem metit, hunc a poplite sectum,
> cuspide non missa <u>Chromin</u> <u>Iphinoum</u>que <u>Sagen</u>que
> intonsumque <u>Gyan</u> sacrumque <u>Lycorea</u> Phoebo   715
> (inuitus: iam fraxineum demiserat hastae
> robur, et excussis apparuit infula cristis),
> <u>Alcathoum</u> saxo, cui circum stagna Carysti
> et domus et coniunx et amantes litora nati.
>
> (Stat. *Theb.* 7.711–719)

With javelin he slays Phlegyas, with javelin proud Phyleus, with scythed chariot mows down Clonis and Chremetaon (one standing to face him, the other severed from the knee), Chromis with a spear thrust and Iphinous and Sages and unshorn Gyas and Lycoreus sacred to Phoebus (him unwilling; he had already plunged the strength of his ashen spear when the crest was shaken off and the fillet came to view), Alcathous with a stone, who had home and wife and shore-loving children by the pools of Carystos.

As William Dominik has observed here, "this pathetic vignette, with the rapid succession of deaths and the different weapons employed in the slayings, underlines the purely destructive nature of war."²⁹ Amphiaraus' victims die in quick succession but in varying degrees of attention from the narrator who passes some over while dwelling on others, such as the last one, Alcathous.³⁰ The name Chremetaon occurs only here in the *Thebaid*,³¹ reminiscent of Hypetaon from the Valerian passage, but the effect of the name listing here is unique: it seems to consist of internal repetition of sounds and names such as Phle-gyas, Cl-onis, Chr-omis, Sa-ges, Gyas. Such repetition would reinforce the notion of commonality, since these are common epic names of minor characters dying an otherwise insignificant death in the hands of the epic hero performing an *aristeia*, such as

---

28 Spaltenstein (2005) 184: "aucun des noms … n'évoque quoi que ce soit de précis …, à l'exception peut-être de celui de Thydrus …, qui pourrait faire écho à *hydr-* avec un calembour ingénieux pour ce servant d'un fleuve."
29 Dominik (1994) 105.
30 See Smolenaars (1994) 342 on the Homeric and Virgilian name.
31 For the type of death, cf. Verg. *Aen.* 10.697–700.

Amphiaraus here.[32] And yet the sound effect and repetition of syllables adds a distinct significance to each one of those names, as the narrator chooses or not to provide further information on them.

Furthermore, this intertextual exercise in name listing may also have intratextual resonances within Statius' epic, if we consider the list of dying young men on Lemnos:

> quod te, flaue Cydon, quod te per colla refusis   220
> intactum, Crenaee, comis (quibus ubera mecum
> obliquumque a patre genus), fortemque, timebam
> quem desponsa, Gyan uidi lapsare cruentae
> uulnere Myrmidones, quodque inter serta torosque
> barbara ludentem fodiebat Epopea mater.   225
> flet super aequaeuum exarmata Lycaste
> Cydimon, heu similes perituro in corpore uultus
> aspiciens floremque genae et quas finxerat auro
> ipsa comas, cum saeua parens iam coniuge fuso
> astitit impellitque minis atque inserit ensem.   230
>
>   (Stat. *Theb.* 5.220–230)

I saw you fall, blond Cydon, and you, Crenaeus, with your untouched locks flowing down your neck; you were my foster brothers, my father's sons on the side. You too, strong Gyas, my betrothed whom I feared, I saw fall by the stroke of bloody Myrmidone, and how his barbarous mother stabbed Epopeus as he played among the chaplets and couches. Lycaste weeps disarmed over her brother of equal age, Cydimus, watching the face alas so like her own upon his doomed body, and the bloom on his cheek and the locks she had herself twined with gold, when their savage mother, who had already slain her husband, takes stand beside her, urging her with threats and putting the sword in her hands.

The Theban Gyas in book 7 is *intonsus*, a marker of his young age. Hypsipyle's Gyas in book 5, presented as her fiancé, dying at the hands of Myrmidone, is cast as *fortis*, a strong man, whom the narrator of the slaughter herself fears very much. Is it because the Greek name of Gyas derives from the word for limbs, γυῖα, and thus could refer to Gyas' tall stature or muscular strength? But this list is intriguing since it starts with blond Cydon, whose name derives from the color of quinces (κυδώνια μῆλα), and the emphasis of colorful hair continues with Crenaeus' *comae*, rich hair flowing down his neck and shoulders; the list is rounded off with Cydimos, whose hair his mother had arranged, and whose name is meant to recall part of Cydon's.

---

[32] For Phlegyas, cf. Val. Fl. 3.124–137; for Clonis, cf. *Theb.* 7.369; for Chromis, see Verg. *Aen.* 11.675 and *Theb.* 1.613, 3.13, 4.597, 8.476, 9.252.

In our last example from Statius' *Thebaid*, we shall see an illustration of how a name prefigures the hero's death:

> attamen Olenium Lamyrumque, hunc tela pharetra
> promentem, hunc saeui tollentem pondera saxi
> deicit, et triplici confisos robore gentis
> Alcetidas fratres, totidem quos eminus hastis
> continuat; ferrum consumpsit pectore Phyleus,   745
> ore momordit Helops, umero transmisit Iapyx.
>
> (Stat. *Theb.* 12.741–746)

> All the same he brings down Olenius and Lamyrus, the one as he takes arrows from his quiver, the other lifting the weight of a cruel rock, and the sons of Alcetus, brothers trusting in their family's triple strength, whom one after another he slays from a distance with as many spears: Phyleus consumed the steel in his chest, Helops bit it with his mouth, Iapyx passed it through his shoulder.

This is part of the last book's *aristeia* of "sea-born" Theseus (*aequoreus*, 12.730), the son of the sea god, Poseidon. As Karla Pollmann notes, "the fact that Statius gives a name to all of Theseus' victims ... indicates a more honourable 'man-to-man' conflict."[33] Theseus destroys each one in sequence, with more emphasis on the Alcetidae than on the others. But the death of Helops seems hardly coincidental: the name is recycled from Ovid's Centauromachy in *Metamorphoses* 12.334–335; the name *helops* is used of a fish, a rare delicacy (Greek, ἔλλοψ), as seen in Lucilius, Ovid, and Columella among others.[34] And Helops here dies like a fish hit by the son of Poseidon: he bit the steel with his mouth, like a fish biting the fisherman's bait!

Let us finally turn to Silius Italicus' *Punica*, a poem that follows in the footsteps of the epic tradition but with significant changes and adaptations. The first scene we will examine comes from the siege of Saguntum, a series of Hannibal's victims:

> iamque Hostum rutilumque Pholum ingentemque Metiscum,
> iam Lygdum Duriumque simul flauumque Galaesum
> et geminos Chromin atque Gyan demiserat umbris.
>
> (Sil. 1.437–439)[35]

---

33 Pollmann (2004) 268.
34 *OLD* s.v. with Lucil. 1276, Ov. *Hal.* 96, Columella *Rust.* 8.16.9.
35 For Silius Italicus, I follow the Latin text of Delz (1987) and have modified the translation from Duff (1934).

> Already Hannibal had sent down to Hades Hostus and Pholus the Rutulian and huge Metiscus, and, with them, Lygdus and Durius and fair-haired Galaesus, and a pair of twins, Chromis and Gyas.

As expected, geography plays an important role in choosing the names of these peripheral characters: Durius and Galaesus are named after rivers, Durius after a Spanish (1.324) and Galaesus after an Italian one.[36] The Saguntines are after all an amalgam of people, immigrants from the Greek island of Zacynthus and the Italian city of Ardea.[37] And Silius' nod to Virgil in naming Galaesus begins with Metiscus, who is Turnus' charioteer (*Aen.* 12.469–472). We have already seen the employment of names such as Chromis and Gyas by Statius in *Todeskette*, in *Thebaid* 7 above. But the name of Hostus is unique, recalling Latin names such as Hostius or Hostilius,[38] alternating Greek and Latin names to underscore the hybrid nature of the Saguntines.[39] The common Greek name Pholus recalls the eponymous Centaur,[40] but as a *jeu* Silius switches the adjective *ingens*, expected for the Centaur Pholus, to apply it to Metiscus.

Silius' penchant for geography and recherché references is evident in such lists elsewhere too, as in the battle at the Ticinus river:

> Crixus Picentem Laurumque, nec eminus ambo   175
> sed gladio Laurum; Picenti rasilis hasta,
> ripis lecta Padi, letum tulit.
>   [...]
> idem sanguinea Venuli ceruice reuellens
> sternit praecipitem tepido te, Farfare, telo
> et te sub gelido nutritum, Tulle, Velino,
> egregium Ausoniae decus ac memorabile nomen,
> si dent fata moras aut seruent foedera Poeni,   185
> tum Remulum atque, olim celeberrima nomina bello,

---

[36] In Sil. 5.323 and 16.366, Durius is used for Spanish men. For Galaesus, cf. the famous Virgilian counterpart in *Aen.* 7.535–539 and 575.
[37] On Saguntine identity and for further bibliography, see Augoustakis (2010) 113–136. Lygdus is a Greek name, also used by Statius in *Theb.* 9.764.
[38] Spaltenstein (1986) 73. Silius uses the name Hostus for the son of Hampsagoras of Sardinia in 12.347.
[39] Spaltenstein (1986) 73: "Sil. étant attentif à alterner les nationalités des Sagontins."
[40] Cf. Verg. *Aen.* 8. 294, Ov. *Met.* 12.306, Val. Fl. 1.338. In Stat. *Theb.* 8.476, in a *Todeskette*, the death of Pholus is followed by that of Chromis, another instance of a generic grouping of such names closely together.

Tiburtes <u>Magios</u> Hispellatemque <u>Mataurum</u>
et <u>Clanium</u> dubia meditantem cuspide uulnus.

(Sil. 4.175–177, 181–188)

Crixus slew Picens and Laurus, but not both from a distance; for Laurus fell by the sword, but Picens was slain by a polished spear, once cut on the banks of the Po. Crixus also plucked his weapon from the gory neck of Venulus and, while it was still warm, laid low Farfarus with it, and Tullus who was reared near cold Velinus—a proud boast of Italy he would have been and a famous name, if the Fates had granted him longer life or the Carthaginians had adhered to the treaty. Next Crixus slew Remulus, and warriors whose names were once famous in arms—the Magii of Tibur, Metaurus of Hispellum, and Clanius—and aimed his blow with a spear which doubted whom to strike.

The Celt king, Crixus, lays low a number of men whose names are associated with their respective places. Picens, Laurus, Venulus,[41] Farfarus, and Remulus[42] are linked to Italy; and Farfarus and Tullus are associated because of rivers: Farfarus is the name of a Sabine river, and Tullus was reared in the Velinus, another lake in Sabine territory, but which tantalizingly echoes in repetition almost the name of the previous victim, Venulus.[43] Cold and warm are juxtaposed, in the warm spear (*tepido*) and the icy cold waters of the lake (*gelido*). The fascination with river names continues in Mataurus, whose name slightly changed evokes the Metaurus, the Umbrian river (and Hispellum is city in Umbria), while Clanius is a river in Campania (8.535). It is fitting after all to import such names from the epic tradition, combined with geographic places, in a battle that takes place at the river Ticinus.

Similarly, in Fabius' *aristeia* in book 7, Silius creates names that sound Punic or African to accommodate the needs of the narrative:

> Inde ruens <u>Thurin</u> et <u>Buten</u> et <u>Narin</u> et <u>Arsen</u>
> dat leto fisumque manus conferre <u>Mahalcen</u>,
> cui decus insigne et quaesitum cuspide nomen.   600
> tum <u>Garadum</u> largumque comae prosternit <u>Adherben</u>
> et geminas acies superantem uertice <u>Thulin</u>,
> qui summas alto prensabat in aggere pinnas,
> eminus hos. gladio <u>Sapharum</u> gladioque <u>Monaesum</u>
> et <u>Morinum</u> pugnas aeris stridore cientem,   605
> dexteriore gena cum sedit letifer ictus,
> perque tubam fixae decurrens uulnere malae
> extremo fluxit propulsus murmure sanguis.

---

41 For Venulus, cf. Verg. *Aen.* 8.9 and 11.242, 742; Ov. *Met.* 14.457 and 512.
42 Verg. *Aen.* 9.360 and 593; Ov. *Met.* 14.617.
43 For Farfarus, cf. Ov. *Met.* 14.330; for Velinus, cf. Verg. *Aen.* 7.517 and 712.

> proximus huic iaculo Nasamonius occidit Idmon.
> namque super tepido lapsantem sanguine et aegra   610
> lubrica nitentem nequiquam euadere planta
> impacto prosternit equo trepideque leuantem
> membra adflicta solo pressa uiolentius hasta
> implicuit terrae telumque in caede reliquit.
> haeret humi cornus motu tremefacta iacentis   615
> et campo seruat mandatum affixa cadauer.
>
> (Sil. 7.598–616)

On he rushed and slew Thuris and Butes, Naris and Arses, and Mahalces who had dared to face him, a famous warrior who had gained glory by his spear. Then he laid low Garadus and Adherbes of the long hair, and Thulis who towered above both armies and could grasp the top battlements on a lofty wall. These he slew from a distance; and his sword accounted for Sapharus and Monaesus, and for Morinus, as he stirred the hearts of the combatants with the trumpet's blare; the fatal blow struck his right cheek, and the blood, running down through the trumpet from the wound in his face, flowed forth, expelled by his dying breath. Close by him fell Idmon, a Nasamonian, slain by a javelin. For as he slipped on the warm blood and was vainly striving to plant his unsteady feet on firm ground, the Dictator's horse struck him down; and, when he tried in haste to lift his bruised limbs from the ground, Fabius pinned him to the earth by a strong thrust of his spear and left the weapon in the deadly wound. Sticking in the ground, the spear quivered as the dying man moved, and kept guard on the plain over the corpse consigned to it.

As Joy Littlewood notes, "the poet appears to have made up this string of disyllabic names, which may bear some resemblance to Punic-sounding names ... Adherbes and Mahalces are variants of the historical Adherbal ... and Maharbal ..., Garadus resembles Garamas."[44] The parechesis of the final syllables -en or -in in the first six lines of the passage is striking, perhaps emphasizing the quick succession of victims that sound almost the same, and, as we have seen before, the list includes two warriors whose name is simply varied by a consonant, *Thurin* and *Thulin*. But admittedly the geographic range evoked here is wide: Butes is a Greek name,[45] while Thulis recalls the island Thule, and Monaesus has Parthian or Colchian connections.[46] Arses is of Persian provenance, while Morinus recalls a Belgian tribe,[47] and Nar is a river in Umbria.[48] And last comes Idmon, a name familiar from the Argonautic saga as the helmsman of the Argo, metamorphosed

---

[44] Littlewood (2011) 220.
[45] Cf. Verg. *Aen.* 5.372, 9.647, 11.690; Ov. *Met.* 7.500; Val. Fl. 1.394; Stat. *Theb.* 8.484.
[46] Cf. Val. Fl. 6.651.
[47] Cf. Verg. *Aen.* 8.727 and Sil. 15.723.
[48] Cf. Sil. 8.451.

here into a Nasamonian warrior:[49] Joy Littlewood correctly notes that "Seneca (*Med.* 652–653) has Idmon slain by a Libyan serpent, which may account for Silius' associating him with Africa."[50] But it is quite possible that Silius has in mind also Idmon's death in Valerius' *Argonautica*: Silius' Idmon slips (*lapsantem*), as he also does in Valerius, in a metaphor for dying, *Idmon / labitur* (5.2–3). This allusion may be combined with Statius' Idmon, who is good with medicinal herbs (*tepentibus herbis*, Stat. *Theb.* 3.399–400), possibly echoed here in the warm blood which proves to be lethal for Silius' namesake (*super tepido … sanguine*).

In our final example, we shall consider a groundbreaking Silian innovation, the transferral of *Todeskette* from humans to ships in the naval battle of Syracuse:

> ardet nota fretis Cyane pennataque Siren.
> ardet et Europe, niuei sub imagine tauri
> uecta Ioue ac prenso tramittens aequora cornu,
> et quae fusa comas curuum per caerula piscem   570
> Nereis umenti moderatur roscida freno.
> uritur undiuagus Python et corniger Hammon
> et, quae Sidonios uultus portabat Elissae,
> bis ternis ratis ordinibus grassata per undas.
> at uinclis trahitur cognata in litora Anapus   575
> Gorgoneasque ferens ad sidera Pegasus alas.
> ducitur et Libyae puppis signata figuram
> et Triton captiuus et ardua rupibus Aetne,
> spirantis rogus Enceladi, Cadmeaque Sidon.
>
> (Sil. 14.567–579)

Among the burning ships was the Cyane, well known to those waters, and the winged Siren; Europa too, who rode on the back of Jove disguised as a snow-white bull, and grasped one horn as she moved over the water; and the watery Nereid with floating hair, who drove a curving dolphin over the deep with dripping rein; the sea-traversing Python was burnt, and horn-crowned Ammon, and the vessel that bore the likeness of Tyrian Dido and was propelled by six banks of oars. The Anapus, on the other hand, was towed to her native shore, and the Pegasus who raised to heaven his wings born of the Gorgon; and other ships were carried captive—that which bore the likeness of Libya, and the Triton, and Etna of the rocky peaks, the pyre that covers living Enceladus, and Sidon, the city of Cadmus.

Homer's catalogue of ships begins the epic trope in the ancient tradition: a list of ships that guides the reader to know the who is who in the narrative that follows; in Virgil's *Aeneid* 5, the Trojan mothers set the ships on fire trying to put an end to an otherwise endless voyage. In Silius' *Punica* 14, the foreign ships are burned

---

49 A common name; cf. Verg. *Aen.* 12.75, Ov. *Ib.* 502, Stat. *Theb.* 3.398.
50 Littlewood (2011) 221.

in an effort to annihilate the Carthaginian forces towards the end of a long war. And the names fittingly and clearly point to the origins of the Carthaginian race in Phoenicia from the tale of Cadmus and Europa onwards: Europe, Elissa, Libya, Sidon. Hammon and Pegasus are also linked to Africa.[51] But Silius blends the Carthaginian and Sicilian in this catalogue as well: Cyane is the name of the well-known Syracusan spring, crucial in the myth of Proserpina,[52] marked here by *nota fretis*, a gesture towards an 'epitaphization' of the catalogue. Aetna recalls the volcano, while Anapus is a Syracusan river (14.515), and the Sirens are placed in Sicily by Silius (14.473). The burning and enslavement of the ships marks a departure from the trope of *Todeskette* we have studied so far: Silius creates his own epitaph for these ships in a display of originality and creative use of the tradition.

In my short and selective examination of lists of dying men (and ships!) in Flavian epic, I have demonstrated how the Flavian poets insightfully recycle the epic tradition, by using *Todeskette* as miniature catalogues that highlight their poetic craft: these deaths are anything but banal, as they often resort to the treasure trove of the epic tradition in an endless intertextual game of sorts, whereby the poets refashion existing scenes and recycle common names to claim their own standing within a line of authors. This exercise in intertextuality opens new avenues for interpretation, only facilitated by modern technology and advances in how we conduct word searches and hunt for parallels.

Bibliography

Augoustakis, Antony (2010), *Motherhood and the Other: Fashioning Female Power in Flavian Epic*, Oxford.
Baier, Thomas (2001), *Valerius Flaccus*, Argonautica Buch VI: Einleitung und Kommentar, Munich.
Beye, Charles R. (1964), "Homeric Battle Narrative and Catalogues", in: *HSPh* 68, 345–373.
Delarue, Fernand/Georgacopoulou, Sophia/Laurens, Pierre/Taisne, Anne-Marie (eds.) (1996), *Epicedion: Hommage à P. Papinius Statius, 96–1996*, Poitiers.
Delz, Josef (1987), *Silius Italicus*, Punica, Stuttgart.
Dewar, Michael (1991), *Statius*, Thebaid IX, Oxford.
Dominik, William J. (1994), *The Mythic Voice of Statius: Power and Politics in the* Thebaid, Leiden.
Duff, James D. (1934), *Silius Italicus, I-II*, Cambridge, MA.
Ehlers, Widu-Wolfgang (1980), *Valerius Flaccus*, Stuttgart.

---

51 Medusa's connection with Africa legitimizes Pegasus' also; see Spaltenstein (1990) 329.
52 Cf. Ov. *Met.* 5.409–412.

Fucecchi, Marco (2006), *Una guerra in Colchide: Valerio Flacco*, Argonautiche *6, 1–426*, Pisa.
Georgacopoulou, Sophia (1996), "Ranger/Déranger: Catalogues et listes de personnages dans la *Thébaïde*", in: Delarue *et al.* (1996) 93–129.
Greene, Thomas (1963), *The Descent from Heaven: A Study in Epic Continuity*, New Haven.
Hardie, Philip R. (1994), *Vergil*, Aeneid *Book IX*, Cambridge.
Hill, Donald E. (1996), *P. Papini Stati* Thebaidos *Libri XII*, 2nd ed., Leiden.
Hopkinson, Neil (2000), *Ovid*, Metamorphoses *Book XIII*, Cambridge.
Hulls, Jean-Michel (2006), "What's in a Name? Repetition of Names in Statius' *Thebaid*", in: *BICS* 49, 131–144.
Kirk, Geoffrey S. (1990), *The* Iliad: *A Commentary. Volume II: Books 5–8*, Cambridge.
Kühlmann, Wilhelm (1973), *Katalog und Erzählung: Studien zu Konstanz und Wandel einer literarischen Form in der antiken Epic*, Freiburg.
Liberman, Gauthier (2002), *Valerius Flaccus*, Argonautiques *Chants V–VIII*, Paris.
Littlewood, R. Joy (2011), *A Commentary on Silius Italicus'* Punica *7*, Oxford.
Manuwald, Gesine (2015), *Valerius Flaccus:* Argonautica *Book III*, Cambridge.
Miller, Frank J./Goold, Georg P. (1984), *Ovid*, Metamorphoses, *I-II*, Cambridge, MA.
Mozley, John H. (1934), *Valerius Flaccus*, Argonautica, Cambridge, MA.
Murray, Augustus T./Wyatt, William F. (1999), *Homer*, Iliad, *I-II*, Cambridge, MA.
Pollmann, Karla F.L. (2004), *Statius*, Thebaid *12*, Paderborn.
Shackleton Bailey, David R. (2003), *Statius, I-III*, Cambridge, MA.
Smolenaars, Johannes J.L. (1994), *Statius,* Thebaid *7: A Commentary*, Leiden.
Spaltenstein, François (1986), *Commentaire des* Punica *de Silius Italicus (livres 1 à 8)*, Geneva.
Spaltenstein, François (1990), *Commentaire des* Punica *de Silius Italicus (livres 9 à 17)*, Geneva.
Spaltenstein, François (2004), *Commentaire des* Argonautica *de Valérius Flaccus (livres 3, 4 et 5)*, Brussels.
Spaltenstein, François (2005), *Commentaire des* Argonautica *de Valérius Flaccus (livres 6, 7 et 8)*, Brussels.
Strasburger, Gisela (1954), *Die Kleinen Kämpfer der* Ilias, Frankfurt am Main.
Tarrant, Richard (2012), *Virgil*, Aeneid *Book XII*, Cambridge.

Mark Heerink
Replaying Dido: Elegy and the Poetics of Inversion in Valerius Flaccus' *Argonautica*

1 Introduction: Dido as an Elegiac Moment in *Aeneid* 4 and 7

One of the ways in which the Roman love elegists defined their poetry was their self-conscious opposition to epic: their genre was all about women and love, not about men and war. At the very beginning of his *Aeneid*, Virgil follows suit by stating that his epic will deal with *arma virumque*. As part of this set-up generic tension, Dido's passion for Aeneas is described in elegiac terms, and in fact the entire episode, despite its firm roots in the epic tradition, is marked by Virgil as an elegiac delay in Aeneas' epic mission.[1]

Halfway through the *Aeneid*, in book 7, Virgil picks up on the elegiac play in the Dido episode and goes one step further: on the eve of the war in Latium his epic is about to turn into *arma virumque* proper, "essential epic", to use Stephen Hinds' term.[2] As Michael Putnam has shown, this transition to epic war can be read in metapoetical terms, as elegy turned into epic, and Dido plays an important role in this respect.[3]

In Valerius Flaccus' *Argonautica*, several scenes and characters evoke Roman love elegy as well, most strikingly the Lemnos and Hylas episodes in the first half of the epic,[4] and Medea and her passion for Jason in the second half. At the same time, several characters clearly evoke Virgil's Dido, in particular Hypsipyle in the Lemnos episode, Heracles in the Hylas episode, and Medea. Interestingly, Valerius' allusions to elegy and Virgil's Dido seem to coincide, which suggests that Valerius reacts to Virgil's metageneric use of elegy in his epic.

---

1 For the influence of Roman love elegy on *Aeneid* 4, see e.g. Hinds (1987) 134–135; Cairns (1989) 135–150 (= Ch. 6: "Dido and the elegiac tradition"); Hardie (1998) 61–62; Harrison (2007) 208–214.
2 Hinds (2000).
3 Putnam (1995) = (1998) 97–118, on which much of what is discussed below is based. Incidentally, Putnam also sees this generic transition as one from bucolic to epic, on which see also Hardie (1998) 61; Heerink (2015a) 119, 123–125.
4 See for instance Colton (1964), who discusses Propertius' influence on Valerius Flaccus and detects most parallels (and the most striking ones) in the Lemnos and Hylas episodes.

After outlining this metapoetical shift in the *Aeneid*, I will argue in the remainder of this chapter that the *Argonautica* exploits the elegiac link between *Aeneid* 4 and 7, as both the Lemnos and Hylas episodes in the first half of the epic are connected to Medea's role in the second half of the epic. Whereas the *Aeneid* moves from elegy to epic, however, Valerius inverts Virgil's generic transition, which has consequences for the way we read the Flavian epic.

2 From Elegy to Epic in *Aeneid* 7

In book 7 of the *Aeneid*, just before war breaks out between the Trojans and the indigenous Italians, Latium is associated with Roman love elegy. The relationship between the native girl Silvia and her pet stag, for instance, gets an elegiac dimension through the use of vocabulary:[5]

> cervus erat forma praestanti et cornibus ingens,
> Tyrrhidae pueri quem matris ab ubere raptum
> nutribant Tyrrhusque pater, cui regia parent   485
> armenta et late custodia credita campi.
> adsuetum imperiis soror omni Silvia <u>cura</u>
> <u>mollibus</u> intexens ornabat cornua <u>sertis</u>,
> pectebatque ferum <u>puroque in fonte</u> lavabat.
> ille manum patiens mensaeque adsuetus erili   490
> errabat silvis rursusque ad limina nota
> ipse domum sera quamvis se nocte ferebat.
>
> (Verg. *Aen.* 7.483–492)

It was a huge and beautiful stag with a fine head of antlers, which had been torn from the udders of its mother and fed by Tyrrhus and his young sons—Tyrrhus looked after the royal herds and was entrusted with the wardenship of the whole broad plain. Silvia, the boys' sister, has given this wild creature every care and trained it to obey her. She would weave soft garlands for its horns, combing and washing it in clear running water. It became tame to the hand and used to come to its master's table. It would wander through the woods and come back home of its own accord to the door it knew so well, no matter how late the night.[6]

---

5 Cf. Putnam (1995) 128 (= [1998] 114) on the "understated eroticism of the description."
6 Translations of the *Aeneid* are adopted from West (1991); translations of the Argonautica are adapted from Mozley (1934).

First of all, the word used to describe Silvia's love for the stag, *cura*, is very common in Latin love elegy.[7] Furthermore, *mollis* is an elegiac buzzword that here, in its connection with the weaving of garlands, recalls the intertextually connected scenes in *Eclogue* 2 (*intexens*, 49) and *Eclogue* 10 (*serta mihi Phyllis legeret*, 41), where garlands were associated with elegiac poetry, contributing to the depiction of Corydon and Gallus respectively as elegiac lovers in a bucolic landscape.[8] The elegiac resonance of the "soft garlands" is reinforced by their occurrence in Propertius' programmatic elegy 3.1.[9] When the poet addresses the Muses, he opposes his Callimachean, elegiac poetry, as symbolized by the garlands, to "harsh" epic:[10]

> mollia, Pegasides, date vestro serta poetae:
> non faciet capiti dura corona meo.
>
> (Prop. 3.1.19–20)
>
> Daughters of Pegasus, give your poet soft garlands: an epic wreath will not do for my head.[11]

This intertextual contact between Virgil's passage and this Propertian poem is strengthened by the mention of a limpid spring in the next line (*puroque in fonte*, 489), as this recalls the beginning of Propertius' elegy 3.1:

---

7 Cf. Harrison (2007) 211 (on elegiac elements at the beginning of *Aeneid* 4): "Especially elegiac is the use of *cura(e)* ... for the anxiety of love (Propertius 1.5.10, 1.10.17, 2.18.21, 3.17.4), and the climactic picture of the lover's consequent sleeplessness (Propertius 1.1.33, 1.11.5, 2.7.11, Tibullus 1.2.76, 2.4.11, Ovid, *Am*. 1.2.1)."
8 See Heerink (2015a) 92–100. Cf. Putnam (1995) 118–123 (= [1998] 106–109) for these and other parallels with the *Eclogues*. See also e.g. Prop. 4.1.61 for the poetic associations of garlands: *Ennius hirsuta cingat sua dicta corona*, "Let Ennius crown his words with a shaggy garland." (See Hinds 1998, 66 for the way Ennius is depicted here and in other Augustan poetry as an archaic poet.)
9 The intertextual contact between the ekphrasis and Propertius 3.1 is discussed by Putnam (1995) 126–128 (= [1998] 113–115). With Putnam I agree that, although the relative chronology of the two texts cannot be determined, "imaginative interaction can shed light on both poets" (p. 126 (=113)).
10 For the elegiac poets' association of *durus* with epic and the contrasting association of *mollis* with their own elegiac poetry, see e.g. Baker (2000) 102 (on Prop. 1.7.19); Tzounakas (2012) 173, notes 44 and 45.
11 Translations of Propertius are adopted (and sometimes slightly adapted) from Heyworth (2007).

> primus ego ingredior puro de fonte sacerdos
> Itala per Graios orgia ferre choros.
>
> (Prop. 3.1.3–4)

> I am the first priest from the pure spring to begin bearing Italian sacraments to the accompaniment of Greek music.

Dealing with the poet's inspiration in an explicitly programmatic context, Propertius' *fons* has a clear metapoetic dimension, and the spring in *Aeneid* 7 can accordingly be read—even retrospectively, if Propertius' poem would postdate the *Aeneid*—as evoking Roman love elegy and as reinforcing the elegiac nature of the poetic world of pre-war Latium and Silvia and her stag in particular.

The elegiac resonances of this world are reinforced by the intertextual contact with Dido's "elegiac love" for Aeneas in *Aeneid* 4,[12] and in particular the famous simile comparing the lovesick Dido to a wounded deer and, by implication, Aeneas to the hunter:

> uritur infelix Dido totaque vagatur
> urbe furens, qualis coniecta cerva sagitta,
> quam procul incautam nemora inter Cresia fixit   70
> pastor agens telis liquitque volatile ferrum
> nescius; illa fuga silvas saltusque peragrat
> Dictaeos; haeret lateri letalis harundo.
>
> (Verg. *Aen.* 4.68–73)

> Dido was on fire with love and wandered all over the city in her misery and madness like a wounded doe which a shepherd hunting in the woods of Crete has caught off guard, striking her from long range with steel-tipped shaft; the arrow flies and is left in her body without his knowing it; she runs away over all the wooded slopes of Mount Dicte, and sticking in her side is the arrow that will bring her death.

This simile resembles Ascanius' hunting of the deer, which is described immediately after the ekphrasis of Silvia's stag, as the underlined words indicate:[13]

---

12 Like the love of Silvia for her stag, Dido's love is not typically elegiac. See Harrison (2007) 211: "In elegy it is almost always the tormented male lover who describes himself as feeling the symptoms of love and suffering rejection and abandonment; in the *Aeneid* it is Dido who is depicted as enduring this range of emotions, while Aeneas steadfastly keeps his (genuine) feelings under control ... and suffers insomnia only in the manner of a good leader." See also note 1 above for bibliography on the influence of Roman love elegy on *Aeneid* 4.
13 For a comparison between Ascanius' hunt in *Aeneid* 7 and the simile in *Aeneid* 4, see also Griffin (1986) 180–182; Putnam (1995) 111–112 (= [1998] 100–102). See Horsfall (2000) 321 (on *Aen.* 7.525–539) for more bibliography.

```
hunc procul errantem rabidae venantis Iuli
commovere canes, fluvio cum forte secundo
deflueret ripaque aestus viridante levaret.                495
ipse etiam eximiae laudis succensus amore
Ascanius curvo derexit spicula cornu;
nec dextrae erranti deus afuit, actaque multo
perque uterum sonitu perque ilia venit harundo.
saucius at quadripes nota intra tecta refugit             500
successitque gemens stabulis, questuque cruentus
atque imploranti similis tectum omne replebat.
```
(Verg. *Aen.* 7.493–502)

This is the creature that was roaming far from home, floating down a river, cooling itself in the green shade of the bank when it was startled by the maddened dogs of the young huntsman Iulus. He himself, Ascanius, burning with a passionate love of glory, bent his bow and aimed the arrow. The god was with him and kept his hand from erring. The arrow flew with a great hiss and passed straight through the flank into the belly. Fleeing to the home it knew so well, the wounded stag came into its pen moaning, and stood there bleeding, and filling the house with its cries of anguish, as though begging and pleading.

Once the intratextual contact between the two passages has been established, more parallels can be discerned that give the later passage an elegiac colouring: like Dido in the first line of book 4, the stag is wounded (*saucius*, 500),[14] and like the elegiac *questus* of Dido in her soliloquy (*tantos ... questus*, *Aen.* 4.553), the wounded stag is also complaining (*questu*, 501).[15]

The difference between the two passages, of course, is that the hunting in book 4 is metaphorical, whereas Ascanius is literally hunting a stag, but another verbal parallel between the two texts reveals that both Aeneas' metaphorical wounding of the elegiac Dido and Ascanius' shooting of Silvia's stag are comparable from a metapoetical point of view. Immediately before the ekphrasis of the stag, Virgil's comments on Allecto's rousing of Ascanius' hounds as "the first cause of suffering" and the beginning of war in Latium (*quae prima laborum / causa fuit belloque animos accendit agrestis*, 481–482). This recalls another famous scene in *Aeneid* 4, the marriage of Aeneas and Dido in the cave, which is

---

14 Putnam (1995) 112 (= [1998] 101). For the metaphor of love as wound, see e.g. Harrison (2007) 211, adducing Tibullus 2.5.109; Ov. *Am.* 1.2.9; 2.19.5 as instances of elegiac use of *saucius*.
15 Putnam (1995) 112 (= [1998] 101). For the elegiac ring of *questus*, see e.g. Barchiesi (1993) 365: "There is a strong tradition in Roman culture (not, apparently, in Alexandria) connecting the birth of elegy with lament, *querela*, ἒ ἒ λέγειν and the like." Incidentally, one of Dido's complaints—that she was not allowed to live her life *more ferae*, "like a wild animal" (551)—further strengthens the contact between Dido and Silvia's stag, a literal "wild animal", which is (like Dido) disturbed and wounded by a Trojan (Putnam [1995] 112 = [1998]).

also commented on by the authorial narrator, in similar terms: *ille dies primus leti primusque malorum / causa fuit*, "That day was the first cause of death and the first of disaster." So the misery and death of Dido, to which this marriage will eventually lead, and the war in Latium are associated with each other, a link that is described by Putnam as follows: "Had circumstances been otherwise and Aeneas not impinged upon her world, she [Dido] might have continued through life with a type of freedom similar to that which Virgil allots both the Latins and Silvia's stag."[16] In metapoetical terms, this implies that the two poetic, elegiac worlds that oppose the epic mission of the *Aeneid*, that of Dido and that of Silvia and her stag, yield to their opposite—heroic epic—as represented by two male epic heroes, Aeneas and his son Ascanius.[17]

As I will show in what follows, this poetic transformation is reversed in Valerius Flaccus' *Argonautica*.

3 The Massacre at Lemnos

On a structural level, the Lemnos episode, as the Argonauts' first stopover and coming after the storm in book 1, corresponds to Aeneas' stay in Carthage in the *Aeneid*. This is not surprising as Lemnos and Hypsipyle in Apollonius' *Argonautica* were already main models for Carthage and Dido in the *Aeneid*.[18] On the basis of the metapoetical play with elegy in the *Aeneid*, one would perhaps expect an "elegiac excursion", which will eventually be left behind by the Argonauts, and in fact this is what will happen when the Argonauts arrive and get engaged with the Lemnian women. First there is a surprise, however, when Valerius extensively tells about the horrible pre-history of the situation on Lemnos and describes a perversion of civil war, as the Lemnian women kill their husbands (2.216–241), led on by a Fury-like Venus (2.196–215).[19] This passage clearly evokes the war in Troy in *Aeneid* 2,[20] which will get a sequel later in the Lemnos episode,

---

16 Putnam (1995) 112 (= [1998] 101).
17 Cf. Hardie (1998) 61–62: "[O]ne way of viewing the situation in *Aeneid* 4 is as the interference of the values of the world of love elegy in the Roman (and epic) mission of Aeneas."
18 See e.g. Nelis (2001) 160, with note 151 for more bibliography.
19 On the Lemnian massacre as a civil war of sorts, see e.g. McGuire (1997) 104–108; Hershkowitz (1998) 137; Seal (2014) 130. For Venus as a Fury, see in particular Hardie (1989) 7 and Schimann (1997) 106–107.
20 On these allusions see e.g. Garson (1964) 273.

when Hypsipyle rescues her father Thoas as Aeneas rescues his father from burning Troy in *Aeneid* 2, on which more below.

Elegy is brought in through a complicated intertextual strategy. On the one hand, the expected intertext, the Dido episode in *Aeneid* 1 and 4, is clearly evoked already at the very beginning of the episode, when Venus descends to earth to ask Fama to stir up the Lemnian women against their husbands:

> cum dea se piceo per sudum turbida nimbo
> praecipitat Famamque vaga vestigat in umbra,
> quam pater omnipotens digna atque indigna canentem
> spargentemque metus placidis regionibus arcet
> aetheris.
>
> (Val. Fl. 2.115–119)

> Then the goddess in frenzy throws herself in a pitchy cloud through the clear sky, and in the darkness tracks wandering Rumour, her whom the almighty Father keeps away from his peaceful world of heaven, as she sings of foul things and spreads panic.

This brings to mind Fama entering the stage in *Aeneid* 4 (173–195), and this intertextual contact is reinforced a few lines later by the clear allusion to the same scene in the *Aeneid*:[21]

> adfore iam luxu turpique cupidine captos
> fare viros carasque toris inducere Thressas.
>
> (Val. Fl. 2.131–132)

> Say that the men are coming, enslaved by debauchery and shameful lust, and are bringing women from Thrace to share the bed of love."

> nunc hiemem inter se luxu, quam longa, fovere
> regnorum immemores turpique cupidine captos.
>
> (Verg. *Aen*. 4.193–194)

> How they were even now indulging themselves and keeping each other warm the whole winter through, forgetting about their kingdoms and becoming the slaves of lust.

Another Virgilian intertext is relevant here, as the actions of the Fury-like Venus (later disguised as the Lemnian Dryope), with the help of Fama, against the Lemnian women evoke Juno and the Fury Allecto in *Aeneid* 7.[22] There, in Latium, these goddesses stir up a civil war as well and attack Amata as well as the other Latin

---

[21] For these allusions, see Hardie (1989) 7. Cf. Poortvliet (1991) 92, 99.
[22] For the allusions to Virgil's Juno and Allecto, see esp. Hardie (1989) 6–7.

matrons (*Aeneid* 7.323–405).²³ The Fury Allecto's attack on Amata has been read by scholars metapoetically, as an elegiac allegory of sorts, grounded in the metaphorical meaning of *furia* as the madness of being in love as well as in the recurring pun on Amata's own speaking name ("beloved"): Amata under attack can also be read as being madly in love.²⁴ The elegiac nature of the Amata passage is underlined by the close intratextual connection to Dido and her passionate love for Aeneas.²⁵

There is, however, another elegiac connection between *Aeneid* 4 and 7, as already mentioned: the scene with Silvia and her stag recalls the comparison of Dido with a wounded deer. Valerius seems to have seen this close connection between Carthage and Latium—so between Dido's metaphorical fury of love, which is left behind by Aeneas and Virgil eventually, and the literal Fury Allecto who initiates war in Latium and thus starts Virgil's essential epic, which leaves the elegiac world of Silvia and her stag behind. When Amata is then somewhat later in *Aeneid* 7 allusively associated with elegy, we are in fact not dealing with elegiac passion anymore, but with a *furia* that is placed by Juno and Allecto in service of the war in Latium.

So by combining allusions to these passages in his Lemnos episode, Valerius has exploited the elegiac connection between *Aeneid* 4 and 7 and their mirroring. The civil war on Lemnos with an Allecto-like Venus and with Amata-like Lemnian women is more similar to the situation in Latium than to that in Carthage, but that is not all.

4 Hypsipyle

In the scene following the massacre, the same three Virgilian intertexts that played a role before are evoked again. First *Aeneid* 2, for Hypsipyle saves her father (2.242–305) as Aeneas saves Anchises from Troy.²⁶ She hides Thoas and dresses him up as Bacchus, a passage which recalls Amata hiding Lavinia and then invoking Bacchus in *Aeneid* 7.²⁷ The third intertext, *Aeneid* 4, comes into play in the next and final part of the Lemnos episode, the arrival and stay of the Argonauts on the island (2.311–427), which clearly evokes the sojourn of the Trojans

---

23 Hardie (1989) 7. Cf. Poortvliet (1991) 92.
24 Lyne (1987) 13–17; Hardie (1989) 6; Harrison (2007) 212–214.
25 Harrison (2007) 213–214.
26 See e.g. Hershkowitz (1998) 137–138 for the intertextual contact.
27 Cf. Poortvliet (1991) 159 (on Val. Fl. 2.265ff.).

in Carthage, just as Hypsipyle evokes Dido.[28] But there are some striking differences with this Virgilian intertext (and incidentally with Apollonius' version as well), as Hypsipyle's *pietas* is emphasized a striking amount of times.[29] This makes her in fact resemble Aeneas and *not* Dido, who of course gets carried away by her elegiac passion, neglecting her duties as *regina*.

At the end of the Lemnos episode, the contrast between the two queens becomes even stronger. Although Hypsipyle, as well as the other Lemnian women, mourn the departure of the Argonauts, the Lemnian queen's reaction is ultimately completely unlike Dido's, as she proceeds to give Jason gifts: a beautiful, richly decorated cloak and the sword of her father Thoas (2.408–418). This latter gift underlines the contrast with Dido, who kills herself with the sword given to her by Aeneas (*Aen.* 4.645–647).[30] Hypsipyle's accompanying farewell speech to Jason also differs greatly from its intertext, Dido's final, cursing words to Aeneas:[31]

> 'accipe' ait, 'bellis mediaeque ut pulvere pugnae
> sim comes, Aetnaei genitor quae flammea gessit   420
> dona dei, nunc digna tuis adiungier armis.
> i, memor i terrae, quae vos amplexa quieto
> prima sinu, refer et domitis a Colchidos oris
> vela per hunc utero quem linquis Iasona nostro.'
>
> (Val. Fl. 2.419–424).

'Take this', she said, 'that I may be by your side in wartime and in the dust of battle's heat, the flaming gift of Aetna's god that my father bore, worthy to be worn now along with your own arms. Go now, go, but do not forget the land that first folded you to its peaceful bosom; and bring back your sails from Colchis' conquered shores, I beg you by this Jason whom you leave behind in my womb.'

Dido, by contrast, ends her first speech to Aeneas by wishing he would at least have given her a *parvulus Aeneas*, who would have allowed her to create a kingdom and dynasty:

> quid moror? an mea Pygmalion dum moenia frater   325
> destruat aut captam ducat Gaetulus Iarbas?
> saltem si qua mihi de te suscepta fuisset

---

[28] For Hypsipyle and Dido, see esp. Hershkowitz (1998) 138–146.
[29] See conveniently Schimann (1997) 104–105 for a survey of all these instances.
[30] Harper Smith (1987) 183 (on Val. Fl. 2.424); Poortvliet (1991) 230 (on Val. Fl. 2.423–424.); Hershkowitz (1998) 143.
[31] Poortvliet (1991) 229–230; Hershkowitz (1998) 143.

> ante fugam suboles, si quis mihi parvulus aula
> luderet Aeneas, qui te tamen ore referret,
> non equidem omnino capta ac deserta viderer. 330
>
> (Verg. *Aen.* 4.325–330)

> What am I waiting for? For my brother Pygmalion to come and raze my city to the ground? For the Gaetulian Iarbas to drag me off in chains? Oh if only you had given me a child before you abandoned me! If only there were a little Aeneas to play in my palace! In spite of everything his face would remind me of yours and I would not feel utterly betrayed and desolate.

This is precisely what happens to Hypsipyle, who uses this elegiac *mora* of the Argonauts to get what she wants: offspring for herself and the other Lemnian women to repopulate the kingdom and create a dynasty.[32] Unlike Dido, Hypsipyle is truly *pia*, taking care of both her father and her fatherland, in a "unique depiction of orderly political succession",[33] which is not unlike the situation in the early Roman principate.

5 Lemnos and Colchis

If someone is like Dido in the Lemnos episode it is rather Jason, who gets carried away by (the wrong kind of) *amor*, for which Hercules reproaches him in a speech that recalls Mercurius' admonition to Aeneas to leave elegiac Carthage behind (*Aen.* 4.265–295):[34]

> ... me tecum solus in aequor
> rerum traxit amor, dum spes mihi sistere montes
> Cyaneos vigilemque alium spoliare draconem.
>
> (Val. Fl. 2.380–382)

> Sheer love of action drew me to sea with you, while I had hope to stay the Cyanean mountains and to despoil another vigilant dragon.

Hercules saves the day for the moment, as his words spur Jason into action and, as Denis Feeney has it, "the epic is saved from elegiac sloth."[35] Incidentally, as

---

[32] For the elegiac nature of the stay, cf. Val. Fl. 2.356: *et deus ipse moras spatiumque indulget amori*, "And the god himself [*scil.* Jupiter] / concedes a span of time to linger in love." See also note 36 below.
[33] Zissos (2009) 361, note 39.
[34] E.g. Harper Smith (1987) 164 (on Val. Fl. 2.373); Poortvliet (1991) 210 (on Val. Fl. 2.373–374).
[35] Feeney (1991) 323.

Feeney has noted, this restart of the epic, as Tiphys gets ready to depart, is also marked by an allusion to the first words of the *Aeneid* a few lines later:[36]

> ... petit ingenti clamore magister
> <u>arma viros</u> pariter sparsosque in litore remos.
> (Val. Fl. 2.391–392)
>
> ...With a loud shout the helmsman seeks the tackle and his crew, and the oars that lie scattered on the beach.

In the second half of the epic, however, it becomes apparent that Medea's elegiac *amor* for Jason is crucial for the mission to succeed.

In this sense the Lemnos episode prefigures Colchis,[37] a link that is reinforced by the sharing of intertexts, as Carthage and Dido are obvious models for Colchis and Medea respectively.[38] As in the case of the Lemnos episode, however, Allecto's actions against Amata are also evoked, when Juno, disguised as Chalciope, attacks Medea with Venus' necklace to make her fall in love (6.477–506, 575–601, 657–680), and when Venus, in the guise of Circe, gives her the final push by making her help Jason (7.210–291).[39] At the same time, the (perversion of) civil war in Lemnos is evoked as well, as the Argonauts help Aeetes in his fight against his brother Perses in exchange for the Golden Fleece. This is again a kind of civil war,[40] and a useless one in the sense that Aeetes does not keep his promise and the Argonauts are helping the wrong person, the bad guy. Again, this war is orchestrated and manipulated by the gods, Venus and Juno, the same goddesses that are in charge of the Lemnos episode and the epic's third major elegiac moment, the Hylas episode, respectively.

---

36 Feeney (1991) 323, also for similar metapoetical markers of the Lemnos episode as an elegiac delay.
37 Cf. Hardie (1990) 6, who establishes Venus' affair with Mars as a link between the two episodes: "[F]or Venus' hatred of Lemnos stems from the fact that after her adultery with Mars her altars have lain cold on the island dear to Vulcan. Her willingness to cooperate in the disastrous infatuation of Medea at 6.467ff. is based on the same grievance, for thus she will be able to hit at the Colchian race of the Sun." See Heerink (2015a) Ch. 1 for the way this is already the case in Apollonius' *Argonautica*.
38 For Valerius' Colchis and Virgil's Carthage, and in particular Valerius' many allusions to *Aeneid* 1 in *Argonautica* 5, see e.g. esp. the commentaries by Wijsman (1996) and Spaltenstein (2004) *ad loc.* and the convenient discussion by Manuwald (1998) 316–317. For Medea and Dido, see Hershkowitz (1998) 99–100 (with 99, note 42 for more bibliography).
39 Hardie (1989) 7–8.
40 See e.g. McGuire (1997) 111; Buckley (2010); Bernstein (2014) 164–165 on this war as a civil war.

As Juno makes clear, her sole purpose for the war in Colchis is to make Medea fall in love with Jason:[41]

> talia certatim Minyae sparsique Cytaei
> funera miscebant campis Scythiamque premebant,
> cum Iuno Aesonidae non hanc ad vellera cernens
> esse viam nec sic redditus regina parandos,   430
> extremam molitur opem.
>   [...]
> sola animo Medea subit, mens omnis in una
> virgine, nocturnis qua nulla potentior aris.
>
> (Val. Fl. 6.427–431; 439–440)

> Thus in rivalry were the Minyae and scattered Cytaei dealing death upon the plains and putting Scythia to rout, when queen Juno, seeing that this was no way for Aesonides to win the fleece or accomplish his return, contrives a last resource ... Medea alone comes to her mind, all her thoughts are centred on the maiden only; no one is more potent at the nightly altars than her.

So the fighting is in service of *amor*, which in a sense was the case on Lemnos as well, with Venus stirring up and leading the war. The civil war at Colchis is thus quite unlike the second half of the *Aeneid*, its main intertext, which can eventually be said to lead to something positive, i.e. the Roman empire. In fact, the situation in Virgil's Latium is more similar to that on Lemnos, where also a goddess and a Fury—in fact Venus *as* a Fury—were pulling the strings and where there eventually is a happy end—not for the Argonauts but for the Lemnian women, who are able to reconstruct their kingdom. Whereas the Lemnos episode more closely resembles the second half of the *Aeneid*, what happens to Medea in Colchis is ultimately more similar to the situation in Virgil's Carthage. This inversion of Virgil's *Aeneid* on a macro-level seems significant. Whereas the interconnected allusions to elegy in the *Aeneid* (in Carthage and Latium) suggest that the *Aeneid* will leave elegy behind, as we have seen above, Valerius' reworking of Virgil's intratextual parallel in his Lemnos and Colchis episodes suggests rather the opposite, i.e. that the epic is moving towards elegy and Virgil's Dido, as it were, as Medea's love is essential for the mission to succeed.

The ending of the *Argonautica* as it has been transmitted becomes quite significant from this perspective, as the epic breaks off at a crucial and very striking

---

41 Cf. Feeney (1991) 326: "The poem's great set-piece battle book is undermined, to become only an occasion for the girl to fall in love with her future husband; Jason's greatest moment of heroic action is engineered by Juno in order to impress Medea (6.600–620)."

point. The literary tradition of the Argonautic myth of course prescribes that Jason and Medea will get married and stay together until Jason leaves her in Corinth, with horrible consequences. In book 8 of Valerius' epic, however, a different course of events is suggested, as the wedding ceremony of Jason and Medea is interrupted, when the party is attacked by Colchians and the Argonauts prepare for battle (8.259–317). Then, as Juno suspends the action by raising a storm (8.318–368), the Argonauts persuade Jason to leave Medea behind and continue their voyage home (8.385–404), and Jason is actually on the verge of bringing her this bad news when the epic breaks off (8.467).

The allusions to *Aeneid* 4, which have played a role in the entire second half of the epic, continue here, as Jason and Medea evoke Aeneas and Dido again.[42] These allusions actually suggest that Jason will leave Medea behind like a Dido, and that the epic will continue, leaving elegy behind, as was the case in *Aeneid* 4. We know, however, that this will (probably) not happen: Jason and Medea will stay together, as literary tradition dictates and several flashforwards also make clear.[43] The *Argonautica*—or rather its projected sequel, beyond the boundary of the epic proper—will in a sense move towards elegy as well as tragedy, which is not coincidentally a generic feature of the Dido episode as well.[44] Again, the elegiac agenda of the *Aeneid* is inverted, which reinforces the idea that Valerius' epic is generically moving in a direction opposite to that of the *Aeneid*, away from epic and towards elegy. From this meta-elegiac point of view, the ending of the *Argonautica* as we have it is rather fitting, as the moment where Jason—and Valerius—decide what kind of epic the *Argonautica* will turn out to be, an *Aeneid* or rather an elegiac inversion of it, is suspended.

6 Hylas

A similar inversion of the elegiac agenda of the *Aeneid* can be detected in the Hylas episode, as I have argued elsewhere.[45] In an episode that is set up as a miniature *Aeneid*, orchestrated by Juno, who is persecuting a single hero (Hercules) as she did in Virgil's epic, Hylas is initially presented as a potentially epic hero,

---

42 See e.g. Pellucchi (2012) 393–394 for the allusions to *Aeneid* 4 in this episode.
43 See esp. Hershkowitz (1998) Ch. 1 for the way the *Argonautica* foreshadows events to come. Cf. also the chapter by Battistella and Galli Milić in this volume.
44 For the Dido episode as a tragedy, see conveniently Hardie (1998) 62–63; Harrison (2007) 208–210, also for more bibliography.
45 What follows is based on Heerink (2015a) 113–139, 157.

through allusions to *Aeneid* 7. As we have seen, Ascanius' shooting of Silvia's stag there sets in motion the chain of events that leads to war in Latium, thus starting Virgil's "essential epic" and ending the bucolic and in particular elegiac world that Latium was. When Hylas is chasing a stag in Valerius' *Argonautica*, he initially clearly resembles Ascanius, but unlike his epic predecessor, Hylas fails to shoot the animal. Furthermore, through Valerius' suggestive use of imagery, Hylas' initially epic hunting is transformed into an erotic, elegiac hunt, that eventually is more similar to the famous comparison of Dido with a wounded deer in *Aeneid* 4 than to Ascanius' hunt in *Aeneid* 7. Exploiting the intertextual contact between *Aeneid* 4 and 7, Valerius has reversed Virgil's transformation from elegy to epic in Latium.

Hylas' hunt culminates in the rape of the boy by a nymph called Dryope, who, ordered by Juno, pulls Hylas into the water. Allusively, the nymph is associated with Juno's assistant Allecto in *Aeneid* 7, but Valerius' "Fury of love" is metapoetically the opposite of Virgil's Fury, as she elegizes a potential epic instead of turning an elegiac world into an essential-epic war. It is not a coincidence, I think, that Valerius' nymph carries the same name as Venus' avatar Dryope, who similarly evokes Virgil's Allecto when she incites the other Lemnian women to kill their husbands in an episode where epic and elegy are confounded.

But Hylas is not the only one who is elegized. Through his abduction the boy becomes the unattainable elegiac beloved of Hercules, who is consequently also transformed, from an epic hero into an elegiac lover, stricken by elegiac *amor*. In this respect he is also compared to a wounded lion (3.587–591), which makes him resemble the lovesick, elegiac Dido compared to a wounded deer. Later in the episode, when it is said that "his love burns" (*urit amor*, 3.736), Hercules's *amor* again resembles Dido's elegiac passion, for which the fire metaphor is continuously employed, for instance in *Aen.* 4.68, just before Dido is compared to the deer: *uritur infelix Dido*, "unhappy Dido burns."

The elegiac nature of Hercules' love is made even clearer when Hylas addresses Hercules in the aftermath of the episode, at the beginning of book 4, and describes his love as *questus* ("complaint"), a word that is often used to denote Roman love elegy, by reference to the genre's supposed origin:[46] *quid, pater, in vanos absumis tempora questus*?, "Why, father, do you waste time in vain lament?" (Val. Fl. 4.25).

By thus transforming a potential *Aeneid* into an elegiac world, Valerius inverts Virgil's poetical move to essential epic in *Aeneid* 7. Furthermore, as was the case in the Lemnos episode, the Hylas episode can also be seen to prefigure the

---

46 See note 15 above.

way that the *Argonautica*, for which the elegiac love of Medea is crucial, will go, and the elegizing of the *Aeneid* can thus be seen as a metapoetical statement about the entire epic: Valerius' *Argonautica* is an elegized *Aeneid*.

7 Conclusion

So what is the point of these allusions to and inversions of Virgil's *Aeneid* and of the role of elegy in this respect? By the time Valerius wrote his *Argonautica*, Virgil's perfect, Augustan picture of a future Rome, as emblematically envisaged on the Shield of Aeneas, had been shattered by Nero and the ensuing civil wars of 68–69.[47] These civil wars are actually evoked in the well-known comparison of the war in Colchis to Roman legions fighting each other (6.402–409), and are behind all the useless and perverted civil wars that feature in the *Argonautica*, including the one on Lemnos.[48] These and other episodes testify to a pessimistic and disappointed worldview; Valerius does not believe in an *imperium sine fine*, "an empire that will know no end" as famously prophesied by Jupiter in the *Aeneid* (1.254–296) any more. In fact, Jupiter seems not to be in full control anymore, and he strikingly does not mention the Romans as the new rulers of the world in his prophecy in *Argonautica* 1 (531–567), which is clearly modelled on that of Virgil's Jupiter.[49] Writing under Vespasian, who fashioned himself as a new Augustus, Valerius at first sight seems to follow suit and replay the *Aeneid* when he addresses the emperor in his proem and associates him with Jason and the Argonauts, just like Virgil associates Aeneas with Augustus. But Valerius is not following Virgil; his *Argonautica*, which initiates a new but harsh Iron Age, reveals a disappointed attitude concerning the Principate, and by inverting and elegizing the *Aeneid* in several ways, Valerius seems to emphasize that an *Aeneid* in the Flavian age is no longer possible. One can understand the optimism of the Au-

---

[47] What follows is partly based on Heerink (2014) 95.
[48] On Valerius' pessimistic reaction to the civil wars of 68–69, see esp. McGuire (1997) 88–146. For an optimistic interpretation of Valerius' engagement with these wars, see Stover (2012) 113–148, with Heerink (2015b) for a critical assessment.
[49] Cf. e.g. Bernstein (2014) 160. See Stover (2012) 27–77 (Ch. 2: "The Inauguration of the 'Argonautic moment'") for a different, i.e. optimistic, interpretation of the "Jovian programme" (p. 28) in Valerius' *Argonautica*, including Jupiter's prophetic speech and the transition from the Golden to the Iron Age.

gustan age, when the first *princeps* had ended more than half a century of traumatic civil wars, but one can equally understand Valerius in not believing in the Augustan dream anymore.

Bibliography

Augoustakis, Antony (ed.) (2014), *Flavian Poetry and its Greek Past*, Leiden.
Baier, Thomas/Schimann, Frank (eds.) (1997), *Fabrica: Studien zur antiken Literatur und ihrer Rezeption*, Stuttgart.
Baker, Robert (2000²), *Propertius I*, Warminster.
Barchiesi, Alessandro (1993), "Future Reflexive: Two Modes of Allusion and Ovid's *Heroides*", in: *HSPh* 95, 333–365.
Bernstein, Neil (2014), "*Romanas veluti saevissima cum legiones Tisiphone regesque movet*: Valerius Flaccus' *Argonautica* and the Flavian Era", in: Heerink/Manuwald (2014) 154–169.
Buckley, Emma (2010), "War-Epic for a New Era: Valerius Flaccus' *Argonautica*", in: Kramer/Reitz (2010) 431–455.
Cairns, Francis (1989), *Virgil's Augustan Epic*, Cambridge.
Colton, Robert (1964), "Influence of Propertius on Valerius Flaccus", in: *CB* 40.3, 35–42.
Dominik, William/Garthwaite, John/Roche, Paul (eds.) (2009), *Writing Politics in Imperial Rome*, Leiden.
Eigler, Ulrich/Lefèvre, Eckard/Manuwald, Gesine (eds.) (1998), Ratis omnia vincet. *Neue Untersuchungen zu den* Argonautica *des Valerius Flaccus*, Munich.
Feeney, Denis (1991), *The Gods in Epic: Poets and Critics of the Classical Tradition*, Oxford.
Garson, Ronald W. (1964), "Some Critical Observations on Valerius Flaccus' *Argonautica* I", in: *CQ* 14, 267–279.
Griffin, Jasper (1986), *Latin Poets and Roman Life*, Chapel Hill.
Hardie, Philip (1989), "Flavian epicists on Virgil's epic technique", in: *Ramus* 18, 3–20.
Hardie, Philip (1998), *Virgil*, Oxford.
Harper Smith, Alison (1987), *A Commentary on Valerius Flaccus'* Argonautica *II*, Diss. Oxford.
Harrison, Stephen (2007), *Generic Enrichment in Vergil and Horace*, Oxford.
Heerink, Mark (2014), "Valerius Flaccus, Virgil and the Poetics of Ekphrasis", in: Heerink/Manuwald (2014) 72–95.
Heerink, Mark/Manuwald, Gesine (eds.) (2014), *Brill's Companion to Valerius Flaccus*, Leiden.
Heerink, Mark (eds.) (2015a), *Echoing Hylas: A Study in Hellenistic and Roman Metapoetics*, Madison.
Heerink, Mark (2015b), "Virgil, Lucan, and the Meaning of Civil War in Valerius Flaccus' *Argonautica*", in: *Mnemosyne* 69, 511–525.
Hershkowitz, Debra (1998), *Valerius Flaccus'* Argonautica: *Abbreviated Voyages in Silver Latin Epic*, Oxford.
Heyworth, Stephen (2007), *Cynthia: A Companion to the Text of Propertius*, Oxford.
Hinds, Stephen (1987), *The Metamorphosis of Persephone: Ovid and the Self-Conscious Muse*, Cambridge.
Horsfall, Nicholas (2000), *Virgil, Aeneid 7: A Commentary*, Leiden.

Kramer, Norbert/Reitz, Christiane (eds.) (2010), *Tradition und Erneuerung: Mediale Strategien in der Zeit der Flavier*, Berlin.
Lyne, Oliver (1987), *Further Voices in Vergil's* Aeneid, Oxford.
Manuwald, Gesine (1998), "Die Bilder am Tempel in Kolchis", in: Eigler *et al.* (1998) 307–318.
Nelis, Damien P. (2001), *Vergil's* Aeneid *and the* Argonautica *of Apollonius Rhodius*, Leeds.
McGuire, Donald (1997), *Acts of Silence: Civil War, Tyranny, and Suicide in the Flavian Epics*, Hildesheim.
Mozley, John (1934), *Valerius Flaccus*, Argonautica, Cambridge, MA.
Pellucchi, Tiziana (2012), *Commento al libro VIII delle* Argonautiche *di Valerio Flacco*, Hildesheim.
Poortvliet, Harm (1991), *C. Valerius Flaccus'* Argonautica, *Book II: A Commentary*, Amsterdam.
Putnam, Michael (1995), "Silvia's Stag and Virgilian Ekphrasis", in: *MD* 34, 107–133.
Putnam, Michael (1998), *Virgil's Epic Designs: Ekphrasis in the* Aeneid, New Haven.
Schimann, Frank (1997), "Feuer auf Lemnos: Feuer und Furie in den *Argonautica* des Valerius Flaccus", in: Baier/Schimann (1997) 103–128.
Seal, Carey (2014), "Civil War and the Apollonian Model in Valerius' *Argonautica*", in: Augoustakis (2014) 113–135.
Spaltenstein, François (2004), *Commentaire des* Argonautica *de Valérius Flaccus (livres 3, 4 et 5)*, Brussels.
Stover, Tim (2012), *Epic and Empire in Vespasianic Rome: A New Reading of Valerius Flaccus'* Argonautica, Oxford.
Tzounakas, Spyridon (2012), "Further Programmatic Implications of Valerius Flaccus' Description of the Construction of the Argo (1.121–9)", in: *SO* 86, 160–177.
West, David (1991), *Virgil, The* Aeneid, London.
Wijsman, Henri (1996), *Valerius Flaccus*, Argonautica, *book V: A Commentary*, Leiden.
Zissos, Andrew (2009), "Navigating Power: Valerius Flaccus' *Argonautica*", in: Dominik *et al.* (2009) 351–366.

Chiara Battistella/Lavinia Galli Milić
Foreshadowing Medea: Prolepsis and Intertextuality in Valerius Flaccus

1 Introduction

The Medea of Valerius Flaccus has received much attention in recent years, far more than the male protagonist of the story narrated in the Roman *Argonautica*,[1] and she has been recognized by scholars as a deeply intertextual character.[2] On the one hand, this assumption may be inevitably tied to the belatedness of the author, coming in a long tradition of pre-Vergilian, Augustan, and post-Vergilian epic, and activating an intense dialogue with the numerous female characters of his predecessors (especially Homer, Euripides, Apollonius Rhodius, Catullus, Vergil, Ovid, Lucan and Seneca), as well as with the narrative context in which these characters evolve.[3] On the other hand, we would like to argue that the intertextual nature of the Flavian Medea can be interpreted in light of Valerius Flaccus' literary programme of de- and reconstruction of the epic genre. We agree with Denis Feeney that Valerius practises "a creative transgression of the expected bounds of epic,"[4] and we believe that this statement can easily be applied to Medea as an epic character.

Intertextuality as a means of shaping a character occurs at the level of the narrative as well as at the level of the speeches uttered by the characters themselves. Instead of providing a general overview of this trend, in this paper we will raise the question of the role played by intertextuality in the creation of the Valerian Medea from a specific perspective, and we will consider how proleptic passages may allow for intertextual undercurrents and insights into the problem of the character's portrayal.

---

[1] On the character of Jason in Valerius Flaccus' *Argonautica* see nonetheless Ripoll (2003), Stover (2003), Dubrana (2008), and Castelletti (2014).
[2] On the intrinsically intertextual nature of Medea's character see Hinds (1993) 46 and passim. The multi-faceted nature of Medea—maiden, priest, spouse, mother, princess, magician and murderer—makes particularly true the following statement of Don Fowler (1997, 17): "One area in which intertextuality comes to play a central role [...] is that of the construction of character."
[3] See for example Wijsman (1996) 166 and ad 5.378–390 (Nausicaa), Hershkowitz (1998) 95–100 (Helen and Dido), Salemme (1991) 25–46 and Keith (2014) 275–280 (Ovidian Proserpina), Roux (2015) (Ariadne and other female figures in the Ovidian *Heroides*), and again Hershkowitz (1998) 95, n. 231 for additional bibliography.
[4] Feeney (1993) 321.

Several scholars have already noted that Valerius Flaccus is obsessed with *prolepsis*.[5] As a narrative device, *prolepsis* disrupts the chronological order of the narrative by anticipating future events in the story.[6] In Valerius Flaccus' poem some of these *prolepseis* are homodiegetic and internal, as they foreshadow dark events *inside* the Argonautic plot, which is fundamentally an "epic" plot.[7] But most of them are external *prolepseis*. Whereas the action of the poem concerns solely the Argonautic plot,[8] these *prolepseis* aim at foreshadowing Medea's future as featured in the tragic/Euripidean sequel to the story,[9] in a manner similar to that found in Apollonius, although the Hellenistic poet exploits this kind of *prolepsis* to a lesser degree.[10]

According to Peter Davis, Valerius uses *prolepsis* to make his readers aware of the whole story of Medea and also "to underline Medea's role in the divine plan for world history, including the Trojan War, and in the poem's ideological structure."[11] As for us, we assume that Valerius employs this forward-looking device as a strategic place to urge a confrontation with past authors (within the epic genre and beyond) and with other Medeas and literary female characters. More

---

[5] Most recently, Buckley (2014) 307.
[6] Genette (1972) 105–115; de Jong (2001) xvi. On the function of *prolepsis* in ancient epic poetry, see, for example, Duckworth (1933), de Jong (2014) 78–87.
[7] For instance, Val. Fl. 1.546–548 (Jupiter's speech) *nec vellera tantum / indignanda manent propiorque ex virgine rapta / ille dolor,* "Nor is it the fleece alone that is fated to rouse resentment and the still closer pang that comes from a ravished maid" (Mozley); 5.219–221 (a proem in the middle) *ventum ad furias infandaque natae / foedera et horrenda trepidam sub virgine puppem; / impia monstriferis surgunt iam proelia campis,* "We are come to the madness and unholy compact of the princess, and how the vessel shuddered beneath the terrible maid; the accursed contests on the portent-bearing fields arise before me" (Mozley).
[8] The Valerian *Argonautica* is an incomplete work, but even if the scholars have not found an overall agreement on its original length (8, 9, 10, 12 books?), there is no doubt that this poem was intended to conclude without developing the further Corinthian events of Medea's myth.
[9] For instance, Val. Fl. 1.224–225 (Mopsus' prophecy) *quaenam aligeris secat anguibus auras / caede madens?,* "What woman is this, drenched with slaughter, that cleaves the air upon winged serpents" (Mozley); 4.13–14 *dabit impia poenas / virgo nec Aeetae gemitus patiemur inultos,* "[P]unished shall be the sinful maid, nor shall we suffer Aeetes' sorrow to go unavenged" (Mozley). Cf. Zissos (2012) 98, who challenges this traditional point of view by claiming that "Valerius clearly invites the reader to look beyond *that* Medea [i.e. Euripidean Medea] to a 'Pacuvian' Medea—to a more distant chronological horizon that holds out a prospect not of desolation but of redemption." We are far from agreeing with his thesis.
[10] Fusillo (1985), Hurst (2012).
[11] Davis (2014) 199.

than arousing the reader's curiosity,[12] Valerian *prolepseis* open an intertextual "window" whose function is similar to that fulfilled by Barchiesi's "intertextual tropes" (dreams, prophecies, *ekphraseis*, etc.) some of which have of course proleptic nature.[13] They can also convey metapoetic meaning as Mark Heerink has pointed out in his analysis of two proleptic *ekphraseis* in the poem (the descriptions of the Argo's keel, Val. Fl. 1.130–148, and of the temple of the Sun, 5.415–454).[14]

In what follows, we will especially focus on two passages in order to illustrate our thesis: the first appearance of Medea in the poem and her meeting with Jason (5.329–398), and Hecate's monologue (6.495–502).[15]

2 When She Meets Him (Val. Fl. 5.329–398): Combining Small-scale Narrative Patterns

The reader meets Medea as an acting character for the first time at Val. Fl. 5.329. Until this line, there are only allusive references to Medea, which shed a gloomy light on her, for she is given a rather ominous depiction.[16] Andrew Zissos argues that such a presentation of Medea's character is rather misleading, for the person the Argonauts will meet does not seem to correspond to the one sketched early on in the narrative.[17] And it is also noteworthy that the discrepancy between the acting character and these proleptic depictions occurs throughout the poem.[18] The question thus arises why Valerius scatters these proleptic "dark" depictions of Medea through the narrative, when he persistently presents us with the picture

---

12 That is the ancient point of view on the function of *prolepsis*, see for instance *Schol. ad Hom. Il.* 11.604 cited by de Jong (2001) xvi.
13 On this see Barchiesi (1995).
14 Heerink (2014).
15 While writing this paper, the authors have been consistently collaborating and have drafted together the introduction and conclusion. Lavinia Galli Milić is specifically the author of section 2 and Chiara Battistella of section 3. The paper was conceived in the framework of a FNS project entitled *Intertextuality in Flavian Epic Poetry* and led by Damien Nelis. We would like to thank him for his invaluable advice and comments.
16 Corrigan (2013) 198 regards these repetitive allusions as a manner for Valerius "to keep Medea in the forefront of readers' minds."
17 Zissos (2012) 96.
18 For proleptic passages after Medea's coming into the story see, for instance, Val. Fl. 5.433–454, 6.43–47, 6.497–502, 6.584–586, 7.249–250, 7.309–311, 7.339–340, 7.485–486, 7.501–510, 8.77, 8.108, 8.204–206, 8.236, 8.248–251, 8.316–317, 8.420–422, 8.459–441.

of a *virgo*—torn between her love for her father (*pudor*) and her passion for Jason (*amor*)—rather than a *virago*. This has been interpreted in a number of ways and can be due to the intrinsic contradictions of Medea, a character with an extraordinarily rich literary biography, built up over time and across different literary genres. But it seems not unreasonable to us to assume that Valerius in this way was heightening awareness among his readers of the weight of the tradition on this character (and on him as a belated poet) while challenging different narrative perspectives at the interplay between epos and tragedy.

The first appearance of the character plays thus a major role in asserting the Valerian Medea's distinguishing traits.[19] Here is a synopsis of this well-known passage, which we will read from a proleptic perspective (Val. Fl. 5.329–398):

329–332   Medea wakes up and heads for the river Phasis [Phasis 1]
333–340   Description of her proleptic nightmare
341–342   Medea heads for the river Phasis with her companions [Phasis 2]
343–349   Simile: Medea/Proserpina
350–352   Before arriving at the Phasis, Medea sees the strangers and is scared [Phasis 3]
353–363a *Dialogue between Medea and her nurse Henioche*
363b–367 Juno beautifies Jason
368–372   Simile: Jason/Sirius
373–375a Medea is scared but admires Jason
375b–377 Jason admires Medea
378–396   *Dialogue between Jason and Medea*
397–398   Medea finally arrives at the river Phasis [Phasis 4]

These 70 lines should be considered as a whole, because they display a strong structural unity, owing to symmetric scenes such as the two similes, the two dialogues, and the description of the two protagonists admiring each other alternately (5.375 *[mirata] in solo stupuit duce*, "[She] gazed marvelling at the chief, and at him alone" and 5.376–377 *haeret in una / defixus*, "[He] is entranced by her alone" (Mozley)). Furthermore, these lines are designed in the shape of a *Ringkomposition*: the passage starts with a description of Medea getting ready to move to the Phasis and it ends with Medea' sacrificing on its shores. Readerly attention is thus focused on the space in-between, which should be regarded as a "freeze

---

19 Hershkowitz (1998) 95: The "first appearance [of Medea] in the narrative provides a good illustration of many of the literary dynamics contributing both to her conception as a character in particular and to Valerian intertextuality in general."

frame," a sort of "achrony"[20] fixing the nature of the main character. And, as we will see, intratextuality intervenes to relate these lines to the whole poem.

2.1 More than Just an Apollonian Medea: Nausicaa, Dido, Proserpina but also Diana/Hecate and Venus

When Medea first enters the epic action, she is immediately *territa* and *rapta*.[21] These will be the dominant features of the Valerian Medea[22] despite her status of sorceress, to which Valerius gives some prominence right from the first allusion to Medea (Val. Fl. 1.60–63) and then all through the poem.[23] Valerius gives us the reasons for her emotional state by describing the nightmare Medea has had the previous night and creates an eerie atmosphere right from her first appearance in the story.

Alessandro Perutelli, pointing out that Valerius Flaccus blends here two Apollonian *loci*, Ap. Rhod. *Argon.* 3.616–635 (Medea's dream) and Ap. Rhod. *Argon.*

---

[20] We employ the word "achrony" in its etymological sense. In narratology, it denotes instead "a deviation of time that cannot be analysed any further" (Bal 1997, 97).

[21] Val. Fl. 5.329–331 *Forte deum variis per noctem territa monstris / senserat ut pulsas tandem Medea tenebras / rapta toris*, "It chanced that Medea, alarmed in the night by heavenly portents, had sprung from her couch as soon as she saw the shadows fled" (Mozley). Even if the syntax of the line clearly makes the readers understand *rapta* in connection with *toris* (i.e., "snatched from her bed") the use of this participle, highlighted by its position at the beginning of the line, is meaningful in light of what follows. Furthermore, at a metaphorical level, *rapta toris* might be referred to the change of social status from *virgo* to *matrona*.

[22] Fear is a recurring feature describing Medea in our passage (Val. Fl. 5.335 *pavens*; 5.339 *trementem*; 5.352 *timore*; 5.358 *trepidam*; 5.373 *pavor*; 5.391 *trepidam*; 5.392 *metu*) and Pederzani (1987) 112–124 regards it as a structural emotion of the Valerian *Argonautica*. In Seneca's *Medea*, *metus* is a key word "to refer to the protagonist as a source of fear," as pointed out by Chiara Battistella *infra*: may we read the focus Valerius give to this emotion as an attempt to present the epic and the tragic Medea in a opposite specular way? As regards *rapta*, see for example Val. Fl. 1.547 *virgine rapta* (Jupiter foretells Medea's abduction); 6.439–448; 6.498 (Hecate says that she will punish Jason for the rape of her servant); 8.265–266 (Absyrtus sees Jason as a *raptor*); 8.392–393 (the Argonauts define the marriage between Jason and Medea as *raptis coniugiis*). *Contra* Davis, who underlines the ambiguity of Medea who "is and is not raped" (2014, 197), just like Thetis whose marriage is painted on the Argo's hull at 1.130–132.

[23] On the dual role of Medea and Valerius Flaccus' satisfactory or unsatisfactory way of dealing with it, see Hull (1975) 18–19. Corrigan (2013) 200, n. 30 admits that Valerius "places more emphasis on her sorceress elements than Apollonius in order to answer the demands of the Silver Age," although she recognizes that, in the Roman *Argonautica*, "it is the girl who emerges and not the witch."

4.662–671 (Circe's dream), has highlighted the similarities and differences between these three passages.[24] The dream, a typical epic device, serves here the psychological description of the character. At the same time, the lines of Valerius subtly hint at the description of a sleepless Dido, burning with unseen fire (Verg. *Aen.* 4.1–9).[25] May we go further? We would like to draw attention to the difference of content and narrative chronology between the Hellenistic and the Roman *Argonautica*. Unlike Ap. Rhod. *Argon.* 3.616–636 (and Verg. *Aen.* 4.1–9), where Medea has already fallen in love with Jason (and Dido with Aeneas) and is dreaming that she has chosen to leave with the stranger, Valerius Flaccus describes a premonitory dream at the very moment in which his readers meet the Valerian Medea and she is about to meet Jason, in both cases for the first time:

> dum premit alta quies nullaeque in virgine curae,
> visa pavens castis Hecates excedere lucis   335
> dumque pii petit ora patris, stetit arduus inter
> pontus et ingenti circum stupefacta profundo,
> fratre tamen conante sequi: mox stare paventes
> viderat intenta pueros nece seque trementum
> spargere caede manus et lumina rumpere fletu.   340
>
> (Val. Fl. 5.334–340)

[W]hile ... deep quiet held [her limbs] and no trouble was in her maiden heart, she seemed to her terror to be stepping forth from Hecate's holy grove, and when she sought her loving father's presence, the tall sea stood between them and she was aghast at the vast deep all around, yet her brother assayed to follow; then had she seen children stand terror-stricken at the threat of sudden death, and herself as they trembled stain her hands with their murder, while tears burst from her eyes.

(Mozley)

---

[24] Perutelli (1994). Mainly on their differences see Davis (2014) 193–195; cf. also Walde (1998) 101–106.

[25] Perutelli (1994) 37–38 refers to Verg. *Aen.* 4.1–9 only as the text source of the description of a second dream by Medea, Val. Fl. 7.141–152. The awareness that this Vergilian passage is already a reworking of Ap. Rhod. *Argon.* 3.616–635 (Nelis 2001, 136–137) and that the Ur-scene of all these scenes is naturally the dream of Nausicaa in Hom. *Od.* 6.25–40, where a disguised Athena invites the maiden to go to the river in order to wash the dowry for her marriage, would shed light on the complexity of Valerius' allusive strategies both at a verbal and structural level. Studies on Vergil as one of the key models for Valerius include Hardie (1990), Hardie (1993), Hershkowitz (1998), Zissos (2008), Heerink (2014). In particular, Nelis (forthcoming) and Nelis' paper in this volume put convincingly an emphasis on the meaningfulness of some structural similarities between Apollonius, Vergil and Valerius. See also Heerink in this volume on Valerius Flaccus' allusions to elegiac moments in the *Aeneid*.

And the aware reader understands that from now on, that is to say from the entry of Jason into the life of Medea, the carefree maiden (5.334 *nullaeque in virgine curae*)[26] will lose her status of priestess and *virgo* (5.335),[27] of pious daughter (5.336–337), and of sister (5.338 *fratre tamen conante sequi*), before sinking into "canonical" tragedy (5.338–340). On the one hand, the intertextual relation with Apollonius and Vergil ensures that Valerius is challenging the tradition about Medea and embedding in it the tragic/elegiac influences at work on Apollonian/Vergilian epic. On the other hand, these proleptic moments, before being an anticipation of Medea's behaviour in tragedy, point out the nature of this character who is *already* tragic *inside* the epic. The Valerian Medea is a scared maiden unaware that she is designed for and will accomplish evil deeds. In highlighting that, Valerius claims that her actions in Colchis do not have simply an epic nature. There is a continuity between his epic Medea and the tragic one and the boundary between the two has to be settled at the very moment of the arrival of Jason in her life.

The following lines (5.343–349) contain a simile that has strong Homeric colours, recalling especially the meeting between Odysseus and Nausicaa in Hom. *Od.* 6.102–108 (Nausicaa ~ Artemis), as well as the reworking of this scene in Ap. Rhod. *Argon.* 3.878–884 (Medea ~ Artemis) and Verg. *Aen.* 1.498–504 (Dido ~ Diana).[28] Stover has rightly highlighted that these multiple layers of intertextuality illustrate the incursion of *eros* into the Latin *Argonautica* and "the potential enervation of the epic's hero."[29] Without rejecting this reading nor denying the importance of these passages for the construction of the Valerian Medea (and Jason), we would like to consider them as an essential background also insofar as they point out the *dissimilarity* between Valerius' main character and his models. Furthermore, we would argue that these lines involve metapoetical concerns:[30]

florea per verni qualis iuga duxit Hymetti
aut Sicula sub rupe choros hinc gressibus haerens

---

[26] On *curae* having erotic meaning and elegiac connotation see Pichon (1902) 120.
[27] This loss implies that she will abandon her father's home, cf. the similar structure and sound in Val. Fl. 7.440 *si patriis timuissem excedere tectis*, "had I feared to leave my father's house" (Mozley).
[28] For detailed references and comments see Hull (1975), Bessone (1991) 82–84, Gärtner (1994) 137–146, Hershkowitz (1998) 95–100, Manuwald (2002), Caviglia (2002), Corrigan (2013) 202–204. Cf. also Buckley (2016) 77–78 and n. 39.
[29] Stover (2003) 124 and Stover (2012) 187–206.
[30] On the potential metapoetic force of the simile in the Hellenistic poetry see Cusset (2012) 104–107. In our view, the same observations can be made regarding the Augustan and the Flavian epic poetry. On similes as part of the resources of the epic voice, see Lyne (1987) 224–225.

> Pallados, hinc carae Proserpina iuncta Dianae, 345
> altior ac nulla comitum certante, priusquam
> palluit et viso pulsus decor omnis Averno;
> talis et in vittis geminae cum lumine taedae
> Colchis erat nondum miseros exosa parentes.
> ut procul extremi gelidis a fluminis undis 350
> prima viros tacito vidit procedere passu,
> substitit ac maesto nutricem adfata timore est.
>
> (Val. Fl. 5.343–352)

> As Proserpine in springtime led the dance over Hymettus' flowery ridges or beneath the cliffs of Sicily, on this side stepping close by Pallas, on that side hand in hand with her beloved Diana, taller than they and surpassing all her fellows, ere she grew pale at the sight of Avernus and all her beauty fled: so fair also was the Colchian in her sacred fillets by the twin torches' light, while yet she hated not her hapless parents. When first she saw, at a distance from the cool waters of the river-side, men proceeding with silent pace, she stopped, and called to her nurse in dismay and fear.
>
> (Mozley)

The Colchian maiden is compared to Proserpina, dancing in a ring with her companions in a natural setting. At 5.346–347 the reference to the future paleness of Proserpina and to her descent into Avernus casts a shadow on this idyllic landscape, bringing into the picture her rape by the god Pluto.

At lines 5.348–349 *talis ... Colchis erat* is doubtless a reworking of Verg. *Aen.* 1.503 (*talis erat Dido*), a line which takes place in the first meeting between Dido and Aeneas and which introduces the comparison between the Carthaginian queen and Diana.[31] Nevertheless, the focus of the Valerian simile has not been placed on the beauty of the girl.[32] Valerius is stressing the chronological order of Medea's story. At this stage, she is a maiden, a priestess of Hecate (5.348 *vittis, taedae*), she is the "prior" Medea (5.346 *priusquam*; 5.349 *nondum*).[33] The meeting

---

[31] By combining allusions to Verg. *Aen.* 1 and 4 in the passage of the meeting between Medea and Jason, Valerius points to the relationship which he recognizes between these two Vergilian scenes, cf. also infra. On this kind of combinatorial imitation that mirrors Vergil's own literary practices see Hardie (1990).

[32] As, by contrast, in Hom. *Od.* 6.107–108 πασάων δ' ὑπὲρ ἥ γε κάρη ἔχει ἠδὲ μέτωπα, / ῥεῖά τ' ἀριγνώτη πέλεται, καλαὶ δέ τε πᾶσαι·, "[H]igh above them all Artemis holds her head and brows, and easily may she be known, though all are beautiful" (Murray) and Verg. *Aen.* 1.496 *pulcherrima Dido*. Apollonius emphasizes rather the motion of the group of young girls.

[33] Chiara Battistella has suggested to me that this attention to a temporal sequence is quintessentially Ovidian, see for instance Ov. *Met.* 8.372 and Esposito (2003). Valerius would depict the past of Medea as a pre-metamorphic condition.

with Jason is in the eyes of Valerius the pivotal moment in Medea's story from her past to her future condition of *rapta* and her fatal betrayal of family bonds (5.349 *miseros exosa parentes*). The intratextual connexion generated by the reuse of *video* draws a parallel between Proserpina's descent into the underworld (5.347 <u>viso</u> *Averno*) and the first gaze of Medea towards the Argonauts (5.351 *prima viros tacito <u>vidit</u> procedere passu*). By modifying the point of comparison of his models (Proserpina instead of Diana), Valerius is adapting the simile to his poem, where the maiden Medea is linked to the Underworld as Hecate's priestess and, as we have already seen, is presented as a *virgo rapta*, perhaps because of Seneca.[34]

As it has been noted, the reference to Proserpina has to be considered an Ovidian intrusion into this recurring epic encounter between an unmarried maiden and a foreign hero:[35]

> haud procul <u>Hennaeis</u> lacus est <u>a moenibus</u> altae,   385
> nomine Pergus, aquae; non illo plura Caystros
> carmina cygnorum labentibus audit in undis.
> silva coronat aquas cingens latus omne suisque
> frondibus ut velo Phoebeos submovet ictus.
> frigora dant rami, Tyrios humus umida <u>flores</u>:   390
> perpetuum <u>ver</u> est. quo dum <u>Proserpina</u> luco
> ludit et aut violas aut <u>candida lilia</u> carpit,
> dumque puellari studio calathosque sinumque
> inplet et <u>aequales certat superare</u> legendo,
> paene simul <u>visa</u> est dilectaque raptaque Diti.   395
>
> (Ov. *Met.* 5.385–395)

Not far from the walls of Henna there is a lake of deep water, Pergus by name; Cayster hears no more songs from the swans upon its gliding waves than does that lake. A wood crowns the waters, ringing them on every side, and with its leaves like an awning keeps out Phoebus' blows. The branches give coolness and the damp earth a variety of flowers; there is perpetual spring. While Proserpina played in this grove gathering either violets or white lilies and was filling up her baskets and her lap with girlish enthusiasm striving to outdo

---

34 Cf. Sen. *Med.* 12 *fide meliore raptam* (referring to Proserpina compared to Medea), 607–615 (Medea's departure is equated with the theft of the Golden Fleece), 982–985 *virginitas rapta*.

35 See McIntyre (2008) 215–141, Davis (2014), and Keith (2014) 275: "Valerius flags the setting as an Ovidian topos when he introduces it by comparing the banks of the Phasis to the site of Proserpina's rape in Sicily." Keith highlights that these Ovidian lines are also a meaningful hypotext for Val. Fl. 6.492 *lilia per vernos lucent velut alba colores*, where Medea scaling the town ramparts is compared to a lily. The characterisation of Medea through similes is indeed consistent.

her companions in collecting them, almost in one moment she was seen, adored and ravished by Dis (so hurried was his love).

(Hill)

Valerius in fact shapes his simile by referring verbally to the Ovidian landscape of the rape of Proserpina where the charm of the *locus amoenus*, representing symbolically the beauty of the maiden, is suddenly violated by the intrusion of *eros* (Ov. *Met.* 5.395). Even the mention of Pallas and Diana together seems borrowed from Ovid. Some lines earlier (Ov. *Met.* 5.375–376), the narrator quotes a speech from Venus where Pallas and Diana are referred by the goddess as *virgines* beyond her power and serve to introduce the opposite destiny of Proserpina. Nevertheless once again the model is redesigned: Diana and Pallas become in Valerius the companions of Proserpina (Val. Fl. 5.344–345), about whom he says that no one surpasses her (5.346 *nulla comitum certante*).[36] Assuming that Valerius is combining references to Ovid and at the same time to Homer, Apollonius, and Vergil, the switch from Diana to Proserpina modifies the scope of the simile and may have metapoetic implications. As Ovid's Proserpina outperforms her companions in picking flowers (Ov. *Met.* 5.394), Valerius Flaccus' character is said to outperform Diana (Val. Fl. 5.346), who is the point of comparison in the analogous Homeric, Apollonian and Vergilian scenes.[37] Consequently, the Valerian Medea, shaped partly along, partly beyond the lines established by the tradition for this kind of scenes, is emerging definitely as a character outshining her predecessors. She is thus like the Flavian poet, asserting proudly his *aemulatio* in constructing his proper character.

The analogy between Diana and Medea, however, is recovered some lines later by Valerius, where Jason addresses the maiden for the first time:

'si dea, si magni decus huc ades' inquit 'Olympi,
has ego credo faces, haec virginis ora Dianae,
teque renodatam pharetris ac pace fruentem   380
ad sua Caucaseae producunt flumina nymphae.
si domus in terris atque hinc tibi gentis origo,
felix prole parens olimque beatior ille,
qui tulerit longis et te sibi iunxerit annis.
sed fer opem, regina, viris! nos hospita pubes   385
advehimur, Graium proceres tua tecta petentes.
duc, precor, ad vestri quicumque est ora tyranni

---

[36] Despite Spaltenstein (2004) 478, who prefers to understand *comites* as the nymphs.
[37] The idea of prominence is already in Verg. *Aen.* 1.501 *[Diana] gradiensque deas supereminet omnis*, "and ... she [Diana] treads overtops all the goddesses" (Fairclough/Goold).

```
ac tu prima doce fandi tempusque modumque.
nam mihi sollicito deus ignaroque locorum
te dedit, in te animos atque omnia nostra repono.'                    390
```
(Val. Fl. 5.378–384)

'If thou are a goddess,' he says, 'a glory of great Olympus come to earth, these are the torches, I ween, and this the face of virgin Diana, and thy Nymphs escort thee, at peace and thy quiver-string unloosed, to their Caucasian streams. But if thy home is on earth and thy race hath here its origin, happy thy parents in their offspring, and happier one day he who will bear thee away and join thee to himself in long-enduring union. But, O queen, give succour to heroes. Strangers are we, who have sailed hither, Grecian princes in search of thy house. Lead us, I pray, to the presence of your lord, whoe'er he be, and do thou first instruct us in the time and manner of address. For heaven hath sent thee to me, bewildered as I am and ignorant of this region; to thee I entrust our purpose and our all.'

(Mozley)

In a flattering manner, Jason points out the resemblance between her and Diana, before noticing that, if she is a mortal, her parents should be delighted to have such a child. Then he declares to which nation he belongs and asks Medea for help, by telling her that he does not know where he is. The speech of Jason closely reenacts the archetype of this kind of scene, Hom. *Od.* 6.150–185.[38] Nevertheless in Homer this speech is qualified as crafty (Hom. *Od.* 6.148 μειλίχιον καὶ κερδαλέον φάτο μῦθον, "he made a speech both winning and crafty" (Murray)), whereas Valerius stresses that the meeting actually triggers love at first sight (Val. Fl. 5.375 *in solo stupuit duce* and 5.376–377 *haeret in una / defixus*). The Flavian poet describes this exchange of admiring glances by interweaving three Vergilian passages, two of which are linked only implicitly to erotic themes, Verg. *Aen.* 10.446 ([Pallas] *stupet in Turno*, "stands amazed at Turnus" (Fairclough/Goold)) and Verg. *Aen.* 1.495 (*dum stupet obtutuque haeret defixus in uno*, "while in amazement he hangs rapt in one fixed gaze" (Fairclough/Goold)) where Aeneas is staring at the images on the Carthago's temple when Dido arrives.[39] As for Verg.

---

38 A similar scene is not found in Apollonius Rhodius who imagines the first dialogue between Medea and Jason later in the story when Medea has agreed to help the Greek hero by giving him a drug (Ap. Rhod. *Argon.* 3.975–1145). One is tempted to compare the intertextual attitude of the narrator to that of the character in the Latin *Argonautica*. Whereas the narrator leaves out the traditional comparison between the maiden and Diana, the male character complies entirely with similar Homeric and Vergilian passages. Is this a way to show the various manners of dealing with the literary tradition?
39 The use of the verbs *defixus* and *haeret*, both in Vergil and Valerius, may point to the rejection by the two poets of the traditional intervention of Eros—causing characters to fall in love by piercing them with his arrow, cf. Ap. Rhod. *Argon.* 3.275–298. At the same time, Valerius could have in mind the simile between Dido burning with passion and a wounded deer: Verg. *Aen.*

Aen 1.613 (*obstipuit primo aspectu Sidonia Dido*, "Sidonian Dido was amazed, first at the sight of the hero" (Fairclough/Goold)), it describes the astonishment of the queen at the appearance of Aeneas.[40] Valerius brings also into the picture the Vergilian Aeneas addressing his mother Venus:

> 'nulla tuarum audita mihi neque visa sororum,
> o quam te memorem, virgo? namque haud tibi voltus
> mortalis, nec vox hominem sonat. o, dea certe
> –an Phoebi soror? an nympharum sanguinis una?
> –sis felix, nostrumque leves, quaecumque, laborem,   330
> et, quo sub caelo tandem, quibus orbis in oris
> iactemur, doceas. ignari hominumque locorumque
> erramus, vento huc vastis et fluctibus acti:
> multa tibi ante aras nostra cadet hostia dextra.'

(Verg. *Aen.* 1.326–334)

> 'None of your sisters have I heard or seen—but by what name should I call you, maiden? for your face is not mortal nor has your voice a human ring; O goddess surely! sister of Phoebus, or one of the race of Nymphs? Show grace to us, whoever you may be, and lighten this our burden. Inform us, pray, beneath what sky, on what coasts of the world, we are cast; knowing nothing of countries or peoples we wander driven hither by wind and huge billows. Many a victim shall fall for you at our hand before your altars.'

(Fairclough/Goold)

In our opinion the Vergilian model brings into the hypertext tragic irony and proleptic undertones, which were absent from the Homeric lines.[41] Aeneas, who really has not recognised the maiden as his mother, declares that he will sacrifice victims to her. The Vergilian reader is, thus, immediately invited to consider the erotic connotation of Venus and to have in mind the sacrifice of Dido at the end of *Aeneid* 4.[42] As for Jason, he is pronouncing a *makarismos* towards the future

---

4.69–73 ... *qualis coniecta cerva sagitta, / quam procul incautam nemora inter Cresia fixit / pastor agens telis liquitque volatile ferrum / nescius, illa fuga silvas saltusque peragrat / Dictaeos, haeret lateri letalis harundo,* "even as a hind, smitten by an arrow, which, all unwary, amid the Cretan woods, a shepherd hunting with darts has pierced from afar, leaving in her the winged steel, unknowing: she in flight ranges the Dictaean woods and glades, but fast to her side clings the deadly shaft" (Fairclough/Goold). On the latter see Harrison (1972–1973).
40 On the meaning of *obstipuit* in the Vergilian passage as echoing the sudden cry of Medea in Ap. Rhod. *Argon.* 3.253 (ἀνίαχεν) and, thus, foreshadowing her overwhelming passion see Knox (1984), Nelis (2001) 89.
41 This is also true as regards Verg. *Aen.* 1.613, see n. 40 above.
42 On the recurring representation of Dido as a sacrificial victim, see Spencer (1999) 83–85, Panoussi (2009) 45–56, Galli Milić (2011) 160–161. The whole passage of the appearance of Venus

husband of Medea, unaware that he is referring to himself and, also, that his prophecy is completely misleading.[43] This allows the reader to apply an ironic reading to the whole speech.[44]

Firstly, the traditional similarity with Diana can be extended to the chthonian Hecate (cf. Val. Fl. 5.335 *castis Hecates ... lucis*), one of the facets of this deity, who will be an ally of the tragic Medea.[45] In fact, we can reasonably assume that the proleptic implications of the assimilation between Diana/Hecate/the Moon were already implicit in this passage of Vergil as well as in other lines of the *Aeneid*[46] and, maybe, also in the narrative of Apollonius.[47]

Secondly, we can assume that, via the Vergilian hypotext, Valerius is establishing an analogy between Medea and Venus, a goddess that the Valerian reader has previously met at Lemnos as a frightening double character, a foster parent but above all a Fury:[48]

> quocirca struit illa nefas Lemnoque merenti
> exitium furiale movet. neque enim alma videri

---

disguised as a huntress has to be read in relation to the Dido's tragedy of book 4, Harrison (1972–1973).

43 The tragic irony of this passage is increased by verbal and structural references to the episode of the rape of Hermaphroditus by Salmacis (Ov. *Met.* 4.317–328) as established by Stover (2003) 127–133.

44 The previous speech of the nurse Henioche, too, contains elements to be considered as moments of tragic irony (Val. Fl. 5.359–360): This "aged guardian of the maiden's honour, to whom was entrusted her girlhood's upbringing" reassures the frightened maiden, *non tibi ab hoste minae nec vis ... ulla propinquat / nec metus*, "No enemy's threat, no violence or cause of fear draws nigh thee" (Mozley). This character is completely misunderstanding the situation and therefore brings Medea to ruin. The name Henioche, chosen by Valerius for the nurse, is interesting and may be considered as a further dramatic ironic element, for it is also an *epiklesis* of Juno (see PW VIII.1 258.2 s.v. Henioche), the goddess supporting Jason. In the Valerian *Argonautica*, familiar people surrounding Medea are different in nature from what they are like (as Chalciope/Juno at book 6 and Circe/Venus at book 7).

45 The connection between Medea and Hecate will be discussed by Chiara Battistella in section 3 below.

46 In the Underworld, Dido will appear to Aeneas in the likeness of the Moon, another aspect of Diana (*Aen.* 6.453–454). On the assimilation of Dido/Aeneas with the Moon/the Sun (Apollo) see Hardie (2006) 29–31.

47 See for instance Nelis (1991a) referring to Ap. Rhod. *Argon.* 1.311–316 (the Iphias episode).

48 On the meaning of the Lemnian episode in the Latin *Argonautica* as "oblique visualisation of future tragedy" see Buckley (2013) 81. Cf. also Finkmann (2015) who argues that the "Argonauts' arrival (VF. 2.311–312a ~ VF. 5.325–328) and Jason's first encounter with Medea and her elderly nurse Henioche (VF. 5.325–398) resemble the Argonauts' arrival at Lemnos and Polyxo's instructions for Hypsipyle and the Lemnian women (VF. 2.311–331)."

> tantum: eadem tereti crinem subnectitur auro
> sidereos diffusa sinus, eadem effera et ingens
> et maculis suffecta genas pinumque sonantem   105
> virginibus Stygiis nigramque simillima pallam.
>
> (Val. Fl. 2.101–106)

For this cause she is plotting evil and scheming destruction for guilty Lemnos like some Fury; for she hath not only a gracious aspect when she binds her hair with golden pin, her bright robes falling loose about her; it is the same goddess that, fierce and huge, her cheeks blotched and dark, seems like a Hell-maid with her crackling torch and black mantle.

(Mozley)

2.2 Beautifying the Hero: Beyond the Epic Motif

Let us come back now to the passage coming before the verbal exchange between the protagonists and where the Greek hero is beautified by Juno and compared to the star Sirius:

>   at Iuno, pulchrum longissima quando
> robur cura ducis magnique edere labores,
> mole nova et roseae perfudit luce iuventae.   365
> iam Talaum iamque Ampyciden astroque comantes
> Tyndaridas ipse egregio supereminet ore.
> non secus autumno quam cum magis asperat ignes
> Sirius et saevo cum nox accenditur auro
> luciferas crinita faces, hebet Arcas et ingens   370
> Iuppiter. ast illum tanto non gliscere caelo
> vellet ager, vellent calidis iam fontibus amnes.
>
> (Val. Fl. 5.363–372)

But Juno, since long anxiety and heavy toil had taken from the leader the beauty of his strength, shed over him new might and the sheen of roseate youth. And now in peerless aspect doth he outvie Talaus and Ampycides and the sons of Tyndareus with star-illumined hair; just as when Sirius in autumn sharpens yet more his fires, and his angry gold gleams in the shining tresses of the night, the Arcadian and great Jupiter grow dim; fain are the fields that he would not blaze so fiercely in heaven, fain too the already heated waters of the streams.

(Mozley)

The commentators have already noticed that Valerius is combining here two passages of Apollonius taken from the account of the meeting between Medea and Jason at Hecate's temple (Ap. Rhod. *Argon.* 3.919–923 and 3.956–961) and, at the same time, bringing into the picture Hom. *Od.* 6.232–235 (Ulysses beautified by

Athena) and Hom. *Il.* 22.25–32 (Achilles compared to Sirius).⁴⁹ In general, the scholars agree that these intertexts are all about the leadership of Jason.⁵⁰ Stover (2003) focuses on the rare verb *supereminet* as a verbal echo of Verg. *Aen.* 1.501 (Dido)⁵¹ and Ov. *Met.* 3.182 (Diana, when Actaeon gazes at her) and argues rather in favour of a destabilisation of the heroic paradigm at this moment of the narrative, which introduces uncertainty about how the story will continue, because of Medea's arrival in it.⁵² It is worth asking the same question in relation to Medea: what are the implications of this meeting for her? We would like to tackle this issue by discussing some potential hypotexts for this passage which have previously gone unnoticed, as far as we know.⁵³ Valerius' description of the transformation of Jason echoes some Senecan lines from the first chorus of the *Medea*. Performing a sort of *epithalamion* sung in honour of the new bride and bridegroom, the chorus praises the brilliant beauty of Jason with these words:

> ostro sic niveus puniceo color
> perfusus rubuit, sic nitidum iubar
> pastor luce nova roscidus aspicit.
>
> (Sen. *Med.* 99–101)

> So snowy whiteness blushes, suffused with Punic purple, so dawn's bright rays are viewed by the dewy shepherd.
>
> (Boyle)

Jason has been furthermore said to be superior to the Tyndarides (Sen. *Med.* 88–89 *cedet Castore cum suo / Pollux* "[he will] surpass … Pollux with his Castor"

---

49 On the simile between Jason and Sirius see also Gärtner (1994) 146–153.
50 The researchers are almost unanimous in thinking that the heroic nature of Jason is enhanced in the Latin *Argonautica*, unlike in Apollonius' poem. See Hershkowitz (1998) 105–189 and Castelletti (2014) 173 for a *status quaestionis*.
51 It would be useful, however, to take into account the combination of this allusion with Verg. *Aen.* 4.150 *egregio decus enitet ore*, "beauty shines forth from his noble face" (Fairclough/Goold) (cf. the second half line of Val. Fl. 5.367 *egregio supereminet ore*), quoted by Wijsman (1996) *ad loc.* and referring to Aeneas compared to Apollo.
52 Stover (2003) 130–133.
53 These verbal echoes have been found by using the Tesserae tool (http://tesserae.caset.buffalo.edu), obtaining scores between 7 and 9 (about the criteria on which the scoring system is based see http://tesserae.caset.buffalo.edu/help_results.php).

(Boyle), cf. Val. Fl. 5.366–367). Assuming that Valerius is actually alluding to Seneca,[54] the traditional beautification of the hero performs a different function and can be read as anticipating the betrayal of the male protagonist.

The same applies to subsequent portions of the text. At Val. Fl. 5.370 *luciferas faces* are the stars shining in the dark night. This *iunctura* is already employed by Seneca (and by him solely) to describe the torchlight of Hecate:

> vota tenentur: ter latratus
> audax Hecate dedit et sacros
> edidit ignes face lucifera.

(Sen. *Med.* 840–842)

> My prayers are granted. Three times bold Hecate howled, and shot sacred flames from her shining torch.

(Boyle)

These are the last lines of a long prayer to Hecate/the Moon (Sen. *Med.* 750–842) by which Medea is asking the goddess to assist her in her revenge, in particular about the murder of Glauce, Jason's new bride, with fire.[55] The goddess signals that she has provided a favorable response to this prayer by lighting the torches. At the very moment of the first meeting between the two main characters, Medea's tragic future has already been foreshadowed in the portrait of Jason.[56] The same may be said of the phrase *magis asperat ignes* (Val. Fl. 5.368). Even though fire is indeed a metaphor appropriate to an astronomical context, this phrase takes on further connotations if read through the prism of a two-tier allusion. In

---

54 The influence of Seneca on the Valerian *Argonautica* has been recognised since the 19th century, cf. the bibliography quoted by Buckley (2014) 307–308, n. 3. We entirely agree with Buckley that the intertextual engagement with Seneca's tragedies has to be intended not only to "enrich our understanding of the *Argonautica* as a carefully wrought, highly artificial and mannered poem, but also suggests that Valerius is using a central generic tension between tragedy and epic to articulate the compositional 'fracture' the epic suffers" (Buckley 2014, 308).

55 Sen. *Med.* 833–839 *Adde venenis stimulos, Hecate, / donisque meis semina flammae / condita serva: fallant visus / tactusque ferant, meet in pectus / venasque calor, stillent artus / ossaque fument vincatque suas / flagrante coma nova nupta faces*, "Spur on the poisons, Hecate and keep the seeds of flame concealed inside my gifts. May they cheat the eyes and bear the touch, may heat invade her heart and veins. May the limbs melt and the bones smoke and the new bride's blazing hair surpass her torches" (Boyle). The polysemic *fax* is always ambiguous when referred to the story of Medea and conveys at least three layers of meaning: wedding torch, religious practice and devastating fire.

56 On the intertextual engagement of Apollonius with the Attic tragedy and Euripides' *Medea* in particular see Knight (1991), Schmakeit (2003), Sistakou (2016) 141–167.

Ov. *Met.* 4.64 (*magis* tegitur, tectus *magis aestuat ignis*, "[T]he more they covered up the fire, the more it burned" (Miller)) the phrase denotes the fatal passion between Pyramus and Thisbe, growing because forbidden, and in Sen. *Med.* 889–890 (*alit unda flammas, quoque prohibetur magis, / magis ardet ignis*, "Water feeds the flames. The more the fire's checked, the more it burns" (Boyle)) the messenger tells the chorus that the palace is on fire and that, for some unexplainable reason, the more the water tries to extinguish the flames the more the fire burns. The repeated anaphora of *magis* suggests that Seneca is adapting the Ovidian text, by reshaping the erotic passion into a devastating one, and intertwining a reference to Medea's power over nature. One cannot exclude the possibility that Valerius relies on the ability of the audience to recognise a relationship between the three passages that casts a dark shadow on an essential epic pattern. Bearing in mind that Valerius has anticipated the simile between Jason and Sirius with respect to the chronological order of the story in Apollonius, Jason appears as the catalyst of Medea's criminal activities at the very beginning of their story.

Therefore the Greek hero will have devastating effects on Medea, like Sirius (Val. Fl. 5.369 *saevo auro*), a star belonging to the constellation of the *Canicula* (or *Canis Maior*) and related to the oppressive heat of the summer. The previous texts to which Valerius is alluding are very explicit on this point; the Dog Star has harmful effects on men and animals.[57] At 5.371–372 Valerius mentions fields and rivers as the victims of the Dog Star, with reference to the possible drying up of the rivers. This motif is traditional,[58] but in our opinion it has to be seen in light

---

[57] Hom. *Il.* 22.30–31 λαμπρότατος μὲν ὅ γ' ἐστί, κακὸν δέ τε σῆμα τέτυκται, / καί τε φέρει πολλὸν πυρετὸν δειλοῖσι βροτοῖσιν·, "Brightest of all is he, yet he is a sign of evil, and brings much fever on wretched mortals" (Murray); Ap. Rhod. *Argon.* 3.958–959 ὅς δ'ἤτοι καλὸς μὲν ἀρίζηλός τ'ἐσιδέσθαι / ἀντέλλει, μήλοισι δ'ἐν ἄσπετον ἧκεν ὀιζύν·, "… which rises beautiful and bright to behold, but casts unspeakable grief on the flocks" (Race). Stover (2003) 133–141 put rather an emphasis on the ambiguity of this star, mentioned in some poems in order to enhance the elegiac lifestyle against the martial engagement.

[58] See for instance Verg. *G.* 4.425–428 *iam rapidus torrens sitientes Sirius Indos / ardebat, caelo et medium sol igneus orbem / hauserat; arebant herbae et cava flumina siccis / faucibus ad limum radii tepefacta coquebant*, "And now the Dog Star, fiercely parching the thirsty Indians, was ablaze in heaven, and the fiery Sun had consumed half his course; the grass was withering and the hollow streams, in their parched throats, were scorched and baked by the rays down to the slime" (Fairclough/Goold); *Aen.* 3.141–142 *tum sterilis exurere Sirius agros; / arebant herbae*, "Sirius, too, scorched the fields with drought; the grass withered" (Fairclough/Goold); *Aen.* 10.272–275 (comparing the glittering shield of Aeneas to Sirius) *non secus ac liquida si quando nocte cometae / sanguinei lugubre rubent, aut Sirius ardor / ille sitim morbosque ferens mortalibus aegris / nascitur et laevo contristat lumine caelum*, "even as when in the clear night comets glow blood-

of (a) the Senecan hypotext quoted above, Sen. *Med.* 889–890, where the paradox of water fueling the fire is described (Valerius is describing the reverse natural phenomenon); and (b) the frequent reference to the Phasis in our passage (Val. Fl. 5.332; 5.341; 5.350; 5.397).

According to Valerius, this river plays an important role in the mythical past of Colchis, as we can see by reading the *ekphrasis* of the temple of the Sun which follows our passage (5.407–454). At 5.427, *virgineo turbata metu*, "in maiden distress and panic" (Mozley) is echoing 5.392 (Medea answering Jason) *virgineo cunctata metu*, "hesitating in maiden fear" (Mozley). The maiden frightened and upset is Ea, a nymph who gave her name to the geographical region where Aeëtes lives and who is a sort of double of Medea.[59] As far as we know, Valerius is the only one to mention this nymph.[60] He has imagined that she was raped by the Phasis and in this way he links the rape to the landscape of the story of his female character. Furthermore, this river has been already connotated in the poem as favouring the Argonauts. Jason has invoked his help at 5.205 and received from him a positive reply in the form of an *omen*: in fact, the ship Argo turns its own bow towards the river mouth, thereby confirming that the heros will return home one day.

With this in mind, the reader can fully appreciate the dramatic irony at the end of the passage which we have focused on (5.397–398): *dixerat haec patrium<que> viam detorquet ad amnem / sacraque terrificae supplex movet inrita Nocti*, "So she spoke, and turned her steps toward her native stream, and begins her fruitless sacrifice to terror-bringing Night" (Mozley). At 5.397 Medea finally arrives at her *patrius amnis*, but the narrator has pointed to the futility of the ritual which will follow by means of inter- and intratextuality. Medea is trying to

---

red in baneful wise; or even as fiery Sirius, that bearer of drought and pestilence to feeble mortals, rises and saddens the sky with baleful light" (Fairclough/Goold); Sen. *Oed.* 39–41 *sed ignes auget aestiferi canis / Titan, leonis terga Nemeaei premens. / deseruit amnes humor atque herbas color*, "[B]ut Titan augments the scorching dog-star's fires, close-pressing upon the Nemean Lion's back. Water has fled the streams, and from the herbage verdure" (Miller).

59 *Pace* Spaltenstein (2004) 499.
60 Cf. *PW* I 920.30 s.v. *Aia* [Escher 1893]. From a similar perspective, the choice of Peuce as the island where the wedding between Medea and Jason takes place (Val. Fl. 8.217–219) is meaningful, because Peuce too was a nymph raped by a river, the Hister (Val. Fl. 8.256 *Hister anhelantem Peucen quo presserat antro*, "where ... within her bower Hister had caught the panting Peuce to his breast" (Mozley)). Scott (2012) 76–91 highlights the many correspondences between this scene and the first meeting of Medea and Jason and analyses these images of landscape violation as transformative moments.

purify herself in the water of a river, symbolically dried up, who is himself a mythical rapist and who favours the (future) *raptor* Jason whom Medea is now encountering.

To sum up, Valerius has redesigned the meeting between the male and female figures, which is an essential scene of epic poetry to illustrate that the arrival of Jason in the story of Medea is the pivotal point between the current condition of the maiden and her inescapable metamorphosis. The Flavian poet has conceived these lines as a freeze frame which we have suggested to read as a proleptic space and in the light of some Vergilian, Ovidian and Senecan passages. Freely alluding to similar scenes in previous epic and exploring the multiple narrative perspectives offered by his main character at a generic crossroad between epic and tragedy, Valerius provides the reader with his Medea's portrayal while displaying the challenge of constructing such a complex and literary long-living character. Furthermore, by referring to this multiplicity of models (Nausicaa, Dido, Proserpina, Diana/Hecate, Venus and possibly others),[61] Valerius perhaps suggests that his Medea is, in a sense, an unparalleled figure.[62]

3 The sympathetic Hecate of Book 6

We set out now to discuss another proleptic moment, a monologue by Hecate weeping over Medea's departure in book 6 of Valerius' *Argonautica* (Val. Fl. 6.495–502). This is a notable passage for at least two reasons: the first is the place it occupies within the book, since, as will be argued below, Hecate's lamentation comes as a bit of a surprise within book 6, given that Medea will leave Colchis only in book 8. The second reason concerns Hecate's role in the narrative of this book and, more broadly, in Valerius' poem.

---

[61] We think for instance of Hypsipyle, Helen or Lavinia. The reference to Lavinia would be particularly meaningful and would support Nelis' claim of Valerius' deep sensitivity to the strong relationship between books 1, 4 and 7 of the *Aeneid*, cf. Nelis (2001) 275–280 and Nelis' paper in this volume.

[62] We twist into a metapoetical meaning the idea that Medea is an unparalleled mythic figure. See Stover (2011) 172, who examines "how Medea's radical singularity affects Venus's attempt to offer the Colchian maiden models to follow [*scil*. Circe, Hippodamia, Ariadne] in book 7 of Valerius's *Argonautica*."

Hecate is a complex divinity both in religion and in literature, encompassing a variety of figures and powers because of her multiple identities (Hecate, Artemis, the Moon).[63] However, her main function in connection with the character of Medea in the Argonautic saga in Colchis and in the sequel to the story set in Greece revolves around the practice of magic, especially black magic, for she is first and foremost a chthonian divinity.

Halfway through book 6, we encounter Juno planning to involve Medea in Jason's destiny (6.427–494),[64] so that he may get help from her, whom she knows to be *tremenda* thanks to her magical arts (6.449).[65] Thus, after borrowing Venus's weapons (probably her necklace) and descending from heaven disguised as Medea's sister Chalciope, she takes the girl to the summit of the walls for the *teichoskopia* to make her fatally fall in love with the Greek hero.[66] In the meantime Hecate, reacting helplessly to Juno's scheming plan in her grove, pours tears of pain over her protégée, being aware that Medea will soon relinquish her *lucus* to wander unwillingly (*haud sponte*)[67] to the cities of Greece:

> hanc residens altis Hecate Perseia lucis   495
> flebat et has imo referebat pectore voces:
> 'deseris heu nostrum nemus aequalesque catervas,
> a misera, ut Graias haud sponte vageris ad urbes.
> non invisa tamen neque te, mea cura, relinquam.
> magna fugae monumenta dabis, spernere nec usquam   500
> mendaci captiva viro meque ille magistram
> sentiet et raptu famulae doluisse pudendo.'

(Val. Fl. 6.495–502)

---

[63] For an overview of this figure, see the recent volume by Serafini (2015). Cf. also our n. 73 below.

[64] Cf. Fucecchi (2014) 225.

[65] Note that the term *trEMEnDAm* has the name of Medea in it, for which cf. also Sen. *Med.* 46–47 *tremenda caelo pariter ac terris mala / mens intus agitat*, "my mind urges things ... evil, dreadful to sky and earth" (Boyle).

[66] On the function of *teichoskopia* in relation to women's gaze cf. Fuhrer (2015).

[67] Obviously from Hecate's viewpoint, but cf. also Ap. Rhod. *Argon.* 4.1021–1022 (Medea to the queen Arete): μὴ μὲν ἐγὼν ἐθέλουσα σὺν ἀνδράσιν ἀλλοδαποῖσιν / κεῖθεν ἀφωρμήθην, "[N]ot willingly did I leave that place with foreign men" (Race). Medea calls Hecate's rites to bear witness. By contrast, in Valerius' poem, when Medea's mother disapproves of her flight, she seems to suggest that Medea is willing to flee (Val. Fl. 8.159): *ipsa fugit tantoque (nefas!) ipsa ardet amore*, "She herself willed to flee, and avows (ah, horror!) the passion that consumes her" (Mozley). Valerius' Hecate shows almost maternal affection for Medea, which is somehow new in comparison with Apollonius' corresponding goddess, the Moon (see further). Interestingly, Diodorus Siculus (4.45–46) presents Hecate as Medea's mother.

499 iniussa ω; invisa *Baehrens*; inlusa *Strand*; invita *Liberman*; inrisa *Fucecchi*

> Persean Hecate dwelling in her lofty groves bewailed her, and from the depth of her heart uttered these words: 'Alas! thou dost leave our woodland and thy maidens' bands, unhappy girl, to wander in thy own despite to the cities of the Greeks. Yet not unbidden goest thou, nor, my dear one, will I forsake thee. A signal record of thy flight shalt thou leave behind, nor though a captive shalt thou ever be despised by thy false lord, nay, he shall know me for thy teacher, and that I grieved with shame that he robbed me of my handmaid.'
>
> (Mozley)

These lines may be considered proleptic, in that Hecate's words give us a taste of Medea' future away from Colchis, by referring to her memorable escape (6.500 *magna fugae monumenta dabis*)[68] and her marriage (or rather her captivity) to Jason, the *mendax vir* (6.501).[69] In Hecate's lamentation Medea is depicted as a "war captive" shamefully snatched by Jason: the phrasing *raptu ... pudendo* (6.502), put in Hecate's mouth, evokes another *raptus*, that of Proserpina, whose figure frequently overlaps with Hecate's as a syncretised underworld deity.[70] The goddess also promises that she will not abandon Medea[71] and will save her from being despised (6.500 *spernere nec usquam*) by her lying husband. Hecate sheds negative light upon Jason, who is portrayed as her antagonist and a source of pain (*doluisse*) and who will also become the target of her revenge, as may be assumed

---

68 On *monumenta* cf. Fucecchi (1997) *ad loc.*; Dinter (2009) 556 points out that *monumenta* is a metapoetic self-reference by Valerius to his *Argonautica* with regard to previous literary tradition of the Medea-myth. Absyrtus' murder is certainly a momentous event of Medea's escape, but *magna monumenta* might also contain an ominous allusion to the infanticide (Zissos 2012, 107). Buckley (2016) 79 sees epic rather than tragic undertones in the expression. It is also worth noting that Apollonius in Book 4, thus during the Argonauts' *nostos*, which corresponds to Medea's flight from Colchis, mentions the building of a sanctuary in Paphlagonia in honour of Hecate (246–252).
69 On *captiva* cf. Baier (2001) 220. We find it tempting to identify the *magnae Perseidos* of Val. Fl. 7.238 with Hecate, despite Stover (2009), who prefers the identification with Circe. Medea is talking to Venus disguised as her aunt Circe and promises her that she will not be forgetful of great Perseis and will avoid an unsuitable marriage to a Colchian or barbarian, as Circe herself did, for she left Colchis and married Picus in Ausonia (7.238–239): *non ita me immemorem magnae Perseidos ... / cernis ut infelix thalamos ego cogar in illos*, "Not so forgetful of great Perseis dost thou see me as to be driven, a hapless victim, into such wedlock" (Mozley). There is a double ironic point here, since she will become *infelix* because of a non-barbarian marriage and will also prove *immemor* of Hecate, the great daughter of Perses, whose *lucus* she will abandon to follow the Greek hero.
70 Cf. discussion above.
71 We accept Baehrens' correction *invisa* to be construed as *non invisa mihi eris*: "I will not hate you or abandon you, although you went away."

from the ominously hostile tone of her prophecy: *meque ille magistram / sentiet* (6.501–502). Hecate's words will prove effective in Corinth, that is in the tragic sequel to the story, so that their proleptic value lets a different generic voice enter the epic narrative at this point.

The main commentators to book 6 have already duly signalled two major models Valerius Flaccus had certainly in mind for the Hecate scene, Apollonius and Vergil.[72] Apollonius has the Moon[73] utter her monologue in the last book of the poem, when Medea is about to leave Colchis for good:

> τὴν δὲ νέον Τιτηνὶς ἀνερχομένη περάτηθεν
> φοιταλέην ἐσιδοῦσα θεὰ ἐπεχήρατο Μήνη   55
> ἁρπαλέως, καὶ τοῖα μετὰ φρεσὶν ᾗσιν ἔειπεν·
> 'οὐκ ἄρ' ἐγὼ μούνη μετὰ Λάτμιον ἄντρον ἀλύσκω,
> οὐδ' οἴη καλῷ περιδαίομαι Ἐνδυμίωνι·
> ἦ θαμὰ δὴ καὶ σεῖο κλύον[74] δολίῃσιν ἀοιδαῖς,
> μνησαμένη φιλότητος, ἵνα σκοτίῃ ἐνὶ νυκτὶ   60
> φαρμάσσῃς εὔκηλος, ἅ τοι φίλα ἔργα τέτυκται.
> νῦν δὲ καὶ αὐτὴ δῆθεν ὁμοίης ἔμμορες ἄτης·
> δῶκε δ' ἀνιηρόν τοι Ἰήσονα πῆμα γενέσθαι
> δαίμων ἀλγινόεις. ἀλλ' ἔρχεο, τέτλαθι δ' ἔμπης,
> καὶ πινυτή περ ἐοῦσα, πολύστονον ἄλγος ἀείρειν.'   65
>
> (Ap. Rhod. *Argon.* 4.54–65)

> And when the Titanian goddess, the Moon, newly rising above the horizon, saw her wandering in distress, she exulted gleefully over her and spoke these thoughts to herself: 'So I am not the only one, after all, to flee to the Latmian cave, nor alone in burning for handsome Endymion. How often indeed I, mindful of love, listened to your crafty incantations, so that in the dark of night you could calmly work the spells that are dear to you. But now it appears that you too have been allotted a similar obsession, for a cruel god has given you Jason as a grievous affliction. Go on, and in spite of your cleverness bring yourself to endure pain full of tears.'
>
> (Race, slightly modified)

The Moon's monologue too has a proleptic function, despite the different tone of her words, full of *Schadenfreude* rather than compassionate pity for Medea and hate for Jason as in Valerius. In Apollonius the goddess revels in the thought of Medea who will endure suffering because of Jason and certainly alludes to the events that will occur in Corinth (Ap. Rhod. *Argon.* 4.63–65). Also, the place the

---

72 Fucecchi (1997), Baier (2010), Wijsman (2000), and Spaltenstein (2005), *ad loc.*
73 The Moon is one of three facets of the goddess: Selene in the heavens/Artemis on earth/Hecate in the underworld. Cf. Brunel (1996) 130–131.
74 We print Fantuzzi's conjecture, for which see Fantuzzi (2007) 91–93.

Moon's monologue occupies in Apollonius' poem apparently makes more sense than Hecate's equivalent lament in Valerius: in Apollonius one final undertaking, the capture of the Golden Fleece, awaits Medea, who will then immediately flee from Colchis with the Argonauts. By contrast, Hecate's monologue in the Valerian epic comes much earlier within the narrative, even before Medea's resolve to help Jason, showing Valerius' flexibility in handling the order of events of the Greek model.

Valerius portrays Hecate as a character sympathetic to Medea, which the Moon in Apollonius is not, as proved by her cruel joy in seeing Medea wandering in distress (Ap. Rhod. *Argon.* 4.55–56). Therefore, another text has to be brought into picture as a model for Hecate's thoughtful attitude towards her acolyte, Vergil's *Aeneid*:

> at Triviae custos iamdudum in montibus Opis
> alta sedet summis spectatque interrita pugnas.
> utque procul medio iuvenum in clamore furentum
> prospexit tristi mulcatam morte Camillam,
> ingemuitque deditque has imo pectore voces: 840
> 'heu nimium, virgo, nimium crudele luisti
> supplicium Teucros conata lacessere bello!
> nec tibi desertae in dumis coluisse Dianam
> profuit aut nostras umero gessisse pharetras.
> non tamen indecorem tua te regina reliquit   845
> extrema iam in morte, neque hoc sine nomine letum
> per gentis erit aut famam patieris inultae.
> nam quicumque tuum violavit vulnere corpus
> morte luet merita.'

(Verg. *Aen.* 11.836–849)

'Fair Opis, keeping guard for Trivia in patient sentry on a lofty hill, beheld unterrified the conflict's rage. Yet when, amid the frenzied shouts of soldiery, she saw from far Camilla pay the doom of piteous death, with deep-drawn voice of sight she thus complained: 'O virgin, woe is me! too much, too much, this agony of thine, to expiate that thou didst lift thy spear for wounding Troy. It was no shield in war, nor any vantage to have kept thy vow to chaste Diana in the thorny wild. Our maiden arrows at thy shoulder slung availed thee not! Yet will our Queen divine not leave unhonored this thy dying day, nor shall thy people let thy death remain a thing forgot, nor thy bright name appear a glory unavenged. Whoe'er he be that marred thy body with the mortal wound shall die as he deserves.'

(Williams)

The lines revolve around the episode of Camilla's death, Diana's protégée, whom Opis, Diana's agent, sent to avenge her, pities and mourns. She weeps over Camilla (*ingemuit*), as Hecate does in Valerius over Medea (*flebat*), but also promises to exact immediate revenge by killing Arruns, the man responsible for the girl's death, on the battlefield,[75] unlike Hecate, who only obscurely foretells Jason's future punishment. Despite being overall situationally different, the two episodes have a few lexical elements in common: apart from the goddesses' shedding tears[76] (Val. Fl. 6.496 and Verg. *Aen.* 11.840), both Diana and Hecate ensure that they will not abandon their protégées (*non invisa tamen neque te ... relinquam* of Val. Fl. 6.499 recalls Verg. *Aen.* 11.845 *non tamen indecorum tua te regina reliquit*). Also, both Hecate and Opis are depicted as sitting in their respective places (*hanc residens altis Hecate Perseia lucis* of Val. Fl. 6.495 evokes Verg. *Aen.* 11.837 [*in montibus*] *alta sedens summis spectatque interrita pugnas*),[77] further pointing to lexical commonalities between the passages.

Although Vergil's passage does not have proleptic content,[78] it represents, however, the exemplary model on which Valerius likely drew Hecate's sympathetic portrait characterised by strong affection for Medea.

As already said, Hecate and Medea are strongly connected in the literary tradition, in which they end up becoming almost inseparable in the practice of black magic and infernal rites.[79] In Apollonius' *Argonautica* Medea is presented as Hecate's priestess:

> πρὶν δ' οὔτι θάμιζεν
> ἐν μεγάροις, Ἑκάτης δὲ πανήμερος ἀμφεπονεῖτο
> νηόν, ἐπεί ῥα θεᾶς αὐτὴ πέλεν ἀρήτειρα
>
> (Ap. Rhod. *Argon.* 3.250–252)

[B]efore that she was not often in the palace, but spent all day tending's temple, since she herself was the priestess of the goddess.

(Race)

---

[75] Vergil establishes parallels between the figures of Camilla and Turnus and those of Arruns and Aeneas. The passage of Book 11 (785–867) on Arruns' early death seems to hint at a similar destiny for Aeneas too: on this cf. Kepple (1976) (we thank Robert Cowan for pointing out this article to us). Arruns' death might be considered somehow proleptic in this respect.

[76] In Vergil Opis' and Diana's intervention looks like a sort of joint-action. It may be noticed that *Diana Trivia* is assimilated in the Greek world to Hecate.

[77] The following link may be usefully consulted: http://tesserae.caset.buffalo.edu/cgi-bin/read_bin.pl?session=0000345b.

[78] But cf. our n. 75 above.

[79] Cf. Boyle (2014) 107. As will be shown further on, Medea usually invokes Hecate before getting ready for action. Cf. for example Ov. *Met.* 7.177–178, in which Medea is about to rejuvenate Jason's father, but first she prays to Hecate to secure her help: *modo diva triformis / adiuvet et praesens ingentibus adnuat ausis*, "if only the three-formed goddess will help me and grant her present aid in this great deed which I dare attempt" (Miller).

Jason, for his part, learns about Medea from his companion Argo, who describes her as (Ap. Rhod. *Argon*. 3.478) κούρην δή τινα ... / φαρμάσσειν Ἑκάτης Περσηίδος ἐννεσίῃσιν, "a certain girl who concocts drugs with the guidance of Hecate, daughter of Perses" (Race). A few hundred lines later, Argo, who is also the son of Medea's sister Chalciope, speaks again about Medea, addressing his fellows:

κούρη τις μεγάροισιν ἐνιτρέφετ' Αἰήταο
τὴν Ἑκάτη περίαλλα θεὰ δάε[80] τεχνήσασθαι
φάρμαχ', ὅσ' ἤπειρός τε φύει καὶ νήχυτον ὕδωρ.

(Ap. Rhod. *Argon*. 3.528–530)

There is a certain girl being raised in Aeetes' palace, whom the goddess Hecate has taught to employ with exceeding skill all the drugs that the land and full-flowing waters produce.

(Race)

"A certain girl" rings obviously ironic, even though it is unwitting irony on Argo's part, if one considers the extraordinary role Medea will have in the remainder of the poem. In Apollonius' epic Hecate does not utter a word; however, she is admittedly not upset about Medea's decision to help Jason capture the Golden Fleece. In this respect, it is significant that Jason himself sacrifices and performs his prayer to Hecate later on in book 3 before fighting with the fire-breathing bulls and the earthborn men, as recommended by Medea (3.1030–1036), to render Hecate propitious. Thus, Jason, after sacrificing a sheep, calls on Hecate Brimo, "the roarer," to ask for her help in the imminent contest (Ap. Rhod. *Argon*. 3.1211): Βριμὼ κικλήσκων Ἑκάτην ἐπαρωγὸν ἀέθλων, "as he invoked Hecate Brimo to be a helper in the contests" (Race). The goddess comes forth to accept Jason's offering and the barking of her dogs is heard, which is a standard marker of her favourable response.[81] In the Greek poem, Hecate gives her full consent to Jason's mission without manifesting any signs of disapproval or resentment. Overall, her presence in the poem appears to be, so to speak, non-problematic.

Valerius' passage in book 6 returns us a completely different picture of Hecate's relation to Jason. Her complaining monologue features sadness for Medea's departure and hostility towards the *mendax vir*, even before her protégée is persuaded to grant him her help, of which Hecate clearly does not approve. Valerius turns her into a lesser goddess, somewhat diminished in power, who will make no attempt to oppose the plot of Juno and Venus or interfere with their plans

---

[80] Hecate calls herself *magistra* in Val. Fl. 6.501 quoted above.
[81] The epithet "roarer" refers to her noisy appearances.

meant to encourage Medea to fall in love with and protect Jason, as shown by lines 182–185 of book 7. Venus talks confidently to Juno and reassures her that, once Jason and Medea will meet at Diana's temple, everything will turn out well and Medea will finally capitulate. Juno need not be afraid of Hecate:

> nec te nunc Hecates subeat metus aut mea forte
> impediat ne coepta time. quin audeat opto:
> continuo transibit amor cantuque trilingui
> ipsam flammiferos cogam compescere tauros.[82]

(Val. Fl. 7.182–185)

> Nor let dread of Hecate now come over thee; fear not lest she hinder my efforts. Nay, let her even venture: straightway will the passion pass to her, and I will compel her herself to subdue with triple chant the fire-breathing bulls.

(Mozley)

If we go back now to the Hecate-scene in book 6, from which we started, it may be useful to consider briefly its immediate context too:

> ducitur infelix ad moenia summa futuri   490
> nescia virgo mali et falsae commissa sorori,
> lilia per vernos lucent velut alba colores
> praecipue, quis vita brevis totusque parumper
> floret honor, fuscis et iam Notus imminet alis.
> hanc residens altis Hecate Perseia lucis   495
> flebat et has imo referebat pectore voces:
> 'deseris heu nostrum nemus aequalesque catervas,
> a misera, ut Graias haud sponte vageris ad urbes.
> non invisa tamen neque te, mea cura, relinquam.
> magna fugae monumenta dabis, spernere nec usquam   500
> mendaci captiva viro meque ille magistram
> sentiet et raptu famulae doluisse pudendo.'
> dixerat. ast illae murorum extrema capessunt
> defixaeque virum lituumque fragoribus horrent,
> quales instanti nimborum frigore[83] maestae   505
> succedunt ramis haerent<que> pavore volucres.

(Val. Fl. 6.490–506)

---

82 On this passage cf. also Zissos (2012) 117, n. 56.
83 For this reading cf. Fucecchi (1997) 137; cf. also Augoustakis (2013) 160, n. 10 who prefers the reading *fulgore*, "the flash of storm-clouds."

Ignorant of future ill, surrendering herself to her feigned sister, the hapless maid is led to the summit of the walls: even as white lilies gleam conspicuous through the hues of springtime, lilies whose life is short and their glory reigns but for a while and already the dark pinions of the South wind hover near. Persean Hecate dwelling in her lofty groves bewailed her, and from the depth of her heart uttered these words: 'Alas! thou dost leave our woodland and thy maidens' bands, unhappy girl, to wander in thy own despite to the cities of the Greeks. Yet not unbidden goest thou, nor, my dear one, will I forsake thee. A signal record of thy flight shalt thou leave behind, nor though a captive shalt thou ever be despised by thy false lord, nay, he shall know me for thy teacher, and that I grieved with shame that he robbed me of my handmaid.' She spoke; but they gaining the extremity of the walls listen motionless and in fear to the cries of men and the trumpet's blaring; even as birds dismayed at the oncoming chill of the storm-clouds flock to the branches and cling to them in terror.

(Mozley)

Hecate's monologue is framed by two similes,[84] which both contribute to bestowing an ominous prophetic overtone upon Hecate's words. The comparison of *infelix* Medea with the white lilies threatened (*imminet*) by dark-winged Notus (6.492–494) clearly conjures up images of violence intrinsically linked to the lily's symbolism, often associated with rape, as in Proserpina's episode in Ov. *Met.* 5.391–392.[85] Interestingly, Medea herself will turn from a vulnerable character into a sort of menacing Notus in the sequel to the story, the one set in Corinth, as is well known, especially from Seneca's text. In the epilogue to that tragedy, after killing the first of her two children, Medea appears on top of the house with Jason pointing his finger at her (Sen. *Med.* 995): *en ipsa tecti parte praecipiti imminet*, "[T]here she is poised on the edge of the roof" (Boyle). The verb, which conveys a threatening nuance, is attested in this form only once in Seneca's *Medea* and, notably, just twice in Valerius' poem. Aside from Val. Fl. 6.494, where it is referred to the wind Notus, the other occurrence is shortly afterward, where it is applied to Medea herself, whom Juno's *fraus*, dismantling the girl's *extremus pudor* (6.674), has made bolder (6.681): *imminet e celsis audentius improba muris* [*virgo*], "[M]ore boldly now leans the reckless girl from the high walls" (Mozley). She leans forward from the high walls, but the verb also means "to rise". In our view, this is a suggestive prelude to the towering role she will have in the tragic sequel to the story and in this regard may be, therefore, considered proleptic.

The second simile compares Medea and the false Chalciope, who shudder motionless struck by the cries of men and trumpets on the battlefield, with birds that cling to the branches afraid of the oncoming storm. This simile too, which,

---

84 The standard reference is Gärtner (1994), in particular 156–161.
85 On the lily's symbolism and sexual violation cf. Davis (2014) 209–210; also our n. 35 above.

like the previous, has quasi-narrative status and aims at bringing forward the fragility of Medea's character so far, seems to have a predictive function.[86] Fear is a recurrent element in the whole of the Medea narrative both in Colchis and in Greece, but it receives absolute priority in Seneca's play, in which Medea herself instils this feeling in all characters around her. *Metus* is a key word in the Senecan text to refer to the protagonist as a source of fear (cf. for example Sen. *Med.* 185; 270; 516; 872). In Sen. *Med.* 670, in particular, the Nurse appears on stage visibly overwhelmed by fear (*pavet animus, horret*, "my soul quivers with fear" (Boyle)), being well aware that her mistress is up to something hideous and *maius* (Sen. *Med.* 674). The Nurse's fear also develops that of the preceding Chorus, as Boyle points out.[87] Some lines later, at Sen. *Med.* 738, she observes that Medea's words are not less *metuenda* than her magic philtres. Medea will thus go, in the timeline of her story, from undergoing fear to inflicting it in memorable ways.

Both similes, together with Hecate's monologue, therefore contribute to foreshadowing the tragic potential of the story, allusively toying with the well-known notion of "future past" in literary chronology, with which the reader of Silver Latin poetry is certainly familiar (cf. below).

3.1 Foreshadowing Seneca's Hecate

It is now time to bring in another text, which has in fact already cropped up above and may help further clarify to what extent Hecate's monologue in Valerius' book 6 has proleptic content.

Seneca's *Medea* has an extraordinary passage (Sen. *Med.* 740–848) that effectively showcases how close Medea and Hecate are. In her last monologue, the protagonist describes in detail the preparation of the magical potion she will administer to Creusa through the robe. It is indeed one of the dramatic high-spots of the tragedy, in Boyle's words "a black mass, an incantation scene unique in extant Greek and Roman tragedy",[88] in which Hecate is invoked by Medea, acting as her priestess, and conjured up under her many identities (Phoebe, Trivia, Dictynna, Perseis).[89] The goddess is key to the protagonist's revenge plan, for Medea needs her assent to achieve her goals. Strikingly, Euripides has no equivalent

---

[86] Fucecchi (1997) 137 spots a Vergilian intertext here, that of Orpheus's song stirring the *umbrae* of the underworld in Verg. *G.* 4.471–474.
[87] Boyle (2014), *ad loc.* See also Battistella (2018).
[88] Boyle (2014), cxi.
[89] Medea also begins her prayer asking Hecate to approach *pessimos induta vultus, fronte non una minax* (Sen. *Med.* 751), "display doom and menace in every face" (Boyle).

scene, aside from an invocation to the goddess at Eur. *Med.* 395–400, in which Hecate is called upon by Medea as her mistress and helper (συνεργός), that is as an ally against Jason and his new bride. Such an invocation is a prelude to the poison-plan, which however does not result in a proper incantation scene as in Seneca's rewriting[90] (in fact, there seems to be an oversight on Euripides' part in his play, since Medea announces her intention to smear the gifts for the princess at 789, but will not leave the scene until the infanticide).

Earlier on, it has become immediately clear to Seneca's Medea, after an exchange between her and Jason, how to hit him at his weak point, that is their children (Sen. *Med.* 549–550). She thus delivers a short *Trugrede* making Jason believe she will not hurt anybody and, once he leaves, gets ready for revenge. The invocation to Hecate, whom Medea addresses in the presence of the Nurse, is the first step to sanction her murderous plan (Sen. *Med.* 577–578): *vocetur Hecate. sacra letifica appara: / statuantur arae, flamma iam tectis sonnet*, "Hecate must be invoked. Prepare death rites. Build an altar. Let the house now scream with fire" (Boyle).

At the beginning of the fourth act we find a terrified Nurse alone on stage (Sen. *Med.* 670–739, cf. also above) describing the preparation of Medea's magic rites, until Medea herself is brought into view intent to perform her black mass (Sen. *Med.* 740–840). The whole scene takes place before Hecate, whom Medea invokes and whose presence she attests until the final summons aimed at poisoning the gift for Creusa. Hecate listens to Medea's prayer and grants her favour (Sen. *Med.* 843–848). This is an extraordinary passage, whose length and complex internal articulation points to the prominent role attributed to Hecate in that scene.[91]

Although Medea at the onset of her prayer summons various entities, Hecate is given absolute priority. The frequency of second-person pronouns (see Sen. *Med.* 752; 771; 773; 797; 800; 801–802; 804; 806; 817), adjectives and imperatives related to the goddess brings to the fore a very special relationship between her and her protégée (see for example Sen. *Med.* 785–786 *sonuistis, arae, tripodas agnosco meos / favente commotos dea*, "[Y]ou roared, altar! My cauldrons tremble. I recognize the god's assent" (Boyle)). For Hecate Medea performs the sacred rites

---

[90] We know nothing about Ovid's *Medea*. However, given the relevance magic has in the Medea-episode in Ov. *Met.* 7.1–424 (on which cf. Williams 2012), an incantation scene is likely to have been present also in Ovid's lost tragedy. The theme of Medea's sorcery is especially emphasized by Apollonius and Ovid.
[91] In general, on the hymn's structure and its innovations cf. La Bua (1999) 314–316.

on bloody turf, for her she rips her clothing, exposing her breast, for her she gruesomely slashes her arms letting her blood drip on the altar (Sen. *Med.* 797–810; cf. the hammering iteration of *tibi*). Medea also strikingly apologises to the goddess for invoking her so often:

> quodsi nimium saepe vocari
> quereris votis, ignosce, precor.
> causa vocandi, Persei, tuos
> saepius arcus una atque eadem est   815
> semper Iason.
>
> (Sen. *Med.* 812–816)

> If thou dost protest I pray to thee too often, please forgive me. The reason, Perseis, for invoking thine arc so much, is one and the same always: Jason.
>
> (Boyle)

During the magic spell, the altars make a sound (Sen. *Med.* 785 *sonuistis arae*), but the true novelty of this incantation scene is that Hecate in person is heard barking in positive reaction to Medea's requests and not, as usual, her dogs (Sen. *Med.* 840–841 *ter latratus / audax Hecate dedit*, "[T]hree times bold Hecate howled" (Boyle)).[92] Notwithstanding that she does not articulate a proper speech or monologue as in Valerius, she manifests her assent in non-verbal, yet powerful ways. Medea needs Hecate's help to take successful revenge on Jason, the *causa vocandi*, which is also *una atque eadem ... semper* (Sen. *Med.* 814–816). Even before learning this from Medea's mouth, Hecate already gives her first assent at Sen. *Med.* 786 (*favente ... dea*). The phrase *causa vocandi* hints at quasi-legal argumentation, but it may also gesture towards elegiac language: *causa* is a sort of keyword of Roman elegy to point to the beloved as the cause of someone's pain or death.[93] Hecate's behaviour in Seneca is suggestive of her care towards Medea, which Valerius, in his epic narrative, turns into verbal tenderness in the goddess' monologue (Val. Fl. 6.495–502), the prequel to the story, almost transforming Hecate into a nurse figure of tragedy.[94] As we have already seen, in Apollonius' *Argonautica* Hecate is willing to help both Medea and Jason. By contrast, Hecate's monologue in Valerius conjures up a completely different scenario. She will not dare interfere with Juno's and Venus' plans so as to prevent Medea from falling in love with Jason, but she does not hide her hostility towards the Greek hero

---

[92] This is an *unicum*, cf. Boyle (2014) 335. On this cf. also Secci (2000) 252–253.
[93] There are, for example, 13 occurrences of *causa mortis* only in Ovid's *Heroides*. On this cf. e.g. Battistella (2010) 105.
[94] Cf. Corrigan (2013) 209.

either, while promising to stay faithful to Medea. Hecate's "glimpse" into Medea's future seems to imply that, despite being deprived of her authority in Colchis, she will fully regain it in that part of the story yet to come. In this regard, the goddess' hatred for Jason is in line with the idea expressed by the Chorus in Seneca's play that the Argonautic expedition is nothing but a source of destruction and corruption (Sen. *Med.* 301–363; 603–669), even though Hecate sees Medea as a victim[95] and the Senecan Chorus sees her as a *malum* brought about by that baleful expedition (Sen. *Med.* 362 *maiusque mari Medea malum*, "Medea, more monstrous than the sea" (Boyle)).

Hecate's prophetic words will prove true in Corinth. Jason will behave as a *mendax vir* (Val Fl. 6.501) and will do injustice to Medea, who, however, will rebel against him. Consequently, Hecate's promise will also come true, in that she will then take care of her protégée by not letting her be despised and making Jason know her for Medea's teacher (6.500–502). Medea will in fact be rid of her rival by means of black magic, therefore acting as Hecate's pupil. Both Medea and Hecate are portrayed by Valerius as powerless and passive characters controlled by aggressive forces like Juno and Venus.[96] Seneca's text stages, on the contrary, a Medea in full control of her actions, as much as Hecate thrives in her role as helping goddess on Medea's side.

If we look at the way literary chronology works, being based, as it is, on the idea that characters can have a future that has already been written down somewhere else,[97] Valerius' Hecate is endowed with foreknowledge obviously not only because she is a goddess,[98] but also since she has already come to the aid of Medea in previous texts (Euripides, Ovid,[99] and especially Seneca). Therefore, once in Valerius' poem Juno's plan starts to take shape, as she drags Medea to the ramparts of the city disguised as Chalciope, Hecate cannot but give in to the divine

---

95 On the role of Medea as a victim of powerful, even oppressive, supernatural forces in Valerius' poem cf. Zissos (2012), in part. 106–107.
96 On this cf. especially Zissos (2012) 105: "Valerius leaves the reader with little doubt that, left to her own devices, Medea would not have forsaken father and fatherland to Jason."
97 For the notion of "future reflexive" Barchiesi (1993) remains the standard reference.
98 Hecate in Valerius is presented as omniscient; it is striking that Juno, by contrast, is described as *adhuc ignara futuri* ("ignorant yet of what will befall") in 7.192, on which cf. Perutelli (1997) 262: "Risulta anomalo [...] l'atteggiamento di Giunone [...] per le sue troppo umane incertezza e ansia nei confronti del futuro." This serves the purpose of producing a pathetic effect. The role Juno and Venus have in the poem, especially their prolonged masquerades, lets them affect decisive changes in their victim Medea. Apollonius, on the other hand, grants much more independent roles to his human characters (cf. Bernstein 2008, 55).
99 At least Ov. *Met.* 7.1–424; cf. also our n. 90 above.

machinery of superior deities and wait for another literary space to come, in which she will eventually be able to support her protégée. In fact, such a literary space already exists and is represented, in our view, specifically by Seneca's play, where Medea and Hecate end up having no rivals.

We suggest, therefore, that Seneca's incantation scene, strongly focused, as it is, on the manifestation of Hecate's power, may be taken as the textual backdrop against which Hecate's lamentation in Valerius has to be construed. As Buckley has shown,[100] pieces of tragic extra-narrative are copiously scattered across the poem, amongst which Seneca's tragedy especially stands out as a generic undercurrent alternative to epic. Both Medea's character and her story certainly lend themselves well to intergeneric and intertextual games in texts, given the status of "intertextual heroine" at home in different genres that has been rightly bestowed on her.[101] Valerius' poem hints, through Hecate's monologue, at Medea's future reflected in the mirror of one model in particular, which the reader is invited to select and recollect. In doing so, the poet, carving out his own niche in a well-established literary tradition, injects new life into Hecate's character, who is presented for the first time in the Medea-myth as deeply attached to her protégée. Even though she cannot interfere with future events, which are already predetermined (and, of course, written down elsewhere), she is at least allowed to express herself in an unprecedented manner, *hic et nunc*, in the present time of Valerius' epic. The goddess' manifestation of affection paves the way to the unconditioned favour guaranteed by her to Medea in Corinth, that is in Seneca's play; in other words, her lamentation is a prelude to an act of revenge that, as a matter of fact, has already been accomplished in Seneca's play. Acknowledging the textual contact we have tried to delineate above between Hecate's monologue in Valerius' book 6 and Medea's incantation scene in Seneca may, thus, help us clarify the proleptic significance of the goddess' words: they let us see tragedy behind epic, while positing it as a disturbing generic undercurrent that crops up in Valerius' narrative with ominous potential.

---

100 Cf. Buckley (2014); cf. also Grewe (1998). For tragic (Euripidean) foreshadowing in Apollonius' poem cf. Knight (1991), Hurst (2012).
101 Cf. Hinds (1993); cf. also Bessone (1998); Stover (2003); Boyle (2012); Walsh (2012).

4 Conclusion

As we hope to have made clear, the passages discussed above aim to show how the combination of intertextual and proleptic moments let further generic voices enter Valerius' epic, giving it a new flavour and a more dynamic narrative texture. As well as shaping characters who are massively intertextual (multi-layered intertextuality is certainly key to his poetry, as it is to Flavian poetry in general), he also resorts to the device of prolepsis by toying with the timeline of the Argonautic saga as recounted in his models, especially Apollonius Rhodius' poem, but also with the timeline of the Dido story. Moreover, he appears to be particularly interested in hinting at those passages, in his models, already having a proleptic tone, as shown above with Vergil's *Aeneid*. By means of anticipation, Valerius comes to bestow upon his characters a multifaceted generic profile, which, far from deriving exclusively from the Argonautic epic, gestures towards several other source-texts, such as Homer's *Odyssey* and *Iliad*, Vergil's *Aeneid*, Ovid's *Metamorphoses*, Seneca's tragedy *Medea*. Medea, in particular, owing to her repeated and recurring presence in the literary tradition and to her well-established status as an intertextual heroine, lends herself well to representing the perfect character for Valerius, a poet literally obsessed with secondariness, to experiment new ways of portraying her with a view to challenging the tradition. However, we have seen that also the characterisation of Jason and Hecate in the passages examined above becomes more meaningful in light of the proleptic moments we have tried to single out. Both the comparison of Jason with Sirius and Hecate's sympathetic monologue in a surprisingly early section of the poem subtly and allusively disrupt the traditional chronological order of the narrative, inviting readers to play with their knowledge of the Argonautic saga in Greek and Latin texts, so as to recall how Jason and Hecate will "truly" act in the sequel to the story. We all know that the epilogue belongs to a different genre, tragedy, especially Seneca's tragedy *Medea*, in which Jason receives terrible punishment for having abandoned Medea, while Hecate appears to be again in full control of her chthonian powers. Proleptic elements in the narrative can destabilise the main epic plot and set in motion narrative undercurrents that allow the reader to see into the future lives of Valerius' characters and think in advance of the impending catastrophe that will put an end to Medea' and Jason's story.

Bibliography

Augoustakis, Antony (2013), "Teichoskopia and Katabasis. The Poetics of Spectatorship in Flavian Epic", in: Heerink/Manuwald (2014) 157–176.
Baier, Thomas (2001), *Valerius Flaccus*, Argonautica. *Buch VI*, München.
Bal, Mieke (1997), *Narratology. Introduction to the Theory of Narrative*, 2nd ed., Toronto/Buffalo/London.
Barchiesi, Alessandro (1993), "Future Reflexive: Two Modes of Allusion and Ovid's *Heroides*", in: *HSCP* 95, 333–65.
Barchiesi, Alessandro (1995), "Figure dell'intertestualità nell'epica romana", in: *Lexis* 13, 49–67 (now available in English translation in: Alessandro Barchiesi, *Speaking Volumes. Narrative and Intertext in Ovid and other Latin Poets*, London, 2001, 129–140).
Battistella, Chiara (2010), *P. Ovidii Nasonis Heroidum Epistula 10: Ariadne Theseo*, Berlin/New York.
Battistella, Chiara (2018), "*Pavet animus, horret*: la paura nella *Medea* di Seneca", in: De Poli (2018) 357–380.
Bernstein, Neil W. (2008), *In the Image of the Ancestors. Narratives of Kingship in Flavian Epic*, Toronto/Buffalo/London.
Bessone, Federica (1991), "Valerius, Apollonios und die Gleichnisse: Umformung der Vorlage und Kompositionstechnik", in: Korn/Tschiedel (1991) 73–87.
Bessone, Federica (1998), "Valerius Flaccus und die Medeen des Ovid", in: Eigler *et al.* (1998) 141–171.
Boyle, Anthony J. (1990), *The Imperial Muse. Ramus Essays on Roman Literature of the Empire: Flavian Epicist to Claudian*, Bendigo, Victoria.
Boyle, Anthony J. (2012), "Introduction: Medea in Greece and Rome", in: *Ramus* 41.1–2, 1–32.
Boyle, Anthony J. (2014), *Seneca*, Medea, Oxford.
Brunel, Pierre (ed.) (1996), *Companion to Literary Myths, Heroes and Archetypes*, London/New York.
Buckley, Emma (2013), "Visualizing Venus: epiphany and *anagnorisis* in Valerius Flaccus' *Argonautica*", in: Lovatt/Vout (2013) 78–98.
Buckley, Emma (2014), "Valerius Flaccus and Seneca's tragedies", in: Heerink/Manuwald (2014) 307–325.
Buckley, Emma (2016), "Over Her Live Body: Marriage in Valerius Flaccus' *Argonautica*", in: Manioti (2016) 61–88.
Castelletti, Cristiano (2014), "A Hero with a Sandal and a Buskin: The Figure of Jason in Valerius Flaccus' *Argonautica*", in: Heerink/Manuwald (2014) 173–191.
Caviglia, Franco (2002), "Similitudini in Valerio Flacco: sotto il segno di Medea", in *Aevuum Antiquum* 2, 3–34.
Cusset, Christophe (2012), "The metapoetics of simile in hellenistic poetry", in: *PP* 67 (n. 383), 104–117.
Corrigan, Kirsty (2013), *Virgo to Virago: Medea in the Silver Age*, Cambridge.
Davis, Peter J. (2014), "Medea: from Epic to Tragedy", in: Heerink/Manuwald (2014) 192–210.
De Poli, Mattia (ed.) (2018), *Il teatro delle emozioni: la paura*, Padua.
Dinter, Martin T. (2009), "Epic from Epigram: The Poetics of Valerius Flaccus' *Argonautica*", in: *AJPh* 130.4, 533–566.

Dubrana, Marie (2008), "L'autorité de Jason dans les *Argonautiques* de Valerius Flaccus", in: *Camenulae* 2, http://www.paris-sorbonne.fr/IMG/pdf/M_Dubrana.pdf (seen 02.05.2014)
Duckworth, Georg Eckel (1933), *Foreshadowing and Suspense in the Epics of Homer, Apollonius, and Vergil*, New York.
Eigler, Ulrich/Lefèvre, Eckard/Manuwald, Gesine (eds.) (1998), *Ratis omnia vincet II. Neue Untersuchungen zu den* Argonautica *des Valerius Flaccus*, München.
Esposito, Paolo (2003), "I segnali della metamorfosi", in: Landolfi/Monella (2003) 11–28.
Fabre-Serris, Jacqueline/Keith, Alison (eds.) (2015), *Women and War in Antiquity*, Baltimore.
Fantuzzi, Marco (2007), "Medea maga, la luna, l'amore (Apollonio Rodio 4,50–65)", in: Martina/Cozzoli (2007) 77–95.
Feeney, Denis C. (1993), *The Gods in Epic. Poets and Critics of the Classical Tradition*, Oxford.
Finkmann, Simone (2015), "Polyxo and the Lemnian Episode – An Inter- and Intratextual Study of Apollonius Rhodius, Valerius Flaccus, and Statius", in: *Dictynna* 12, http://dictynna.revues.org/1201 (seen 10.05.2016)
Fowler, Don (1997), "On the Shoulders of Giants: Intertextuality and Classical Studies", in: *MD* 39, 13–34.
Fratantuono, Lee/Stark, Caroline (eds.) (forthcoming), *A Companion to Latin Epic, 14–96 CE*, Malden, MA.
Fucecchi, Marco (1996), "Il restauro dei modelli antichi: tradizione epica e tecnica manieristica in Valerio Flacco", in: *MD* 36, 101–165.
Fucecchi, Marco (1997), *La teichoskopia e l'innamoramento di Medea. Saggio di commento a Valerio Flacco* Argonautiche *6,427–760*, Pisa.
Fucecchi, Marco (2014), "War and Love in Valerius Flaccus' Argonautica", in: Heerink/Manuwald (2014) 115–35.
Fuhrer, Therese (2015), "Teichoskopia: Female Figures Looking on Battles", in: Fabre-Serris/Keith (2015) 52–70.
Fusillo, Massimo (1985), *Il tempo delle* Argonautiche. *Un'analisi del racconto in Apollonio Rodio*, Roma.
Galli Milić, Lavinia (2011), "Iphigénie, Polyxène et Didon à Rome, ou le mariage manqué dans la représentation pathétique de la victime au féminin", in: Prescendi/Nagy (2011) 154–166.
Gärtner, Ursula (1994), *Gehalt und Funktion der Gleichnisse bei Valerius Flaccus*, Stuttgart.
Genette, Gérard (1972), "Discours du récit: essai de méthode", in: Gérard Genette, *Figures III*, Paris, 65–273 (now available in English translation as Gérard Genette, *Narrative discourse: An essay in method*, Ithaca, NY, 1980).
Grewe, Stefanie (1998), "Der Einfluss von Senecas Medea auf die Argonautica des Valerius Flaccus", in: Eigler *et al.* (1998) 173–190.
Hardie, Philip (1990), "Flavian Epicists on Virgil's Epic Technique", in: Boyle (1990) 3–20.
Hardie, Philip (1993), *The epic successors of Virgil. A study in the dynamics of a tradition*. Cambridge.
Hardie, Philip (2006), "Virgil's Ptolemaic Relations", in: *JRS* 96, 25–41.
Harrison, Edward L. (1972–1973), "Why Did Venus Wear Boots? Some Reflections on *Aeneid* 1.314 f.", in: *PVS* 12, 10–25.
Heerink, Mark (2014), "Valerius Flaccus, Virgil and the Poetics of Ekphrasis", in: Heerink/Manuwald (2014) 72–95.
Heerink, Mark/Manuwald, Gesine (eds.) (2014), *Brill's Companion to Valerius Flaccus*, Leiden/Boston.

Hershkowitz, Debra (1998), *Valerius Flaccus'* Argonautica. *Abbreviated Voyages in Silver Latin Epic*, Oxford.
Hinds, Stephen (1993), "Medea in Ovid: Scenes from the Life of an Intertextual Heroine", in: *MD* 30, 9–47.
Hull, Kathleen W.D. (1975), "Medea in Valerius Flaccus' *Argonautica*", in: *Proceedings of the Leeds Philosophical and Literary Society* 16.1, 1–25.
Hurst, André (2012), "Préfigurations de Médée", in: *Gaia* 15, 81–95.
de Jong, Irene J.F. (2001), *A Narratological Commentary on the* Odyssey, Cambridge.
de Jong, Irene J.F. (2014), *Narratology and Classics. A Practical Guide*, Oxford.
Keith, Alison (2014), "Ovid and Valerius Flaccus", in: Heerink/Manuwald (2014) 269–289.
Kepple, Laurence R. (1976), "Arruns and the Death of Aeneas", in: *AJPh* 97, 344–360.
Knauer, Georg Nicolaus (1979[2]; 1964), *Die* Aeneis *und Homer. Studien zur poetischen Technik Vergils mit Listen der Homerzitate in der* Aeneis, Göttingen.
Knight, Virginia (1991), "Apollonius, *Argonautica* 4.167–70 and Euripides' *Medea*", in: *CQ* 41, 248–250.
Knox, Peter E. (1984), "A note on *Aeneid* 1.613", in: *CPh* 79, 304–305.
Korn, Matthias/Tschiedel, Hans Jürgen (eds.) (1991), *Ratis omnia vincet. Untersuchungen zu den Argonautica des Valerius Flaccus*, Hildesheim/Zürich/New York.
La Bua, Giuseppe (1999), *L'inno nella letteratura poetica latina*, San Severo.
Landolfi, Luciano/Monella, Paolo (eds.) (2003), Ars adeo latet arte sua. *Riflessioni sull'intertestualità ovidiana. Le Metamorfosi*, Palermo.
Lyne, R.O.A.M. (1987), *Further Voices in Vergil's* Aeneid, Oxford.
Lovatt, Helen/Vout, Caroline (eds.) (2013), *Epic Visions. Visuality in Greek and Latin Epic and its Reception*, Cambridge.
Manioti, Nikoletta (ed.) (2016), *Family in Flavian Epic*, Leiden/Boston.
Manuwald, Gesine (2002), "The narrative function of the similes in Valerius Flaccus' *Argonautica*. Comment on Franco Caviglia's article", in: *Aevum Antiquum* 2, 63–72.
Manuwald, Gesine (2013), "Medea: Transformations of a Greek figure in Latin literature", in: *G&R* 60, 114–135.
Martina, Antonio/Cozzoli, Adele-Teresa (eds.) (2007), *L'epos argonautico*, Rome.
McIntyre, James Stuart (2008), *Written into the Landscape: Latin Epic and the Landmarks of Literary Reception*, PhD Thesis, St. Andrews, http://hdl.handle.net/10023/543 (seen 10.05.2016)
Nelis, Damien P. (1991a), "Iphias: Apollonius Rhodius, *Argonautica* 1.311–16", in: *CQ* 41, 96–105.
Nelis, Damien P. (1991b), "Apollonius Rhodius, *Argonautica* 4.12", in: *CQ* 41, 250–251.
Nelis, Damien P. (2001), *Vergil's* Aeneid *and the* Argonautica *of Apollonius Rhodius*, Leeds.
Nelis, Damien P. (forthcoming), "Valerius Flaccus, Vergil and Apollonius Rhodius: the intertextual strategies of a Flavian poet", in: Fratantuono/Stark (forthcoming).
Panoussi, Vassiliki (2009), *Greek Tragedy in Vergil's* Aeneid: *Ritual, Empire, and Intertext*, Cambridge.
Pederzani, Ombretta (1987), "*Curiositas* e classicismo nelle Argonautiche di Valerio Flacco", in: *MD* 18, 101–129.
Perkell, Christine (1999), *Reading Vergil's* Aeneid. *An interpretive Guide*, Norman.
Perutelli, Alessandro (1994), "Il sogno di Medea da Apollonio Rodio a Valerio Flacco", in: *MD* 33, 33–50.
Perutelli, Alessandro (1997), *C. Valerii Flacci,* Argonauticon Liber VII, Florence.

Pichon, René (1902), *Index verborum amatoriorum*, Hildesheim.
Prescendi, Francesca/Nagy, Agnès A. (eds.) (2011), *Victimes au féminin*, Geneva.
Ripoll, François (2003), "Jason héros épique et tragique au chant VII des *Argonautiques* de Valérius Flaccus", in: *VL* 169, 70–82.
Roux, Magalie (2015), "*Sis memor, oro, mei*: la composition intertextuelle d'un faux discours d'adieu (Valerius Flaccus, *Argonuatiques*, VII, 472–489)", in: *Dictynna* 12, http://dictyn na.revues.org/ 1201 (seen 20.04.2016)
Salemme, Carmelo (1991), Medea. *Un antico mito in Valerio Flacco*, Naples.
Schmakeit, Iris Astrid (2003), *Apollonios Rhodios und die attische Tragödie: Gattungs-überschreitende Intertextualität in der alexandrinischen Epik*, Diss. Groningen.
Scott, Beverley (2012), *Aspects of Transgression in Valerius Flaccus' Argonautica*, PhD Thesis, Liverpool, http://repository.liv.ac.uk/10035/ (seen 15.05.2016)
Serafini, Nicola (2015), *La dea Ecate nell'antica Grecia: una protettrice dalla quale proteggersi*, Rome.
Secci, Elisabetta (2000), "*Non movent divos preces (Phaedr.* 1242): aspetti delle invocazioni agli dèi nelle tragedie di Seneca (parte II)", in: *Prometheus* 26, 241–266.
Sistakou, Evina (2016), *Tragic Failures: Alexandrian Responses to Tragedy and the Tragic*, Berlin/Boston.
Spaltenstein, François (2004), *Commentaire des Argonautica de Valérius Flaccus (livres 3, 4, et 5)*, Brussels.
Spaltenstein, François (2005), *Commentaire des Argonautica de Valérius Flaccus (livres 6, 7 et 8)*, Brussels.
Spencer, Sarah (1999), "*Varium et Mutabile*. Voices of Authority in *Aeneid* 4", in: Perkell (1999) 80–95.
Stover, Tim (2003), "Confronting Medea: Genre, Gender, and Allusion in the *Argonautica* of Valerius Flaccus", in: *CPh* 98.2, 123–147.
Stover, Tim (2009), "*Magna Perseis*: A Note on Valerius Flaccus, *Arg.* 7.238", in: *CJ* 104.4, 321–327.
Stover, Tim (2011), "Unexampled Exemplarity: Medea in the *Argonautica* of Valerius Flaccus", in: *TAPhA* 141, 171–200.
Stover, Tim (2012), *Epic and Empire in Vespasianic Rome. A New Reading of Valerius Flaccus' Argonautica*, Oxford.
Walde, Christine (1998), "Traumdarstellungen in den *Argonautica* des Valerius Flaccus", in: Eigler *et al.* (1998) 87–106.
Walsh, Lisl (2012), "The Metamorphoses of Seneca's Medea", in: *Ramus* 41.1–2, 71–93.
Wijsman, Henri J.W. (1996), *Valerius Flaccus, Argonautica. Book V. A Commentary*, Leiden.
Wijsman, Henri J.W. (2000), *Valerius Flaccus, Argonautica. Book VI. A Commentary*, Leiden.
Williams, Gareth (2012), "Medea in *Metamorphoses* 7: Magic, Moreness and the Maius Opus", in: *Ramus* 41.1–2, 49–70.
Zissos, Andrew (2008), *Valerius Flaccus' Argonautica Book 1. A Commentary*, Oxford.
Zissos, Andrew (2012), "The King's Daughter: Medea in Valerius Flaccus' *Argonautica*", in: *Ramus* 41.1–2, 94–118.

François Ripoll
Ulysses as an Inter (and Meta-)textual Hero in the *Achilleid* of Statius

Whereas Ulysses was the hero of the first Latin epic, the *Odyssia* of Livius Andronicus, the *Achilleid* of Statius is the only extant ancient epic putting him on stage as a forefront character.[1] In this unfinished poem, the Flavian epicist has drawn his inspiration from a tradition derived from the *Cypria* and notably represented by the *Skyrioi* of Euripides.[2] According to this tradition, the king of Ithaca was sent by the Greeks to Scyros in order to discover Achilles hiding in a womanly disguise among the daughters of king Lycomedes, and to persuade him to join the Achaean expedition against Troy. Even if many elements of Statius' narrative are borrowed from the play of Euripides, the epic frame gave him the occasion to enhance the character of Ulysses with many details of his own and to keep up a kind of dialogue with his epic predecessors (from Homer to Ovid) by playing with intertextual allusion. Critics generally assume that the Flavian poet provides us with a stylized and impoverished image of the Homeric hero.[3] That is not untrue from a psychological point of view, but it needs to be qualified by taking into account the intertextual strategy of Statius, which makes this character quite emblematic of the project of the *Achilleid* as a whole. What I intend to demonstrate here, is that Statius, feeling for this hero a kind of sympathy quite unprecedented in Latin Literature, uses him in order to provide his readers with a threefold intertextual pleasure: the one of ethical[4] recognition, the one of allusive prefiguration, and the one of critical distantiation. This 'intertextual' Ulysses is thus, as the same time, a 'super-Ulysses', a 'proto-Ulysses', and a 'meta-Ulysses'.[5]

---

[1] I put aside the debate between Ulysses and Ajax in Ovid's *Metamorphoses* (13.1–381), to which I shall come back at the end of this article. On the character of Ulysses in Latin Literature, see Stanford (1963); Perutelli (2006); Jouanno (2013) 81–239.
[2] About the *Skyrioi* of Euripides as the main source for the *Achilleid*, see Jouan (1966); Jouan (2002); Aricò (1981).
[3] That is the overall impression given by Perutelli (2006) 30–42.
[4] I take this adjective in an Aristotelian sense, i.e. referring to the character, the *ethos* of the hero.
[5] The content of this article is partly drawn from the notes I have written in Ripoll/Soubiran (2008). The translations are mostly borrowed from Shackleton Bailey (2003).

1 A 'Super-Ulysses' or: The Pleasure of Ethical Recognition

One of Statius's aims is to make the reader enjoy the pleasure of recognizing the most typical traits of Ulysses' *ethos* in the whole literary tradition—a tradition based mainly upon the Homeric poems, but including the reflections of the Homeric hero by subsequent Greek and Latin authors. His method rests on two principles: selection and amplification. On the one hand, Statius reduces Ulysses' personality to a couple of dominating traits: craftiness and eloquency. On the other hand, starting from motives already present in Homer, he accentuates these two traits by inventing some episodes or narrative details which exemplify them in a vivid manner, or even add some new modulations to them. The purpose of the Flavian poet is, in a way, to outdo the Ulysses of Homer and his followers by contaminating, transposing and reinterpreting different elements from the tradition in order to produce an Ulysses looking more 'Ulysses-like' (at least according to the Roman reader) than any of his predecessors. That is what I call a 'super-Ulysses'.

I shall take firstly an example of what I would call a 'purification' of Homer, intending to put in better relief Ulysses' craftiness by eliminating some other traits of the Homeric character which might compete with it. This process is at work in the scene of the designation of the Greek delegation to Scyros (*Ach.* 1.538–559), directly inspired by the preliminary episode of the Homeric Dolonia[6] (*Il.* 10.180–217). In both epics, Diomedes volunteers for the mission and chooses Ulysses as a partner. In the Homeric model, Diomedes praises Ulysses' boldness, then the protection granted to him by Pallas, and finally, his craftiness (*Il.* 10.242–247). In the *Achilleid*, Diomedes relies only upon Ulysses' craftiness, which he praises in a more emphatic manner than in Homer (*Ach.* 1.539–545), and Ulysses politely replies by paying homage to Pallas' favour ... for Diomedes (*Ach.* 1.546–547). It implies that Ulysses' craftiness makes him so self-sufficient that he does not seem to need any divine help. So we see here a process both of reduction and amplification in order to make craftiness appear as the master trump (and in fact, the only one) of Ulysses.

But, as I said above, Statius also adds to elements stemming directly from Homer some traits borrowed from the posthomeric tradition, in order to make his

---

[6] In the *Cypria*, which are the primal source for the episode of Achilles at Scyros, the Achaean ambassadors were Ulysses, Phoenix and Nestor, but Euripides, in his *Skyrioi*, had replaced the two latters by Diomedes under the influence of the Homeric Dolonia.

Ulysses even more 'Ulysses-like' than the one of Homer. My second example will put into relief another kind of 'correction' of Homer, in the same episode. At this time, the purpose of the poet is to illustrate the cautiousness which is supposed to be one of the aspects of Ulysses' shrewdness. In the tradition coming probably from the *Cypria*, and echoed notably by Ovid,[7] Ulysses was anything but enthusiastic about the idea of going to war, and even tried to simulate insanity in order to avoid it. It seems to me that something of this propensity for shying away appears in Statius. Whereas the Ulysses of Homer's Dolonia spontaneously volunteers for the mission (*Il.* 10.213–232), the one of Statius hesitates (1.538 *haerentem*) to throw himself into the adventure, and needs to be encouraged by Diomedes, because he is afraid of a shameful failure and return (1.549). By eliminating the boldness of the Homeric Ulysses (and thus, accentuating the contrast between the bold Diomedes and the cautious Ulysses), Statius seems to have privileged a posthomeric image of the hero, according to which his shrewdness is more coloured by cautiousness than in the *Iliad*. So the Roman reader, aware of the posthomeric tradition, might have the impression that this Ulysses, less bold than his Iliadic avatar and inspiring confidence mostly by his craftiness, is perhaps more coherent and more in accordance with his previous attitude in the preliminary episodes of the war.

This tendency to 'unify' the image of Ulysses around the topic of cunning can also be observed in a simile inspired by another passage of the Homeric Dolonia. In *Ach.* 1.704–708, Ulysses and Diomedes arriving at Scyros are compared with two wolves walking through a winter night. The original idea stems from *Il.* 10.296–298, where the two heroes are compared with a pair of lions, but Statius, contaminating this passage with Virgil, *Aen.* 2.335–360 substituted wolves to lions in order to enhance the idea of dissimulation.[8] Once again, the purpose here is to improve on Homer by a 'correction' supposed to suit better the typical *ethos* of Ulysses.

After the episode at Aulis, the other important scene for the characterization of Ulysses is the audience at Lycomedes' palace, where the poet stresses both Ulysses' shrewdness and eloquency by alluding to different elements of the literary tradition. Let us begin with the former before coming to the latter.

One of the most conspicuous traits of Ulysses in the *Odyssey* (and an aspect of his shrewdness) is his curiosity and his perceptive glance.[9] In the scene of the audience, Statius lays much emphasis on the motive of the observant glance, by

---

[7] Cf. Ov. *Met.* 13.34–42; Apollod. *Epit.* 3.7.
[8] For the idea, see Ov. *Met.* 14.778 *tacito more luporum*.
[9] Cf. Hom. *Od.* 1.3; 11.566–567.

applying it to the 'inquisitorial' attitude of Ulysses in search of Achilles. What is most remarkable here, is the recurrence of the vocabulary of looking as soon as the hero enters the palace (1.741 *uisu perlustrat* ... / *scrutaturque*; 748 *uideat*). Statius had probably in mind the arrival of Ulysses at the palace of Alcinous, where the hero admires everything around him (*Od.* 7.133–134),[10] but with an original reinterpretation: here (*Ach.* 1.742–746), Ulysses *feigns* to admire (*ceu miretur*) the surroundings in order to dissimulate his searching intent. So Statius diverts the homeric motive of the admirative glance on the palace in order to suggest Ulysses' ability to conceal his real aims, which is an aspect of his cleverness also in Homer, but in other circumstances: notably his arrival at Ithaca and his entry into his own palace in *Od.* 14–15.[11]

Later on (*Ach.* 1.761–766), we see again the searching look of Ulysses upon the daughters of Lycomedes (761–762 *intentus* ... *perlibrat uisu*), then we see him staring at Achilles (766 *defigit*) and glancing at Diomedes (*ibid. obliquo lumine monstrat*), and later on, watching (794 *aspicit*) the effects of his speech upon the princesses. So the motive of the observant glance is a good example of the way Statius takes up a typical trait of the hero by Homer, accentuates it (drawing here a very lively and dramatic scene based upon an exchange of attentive looks), and even reinterprets it in order to stress the famous shrewdness of Ulysses by alluding to another Homeric motive, namely his *dissimulatio*. The curiosity of Ulysses by Alcinous and the dissimulation of Ulysses at Ithaca merge in Scyros so as to produce a new image of the hero: the one of a 'super-investigator'.[12] This specific talent appears thus as a natural extension of his abilities displayed in the Homeric tradition.

There is finally another characteristic of Ulysses indirectly related to his shrewdness *via* his thoughtfulness, which is his sleeplessness: Ulysses is often portrayed as a sleepless hero in Homer,[13] and Statius alludes to this in *Ach.* 1.816–817, with a specific hint at *Od.* 19.336–342, as noticed by A. Sacerdoti.[14]

I shall end this first section by examining the different terms denoting Ulysses' craftiness in the *Achilleid*, which are sustained by an interesting network of intertextual reminiscences. The most frequent epithet is *prouidus* (1.542, 689),

---

10 For the same *topos*, see also Ap. Rhod. *Argon.* 3.215–241 and Verg. *Aen.* 1.494–495.
11 For the observant glance of Ulysses at Ithaca, see also *Od.* 18.343, with an 'inquisitorial touch'.
12 Cf. Dilke (1954) 18: "... the crafty Ulysses, the Sherlock Holmes who had Diomedes as his Dr Watson".
13 Cf. *Od.* 10.476–481; 12.31–35; 20.1–97.
14 Sacerdoti (2014).

which was applied to Ulysses by Horace, *Epist.* 1.2.19, as an approximative equivalent to the Homeric *polytropos*[15] (or *polymetis*), but with a more positive connotation than the *uorsutus* of Livius Andronicus:[16] it does not denote only craftiness, but also a capacity for foresight naturally expected from a leader.[17] This foresight is notably illustrated in *Ach.* 1.698–699 when Ulysses, who has just landed on Scyros, decides to conceal the main body of his troops and to go on reconnaissance with only one companion, like Aeneas at Carthage (*Aen.* 1.305–313), but for a different reason; in fact, he does not fear the natives like Aeneas, but he wants to avoid frightening them, as Aeneas did when he showed himself to Evander and his men surrounded by his whole crew (*Aen.* 8.107–110). Everything happens as if Ulysses, having read the *Aeneid*, wanted to appear shrewder than Aeneas, both by imitating his cautiousness in *Aeneid* 1 and avoiding his clumsiness in *Aeneid* 8: this 'precedent' fosters, in a way, his *prouidentia*.

Another adjective applied to Ulysses is *uarius* ("with different faces"), in a context which is apparently derogatory[18] (1.846–847). This is another equivalent of *polytropos*,[19] but loaded with a negative connotation, based on the allusion to a Virgilian intertext (*Aen.* 2.43–44) to which I shall come back later on, and on the value of this adjective in another famous text, namely the portrait of Catilina by Sallust (*Cat.* 5.4 *animus ... subdolus, uarius*).[20]

There is a third epithet applied to Ulysses in the *Achilleid*, *sollers* (1.784), which was previously used about him by Ovid:[21] it denotes nothing but cleverness, with no positive or negative moral connotation.[22]

---

15 Cf. Préaux (1968) 51.
16 Ancient authors generally used to interpret the Homeric epithet *polytropos* as alluding to Ulysses' craftiness rather than to his wanderings (as the Moderns often do): cf. Clay (1983) 29–30.
17 With, in Horace, a Stoic connotation linked to the general topic of the *Epistle*, which is not the case in the *Achilleid*.
18 Even if this reprobation is not of serious intent, as we shall see below.
19 Nuzzo (2012) 151 proposes rather to bring this epithet close to the one of *poïkilophrôn* applied to Ulysses in Eur. *Hec.* 131.
20 The correction of *uariumque* into *uafrumque* proposed by Heinsius, and adopted by Shackleton Bailey, is unnecessary: *uarius* with its 'Catilinian' meaning suits very well here, because it might be understood as a derogatory equivalent for *polytropos* (or *poïkilophrôn*). The same epithet was already applied to Catilina by Cic. *Cael.* 14. For this meaning in a juridical context, see also Ulp. *dig.* 4.3.1.
21 *Ars* 2.355; *Pont.* 4.14.35.
22 It is perhaps more specifically the equivalent of the Homeric epithet *polymétis*; see Gavoille (2008).

The fourth epithet is *sagax* (1.817), which bears no specific moral connotation in the context,[23] but, since it is often applied to seers in Latin epic,[24] it might point obliquely to Ulysses' *prouidentia*.

In fact, the poet seems to have intended to present, in a quite playful way, different possible equivalents for the Homeric *polytropos/polymetis* (without making a clear choice which would have been also a moral one): the first one endowed with a positive connotation (*prouidus*), the second one with a negative connotation (*uarius*), and the two other ones rather neutral (*sollers, sagax*). Maybe it suggests the relativity of any moral judgement[25] to be passed on the astute personality of the hero.[26]

The other topical trait of Ulysses which Statius strived to enhance is his eloquency.[27] It is well known that in the tradition of the schools of rhetoric, Ulysses' eloquency had become a paradigm for the Great Style (*genus grande*), characterized by oratory strength and impetuosity, and particularly aiming at *mouere*.[28] The Ulysses of Statius obviously strives to be equal to his reputation.

In his three main speeches (1.728–802; 1.867–874; 2.32–83), he displays a performative rhetoric, aiming at waking up Achilles' martial spirit and strengthening his warlike vocation by appealing to emotions:[29] shame about his womanly disguise,[30] proudness about his ancestors,[31] confidence in his own destiny,[32] longing

---

23 It suggests that Ulysses, who has carefully planned what is going to happen the next day (and so, who 'foresees' the future, hence *sagax*) is eager to see the coming of that day.
24 Cf. Ov. *Met.* 5.46; Stat. *Theb.* 4.407; Sil. *Pun.* 3.344. Ulysses himself is characterized as a kind of seer by Diomedes at *Ach.* 1.544–545.
25 About the 'amoralism' of the *Achilleid*, see Méheust (1971) xxxvi.
26 Let us notice finally that there is another character labelled *prouidus* in the *Achilleid*: Deidamia, when she succeeds in delaying for a time Ulysses' plot (1.802–805). Perhaps we can see in this *prouida Deidamia* delaying the recognition of Achilles an indirect prefiguration of the *periphron Penelopea* who will delay another recognition, the one of Ulysses himself at Ithaca.
27 See notably Jouanno (2013) 165–190.
28 Cf. Quint. *Inst.* 12.10.64.
29 In a way, Ulysses plays the part of an 'epic consciousness' of Achilles, removing him from the comico-elegiac temptation of the life at Scyros, and sending him back to his 'natural' epic destiny.
30 2.35.
31 1.796, 868–869.
32 1.869–971; 2.32–33, 57.

for glory,[33] panhellenic patriotism,[34] indignation towards wickedness,[35] attachment to justice.[36] Thus, he resorts to most of the rhetorical figures typical of the Great Style, as we can see notably in 1.785–793: rhetorical question, hyperboles, numerous metaphors, asyndeton, final *sententia*. It sounds very much like a Roman *cohortatio*; and in many ways, this Ulysses seems to assume the *persona* of a Roman orator[37] upon his identity of Greek hero.[38]

But this martial eloquency goes hand in hand with a display of craftiness in the field of rhetorical manipulation which reflects another typical trait of the character in the tradition, namely his *facundia*.[39] Throughout his speeches, we see a Ulysses remarkable for his opportunism and adaptability, able to use oblique discourse[40] and ironical double-entendre,[41] to grasp an opportunity,[42] to modify his strategy in accordance with the situation,[43] and to manipulate the legendary tradition so as to make it serve his purpose.[44] He also displays a fine knowledge of the psychology of his interlocutor, especially in 1.792–802, where, without knowing Achilles personally, he is able to find the most fitting arguments to deeply move the young hero, as if he had heard his monologue a few verses before (1.619–639).[45] This ability to adopt the rhetorical strategy most suited to his interlocutor recalls precisely the Ulysses of Homer facing Nausicaa in *Od*.

---

[33] 1.791–793, 801. This trait is in accordance with the Homeric Achilles' desire for *kleos*.
[34] 1.63–64. This unhomeric presentation owes much to the reinterpretations of the Persian wars in classical Greece.
[35] 2.60–78.
[36] 1.788; 2.48.
[37] I think particularly to the topic of the *bellum iustum*, which Statius puts into the forefront (1.403–404, 788; 2.48) instead of the oath of Helen's suitors present in Euripides. This may be considered as a typical 'Roman touch'.
[38] See Barchiesi (2005) 64–67, who analyzes the speech of 1.866–876 and the alliterations in -*t* sounding like a martial trumpet (cf. Enn. *Ann.* 451 Skutsch).
[39] See notably Gavoille (2008) and Jouanno (2013) 171–175.
[40] Notably, feigning to address Lycomedes while, in fact, speaking to Achilles above the head of the former.
[41] 1.811.
[42] 1.784 *arrepto tempore*.
[43] 1.806.
[44] 1.60–62; on which see my commentary below.
[45] The argument of the noble origin (*quisquis proauis et gente superba*, 796) fits peculiarly well with the dynastic pride of Achilles (cf. 655–656). The hint at horse-riding, javelin and archery (797) recalls the passage where Achilles, fed up with his womanly disguise, longed for his bow, his javelin and his horses (632–633). Besides, Ulysses' allusion to the fearful mothers of the heroes (*timidae matres*, 799) recalls the expression used by Achilles about his own mother in the same monologue (*timidae ... parentis*, 624).

6.141–148; so Statius, as usual, has expanded a suggestion already present in the tradition. And the *sententia* of Ulysses about the sterile old age of the one who misses the occasion for glory (1.800–802) is an obvious allusion to the homeric theme of the two paths opened to Achilles: the one of a long and obscure life and the one of a short but glorious existence (*Il.* 9.410–416). So this Ulysses seems to have a good 'intuitive' knowledge of Achilles' literary biography.

As well as for Achilles, whom Statius intends to show, as he said in the prologue, "as a whole" (1.4–5 *omnem ... heroa*), the Flavian poet makes a point of showing *omnem Ulyxen*, by illustrating at least the most famous aspects of his *ethos*, as we have just seen it from a synchronic point of view. But there is also a diachronic aspect in this delineation of the character, as we will see below.

To sum up, the pleasure of ethical recognition consists in recognizing the most familiar and basic aspects of the personality of the hero, vividly illustrated and enhanced by some new variations and modulations which seem to bring him to a degree of 'perfection' never reached before.

2 A 'Proto-Ulysses' or: The Pleasure of Anticipative Allusion

Throughout *Achilleid* 1, Statius weaves a network of allusive connections between the unhomeric episode of the reception at Scyros and some passages of the *Iliad* or the *Odyssey* in order to prefigure the forthcoming adventures of Ulysses, sometimes with anticipative irony. The aim is to convey to the reader the pleasure of recognizing the future hero of the Homeric poems, so as to make the *Achilleid* look like a 'prequel' of the *Iliad* and the *Odyssey*.

For instance, the designation of the ambassadors (1.536–559), based on the model of the Dolonia (*Il.* 10.218–253), seems to be, retrospectively, a precedent for the engagement of Ulysses and Diomedes in the nocturnal expedition at Troy. And if we read Homer after Statius, i.e. following the 'chronological' order of the story, we may rebuild a kind of psychological coherence between the two different images of Ulysses: the reluctant hero of *Ach.* 1 and the daring one of *Il.* 10. In fact, we may guess that Ulysses does not hesitate any longer to volunteer in the Dolonia because he has been encouraged by his previous success at Scyros, which made him more self-confident than he was at the beginning of the Trojan war. So the fact that the Homeric scene is shorter than the Statian one may be due to the fact that the decision to volunteer is easier to take since such a situation has already taken place 'before'.

We may also detect a strategy of anticipative allusion, with a different effect, in the scene of the audience by Lycomedes (1.726–818), which is interwoven with intertextual reminiscences, among which the archetype is the reception of Ulysses at the palace of Alcinous (*Od.* 7–8). Despite the abundance of intertexts, this primal one is still detectable at some moments. For instance, the spectacle of dancing displayed to the guests by the daughters of the king (v. 819–840), probably invented by Statius, must draw his inspiration from the one offered to Ulysses by the sons of the Phaeacian king (*Od.* 8.370–380). Besides, the attitude of Ulysses towards the Scyrian princesses, with a mixture of respect and admiration (*Ach.* 1.810), resembles the one of the Homeric hero towards Nausicaa (*Od.* 6.168). We come even closer to Homer when we understand that Lycomedes secretly hopes to marry his daughters to the Achaean ambassadors (1.780–783),[46] which inevitably reminds us of Alcinous and ... Ulysses (*Od.* 7.311–314).[47] So the reader enjoys seeing Ulysses (who feigns not to have understood what the old king has in mind) in the position of a virtual son-in-law, which 'anticipates', with an effect of irony, the situation he will experience 'again' at the court of Phaeacia. *Bis repetita*.

The allusive game reaches its highest degree of irony when Ulysses addresses Lycomedes as follows (1.785–787): *Quis enim non uisere gentes / innumeras ... / ardeat?*, "But who would not burn to see the countless peoples?" This may be easily identified by the readers as an allusion to *Od.* 1.3 (about the wanderings of Ulysses):[48] so Ulysses does not guess, when enunciating this *sententia*, that it will apply to himself more than to anyone. The reader, knowing the whole story, may enjoy his superior knowledge and smile at the expense of the character. This is in fact one of the rare instances where the reader gets the impression of being more *prouidus* than Ulysses himself.

We can see finally a direct anticipation of the *Odyssey* when Neptune promises to Thetis that he will help her to take revenge on Ulysses one day (1.94 *dirum*[49] *pariter quaeremus Vlixen*). The sea-god speaks as if he knew what Ulysses will do to his son Polyphemus, which brings him close to the goddess, whose son Achilles will be sent to death by the man of Ithaca; in fact, the whole *Odyssey* is already latent in the *Achilleid*.

---

46 See Heslin (2005) 145–155.
47 Such is also the case of Polynices by Adrastes and Aeneas by Latinus, and these intertexts are also present here, but Statius is closer to Homer on two points: 1) Ulysses is involved both in *Ach.* 1 and *Od.* 7; 2) There is no divine oracle about a son-in-law at stake within these two epics.
48 Cf. also Hor. *Epist.* 1.2.19 and *Ars P.* 141–142.
49 *Dirus* is used by the Trojans about Ulysses in Verg. *Aen.* 2.261, 762. So the Neptune of Statius adopts the point of view of the victims of the hero in Virgil.

In order to be inclusive about this topic, I shall quote another instance of anticipative irony, based on an allusion to the posthomeric Ulysses, the one of the Trojan horse, and more precisely, the treacherous character of the *Aeneid*.[50] When the old Lycomedes, deceived by Ulysses' trick, presents his daughters with the ambassadors' gifts, the narrator exclaims in a (falsely) pitiful manner (846–847):

> heu simplex nimiumque rudis, qui callida dona
> Graiorumque dolos uariumque ignoret Vlixen!
>
> Alas, too simple and inexperienced, he knows not of cunning presents and Grecian wiles and shifty Ulysses!

This is an obvious allusion to the exclamation of Laocoon about the treacherousness of the Greeks in the episode of the Trojan horse, *Aen.* 2.43–44 ... *aut ulla putatis / dona carere dolis Danaum? Sic notus Vlixes?* In the *Achilleid*, it is Lycomedes who is the victim of the poet's irony: one might say that the Scyrian king can be so easily deceived by the man of Ithaca because he has not read the *Aeneid*. But the recontextualization of this motive completely modifies its affective value. Far from having for Lycomedes the same dramatic consequences as for Priam, Ulysses' trick will, at the end of the episode, provide the old king with the son-in-law whom he was secretly expecting from the start![51] So the *pathos* of this exclamation is not to be taken seriously. In fact the narrator, with a kind of smiling casualness, dedramatizes the threatening aspect of the Virgilian Ulysses.

So it is not only some parts of the *Iliad* and the *Odyssey*, but also of the *Aeneid*, which are virtually present in the *Achilleid* through the character of Ulysses. But the general meaning and the affective colouring of the allusions may differ. Firstly, the *Achilleid* appears as a prelude to the *Iliad*, where Ulysses will develop (quite like Achilles, although to a lesser degree) a daring temper he has not fully acquired yet. Secondly, the *Achilleid* looks like an anticipative repetition of the *Odyssey*, where the hero is doomed to experience almost the same situations for the 'second time'; hence an effect or irony. Thirdly, the *Achilleid* is a dedramatized 'response' to the *Aeneid*, the dark side of the Virgilian hero being attenuated by the less dramatic context and the relativization of any moral judgement on the character.

---

50 On this, see Stanford (1963) 128–137 and Perutelli (2006) 30–42.
51 By making Achilles recover his masculine identity and regularize his love affair with Deidamia.

The intertextual pleasure of allusive prefiguration consists thus in establishing some new diachronic connections between different elements of the tradition and different images of the hero, whether to make a new coherence appear between them, or to project a new light on to some of them.

3 A 'Meta-Ulysses' or: The Strategy of Critical Distantiation

I shall now examine a few passages where Statius seems to use Ulysses as a spokesman or a 'double' in order to comment upon the tradition and justify some 'improvements' introduced in the *fabula* by the Flavian poet.

My first example of a 'metaliterary' treatment of Ulysses' voice is the conversation between Diomedes and Ulysses on their arrival at Scyros (1.709–725). Here, Diomedes plays the part of the reader, curious to know which trick the man of Ithaca is going to use to recognize Achilles among the daughters of Lycomedes. In fact, the tradition proposed a couple of possibilities well known to the readers: whether the shield and the spear disposed among the presents destined for the princesses, like in the *Cypria*, or the blow of a trumpet, like in the *Skyrioi* of Euripides.[52] But Statius creates an effect of surprise by making Diomedes allude to Bacchic instruments gathered by Ulysses (712–717), which are not part of the tradition, and about which Diomedes' astonishment reflects that of the reader. In reply, Ulysses' attitude is the one of a 'Master of the game', or, we might say, of the author himself. Speaking with an air of benevolent (and quasi Jovian) superiority to his interlocutor (*illi subridens*, 718),[53] he keeps the suspense going by announcing that he will use all the accessories of the recognition previously mentioned in the tradition (i.e. the weapons *and* the trumpet), and that he will add to them the mysterious Bacchic instruments which are an innovation of his own. By doing so, he teases the curiosity of Diomedes/the reader, who is eager to know how Ulysses/Statius will combine all these elements to produce a new version of the story, both incorporating the ones of all his predecessors and breaking new ground in comparison with them.

Let us consider another example, in the speech of Ulysses to Achilles in *Ach.* 2.49–83. The strategy of Ulysses consists of stressing the wickedness of Paris in

---

52 On this, see Ripoll (2012).
53 This *iunctura* comes from Verg. *Aen.* 1.254; 12.829 (about Jupiter speaking to a goddess). Besides, the motive of Ulysses' smile has some Homeric antecedents: cf. *Od.* 20.301; 21.371; 23.111.

order to stimulate the wrath of Achilles against the Trojans. On this occasion, a new detail in the story appears in the mouth of Ulysses: Paris is said to have felled a sacred grove in order to build his fleet (2.60–62): *Ille Phrygas lucos, Matris penetralia caedit / turrigerae* ... No other author mentions this sacrilege, which rather recalls the myth of Erysichthon (Ov. *Met.* 8.741–776). Do we have to consider this as a mere forgery from Ulysses, aiming at calumniating Paris? Not necessarily. In fact, in the *Heroides* of Ovid, 16.107–110, Paris prides himself on having felled all the big trees of Mount Ida to build his fleet (without mentioning any sacred grove). In Virgil, *Aen.* 9.85–89, we learn that Cybele owned a sacred grove on the Ida, which, in this particular instance, she allowed Aeneas to fell so as to permit him to build his fleet; this is most probably an invention of Virgil, which became canonical afterwards.[54] Thus, if Paris has told the truth in the *Heroides*, he must have felled also, without permission, at least some part of the 'famous' sacred grove of Cybele,[55] although he has 'avoided' to mention it at that time.

So in the *Achilleid*, Ulysses is, in fact, matching up the indications of Ovid with those of Virgil; and so, through the voice of the hero, Statius provides us with the 'complete story' of the grove on Mount Ida. This is thus another example of how Ulysses/Statius merges different elements from the tradition to produce a new and comprehensive version of the legend, complementing and/or correcting the ones of his predecessors.

My following example will put into relief another kind of 'correction' of a predecessor by Ulysses/Statius. In Ovid's *Metamorphoses*, 13.166–170, Ulysses tells retrospectively how he delivered a speech to Achilles in order to persuade him to join the Achaean army:[56]

> ... neque adhuc proiecerat heros
> uirgineos habitus, cum parmam hastamque tenenti:
> 'nate dea', dixi 'tibi se peritura reseruant
> Pergama; quid dubitas ingentem euertere Troiam?'
> iniecique manum fortemque ad fortia misi.

> ... The hero still wore girls' clothing when, as he laid hands on shield and spear, I said to him: 'O son of a goddess, Pergama, doomed to perish, is keeping herself for you! why do

---

[54] Cf. Ov. *Fast.* 4.273–274.
[55] At least, as he says, the tallest ones, so that Aeneas could use the survivors eighteen years later; but this technical detail is of little importance.
[56] Such a speech must have taken place in the *Skyrioi* of Euripides, as we know from two extant fragments (frg. 5 and 6 ed. Jouan (2002) 51–71). But Statius had obviously Ovid in mind, as we may infer from the numerous similarities between *Ach.* 1 and *Met.* 13.102–170.

you delay the fall of mighty Troy?' And I laid my hand on him and sent the brave fellow forth to do brave deeds.

The Ulysses of Statius *Ach.* 1.867–874, gives us that is supposed to be the 'real' speech, pronounced at that very moment:[57]

> 'quid haeres?
> scimus', ait, 'tu semiferi Chironis alumnus,
> tu Caeli pelagique Nepos, te Dorica classis,
> te tua suspensis exspectat Graecia signis,   870
> ipsaque iam dubiis nutant tibi Pergama muris.
> heia, abrumpe moras! Sine perfida palleat Ide,
> et iuuet haec audire patrem, pudeatque dolosam
> sic pro te timuisse Thetin'.

'Why do you hesitate?' he says. 'We know. You are half-beast Chiron's fosterling, grandson of Sea and Sky. The Dorian fleet attends you, your Greece expects you with flying standards and Pergamus herself nods to you with walls already tottering. Up now, no more delay! Let treacherous Ide turn pale, let your father rejoice to hear the news and wily Thetis be ashamed to have so feared for you'.

In Statius, Ulysses' speech is not only more fully developed than in Ovid; it is also, in a way, more clever. The Ulysses of Ovid, drawing from Mercury's speech to Aeneas in *Aeneid* 4, had addressed Achilles as *nate dea*[58] (Ov. *Met.* 13.168: cf. *Aen.* 4.560). But Statius must have felt that it would have been quite awkward, coming from Ulysses, to address Achilles by mentioning his mother in a speech aiming precisely at removing him from her influence; that is why his Ulysses prefers to put in the foreground the fierce Chiro and the godlike ancestors of the hero, reserving Thetis for a brief and depreciating mention at the end of the tirade. He also chooses to take up another expression from Mercury's speech to Aeneas, more in keeping with the general mood of his own speech: *Heia, abrumpe moras* (*Ach.* 1.872); which recalls *Aen.* 4.569 *Heia age, rumpe moras*, and enhances the martial tone of the tirade. To sum up, the Ulysses of Statius, on the one hand, 'corrects' what might appear as an awkwardness from the one of Ovid, resulting from an 'inappropriate' borrowing from Virgil, and, on the other hand, introduces another borrowing from the same Virgilian text, fitting better to the context.

---

57 See Davis (2006) 137–139.
58 This apostrophe is present elsewhere in the *Aeneid*, but here, the context is much closer to *Aeneid* 4, since in both cases, a messenger comes to 'wake up' a hero who was about to forget his 'mission'.

Through the voice of his hero, Statius displays a kind of critical emulation towards Ovid about the better way of using and adapting a Virgilian intertext.

This latent 'criticism' of Ovid may also be detected in another passage, when Ulysses tells Achilles that, had he not intervened, the young man would have come to war anyway, because he was doomed to it (2.41–42):

> 'Nec nostrum est, quod in arma uenis sequerisque precantes;
> uenisses'.

> 'Tis not our doing that you come to arms and follow our entreaties. You would have come'.

This is in utter contradiction with what Ulysses says in Ovid, *Met.* 13.170–180, where he proudly claims for himself the merit to have persuaded Achilles to join the expedition, implying that, had he not intervened, the hero would never have come. How must we interpret this discrepancy? One the one hand, it might point to the boastfulness of the Ovidian Ulysses, and invite us to reread with a very critical eye his tendancious speech in the *Metamorphoses*.[59] But on the other hand, one may not exclude the idea that the Ulysses of the *Achilleid* exaggerates his modesty and minimizes his own part in order to flatter Achilles.[60] In fact, both interpretations may be valid, and no matter which Ulysses is closer to the 'truth', since this contradiction is rather intended to point to the craftiness and duplicity of Ulysses in his manipulation of argumentative rhetoric in general, with an effect of smiling distantiation towards both images of the hero.

I shall end with a last remark about the main argument of Ulysses in this passage, namely the predestination of Achilles to play a decisive part in the Trojan war. In the posthomeric tradition, this predestination resulted from an oracle, mentioned in the *Hypothesis* of the *Skyrioi*.[61] In the *Achilleid* however, the narrator did not mention this oracle explicitly anywhere.[62] So we do not know on what occasion Ulysses could have heard of the *diuum oracula* he mentions in 2.32 ...

---

[59] This is the interpretation of Davis (2006) 138.
[60] Ulysses himself was not so confident about the *fata* in 1.549... But this apparent lack of self-confidence had mainly an ethical fonction: to stress the cautiousness of the character (see above).
[61] Cf. also Apollod. *Bibl.* 3.13.8. This detail is absent from the Homeric poems.
[62] The allusion of 1.475–476 is indirect and rather vague: ... *Illum unum Teucris Priamoque loquuntur / fatalem*. It might be just a rumour, lying only upon the natural skills of the hero (as enumerated in 476–482).

unless he has read the *Skyrioi* of Euripides.⁶³ This apparent inconsistency is probably not meant to suggest that Ulysses is merely inventing this oracle at that very moment, since it is well attested elsewhere in the tradition, but it gives rather the impression that he (alone among the human characters of the *Achilleid*)⁶⁴ enjoys a superior knowledge of the story,⁶⁵ resulting from a kind of 'intertextual' learning ... which is, in fact, the one of the author.⁶⁶

Thus, in order to rise the intertextual pleasure of critical distantiation, Statius incites the reader to reread some famous texts of other authors with a critical eye, so as to suggest that his own version of the myth is, by comparison, the most clever and elaborate one, since his Ulysses is, by comparison, the shrewdest of all.

It is time to conclude. Statius seems to have delineated his Ulysses through a network of intertextual allusions which make him a comprehensive character, both uniting and overriding all the Ulysses of the tradition, not without any critical, and sometimes, ironical distantiation. But there is possibly, in a more diffuse way, another model for this 'supra-Ulysses', who might be ... Statius himself. This quite sympathetic manipulator, *uarius* and *facundus*, who displays his ability to play the epic trumpet, to use martial rhetoric with a consummate artistry, to deliver 'Roman-like' *cohortationes* with the cleverness of a Greek, to 'invent' mythical traditions by contaminating ancient and recent poetical sources, looks very much like Papinius Statius, the Neapolitan poet impregnated with Greek and Roman culture. Besides, Ulysses' fatherlike attitude towards Achilles⁶⁷ resembles the one which the poet claims for himself in the prologue, when he announces

---

63 Inconsistencies of this kind are notoriously recurrent in the *Aeneid* (for a survey, see O'Hara 2007), and may be interpreted in different ways. It seems to me that putting the problem only in terms of logical inconsistency is to miss the point. What matters most, I think, is the affective effect produced upon the reader in each case. On this, see the very clever analysis of Rohman (2013) 294–309.
64 It is all the more striking since the 'prophecy' of Tiresias (1.526–536) concerns only the past and the present, and says nothing about the future.
65 It was already obliquely suggested by the praise of Ulysses' 'seer-like' qualities by Diomedes in 1.544–545: if we admit that *fata* is an equivalent for the *fabula*, we come to the suggestion that Ulysses is considered as the one who knows the whole 'plot' of the story, like the author himself.
66 The same impression is conveyed by the *sententia* of 1.800–802 (on which see my comment above).
67 Cf. Heslin (2005) 292. By the end of *Ach.* 1 and the beginning of *Ach.* 2, Ulysses replaces, in a way, both the absent Peleus and the removed Chiro. For his 'didactic' attitude, see notably 2.12 *ita namque monebat Vlixes*.

his intention to accompany the young hero like a *paedagogus* throughout the Trojan war: *tota iuuenem deducere Troia* (1.7);[68] which is precisely what Ulysses is going to do on the intradiegetical level, acting 'by proxy' for the author, so to speak.[69] So one can understand better the obvious sympathy of Statius for the man of Ithaca, to whom he must have identified himself spontaneously with a touch of self-reflexive humour, and thus who resembles him like a brother.[70]

Bibliography

Aricò, Giuseppe (1981), "Contributo alla ricostruzione degli *Skyrioi* euripidei", in: Gallo (1981) 215–230.
Augoustakis, Antony (ed.) (2014), *Flavian Poetry and its Greek Past*, Leiden/Boston.
Barchiesi, Alessandro (2005), "Masculinity in the 90's: The Education of Achilles in Statius and Quintilian", in: Paschalis (2005) 47–75.
Clay, Jenny S. (1983), *The Wrath of Athena: Gods and Men in the Odyssey*, Princeton.
Davis, Peter J. (2006), "Allusion to Ovid and others in Statius' *Achilleid*", in: *Ramus* 35, 129–143.
Dilke, Oswald A.W. (1954), *Statius, Achilleid, Edited with Introduction, Apparatus Criticus and Notes*, Cambridge.
Fontanier, Jean-Michel (ed.) (2008), Amor Romanus. *Amours romaines. Etudes et anthologie*, Rennes.
Gallo, Italo (ed.) (1981), *Studi Salernitani in memoria di Raffaele Cantarella*, Salerno.
Gavoille, Elizabeth (2008), "Du soldat de Tibulle à l'amant ovidien: *facundus Vlixes*", in: Fontanier (2008) 119–133.
Heslin, Peter J. (2005), *The Transvestite Achilles. Gender and Genre in the Achilleid*, Cambridge.
Jouan, François (1966), *Euripide et les légendes des chants cypriens*, Paris.
Jouan, François (2002), *Euripide*, Tragédies. Tome VIII, 3e partie, Paris.
Jouanno, Corinne (2013), *Ulysse. Odyssée d'un personnage d'Homère à Joyce*, Paris.
Méheust, Jean (1971), *Stace*, Achilléide, Paris.
Nuzzo, Gianfranco (2012), *Publio Papinio Stazio*, Achilleide, Palermo.
O'Hara, James J. (2007), *Inconsistency in Roman Epic*, Cambridge.
Paschalis, Michael (ed.) (2005), *Roman and Greek Imperial Epic*, Rethymnon.
Perutelli, Alessandro (2006), *Ulisse nella cultura romana*, Florence.
Préaux, Jean (1968), *Q. Horatius Flaccus,* Epistulae, Liber Primus, Paris.
Ripoll, François (2012), "La découverte d'Achille à Scyros dans l'*Achilléide* de Stace: de l'iconographie à l'anthropologie", in: *Latomus* 71, 116–132.

---

68 For the meaning of *deducere* here, cf. Cic. *Fam.* 10.12.2; *Mur.* 70; Hor. *Sat.* 1.9.59. See also my commentary *ad loc.*
69 One may think that, had the *Achilleid* been completed, the poet would have kept on laying the stress on the pedagogical role of Ulysses towards Achilles.
70 I wish to express my gratitude to my English-speaking friends John and Adrienne Hoyle for their careful rereading and their corrections.

Marco Fucecchi
Constructing (Super-)characters: The Case Study of Silius' Hannibal

1 Introduction: Silius' Hannibal as Example of 'Multiple Intertextuality'

The phenomenon usually labelled as 'multiple intertextuality' is a fundamental feature of imperial literature, which programmatically undertakes the deconstruction of the great models of the past in order to create new patterns by recurring to sophisticated techniques of combination and 'hybridization'. In the last decades, Flavian epic poetry has become a privileged field for research on intertextuality,[1] which can now take advantage of the (quantitatively impressive) evidence produced by the modern technological devices.[2]

In fact, multiplicity of models as well as their deconstruction (and reconstruction) are sides of the same coin. Processes of recollecting series and tracing 'genealogies' of patterns necessarily imply fragmentation and close analysis of details, which both serve to highlight affinities and establish relationships between characters, often displayed through the synthetic form of window-reference.[3] Sometimes, however, an even more creative and suggestive negotiation between conflicting patterns may take place, which invites us to go beyond the surface of their reciprocal opposition and discover unexpected signs of 'unity in diversity'. For example, detecting similarities within pairs of epic (and/or historical) antagonists leads the poet to deal with the difficult task of (re)constructing multi-faceted characters and giving coherence to their individual profiles. The epigonal, belated 'matrices' which result from such operations may even claim to reach the peculiar status of *a posteriori* archetypes of their own models.

---

[1] Its manifestations as well as its theory: Hinds (1998) and Barchiesi (2001); for insightful remarks see already Fowler (1997), esp. 20–25.
[2] On these new approaches, see Bernstein *et al.* (2015) and Chaudhuri *et al.* (2015). Coffee and Gawley, in this volume, provide a case study as well as further bibliography.
[3] On this imitative technique, also named 'double allusion', which originates in Alexandria and is widely diffused in Roman poetry, see at least DuQuesnay (1977) 54–55; Cairns (1979) 36–63; Thomas (1986); McKeown (1987) 37–45 and Clausen (1987) 20–21 and 61–69.

Silius' *Punica*, in particular, develops an inclusive relationship with literary tradition, in that it aims to saturate the paradigm of heroism through the systematic reuse of elements from different (sometimes even opposite) matrices.[4] The Flavian Hannibal provides an illuminating example of this artistic challenge, which seeks to enrich the semantic potential of the epic tradition. The strong influence of the historical portrait of the Carthaginian[5] is enhanced through the careful recollection of traits belonging to the greatest epic champions, such as Homer's Achilles, Hector and Ulixes or Virgil's Aeneas and Turnus, as well as the most famous couple of Roman antagonists, directly stemming from Lucan's counter-epic: Caesar and Pompey.[6] The internal tension produced by these reciprocally contrasting influences might cause the container to explode, were it not for a simultaneous reduction of their respective polarity. Once included as parts of the same individual, the components of each pair (or triad) of models seem to gradually attenuate their opposition, until finding even points of convergence. We are thus invited to discover unexpected relationships connecting patterns which, in their respective original contexts, stand on reciprocally opposite sides, as well as appreciate the poet's attempt to increase the 'problematic' depth and complexity of the narrative characters relying on his own literary competence.

Hannibal is undoubtedly the arch-enemy of the Romans, the symbol of atavistic hatred, which traces back to Dido's curse against Aeneas and his descendants.[7] Nonetheless, in the *Punica* he ends up embodying the maniacal 'suitor' of Rome, whose obsessive image sometimes makes him almost oblivious of his own homeland, to the point that it is sometimes difficult to understand the very nature of such a concentration of evil and passion. Hannibal as the (foreign) historical archetype of cruelty, treachery and lust for power, is anything but unfamiliar to the readers of Roman epic in the 1st century CE, who can easily compare the Carthaginian with Lucan's 'imperial' recollections of the masters of war dominating the political scene during the last decades of the Republic.

---

4 On Silius' 'multiple intertextuality' see Manuwald (2007), centred on the representation of the poet as an epic character.
5 Livy has long been recognized as the most important source text for Silius' Hannibal. As regards the possible contribution of other Latin historians (such as the Annalists), see Lucarini (2004) and the response by Spaltenstein (2006). However, Silius also draws on Polybius, Cornelius Nepos, Cicero, Valerius Maximus and Seneca. Up-to-date surveys of this topic are offered by Pomeroy (2010) and Stocks (2014) 13–44.
6 Stocks (2014) 53–79.
7 On the famous scene of the young Hannibal's oath in Dido's temple (Sil. 1.99–119) see the recent assessment by Ganiban (2010) 78–83.

The principal aim of this chapter is to focus on the influence exerted on Silius' Hannibal by the main characters of the *Bellum Civile*, Caesar and Pompey: two polar extremes, who—as literary models—may (for once) even 'concur' together so as to highlight the inner contradictions of the *Punica*'s 'dark' hero.[8] A first approximation to this technique (though still not an actual example), which mobilizes the resources of poetic invention in order to stress the pathos of crucial moments in the narrative, can already be considered Hannibal's farewell to his wife Imilce in Book 3 (Sil. 3.61–162): like Pompey's wife Cornelia, Imilce tries to resist being separated from her husband, but the way she describes Hannibal's titanic rage and absolute contempt for danger rather makes him resemble Lucan's Caesar.[9]

This phenomenon becomes more evident and symptomatic in the last phase of Hannibal's military campaign in Italy, when the Carthaginian leader—after reaching the zenith of his achievement at Cannae—has to deal with unrelenting decline. Therefore, I wish to concentrate on the final scenes of *Punica* Book 17 recounting Hannibal's departure from Italy and his flight from the battlefield at Zama. As further objects of analysis, I will take into consideration the endings of Book 2 and 13, both giving anticipations of an event which is excluded from the poem's diegetic horizon: Hannibal's death in exile.

2 After Zama: Hannibal's Last Words

Much has already been said about the 'inversion' that takes place towards the end of the poem, when Hannibal—progressively forced to withdraw into a narrow part of South Italy and finally obliged to leave for Africa—no longer reminds us of his previous Lucanian model, the 'fortunate' and demonic Caesar, but rather resembles the defeated Pompey.[10] However, we should not think that, starting from a certain point in the narrative, a radical change suddenly happens that necessarily leads to a mechanical substitution of one primary model (the villain's character) with the opposite one (the resigned victim of fate). On the contrary, more than featuring a mere reversal of situation, Silius' last book illustrates how the two extreme poles seem in fact to approach each other, how they negotiate their respective functions and even how they 'collaborate' in constructing a new

---

8 I borrow this definition from Rosati's chapter on Capaneus in this volume.
9 On the episode, see Bruère (1951) and (1952); La Penna (1981); Augoustakis (2010a) 198–199.
10 Stocks (2014) 67–70; on Silius and Lucan, see Marks (2010), Brouwers (1982) and Meyer (1924). As for the relationship between Silius' Hannibal and Lucan's Caesar in particular, see also Bernstein in this volume.

pattern: the 'late' Hannibal looks indeed like a syncretic figure, into which—among others—both Lucanian characters, the winner and the loser, are merged.

Despite his final defeat, the Flavian Hannibal does not abandon his proverbial *ira* as he did at the end of Livy's third decade and at the beginning of the fourth, where he rather displays a form of superior awareness, if not proper resignation.[11] On the contrary, according to Silius—after momentarily considering suicide as a means of escape during the battle of Zama (Sil. 17.566 *spectabat dextram ac leti fervebat amore*, "he looked to the sword in his right hand in his passionate desire for death")[12]—the Carthaginian switches again to become the titanic rebel whom we have known from the outset: i.e. the rebel against Rome and Jupiter's power. Before definitively leaving the stage, Hannibal declares himself proud of the feats accomplished (the great victory at Cannae, above all), which will grant him eternal fame—longer than Jupiter's reign—, and even shows he is still yearning for (or, better, dreaming of) revenge on Rome:

> ... caelum licet omne soluta
> in caput hoc conpage ruat terraeque dehiscant
> non ullo Cannas abolebis, Iuppiter, aevo,
> decedesque prius regnis, quam nomina gentes
> aut facta Hannibalis sileant. Nec deinde relinquo   610
> securam te, Roma, mei, patriaeque superstes
> ad spes armorum vivam tibi. nam modo pugna
> praecellis, resident hostes: mihi satque superque
> ut me Dardaniae matres atque Itala tellus,
> dum vivam, expectent nec pacem pectore norint.   615
>
> (Sil. 17.606–615)

... though the earth yawn asunder, though all the framework of heaven break up and fall upon my head, never shalt thou, Jupiter, wipe out the memory of Cannae, but thou shalt step down from thy throne ere the world forgets the name or achievements of Hannibal. Nor do I leave you, Rome, without dread of me: I shall survive my country and live on for you in the hope of warring against you. You win this battle, your foes are lying low: that is all for

---

11 Stocks (2014) 45–46 observes that in the *Punica* we have the exact reversal of the closural image of Hannibal in Livy's Book 30 (e.g. 30.30.29 *Hannibal peto pacem*, "now it's me, Hannibal, who seeks peace"), who looks "quietly and apparently subjected", i.e. characterized by a 'superior', almost detached resignation (an attitude which may remind us of Lucan's Pompey).

12 Juno's intervention prevents him from killing himself in a scene that parallels Scipio the Younger's attempt to commit suicide during the battle of Ticinus (an attempt failed because of the intervention of Mars: 4.454–460). On the whole scene of Book 17, see Fucecchi (2006 [=2010]) 325–331 and 342–344.

now. Enough, and more than enough for me, if Roman mothers and the people of Italy dread my coming while I live, and never know peace of mind.

(transl. by J.D. Duff)

In the first half of the speech (Sil. 17.606–610a), the Carthaginian leader seems well aware that he has provided abundant matter for literature (both history and poetry) and built a *monumentum Iove perennius*.[13] Both the present defeat at Zama as well as the previous, failed attempt to conquer Rome, which was rejected by Jupiter's lightning, are completely forgotten, almost erased. Rather, Hannibal powerfully conjures up the victory at Cannae as an event whose memory not even Jupiter will be able to wipe out and that will last longer than the reign of the Olympian dynasty. Playing his titanic role for the last time, Hannibal suggests the return of Chaos as the consequence of Jupiter's extreme attempt to defend his own power. Cosmic destruction (Sil. 17.606–607 *soluta* ... / *conpage*) reminds us of the scenario already evoked by Lucan in the *Laudes Neronis* as a metaphor for civil war: this might be interpreted as a sinister omen for the future of Rome:

> ... sic, cum <u>conpage soluta</u>
> saecula tot mundi suprema coegerit hora
> antiquum repetens iterum chaos ...
>
> (Luc. *BC* 1.72–74)
>
> ... even so, when the framework of the world is dissolved and the final hour, closing so many ages, reverts to primeval chaos ...
>
> (transl. by J.D. Duff)[14]

Thus, the world's end, that Silius' Hannibal imagines by recurring to the (Lucanian) vocabulary of Stoic *ekpyrosis*, would catch the king of the gods still engaged in the (vain) effort to erase the memory of *Cannae*. Finally, however, nothing will avert his abdication, while the fame of the Carthaginian is destined to survive.

The second part of Hannibal's last speech (Sil. 17.610b–615) gives a further, even more interesting clue. The Carthaginian leader leaves Jupiter aside, and concentrates on Rome as his privileged target. He, Hannibal, is still living and Rome has won a battle, not the whole war: or, better, Rome has gained victory over Carthage, not over Hannibal. Yet, the following, menacing prophecy (612 *ad spem*

---

13 Stocks (2014) 229–230.
14 Roche (2009) 152 *ad loc*. The same phrasing occurs in Statius' *Thebaid*, where Hades describes the unexpected arrival of the still living Amphiaraus in the underworld (*Theb.* 8.31): see Augoustakis (2016) 76 *ad loc*. Claudian uses this expression in *Rapt.* 1.115, when it is Hades himself who threatens to break the boundaries between the lower and the upper world.

armorum vivam etc., 614 *dum vivam*) sounds rather vague and does not manage to suggest the actual risk of a military revenge: Hannibal only aims at becoming a perennial nightmare for the Romans.

3 Silius' Late Hannibal between Caesar and Pompey

As is well known,[15] the last words pronounced by the Carthaginian leader in Silius' *Punica* are strongly reminiscent of the episode in Lucan's Book 5, where Caesar, while dealing with a terrible sea-storm aboard Amyclas' little vessel, proudly declares that he is ready to die and challenges both Jupiter and the Olympian gods:

> ... 'quantusne evertere' dixit
> 'me superis labor est, parva quem puppe sedentem   655
> tam magno petiere mari? si gloria leti
> est pelago donata mei bellisque negamur,
> intrepidus quamcumque datis mihi, numina, mortem
> accipiam. licet ingentis abruperit actus
> festinata dies fatis, sat magna peregi'.   660
>
> (Luc. *BC* 5.654–660)

...'is it a labour so great', says he, 'with the gods above to overwhelm me, whom, sitting in a little bark, they have assaulted me with seas so vast? if the glory of my end has been granted to the deep, and I am denied to the warfare, fearlessly will I receive whatever death, ye Deities, you send me. Although the day hurried on by the Fates should cut shorts my mighty exploits, things great enough have I done'.

(transl. by J.D. Duff)[16]

After pointing to the gods' intense (almost disproportionate) effort to destroy his *parva puppis*,[17] Caesar says that their attempt, be it successful or not, will not

---

15 Brouwers (1982); Fucecchi (1990); Marks (2010) and Stocks (2014).
16 The concessive clause introduced by *licet* at 659–660 matches the similar construction in Sil. 17.606–608 (quoted above), which nonetheless seems to display more preoccupation with the future (*non ... Cannas abolebis, Iuppiter*). For the use of *peregi*, see also Dido in Verg. *Aen.* 4.653 *vixi et quem dederat cursum Fortuna peregi*.
17 This looks as an anticipation of Pompey's destiny after Pharsalus (Luc. *BC* 8.258 *parva puppe fugit*). For the relationship of this image with Hannibal's exile, previously announced at the end of *Punica* Book 2 and 13, see below.

manage to erase the memory of his glorious deeds, which will last forever. Absolutely fearless of unheroic death at sea,[18] Caesar only cares to have *Fortuna* as witness (665–666) and, in his claims, he goes as far as to take advantage of that circumstance by meaningfully replaying *cum variatione* Atreus' famous phrase, *oderint dum metuant*:

> '... mihi funere nullo
> est opus, o superi: lacerum retinete cadaver
> fluctibus in mediis, desint mihi busta rogusque, –
> dum metuar semper terraque <u>expecter</u> ab omni'.
>
> (Luc. *BC* 5.668–671)

> 'I ask no burials of the gods: let them leave my mutilated corpse amid the waves; I can dispense with grave and funeral pyre, provided I am feared for ever and my appearance is dreaded by every land'.
>
> (transl. by J.D. Duff)

In the polemical self-eulogy delivered while fleeing from the battlefield of Zama, Hannibal too looks back at his own great deeds of the (relatively recent) past, which will ensure him eternal survival in glory. As a matter of fact, however, the Carthaginian's last words do not leave room for future victory nor will they be followed by actual revenge.[19] Unlike the 'demonic' protagonist of Lucan's *Civil War*—who, after being saved from the storm, will manage to win at Pharsalus with the help of *Fortuna*—Silius' late Hannibal, after the decisive defeat, can only try to bolster his self-confidence in the future, but will not be able to come back again. Therefore, he looks like both a degraded/diminished copy of himself as well as a failed imitation of Lucan's Caesar.

Moreover, we should not forget that the *Punica*'s ideological system is based upon the paradoxical assumption that Cannae represents the very turning point

---

18 Caesar's speech, like an apotropaic spell, subverts the words pronounced by Aeneas during the storm in Verg. *Aen.* 1.94–101, when—according to the epic code—the hero regrets not having died by the walls of Troy. Like Aeneas, however, Caesar will survive the storm and accomplish other major feats, such as the victory itself at Pharsalus. By contrast, the attitude of Silius' Hannibal, during the storm definitively averting him from Italy, looks completely different. The *makarismos* of his brother Hasdrubal (Sil. 17.260–267), who died in the battle of Metaurus, largely draws on Aeneas' speech in Virgil's *Aeneid* Book 1.

19 As we have seen above, despite his titanic rebellion, Hannibal almost seems to 'console' himself with the image of Roman mothers constantly fearing his return in the future (Sil. 17.613–615 ... *mihi satque superque / ut me Dardaniae matres ... / ... <u>expectent</u>*).

of the war, the nadir after which Rome will reach the zenith.[20] Such an assumption already makes Hannibal's (self-consolatory) pride sound unrealistic at the very least. The crude reality condemns him to rely on his past deeds only, i.e. his *nomen*, as is the case for Lucan's Pompey.

Thus, the way Silius' late Hannibal displays his (residual) vein of titanism brings closer together his irredeemable defeat with the destiny of Pompey. As already observed by Emanuele Narducci, Hannibal's last words in the *Punica* are largely indebted to Pompey's monologue when he heroically faces death (Luc. *BC* 8.622–635).[21] On that occasion, Pompey shows, perhaps for the first time in the poem, the greatness hinted at by his surname *Magnus* and proves that his posthumous fame will be a κτῆμα ἐς αἰεί: the way he faces death offering himself to Achillas' sword will add to his own glory more than all previous successful feats as a military and political leader.[22] Moreover, his display of self-awareness, deeply tinged with Stoicism, also seems to challenge the power of the gods, being as it is an attack against their cruel providence:

> ... spargant lacerentque licebit,
> sum tamen, o superi, felix, nullique potestas
> hoc auferre deo.
>
> (Luc. *BC* 8.629–631)

> ...though they should rend and tear me, still, o gods of heaven, I am happy and no god has the power to deprive me of that.
>
> (transl. by J.D. Duff)

According to the axiological system of Lucan's *Civil War*, Pompey's last words (or, rather, last thoughts), when he is about to die on the Egyptian shore, represent the ideal counterpart to those boastfully pronounced by Caesar during the storm. By picking up on and highlighting this contrast, Silius makes these two narratives converge into Hannibal's last speech and complement each other.

---

20 Sil. 9.350–353, see also Jupiter's words at 3.584–590.
21 Narducci (2002) 363, n. 170. On the challenging tone of this speech, see Narducci (2002) 441–447 and already Jal (1962) 188.
22 We are not so far from the eulogy of the sacrifice of the great Roman leaders in Silius' *Punica* (e.g. 3.584–590 and 9.350–351 *adora vulnera laudes / perpetuas paritura tibi*, "bless those wounds which shall bring you eternal glory").

4 Hannibal's Obsession with Rome: Other Concurrent Influences

As we have seen, more than suggesting an effective return, an actual military revenge, the defeated Hannibal, when fleeing from Zama, seems already to assume that he will survive mostly as a terrifying legend. Despite his sustained will to keep up with fate, while being preoccupied with the future and anxiety about survival, the Carthaginian general cannot but look like a diminished version of Lucan's Pompey himself, who is characterized, on the contrary, by an extraordinary capacity to endure adversity (Luc. *BC* 8.627 *adversa pati*) as well as a supreme indifference towards the strokes of destiny.

In the eyes of an informed reader, Hannibal's last, boastful, words as well as his pretentious promise to survive sound rather as a pathetic farewell, if not a self-epitaph. More exactly, they still lay emphasis on fame, survival in memory and, particularly, on the fear which Hannibal's name will raise forever:

> ... nec deinde relinquo   610
> securam te, Roma, mei, patriaeque superstes
> ad spes armorum <u>vivam tibi</u>. nam modo pugna
> praecellis, resident hostes: mihi satque superque
> ut me Dardaniae matres atque Itala tellus,
> dum <u>vivam</u>, expectent nec pacem pectore norint.   615
>
> (Sil. 17.610b–615)

... nor do I leave you, Rome, without dread of me: I shall survive my country and live on for you in the hope of warring against you. You win this battle, your foes are lying low: that is all for now. Enough, and more than enough for me, if Roman mothers and the people of Italy dread my coming while I live, and never know peace of mind.

(transl. by J.D. Duff)

The first *vivam* (612), strongly packed with pride, seems to gesture towards other occurrences of the term, which is also employed in a similar way by the Augustan poets, as is well known. Stocks, in particular, recalls the close of Ovid's *Metamorphoses* (15.879 *vivam*),[23] but a further Ovidian intertext might be at work here. I am referring to Ovid's *Amores* 1.15.41–42, where the poet is confident that he will

---

23 Stocks (2014) 229, n. 23; and also Tipping (2010) 104 for a metapoetic nuance in Hannibal's last words. See also e.g. Prop. 3.7.19–20; Luc. *BC* 9.985–986 *Pharsalia nostra / vivet*, "our Pharsalia shall live on"; until the finale of Statius' *Thebaid* (12.816 *vive, precor*). For another possible intertextual link to *vivam*, see below in the text. More generally, for the immortalizing power of poetry, see Hor. *Carm.* 3.30.6–7 and Tib. 1.4.65–66.

survive his own death: *ergo etiam cum me supremus adederit ignis, / vivam, parsque mei multa superstes erit*, "I too, when the final fires have eaten up my frame, shall still live on, and the great part of me survive my death" (transl. by G. Showerman).[24]

As well as carrying a metapoetic value, Hannibal's words also exhibit another outstanding feature. By means of a direct apostrophe to Rome (*Roma*) and owing to the presence of *tibi* (612), *dativus (in)commodi* strictly related to *vivam* ("I shall live on for you"), they hint that Rome remains Hannibal's private obsession, the only target of his persecutory desire.[25] Thus, Hannibal's threat against the enemy city also ends up sounding like the delirious message of a passionately faithful 'lover' who has been rejected, almost a maniacal suitor or, rather, persecutor of the *Urbs*.

It is probably worth observing that there is another occurrence of *vivam tibi*, which also occupies the same, central, position in the verse, i.e. at the end of the hexameter's fourth foot. This occurrence comes from the speech addressed by the dying Maecenas to Augustus in the second *Elegy for Maecenas* of the *Appendix Vergiliana*. Maecenas, close to death, would have liked to receive his beloved wife's embrace, but she was not there (*El. Maec.* 2.153–154). Therefore, his last thought goes to his closest friend, the *princeps*, in the hope that he will keep dear his friend's memory:

> hoc mihi contingat, iaceam tellure sub aequa;
>   nec tamen hoc ultra te doluisse velim,   160
> sed meminisse velim: vivam sermonibus illic;
>   semper ero, semper si meminisse voles.

---

[24] Ovid's proud self-awareness is shared by the first imperial followers (and critics) of the Augustan poets. Lucan's *Civil War* already offers us a remarkable parallel in the narrator's final comment on Caesar's visit at Troy (Luc. *BC* 9.980–986): *o sacer et magnus vatum labor! omnia fato / eripis et populis donas mortalibus aevum. / invidia sacrae, Caesar, ne tangere famae; / nam, siquid Latiis fas est promittere Musis, / quantum Zmyrnaei durabunt vatis honores, / venturi me teque legent; Pharsalia nostra / vivet, et a nullo tenebris damnabimur aevo*, "how mighty, how sacred is the poet's task! He snatches all things from destruction and gives to mortal men immortality. Be not jealous, Caesar, of those whom fame has consecrated; for, if it is permissible for the Latin Muses to promise aught, then, as long as the fame of Smyrna's bard endures, posterity shall read my verse and your deeds; our Pharsalia shall live on, and no age will ever doom us to oblivion." (transl. by J.D. Duff)

[25] I do not share the doubts manifested by Delz (1987) regarding the authenticity of *tibi*, whose relevance to the context I shall try to illustrate below.

> et decet et certe vivam tibi semper amore,
> nec tibi qui moritur desinit esse tuus.
>
> (*El. Maec.* 2.159–163)

This be my lot, to lie beneath the impartial earth: nor yet would I have you longer grieve for this. But I would wish for remembrance: there in your talk would I live; for I shall always exist, if you will always remember me. It is fitting so, and I shall surely live for you in affection ever; your dying friend ceases not to be your own.

(transl. by J.D. Duff)

The power of memory is here celebrated in that it corresponds to perennial friendship: Maecenas' words highlight the close tie connecting him to Augustus, which will last well beyond the limits of human life. It is tempting to guess that Silius may have drawn on this image too and perverted its meaning so as to represent Hannibal's obsession with Rome as well as the paradoxical idea of an everlasting persecution.

The phrasing *vivam tibi*, in the same verse position, also recurs in another text: Lucan's *Civil War*. When the moment of the decisive battle approaches, Pompey decides to leave Cornelia in safe keeping on Lesbos: she tries in vain to dissuade him, for she cannot bear the thought of surviving war while being unaware of Pompey's death:

> ... secura videtur
> sors tibi, cum facias etiamnunc vota, perisse?
> ut nolim servire malis sed morte parata
> te sequar ad manes: feriat dum maesta remotas
> fama procul terras, vivam tibi nempe superstes.
>
> (Luc. *BC* 5.771–775)

Do you think it is an easy lot for me to have already perished while you are still praying for success? Suppose I refuse to be mastered by misfortune, and follow you to the nether world by a prompt death; yet, until the sad news falls on regions far away, I shall surely live on after you are dead.

(transl. by J.D. Duff)

In this passage, in addition to *vivam tibi*, we also come across the term *superstes*, as we have seen in Silius 17.611–612 and Ovid *Am.* 1.15.42. In Lucan, however, *tibi* goes with *superstes*, not with *vivam*. Hannibal and Maecenas are both confident that they will live in the memory of their (more or less direct) interlocutors. Cornelia, on the contrary, fears that her husband may die in war: her words imply that surviving Pompey represents for her the worst of all nightmares. However, despite the differences, Hannibal's menacing words and Maecenas' hopeful confidence, not least Cornelia's prayer, all express a fundamentally similar wish.

Each character hopes to 'accompany' his/her respective addressee and share his/her destiny until and even beyond the end: the first two by surviving in their memory at least, the third by staying together and eventually dying with him. With regard to Hannibal in particular, he will never allow Rome to feel like a *relicta*; thus his threatening promise 'to live for Rome' seems to be brought about by a dangerous combination of ancestral hatred and obsessive 'passion'.

5 Hannibal's Fighting for Rome (against Fate)

Therefore, although in a 'negative' manner, Silius' Hannibal draws on the two Lucanian patterns of Caesar and Pompey, which are combined so as to explore new possibilities in character construction. Hannibal's relationship with Rome and Italy is a case in point, which demonstrates the extent to which the Flavian poets may deconstruct their models in order to inject new life into them. The image of Rome, identified with Jupiter's power, still represents the major obsession of the general, defeated at Zama and exacerbated by his previous frustrated attempts to conquer the *Urbs* and keep control of Italy. Hannibal thus combines a sort of Caesarean behaviour, characterised by indomitable energy, impatience and anxiety about success, with some distinctive features of Pompey's ethos, such as nostalgia and deep love for his homeland. This merging results in a paradoxical attitude: by replacing Carthage, his real *patria*, with Rome, Hannibal is also forced into the role of 'rejected suitor' of Rome itself.

In the last part of this chapter, I set out to argue that noticeable traces of this sort of paranoid schizophrenia can already be spotted before Hannibal's departure from Italy. Lines 149–291 of Silius' Book 17 are centred on the contrast between Carthage's pathetic prayer for Hannibal's return and the latter's reluctance to respond to his homeland's call for help. Carthage still looks at Hannibal as its greatest champion and its last 'rampart' (Sil. 17.149–150 *stabat Carthago, truncatis undique membris / uni innixa viro*, "now that all her limbs were severed, Carthage depended entirely upon one man for support"). By contrast, Hannibal does not properly incline to play the role equivalent to Trojan Hector and, as the poet points out, this is not because of his lack of good will. In fact, Hannibal's fortune has changed over time and he cannot provide the help his homeland is expecting from him. The truth is that he has lost much of his previous strength: only his *nomen* is left in support of his country (17.150–151): *tantoque fragore ruentem / Hannibal absenti retinebat nomine molem*, "the great name of Hannibal, even in his absence, kept the edifice of her greatness from falling in utter ruin".²⁶ Thus, Hannibal's portrayal in the last books of the *Punica* clearly depends upon the introduction of Pompey in Lucan's *Civil War* (Luc. *BC* 1.135 as *magni nominis umbra*, "the mere shadow of a mighty name"), followed by the famous comparison between Magnus with a grand old oak which is no longer firmly rooted in the soil (1.136–143).²⁷

Finally, Hannibal decides to come to the aid of Carthage, giving up his resentment towards many of his fellow citizens, who belittled his deeds and denied him the help he needed. However, the narrator does not fail to stress how difficult this choice is for Hannibal. The pathos reaches its climax with Hannibal's departure from Italy, which recalls that of an *exul* leaving his beloved homeland:

> ductor defixos Itala tellure tenebat
> intentus vultus, manantesque ora rigabant
> per tacitum lacrimae, et suspiria crebra ciebat;
> haud secus ac patriam pulsus dulcisque penatis
> linqueret et tristis exul traheretur in oras.
>
> (Sil. 17.213–217)

> ... while all the Carthaginians soldiers bent their gaze upon the sea, Hannibal kept his eyes steadily fixed on the Italian coast; the silent tears flowed down his cheeks, and again and again he sighed, like an exile driven to a dismal shore, who leaves behind his native land and the home he loves.²⁸
>
> (transl. by J.D. Duff)

---

26 See also Sil. 16.17–19 ... *proque omnibus armis / et castrorum opibus dextrisque recentibus unum / Hannibalis sat nomen erat*, "the name of Hannibal was enough: it took the place of all weapons and camp-equipments and fresh recruits"; Fucecchi (1990), 156 and 159.

27 See also Luc. *BC* 8.449–450 *quis nominis umbram / horreat?*, "who would dread a mere empty name?"

28 Cf. Livy 30.20.7 *raro quemquam alium patriam exsilii causa relinquentem tam maestum abisse ferunt quam Hannibalem hostium terra excedentem; respexisse saepe Italiae litora ...*, "seldom, according to the accounts, has any one left his native country to go into exile in such gloomy sorrow as Hannibal manifested when quitting the country of his foes. It is stated that he often looked back to the shores of Italy ..." (transl. by C. Roberts). Hannibal's sorrow is in sharp contrast with his soldiers' desire for African coasts (17.211–212) as well as with the (enthusiastic) incredulity of Italian people (17.203–211; cf. also the Trojans' surprise in discovering the (false) departure of the Greeks in Verg. *Aen.* 2.25–30). This time, however, the enemy will not come back: the storm raised by Neptune will prevent him from reaching the Italian shore again.

There are various textual contacts both with Lucan and Virgil, over which I will not linger, as they are well known.[29] However, one detail deserves special attention. Unlike his main poetic antecedents (Aeneas, Pompey), who are depicted as undergoing their fate with virile resignation to a greater or lesser degree, Hannibal displays a peculiarly rebellious character. He is a 'resistant exile', who does not accept his destiny without a struggle, as is well shown by his further attempt to regain the Italian shore, shortly after leaving for Africa (Sil. 17.218–235). This crucial passage, which is followed by the sea-storm raised by Neptune, marks the strongest difference with Pompey's sad and resigned departure from Brundisium at the opening of *Civil War* Book 3. Although Hannibal, like Pompey, will no longer see the Italian shore, his intention to go back and challenge the gods' will inevitably recalls Caesar's obstinate fight against the sea-storm in *Civil War* Book 5, but with the fundamental difference that, while Caesar is rejected on the Greek shore (and thus literally 'preserved' by Fortune for his future success in war), Hannibal is pushed towards Africa, his proper homeland, only to undergo a decisive defeat.

Hannibal looks at Italy as if it were his own homeland (as is actually the case with Pompey). But such attraction turns into an obsessive, compulsive sentiment that even induces the Carthaginian general to forget his duties, and even his identity. Displaying a perverse affection towards the enemy land, he almost goes as far as to abandon his role of national hero, that of Dido's and Hamilcar's avenger.

6 An Instinctive Rebellion (and a Puzzling Verb)

Now, let us take a closer look at the introductory lines of Hannibal's monologue: this will help us appreciate some further effects of tension between his two opposite Lucanian models:

---

[29] Silius draws on very famous scenes like Aeneas' departures from Troy (Verg. *Aen.* 3.10–12) and Carthage respectively (Verg. *Aen.* 5.1–6) as well as on Pompey's flight from Italy in Luc. *BC* 2.725–731 and above all 3.1–7 (see von Albrecht (1964); Fucecchi (1990) etc.). The whole scene may also be reminiscent of the pathetic account in Ov. *Tr.* 1.2 (e.g. 14–16 *ipsa graves spargunt ora loquentis aquae, / terribilisque Notus iactat mea dicta, precesque / ad quos mittuntur, non sinit ire deos*, "my very lips, as I speak, are sprayed by the heavy waves, and dread Notus hurls away my words nor suffers my prayers to reach the gods to whom they are directed" (transl. by A. Wheeler); cf. Sil. 17.258 *super ora*). At the beginning of Lucan's Book 7, we read that Pompey will be able to see Rome again only in his dreams: see Luc. *BC* 7.23–24 with Lanzarone (2016) 102–105 *ad loc.*

... mentisne ego compos et hoc nunc
indignus reditu, qui memet finibus umquam
<u>amorim</u> Ausoniae? flagrasset subdita taedis
Carthago, et potius cecidisset nomen Elissae.

(Sil. 17.221–224)

... am I mad? do not I deserve to return thus, as a punishment for ever leaving Italy? Better that Carthage had been burned with fire, and the name of Elissa been blotted out forever!

(transl. by J.D. Duff)[30]

Hannibal suddenly feels ashamed and reproaches himself for abandoning in such a dishonourable way the land where he has spent a great part of his life. It would seem a matter of wounded pride: nobody will probably think of nostalgia nor frustrated affection for an 'adoptive homeland'.

Yet, we should perhaps pay more attention to *amorim*, an awkward verb to be sure, which strangely enough has not raised particular doubts or suspicions.[31] In fact, this syncopated form for *amoverim* is a hapax. Moreover, while the most

---

30 In Duff's translation the relative clause with subjunctive mood is given causal sense in support of the preceding rhetorical questions (see also the French translation in Nisard's collection: "Suis-je donc maître de ma raison? n'ai-je pas mérité la honte de ce retour, pour avoir pu me décider à quitter l'Italie? N'eût-il pas mieux valu laisser périr le nom d'Élise dans les ruines fumantes de Carthage?"): as it were, 'decidedly, I am mad and I do deserve such a shameful return, if I can leave Ausonia in this way'. In order to stress the rhetorical character of the whole passage, Stocks (2014) 204 treats the relative clause as if it were a further interrogative ("should I ever have removed myself from the borders of Italy?"). In slightly different way, according to Vinchesi (2001) 957, Hannibal's words would express a note of serious regret rather than bitter self-irony ("sono io sempre Annibale? e non sono ora io indegno di questo ritorno, io che non mi sarei mai allontanato dai confini di Ausonia?") and the relative-causal clause (where *umquam* is treated as equivalent to *numquam*) should explain the reason of such an 'indignity' ('I would never have left Ausonia'). Be it as it may, Hannibal's thought follows two steps. At first, we read the recrimination against his own decision to leave Italy and for not having immediately attacked Rome after *Cannae* (225–229; see Livy 30.20.7 ... *et deos hominesque accusantem in se quoque ac suum ipsius caput exsecratum quod non cruentum ab Cannensi victoria militem Romam duxisset* etc., "accusing gods and men and even cursing himself for not having led his soldiers reeking with blood from the victorious field of Cannae straight to Rome", transl. by C. Roberts). Then, we have a further (elsewhere unattested) access of fury (230–231): "but there's still time: why not try again?" The motif of the 'bad return' also reminds us of Hannibal's polemics against the Carthaginian senate (e.g. Livy 30.20.4 *neque hac deformitate reditus mei tam Scipio exsultabit atque efferet sese quam Hanno* etc., "it is not Scipio who will pride himself and exult over the disgrace of my return so much as Hanno ...", transl. by C. Roberts).
31 For a first, cursory, glance at this issue, see Fucecchi (2006 [=2010]) 329, n. 58.

common type of internal cut consists of the loss of the temporal suffix -*vi*- juxtaposed to the present stem,[32] in the form *amorim* it is part of the word's semantic root which falls at the same time.[33] The case attested in Silius is not the only one in Latin literature, as is shown by at least two instances of *commorit* (= *commoverit*: *Rhet. Her.* 4.60; Cic. *Fam.* 8.15.1); three of *commorat* (= *commoverat*: Ter. *Phorm.* 101; Turpil. *Com.* 30 Ribbeck; Cic. *QFr.* 2.1.1); two of *promorat* (= *promoverat*: Hor. *Epod.* 11.14; Phaedr. 4.26); one of *admoram* (= *admoveram*: Prop. 3.3.5, the only other case in the 1st person), *admorat* (= *admoverat*: Ov. *Am.* 3.8.38) and *remorant* (= *removerant*: Hor. *Sat.* 2.1.71).

Finally, apart from its morphological uniqueness, *āmorim* is also puzzling because it may recall *ămor*, a word which cannot stand at the beginning of the dactylic hexameter, due to its initial short *ă*- (unless we assume a wordplay like this). At the same time, by virtue of the synaloepha (here reinforced by alliteration), *amorim* seems almost to merge into the following *Ausoniae*. I am perfectly aware that this last suggestion would imply an artistic intention which is obviously impossible to demonstrate. Nonetheless, in my opinion, the curious phonosemantic effect produced by the juxtaposition of the two words at the beginning of Silius' line, in this particular context, deserved a brief mention at least.

A further clue in that sense might come from intertextuality: precisely from Lucan's Pompey again. The night before the battle of Pharsalus, Magnus dreams of being in his theatre, in Rome, where people enthusiastically praise his name with loud applause and triumphal shout (Luc. *BC* 7.7–19). Then, the narrator lists three possible explanations of the dream (7.19–24), which are followed by some pathetic considerations about Pompey's fate of dying far from Rome (7.24b–44), the city to which he was tied by a passionate reciprocal love:

> o felix, si te vel sic tua Roma videret!
> donassent utinam superi patriaeque tibique   30
> unum, Magne, diem, quo fati certus uterque
> extremum tanti fructum raperetis <u>amoris</u>.
> tu velut <u>Ausonia</u> vadis moriturus <u>in urbe</u>,
> illa rati semper de te sibi conscia voti

---

32 E.g. *laudarim* = *laudaverim*: e.g. Cic. *Fam.* 1.9.4; *probarim* = *probaverim*: e.g. Cic. *Verr.* 2.2.142.
33 In fact *movi* is usually considered a case of perfect with suffix -*vi* (*mōvi* < **mov-vi*): Ernout (1914) 296–297. Nonetheless, in the case of *amorim* the fall of part of the word's stem (together with the suffix) is undeniable. Instead, forms like *norim* (= *noverim*: Varro *Ling.* 7.4.5; Cic. *Att.* 5.6.2; Livy 23.42.12; Prop. 3.15.1 *sic ego non ullos iam norim in amore tumultus*, "so may I know no further storms in my love") and its compound *cognorim* (= *cognoverim*: e.g. Cic. *Fam.* 6.9.2; 8.16.1) only exemplify the fall of a suffix -*vi*.

> hoc scelus haud umquam fatis haerere putavit,   35
> sic se dilecti tumulum quoque perdere Magni.
>
> (7.29–36)
>
> Fortunate had been the Rome he loved, if she had seen him even in a dream. One day at least the gods should have granted to him and to his country, on which each, with full knowledge of the future, might have snatched the last enjoyment of their great <u>love</u> for one another. He goes forth, believing that he is destined to die in the Ausonian city; hile she, knowing that her prayers for him had always been answered, refused to believe that this horror was written in the book of destiny—that she should thus lose even the grave of her beloved Magnus.
>
> (transl. by J.D. Duff)

Pompey's glorious past has become nothing but a dream, where the joyful atmosphere of the triumph can neither sweeten the bitterness of the present nor the tragedy of imminent defeat. The painful regret for what did not (and will no longer) happen pervades the whole passage. In such a nostalgic evocation of the love theme (*amor*), dominated by a sense of unattainable happiness, the notion of Pompey's actual distance from the city (*Ausonia ... in urbe*) plays an important role. War crisis and his own Eastern connections led Pompey to leave his homeland and now—just before the decisive (and unlucky) battle—we find him dreaming of an eventual (even triumphal) return. Unfortunately, however, the two lovers will not meet again and Pompey will die abroad, not *in urbe Ausonia*.

Such a generic designation for Rome is worthy of our attention. It well fits the viewpoint (if not the very words) of an *exul*; especially if we think that Ovid uses it twice in the *Epistulae ex Ponto* to highlight his own distance (geographical as well as cultural) from Rome itself (*Pont*. 3.2.101–102 *quid facere Ausonia geniti debetis in urbe, / cum tangant duros talia facta Getas?*, "what ought ye to do, born in the Ausonian city, when such deeds move the stern Getae?"; *Pont*. 4.8.85–86 *... ut ponar in ullo / qui minus Ausonia distat ab urbe loco*, "may I be set in a place less distant than this from the Ausonian city").[34] In Lucan's passage the only relative proximity of *amor* and *Ausonia* (*in urbe*) could serve to stress Pompey's definitive separation from Rome and thus increase pathetic tension. When narrating Hannibal's painful sea voyage back to Africa and his momentary hesitation between (resigned) sadness and (titanic) anxiety of revenge, Silius may also have been influenced by Pompey's dream on the eve of the battle of Pharsalus. In the *Punica*, however, the closer juxtaposition *amorim Ausoniae*, covering the first

---

34 The two Ovidian parallels are registered by Lanzarone (2016) 116 *ad loc.*, together with Mart. *Spect*. 5.1 [4.5] *exulat Ausonia profugus delator ab urbe*, "the informer is a fugitive in exile from the Ausonian city" (transl. by D.R. Shackleton Bailey).

half of line 223 until the primary caesura, rather emphasizes the moment when Hannibal's further rebellion to fate is set off and provides it indirectly with a paradoxical motivation.

It is worth noting that a few lines before hinting at the second of Pompey's dreams in the *Bellum civile*, Silius has referred to a previous dream of Pompey's. In fact, Hannibal's nightmare, when he sees himself attacked with drawn swords by the ghosts of Flaminius, Gracchus and Paulus,[35] is certainly reminiscent of Caesar's dream after the battle of Pharsalus (Luc. *BC* 7.776 *omnes in Caesare manes*, "all the ghosts alike attack Caesar", and 781–783 *hunc omnes gladii, quos aut Pharsalia vidit / aut ultrix visura dies stringente senatu, / illa nocte premunt, hunc infera monstra flagellant*, "all the swords that Pharsalia saw, and all that the day of vengeance was to see drawn by the Senate, were aimed at Caesar's breast that night"). However, it also links up with Pompey's first dream, during the journey to Greece, when Magnus saw the ghost of his dead wife, Julia, menacingly standing amid the flames of her funeral pyre like an infernal Fury (Luc. *BC* 3.9–11 ... *diri tum plena horroris imago / visa caput maestum per hiantis Iulia terras / tollere et accenso furialis stare sepulchro*, "[Julia] a spectre full of dread and menace, raised her sorrowful head above the yawning hearth and stood in the guise of a Fury amid the flames of her funeral pyre").[36] Pompey's second dream, on the contrary, is not based upon the sense of guilt: the image of his public acclamation in the theatre is interpreted as the typical manifestation of an unconscious desire. For that reason, it perfectly suits Hannibal's nostalgia for his own deeds of the recent past and may also account for his sudden emotive reaction.

---

35 Sil. 17.160–163 *namque gravis curis carpit dum nocte quietem, / cernere Flaminium Gracchumque et cernere Paulum / visus erat simul adversos mucronibus in se / destrictis ruere atque Itala depellere terra* ..., "while resting at night from his burden of anxiety, he dreamed that Flaminius, Gracchus and Paulus were all attacking him at once with drawn swords and driving him off the soil of Italy". Something similar apparently happens to the late, exiled, Hannibal (Sil. 2.704–705 *saepe Saguntinis somnos exterritus umbris / optabit cecidisse manu* etc., "often, startled in his sleep by the ghosts of Saguntum, he shall wish that he had fallen by sword").
36 See in part. Luc. *BC* 3.14–15 (the Furies who brandish torches against the armies of the rivals) and the final claustrophobic image of persecution (30–32 ... *veniam te bella gerente / in medias acies. numquam tibi, Magne, per umbras / perque meos manes genero non esse licebit*, "when you fight battles, I shall appear in the centre of the fray: never shall my shade, my ghost, suffer you to forget that you were husband to Caesar's daughter").

7 Hannibal's Final Defeat and His Exile

After the forced and traumatic *discidium* from Italy, Hannibal suffers the humiliating defeat at Zama and soon he undergoes exile in the proper sense. In fact, this last chapter of his life remains outside the chronological range of the Flavian *Punica*, which—just like Livy's third decade—stops with Scipio's triumph, at the end of 3rd century BCE. Nonetheless, following its taste for digression (as well as the sake of completeness), Silius' poem anticipates the tragic end of the years spent by Hannibal in Asia Minor, first, at the court of the Syrian king Antiochus III at Ephesus, and then at Nicomedia, hosted by Prusias I, king of Bithynia, who finally decides to surrender him to the Romans.[37]

Such anticipations, in form of rapid extradiegetic allusions, are placed at crucial points of the narrative: at the end of Book 2, on the fall of Saguntum,[38] and at the end of Scipio's katabasis in Book 13, where the Sybil—at the same time—announces the exile of Carthage's future conqueror from the ungrateful Rome (Sil. 13.868–893). By focusing on the image of the exiled Carthaginian, who finally commits suicide in order to avoid being captured by the Romans,[39] these allusions serve both as reminders of the ultimate power of *fides*[40] and reassure the internal audience (Scipio) as well as readers about the efficacy of divine retributive justice.[41]

For my purpose, however, I wish to highlight the exile theme as a (more or less immediate) consequence of the military defeat, which also weakens Hannibal's political authority, favouring the internal aristocratic opposition. The great leader pays for his trickery once and for all: he has left his wife and son at Carthage (Sil. 13.879–880 ... *desertis coniuge fida / et dulci nato linquet Carthaginis*

---

[37] Hannibal's exile goes from 195 BCE until the death (between 183 and 181 BCE).
[38] Sil. 2.696–707 (see above n. 35) where the narrator's comment on the fall of the city symbol of *fides* is stressed by the praise of its citizens (*venerabile vulgus*).
[39] Sil. 2.705–707 ... *ferroque negato / invictus quondam Stygias bellator ad undas / deformata feret liventi membra veneno*, "the steel will be denied him, and the warrior once invincible in earlier years shall carry down to the waters of Styx a body disfigured and blackened by poison", and 13.890–892 ... *perstantibus inde / Aeneadis reddique sibi poscentibus hostem / pocula furtivo rapiet properata veneno*, "then, when Rome persists in demanding the surrender of her foe, in hasty stealth he will swallow a draught of poison".
[40] Sil. 2.700–701 *audite, o gentes, neu rumpite foedera pacis / nec regnis postferte fidem* ..., "hear it, ye nations, and break not treaties of peace nor set power above loyalty!"
[41] Sil. 13.874–875 the Sybil announces Hannibal's final punishment to Scipio: '*ne metue!*' *exclamat vates 'non vita sequetur / inviolata virum*', "'Fear not,' cried the priestess, 'no life of untroubled prosperity shall be his'".

arces, but see also 3.61–65, above), and begins his tour all around the East Mediterranean aboard one ship only (13.881–882 *atque una profugus lustrabit caerula puppe. / hinc Cilicis Tauri saxosa cacumina uiset*, "he flees across the sea with a single ship. Next he will visit the rocky heights of Mount Taurus in Cilicia").[42] Hotly pursued by the Romans, he is obliged to recommend himself to his tyrannical hosts, but is always afraid of being surrendered to the enemy. Thus, Hannibal becomes an example of how difficult it is to die at the right time:

> Assyrio famulus regi falsusque cupiti
> Ausoniae motus dubio petet aequora velo,
> donec Prusiacas delatus segniter oras
> altera servitia imbelli patietur in aevo
> et latebram munus regni.
>
> (13.886–890)

He will serve a Syrian king and, cheated of his hope to make war against Rome, he will put to sea with no certain destination, and at last drift idly to the land of Prusias, where, too old to fight any more, he will suffer a second slavery and find a hiding-place by the king's favour.

(transl. by J.D. Duff)

In this sense, his fate mirrors that of Pompey again, as we see him after being defeated at Pharsalus in Lucan's poem. Magnus himself sails on board a small vessel along the Cilician coast (Luc. *BC* 8.257–258 ... *Cilicum per litora tutus / parva puppe fugit*, "he flees unharmed along the coasts of Cilicia in his litle vessel") and, before the Roman senate gathers abroad, he declares his intention to ask the Parthians for help against Caesar.[43] But Lentulus finally persuades him not to become the servant of Crassus' killers (Luc. *BC* 8.339 *Parthorum famulus*) and points rather to Egypt, whose king, Tolomeus VI, looks more like a reliable host. There, Pompey encounters a tragic end, which however prevents him from humiliation and slavery, at least.[44] Indeed he delivers exemplary virtue before the eyes of his

---

42 See already Sil. 2.701–702 *vagus exul in orbe / errabit toto patriis proiectus ab oris*, "banished from his native land, he shall wander, an exile, over the whole earth".
43 Pompey's flight in a *parva puppis* echoes the image of Caesar's *exigua carina* amid the storm (5.503): see above.
44 Death is also a way to avoid being prosecuted by nightmares, like the ghosts of the dead at Pharsalus (Luc. *BC* 8.505–509 ... *rapitur civilibus umbris. / nec soceri tantum arma fugit: fugit ora senatus, / cuius Thessalicas saturat pars magna volucres, / et metuit gentes quas uno in sanguine mixtas / deseruit, regesque timet quorum omnia mersit*, "he is dragged down by the ghosts of those who fell in civil war. It is not mere Caesar's sword that he flies from: he flies also from the face of the senators, of whom so many are now glutting the vultures of Thessaly; he fears the foreign

wife and his son: the old big oak turns out to be perfectly aware of the greatness of his *nomen* (Luc. BC 8.629–631 ... *spargant lacerentque licebit, / sum tamen, o superi, felix, nullique potestas / hoc auferre deo*, "though men scatter and mutilate my limbs, nevertheless, ye gods, I am a fortunate man, and of this no god can deprive me").

8 Conclusion

In this chapter centred on Hannibal, probably the most prominent individual of Silius' *Punica*, I have tried to illustrate the sophisticated technique adopted by the Flavian epicist in constructing a complex character through the conflation of traditionally opposite patterns. The choice of the couple Caesar/Pompey, the two main antagonists of Lucan's poem on civil war, as privileged antecedents for the poetic recollection of the 'late' Hannibal, has given us the opportunity to reconsider the actual meaning of their opposition within the text-model, as well as to explore other possible forms of relationship between them.

At the same time, we have seen how a belated, exquisitely intertextual character like the Carthaginian leader (Rome's enemy *par excellence*)—thanks to his composite nature—may feature as an 'a posteriori' archetype of the two greatest masters of war of the late republic. Thus, in this specific case, such a technique leads in an indirect way to inviting readers to appreciate the perpetuation of Hannibal's most 'familiar' traits in a Roman political (as well as literary) context. From the vantage point of his 'belatedness', which helps him problematize the use itself of the intertextual device, Silius is thus legitimizing his own right to stand as a critic of a whole literary tradition.

---

nations, whom he forsook and left weltering in blood together; he dreads the kings, whose all he destroyed"). Similar terrific visions, the night after the carnage of Pharsalus, disturbed Caesar and his soldiers (7.772–773 ... *umbra perempti / civis adest; sua quemque premit terroris imago*, "the ghost of a slain countryman stands by the bed; each man has a different shape of terror to haunt him" and "all the swords that Pharsalia saw", and 776 ... *omnes in Caesare manes*, "all the ghosts alike attack Caesar"): see already above, § 6.

Bibliography

von Albrecht, Michael (1964), *Silius Italicus. Freiheit und Gebundenheit römischer Epik*, Amsterdam.
Augoustakis, Antony (2010a), *Motherhood and the Other. Fashioning Female Power in Flavian Epic*, Oxford.
Augoustakis, Antony (ed.) (2010b), *Brill's Companion to Silius Italicus*, Leiden/Boston.
Augoustakis, Antony (2016), *Statius*, Thebaid *8*, Oxford.
Barchiesi, Alessandro (2001), "Genealogie letterarie nell'epica imperiale: fondamentalismo e ironia", in: Schmidt (2001) 315–362.
Bernstein, Neil/Gervais, Kyle/Lin, Wei (2015), "Comparative rates of text reuse in classical Latin hexameter poetry", in: *Digital Humanities Quarterly* 9.3, http://www.digitalhumanities.org/dhq/vol/9/3/000237/000237.html (seen 1.4.2018).
den Boeft, Jan/Kessels, Antonius H.M. (eds.) (1982), *Actus. Studies in Honour of H.L.W. Nelson*, Utrecht.
Brouwers, Johann H. (1982), "Zur Lucan-Imitation bei Silius Italicus", in: den Boeft/Kessels (1982) 73–87.
Bruère, Richard T. (1951), "Lucan's Cornelia", in: *CPh* 46, 221–236.
Bruère, Richard T. (1952), "Silius Italicus, Punica 3.62–162 and 4.763–822", in: *CPh* 47, 219–227.
Cairns, Francis (1979), *Tibullus: A Hellenistic Poet at Rome*, Cambridge.
Chaudhuri, Pramit/Dexter, Joseph P./Bonilla Lopez, Jorge A. (2015), "Strings, Triangles, and go-betweens: Intertextual Approaches to Silius' Carthaginian Debates", in: *Dictynna* [En ligne], 12 (mis en ligne le 17 mai 2016). URL: http://dictynna.revues.org/1156 (seen 7.10.2017).
Clausen, Wendell (1987), *Virgil's* Aeneid *and the Tradition of Hellenistic Poetry*, Berkeley/Los Angeles.
Delz, Josef (1987), *Silius Italicus, Punica*, Stuttgart.
DuQuesnay, Ian M. Le M. (1977), "Vergil's Fourth Eclogue", in: *PLLS* 1, 25–99.
Ernout, Alfred (1914), *Morphologie historique du latin*, Paris.
Fowler, Don (1997), "On the Shoulders of Giants: Intertextuality and Classical Studies", in: *MD* 39, 13–34.
Fucecchi, Marco (1990), "Il declino di Annibale nei *Punica*", in: *Maia* 42, 151–166.
Fucecchi, Marco (2006 [= 2010]), "*Ad finem ventum*. Considerazioni sull'ultimo libro dei *Punica*", in: *Aevum* n.s. 6, 311–345.
Ganiban, Randall T. (2010), "Virgil's Dido and the Heroism of Hannibal in Silius' *Punica*", in: Augoustakis (2010b) 73–98.
Hinds, Stephen (1998), *Allusion and Intertext. Dynamics of Appropriation in Roman Poetry*, Cambridge.
Jal, Paul (1962), "Les dieux et les guerres civiles dans la Rome de la fin de la République", in: *REL* 40, 170–200.
La Penna, Antonio (1981), "Tipi e modelli femminili nella cultura dell'epoca dei Flavi", in: *Atti del Congresso Internazionale di Studi Vespasianei, Rieti, settembre 1979*, I, Rieti, 223–251.
Lucarini, Carlo Martino (2004), "Le fonti storiche di Silio Italico", in: *Athenaeum* 92, 103–126.
Manuwald, Gesine (2007), "Epic poets as characters: On poetics and multiple intertextuality in Silius Italicus' *Punica*", in: *RFIC* 135, 71–90.
Marks, Raymond (2010), "Silius and Lucan", in: Augoustakis (2010b) 127–153.

McKeown, James C. (1987), *Ovid*, Amores. *Vol. I: Text and Prolegomena*, Leeds.
Meyer, Kurt (1924), *Silius und Lucan*, Diss., Würzburg.
Narducci, Emanuele (2002), *Lucano. Un'epica contro l'impero. Interpretazione della* Pharsalia, Rome/Bari.
Pomeroy, Arthur (2010), "To Silius through Livy and his Predecessors", in: Augoustakis (2010b) 27–45.
Roche, Paul (2009), *Lucan,* De Bello Civili *Book I. Edited with Introduction, Text and Commentary*, Oxford.
Schmidt, Ernst A. (ed.) (2001), *L'histoire littéraire immanente dans la poésie latine*, Vandœuvres-Geneva.
Spaltenstein, François (1986), *Commentaire des* Punica *de Silius Italicus (livres 1 à 8)*, Geneva.
Spaltenstein, François (1990), *Commentaire des* Punica *de Silius Italicus (livres 9 à 17)*, Geneva.
Spaltenstein, François (2006), "A propos des sources historiques de Silius Italicus: une réponse à Lucarini", in: *Athenaeum* 94, 717–718.
Stocks, Claire (2014), *The Roman Hannibal. Remembering the Enemy*, Liverpool.
Thomas, Richard F. (1986), "Virgil's *Georgics* and the Art of Reference", in: *HSCPh* 90, 171–198.
Tipping, Ben (2010), *Exemplary Epic. Silius Italicus'* Punica, Oxford.
Vinchesi, Maria Assunta (2001), *Silio Italico,* Le Guerre Puniche, *I-II*, Milan.

Gianpiero Rosati
The Redemption of the Monster, or: The 'Evil Hero' in Ancient Epic

The goal of this paper is to reconstruct the network of intertextual connections that in ancient epic poetry link the most important evil heroes, from Homer's Cyclops to Vergil's Mezentius and Statius' Capaneus, and to investigate the functions of this typological model in the value system of the epic genre.[1] Through the character of the villain, and his final, if partial, redemption, epic poetry reflects on the (not always clear-cut) boundaries between good and evil, and invites its readers to broaden and deepen the understanding of the complexity of human nature.

1 Sympathy for the Monster: Capaneus and His Fellows

> Hostility, or even detestation of wickedness, is not incompatible with admiration of courage: Hagen in the *Nibelungenlied* treacherously murdered Siegfried but became the hero of the last fight.
>
> J.B. Hainsworth, *The Idea of Epic*

In literature, as in other forms of artistic expression (especially cinema), there is a type of character that can be summarily defined as the 'dark' hero, or the 'villain.' A figure of heroic stature, endowed with qualities like courage and exceptional physical strength, who overshadows those around him and dominates the context (and thus differs from the anti-hero, the Thersites-type who demeans and 'drags down' the heroic characters), but who has very negative distinguishing moral traits that go against the ethical code of the world that the author and the readers live in. Usually, the primary element by which this disparity is gauged is religion or the gods (of whom the villain is a scorner, a *contemptor deorum*), understood as a system of moral values that a society shares and acknowledges as its unifying feature. The 'war with god' is thus the most common expression of

---

[1] Some analogies with my pages can be found in Marco Fucecchi's paper in this volume on Hannibal's '(Super-)character', which deals with Silius' "difficult task of (re)constructing multi-faceted characters and giving coherence to their individual profiles" (p. 259).

https://doi.org/10.1515/9783110602203-013

his moral difference. In short, the dark hero is generally also, or perhaps above all, a *theomachos*.[2] This category includes an 'extreme' character from ancient literature, Capaneus, known to us mainly from Statius' *Thebaid*, but who, as an emblem of the blasphemous rebel who defies the gods, has also had a considerable afterlife in modern literature (from Dante to Dryden to D'Annunzio).

But before we focus on Capaneus, we should better define the qualifying traits of the champion of evil, or evil hero, as I would call a figure typically present with an important role in epic poetry. In Propp's functionalistic terms, the evil hero serves as an antagonist of forces for good, or of the main hero, and embodies a series of negative values that set him in opposition to his context, in a conflict that further constitutes a clash between the forces of civilization and those of a hostile, savage, even primordial world. His role is clearly that of a 'reagent' eliciting a moral and emotional response from the audience: the dark hero strikes fear in readers' hearts, leading them to align themselves against him, to shore up their collective solidarity with the forces of good, which are usually led by the poem's protagonist-hero or, in epic mythology, are represented by a figure like Jupiter, father and leader of the gods as well as the guarantor of moral order on earth. Obviously, the evil hero must be defeated in the end; this is in fact the reason for which he was invented. And yet—and this is the point I wish to emphasize—, at the moment when the evil hero begins to succumb, as he customarily does, and his downfall appears imminent, just when the emotional tension ebbs because good is finally prevailing over evil, we see the dark hero undergo a (at least partial) metamorphosis, a maturation that alters his image, ennobling and to a certain degree redeeming him. So it seems evident that, once the clash between good and evil has come to its conclusion with the triumph of the former, the epic poet wants to render 'the honors of war' to the defeated hero, to make him less hateful and hostile, less incompatible with and distant from the victorious collectivity and its values. The reader's sympathy for the losing hero is aroused *a posteriori* when the armor that made him impermeable to the morals of the world around him cracks, exposing a weak spot that links him to the very values he rejected or scorned.

Now I would like to delve into this same dynamic by analyzing the figure of Statius' Capaneus, and his intrinsically ambiguous nature. That is to say, I intend to both examine his connections with other constituents of the category of evil heroes, and attempt to demonstrate how Statius elaborates and develops this critical component in his models to extract and render explicit the meaning they somehow presupposed.

---

[2] Chaudhuri's important 2014 essay is dedicated to this specific theme.

I shall begin with what can justifiably be considered the ancient-literature archetype of the 'monster' I have just described: Homer's Cyclops. A moral monster, certainly, but also a physical one, because, as we shall see, the exceptionality that isolates the character from his context is also due to his abnormal physical traits. The Cyclops—whose name itself declares the anomaly, the single giant eye, that renders him monstrous and divergent from the human condition—encapsulates many of the negative values that would become characteristic of the epic anti-hero (Hom. *Od.* 9.116–566). Terrifying in appearance with his gargantuan size (the description of him by Virgil's character Achaemenides in *Aen.* 3.619–620 *ipse arduus, altaque pulsat / sidera (di talem terris avertite pestem!)*, "he is gigantic, and strikes the stars on high (ye gods, rid the earth from such a pest!)", seems to allude to a sort of 'attack on the heavens')[3] and his brutish features, he is also distinguished by his rejection of any sort of human behavior, beginning with respect for guests, and the recourse he makes with apparent pleasure to ruthless violence and horrible atrocities, culminating in cannibalism.[4] Another key element for his inclusion in this category of monsters is his contempt for the gods (9.273–278), arrogantly contrasting with the *pietas* invoked by Odysseus (9.269–271); Ovid also presents him as *magni cum dis contemptor Olympi*, "who despised great Olympus and its gods" (*Met.* 13.761). Naturally, the world of Polyphemus and the Cyclopes lacks any form of social or civilized life,[5] except for a sort of automatic, primordial solidarity;[6] and yet, in this universe ruled by the callous laws of brute force and impulse, he reveals a certain affection for one of the animals in his flock. It is, specifically, the ram Odysseus uses to escape the monster, and the fact that this particular animal becomes the vehicle of the hero's ploy also contributes to stirring a modicum of the reader's sympathy for the ruse's victim Polyphemus, in spite of his culpability. Virgil himself, in the words of Achaemenides—the companion Odysseus involuntarily abandons on the island in

---

[3] In a similar manner, like a telluric shock of the sort produced by Giants, his reaction to the escape of Ulysses and his men is configured in *Aen.* 3.672–674 *clamorem immensum tollit, quo pontus et omnes / intremuere undae, penitusque exterrita tellus / Italiae curvisque immugiit Aetna cavernis.* Cf. Hardie (1986) 284–285.
[4] Cf. Hom. *Od.* 9.288–293, 311, 344, 373–374; *Aen.* 3.622–627.
[5] Cf. Hom. *Od.* 9.118–135; Verg. *Aen.* 3.621 nec visu facilis nec dictu adfabilis ulli.
[6] Cf. Verg. *Aen.* 3.675–679, in which their *concilium horrendum* (679) summoned by Polyphemus' cries is compared not to an assembly of human beings (of the sort Homer expressly states is unknown to them, *Od.* 9.128–129) but to gigantic trees, almost a grotesque anti-*concilium deorum* (and again, they seem to challenge the heavens with their stance (677–678): *astantis nequiquam lumine torvo / Aetnaeos fratres caelo capita alta ferentis*).

his flight—, grasps the nature and importance of this bond of affection, strengthened by the humiliation Polyphemus has suffered (*Aen.* 3.660–661 *lanigerae comitantur oves; ea sola voluptas / solamenque mali*, "the fleecy sheep go with him—they are his only joy, the only consolation in woe!"). Just when the monster appears to be defeated, the reader is afforded a glimpse into a previously unsuspected psychological dimension that renders him less distant and repugnant, less 'other' and more linked to human nature and the human condition.

A few of Polyphemus' essential traits are also found in the Virgilian figure of Mezentius.[7] This Etruscan tyrant, a more 'evolved' monster than the primordial Cyclops (the latter has a closer counterpart in the *Aeneid*—the other monster-giant Cacus, who is defeated by Hercules, the civilizing hero),[8] is a giant of evil, surrounded as he is by a mankind that has endured the cruelty of his tyranny, and in return harbors an immeasurable hatred for him—in fact, it could be said that Mezentius seeks to affirm his own heroic stature in the absoluteness of said hatred. His is a savage cruelty that finds satisfaction in concocting extreme 'technological' expedients (like the *longa mors*, the slow death by contagion inflicted on his victims: *Aen.* 8.485–488), which, with its gratuitous pleasure in evildoing, confirms his nature as a tyrant isolated from normal humanity. The only chinks in his armor of inhuman monstrosity are his love for two figures that share his grandiose solitude. The first is an animal, the horse Rhaebus, the faithful companion in battle who Mezentius (like Polyphemus with the ram)[9] apostrophizes as someone with whom to share not only his feelings (*maerentem*), but also his desire for vengeance against his enemy,[10] and solidarity in death as in life:

> ... adloquitur maerentem et talibus infit: 860
> 'Rhaebe, diu, res si qua diu mortalibus ulla est,
> viximus. Aut hodie victor spolia illa cruenti
> et caput Aeneae referes Lausique dolorum
> ultor eris mecum, aut, aperit si nulla viam vis,

---

7 Cf. esp. Glenn (1971).

8 Cacus is, after all (even in terms of his name), an absolute champion of evil, as other monsters defeated by Hercules, who unlike Polyphemus and his 'heirs' is never redeemed. On similarities and differences between Cacus and Polyphemus cf. Hardie (1986) 115–116 (with previous bibliography).

9 Cf. Glenn (1971) 140–149; Harrison (1991) 275.

10 On this further trait in common with the Homeric Polyphemus, who imagines the ram is saddened by his blinding (*Od.* 9.452–453) and seeks vendetta like his master (456–457), cf. Glenn (1971) 141–144.

> occumbes pariter; neque enim, fortissime, credo,   865
> iussa aliena pati et dominos dignabere Teucros.'
>
> (Aen. 10.860–866)

He addresses the sorrowing beast and accosts it thus: 'Rhaebus, we have lived long, if anything can be long for mortals. Today you shall either bear back in victory those bloody spoils and the head of Aeneas, and avenge with me the sufferings of Lausus, or, if no force opens a way, you shall die with me; for you, gallant steed, will not deign, I think, to endure a stranger's bidding and a Trojan lord!'

But obviously, what somehow compensates for Mezentius' inhumanity most of all, attenuating his bloodthirsty, brutal persona, is the bond of affection he has with his son Lausus. The narrator introduces the latter from the outset as flanking his father in battle, but at the same time clearly differentiates him from Mezentius, exalting his physical beauty as well as a moral nobility later borne out by his behavior, and placing him in the category of young heroes destined for a generous and premature end:

> Primus init bellum Tyrrhenis asper ab oris
> contemptor divum Mezentius agminaque armat.
> Filius huic iuxta Lausus, quo pulchrior alter
> non fuit excepto Laurentis corpore Turni;   650
> Lausus, equum domitor debellatorque ferarum,
> ducit Agyllina nequiquam ex urbe secutos
> mille viros, dignus patriis qui laetior esset
> imperiis et cui pater haud Mezentius esset.
>
> (Aen. 7.647–654)

First into the war comes, from Tuscan coasts, fierce Mezentius, scorner of the gods, and arrays his men. At his side is his son Lausus, who excelled all others in beauty save Laurentine Turnus—Lausus, tamer of horses and vanquisher of beasts. From Agylla's town he leads a thousand men, that followed him in vain; one worthy to be happier in a father's rule, a father other than Mezentius!

Lausus too, devoted as he is to a father who does not deserve his devotion, and for whom he courageously sacrifices his life, becomes a paradigm of *pietas* capable of moving his enemy Aeneas, who tries to dissuade him from engaging in a battle that will clearly be unequal and ultimately fatal (8.811–812 *quo moriture ruis maioraque viribus audes? / fallit te incautum pietas tua*, "where are you rushing to death, with your daring beyond your strength? Your love betrays you to your ruin"), and earns the admiration of the epic's narrator, who guarantees him the immortality granted to great heroes destined for death *ante diem*, like Pallas or the pair of friends Euryalus and Nisus. The apostrophe of verses 8.791–793 (*hic mortis durae casum tuaque optima facta, / si qua fidem tanto est operi latura vetustas, / non equidem nec te, iuvenis memorande, silebo*, "and here death's cruel gloom and your most glorious deeds—if at all ancient days can win belief in such prowess—I will not leave unsung, nor yourself, young man, so worthy to be sung!") places him unambiguously on a par with the two ill-fated young heroes of the famous allocution in 9.446–449 (*Fortunati ambo! si quid mea carmina possunt, / nulla dies umquam memori vos eximet aevo, / dum domus Aeneae Capitoli immobile saxum / accolet imperiumque pater Romanus habebit*, "Happy pair! If my poetry has any power, no day shall ever blot you from the memory of time, so long the house of Aeneas shall dwell on the Capitol's unshaken rock, and the Father of Rome keeps his power!").

The typological analogies between Mezentius and Polyphemus are well known, as are those that link Mezentius and Capaneus,[11] the monstrous "supergiant"[12] of Flavian epic, who in many ways seems an outgrowth and an amplification of the Virgilian 'giant.' It is almost as if, in constructing the figure of Capaneus, Statius sought to engage in a duel with his venerated model Virgil, taking the paradigms of evilness developed in earlier literary tradition to the point of paroxysm. Capaneus' 'monstrous' exceptionality is highlighted from the very beginning of the *Thebaid*: when in the proem Statius ponders what order to follow in illustrating his heroes, the list of great Argives (Tydeus, Amphiaraus, Hippomedon, Parthenopaeus) ends with Capaneus, in terms that proclaim his exceptionality (1.41–45): *atque alio Capaneus horrore canendus*, "and sing Capaneus in consternation never felt before" (the same terms that will introduce his aristeia in 10.827–836). The horror required to tell the story of Capaneus is the poetic horror of the author, who is aware of the difficulty of his task, but also reveals the moral anomaly and grandiose stature of this evil hero, establishing a link between the 'monstrosity' of the character and the aesthetic creativity of the poet who sings of him.[13] When Statius brings Capaneus onto the scene in the third book (from v. 598), he delineates his intertextual genealogy as *superum contemptor* (3.602), recalling his literary precursors as champions of blasphemous impiety with the "my god is my sword, and force is the only law I know" maxim (*virtus mihi numen et ensis / quem teneo*, 3.615–616). The models Capaneus thus aligns himself behind include the Argive hero Parthenopaeus of Aeschylus' *Seven* (529–530 "by his spear he swears, which, as he grasps, he dares to venerate more than a god, and

---

11 Cf. Caiani (1990); Ripoll (1998) 340–348.
12 Cf. Fucecchi (2013) 112.
13 For a metapoetic reading of monstrosity cf. Lowe (2015), who, however, discusses monsters and monstrosities only understood in a physical sense. Cf. also Leigh (2006).

dearer to his eyes"), Apollonius Rhodius' sacrilegious Idas, who puts his own lance before Zeus (1.466–468 "Let my rushing spear be witness now, with which beyond all others I carry off glory in wars nor does Zeus aid me so much as my spear"), and above all Virgil's Mezentius, who represents Latin epic's paradigm of negative, perverse heroism. Contempt for the gods is one of the qualifying traits of Mezentius (*Aen.* 7.648 *contemptor divum Mezentius*; 8.7 *contemptorque deum Mezentius*) who—along the same lines as Idas—made an analogous blasphemous declaration, invoking his own right hand and the lance it held as the only divinity to appeal to for support (*Aen.* 10.773–774 *dextra mihi deus et telum, quod missile libro, / nunc adsint!*, "may this right hand, my deity, and the hurtling dart I poise, now aid me!"). This motif is picked up in an even more marked way by Capaneus, who, sarcastically echoing the stylistic elements of religious language, underscores the invocation of his right hand, his sole *numen*, reiterating his disdain for traditional gods:

> 'ades o mihi, dextera, tantum
> tu praesens bellis et inevitabile numen,
> te voco, te solam superum contemptor adoro.'
>
> (*Theb.* 9.548–550)
>
> 'Help me, right hand, my only present and inevitable deity in battle, I call upon you; you only I, scorner of the High Ones, adore.'

An absolute, fanatically religious faith in the principle of force accentuates the Titanism of the Statian figure, whose own armor (with the image of a Giant "hurling himself" from his helmet: *prominet Gigas*, 4.176) represents his identifying trademark, condensed in the symbolic gesture of the attack.[14] And what is more, the simile in the third book with which he is introduced into the poem's narrative likens him to Giant-figures like Centaurs and Cyclopes (3.604–605 *unus ut e silvis Pholoes habitator opacae / inter et Aetnaeos aequus consurgere fratres*, "like a denizen of darkling Pholoë from out the forest or one that might rise equal among Aetna's brethren"), while the one in the tenth book, in the aristeia that has him scaling the city wall of Thebes, expressly compares him to Giants in the act of attacking the heavens:[15]

---

14 Cf. Micozzi (2007) *ad loc.*
15 A characterization already made explicit in Aesch. *Sept.* 427–431. Cf. also McNelis (2007), 142–143. On the figures of Tydeus, Capaneus and Hippomedon as champions of de-humanizing violence and *immanitas*, compared to Cyclopes, Centaurs and Giants, cf. Franchet d'Espèrey (1999) 190–205.

> quales mediis in nubibus aether
> vidit Aloidas, cum cresceret impia Tellus
> despectura deos nec adhuc inmane veniret
> Pelion et trepidum iam tangeret Ossa Tonantem.
>
> (*Theb.* 10.849–852)

> So the ether saw the Aloidae amid the clouds when the impious earth was growing as though to look down upon the gods; vast Pelion was not yet come and already Ossa touched the frightened Thunderer.

The heroic grandiosity of the character is thus made plain by the magnitude of the challenge he launches to the gods, whose very existence he repeatedly calls into question (note for example the scornful tone he uses when speaking of Apollo at 3.611–613 *non si ipse cavo sub vertice Cirrhae / (quisquis is est, timidis famaeque ita visus) Apollo / mugiat insano penitus seclusus in antro*, "were Apollo himself, whoever he is (cowards and Rumour so think of him), to bellow under Cirrha's hollow peak, deep withdrawn in his frenzied cavern" and at 10.847 *experiar quid sacra iuvent, an falsus Apollo*, "I shall try what sacrifice avails, whether Apollo be false"). The atheistic/blasphemous rationalism of Capaneus, who challenges the gods to demonstrate their inexistence or their impotence in the face of the clash toward which his courage impels him, is tinged with strikingly Epicurean, or more specifically Lucretian tones (cf. esp. 3.659–661 *miseret superum, si carmina curae / humanaeque preces. Quid inertia pectora terres? / primus in orbe deos fecit timor!*, "Tis pity of the High Ones if they take heed of spells and human prayers. Why frighten you untutored hearts? Fear first made gods in the world"), and here as well the Statian 'giant' seems to develop and explicate ideas already present in model-figures from the intertextual network described above.[16] Capaneus, in short, is a Mezentius with an intellectual awareness that enriches and empowers his stature as a champion of force and courage. As has been noted, he transfers onto the physical plain the intellectual battle waged by the Lucretian hero Epicurus.[17]

Capaneus is thus an extreme figure, and yet, although he represents a sort of quintessence of evil, a champion of omnipotent impiety, he undergoes a redemption which, especially at the moment of his death and in virtue of the heroism said death proves, ennobles his persona on the whole. It is quite evident that the

---

[16] On Mezentius cf. especially Kronenberg (2005). On Epicurean traits in Capaneus cf. Taisne (1999); Chaudhuri (2014) 268–271; Pontiggia (2018).
[17] Cf. Pontiggia (2018).

representation of this emblem of evil is by no means uniform or drawn in exclusively dark tones: beginning with his initial presentation, the poet's intrinsic admiration for the character's noble heroism emerges (cf. for example 3.600–602 *huic ampla quidem de sanguine prisco / nobilitas; sed enim ipse manu praegressus avorum / facta*, "ample nobility was his from ancient blood, but he himself had outstripped the doughty deeds of his forebears. Long had he despised the High Ones with impunity, impatient of justice and prodigal of life if anger urged"),[18] as well as for the courage of his anti-theological challenge.

The epic narrator of the *Thebaid* repeatedly ponders Capaneus' motivation: whether it is *virtus egressa modum*, "valour past bounds" (10.834), or *gloria praeceps*, "reckless thirst for glory", or *virtus iniqua*, "excessive valour" (11.1), he acknowledges that it is in any case inspired by a noble impulse (confirmed by the character's own voice: *me iubet ardua virtus / ire*, "this way my mounting valour bids me go", 10.845–846), an impulse expressed in the compressed formulation of an oxymoron that cannot be quashed by the moral judgment implicit in epithets (heroism is *iniquus*, unjust and culpable, but is nonetheless *virtus*). In fact, Capaneus seems to become the paradigm of this form of perverse, inhuman heroism precisely for his lack of bounds, an attribute that typifies other figures in Flavian epic as well, foremost among them Silius Italicus' Hannibal. He is the champion of a *barbara virtus*, "barbaric valour" (10.146), a destructive force that knows no moral correctives and bears the traits of an ethnic-cultural matrix:[19] his characterization makes his an *improba virtus*, "evil valour" (1.58), a degraded and negative value. Here again, the use of a conceptual oxymoron conveys the perversion of a quality for which the author cannot fully mask his admiration.[20]

And in the case of Capaneus, the narrator's admiration is bolstered on the diegetic level, almost as if to legitimize his objectivity, by the respect afforded the hero by the target of his challenge, Jupiter: when the latter receives grateful homage from the other gods for having saved world order by triumphing in this new Gigantomachia (11.7–8 *gratantur superi, Phlegrae ceu fessus anhelet / proelia et Encelado fumantem impresserit Aetnen*, "the High Ones congratulate him as though he were wearily panting the battles of Phlegra and had piled Aetna on

---

18 On Capaneus' *pietas* cf. Caiani (1990) 269–274.
19 Cf. Fucecchi (1990); Ripoll (1998) 332–336 and 342–344.
20 Ripoll (1998) 347 speaks of "fascination ambiguë pour les 'héros négatifs', pour les 'beaux monstres'". Cf. Fucecchi's analysis in this volume of Hannibal's complex character constructed by Silius "through the conflation of traditionally opposite patterns", that is primarily Lucan's Caesar and Pompey.

smoking Enceladus"), the defeated enemy—a *magnanimus* (11.1) symbolically depicted in the mad act of attack—is given the honors of war by the victor:

> ille iacet lacerae complexus fragmina turris,
> torvus adhuc visu memorandaque facta relinquens
> gentibus atque ipsi non inlaudata Tonanti.[21]
>
> (*Theb.* 11.9–11)
>
> Capaneus lies grasping fragments of the broken tower, still grim of visage, leaving to the nations memorable deeds not unpraised of the Thunderer himself.

In addition to acknowledgement of the loser's heroic courage, which guarantees him the 'right to memory' ensured by the epic poem (*memoranda*), there is an external agent in this case as well, an emotional tie that contributes in a decisive way to altering for the better—in fact, almost rehabilitating—Capaneus' image: his wife, Evadne, who in the final book of the poem argues Capaneus' cause and his right to proper burial before Theseus. But before moving on to Evadne's speech in 'defense of the monster' (and, in parallel, Deipyle's peroration for her husband Tydeus), I would like to consider the possibility of including another figure from myth and literature in this category of 'monsters' who are redeemed, or at least partially rehabilitated, before the curtain falls.

That figure is Geryon, protagonist of the Stesichorus poem (6th c. BCE) to which he lent his name, the *Geryoneis*, of which we have only fragments that have been the object of scholars' attention in recent years. The composition, although it is formally a choral ode, if only in terms of its anomalous length (more than 1,500 verses), seems more like an epic text in its narrative structure; it is in any case well known that ancient critics lauded Stesichorus for his epic qualities. The Anonymous *Peri Hypsous* (13.3) defines him as *Homerikótatos*, "very Homer-like", while Quintilian (*Inst.* 10.1.62) grasps the specifically epic essence of his poetry both in terms of content (great wars and illustrious heroes) and narrative techniques equal to the loftiness of said content:

> maxima bella et clarissimos canentem duces et epici carminis onera lyra sustinentem. Reddit enim personis in agendo simul loquendoque debitam dignitatem, ac si tenuisset modum videtur aemulari proximus Homerum potuisse.[22]

---

[21] A hint of admiration for the enormity of the challenge comes through in the god's words at 11.123–124 *impia bella / unus init aususque mea procumbere dextra*.
[22] For a thoughtful comparative evaluation of the judgments of Quintilian and Dionysius cf. Arrighetti (1995b).

He sings of great wars and famous leaders and makes his lyre bear the weight of epic. He gives his characters due dignity of action and word, and, if he had exercised restraint, he might have been Homer's nearest rival.

(transl. Russell)

Analogously, Dionysius of Halicarnassus (*De imit.* 2.7) sees the psychological and moral characterization of characters, in particular their "dignity" (ἀξιώματα), as a distinctive trait of his poetry. And so it must have been, we may suppose, even when the character was a monster.

Geryon is a monster in the true sense of the word, that is, in physical terms: he has three bodies, with six hands and feet and wings, and is proverbially gigantic;[23] he is the son of Chrysaor, who was in turn born of Medusa; and he also lives at the edge of the world, on the island of Eritheya in the far west. His story is part of the saga of Hercules, who as his tenth labor captured Geryon's oxen, first killing their two-headed guard dog—Orthros, the son of Echidna and brother of Cerberus and Chimaera—, as well as their guardian Eurythion, the bellicose son of Ares, and finally Geryon himself. Geryon's genealogical network, along with his physical appearance and geographically remote environment, qualify him as a monstrous character, an 'extreme' figure in various ways, and thus destined to fall victim to the civilizing hero Hercules.

From the few fragments we have of the *Geryoneis* it is not easy to reconstruct a precise outline of the story it narrated, i.e. the arrival of Hercules, the theft of Geryon's livestock, the killing of their guardians and then that of Geryon himself, prior to the hero's return to Greece. Above all, we are not given to know whether the poet justified Geryon's death on a moral level as punishment for some wrong, and thus in the name of justice or order as represented by Hercules, or whether it was instead viewed as the natural consequence of his condition as a mortal destined to succumb in the clash with the great hero. Certainly, in the part of the text that has been left to us, Geryon appears as a victim, steadfastly facing death to defend his land and his property from a marauding and astute invader.

What strikes commentators about the Stesichorus work is the "sympathetic" depiction of the figure, for example the refined Homeric simile that compares one of his heads falling beneath Hercules's blows to a poppy (fr. 12.15–17 Curtis = 19.45–47 Davies/Finglass).[24] But above all, what contributes most in this case to

---

[23] Cf. Gantz (1993) 402.
[24] Cf. Curtis (2011) 147 (an Homeric simile, surely an "unusual one for a monster") and 149, outlining a few analogies with figurative evidence (7th–4th c. BCE) of an apparent attitude of sympathy towards the Minotaur.

'humanizing the monster' is Stesichorus' decision to give him a point of view and allow him to express himself in his own words, to be ennobled through his own voice, in line with the peculiarity revealed by Dionysius of Halicarnassus, mentioned above.[25] It must have been an important innovation, which seems to have modified the traditional manner of conceptualizing monstrosity. The most recent and most prominent example of the success of this interpretation of the monster Geryon is the *Autobiography of Red* by Ann Carson (New York 1998), the story of a sensitive boy who, preoccupied with hiding the wings that cause him shame and lend his red body a monstrous appearance and tormented by desire, falls in love with the young Hercules.

Now, the most obvious opportunity to measure a character's moral status in heroic poetry is surely the moment when he faces death: usually the hero confronts death without fear, knowing that he has no alternative to preserve that highest of values, his dignity. Geryon too, faced with his imminent end at Hercules' hand, declares his choice with extraordinarily noble words, addressing someone (probably Menete, the shepherd of Hades' flocks)[26] who has warned him that Hercules threatens to bring about his death (fr. 7 Curtis = 15 Davies/Finglass):

> Do not hold chill death before me and try to frighten my manly spirit ... But if I am ageless and immortal in race (and partake of?) life on Olympus, better (to fight than leave behind) shameful reproaches ... But if, dear friend, I must come to hateful old age and live among men creatures of a day far from the blessed gods, better by far is it for me now to suffer whatever is my fated portion ...
>
> (transl. Ch. Segal)

This fragment has long been juxtaposed with the verses from the *Iliad* (12.322–328) in which Sarpedon speaks to Glaucus, justifying his decision to accept open conflict with the Greeks and thus risk death: since a mortal cannot elude his destiny, it is best to face it with honor, "whether we shall give glory to another, or another to us" (12.328). Geryon's mother Callirhoe also begs him, for the sake of their mother/son bond, to avoid the clash with Hercules (fr. 6 Curtis = 17 Davies/Finglass; the sequence has been compared to the entreaties Priam and Hecuba address to Hector in *Il.* 22.38–76 and 82–89), and naturally the network of relationships he appears to have contributes greatly to humanizing him.[27]

---

[25] Cf. Franzen (2009) 63: "What is so surprising about Stesichorus' story is that we see it through the eyes of the monster."
[26] Cf. Davies/Finglass (2014) 269; according to others (B. Gentili) the reply was to Hercules.
[27] Cf. Franzen (2009) 65–68.

But what is most distinctive about Geryon is his courageous attitude towards the prospect of death: his composed speech reflects a disenchanted resignation, and a refusal to delude himself regarding the inevitability of the end that awaits all mortals – an attitude that recalls, with obvious differences, Mezentius' last words in response to Aeneas, who is about to kill him:

> Hostis amare, quid increpitas mortemque minaris?
> nullum in caede nefas, nec sic ad proelia veni,
> nec tecum meus haec pepigit mihi foedera Lausus.
>
> (*Aen.* 10.900–902)

> Bitter foe, why do you taunt me and threaten me with death? It is no sin to slay; not on such terms I came to battle, nor is such the pact my Lausus pledged between me and you.

With dignified resolve, Mezentius (just before offering himself up to his enemy's fatal blow: *Haec loquitur, iuguloque haud inscius accipit ensem*, 907) enunciates the harsh reality of war as the locus of death, indignantly contrasting it with ordinary humanity and its 'fine sentiments.'

Without necessarily seeking an echo of Geryon's words in Mezentius' speech or venturing to hypothesize any direct relation between the two figures, nor much less between Virgil and Stesichorus,[28] the strategy adopted by the Sicilian poet to 'humanize the monster' and ennoble him in the manner of an epic hero (and moreover, one destined for defeat, and thus comparable to Hector) is nonetheless interesting. From what we know of the Stesichorus text, Geryon does not seem to be a 'moral monster' like the figures discussed above (Polyphemus, Mezentius, Capaneus and the like). And yet, it seems legitimate to associate him with this category, both because he is involved in one of the labors of Hercules, who kills him (the same Hercules who, journeying back to Greece upon conclusion of the labor, stops in Lazio to eliminate another monster, Cacus, who tries to steal Geryon's oxen from him: *Aen.* 8.201–204), and owing to the divergent traits that distinguish him, making him a figure of the Other, the different and the distant. And what makes the Stesichorus text particularly interesting is precisely the fact that it attributes human psychology and tragic sentiments to the monster, to the point that, as has been observed, "Stesichorus' Geryon was portrayed no less sympathetically than Heracles, and quite possibly more sympathetically than the Greek

---

28 Relationship of which there is no certain proof: cf. nonetheless clues proposed by Lazzeri (2006) 145–151, and Fiorentini (2007) 142–145.

hero."²⁹ In fact, some have come to see in this surprising role reversal—the "transformation of a monster into an exemplary type of ἀγαθός"—, a proposal for a new type of heroism, in which "the two aspects that heroic excellence consists of, namely, physical beauty and martial prowess, are cleaved."³⁰

Whatever the reasons that may have led Stesichorus to depict Geryon in such an unusually sympathetic manner (said reasons have been the subject of scholarly inquiry),³¹ what interests us here is the indication of this episode as a relevant precedent in this intertextual chain running through ancient epic. That is to say, Stesichorus would seem to have been the first (at least in the documentation available to us) to have reflected on the idea of the monster as cultural construction or personification of the anxieties and fears of the society that conceives him, and also to have raised the issue of 'giving the floor' to the monster himself, lending him a personal point of view and listening to his motivations. He thus cleared the path that, two and a half millennia later, would lead Anne Carson to conceive her sensitive, love-struck Geryon.

2 The honors of war

> Tragedy may sometimes present a picture of complete waste:
> in the epic there must be achievement and therefore hope.
>
> J.B. Hainsworth, *The Idea of Epic*

But let us return to Capaneus and the final—or rather, posthumous—metamorphosis of his figure. There is an aspect of this process that I wish to focus on: the use of another character to morally redeem the figure of the 'inhuman' hero, indirectly attributing him human qualities that had seemed completely extraneous to him. In addition to enriching and rendering more complex the characteriza-

---

29 Finglass/Kelly (2015b) 7.
30 Tsitsibakou-Vasalos (1990) 31.
31 Cf. esp. Franzen (2009), who frames the myth within the colonization process (Himera, Stesichorus' homeland, was the westernmost of all of the Greek colonies), in which Geryon "represents a monster of ethnicity, a localization of the fears of the 'other' to Greek primacy" (63), and his hybrid character the multicultural nature of the poet's homeland. Noussia-Fantuzzi (2013) in turn reads Stesichorus' story of Geryon as "a reflection of and reaction to colonial encounters with non-Greeks in the West, both in Himera [...] and in Spain" (234), and "on a symbolic level as a poetic narrative about perceiving diversity" (235).

tion, this phenomenon also has another important function: that of blurring differences, attenuating the primary opposition between the forces of good and evil, inviting the reader to be less schematic and a-critically 'biased,' and more attentive to the motivations on both sides.

In the case of Mezentius, as we have seen, this function is carried out mainly by his son Lausus, who has been taught the heroic code of honor by his father and meets his death in an attempt to save him (*Aen.* 10.815–820), in homage to a *pietas* that certainly does not fit into his father's value system (as the narrator reveals in *Aen.* 7.653–654 and as he himself acknowledges: 8.812). The gap between Mezentius and Lausus, which may make the divergence between the two figures appear excessive, and perhaps implausible—the former an icon of evil and the latter a paradigm of the pious youth destined for premature death—is significantly reduced in the case of Capaneus in Statius. For this 'extreme' character, an emblem of blasphemous arrogance even beyond the ancient world, his wife Evadne has the key role of externally and *a posteriori* humanizing him (to the point that she in turn becomes a paradigm of marital devotion: cf. Prop. 1.15.21–22), aiming to redeem her husband's right to memory and burial so that she can throw herself upon his funeral pyre, thus tying her own destiny to his. Statius thus seems to have been preoccupied with reducing and almost closing the gap between the arrogant, blaspheming, impious man and the more complex and noble image of him offered by Evadne, who probably also voices the feelings of many readers.

Evadne does not come onto the scene until the last book of the *Thebaid*, along with the group of Argive women who travel to Athens to Theseus to invoke the right to bury their husbands' bodies, a right denied by the ruthless new king of Thebes, Creon. In Euripides' *Suppliants* (163–192), Adrastus was the one who went to plead with the king of Athens, but his peroration was made in the name of human decency, and as a generic act of piety towards a group of heroes whose moral profile was never in doubt, much less analyzed on an individual level. The dramatic function of Evadne's speech in Statius (*Theb.* 12.543–586) is quite different; she comes on the scene as a perfect *alter ego* to her husband, both in name (*Capaneia coniunx*) and in terms of becoming a protagonist (*ausa ante alias*) who replicates the proud, even reckless role of the 'giant' Capaneus.[32] The fallen heroes are not exiles, nor are they guilty of anything: they are Argives, a king and

---

32 *Audeo* is the usual verb for indicating the Giants' challenge to the heavens: cf. Rosati (2009) at Ov. *Met.* 5.348. On Capaneus' characterization as a giant cf. Harrison (1992); Chaudhuri (2014) 286.

queen, who have paid the price of their courage (546–551); but this is not the subject of Evadne's lament:

> Nec querimur caesos: haec bellica iura vicesque
> armorum; sed non Siculis exorta sub antris
> monstra nec Ossaei bello cecidere bimembres.
> Mitto genus clarosque patres: hominum, inclute Theseu,   555
> sanguis erant, homines, eademque in sidera, eosdem
> sortitus animarum alimentaque vestra creati,
> quos vetat igne Creon Stygiaeque a limine portae,
> ceu sator Eumenidum aut Lethaei portitor amnis,
> summovet ac dubio caelique Erebique sub axe   560
> detinet. Heu princeps Natura! ubi numina, ubi illest
> fulminis iniusti iaculator? ubi estis, Athenae?
>
> (*Theb.* 12.552–562)

> Neither do we complain of their slaying. That was the law of war and the fortune of battle. They fell in fight, but they were no monsters risen in Sicilian caverns or twiformed creatures of Ossa. I speak not of race and famous ancestry. They were human blood, renowned Theseus, men, created to the same stars, the same living lot, the same nurture as yourselves. Them does Creon forbid the fire and bar from the threshold of the Stygian gate, as though he were father of the Furies or ferryman of Lethe river, keeping them in doubt between heaven and Erebus. Ah primal Nature! Where are the gods, where that hurler of the unjust thunderbolt? Where are you, Athens?

Evadne does not bemoan the fate of Capaneus and his comrades: death, she asserts with the determination of a true *matrona virilis*, is a part of war and of *bellica iura* (words that seem to echo Mezentius' mordant, disenchanted principle of *nullum in caede nefas*, "killing is not a sin"). Rather, she protests against Creon and others who compare those heroes to *monstra* like Cyclopes and Centaurs, undervaluing not only their illustrious lineage, and thus their innate nobility, but even their human nature, to the laws of which Evadne, "the widow of Capaneus, the most inhuman of the heroes" (Feeney 1991, 361), appeals. While in Euripides' *Suppliants* the mother Etra invokes Theseus' intervention in the name of the gods (301–302), Evadne advances her request in the name of the *princeps natura* and of wholly human values,[33] in a secular/Lucretian perspective in which she, *Capaneia coniunx*, like her husband, refuses to acknowledge the rights of a Zeus who casts down his unjust thunderbolts upon Capaneus but tolerates the violation of the most basic laws of humanity.

---

33 Cf. Franchet d'Espèrey (1999) 291–294; Pollmann (2004) 222; Bessone (2013) 160–161.

Evadne's claim that even they, the fallen Argive heroes, were born for "the same nurture" (557) as other men, is formulated so as to be easily rejected by readers who recall the cannibalistic meal that marked Tydeus' exit at the end of the eighth book. And Evadne's assertion of their humanity, as opposed to the wildness of Cyclopes and Centaurs, is not an involuntarily clumsy move on her part,[34] given that throughout the poem, as we have noted, Statius constructs Capaneus as a giant or a Cyclops or a centaur. The contradiction is so obvious precisely because Statius intended for readers to notice it, and explain it through the various points of view expressed by the various 'voices' in the text, that of the narrator and those of the characters. The resulting conflict is meant specifically to make the extremes less extreme, to bring them into dialogue and thus to recognize the humanity even in the 'monster.' Which after all—and this is Evadne's key argument—is what Theseus himself did:

> Tu quoque, ut egregios fama cognovimus actus,
> non trucibus monstris Sinin infandumque dedisti
> Cercyona, et saevum velles Scirona crematum.
> Credo et Amazoniis Tanain fumasse sepulcris,
> unde haec arma refers; sed et hunc dignare triumphum.
>
> (*Theb.* 12.575–579)

> You too, as story tells us of your noble deeds, did not give Sinis or loathly Cercyon to fierce monsters and would fain have had savage Sciron cremated. I believe that Tanais too smoked with Amazonian sepulchres, whence you bring back these arms. But deign this triumph also.

The behavior of the civilizing hero Theseus, who did indeed defeat monsters (Sinis, Cercyon, Scyron) but who also assured them a merciful end, is a model of justice and human clemency juxtaposed with the unjust *iaculator* (562) Jupiter who struck down Capaneus. With her husband, the quintessential *theomachos*, Evadne shares a secular ideology, completely earthly and human, and she wishes to see the values neglected by the celestial Jupiter expressed in the *clementia* of the king of Athens—the emblematic city of civilization and justice.[35]

---

[34] As Feeney (1991) 361, n. 156 seems to suggest: "Evadne is on thin ice in her claim that the Argives were not gigantesque monsters (12.553–554); her husband was doing his best to break into this category (10.849–852)." Also Chaudhuri (2014) 293–294.

[35] On Theseus assuming Jupiteresque functions cf. esp. Bessone (2013) 160–161 (who speaks of "faith in the natural and universal rights of all men, equal among themselves, and trust in the political power which can enforce those rights"); Chaudhuri (2014) 293. For an overall discussion, and a persuasive reading, of the most debated figure of Theseus cf. Bessone (2011) ch. 4.

Alongside Capaneus there is, however, another 'monster,' quite analogous to him, that the *Thebaid* (a poem entirely constructed around the ideal-icon of the double) pairs him with, telling of his feats. He is Tydeus, whose list of exploits ends fittingly with the extreme act of cannibalism,[36] a fratricidal, impious and arrogant hero filled with a bestial rage (*rabidarum more ferarum*, 8.71),[37] in many ways akin and complementary to Capaneus.[38] Tydeus is the wild boar-man who boasts of his origins in the *monstrifera* (1.453) Calydon, the city-kingdom ruled by his father Oeneus ravaged by the monstrous animal from which it is liberated in the hunt led by Tydeus' brother, Meleager. Tydeus is repeatedly compared to a wild boar from his first appearance in the poem (e.g. 1.488–490 *terribiles contra saetis ac dente recurvo / Tydea per latos umeros ambire laborant / exuviae, Calydonis honos*, "set against that, the glorious spoils of Calydon strive to surround Tydeus' broad shoulders, terrible with bristles and backward-curving tusk"), and the animal imagery accompanies him through his exit from the scene with the act of cannibalism, the culmination of his metamorphosis into a wild beast,[39] which fulfills the oxymoron of his *viri feritas* (9.184). In any case, he is by all rights to be included in the category of monsters, to the point that his 'extreme' animal exploit arouses a horrified reaction from Minerva herself, his protector up to that time (8.762–766). And yet, as Tydeus himself had asserted in his initial clash with Polynices, who denied him access to Argo, "even savage monsters have their innate rules, their law" (1.459–460 *sunt et rabidis iura insita monstris / fasque suum*), giving the example of the social structure shared by Centaurs and Cyclopes. In making this claim of a 'natural right' even for monsters, Tydeus anticipated, and in fact extended to all without exception, the argument with which Evadne (12.547–548 and 575–577), and his own wife Deipyle, who accompanies her (12.117–121), support his cause before Theseus. For him, as for Capaneus, redemption comes through the figure of the wife, who, albeit perturbed by Tydeus' savage meal, cannot help but pardon his excesses.

But the entire characterization of the 'monster's wife' is important: through her, in the cases of both Evadne and Deipyle, the force of human feeling redeems the husband's wild ferocity (like Lausus' love for his father Mezentius). This reading thus lends us a clear understanding of the process by which, as we have

---

36 Not coincidentally, *cruentus* is his most frequent epithet: 8.478, 530; 9.1, 545.
37 Cf. Hardie (1993) 69; Ripoll (1998) 330–331.
38 Cf. Ripoll (1998) 330, n. 83 (with bibliography).
39 On Tydeus' metamorphosis to a wild beast, a passage from *virtus* to *efferatio*, cf. also Augoustakis (2016) xxxiii and 345.

noted, Evadne compares herself to her husband Capaneus, openly assuming his anti-theistic attitude of defiance:

> ... magni memor illa mariti
> it <u>torvum</u> lacrimans <u>summisque irascitur astris</u>
>
> (12.127–128)

The other mindful of her great spouse goes <u>grimly</u> weeping <u>in anger at the topmost stars</u>

and later sharing his fate of death by fire on the same pyre:

> turbine quo sese caris instraverit <u>audax</u>
> ignibus Evadne <u>fulmenque in pectore magno</u>
> <u>quaesierit</u>.
>
> (12.800–802)

How Evadne <u>boldly</u> strewed herself on beloved flames, <u>seeking the thunderbolt in the mighty breast</u>.

In the cases of both Capaneus and Tydeus (803–804 *iacens super oscula saevi / corporis infelix excuset Tydea coniunx*, "Tydeus' hapless wife excuses him as she lies over the savage corpse's kisses"), as well as that of another champion of ferocity, Hippomedon (whose wife Nealce seems to take on his aggressive and merciless, 12.121–123 *aspera visu, / ac deflenda tamen, digno plangore Nealce / Hippomedonta ciens*, "Nealce, harsh of aspect but pitiable withal, calling on Hippomedon with fitting lamentation"), it is the wife who *excusat* her husband's inhumanity. While in terms of subjective relationships the character who dies, although guilty, is released from his responsibilities in the eyes of his loved ones (12.120–121 *cuncta iacenti / infelix ignoscit amor*, "luckless love forgives all to the fallen") in the general economy of the text through a positive, pain-stricken figure, the epic narrator seeks to reduce the moral and emotional distance—to 'redeem the monster' and bring him back into the human fold.

According to what Jeffrey Jerome Cohen called 'monster theory',[40] nothing and no-one is intrinsically, 'naturally' monstrous. Monsters do not exist in concrete reality: in his physical shape or his behavior, the monster is the personification of the fears, anxieties, fantasies or desires of the culture that constructs him. Far from being monstrous by nature, the monster is, in short, a cultural

---

[40] Cf. Cohen (1996b). On the recent attention to 'monster theory' in classical studies, Lowe (2015) ch. 1 is now to be read.

product, and is thus presented differently in his various historic configurations:[41] it is a hypostasis of difference, a living representation of it, what we feel is Other or different from us, and which we give a shape to in order to exorcise it. But defining monstrosity is the equivalent of rethinking humanity,[42] our relationships with the Other and with the world around us, and the system of values we identify with, those which—by contrast—we consider fundamental and vital, to the point that they constitute our code of identity.

As we have seen, the archetypal epic poet Homer constructed his monster, Polyphemus, and it is no coincidence that the confrontation/clash with the monster remained a distinguishing element of epic, the genre most committed to representing a society's identity-structuring value system: Mezentius, Capaneus, perhaps Geryon before them, and, in historical epic, Lucan's Caesar and Silius' Hannibal are all in some way personifications of the fear of evil that a society perceives and feels the need to represent. Their function is crucial in setting off a confrontation/clash with the principle of good, but aside from lending a concrete shape to evil, and to the need to exorcise it, it is clear that these figures also express the fascination that evil more or less obscurely exercises, and serve to 'test' the boundaries and border of the two spheres.

Ultimately, the intertextual plot that links the various evil heroes of epic tradition also invites the readers to reflect on epic as the genre that celebrates good's victory over evil and distinguishes the reality it represents on the basis of clear-cut axiological values, and to understand the limitations of this distinction and blur its boundaries. The process thus works as a sort of critical reflection on the genre, and in this sense it seems analogous to a few important cues for thought that Ovid introduces in the *Metamorphoses*, as when Nestor, in the role of epic narrator, openly confesses the partiality of his tales (12.547–548),[43] or when in the contest between the Muses and the Pierides, the poet experiments with a sort of epic told from the losers' point of view (5.319–331).[44] While Ovid questions the epic genre's pretense of being the 'voice of truth,' denouncing its partial, subjective nature as history written by the victors, Statius invites us to reflect on the boundaries between good and evil, and on the ethical-ideological system on

---

[41] We need only think of the degree to which modern technology influence the creation of the most widely- and well-known monsters in today's popular culture.
[42] On the close tie in Statius between reflection on the monster and reflection on human nature cf. Rieks (1967) 211.
[43] Cf. Rosati (2002) 301–303.
[44] Cf. Rosati (2002) 299–301 and Rosati (2009) *ad loc.*

which epic is based. This is why the 'redemption of the monster' acquires its fullest meaning if, behind Capaneus, we read the intertextual watermark that I have tried to reconstruct here, the stories of his precursors and companions: confrontation with the Other goes through ancient epic and interrogates our own human condition.

Bibliography

Andrisano, Angela Maria (ed.) (2007), *Biblioteche del mondo antico*, Rome.
Arrighetti, Graziano (ed.) (1995a), *Poesia Greca*, Pisa.
Arrighetti, Graziano (1995b), "Stesicoro, Quintiliano e la *Poetica* di Aristotele", in: Arrighetti (1995a) 123–136.
Augoustakis, Antony (ed.) (2013), *Ritual and Religion in Flavian Epic*, Oxford.
Augoustakis, Antony (2016), *Statius*, Thebaid 8, Oxford.
Bessone, Federica (2011), *La* Tebaide *di Stazio: epica e potere*, Pisa.
Bessone, Federica (2013), "Religion and Power in the *Thebaid*", in: Augoustakis (2013) 145–161.
Boyd, Barbara W. (ed.) (2002), *Brill's Companion to Ovid*, Leiden/Boston/Cologne.
Caiani, Lucia (1990), "La *pietas* nella 'Tebaide' di Stazio: Mezenzio modello di Ippomedonte e Capaneo", in: *Orpheus* 11, 260–276.
Chaudhuri, Pramit (2014), *The War with God: Theomachy in Roman Imperial Poetry*, Oxford.
Clarke, Michael J./Currie, Bruno G.F./Lyne, R.O.A.M. (eds.) (2006), *Epic Interactions: Perspectives on Homer, Virgil, and the Epic Tradition Presented to Jasper Griffin by Former Pupils*, Oxford.
Cohen, Jeffrey Jerome (ed.) (1996a), *Monster Theory: Reading Culture*, Minneapolis.
Cohen, Jeffrey Jerome (1996b), "Monster Culture (Seven Theses)", in: Cohen (1996a) 3–25.
Curtis, Paul (2011), *Stesichoros'* Geryoneis, Leiden/Boston 2011.
Davies, Malcom/Finglass, Patrick J. (2014), *Stesichorus*, The Poems, Cambridge.
Easterling, Patricia E./Knox, Bernard M.W. (eds.) (1985), *The Cambridge History of Ancient Greek Literature*, Cambridge.
Feeney, Denis (1991), *The Gods in Epic. Poets and Critics of the Classical Tradition*, Oxford.
Finglass, Patrick J./Kelly, Adrian (eds.) (2015a), *Stesichorus in Context*, Cambridge.
Finglass, Patrick J./Kelly, Adrian (2015b), "The state of Stesichorean studies", in: Finglass/Kelly (2015a) 1–17.
Fiorentini, Leonardo (2007), "Lirici greci nella biblioteca di Virgilio: qualche appunto sulla presenza di Saffo, Alceo e Stesicoro nell'*Eneide*", in: Andrisano (2007) 127–145.
Franchet d'Espèrey, Sylvie (1999), *Conflit, violence et non-violence dans la* Thébaïde *de Stace*, Paris.
Franzen, Christina (2009), "Sympathizing with the Monster: Making Sense of Colonization in Stesichorus' *Geryoneis*", in: *QUCC* 92.2, 55–72.
Fucecchi, Marco (1990), "Empietà e titanismo nella rappresentazione siliana di Annibale", in: *Orpheus* 11, 21–42.

Fucecchi, Marco (2013), "Looking for the Giants. Mythological imagery and discourse on power in Flavian epic", in: Manuwald/Voigt (2013) 107–122.
Gantz, Timothy (1993), *Early Greek Myth*, Baltimore.
Glenn, Justin (1971), "Mezentius and Polyphemus", in: *AJPh* 92, 129–155.
Hardie, Philip (1986), *Virgil's* Aeneid: *Cosmos and Imperium*, Oxford.
Hardie, Philip (1993), *The Epic Successors of Virgil: a Study in the Dynamics of a Tradition*, Cambridge.
Harrison, Stephen (1991), *Vergil*, Aeneid *10*, Oxford.
Harrison, Stephen (1992), "The Arms of Capaneus: Statius' *Thebaid* 4.165–77", in: *CQ* 42, 247–252.
Kronenberg, Leah J. (2005), "Mezentius the Epicurean", in: *TAPhA* 135, 403–431.
Lazzeri, Massimo (2006), "I *papavera* di Verg. *Aen.* 9.436, Omero, Stesicoro e Ovidio (con una nota a Servio)", in: *SemRom* 9, 145–160.
Leigh, Matthew (2006), "Statius and the Sublimity of Capaneus", in: Clarke *et al.* (2006) 217–241.
Lowe, Dunstan (2015), *Monsters and Monstrosity in Augustan Poetry*, Ann Arbor.
Manuwald, Gesine/Voigt, Astrid (eds.) (2013), *Flavian Epic Interactions*, Berlin/Boston.
McNelis, Charles (2007), *Statius'* Thebaid *and the Poetics of Civil War*, Cambridge.
Micozzi, Laura (2007), *Il catalogo degli eroi. Saggio di commento a Stazio*, Tebaide 4, 1–344, Pisa.
Noussia-Fantuzzi, Maria (2013), "A Scenario for Stesichorus' Portrayal of the Monster Geryon in the *Geryoneis*", in: *Trends in Classics* 5.2, 234–259.
Poignault, Rémy (ed.) (1999), *Présence de Lucrèce. Actes du colloque tenu à Tours (3–5 décembre 1998)*, Tours.
Pollmann, Karla F.L. (2004), *Statius*, Thebaid 12, Padeborn.
Pontiggia, Ludovico (2018), "La folgore di Giove e la teomachia di Capaneo nella *Tebaide* di Stazio", in: *MD* 80, 165–192.
Rieks, Rudolf (1967), Homo, humanus, humanitas. *Zur Humanität in der lateinischen Literatur des ersten nachchristlichen Jahrhunderts*, Munich.
Ripoll, François (1998), *La morale héroïque dans les épopées latines d'époque flavienne: tradition et innovation*, Leuven/Paris.
Rosati, Gianpiero (2002), "Narrative Techniques and Narrative Structures in the *Metamorphoses*", in: Boyd (2002) 271–304.
Rosati, Gianpiero (ed.) (2009), *Ovidio*, Metamorfosi. *Volume III, Libri V–VI*, Milan.
Santini, Carlo (2014), "La violenza nel Tideo di Stazio: contro l'altro o contro sé stesso?", in: *GIF* 66, 225–244.
Segal, Charles (1985), "Stesichorus", in: Easterling/Knox (1985) 186–201.
Taisne, Anne-Marie (1999), "Le *De rerum natura* et la *Thébaïde* de Stace", in: Poignault (1999) 165–175.
Tsitsibakou-Vasalos, Evanthia (1990), "Stesichorus *Geryoneis*, SLG 15 I–II", in: *Hellenica* 41, 7–31.

Thomas Baier
Flavian Gods in Intertextual Perspective. How Rulers Used Religious Practice as a Means of Communicating

1 Introduction

Flavian epic is often seen as a continuation of and an intertextual play with Virgil's *Aeneid*. In many ways, this is true. But there are significant changes which justify the classification of Flavian literature as an epoch of its own. One significant trait of the age from Nero's demise to Domitian is the "atmosphere of *religio*."[1] Prodigies and all kind of divine intervention play an important role in historical as well as in epic literature. The representation of gods in Valerius and his successors reflects a shift in religious thinking in Rome from the end of the republic to the end of the 1st c. BC. This shift in the conception of the universe comprises the ideas of fate and fortune, of free will and of destiny. There is also evidence that the conception of what is understood as "god" or "gods" underwent a change. My main focus will not be on a theological or metaphysical explanation of what gods actually are, whether they exist and how mighty or influential they are, but rather on how the interaction between god and man is communicated and used as a means of gaining political authority. This will be shown through a discussion of the intertextual similarities as well as differences between Valerius Flaccus' *Argonautica* and texts of various genres such as Tacitus' historical writings and an example of the gospels.

Principally, there are three ways of interpreting divine interventions in ancient epic. They can be seen under a mythological aspect, which the Romans label derogatorily as *religio poetarum* in contrast to *religio philosophorum* and *religio physica*. This perspective, however, is not very helpful in grasping what constitutes a literary work specifically. The second line of interpretation sees divine action in epic as a motif of literary tradition. Scholars who follow this line are interested in intertextuality and source studies. The third and hitherto most productive perspective on gods in epic is the psychological one, in which gods are interpreted as placeholders for emotions, feelings, states of mind. While all three approaches have attracted critical attention in the past, religious practice as a means of communication with fellows and inferiors in epic has, as far as I

---

1 Liebeschuetz (1979) 164.

can see, not yet been thoroughly looked at. My own reading will offer a way to see the political impact of religious practice.

2 Valerius Flaccus

At the beginning of the *Argonautica*, Jason has to carry a complicated burden. Pelias, the tyrant of Iolkos, harbours a malicious plan to destroy him since he sees his own reign threatened by the young hero. Soothsayers (*vates*) and victims at the altar (*pecudum ... per aras / terrifici monitus*, 1.28–29)[2] have repeated fearful warnings and predicted his downfall at the hands of Jason. Furthermore, Pelias fears Jason's prowess and glory. He therefore sends him to Iolkos for the Golden Fleece—with the explicit intent that he may never return. Jason accepts the order, although he clearly knows Pelias' real motif. He places his trust in Juno and Pallas (1.73) and in the force of prayer (1.81–90).[3] This is at least the impression he gives to his underlings. But it is made obvious for the reader that Jason sees his obedience to the gods as a strategy to strengthen his authority. This becomes clear from his free indirect speech (*populumne levem ... advocet an socia Iunone et Pallade fretus ... freta iussa capessat*, "Shall he summon to his aid a fickle populace ...? Or shall he trust rather to the aid of Juno and Pallas and launch forth at the king's command," 1.71–74)[4] and from the way he deals with oracles (1.184–254).[5] In the latter case he deliberately misinterprets prophecies in order to encourage his comrades.[6]

Jason, in dealing with the gods and in fulfilling religious rites shows his abilities as a leader and, in a way, communicates with his troops. Some scholars have already seen this, and they have usually criticized Jason for his behaviour, in particular when comparing him to Virgil's Aeneas. In contrast to his "model," *pius Aeneas*, Jason would appear as a ruthless leader and a prototype of impiety.[7]

---

[2] Dräger (2003) 320 sees an allusion here to the Etruscan augural discipline.
[3] Cf. McDonald (1970) 57: "There is never a feeling that Pelias is simply acting as an agent of the gods. Although Jason suggests here that the expedition will actually further the divine intention that the races of men are to have dealings with each other."
[4] All translations of Valerius Flaccus are taken from Mozley's Loeb edition (1934).
[5] Cf. Lefèvre (1991).
[6] According to Ferenczi (1996) 45 Jason interprets the oracles on the basis of his belief in the gods and with the aim to encourage his comrades.
[7] Examples for this view are Lefèvre (1991), Lefèvre (1998), Elm von der Osten (2007).

But this criticism probably misses the point. It was certainly not Valerius' intention to show us a pious Jason; he rather wanted his readers to perceive him as a strong leader, as a man like Vespasian and the members of the Flavian dynasty, for instance. Among the repertory of such a leader is the enactment of religious rituals aimed at impressing one's comrades.

The touchstone for Jason's attitude is his interpretation of the oracles given by Mopsus and by Idmon (1.205–239). The first one, missing in Apollonius Rhodius, was added by the Roman writer, the second one corresponds to a similar oracle in the Greek *Argonautica* (Ap. Rhod. *Argon.* 1.440–447). Both prophecies convey a sombre and even threatening atmosphere. They are, however, not completely negative or protective. The visions offer a contrasting perspective on the ensuing action. Mopsus foresees many burdens, and he does not know which destiny awaits the Argonauts. Idmon, on the other hand, makes it eminently clear that the ship will overcome the manifold labours in the end (1.235–236): *praeduri plena laboris / cerno equidem, patiens sed quae ratis omnia vincet,* "I behold all our course full of toil and grievous to be borne; yet shall the ship with long suffering overcome all things." In Apollonios' epic the prophetic utterance is embedded into a prayer and into libation scenes, which Valerius at first appears to imitate.[8] But in the Roman *Argonautica* the account has a totally different atmosphere as well as a new function, as Zissos explains: "The scene unfolds according to a careful dialectic of imitation of and deviation from Apollonius' treatment."[9] Idmon's calmness contrasts with Mopsus' agitation. He resembles, as Hershkowitz has pointed out, Lucan's frenzied *matrona* in *Bellum Civile* 1.674–695.[10] And indeed, Valerius might have borrowed the political implications from Lucan's epic: Idmon's inner turmoil is a premonition of how the Argonauts might have reacted, if they had been able to see themselves what the soothsayers see.

The oracles have a psychological impact and a political function. Both aspects are absent in the Greek *Argonautica*. By choosing a significantly different treatment from that of his Greek predecessor, Valerius has also changed Jason's role. The Roman Jason reacts as a statesman who has to avoid an insurrection. Apollonius' mythological hero has turned into a foreseeing, calculating statesman.

Jason, in his interpretation of the oracle, mentions nothing of the predicted hardships and toils. On the contrary, he displays joy and confidence in the presence of his comrades (1.244–245): *non mihi Thessalici pietas culpanda tyranni / suspective doli: deus haec deus omine dextro imperat,* "Not mine is it to blame the

---

8 Cf. Zissos (2004) 320.
9 Zissos (2004) 319.
10 Cf. Hershkowitz (1998a) 26.

Thessalian tyrant for the honour he doth his kin, or his suspected wiles." As Pollini[11] has observed, Valerius follows a Virgilian model, namely Venus' words to her son at the doom of Troy (*Aen.* 2.601–603): *non tibi Tyndaridis facies invisa Lacaenae / culpatusve Paris, divum inclementia, divum / has evertit opes sternitque a culmine Troiam*, "You do not hate the face of the Spartan daughter of Tyndareus, nor is Paris to blame: the ruthlessness of the gods, of the gods, brought down this power, and toppled Troy from its heights."[12] In both cases, the addressees are reminded that they are part of a higher plan and that they should not think in purely human categories of revenge and retribution. There is, however, a clear difference between the Virgilian and the Valerian account. In the *Aeneid*, Venus tries to prevent Aeneas from killing Helena and from letting himself be guided by sheer wrath, for the mere sake of taking blind revenge. The highly pathetic repetition of *divum* reminds him of the fact that there is a divine plan behind the fate of Troy. He learns that there is no point in human intervention. Aeneas' feelings are described as *ira* resulting from *dolor*, his behaviour is characterised as *furere* (2.594–595). This analysis of Aeneas' conduct corresponds to the peripatetic theory describing anger as the product of hurt and mortification. In *De anima* (403 a) Aristotle had defined ὀργή ("wrath") as ὄρεξις ἀντιλυπήσεως ("appetite for retribution"). In response to it, Seneca in *de ira* (3.3) would find the ingenious translation *cupiditas doloris reponendi*. Thus, by the standards of ancient philosophy, both Stoic and Peripatetic, Aeneas' first desire for revenge is unequivocally qualified as evil. We see Aeneas as a human being, tempted by *ira*, the most dangerous affect the Romans knew, but brought to his senses by Venus. The development of his character underlines one of the main topics of the epic, the submission to *pietas*, or, in a broader perspective, the evolution from chaos to order.

By alluding to this very scene, Valerius provokes a comparison between Aeneas and Jason. In contrast to the Virgilian hero, we do not witness any development in Jason's behaviour. From the first moment, Jason is presented as a strategically thinking statesman. For him, the intervention of the gods is not a moral appeal, but an instrument of exerting power. This explains why the words to his troops stand in harsh opposition to his former prayer to Neptunus where he had humbly declared (1.198): *sed non sponte feror*. The allusion to Aeneas' *Italiam non*

---

11 Cf. Pollini (1984).
12 Translated by Kline (2002).

sponte sequor (*Aen.* 4.361) provokes another comparison between the two heroes.[13] Aeneas, stricken by his guilty conscience, uses these words in order to apologize to Dido. Painful though the situation is, he nevertheless tells the truth. Jason, by contrast, does not: when he performs prayers and consults oracles, he fulfils the rites which are required from a military leader. In the prayer, he had presented himself as a victim, but there is no doubt that he had accepted this role out of his own free will.

When he claims that *non mihi Thessalici pietas culpanda tyranni* (1.244), he ironically refers to Pelias' "actions performed 'sub specie pietatis'."[14] We might therefore set *pietas* in inverted commas. His reaction reveals that he even feels relieved by the fact that the necessity to oppose Pelias has ceased. This is why he proclaims, in the name of Jupiter, a new "world order" (1.246–247): *ipse suo voluit commercia mundo / Iuppiter et tantos hominum miscere labores*, "Jupiter himself hath willed the fellowship of men throughout his world, and their union in such mighty tasks." This corresponds to Jupiter's "Weltenplan" (Jovian programme)[15] and is a kind of ethics which shows some similarities with the concept of *labor improbus* in Virgil's *Georgics*.[16]

Virgil's Jupiter promotes the idea of restless activity or, as the Romans put it, the idea of *fortem fortuna adiuvat*. In this optimistic conception of the universe, man relies on the benevolence of a god and "cooperates" with the divine powers. Success is seen as a recompense for piety. The Flavian gods, on the contrary, do not expect subordination but push man into action, take a step back and, in the last consequence, render themselves useless: men take their fate into their own hands and thus replace the gods. Brooks Otis has proposed an aptly ambivalent interpretation of Virgil's *labor*: "There is, in any event, a fatal shadow on the whole picture: man's 'civilization' has a curse on it. The items in it that Virgil selects (135–144) involve at every point the rending and perversion of natural things (i.e. the discovery of fire, navigation, trapping, hunting and fishing, iron and steel tools, and—most important of all—private property)."[17] According to Virgil, the *labor improbus* is necessary for man's survival, but it also implies a sacrilege against the order of nature as instituted by Jupiter himself. It bears pointing out that this was exactly Jupiter's will: making life difficult for man was a pedagogical

---

13 While Aeneas obeys to the *fatum*, Jason follows Pelias' treacherous order. This is the basis on which he is bargaining with Neptunus. The direct comparison between Aeneas and Jason manifest the moral shortcomings of the latter, cf. Lefèvre (1991).
14 Zissos (2008) 203 *ad loc.*
15 Cf. Stover (2012) 28–29; Wacht (1991).
16 Cf. Baier (2007b) 199–202.
17 Otis (1964) 157.

device. Thus, when man subdues nature, he does exactly what Jupiter expects him to do. On the other hand, every human action is a potential transgression and doomed to be sacrilegious. It is therefore at the same time necessary and sinful. Virgil's *labor improbus* is therefore nothing less than a symbol for the ambivalence of the human condition.

Valerius explicitly corroborated this "ideology of activity" and made it the "raison d'être" of the whole universe. It is to be found among the gods as well as among human beings: Jupiter in the "Weltenplan" ("idea of the cosmos") welcomes the opening of the sea (1.545–546). Jason is driven by nothing than by the desire for glory (1.76). But in contrast to the Virgilian model, he is not in harmony with the gods, but rather uses them to corroborate his authority among the other Argonauts. What role, then, does *religio* play in the *Argonautica*? Jason is attracted by the hope of gaining fame by undertaking the enterprise,[18] and, in the end, it is *religio* which drives his decision (1.79–80). But by *religio* he means dealing with oracles in the most practical way. They do not serve so much to guide him, but to show to others that he enjoys divine protection. To some extent, this use of oracles may not have been new. Oracles and prophecies always needed interpretation. One might think of the famous anecdote in which Caesar, landing in Northern Africa, stumbled, fell down and got up again with the words: *teneo te, Africa*.[19] By this witty answer, he had turned a bad oracle into a good one. And he had probably established the tradition of using religion as a means of social communication.[20]

In Valerius, this high-handed way of dealing with the numinous is driven even further. Religion has become an instrument of power, resulting in a new type of ethics: what was traditionally seen as a sacrilege, e.g. seafaring, waging war, etc., is now given a positive connotation. Even Jupiter in his "Weltenplan" (1.531–567) assertively backs this reversal of values.[21] As a matter of course, Jason and the other human protagonists do not know the contents of Jupiter's speech,

---

18 Cf. Manuwald (2009) 592.
19 Suet. *Iul.* 59.1.
20 *Omina* are subject to the arbitrariness of the person who receives them. This is even true for verbal prophecies: the ambiguity of all sorts of oracular responses leads to a "contest of intelligence" (Burkert (2005) 39) between oracle and consultant; the latter may even be tempted to quibble.
21 One might see Jupiter's worldview as a deliberate distortion of Virgil's "empire that will know no end" (*Aen.* 1.279). Heerink, in this volume, has shown the same phenomenon in the use of elegiac elements by both poets.

but they behave as if they did, and they also have learned to see religion as an instrument of governing.[22]

Oracles are mainly present in the first and in the fifth book. In both books Jason has to deal with a tyrant, Pelias and Aeetes respectively. In 5.231–240, dead Phrixus appears to Aeetes and reminds him that he had once welcomed him to Colchis and given him his daughter Chalciope as a wife. He then warns him about the Golden Fleece and its importance for his reign.[23] Concerning Medea, he reveals that she will have to marry a foreigner. This is an allusion to Virgil's *externi venient generi* (*Aen.* 7.98). But the crucial point is that Phrixus' words are ambiguous. Whereas Aeetes has Styrus in mind as son-in-law, the reader already knows that Phrixus is referring to Jason.[24] What is interesting in our context is Aeetes' reaction: he is scared (*socerumque exterruit ingens / prodita vox*, "a great voice spoke forth and struck terror into the father of his bride," 5.232–233), and jumps quivering out of his bed (*membra toris rapit ille tremens*, "trembling the other started from his couch," 5.244).[25] By his behaviour he is clearly characterised as a tyrant. In the following prayer, he does not act as the king known from Greek myth but as a statesman.[26] Once again, a divine intervention is used to characterize a protagonist. Aeetes resembles king Oedipus, who receives many warning hints from several persons but fails to grasp the truth. When a priest advises him to give back the fleece for the sake of his country, he refuses fiercely (5.264–265): *aegro corde negat nec vulgi cura tyranno / dum sua sit modo tuta salus*, "[Aeetes] says nay; the tyrant recks not of his folk, so his own safety be assured."[27] The failure to accept the priest's advice leads to the war against his brother Perses. Political dissent is fought out on the basis of the presumed will of a certain *deus* (5.260) whose name is not even mentioned. But it is clear that the protagonists exploit the divine as a means of politics.[28]

---

[22] Cf. Ganiban (2014) 268: "Thus the worldview of Valerius' Jupiter, military / political supremacy is what is valued most and is reflected in the promotion of his mortal descendants among the Argonauts who will indeed become gods."
[23] Cf. Langen (1896–1897) 361: "Quod apte quidem a Valerio commemoratur ad intellegendum, cur Aeetes ira incensus ne aureum vellus Iasoni daret recusaverit."
[24] For Aeetes this is the most obvious way of reading the prophecy, cf. Manuwald (2013) 44.
[25] Cf. Gärtner (1996) 298–300.
[26] Cf. Lefèvre (1998) 225–226.
[27] Wagner (1805) 162 comments: "Digna tyranno oratio."
[28] Cf. Groß (2003) 123, 243 who seems to imply that divine messages support the character of individuals.

3 Tacitus

This concept, roughly sketched above, can be seen as the "Flavian way" of dealing with religion. There are many examples showing certain parallels between Jason and Vespasian, which cannot be dealt with exhaustively here. One might however compare an anecdote (Tac. *Hist.* 4.81), according to which Vespasian pretends to heal a blind man (an episode very similar to the miracles in the New Testament). The act of healing and thus the adopting of divine qualities are clearly marked as a strategy for securing the emperor's power.[29] Vespasian is at first doubtful whether he should play the game, but then bends to his advisors in the hope of gaining popularity.[30] The whole performance is an enactment of religious piety for the masses or the "audience" around. It is marked by Tacitus as the typical way of a monarch "communicating" with his subjects.[31]

Another aspect in Tacitus' account which deserves mentioning is that he sets the episode in an atmosphere of *multa miracula ... quis caelestis favor et quaedam in Vespasianum inclinatio numinum ostenderetur*, "many miracles ... which proved heaven's favour and divine goodwill for Vespasian" (*Hist.* 4.81). Generally speaking, there is a focus on religious anxiety in the surviving books of his historical works. Liebeschuetz has pointed out that especially at the end of Nero's reign many cases of supernatural "events" were reported: the masses, prone to believe in *prodigia*,[32] saw natural phenomena as a punishment by the gods. While such superstition was not new, of course, the intensity, the frequency and the fact that Tacitus puts so much stress on it are noticeable. In his account, the talent for acting, even the stagecraft of certain rulers had its counterpart in the credulity of the population.[33]

---

29 Cf. Heininger (2009).
30 Tac. *Hist.* 4.81 *atque illis instantibus modo famam vanitatis metuere, modo obsecratione ipsorum et vocibus adulantium in spem induci*, "and he, though on the one hand he feared the scandal of a fruitless attempt, yet, on the other, was induced by the entreaties of the men and by the language of his flatterers to hope for success" (translated by Church/Brodribb [1876] 188–189).
31 Cf. Levick (2017) 65–78. For Vespasian's visit to the Middle East cf. Henrichs (1968) 51–80.
32 Cf. Liebeschuetz (1979) 155–166.
33 Even the *ludibrium falsi Neronis* (Tac. *Hist.* 1.2) can be seen in this context.

4 Statius

Another, even more sublime example of effectively displaying state-craft as stage-craft can be found in Statius' *Thebaid*. After eleven books of hatred and despair, the twelfth book takes an unexpected, reconciling twist, almost giving rise to hope. Argia, Polynices' wife, and Antigone, his sister, bury the dead brothers in defiance of Creon's nefarious orders, choosing to fulfil the divine law instead. The Argive women turn to Theseus of Athens for help, pleading with him to curb the transgressing Creon and to free those deprived of their rights from the tyrant's yoke. Theseus goes to Athens and defeats Creon in single combat. This concluding scene of the epic, by the way a clear parallel to the closure of the *Aeneid*, stands in stark contrast to the previous fighting. The externally visible symbol of the good rule of the king of Athens is the *ara clementiae*, a sanctuary for the "weary and burdened."[34] Statius, however, gives it a specifically Roman and a specifically imperial reinterpretation.[35] The altar is not described as an existing monument, but appears to be removed to the sphere of the symbolic. The *topoi* relating to the altar go back to the Hellenistic period.[36] Neither do the suppliant women invoke the rights that they regard as guaranteed by the altar, nor does Theseus make any reference to the monument in his actions—the *ara* itself is described as *nulli concessa potentum* (12.481): access is denied to the powerful,[37] to whom Theseus belongs as well. The altar is thus not presented as a religious place but as the principle of *clementia*, which is removed from the ruler's grasp. Statius expressed in a poetic image what Seneca tried to provide with a theoretical basis in his philosophical work *On Clemency*: the establishment of *clementia* as a ruler's virtue, which stands unassailable above the arbitrariness of the respective *princeps*. Originally belonging to the fields of jurisprudence and the military, the term *clementia* more and more became an actual or alleged maxim for political action under the principate.

The poet gives two interpretations concerning the erection of the altar. According to the second one (12.499–505), which is presented as more reliable, the

---

34 Cf. Burgess (1972) 343. In 12.175 *clementia* is a significant and distinguishing quality of the Athenian people, cf. Kabsch (1968) 165–169, esp. 166–167.
35 The intertwining of religious and political spheres was characteristic for Domitian's reign, cf. Galimberti (2016) 101.
36 Cf. Bernstein (2013) 147: "The Altar of *Clementia* itself was a rhetorical topos that attracted considerable attention from orators and teachers from the Hellenistic period onwards. It enabled Greek orators to elaborate narratives of an idealized fourth-century Athens."
37 Cf. Burgess (1972) 343 and Baier (2007a) 159–170.

gods themselves founded the shrine when they introduced laws and the new man (*homo novus*, 12.501). The term *homo novus* had a special connotation for Roman ears. It carried a philosophical and a political implication, of which only the latter concerns us here. The self-praise of the tyrant Lycus in Seneca's *Hercules furens* illustrates how *homo novus* was understood in imperial Rome: he characterises himself as a *homo novus* through allusions to famous passages of well-known orations by Cicero, saying that he is not an *ignavus heres*, has no *nobiles avi*, no *inclitum genus* but that he relies on his *clara virtus* (*Herc. f.* 340).[38] He is an ideal ruler due to his own faculties—the *homo novus* as a "self-made man." Using this ambiguous term, Statius might also have intended to pay a little homage to the addressee of the epic, Domitian, or rather his family, for the Flavians were social climbers, too.[39] Domitian's great-grandfather came to Rome during the civil war between Caesar and Pompey and served the former as a centurion. Domitian's grandfather, Vespasian's father, was a tax collector in the province of Asia (Suet. *Vesp.* 1.2). In fact, the Flavians kept harping on their humble origins and alleged poverty, as Suetonius tells us in his *Life of the Emperor Domitian* (1.1). This was part of the Flavian propaganda, especially in the early seventies. Domitian himself was eager to promote the *gens Flavia*'s own achievements—in the *Templum Iovis Conservatoris* or later *Iovis Custodis*, for example.[40] Vespasian's family belonged to the rising *gentes* which replaced the old-established families of the Roman nobility.

In a similar vein, Theseus presents himself as an ideal *princeps*[41] who rules by his own right and his own achievements and who has set up the altar of clem-

---

38 Cf. Billerbeck (1999) 327.
39 Cf. Jones (1992) 2.
40 Cf. Tac. *Hist.* 3.74.1 *modicum sacellum Iovi Conservatori aramque posuit casus suos in marmore expressam; mox imperium adeptus Iovi Custodi templum ingens seque in sinu dei sacravit,* "[he] built a small chapel, dedicated to Jupiter the Preserver, with an altar on which his own adventures were represented in marble. Afterwards, on his own accession to the Imperial power, he consecrated a vast temple to Jupiter the Guardian, with an effigy of himself in the arms of the god" (translated by Church/Brodribb [1876] 133–134). Casus suos refers to Domitian's rescue, when Vitellius' troops assaulted the Roman capitol.
41 The figure of Theseus is disputed among scholars. Fantham (1997) 212 sees in him an impartial judge who is free from animosity against the guilty and "unmoved by envy, anger, fear or [...] hatred." Dominik (1994) 92–110 and Hershkowitz (1998b) 301, on the contrary, see Theseus tainted by signs of madness and cruelty, even if these are hidden under the surface. The debate, whether Theseus is 'positive' or 'negative' tends to forget what is really at stake: Statius gives an illustration of the principle of *clementia*. As Theseus embodies this central virtue of the principate, he is seen as a positive role model for Domitian. It may be true, as Coffee (2009) 226 states,

ency as a symbol for his rule. *Clementia* has replaced the virtue of *pietas*. In Virgil's *Aeneid*, the order is based on the principle that the representatives of *pietas* defeat the *impii*. The differentiation between *pii* and *impii*, however, is not possible any more in the *Thebaid*. The *fraterna bella* in Statius means that everyone becomes guilty; in a world in which every crime tries to trump a previous crime, there is no place for *pietas*. Instead, everybody is dependent on forgiveness.[42] In Statius, *clementia* has replaced *pietas*,[43] a monarchic virtue has outdone a republican one.

As Virgil created Aeneas as a model or archetype for Augustus, Statius created Theseus as a model for Domitian. The reference to Virgil is emphasised not least by the parallel of the epic closures with the "death of the villain." But the times had changed significantly. Virgil's positive order, in which *pietas* was still valid, had given way to a hopeless disorder, in which good and bad, guilty and innocent could no longer be clearly distinguished. They had given way, in other words, to a time which needs *clementia*. It goes without saying, that this concept of *clementia* comes near the Hellenistic idea of φιλανθρωπία or πραότης. Roman *clementia* was originally confined to foreign politics: it meant the display of mercy towards a defeated enemy. In such a case, it was up to the victorious general whether he used mercy or not. Among equals, however, i.e. among Roman citizens, *clementia* had no place. The transfer of *clementia* from foreign to domestic affairs was therefore only possible after the fall of the republic. The use of *clementia* implies a hierarchy of power, a gap between the ruler and his subjects.

---

that, in some scenes of the epic, one notices a "disparity between Theseus and Clementia", the Athenian king being assimilated rather to bellicose Mars than to the mildness of humanity. This once more shows Theseus' aptitude as an emperor who combines the role of a strong warrior with the one of a compassionate ruler. This double-faced behaviour strikingly corresponds with Domitian's, who, according to Suet. *Dom.* 12.1, presented himself *ab initio principatus usque ad exitum ciuilis et clemens.*

42 Cf. Ripoll (1998) 323: It was Statius' intention "de sauvegarder un mythe tragique en le transposant d'une forme d'expression en déclin vers un genre en plein essor."

43 Cf. Baier (2007a) 168: "I protagonisti della Tebaide si assumono una costante colpa, essi sono empi fino alla fine. Essi sono dominati dalle passioni, che rendono loro disumani. La *clementia* li aiuta a trovare di nuovo se stessi e pone l'ordine in modo che colui che possiede la *pietas* vinca sugli *impii*. Nelle *fraterna bella*, per Stazio, tutti sono colpevoli; in un mondo nel quale ogni crimine cerca di farla franca, la *pietas* non ha posto."

Clementia can be humiliating for those who benefit from it.⁴⁴ Nobody has expressed this more clearly than Cicero in his so-called "Caesarian" speeches.⁴⁵ Seneca, in his treatise *On clemency*, has tried to heal the flaw of traditional *clementia* by clearly separating it from *crudelitas* and *feritas* on the one hand and from *misericordia* and *miseria* on the other.⁴⁶ But the real novelty of his approach was to conflate republican *aequitas* and monarchic *clementia*, making thus the latter more acceptable for the Romans.⁴⁷ As a consequence, he sees in the *princeps* the embodiment of law, a νόμος ἔμψυχος or a *lex animata*.⁴⁸ Seneca wanted to shape Nero as a philosopher king.⁴⁹ Statius, in book 12, seems to follow the trail blazed by Seneca.⁵⁰ Maybe Statius perceived himself as a stoic advisor for Domitian. The altar is the medium by which the standard of good rule is communicated. Theseus (and we may infer that Statius meant Domitian) uses this religious symbol as a means of communication with his subjects and as a justification for his one-man-rule.

The two mythological poems mirror the tendency of Flavian rulers to turn religion into politics. There is, however, one difference: while in Valerius Flaccus we can see the practical side of religion with (typically Greek) prophecies, prayers and (typically Tuscan) extispicy, Statius in the twelfth book displays what we might rather call "invisible religion" (according to the definition of Thomas Luckmann), i.e. the ethical content of religion.⁵¹

---

44 Ganiban (2007) 214–217 sees Statius' *clementia* as being "transformed ... into something more like *misericordia* ("pity")" and notes the "dire consequences" that spring from the "conflation of *clementia* and *misericordia*." But it is probably not *misericordia* which Statius has in mind. His reasoning is rather judicial than moral.
45 *Pro Marcello*, *pro Ligario*, *pro Deiotaro rege*. Especially the last speech gives a sombre and shattering impression of the ailing judicature under Caesar, in which all legal procedures were dependant on the dictator himself.
46 Sen. *Clem.* 2.3–4. I shall deal with this problem in an article (Baier (forthcoming)).
47 This has been shown by Fuhrmann (1971) 512–513. The "complicated ... picture of *clementia*" and the "confusion of ideals" asserted by Ganiban (2007) 221 is due to the camouflage of *clementia* as a special form of *aequitas*.
48 Although Seneca does not quote "νόμος ἔμψυχος" literally, he obviously refers to the concept, cf. Griffin (1976) 153. One of the sources may be his contemporary Musonius (*Dissertationum a Lucio digestorum reliquiae* 8.65 = Stob. *Floril.* 4.7.67, p. 283.24 Wachsmuth): δεῖ αὐτόν [sc. τὸν βασιλέα τὸν ἀγαθὸν], ὥσπερ ἐδόκει τοῖς παλαιοῖς, νόμον ἔμψυχον εἶναι.
49 Cf. Braund (2009) 246: "Seneca seems to be replicating the relationship between Stoic adviser and ruler in the guidance, he offers Nero here."
50 Ganiban (2007) 220 rightly sees "Theseus as a representative of Clementia" and makes clear that "his actions draw him closer to the field of imperial *clementia*, as defined in Seneca."
51 Cf. Luckmann (1967) 77–80: "The statement that religion is present in nonspecific form in all societies and all 'normal' (socialized) individuals is, therefore, axiomatic", p. 78.

5 Religion and Power, seen by other sources

We have seen that, in Valerius and Statius, communication with the gods is often a way of ensuring an emperor's power. *Religio* and *imperium* are connected closely. This corresponds with the divinization of emperors and the blending of god and man in the person of the emperor. Especially the Flavian dynasty could not rely on tradition or on ancestors of old. Vespasian and his successors had to provide their legitimacy on their own. The claim of a divine aura could help in this context. This seems all the more natural, if one considers the passage in Tacitus cited above, since it makes clear that at least the eastern parts of the empire expected the emperor to be some sort of "god." The very concept of "god" or "divinity" clearly had undergone a change, probably under Eastern influence. It was this change which enabled the intertwining of the roles of god and the emperor.

The phenomenon described here can also be seen in the gospel of Mark, a text written in the Flavian era as well, normally dated at the beginning of the seventies. As some scholars in New Testament-studies maintain,[52] the gospels display a "political theology," with Jesus Christ characterized as an anti-Emperor. And indeed, the miracles wrought by Jesus correspond in some way to what we have heard about Vespasian. It seems that the evangelist is eager to confirm Jesus' claim that he is a king as well. He is not a king of this world, as a matter of course, but he does have the same attributes and paraphernalia as worldly emperors have. In Mark 8.22–26, Jesus heals a blind man in the same manner as did Vespasian. In 10.46–52 he heals the blind Bartimaeus, the last miracle in this gospel. Bartimaeus cries out:

> 'Thou, son of David have mercy on me.' And Jesus stood still, and commanded him to be called. And they call the blind man, saying unto him: 'Be of good comfort, rise; he calleth thee.' And he, casting away his garment, rose and came to Jesus. And Jesus answered and said unto him: 'What wilt thou that I should do unto thee?' The blind man said unto him: 'Lord, that I might receive my sight.' And Jesus said unto him: 'Go thy way thy faith hath made thee whole.'

This passage has been controversial.[53] I agree with those scholars who see here a parody of an audience scene, in which an emperor receives a supplicant. Bartimaeus addresses Jesus like a sovereign with his "title": "son of David," the sovereign himself asks a question and, in the end, sends him away with a formulaic

---

[52] For the following cf. Ebner (2003), Heininger (2009).
[53] Cf. Ebner (2003) 39 with further bibliography; Neumann (2005) 68–70.

word of discharge and a pledge. This corresponds to the ritualized way of the emperor dealing with underlings. The disciples in this scene act like courtiers.

Jesus also starts his reign as any king would do: he gathers his "troops" or supporters, and preaches the Gospel of the "kingdom" of God (Mark 1.14), τὸ εὐαγγέλιον τῆς βασιλείας τοῦ θεοῦ. The word *euangelion* is a technical term for the enthronement of a new emperor. Flavius Josephus thus writes about Vespasian's accession to the throne: "the news spread more quickly than the thoughts can fly, and every city celebrated the good news, *euangelia*" (*BJ* 4.618 and cf. 658). The authors of the gospels evidently took the technical term from the political system.

Jesus' reign not only begins like an emperor's rule, it also proceeds in a similar way. In the middle of the gospel (Mark 8.27–30) we find Jesus and his disciples in Caesarea Philippi, and he asks them: "Whom say ye that I am?" And Peter answers: "Thou art the Christ." "Christ" is another technical term, referring to the anointing of a king. There are, however, many strange elements about this passage. Why did Jesus, who was on his way from Bethesda to Jerusalem, go to Caesarea Philippi far in the north, only to ask whom his disciples took him for? The reason is that Caesarea Philippi, founded by Herodes' son Philippus (4 BC–34 AD), stood as a symbol for the alliance between a Jewish prince and the Roman emperor, and that Vespasian, after his military triumph in Galilea, went on to Caesarea Philippi, where he spent a winter with Antipas II.[54] There Flavius Josephus surrendered to him voluntarily and of his own will, and made the prophecy that Vespasian was to become emperor. Caesarea Philippi was also a central point in Jewish-Roman affairs.[55] This is why Jesus chose to accept the homage of his disciples at this very place: he took the same route as Vespasian did.[56] Or at least Marcus tells us so, and thereby enacts or presents himself as an Anti-Josephus. After Jesus was crucified, the centurion standing nearby says: "Truly, this man was a son of God" (Ἀληθῶς ὃ ἄνθρωπος οὗτος υἱὸς ἦν θεοῦ). Υἱὸς θεοῦ, *divi filius*, was the official title of the Roman Emperor since the times of Caesar. The centurion does not say, "the" or "the only" son of God, he uses no article.[57] His is obviously not a Christian perspective which would accept only one son of god, but he uses "son of god" in a less specified, pagan sense. He talks from the perspective

---

54 Probably the winter of 67, in the middle of the Jewish war.
55 Cf. Ebner (2003) 31–32.
56 Cf. Ebner (2003) 30, Heininger (2009) 184.
57 Cf. Ebner (2003) 35.

of a Roman soldier. In those days, there were prophecies (or rumours about alleged prophecies) that a new emperor would spring forth from Judaea.[58] The centurion referred these to Jesus; Flavius Josephus referred the same rumours to Vespasian.

We may take this (and other parallels which could be mentioned) as a proof that Jesus was deliberately designed as an Anti-Vespasian and the gospel as an "anti-*euangelion*."[59] Jesus the miracle worker parodies the Flavian pretence of a godlike king. In this sense, the gospel of Marcus functions as a distorting mirror, reflecting the "theology" of Flavian rulers.[60] Even if it was not Marcus' intention to write his gospel as a reflection of Flavian history, his text, as a document of its time, has to be seen in this context. The implicit reproach in the gospel against the Roman Emperor aims at exactly the way of dealing with the gods which we can study in Vespasian, but also in heroes like Jason.

From a Christian point of view, Jason's attitude towards the Gods is an example of abuse of divine authority and of treachery. The Flavians, as a matter of course, did not have this Christian perspective. And they did not have the Christian or Jewish conception of god. For them religion was a social phenomenon, and Vespasian or Jason dealt with it in a way which was compatible with Roman tradition since Caesar, and which seemed perfectly reasonable to them. Two things, however, mark a decisive distance from the Augustan authors like Virgil or Livy: first, fate is not something eternal and reliable any more. Instead, men have continually to fight for their interests, and Jupiter and the other gods do not necessarily foster the Romans, but they grant their goodwill to those who prove to be the strongest. Second, religion is more external and less metaphysical than it was in Virgil. It serves as a means of political communication. Therefore, Valerius' conception of the universe is less optimistic and less ethical than Virgil's one.

---

58 This fits with Suetonius' notice (*Vesp.* 4.5) *percrebruerat Oriente toto vetus et constans opinio esse in fatis ut eo tempore Iudaea profecti rerum potirentur. id de imperatore Romano, quantum postea eventu paruit, praedictum Iudaei ad se trahentes rebellarunt caesoque praeposito legatum insuper Syriae consularem suppetias ferentem rapta aquila fugaverunt*, "there had spread over all the Orient an old and established belief, that it was fated at that time for men coming from Judaea to rule the world. This prediction, referring to the emperor of Rome, as afterwards appeared from the event, the people of Judaea took to themselves; accordingly they revolted and after killing their governor, they routed the consular ruler of Syria as well, when he came to the rescue, and took one of his eagles" (translated by Rolfe [1914]).
59 Cf. Ebner (2003), esp. 33.
60 Cf. Heininger (2009) 181–183.

Bibliography

Augoustakis, Anthony (ed.) (2013), *Ritual and Religion in Flavian Epic*, Oxford.
Baier, Thomas (forthcoming), "Le *princeps* comme figure exemplaire dans le traité *De clementia* de Sénèque", in: Notter *et al.* (forthcoming).
Baier, Thomas (2007a), "L'*ara clementiae* nella *Tebaide* di Stazio (XII 481–518)", in: *Aevum* 81, 159–170.
Baier, Thomas (2007b), "*Labor improbus?* Ist die Arbeit wirklich ein Fluch?", in: Ecker (2007) 189–203.
Bernstein, Neil W. (2013), "*Distat opus nostrum, sed fontibus exit ab isdem*. Declamation and Flavian Epic," in: Manuwald/Voigt (2013) 139–156.
Billerbeck, Margarethe (1999), *Seneca*, Hercules Furens. *Einleitung, Text, Übersetzung und Kommentar*, Leiden/Boston/Köln.
Braund, Susanna M. (2009), *Seneca*, De clementia, Oxford.
Braund, Susanna M./Gill, Christopher (eds.) (1997), *The Passions in Roman Thought and Literature*, Cambridge.
Burgess, John F. (1972), "Statius' Altar of Mercy", in: *CQ* 22 n.s., 339–349.
Burkert, Walter (2005), "Signs, Commands, and Knowledge: Ancient Divination between Enigma and Epiphany", in: Johnston/Struck (2005) 29–49.
Church, Alfred John/Brodribb, William Jackson (eds.) (1876), *The History of Tacitus, translated into English, with notes and a map*, 3rd ed., London.
Coffee, Neil (2009), "Statius' Theseus: Martial or Merciful?", in: *CPh* 104, 221–228.
De Martino, Francesco/Kyriakidis, Stratis (eds.) (2004), *Middles in Latin Poetry*, Bari.
Dominik, William (1994), *The Mythic voice of Statius. Power and Politics in the* Thebaid, Leiden.
Dräger, Paul (2003), *C. Valerius Flaccus,* Argonautica: *Die Sendung der Argonauten, Lateinisch/Deutsch, herausgegeben, übersetzt und kommentiert*, Frankfurt am Main.
Ebner, Martin (2003), "Evangelium contra Evangelium. Das Markusevangelium und der Aufstieg der Flavier", in: *Biblische Nachrichten* 116, 28–42.
Ecker, Hans-Peter (ed.) (2007), *Orte des guten Lebens. Entwürfe humaner Lebensräume*, Würzburg.
Eigler, Ulrich/Lefèvre, Eckard/Manuwald, Gesine (eds.) (1998), Ratis omnia vincet. *Neue Untersuchungen zu den* Argonautica *des Valerius Flaccus*, Munich.
Elm von der Osten, Dorothee (2007), *Liebe als Wahnsinn. Die Konzeption der Göttin Venus in den* Argonautica *des Valerius Flaccus*, Stuttgart.
Erlemann, Kurt/Noethlichs, Karl Leo/Scherberich, Klaus/Zangenberg, Jürgen (eds.) (2005), *Neues Testament und Antike Kultur. Band 2: Familie, Gesellschaft, Wirtschaft*, Neukirchen-Vluyn.
Fantham, Elaine (1997), "'Envy and fear the begetter if hate': Statius' *Thebaid* and the genesis of hatred", in: Braund/Gill (1997) 185–212.
Ferenczi, Attila (1996), "Die Götter bei Valerius Flaccus", in: *WHB* 38, 37–48.
Fuhrmann, Manfred (1963), "Die Alleinherrschaft und das Problem der Gerechtigkeit (Seneca: De clementia)", in: *Gymnasium* 70 (1963), 481–514.
Galimberti, Alessandro (2016), "The Emperor Domitian", in: Zissos (2016) 92–108.
Ganiban, Randall T. (2007), *Statius and Virgil. The* Thebaid *and the Reinterpretation of the* Aeneid, Cambridge.

Ganiban, Randall T. (2014), "Virgilian Prophecy and the Reign of Jupiter in Valerius Flaccus' *Argonautica*", in: Heerink/Manuwald (2014) 251–268.
Gärtner, Ursula (1996), "Träume bei Valerius Flaccus", in: *Philologus* 140, 292–305.
Griffin, Miriam (1976), *Seneca. A Philosopher in Politics*, Oxford.
Groß, Annedore (2003), *Prophezeiungen und Prodigien in den* Argonautica *des Valerius Flaccus*, München.
Heerink, Mark/Manuwald, Gesine (eds.) (2014), *Brill's Companion to Valerius Flaccus*, Leiden/Boston.
Heininger, Bernhard (2009), "'Politische Theologie' im Markusevangelium. Der Aufstieg Vespasians zum Kaiser und der Abstieg Jesu ans Kreuz", in: Mayer (2009) 181–204.
Henrichs, Albert (1968), "Vespasian's Visit to Alexandria", in: *ZPE* 3, 51–80.
Hershkowitz, Debra (1998a), *Valerius Flaccus'* Argonautica. *Abbreviated Voyages in Silver Latin Epic*, Oxford.
Hershkowitz, Debra (1998b), *The Madness of Epic. Reading Insanity from Homer to Statius*, Oxford.
Johnston, Sarah Iles/Struck, Peter T. (eds.) (2005), *Mantikê. Studies in Ancient Divination*, Leiden.
Jones, Brian W. (1992), *The Emperor Domitian*, London/New York.
Kabsch, Edda (1968), *Funktion und Stellung des zwölften Buches der* Thebais *des P. Papinius Statius*, Diss., Kiel.
Kline, Anthony S. (2002), *Virgil. A Translation into English Prose*, www.poetryintranslation.com.
Korn, Matthias/Tschiedel, Hans Jürgen (eds.) (1991), Ratis omnia vincet. *Untersuchungen zu den* Argonautica *des Valerius Flaccus*, Hildesheim/Zürich/New York.
Langen, Peter (1896–1897), *C. Valerii Flacci Setini Balbi Argonauticon libri octo*, Berolini.
Lefèvre, Eckard (1991), "Die Opfer-Szene im ersten Buch (1, 184–254) und das Iason-Bild in Valerius Flaccus' *Argonautica*", in: Korn/Tschiedel (1991) 173–180.
Lefèvre, Eckard (1998), "Der *ordo rerum* in Valerius Flaccus' *Argonautica*", in: Eigler *et al.* (1998) 223–232.
Levick, Barbara (2017), *Vespasian*, 2nd ed., London/New York.
Liebeschuetz, John H.W.G. (1979), *Continuity and Change in Roman Religion*, Oxford.
Luckmann, Thomas (1967), *The Invisible Religion. The Problem of Religion in Modern Society*, New York/London.
Manuwald, Gesine (2009), "What Do Humans Get to Know about the Gods and Their Plans? On Prophecies and Their Deficiencies in Valerius Flaccus' *Argonautica*", in: *Mnemosyne* 62, 586–608.
Manuwald, Gesine (2013), "Divine Messages and Human Actions in the *Argonautica*," in: Augoustakis (2013) 33–51.
Manuwald, Gesine/Voigt, Astrid (eds.) (2013), *Flavian Epic Interactions*, Berlin/Boston.
McDonald, Ian Ritchie (1970), *The Flavian Epic Poets as Political and Social Critics*, Phil. Diss. Ann Arbor, Michigan, Chapel Hill.
Mayer Cornelius (ed.) (2009), *Augustinus – Ethik und Politik. Zwei Würzburger Augustinus-Studientage. Aspekte der Ethik bei Augustinus (11. Juni 2005). Augustinus und die Politik (24. Juni 2006) (Cassiciacum 39,4 = Res et signa. Augustinus-Studien 4)*, Würzburg.
Mozley, John H., (1934), *Valerius Flaccus, with an English Translation*, London/Cambridge, MA, repr. 1972.
Neumann, Josef N. (2005), "2.2.3.2 Behinderung", in: Erlemann *et al.* (2005) 68–70.

Notter, Catherine/Arbo, Agnès/Vix, Jean-Luc (eds.) (forthcoming), *Figures exemplaires du pouvoir*.
Otis, Brooks (1964), *Virgil. A Study in Civilized Poetry*, Oxford.
Pollini, Eva (1984), "Il motivo della *visendi cupido* nel Giasone di Valerio Flacco", in: *Maia* 36, 51–61.
Ripoll, François (1998), "La *Thébaïde* de Stace entre épopée et tragédie", in: *Pallas* 49, 323–340.
Rolfe, John Carew (1914), *Suetonius, with an English Translation*, I-II, London/Cambridge, MA, repr. 2001.
Stover, Tim (2012), *Epic & Empire in Vespasianic Rome. A new reading of Valerius Flaccus' Argonautica*, Oxford.
Wacht, Manfred (1991), *Juppiters Weltenplan im Epos des Valerius Flaccus*, Stuttgart.
Wagner, Johann Augustin (1805), *Commentarius Perpetuus in C. Valerii Flacci Setini Balbi Argonauticon Libros VIII*, Gottingen.
Zissos, Andrew (2004), "Terminal Middle: The *Argonautica* of Valerius Flaccus", in: De Martino/Kyriakidis (2004) 311–344.
Zissos, Andrew (2008), *Valerius Flaccus' Argonautica, Book 1. A Commentary*, Oxford.
Zissos, Andrew (ed.) (2016), *A Companion to the Flavian Age of Imperial Rome*, Chichester, UK/Malden, MA.

Alison Keith
Palatine Apollo, Augustan Architectural Ecphrasis, and Flavian Epic Intertextuality

Architectural ecphrases have long been recognized as an integral feature of classical epic, from Achilles' camp in *Iliad* 24 and Alcinous' palace in *Odyssey* 7 to the palaces of Aeetes in Apollonios' *Argonautica* 3 and Latinus in *Aeneid* 7, and well beyond.[1] In this tradition Ovid's description of the palace of Sol in *Metamorphoses* 2 holds an important position because it has been understood to reflect, and reflect upon, not only the classical epic tradition of palace ecphrases,[2] but also Augustus' spectacular building programme on the Palatine, which conjoined a house fit for a *princeps* with a temple to his tutelary divinity, Apollo.[3] Ovid's interest in the imperial building complex on the Palatine extends throughout his poetic corpus[4] and finds an epic model in Vergil, whose palace of Latinus has been interpreted as a response to Augustus' domestic building there (cf. *Aen.* 7.170 *tectum augustum, ingens, centum sublime columnis*),[5] while his temple of Apollo at Cumae at the opening of *Aeneid* 6 has been understood to respond to the associated complex of the temple of Apollo Palatinus.[6] My study addresses the sophisticated reception of Vergil's Cumaean temple to Apollo and Ovid's palace of the Sun in two architectural ecphrases in Flavian epic: the temple of the

---

1 On Achilles' camp in *Iliad* 24, and its relationship to other Homeric ecphrases of dwellings, see McLeod (1982) 123 ad *Il.* 24.448–456; on Aeetes' palace in Apollonios, see Hunter (1989) 121–126, ad *Argon.* 3.213–248; on Latinus' palace in *Aeneid* 7, and its relationship to both Greek epic literary models and Roman socio-political practice, see Fordyce (1977) 96–104, and Horsfall (2000) 146–149, ad *Aen.* 7.170–191. On Ovid's debts to the tradition of classical epic ecphrasis, see Bömer (1969) 235–237, ad *Met.* 2.1–18. My thanks to Damien Nelis, Neil Coffee, Lavinia Galli Milić, and Christopher Forstall for the invitation to contribute a paper to the original conference, and to my fellow participants for the stimulating discussions both during and after the event. This research was undertaken with the support of the Social Sciences and Humanities Research Council of Canada.
2 On the intertextuality of Ovid's ecphrasis with classical epic models, both in Homer and Vergil, see also Brown (1987). See further Wheeler (2000) 37–40, and Feldherr (2016) on the ecphrasis as a metaphysical reflection on literary representation.
3 See Bömer (1969) 236–237, on the intermediality inherent in Ovid's description of the palace of *Sol* in terms of the Augustan temple of Apollo Palatinus. On the temple itself, see Miller (2009) 185–226, with extensive bibliography.
4 See Miller (2009) *passim*.
5 On the resonance of Augustus' Palatine building programme in Vergil's *tectum augustum ingens*, see Horsfall (2000) 147, *ad loc.*
6 Miller (2009) 134–141.

https://doi.org/10.1515/9783110602203-015

Sun at Colchis in Valerius Flaccus' *Argonautica* 5 and the temple of Apollo at Cumae in Silius Italicus' *Punica* 12. We shall see that the Augustan poets' Flavian successors emulate them in richly intertextual ecphrases that conjoin multiple, many-layered allusions with intermedial poetics and imperial politics.

Before we consider these passages in detail, however, it is appropriate to reflect on this terminology. Throughout this chapter, I treat ecphrasis in the modern sense of "a description of a work of art," a narrower definition than ancient usage of the term, which denotes "a speech that brings the subject matter vividly before the eyes."[7] Classicists, as the contributors to this volume demonstrate, often use the term "intertextuality" interchangeably with that of "allusion" and "reference," and normally define all three as the textual trace of a work's literary sources and models, and it is in this sense that I employ it in my discussion.[8] The term "intermediality" engages cultural systems beyond textual culture: Rippl (2010) defines the concept as "a kind of self-reflexive relationship between two different media" (as, for example an architectural construction described in a literary text), "which ponder their own material characteristics."[9] It will become apparent that the Flavian epic poets' intensive education in, and obsessive attention to, the literary masterpieces of the Augustan age often incline them to represent the architectural monuments of that age in terms indebted to contemporary works of literature, i.e., in a literary reception that is pervasively intertextual.

---

7 Webb (2009) 1, 14. On ecphrasis, ancient and modern, see Fowler (1991); Webb (1999) and (2009); Elsner (2002); Bartsch and Elsner (2007). Friedländer (1912) 1–23, remains the classic discussion of ecphrasis in ancient epic. Vergil's description of a temple celebrating Octavian in the proem to the third *Georgic* is the *locus classicus* of architectural ecphrasis as literary allegory, long interpreted as a statement of the poet's projected epic on Augustus, ultimately instantiated in the *Aeneid*: see, e.g., Wilkinson (1970); Thomas (1988) 2.36–37; and Meban (2008).

8 See, e.g., Conte (1974) and (1986) and Hinds (1998) (on allusion); Edmonds (2001) (on intertextuality); *contra* Thomas (1986) (on reference). Julia Kristeva, who coined the term "intertextuality," argues for wider application of the term in her definition of the concept (1980, 66): "any text is a mosaic of quotations; any text is the absorption and transformation of another" cultural system, whether that be a literary text or any other semiotic system.

9 Rippl (2010); see further Wolf (1998), (1999), (2002a) and (2002b); and Rippl (2015). Dinter (2013) 303–308, offers a helpful introduction for classicists to the theoretical issues involved; he translates the definition offered by Wolf (1998) 238 of intermediality as "an intended and identifiable use or incorporation of at least two usually distinct media in one artefact" (p. 306).

1 The Palace of *Sol* in *Metamorphoses* 2.1–30

Notices in Augustus (*RG* 19), the Augustan poets and later historical writers, as well as the rich surviving archaeological evidence of coins and reliefs, confirm not only Augustus' pride in his temple to Apollo Palatinus but also the enthusiasm that the sacred precinct aroused in his subjects.[10] The earliest extant account attesting the impact of the new complex on the *princeps*' fellow citizens is provided by Propertius, whose elegy 2.31 celebrates the magnificence of the temple precinct:

> tum medium claro surgebat marmore templum,
>   et patria Phoebo carius Ortygia:
> in quo Solis erat supra fastigia currus
>   et ualuae, Libyci nobile dentis opus...
>
> (Prop. 2.31.9–12)
>
> Then in the midst of the complex rose the temple of white marble, dearer to Phoebus than his homeland of Ortygia: on the temple above the attic was Sol's chariot, and the doors were a notable work of Libyan ivory ...

Of particular interest is Propertius' notice that the roof of the temple was adorned with a chariot of the Sun-god *Sol*. Although scholars usually caution that *Sol* and Phoebus Apollo, the deity to whom Augustus dedicated his Palatine temple, were not routinely conflated in this period, it seems clear that the chariot of Sol would have evoked the solar aspect of Phoebus Apollo to a contemporary Roman audience.[11] Propertius' emphasis throughout this elegy on the radiance of the temple certainly implies as much,[12] through sustained play on the etymology of Apollo's epithet "Phoebus" (φοῖβος = "bright") and the propriety of its application to the Sun-god as well as to Apollo.[13]

The radiance of the palace of *Sol* is also the leitmotif of Ovid's ecphrasis:

---

10 Ancient testimony about the temple is collected and discussed in Miller (2009) 185–252.
11 On the implicit syncretism of *Sol* and Apollo Phoebus in Prop. elegy 2.31, see Miller (2009) 199–200; on the scholarly controversy, see Miller (2000) 208–209, esp. 209, n. 46.
12 *Aurea porticus*, 2.31.1; *Poenis columnis*, 2.31.3; *marmoreus* of the God's cult statue, 2.31.6; *uiuida signa*, of Myron's cows, on display in the forecourt, 2.31.8; *claro marmore*, 2.31.9; *Libyci nobile dentis opus*, 2.31.12. Miller (2009) 196–206, esp. 200 well discusses Propertius' emphasis on the brilliance of the temple.
13 The etymology was known to the ancients: see Macr. *Sat.* 1.17.33; Isid. *Orig.* 8.11.54.

> regia Solis erat sublimibus alta columnis,
> clara micante auro, flammasque imitante pyropo:
> cuius ebur nitidum fastigia summa tenebat:
> argenti bifores radiabant lumine ualuae.
>
> *(Met.* 2.1–4)

> The Sun's palace stood high on lofty columns, brilliant with glittering gold and pyrex imitating flames: its gleaming ivory held the highest attic, while double folding-doors of silver shone with light.

In Ovid, the Sun's palace gleams with bright gold and flashy pyrex, just as Propertius describes the newly dedicated temple of Apollo Palatinus shining with brilliant marble (*claro marmore*, 2.31.9), its portico gleaming gold (2.31.1–2): *aurea Phoebi / porticus a magno Caesare aperta fuit*, "Phoebus' golden portico has been opened by great Caesar." The ivory shining on the attic storey of the palace of *Sol*, moreover, recalls the ivory doors of the temple of Palatine Apollo (Prop. 2.31.12, quoted above), while Ovid's reference to an attic storey (*Met.* 2.3 *fastigia summa*) is itself couched in the language of (and placed in the same metrical *sedes* as) Propertius' report of the Sun-god's chariot atop the Palatine temple (2.31.11 *supra fastigia*). Even the brilliant silver double doors of the Sun's palace may evoke the double doors of the temple of Palatine Apollo as Propertius describes it (2.31.12). Ovid's description of the palace of *Sol* thus evokes the features characteristic of a temple[14] and, as we have seen, not just any temple, but the particular temple of Palatine Apollo. The ecphrasis of the palace of the Sun in *Metamorphoses* 2 thus reveals its author's interest not only in Propertius' representation of the temple of Palatine Apollo in elegy 2.31 (evidence of Ovid's poetics of intertextuality, in his literary relations with Propertius), but also in the *princeps'* magnificent temple to Apollo (evidence of Ovid's poetics of intermediality, in his construction of an imperial palace in verse).

The radiance of the Ovidian Sun's palace reflects that of the god's divine person, whose brilliance overwhelms his son Phaethon (*Met.* 2.22–24): *neque enim propiora ferebat / lumina. purpurea uelatus ueste sedebat / in solio Phoebus, claris lucente smaragdis*, "For he was unable to turn his eyes more closely to his father. Clad in purple vestments, Phoebus was sitting on a throne shining with brilliant emeralds." Ovid's emphasis on the divine splendor of the Sun-god's palace continues in the description of the god, surrounded by his attendants, at the centre of his palace, in the posture and location of a cult statue in its temple:

---

14 Cf. Brown (1987) 213–214. On the specific motif of door-ecphrases in Latin poetry, see Wedeniwski (2006).

>   a dextra, laeuaque Dies, et Mensis, et Annus   25
>   Saeculaque, et positae spatiis aequalibus Horae:
>   Verque nouum stabat, cinctum florente corona:
>   stabat nuda Aestas, et spicea serta gerebat:
>   stabat et Autumnus, calcatis sordidus uuis,
>   et glacialis Hiems canos hirsute capillos.   30
>   inde loco medius rerum nouitate pauentem
>   Sol oculis iuuenem quibus aspicit omnia uidit.
>
>   (*Met.* 2.25–32)

On right and left, Day, Month and Year, Centuries and Seasons were positioned at equal intervals: new Spring was standing there, girt with flowering garland; naked Summer was standing there, wearing corn wreaths; Autumn too was standing there, musty from trampled grapes; and icy Winter, hoary with white hair. Then, from his place in the centre, the Sun caught sight of the youth [his son Phaethon], trembling at the strangeness of the palace.

Ovid thus describes the Sun's palace, its decoration and inhabitants, in terms applicable to a god's temple, in his depiction of the impact of an encounter with the divine Sun-god on his mortal son Phaethon at their first meeting.

Many recent commentators have also emphasized the allegorical value of Ovid's ecphrasis as an image of cosmic order, in the tradition of Homeric exegesis on the Shield of Achilles.[15] For one thing, Ovid commends the artistry of the divine craftsman Vulcan, in his guise as Mulciber (the "Softener"),[16] who built the palace of *Sol* (*Met.* 2.5–7): *materiem superabat opus: nam Mulciber illic / aequora caelarat medias cingentia terras, / terrarumque orbem, caelumque quod imminet orbi*, "Its artistry outdid its materials: for Vulcan had engraved on it the seas girdling the lands in their midst, the world, and the sky that overhangs it." As the Roman god of technology, Vulcan was from early times assimilated to the Greek god of smiths, Hephaestus (cf. Vulcan's epithet *ignipotens* at *Aen.* 8.422, 628), the very god who crafts Achilles' shield in *Iliad* 18. Ovid's reference to Vulcan's engraving of the cosmos on the palace doors draws attention to the ecphrasis' direct line of descent from Homer, as does his conclusion of the ecphrasis with the im-

---

15 Brown (1987) 217, following Bartholomé (1935) 75–76. His insight is elaborated by Wheeler (1995) 98 and (2000) 37–40, and Feldherr (2016) 29–35. On the cosmology of the Homeric Shield of Achilles, see Mette (1936) 36–43 (sources) and 177–188 (discussion); Hardie (1985) and (1986) 340–358.
16 The ancients derived Vulcan's title *Mulciber* from *mulceo* or *multo*: see Maltby (1991) 394 ad *Mulciber*. Modern etymological discussion agrees with the derivation from *mulceo*: see Ernout/ Meillet (1994) 418 ad *mulceo*.

ages of heaven and the zodiac (*Met.* 2.17–18): *haec super imposita est caeli fulgentis imago / signaque sex foribus dextris totidemque sinistris*, "Above these was overlaid the image of gleaming heaven and six signs of the zodiac on the right door, and the same number on the left."

Ovid's description of the perfect symmetry and harmonious adornment of the palace of *Sol*, however, contrasts markedly with the thematic impetus of the Phaethon episode as a whole, which moves from cosmic order to chaotic destruction (rather like its Homeric model, whose harmonious representation of the symmetry of the cosmos contrasts markedly with the anarchy of war chronicled by the poet on the battlefield before Troy). The Sun's perfectly proportioned palace is an apt emblem of the cosmic order that will be undone during Phaethon's disastrous chariot-ride.[17] *Sol*'s palace-temple, however, not only reflects the cosmic order of Jupiter's divine dispensation (confirmed by his repair of the fabric of the world after Phaethon's death, *Met.* 2.401–408), but also bears implicit witness to Roman imperial authority, through the interconnection of Roman and divine order emblematized in the contiguity of the Temple of Apollo to the *princeps*' own dwelling on the Palatine. The physical linkage of the temple of Palatine Apollo with the house of Augustus on the Palatine instantiates a symbolic political succession, as Augustus succeeds to the authority of his tutelary divinity (and his divinized father).[18] With the subsequent reification of the alignment of Roman (Augustan) imperial rule with Olympian cosmic order under Augustus' Julio-Claudian successors,[19] Ovid's description of the palace of the Sun became a paradigmatic model for the allegorical significance of divine and imperial architectural ecphrases in later Roman epics. Valerius' *Argonautica* well illustrates not only the thematic and political significance of divine architectural ecphrasis but also the Flavian epicist's special intertextual engagement with Ovid.

---

[17] I am grateful to Dr. Lorenza Bennardo for reminding me (*per litteras*) that in later imperial literature, Phaethon becomes a figure for the 'inexperienced' or 'bad' ruler, even the usurper: see Schmitzer (1990) 89–107; Rosati (2008) esp. 184–193, where he discusses Statius' use of Phaethontic imagery to underline Domitian's legitimacy in the proem to the *Thebaid*; and Rebeggiani (2013) with further bibliography.

[18] Ulrich Schmitzer (1990) 89–107 proposes a counter-interpretation of Ovid's treatment of the myth, in the context of Augustan imperial politics, to argue that Augustus figures as a failed ruler, whose hubristic career illustrates his inability to live up to the divinity of his father.

[19] See Hardie (1986) on the Romans' debt to Pergamene artistic models in this regard.

2 Valerius' Temple of the Sun (*Argonautica* 5.403–456)

When the Argonauts finally reach Colchis in Book Five, Jason is guided to the altar of the Sun in Aeetes' palace by one of Medea's handmaids (*Arg.* 5.399–454), in a passage that rehearses Nausicaa's guidance of Odysseus to her father's palace in the *Odyssey* (6.110–114, 259–322).[20] As the son of Phoebus, the Colchian king Aeetes is rightly to be found dispensing justice at his father's altar:

> ... 'Phoebi genitoris ad aras
> Ventum' ait. 'huc adytis iam se de more paternis
> rex feret; hic proceres audit populosque precantes
> adloquiis facilis: praesens pater admonet aequi.'
>
> (*Arg.* 5.403–406)

> 'We have reached his father Phoebus' altars,' she said. 'The king will come here to his father's shrine according to his custom; here he listens to the leading men and his subjects making petitions, heeding their addresses; his father, by his presence, advises him of what is right.'

Valerius explicitly derives the Colchian king Aeetes' descent from Phoebus at the very moment that his hero Jason reaches the Sun-god's temple in Colchis. There, Aeetes is accustomed to dispense justice to his subjects (*Arg.* 5.404–406), just as the Vergilian Dido had heard her subjects' petitions at the temple of Juno in Carthage (*Aen.* 1.496–508).[21] The Sun's divine authority over the cosmos thus implicitly underwrites his son Aeetes' royal authority in Colchis.

But Valerius, literary heir of Ovid as well as Vergil, draws especially heavily, in his depiction of the Sun-god's temple, on Ovid's description of the palace of the Sun, the destination of another son of Phoebus at the outset of *Metamorphoses* 2:[22]

---

20 Both Wijsman (1996) 196–218 and Spaltenstein (2002) 490–507, *ad loc.*, trace Valerius' many debts in this passage to Homer's account of Odysseus arrival at the palace of Alcinous on Phaeacia, and its description, and to Vergil's report of Aeneas' arrival in Carthage and his description of the temple of Juno admired there by his hero. On the pictures in the temple, see also Manuwald (1998).
21 On the Vergilian Temple of Juno in Carthage, see Williams (1960), Barchiesi (1997), Putnam (1998) 23–54.
22 On Valerius' debt to Ovid in this scene, see Wijsman (1996) 198 ad 407, Spaltenstein (2002) 492–493 ad 406 and 409, Heerink (2014) 90–91, and Keith (2014) 286–289. Harrison (2013) 220–223 and Heerink (2014) 86–94 focus on Valerius' debt, in his description of the temple of *Sol*, to

> dixerat; ast illi propere monstrata capessunt
> limina. non aliter, quam si <u>radiantis</u> adirent
> ora dei uerasque aeterni <u>luminis</u> arces,
> tale iubar per tecta <u>micat</u> ...
>
> (*Arg.* 5.407–410)
>
> Medea's handmaid fell silent, and they hastened to broach the threshold she'd pointed out. Such radiance gleamed through the halls as if they'd approached the face of the shining god and the true citadels of eternal light ...

The Colchian temple of Aeetes' father gleams as brightly as Ovid's palace of *Sol*, as befits another temple-palace belonging to the Sun-god Phoebus: like the Ovidian *Sol*'s palace, which flashes with gold (*micante auro*, *Met.* 2.2) and gleams with the light of silver (*argenti bifores radiabant lumine ualuae*, *Met.* 2.4), the temple of Valerius' Phoebus sparkles with the brilliant light (*tale iubar per tecta micat*, *Arg.* 5.410) of the god's person (*radiantis adirent / ora dei uerasque aeterni luminis arces*, *Arg.* 5.408–409). Indeed, the radiance of Phoebus' temple in Colchis is such that Valerius compares it to the god's "true" home (*Arg.* 5.409), a gleaming citadel like the Augustan temple of Palatine Apollo or its literary transmutation into the palace of *Sol* in *Metamorphoses* 2. We may also compare the splendour of the Ovidian Sun-god, sitting on a throne shining with brilliant emeralds (*Met.* 2.22–24, quoted above). Valerius' simile thus invites interpretation as implicit acknowledgement of the influence of Ovid's *Sol* on his ecphrasis. Indeed, it has been observed that "the Valerian building is so similar to the Ovidian one that it is as if the Argonauts are approaching Sol's palace in *Metamorphoses* 2."[23]

Moreover, the Colchian temple of the Sun, like the palace of *Sol* in *Metamorphoses* 2, surrounds the god with attendants who reflect his stature in the cosmic order:

> ... stat ferreus Atlans   410
> Oceano genibusque tumens infringitur unda;
> at medii per terga senis rapit ipse nitentes
> altus equos curuoque diem subtexit Olympo;
> pone rota breuiore soror densaeque sequuntur
> Pliades et madidis rorantes crinibus ignes.   415
>
> (*Arg.* 5.410–415)

Vergilian ecphrases in *Aeneid* 1 (the temple of Juno), 6 (Apollo's temple at Cumae), and 8 (the Shield of Aeneas).
23 Heerink (2014) 90, n. 66.

> Iron Atlas stands in the Ocean, with the wave swelling and breaking on his knees; and the god himself, on high, seizes his gleaming steeds over the midst of the old man's back and brings daylight over the curving heavens. Behind his sister, the moon, follows with her smaller wheel, along with the crowded Pleiades and the Hyades, their stars dripping with wet hair.

Even Valerius' water imagery may gesture to Ovid's decoration of the double doors of the Sun-god's palace with its brief catalogue of sea-gods (*Met.* 2.8–11): *caeruleos habet unda deos, Tritona canorum / Proteaque ambiguum ballenarumque prementem / Aegaeona suis immania terga lacertis / Doridaque et natas ...*, "The ocean holds the sea-blue gods—sonorous Triton and changeable Proteus; Aegean overpowering the huge expanse of whales with his arms; Doris and her daughters the Nereids ..." Like the palace of the Ovidian *Sol*, the Colchian temple of the Sun-god constitutes an icon of the cosmos, but one that portends the savagery of the Colchian king Aeetes and the underlying violence of his rule. For the Valerian *Sol* seems to drive his chariot over the distant figure of Atlas, standing in the Ocean and holding up the earth, while Phoebus' sister, the moon-goddess, trails him with the constellations of the Pleiades and Hyades in her train. Moreover, where the Ovidian *Sol* was attended in his palace by courtiers, personifications of time and the seasons, the Valerian *Sol* is apparently depicted on the pediment of his temple in the company of some of the other divine inhabitants of the cosmos, whose prone position (Atlas), subdued illumination (*Luna*), and watery demeanour (the rise of the constellations Pleiades and Hyades initiated the Mediterranean rainy season) contrast with his radiance. Valerius thus hints that Aeetes, like his misbegotten mythological brother Phaethon, will fail to live up to the standard of benign rule set by their father *Sol*.[24] Mark Heerink has accordingly argued that "the Valerian context, ... in which Phaethon prefigures Aeetes, suggests an association of Phaethon not with Augustus but with his descendant Nero,"[25] an emperor already associated with the mythological ephebe by Lucan in the proem to his epic (1.51–59), not least because of his well-documented emulation of the Sun-god.[26]

---

[24] Cf. *Arg.* 1.505–527, in which the Sun-god complains to Jupiter about the Argonautic expedition as a threat to his son Aeetes, where he explicitly associates Aeetes with Phaethon.
[25] Heerink (2014) 91; full discussion of the exploitation by the imperial epic poets of the Roman political interpretation of the Phaethon myth at 90–92. For the topos, see further Rosati (2008); Rebeggiani (2013).
[26] Suetonius reports that Nero was celebrated as "the equal of Apollo in music, and of the Sun in driving a chariot" (*Nero* 53). Bergmann (1998) 133–230. documents the widespread use of solar symbolism in connection with the emperor; see also Taylor (1994) 229; Mratschek (2013) 48–50.

Valerius' focus on the artistry of the temple doors may have been inspired, in part, by Vergil's famous representation of Daedalus' artistry on the doors of the temple to Apollo at Cumae in *Aeneid* 6 (14–33, quoted below) as well, perhaps, by his depiction of Vulcan's artistry on the Shield of Aeneas in *Aeneid* 8 (625–728), at the end of which Vergil names the god Mulciber (8.724). For just as the Valerian Jason delights in the varied imagery of the doors (*laetus imagine*, *Arg.* 5.415) so Aeneas rejoices in the decoration of his shield (*imagine gaudet*, *Aen.* 8.730; cf. *Aen.* 8.618). Like Ovid (*Met.* 2.5), moreover, the Flavian epicist specifically attributes the artistry of the double doors of the Colchian temple of the Sun to Vulcan, again in his guise as Mulciber:

> nec minus hinc uaria dux laetus imagine templi
> ad geminas fert ora fores cunabula gentis
> Colchidos hic ortusque tuens ...
>   [...]
> aurea quin etiam praesaga Mulciber arte[27]
> uellera uenturosque olim caelarat Achiuos.
>   [...]
> ... haec tum miracula Colchis
> struxerat ignipotens ...
>
> (*Arg.* 5.416–418, 433–434, 451–452)

And no less happily the leader of the Argonauts surveyed the temple's twin doors with their varied imagery, reviewing here the origins of the Colchian nation ... Why Vulcan even engraved with prophetic artistry the golden fleece and the Greeks who would one day come seeking it ... These wonders the fire-god had crafted for the Colchians ...

The Argonauts, however, are unable to look at the halls of the Valerian Sun-god (*Arg.* 5.455), just like the Ovidian Phaethon in the palace of the Sun, though not because of the brilliance of the decoration but rather out of perplexity (or terror)[28] at the proliferation of scenes inscribed on the shrine's double doors (5.455–456): *quin idem Minyas operum defixerat error / cum se Sole satus patriis penetralibus*

Taylor (1994) 228–31 argues that Valerius' tyrannical Aeetes symbolizes Nero, as distinct from his Jason-Vespasian (223–4) and Hercules-Augustus (222–3).

27 Dr. Bennardo suggests to me that Ovid here alludes to the Vergilian Vulcan's artistry as engraver of the Shield of Aeneas in *Aeneid* 8.612–613 (*en perfecta mei promissa coniugis arte / munera*, "look, the gifts have been completed with my husband's promised artistry"), where the similarity of the word-order after the caesura is bolstered by the similarities in sound-effects and rhythm.

28 Wedeniwski (2006) 164, n. 526 and Heerink (2014) 92 accept the conjectural emendation *horror* (Myncke 1867) in place of the transmitted text's *error*, printed by Ehlers (1980) at *Arg.* 5.455.

infert,²⁹ "But the same uncertainty (about the interpretation) of the artworks rooted the Argonauts in their tracks, when the Sun's offspring betook himself into his father's shrine." Scholars have debated every detail of Valerius' ecphrasis, from the disposition of statuary in the palace (5.410–415) to the number of scenes engraved on the temple doors (5.418–451),³⁰ but one feature of the description on which we may all agree is that the subjects of the works of art in the Colchian Sun-god's temple differ significantly from those that adorn the palace of the Ovidian Sun-god (*Met.* 2.8–18). For the Colchian temple doors depict the origins of Aeetes' people (*Arg.* 5.418–432) and Jason's mythic career from Argonaut to bigamist (*Arg.* 5.433–451), while we have seen that the doors of the palace of the Ovidian Sun, by contrast, are decorated with maritime gods (*Met.* 2.8–16) and cosmic imagery (*Met.* 2.17–18).

Nonetheless, Valerius' decorative scheme of statues and inscribed temple doors seems structurally indebted to the Ovidian ecphrasis of the palace of the Sun, with its inscribed temple doors and temporal personifications in attendance on the god. Moreover, Valerius includes the story of Phaethon on the Colchian Sun-god's temple doors, as the centerpiece of his ecphrasis:

flebant populeae iuuenem Phaethonta sorores
ater et Eridani trepidum globus ibat in amnem.
at iuga uix Tethys sparsumque recolligit axem
et formidantem patrios Pyroenta dolores.

(*Arg.* 5.429–432)

His sisters, poplar-trees, were weeping for young Phaethon, as the black-charred mass went into the terrified stream of Eridanus; but Tethys could scarcely gather up the scattered fragments of yoke and axle, or the remains of the Sun's horse Pyrois, who feared the god's paternal grief.

Valerius' reference to Ovid's Phaethon narrative, in the central panel of his ecphrasis, constitutes pointed acknowledgment of his epic model in a kind of *mise-en-abyme* structure that locates the myth of Phaethon, into which Ovid in-

---

29 The commentators compare Aeneas' amazement at the sight of the panels in the temple of Juno at Carthage in *Aeneid* 1, esp. 1.455–456 and 1.494–495: see Wijsman (1996) 219 *ad* 5.455 and 200 *ad* 5.456; Spaltenstein (2002) 507 ad 5.455.
30 See Wijsman (1996) 199–204, for a summary of the critical debate and further bibliography. The most recent critical discussions of the scene, Harrison (2013) 220–223, and Heerink (2014) focus on the proleptic symbolism of the doors' decorations in relation to Valerius' narrative.

corporates his description of the Sun's palace, at the very centre of his own description of the Colchian temple of the Sun.[31] To be sure, Vergil was the first Latin poet to mention the Heliades' transformation into poplars (*Ecl.* 6.62–63), and Valerius' diction marks his studied debt to Vergil's brief reprise of the myth in the *Aeneid* (10.190): *populeas* inter frondes umbramque *sororum*, "amid the poplar branches and shade of Phaethon's sisters." But Valerius also signals the primacy of his debt in these lines to Ovid's treatment of the Phaethon myth in a number of ways. For example, his emphasis on the Heliades' tears (*flebant, Arg.* 5.429) recalls Ovid's account of the arboreal metamorphosis of Phaethon's sisters, in which he describes their grief at length because their tears explain their transformation into the amber that adorns Roman brides on their wedding day:

> nec minus Heliades lugent et inania morti 340
> munera dant lacrimas et caesae pectora palmis
> non auditurum miseras Phaethonta querelas
> nocte dieque uocant adsternunturque sepulcro.
> [...]
> inde fluunt lacrimae stillataque sole rigescunt
> de ramis electra nouis, quae lucidus amnis 365
> excipit et nuribus mittit spectanda Latinis.
>
> (*Met.* 2.340–343, 364–366)

Nor did the Sun's daughters grieve less [than their mother]; they give the empty gift of tears for his death, beat their breasts with their palms, and night and day they call on Phaethon, who can no longer hear their pitiable plaint, and they cast themselves on his sepulcher ... Thence the trees' tears flow, and from their new branches drops of amber harden in the sun—amber, which the bright stream [of Eridanus] receives and sends to adorn Latin brides.

Valerius retains Ovid's emphasis on the Heliades' mourning (cf., also, *plangorem dederant, Met.* 2.346; *questa est,* 2.347) at the outset of his vignette in the *Argonautica*, in addition to the metrical *sedes* and case form of Phaethon's name (*Met.* 2.342, *Arg.* 5.429).

The unexpected prominence of Tethys in Valerius' passage (*Arg.* 5.431) must also be due to Ovid's treatment of the Phaethon myth. Not only does Ovid represent *Sol* describing to his son the goddess' fear for his own safety when he drives the solar chariot (2.67–69: *ultima prona uia est et eget moderamine certo: / tunc etiam quae me subiectis excipit undis / ne ferar in praeceps Tethys solet ipsa uereri,*

---

[31] Heerink (2014) 88, n. 57, offers a concise history of the term *mise en abyme*, following Dällenbach (1989). First employed by André Gide to denote literary self-reflexivity, the phrase is borrowed from heraldry, "where the technical term denotes the placement of a miniature version of the original shield '*en abyme*', in the centre of it" (*ibid.*).

"the last stage of the journey is downhill and lacks any way to moderate my speed: then even Tethys, who receives me in her underlying waves, is wont to fear lest I am carried headlong"), but he also depicts Tethys opening the gates for her grandson's disastrous ride:

> occupat ille leuem iuuenali corpore currum 150
> statque super manibusque datas contingere habenas
> gaudet et inuito grates agit inde parenti.
> interea uolucres Pyrois et Eous et Aethon,
> Solis equi, quartusque Phlegon hinnitibus auras
> flammiferis implent pedibusque repagula pulsant. 155
> quae postquam Tethys fatorum ignara nepotis
> reppulit et facta est immensi copia caeli
> corripuere uiam ...
>
> (*Met.* 2.150–158)

But Phaethon has already taken possession of the light chariot with his youthful body and stands tall, gleefully handling the reins given into his hands and thanking his unhappy father. Meanwhile the Sun's swift steeds—Pyrois, Eous, Aethon, and Phlegon fourth—fill the air with fiery whinnies and strike the bars with their feet. After Tethys, all unaware of her grandson's destiny, released them and they had free rein throughout the immense expanse of heaven, they careened on their way ...

Valerius highlights Tethys' prominence in the *Metamorphoses* by naming her directly in his vignette, along with the rare name of Sol's horse Pyrois (*Pyroenta*, *Arg.* 5.532), which is otherwise attested in Latin only in Ovid's account of Phaethon's chariot-ride (*Met.* 2.153). In addition, the description of the scattered pieces of the solar chariot (*Arg.* 5.431), which Tethys can scarcely recover let alone repair, echoes Ovid's sketch of the chariot's destruction:

> intonat et dextra libratum fulmen ab aure
> misit in aurigam pariterque animaque rotisque
> expulit et saeuis compescuit ignibus ignes.
> consternantur equi et saltu in contraria facto
> colla iugo eripiunt abruptaque lora relinquunt; 315
> illic frena iacent, illic temone reuulsus
> axis, in hac radii fractarum parte rotarum,
> sparsaque sunt late laceri uestigia currus.
>
> (*Met.* 2.311–318)

Jove thundered and balancing a bolt he hurled it from his right ear against the charioteer, and casting him from the chariot he killed him, and checked the flames with his own savage fires. The horses were terrified, and jumping in opposite directions they snatched their necks from the yoke and abandoned the parted reins; the reins lie there, the axle torn from the pole lies over there; on this side lie the spokes of the broken wheels; and the fragments of the mangled chariot were scattered far and wide.

Ovid emphasizes the horses' fear again, after Phaethon's death, in his description of Phoebus' violent recovery of them out of grief for his son's disastrous ride (*Met.* 2.398–400): <u>colligit</u> amentes et adhuc terrore <u>pauentes</u> / Phoebus equos stimuloque <u>dolens</u> et uerbere saeuit / (saeuit enim) natumque obiectat et imputat illis, "Phoebus recovers his horses, out of their wits and still trembling from fear, and grieving he rages with goad and lash, for he raged, and blamed them for the death of his son." Even Valerius' concluding phrase, *formidantem patrios dolores* (*Arg.* 5.432), clearly looks to his Ovidian model, from which he has also remodeled his verb *recolligit* (*Arg.* 5.431; cf. *colligit*, *Met.* 2.398), with the addition of the prefix "*re-*" fittingly denoting Valerius' reprise of his model's treatment.

Valerius has thus compressed the canonical treatment of Phaethon's myth into a brief but recognizably Ovidian vignette at the very centre of his description of the decoration of the Colchian temple of the Sun. Given the concentrated allusivity of these four lines, I wonder if we may press further the meaning of the verb Valerius uses to describe Tethys' vain efforts to "recover" the youth's chariot, and interpret it as a "self-reflexive annotation"[32] of the poet's own "re-collection" of the scattered fragments of the Phaethon myth in his Augustan models, Ovid and Vergil.[33] Certainly, we can see, in Valerius' sophisticated reworking of their handling of the Phaethon myth, his attention to the political dimension of imperial rule that Latin epic invokes from its origins (whether we locate them in Naevius' *Bellum Punicum* or in Ennius' *Annales*) on, as well as to the literary traditions of classical epic and his own innovative place within it.

3 Apollo's Temple at Cumae (*Punica* 12)

Like his younger contemporary Valerius, Silius too pits his compositional skill against the Augustan masters of classical epic ecphrasis. His craft is on brilliant display in a description of the temple of Apollo at Cumae, visited by Hannibal in

---

[32] On self-reflexive allusion, see Hinds (1998) 6–10.
[33] Dr. Bennardo suggests to me that "*uix* in *Arg.* 5.431 may acquire significance on this 'self-reflexive' reading of Valerius' line." She wonders if it "has been a labour to recollect the 'scattered fragments' or if Valerius is being modest;" and she compares "the theme of 'poetic insufficiency' in the face of marvels at Stat. *Silv.* 2.2.42–44: *uix ... suffecere oculi ... uix suffecere gradus*," with Newlands (2011) *ad loc.*

Punica 12 (*Pun.*12.85–6): *atque hic perlustrans aditus, fulgentia cernit / arcis templa iugo* ("and here, while studying the approaches, Hannibal discerned a shining temple on the summit of the citadel"). Hannibal's visit to this temple rehearses—as it also inverts—that of Aeneas to the self-same temple at the beginning of *Aeneid* 6. Silius' "shining temple" may thus be interpreted as a figure for the literary value and cultural authority of Vergil's masterpiece, which, on this reading, the Flavian epicist aspires to attain, while perhaps acknowledging how far short of the master's standard he himself falls. For Silius draws pointed attention to Hannibal's failure to live up to the model of Aeneas throughout the episode, as the Carthaginian general sees—but ultimately fails to gain access to—the Cumaean landmark.

Vergil's description in *Aeneid* 6 of the temple to Apollo, dedicated by Daedalus at Cumae, is well known to be a densely intertextual ecphrasis:[34]

> at pius Aeneas arces quibus altus Apollo
> praesidet horrendaeque procul secreta Sibyllae,   10
> antrum immane, petit, magnam cui mentem animumque
> Delius inspirat uates aperitque futura.
> iam subeunt Triuiae lucos atque aurea tecta.
> Daedalus, ut fama est, fugiens Minoia regna
> praepetibus pennis ausus se credere caelo   15
> insuetum per iter gelidas enauit ad Arctos,
> Chalcidicaque leuis tandem super astitit arce.
> redditus his primum terris tibi, Phoebe, sacrauit
> remigium alarum posuitque immania templa.
> in foribus letum Androgeo; tum pendere poenas   20
> Cecropidae iussi (miserum!) septena quotannis
> corpora natorum; stat ductis sortibus urna.
> contra elata mari respondet Cnosia tellus:
> hic crudelis amor tauri suppostaque furto
> Pasiphae mixtumque genus prolesque biformis   25
> Minotaurus inest, Veneris monimenta nefandae,
> hic labor ille domus et inextricabilis error;
> magnum reginae sed enim miseratus amorem
> Daedalus ipse dolos tecti ambagesque resoluit,

---

34 See, e.g., Putnam (1998) 75–96; and the discussion of Horsfall (2013) 70–115 *passim*, ad *Aen.* 6.9–76. Like Miller (2009) 134–41, Horsfall (2013) 113–14, ad *Aen.* 6.69–76, emphasizes the importance of the temple of Palatine Apollo for Vergil's conception of Apollo's temple at Cumae. Waszink (1948) surveys the evidence for contemporary interest in the Cumaean Sibyl, the deposition of the *libri Sibyllini* in the Temple of Palatine Apollo, and the restoration of the Temple of Apollo at Cumae by Augustus' partisan Agrippa. On the remains of the temple complex at Cumae, see Smiley (1948) 99–100, Schoder (1971) 104–105.

>   caeca regens filo uestigia. tu quoque magnam   30
>   partem opere in tanto, sineret dolor, Icare, haberes.
>   bis conatus erat casus effingere in auro,
>   bis patriae cecidere manus ...
>
>   (*Aen.* 6.9–33)

> But dutiful Aeneas seeks the citadel over which lofty Apollo presides and the distant secrets of the terrifying Sibyl, whose great mind and spirit the divine Delian seer incites and to whom he discloses things to come, in her huge cavern.
> Daedalus—so the story goes—dared to entrust himself to heaven on swift wings, fleeing Minos' kingdom; he sailed on an unaccustomed journey to the cold north, and at last stood lightly above the Euboean citadel. Restored first to this land, he vowed to you, Phoebus, the oarage of his wings and dedicated a huge temple. On the doors he wrought Androgeus' death; then the Athenians, ordered (alas!) to pay the penalty of seven youths' corpses every year: the urn stands ready for the drawing of the lots. Opposite, standing out from the sea, the land of Crete corresponds [to Athens]: here [are depicted] the love of the cruel bull, Pasiphae set beneath him in secret, and the mixed-race biform offspring is inside, the Minotaur, memorial of unspeakable passion. Here is the famous labour and untraceable wandering of the house; but Daedalus himself, taking pity on the queen's great love, revealed the trick of the passage and solved the difficulties, directing the blind steps with a thread. You too, Icarus, were to have a great part in such a great work, could grief permit. Twice he tried to fashion his son's fall in gold, twice the father's hands fell ...

The golden halls (*aurea tecta*, *Aen.* 6.13) are usually understood to belong to the temple of Apollo at Cumae, rather than the Sibyl's cave, and have been interpreted as inspired by the recently completed temple of Apollo on the Palatine;[35] certainly they are the immediate literary and architectural models for Silius' shining temple (*fulgentia templa*, *Pun.* 12.85–86)[36] that captures Hannibal's attention, though we have seen that Silius' description has still wider significance as an acknowledgement of his literary debt to the Vergilian master text. Vergil's specification of Apollo as the dedicatee of Daedalus' temple has also been connected with the temple of Palatine Apollo, since both temples (literary and historical) seem to reference Apollo in his solar aspect.[37]

Silius signals his Vergilian debts early in his ecphrasis, but diverges soon after to pursue an Ovidian model:

>   atque hic perlustrans aditus, fulgentia cernit   85
>   arcis templa iugo, quorum tum Virrius, altae
>   immitis doctor Capuae, primordia pandit:

---

[35] Miller (2009) 136; cf. *id.* 186.
[36] Spaltenstein (1990) 153, ad 12.85.
[37] Miller (2009) 137.

```
           'non est hoc' inquit 'nostri, quod suspicis, aeui;
           maiores fecere manus. cum bella timeret
           Dictaei regis, sic fama est, linquere terras           90
           Daedalus inuenit nec toto signa sequenti
           orbe dare, aetherias aliena tollere in auras
           ausus se penna atque homini monstrare uolatus.
           suspensum hic librans media inter nubila corpus
           enauit superosque nouus conterruit ales.               95
           natum etiam docuit falsae sub imagine plumae
           attentare uias uolucrum; lapsumque solutis
           pennarum remis et non felicibus alis
           turbida plaudentem uidit freta; dumque dolori
           indulget subito, motis ad pectora palmis,              100
           nescius heu planctu duxit moderante uolatus.'
```
                                                                (*Pun.* 12.85–101)

And here, while studying the approaches, Hannibal discerned a shining temple on the summit of the citadel. Then Virrius, the pitiless general of high Capua, explained its origins: 'This building which you see above us,' he said, 'is not a work of our age: ancestral hands constructed it. When Daedalus, as the story goes, feared the rule of the Cretan king, he discovered how to escape from earth and leave no trace for Minos following him over the whole world. He dared to raise himself into the breezes of the air on wings not his own and to show mankind the skill of flight. Balancing his body, poised in the midst of the clouds, he floated, and the strange winged creature terrified the gods. He taught his son too, beneath semblance of false wings, to attempt the paths of birds; but when the feathered oars melted, he saw him fall and splash the surging sea with his unlucky wings. Yielding to his sudden grief, Daedalus beat his breast, and all unknowing he steered his flight through the modulation of his breast-beating.'

In addition to his description of the gleaming precinct (*fulgentia templa, Pun.* 12.85–86), Silius signals his epigonal relationship to Vergil by opening his ecphrasis with a phrase (*sic fama est, Pun.* 12.90) that takes up the Vergilian tag *ut fama est* from *Aen.* 6.14 (quoted above). So too the Flavian epicist marks the densely allusive construction of his own re-presentation of Apollo's temple at Cumae at the outset of the account offered by Hannibal's host Virrius, a Capuan collaborator, in his report of the temple's antiquity (*Pun.* 12.89): *maiores fecere manus*, "Ancestral hands built it." Silius is scrupulously accurate here in his use of the plural, not only for the construction of the temple but also for the sources of his own literary reconstruction of the temple, as he draws not only on Vergil's ecphrasis in *Aeneid* 6 but also on another epic account of the death of Icarus. For Vergil had famously passed over this part of the myth in his highly allusive treatment of Daedalus' role in Cretan myth (*Aen.* 6.14–33), which emphasizes the father's inability to retrace his son's death (*Aen.* 6.32–33): *bis conatus erat casus effingere in auro, / bis patriae cecidere manus*, "twice he had tried to fashion your fall in gold, and twice his father's hands fell."

Virrius (and Silius) therefore supply the back-story, which Daedalus (and Vergil) leave off the temple doors in *Aeneid* 6, from Ovid's narrative in the central book of the *Metamorphoses*:

> ... postquam manus ultima coepto 200
> imposita est, geminas opifex librauit in alas
> ipse suum corpus motaque pependit in aura
>   [...]
> hos aliquis tremula dum captat harundine pisces,
> aut pastor baculo stiuaue innixus arator
> uidit et obstipuit, quique aethera carpere possent,
> credidit esse deos ... 220
>   [...]
> tabuerant cerae: nudos quatit ille lacertos,
> remigioque carens non ullas percipit auras,
> oraque caerulea patrium clamantia nomen
> excipiuntur aqua, quae nomen traxit ab illo. 230
>   (*Met.* 8.200–202, 217–220, 227–230)

After the finishing touches had been set to the undertaking, the master workman himself balanced his body on two wings and hung poised on the beaten air ... Now some fisherman sees them, angling for fish with his flexible rod, or a shepherd leaning on his staff, or a plowman on his plow-handles, and stands stupefied, and believes them to be gods that they could fly through the air ... The wax melted; his arms were bare as he beat them up and down, but, lacking wings, they took no hold on the air. His mouth, calling to the last his father's name, was drowned in the dark blue sea, which took its name from him.

Bruère has catalogued Silius' pervasive lexical debts to Ovid here.[38] The Silian Daedalus' flight (12.92–95) adapts the Ovidian Daedalus' trial of his new wings (*Met.* 8.201–202); the Silian Daedalus terrifies the gods, who mistake him for a strange new bird (12.95), reversing the amazement of Ovid's fishermen, who take Daedalus and Icarus for gods (*Met.* 8.217–220); and the Silian Daedalus beats his breast in grief over his son's death (12.99–101), in lines that echo the Ovidian Icarus' vain beating of his wings when the Sun has melted the wax that held them together (*Met.* 8.227–230). Bruère views Silius' procedure in this passage "as a compendious one" and so he identifies "few verbal parallels" between the two texts (1959, 235). But we might note, in addition to the numerous lexical reminiscences Bruère himself compiled, just how markedly Ovidian Silius' language is

---

38 Bruère (1959) 235 [= (2016) 374–375]; cf. Wilson (2004) 228; Keith (2014b).

in this passage, in its recuperation of the Augustan poet's lexicon of metamorphosis.[39] Thus, for example, Silius' strange "new" bird (*nouus*, *Pun.* 12.95) perfectly exemplifies the strange new bodies into which shapes are transformed in Ovid's *Metamorphoses*, as we are promised in the proem to the work (*Met.* 1.1–2: *in noua ... corpora*); or, again, the hapless Icarus, transformed "under the semblance of false plumage" (*falsae sub imagine plumae*, *Pun.* 12.96), recalls Ovid's descriptions of Jupiter disguised "in the semblance of a false bull" (*fallacis imagine tauri*, *Met.* 3.1), in order to rape Europa, and Dido's "construction of a pyre on the pretext of a sacred rite" (*inque pyra sacri sub imagine facta*, *Met.* 14.80). In Virrius' description of the temple of Apollo at Cumae, Silius thus renovates a hallowed Vergilian structure to put on display Ovidian mythological learning.[40] He thereby invites us to read the ecphrasis as a figure for the emblematic status not only of Vergil's *Aeneid*, but also of Ovid's *Metamorphoses*, as ancestral literary artefacts in his own day.

***

This study of the impact of Augustan architectural ecphrasis on Flavian epic temples has uncovered numerous points of contact in the linguistic registers of the Flavian poets, with important implications for the thematic and literary interpretation of the Flavian epics. But we may well wonder if there are also implications for our understanding of the political, architectural, and material culture of imperial Rome in the Flavian epicists' temple ecphrases, since Augustus' temple of Apollo on the Palatine supplied such a potent impetus to architectural ecphrasis in the poets of his day. In this regard, I suggest, we see divergent practices in our two Flavian epicists. On the one hand, Valerius' temple of the Sun-god in Colchis is represented—like the Ovidian *Sol*'s palace-temple in *Metamorphoses* 2 and Vergil's temple of Juno at Carthage in *Aeneid* 1 or Latinus' temple-palace in *Aeneid* 7—as the site of the ruler's judicial and political authority, especially in their reception of petitioners. In this context, the ecphrases of the Ovidian Sun-god's palace-temple and of the Valerian Sun-god's temple look closely to the imperial use of temples, particularly the temple of Apollo on the Palatine, for meetings of the senate. Indeed, we have abundant and well-studied evidence for the regular use

---

[39] On Ovid's lexicon of metamorphosis, see Anderson (1963).
[40] Wilson (2004) 231 notes that when Silius incorporates Ovidian intertexts in passages for which "there is a perfectly adequate Virgilian model at hand," as in this passage, he "inevitably" brings both the Virgilian antecedent and the Ovidian intertext "into play at the same time." Thus, he concludes (*ibid.*) that "Silius realigns his narrative choice with the Ovidian version to recount the flight of Icarus and his consequent plunge to his death," only "after evoking the Virgilian context of the temple visited by Aeneas."

of this temple for meetings of the Senate throughout the Julio-Claudian period, from the reign of Augustus (Suet. *Aug.* 29.3) to that of Nero (Tac. *Ann.* 13.5), when the temple was destroyed by fire (64 CE).[41] Moreover, Servius (on *Aen.* 11.235) assumes that Vergil based Latinus' convocation of the Italian "great council" in his palace (*Aen.* 11.234–235: *ergo concilium magnum primosque suorum / imperio accitos alta intra limina cogit*, "and so he convened a great council and summoned the leading men of his realm within his high halls")—which like Augustus' building complex on the Palatine included a *templum* (*Aen.* 7.174)—on the regular convocation of meetings of the senate in the temple of Palatine Apollo during Augustus' reign. Domitian restored the temple of Apollo on the Palatine (Suet. *Dom.* 20), though it is not clear whether he held meetings of the Senate in it.[42] While neither Vespasian nor Titus could have convened the Senate in the temple, there must have been widespread familiarity with the Julio-Claudian practice in the early years of Flavian rule.

In contrast to the official use to which Valerius' "Neronian" Aeetes puts the temple of *Sol*, Silius' temple of Apollo at Cumae is merely glimpsed from afar by Hannibal, who cannot even see the artistry of the temple's decoration (as Aeneas does at *Aen.* 6.14–35), let alone vow the construction of a temple to the god in Rome (as Aeneas does at *Aen.* 6.69–70). Hannibal's failures at Cumae reflect Silius' consistent characterization of the Carthaginian general as an anti-Aeneas, who lacks the attributes of a Roman *princeps* and *imperator*. Nonetheless, the passage in which Hannibal visits the Cumaean temple also seems thoroughly mediated by Silius' extensive reading in, and antiquarian research into, the epics of his Augustan predecessors. Indeed, it is highly likely that Silius saw the temple his Hannibal visits through the filtre of his reading, since notices in Martial and the younger Pliny comment on Silius' habits as an antiquarian and collector, especially of Vergiliana. Martial records Silius' ownership of Vergil's tomb and a villa that had once belonged to Cicero in a short but encomiastic epigram included in his eleventh book:

> Silius haec magni celebrat monimenta Maronis,
>   iugera facundi qui Ciceronis habet.
> heredem dominumque sui tumuliue larisue
>   non alium mallet nec Maro nec Cicero.
>
> (*Epigr.* 11.48)

---

41 Thompson (1981).
42 Thompson (1981) 338.

Silius frequents great Vergil's tomb and possesses the acreage of eloquent Cicero. Neither Vergil nor Cicero would prefer another heir or owner of his tomb or home.

The younger Pliny supplements this picture with the information that Silius revered Vergil's tomb, indeed approached the site almost as if it were a temple, in a celebrated passage of the *Epistles*:

> nouissime ita suadentibus annis ab urbe secessit, seque in Campania tenuit, ac ne aduentu quidem noui principis inde commutus est ... plures isdem in locis uillas possidebat, adamatisque nouis priores neglegebat. multum ubique librorum, multum statuarum, multum imaginum, quas non habebat modo, uerum etiam uenerebatur, Vergili ante omnes, cuius natalem religiosius quam suum celebrabat, Neapoli maxime, ubi monimentum eius adire ut templum solebat.
>
> (*Ep.* 3.7.6–8)

> Most recently at the urging of old age he left the city for retirement in Campania, and he couldn't be brought to return even on the occasion of the new prince's arrival ... He possessed more villas in this part of Italy, and neglected his earlier places, so much had he come to love the new ones. There he had many books, statues and portraits, which he not only owned but even revered, above all those of Vergil, whose birthday he marked more scrupulously than his own, especially at Naples, where he used to approach his tomb as though it were a place of worship.

Both these passages shed considerable light not only on Silius' personal reverence for the two acknowledged masters of the literary forms in which he himself aspired to excel—Ciceronian oratory and Vergilian epic—but also on Roman ancestor worship more generally. In addition, however, the passages invite us to evaluate Silius' description of Hannibal's visit to the temple of Apollo at Cumae in *Punica* 12 as an act of quasi-religious literary reverence to Vergil and Ovid through his allusions to the *Aeneid* and *Metamorphoses* respectively. Silius' intertextual program in the representation of the temple of Apollo at Cumae confirms his admiration for the epic poets of the Augustan age and bears witness to his literary memory of their epics in his verse, as in his life.[43]

Bibliography

Anderson, William S. (1963), "Multiple change in the *Metamorphoses*", in: *TAPhA* 94, 1–27.
Augoustakis, Antony (ed.) (2010), *Brill's Companion to Silius Italicus*, Leiden.
Augoustakis, Antony (ed.) (2016), *Oxford Readings in Flavian Epic*, Oxford.

---

[43] On "literary memory," see Conte (1974), Hinds (1998) and Miller (1993).

Barchiesi, Alessandro (1997), "Virgilian Narrative: Ecphrasis", in: Martindale (1997) 271–281.
Bartholomé, Heinrich (1935), *Ovid und die antike Kunst*, Diss., Münster.
Bartsch, Shadi/Elsner, Jaś (2007), "Introduction: Eight Ways of Looking at an Ekphrasis", in: *CPh* 102.1, i–vi.
Bergmann, Marianne (1998), *Die Strahlen der Herrscher. Theomorphes Herrscherbild und politisch Symbolik im Hellenismus und in der römischen Kaiserzeit*, Mayence.
Bömer, Franz (1969), *P. Ovidius Naso*, Metamorphosen, *Buch I–III*, Heidelberg.
Brown, Robert (1987), "The Palace of the Sun in Ovid's *Metamorphoses*", in: Whitby *et al.* (1987) 211–220.
Bruère, Richard T. (1958), "*Color Ovidianus* in Silius *Punica* 1–7", in: Herescu (1958) 475–499; reprinted in Bruère (2016) 345–364.
Bruère, Richard T. (1959), "*Color Ovidianus* in Silius *Punica* 8–17", in: *CPh* 54, 228–245; reprinted in Bruère (2016) 364–387.
Bruère, Richard T. (2016), "*Color Ouidianus* in Silius' *Punica*", in: Augoustakis (2016) 345–387.
Buckley, Emma/Dinter, Martin T. (eds.) (2016), *Blackwell Companion to the Neronian Age*, Malden, MA.
Clark, Raymond J. (1977), "Vergil, *Aeneid* 6.40ff. and the Cumaean Sibyl's Cave", in: *Latomus* 36.2, 482–495.
Conte, Gian Biagio (1974), *Memoria dei poeti e sistema letterario: Catullo, Virgilio, Ovidio, Lucano*, Turin (translated as Conte (1986)).
Conte, Gian Biagio (1986), *The Rhetoric of Imitation: genre and poetic memory in Virgil and other Latin poets*, Ithaca, NY.
Dällenbach, Lucien (1989), *The Mirror in the Text*, Oxford.
Delz, Josef (1987), *Silius Italicus*, Punica, Stuttgart.
Dinter, Martin (2013), "Inscriptional Intermediality in Latin Literature", in: Liddel/Low (2013) 303–316.
Dominik, William/Newlands, Carole/Gervais, Kyle (eds.) (2015), *Brill's Companion to Statius*, Leiden.
Edmunds, Lowell (2001), *Intertextuality and the reading of Roman poetry*, Baltimore, MD.
Eigler, Ulrich/Lefèvre, Eckard/Manuwald, Gesine (eds.) (1998), Ratis omnia vincet. *Neue Untersuchungen zu den* Argonautica *des Valerius Flaccus*, Munich.
Elsner, Jaś (2002), "Introduction: The Genres of Ekphrasis", in: *Ramus* 31, 1–18.
Emden, Christian/Rippl, Gabriele (eds.) (2010), *The Irreducibility of Images: Intermediality in Contemporary Literary and Cultural Studies*, Oxford.
Ernout, Alfred/Meillet, Antoine (1994), *Dictionnaire étymologique de la langue latine*, 4 rev. J. André, Paris.
Feldherr, Andrew (2016), "Nothing Like the Sun: Repetition and Representation in Ovid's Phaethon Narrative", in: Fulkerson/Stover (2016) 26–46.
Foiltinek, Herbert/Leitgeb, Christoph (eds.) (2002), *Literaturwissenschaft—intermedial, interdisziplinär*, Vienna.
Fordyce, Christian J. (1977), *P. Vergili Maronis*, Aeneidos *Libri VII–VIII*, Oxford.
Fowler, Don (1991), "Narrate and Describe: The Problem of Ekphrasis", in: *JRS* 81, 25–35; reprinted in Fowler (2000) 64–85.
Fowler, Don (2000), *Roman Constructions: Readings in Postmodern Latin*, Oxford.
Friedländer, Paul (1912), *Johannes von Gaza und Paulus Silentiarius: Kunstbeschreibungen justinianischer Zeit*, Leipzig.

Fulkerson, Laurel/Stover, Tim (eds.) (2016), *Repeat Performances: Ovidian Repetition and the Metamorphoses*, Madison, WI.
Hardie, Philip R. (1985), "*Imago Mundi*: Cosmological and Ideological Aspects of the Shield of Achilles", in: *JHS* 105, 11–31.
Hardie, Philip R. (1986), *Cosmos and Imperium*, Oxford.
Harrison, Stephen (2010), "Picturing the Future Again", in: Augoustakis (2010) 279–292.
Harrison, Stephen (2013), "Proleptic *Ekphrasis* in Flavian Epic", in: Manuwald/Voigt (2013) 215–227.
Heerink, Mark (2014), "Valerius Flaccus, Virgil and the Poetics of Ekphrasis", in: Heerink/Manuwald (2014) 72–95.
Heerink, Mark/Manuwald, Gesine (eds.) (2014), *Brill's Companion to Valerius Flaccus*, Leiden.
Herescu, Niculai I. (ed.) (1958), *Ovidiana. Recherches sur Ovide*, Paris.
Hinds, Stephen (1998), *Allusion and Intertext: dynamics of appropriation in Roman poetry*, Cambridge.
Horsfall, Nicholas (2000), *Virgil*, Aeneid 7: A Commentary, Leiden.
Horsfall, Nicholas (2013), *Virgil*, Aeneid 2: A Commentary, Berlin.
Hunter, Richard L. (1989), *Apollonius of Rhodes*, Argonautica Book III, Cambridge.
Keith, Alison M. (2014a), "Ovid and Valerius Flaccus", in: Heerink/Manuwald (2014) 269–289.
Keith, Alison M. (2014b), "*Poetae Ovidiani*", in: Miller/Newlands (2014) 70–85.
Kristeva, Julia (1980), *Desire in Language: A Semiotic Approach to Literature and Art*, New York.
Liddel, Peter/Low, Polly (eds.) (2013), *Inscriptions and their Uses in Greek and Latin Literature*, Oxford.
Lodato, Suzanne M./Aspden, Suzanne/Bernhart, Walter (eds.) (2002), *Word and Music Studies: Essays in Honor of Steven Paul Scher and on Cultural Identity and the Musical Stage*, Amsterdam.
Maltby, Robert (1991), *A Lexicon of Ancient Latin Etymologies*, Leeds.
Manuwald, Gesine (1998), "Die Bilder am Tempel in Kolchis," in: Eigler et al. (1998) 307–318.
Manuwald, Gesine/Voigt, Astrid (eds.) (2013), *Flavian Epic Interactions*, Berlin.
Martindale, Charles (ed.) (1997), *The Cambridge Companion to Virgil*, Cambridge.
McLeod, Colin William (1982), *Homer*, Iliad Book XXIV, Cambridge.
Meban, David (2008), "Temple Building, Primus Language, and the Proem to Vergil's Third *Georgic*", in: *CPh* 103, 150–174.
Mette, Hans Joachim (1936), *Sphairopoiia: Untersuchungen zur Kosmologoie des Krates von Pergamon*, Munich.
Miller, John F. (1993), "Ovidian Allusion and the Vocabulary of Memory", in: *MD* 30, 153–164.
Miller, John F. (2009), *Apollo, Augustus and the Poets*, Cambridge.
Miller, John F./Newlands, Carole (eds.) (2014), *A Handbook to the Reception of Ovid*, Malden, MA.
Mratschek, Sigrid (2013), "Nero the Imperial Misfit", in: Buckley/Dinter (2013) 45–62.
Myncke, Gustav (1867), "Beiträge zur Kritik des Valerius Flaccus", in: *RhM* 22, 362–376.
Nauta, Ruurd R./Van Dam, Harm-Jan/Smolenaars, Johannes J.L. (eds.) (2008), *The Poetry of Statius*, Leiden.
Newlands, Carole E. (2011), *Statius*, Silvae Book II, Cambridge.
Nünning, Ansgar (ed.) (1998), *Metzler Lexikon Literatur-und Kulturtheorie: Ansätze, Personen, Grundbegriffe*, Stuttgart.
Putnam, Michael C.J. (1998), *Virgil's Epic Designs: Ekphrasis in the* Aeneid, New Haven, CT.

Rebeggiani, Stefano (2013), "The Chariot Race and the Destiny of the Empire in Statius' *Thebaid*", in: *ICS* 38, 187–206.
Rippl, Gabriele (2010), "English Literature and its Other: Towards a Poetics of Intermediality", in: Emden/Rippl (2010) 147–65.
Rippl, Gabriele (ed.) (2015), *Handbook of Intermediality: Literature – Image – Sound – Music*, Berlin.
Rosati, Gianpiero (2008), "Statius, Domitian and Acknowledging Paternity: Rituals of Succession in the *Thebaid*" in: Nauta et al. (2008) 175–194.
Schmitzer, Ulrich (1990), *Zeitgeschichte in Ovids* Metamorphosen: *Mythologische Dichtung unter politischem Anspruch*, Stuttgart.
Schmitzer, Ulrich (1999), "*Praesaga ars*: Zur literarischen Technik der Ekphrasis bei Valerius Flaccus", in: *WJA* 23, 143–160.
Schoder, Raymond V. (1971), "Vergil's Poetic Use of the Cumae Area", in: *CJ* 67, 97–105.
Smiley, P. O'R. (1948), "In the Steps of Aeneas", in: *G&R* 17, 97–103.
Spaltenstein, François (1990), *Commentaire des* Punica *de Silius Italicus (livres 9 à 17)*, Geneva.
Spaltenstein, François (2002), *Commentaire des* Argonautica *de Valérius Flaccus (livres 3, 4 et 5)*, Brussels.
Taylor, P. Ruth (1994), "Valerius' Flavian *Argonautica*", in: *CQ* 44, 212–235.
Thomas, Richard F. (1986), "Virgil's *Georgics* and the Art of Reference", in: *HSPh* 90, 171–198.
Thomas, Richard F. (1988), *Virgil*, Georgics, I-II, Cambridge.
Thompson, David L. (1981), "The Meetings of the Roman Senate on the Palatine", in: *AJA* 85.3, 335–339.
Waszink, J.H. (1948), "Vergil and the Sibyl of Cumae", in: *Mnemosyne* 1, 43–58.
Webb, Ruth (1999), "Ekphrasis Ancient and Modern: the Invention of a Genre", in: *Word and Image* 15, 7–18.
Webb, Ruth (2009), *Ekphrasis, Imagination and Persuasion in Ancient Rhetorical Theory and Practice*, Farnham.
Wedeniwski, Esther (2006), *Antike Beschreibungen von Türbildern: Vergil* Georgica 3, *Properz* 2,31, *Vergil* Aeneis 6, *Ovid* met. 2, *Valerius Flaccus* 5 *und Silius Italicus* 3, Marburg.
Wheeler, Stephen M. (1995), "*Imago Mundi*: Another View of the Creation in Ovid's *Metamorphoses*", in: *AJPh* 116.1, 95–121.
Wheeler, Stephen M. (2000), *Narrative Dynamics in Ovid's* Metamorphoses, Tübingen.
Whitby, Michael/Hardie, Philip R./Whitby, Mary (eds.) (1987), *Homo Viator: Classical Essays for John Bramble*, Bristol.
Wijsman, Henri J.W. (1996), *Valerius Flaccus*, Argonautica, *Book V: A Commentary*, Leiden.
Wilkinson, L.P. (1970), "Pindar and the Proem to the Third *Georgic*", in: Wimmel (1970) 286–290.
Williams, Robert D. (1960), "The Pictures on Dido's Temple", in: *CQ* 10, 145–151.
Wilson, Marcus (2004), "Ovidian Silius", in: *Arethusa* 37, 225–249.
Wimmel, Walter (ed.) (1970), *Forschungen zur römischen Literatur: Festschrift zum 60. Geburtstag Karl Büchner*, Wiesbaden.
Wolf, Werner (1998), "Intermedialität", in: Nünning (1998) 238.
Wolf, Werner (1999), *The Musicalization of Fiction: A Study in the Theory and History of Intermediality*, Amsterdam.
Wolf, Werner (2002a), "Intermedialität—ein weites Feld und eine Herausforderung für die Literaturwissenschaft," in: Foiltinek/Leitgeb (2002) 163–192.

Wolf, Werner (2002b), "Intermediality Revisited: Reflections on Word and Music Relations in the Context of a General Typology of Intermediality," in: Lodato *et al.* (2002) 13–34.

Carole Newlands
Statius' Post-Vesuvian Landscapes and Virgil's Parthenope

The *Silvae* are a defiantly new literary form without one specific literary model.[1] True, the title *silvae* evokes Virgil's metaphorical expression for his pastoral poetry, *silvae* (*Ecl.* 4.3). And in his programmatic preface to *Silvae* Book 2 Statius associates his new occasional poetry with epigram (2 *praef.* 15–16). But his poems lack epigram's brevity, and the majority employ the metre associated with epic, the hexameter. The *Silvae* challenge the hierarchy of genre and accommodate to an imperial context epigram's traditional play with contrastive effects—for instance, the smallness of the form versus the intricate labour of poetic production.[2] When Statius published the first three books of *Silvae* at the start of 93 CE, he was at a pivotal moment of his career, having just published his epic poem, the *Thebaid*, the previous year.[3] In this article I shall explore how, in the aftermath of the eruption of Vesuvius in 79 CE, Statius constructs his poetic self within his new, ambitious *Silvae*. His home region of the Bay of Naples was marked both by the monumental presence of the volcano and by the monumental memory of Virgil who had written his early poetry at Naples and was buried there. Through the representation of the physical and cultural geography of the Bay of Naples in several of his *Silvae*, Statius makes claim to the title of successor of Virgil in both "minor" and epic poetry.[4]

The generic lability of the *Silvae* is reflected with particular complexity in Statius' poetic geography of the Bay of Naples. From the late Republic on, the Bay of Naples was commonly imagined as a site of elite withdrawal, of *otium*. Cicero, for instance, famously described the Bay of Naples as *cratera illum delicatum* (*ad Att.* 2.8.2), metaphorically a giant wine bowl associated with self-indulgence and effeminacy (although he himself owned several villas in the region, including his

---

[1] Research on this paper has been helped by the digital resources *Tesserae* and *PHI Latin Texts*. Thanks to Neil Bernstein, to Damien and Lavinia for their invitation to Geneva, and to all my colleagues there for their comments.
[2] On Statius' engagement with epigram's "Hellenistic aesthetic of extremes" see Squire (2011) 269–283; on his engagement in the *Silvae* with epic themes see Gibson (2006b); Newlands (2012).
[3] For the chronology of Statius' works see Coleman (1988) xvi–xx.
[4] Horace, Ovid, and Lucan were also major models for the *Silvae*; see Rosati (2011) 21. But they did not have Virgil's connection with the Bay of Naples.

"Academy").[5] Seneca used his stay on the Bay of Naples to argue that *otium* could be made morally and spiritually productive.[6] But, as Dewar has pointed out, the Bay of Naples was not only a place of leisure; it was also associated with political intrigues and, moreover, with ambitious engineering projects, drastic interventions into the landscape such as the Portus Iulius, a harbour built by Agrippa that connected two lakes to the sea by means of canals (Suet. *Aug.* 16.10).[7] The catastrophic eruption of Vesuvius changed common perceptions of the Bay of Naples as a congenial, safe resort. There were speculations that human society was partly to blame for the eruption. At the start of his *Histories* (2.1–2), Tacitus associates the destruction caused by Vesuvius with rampant corruption in imperial society.[8] Dio Cassius reports that during the eruption of Vesuvius giant figures were seen hurrying on the mountain's slopes, a portent of the coming evil of Domitian's reign (66.22–23).[9] Rimell has recently argued that a central trope of imperial epic is hidden, explosive violence, with "images of eruption, exposure and boundlessness" created from futile attempts to maintain boundaries and contain war.[10] The unexpected, devastating eruption of Vesuvius literalised that central imperial trope. Statius' *Silvae*, on the other hand, counteract it with an "aesthetics of containment", to use Rimell's term, that directs human energies nonetheless to brilliant and joyous effects.[11]

Statius' *Silvae* were written in the aftermath of the eruption, in the early 90's when the region was barely in recovery, and the central coastline remained a long stretch of white ash and mud. Despite Titus' swift response to the immediate emergency, recovery was slow on the Bay of Naples and did not pick up pace until the second century CE under Hadrian.[12] Four years before the publication of Books 1–3 of the *Silvae* in 93 CE, Martial wrote an epitaphic epigram lamenting the destruction of the once fertile landscape (4.4).[13] Yet the poems of the *Silvae* that are centred on Statius' home region of the Bay of Naples, *Silv.* 2.2, 3.1, 3.5, 4.3 and 4.4, assert a narrative of human recuperation and resilience. Through what I call "post-Vesuvian landscapes," they articulate a new form of heroism dedicated

---

5 On Cicero's villas see D'Arms (1970) 198–200; on coastal Campania's reputation for luxury see D'Arms (1970) 39–72.
6 Newlands (2012) 149–153; Dewar (2014) 51–54.
7 Dewar (2014) 7–9, 47–49; Leonard (2015).
8 Damon (2003) 82–83.
9 Connors (2015) 131–134.
10 Rimell (2015) 240–241.
11 Rimell (2015) 30–31.
12 Suet. *Tit.* 8.3–4; Soricelli (2001) 460–461; Taylor (2015) 296–311.
13 For the date of 88 CE or the start of 89 CE see Citroni (1989) 217–220.

to re-establishing a harmonious balance between nature and society that was firmly dissociated from ideas of human guilt or decadence. While they acknowledge the epic violence inflicted by Vesuvius on the Bay of Naples, they are also shaped by a poetic art that directs epic tropes and themes to moral and social and cultural ends.[14] "Landscape," as Alcock comments, is a complex concept whose many meanings "revolve around human experience, perception and modification of the world."[15] Against the volcano's continuing drive to lay waste, Statius' "post-Vesuvian landscapes" display the human commitment to build, order, create new monuments and, above all, write new poetry.

Statius' post-Vesuvian landscapes are alert to literary tradition as well as to contemporary events; Vesuvius, as Statius observes in *Silv.* 4.4.78–86, continues intermittently to erupt. The act of rebuilding is here closely associated with poetic composition, with the challenge of building anew upon poetic tradition. Parthenope, mythical founder of Naples and Virgil's "Muse" of pastoral and georgic poetry (*G.* 4.563–566), plays a strategic role in Statius' restructuring of his poetic self and of his place within the literary history of the Bay of Naples; she will be the focus of this article.

1 The Myth of Parthenope

The Bay of Naples had a deeply storied, mythological past, and epic heroes had left their mark on the landscape. Here Odysseus had sailed past the Sirens, causing their death; here Aeneas had first landed in Italy; here Hercules had battled and crushed the giants and had built a causeway.[16] As Hinds has shown, Statius views many of the sites in the Bay of Naples through a literary, epic lens; heroic exploits and interventions in the landscape are mapped in key landmarks such as Hercules' causeway, or Misenum, with its tomb of a companion of both Odysseus and Aeneas.[17] In the *Silvae*, however, Statius draws not only on the past but also brings myth into the present and makes it topical.[18] The deities that populate his post-Vesuvian landscapes are beneficent. Hercules, for instance, a model of heroic emulation for both Hannibal and Scipio in Silius' *Punica*, here, after the obliteration of Herculaneum by Vesuvius, guards the boundaries of the private

---

14 Newlands (2010).
15 Alcock (2002) 30.
16 Connors (2015) 127–130; Leonard (2015); Prop. 1.11.1–5; Str. 5.4.5–6; Sil. *Pun.* 12.143–146.
17 Hinds (2001) 239–255.
18 Szelest (1972).

estate of Statius' patron, Pollius Felix; he also applies his engineering skills to building a new temple on the estate and improving the land (2.2.23–24; 3.1.163–186).[19] Parthenope, mythical founder of Naples, is less well known than these epic divinities, but she is the deity who is most closely associated with Statius' poetic landscapes and ambitions.

Parthenope was a Siren and thus was associated with beautiful song. Virgil claimed her as the inspiring deity of his "minor poetry" that was composed on the Bay of Naples (G. 4.563–566). In Statius' cultural geography, the Siren unites in one figure the physical city and inspirational poetry. More than a principle of female and civic sovereignty, she also represents literary sovereignty as the founder of a poetic tradition that extends through Virgil to Statius himself. Although she is not traditionally a heroic figure, in the *Silvae*, as we shall see later, she is given a heroic dimension, mediating, as does Statius' poetry, between epic and non-epic tendencies and themes.

Her legend, which belongs to the Hellenistic aetiological tradition of city foundation, can be reconstructed from various sources. The Sirens' song was irresistible to humans, with the exception of Odysseus (Hom. *Od.* 12.39–54, 165–200). They were however doomed to die if anyone successfully passed their shores safely. The Hellenistic poet Lycophron tells us that they committed suicide in the Tyrrhenian sea off Naples, but that one of the Sirens was washed ashore at a new settlement that had been established by Greek colonists from Cumae. She gave her name, Parthenope, to the place, and the local people built a tomb for her.[20] Later, in response to an oracle, the city established an official cult to her, and she was honoured with an annual festival and sacrifices (Lycoph. *Alex.* 712–736).[21] Frederiksen dates the cult of Parthenope to the earliest stage of the city's settlement.[22] It remained a key feature of the city's cultural identity;[23] Strabo in the first century reports seeing her tomb (5.4.7). The myth was bolstered also by the local belief that the Sirens' island was just off the Sorrento promontory, a tradition that Statius adopts in his *Silvae*.[24]

As a founding figure, the Siren lost her destructive powers and became a protector and benefactor of the city. Parthenope's story of death and recovery was

---

19 Stocks (2014) 218–221.
20 Cf. Plin. *Nat.* 3.62.
21 See also Servius on Verg. *G.* 4.563; Livy 8.22.5–6.
22 Frederiksen (1984) 105.
23 Parthenope's head appears on the earliest (4th c. BCE) coins minted in Naples; see Rutter (1979) 42–45.
24 *Silv.* 2.2.1, 116–117; 3.1.64. On the debated location of the Sirens see Str. 1.2.12–13; Bömer (1986) 35–36.

particularly appropriate to Naples after 79 CE. As Alcock has argued of imperial Greek cities, local myths, whether embedded in texts or monuments, were especially important to communities under duress or in a position of resistance to dominant powers.[25] In the *Silvae* Parthenope is a sign of civic and literary continuity and provides a promise of future growth in times of great geographical and cultural stress.

Founding involved a gendered discourse.[26] In contrast to Naples, and indeed to a significant number of Hellenistic cities, Rome's founding myths of the Trojan Aeneas and of Romulus and Remus were violent and bloody, although they also involved divine sanction. Naples' founding myth of the Siren not only legitimated the territorial claims of the Cumaean settlers; it also associated Naples from early on with themes that resonated throughout the city's history to the Roman imperial present: with philhellenism; with poetry and the generative power of myth; with the idea of the city as a peaceful refuge not only for the pleasure-seeker but for the troubled and dispossessed; and with the idea of creative resilience and transformation in the face of trauma.

Lycophron describes Parthenope as "a bird goddess" (οἰωνὸν θεάν, *Alex.* 721), in reference to the Sirens' conventional representation in visual art with bird bodies or feet. Statius, however, avoids any suggestion of the monstrous. He uses the term *Neapolis* for the city only once in the *Silvae* (4.8.6). Otherwise he refers to "Parthenope," usually with a degree of personification. In tying his literary identity to the Siren, Statius develops the Muse-like, creative features of the Siren and her associations with rescue, safety and creative nurture—and with Virgil. For Parthenope's reputation as the crucible of literary excellence was greatly enhanced when Virgil named her in the conclusion to the *Georgics* and laid claim to her power as his Muse of pastoral and georgic poetry (*G.* 4.563–566). Virgil, moreover, was buried in a tomb just outside Naples. As Hinds notes, "the name Parthenope maintains its strong Virgilian resonance in poetic usage through a strongly felt association between the Siren's tomb and the poet's own."[27] Let us therefore turn briefly to Virgil's Parthenope before examining Statius' "poetic usage" of the Siren.

---

25 Alcock (2002) 146–152.
26 Angelova (2015) 5–6.
27 Hinds (2001) 248–249.

2 Virgil's Parthenope

The name Parthenope occurs for the first time in Roman literature at the end of Virgil's *Georgics* to indicate, with slippage between them, both city and Siren. The poet claims that "Parthenope" inspired him to write the *Eclogues* and the *Georgics* while he was flourishing in the pursuit of "ignoble *otium*" (*G.* 4.563–566):

> illo Vergilium me tempore dulcis alebat
> Parthenope studiis florentem ignobilis oti,
> carmina qui lusi pastorum audaxque iuventa,
> Tityre, te patulae cecini sub tegmine fagi.

> At that time Parthenope nurtured me as I flourished in the pursuit of ignoble leisure, I who sang the songs of shepherds and in the boldness of youth sang of you, Tityrus, beneath the shade of a spreading beech tree.

Virgil's close identification between his poetic self and the Siren/founder Parthenope is suggested by a probable translingual, etymological pun on his putative nickname "Parthenias" and "Virgilius/*virgo*."[28] Virgil calls the *otium* offered by Parthenope "ignoble" not simply out of modesty; Thomas comments that the epithet *ignobilis* makes a strong contrast with Octavian's thundering wars on the Roman frontier: [29]

> haec super arvorum cultu pecorumque canebam
> et super arboribus, Caesar dum magnus ad altum
> fulminat Euphraten bello victorque volentes
> per populos dat iura viamque adfectat Olympo.
>
> (*G.* 4.559–562)

> I sang these things about the cultivation of fields and cattle and also trees, while great Caesar thunders in war by the deep Euphrates and as victor gives laws throughout willing peoples and aims at a path to Olympus.

Stärk comments that with this *sphragis* Virgil immortalized Naples not only for poetry but for a way of life.[30] Virgil's passage also carefully demarcates his pastoral and georgic poetry from epic poetry by personifying Parthenope with maternal, non-epic language, *dulcis alebat* (563); *fulminat* (561), on the other hand,

---

28 Hinds (2001) 248, n. 47; Putnam (2016) 144–145 draws a strong link between Virgil's nickname, Parthenope, and Statius' youthful hero of the *Thebaid,* Parthenopaeus.
29 Thomas (1988) 239–241.
30 Stärk (1995) 142.

used here for the first time of a mortal leader, Augustus Caesar, traditionally connotes the epic anger of Jupiter.[31] Virgil, furthermore, uses geographic, spatial divisions to position the matter of war far from Naples, indeed on the frontier of the empire. The effect is thus to sideline the traditional material of epic and, despite the apologetic association with "ignoble leisure", to make Naples central to important forms of new poetry celebrating the arts of peace. The passage thus creates a clash of values that are political and moral as well as generic.

As we shall see, Virgil's sphragis was influential on Statius. By using the old Greek name for Naples, Parthenope, Virgil emphasised the importance of Hellenic culture, in particular the pursuit of philosophy and poetry, to Roman cultural identity and literary traditions; he also thus grants Naples a harmonious identity as a city where Greek and Roman intellectual traditions flourished and intermingled, offering an alternative, cosmopolitan model to imperial, war-mongering Rome. Virgil's Parthenope meant both poetry and a way of life that provided the peace and freedom essential for inspired, creative work in a period of "the utmost political uncertainty."[32]

The cultural prestige that Virgil endowed on Naples by his naming of its mythic founder was enhanced by his burial in a tomb a short distance from the city centre, a tomb which Silius and Statius venerated.[33] In the late first century CE, Virgil's tomb seems to have fallen into neglect; Silius Italicus bought the land on which the tomb was situated and ritually celebrated the poet every year on his birthday (Plin. *Ep.* 3.7.8–9). Like Parthenope's tomb, Virgil's tomb became the object of mystique and cult; it was venerated throughout the Middle Ages and was visited well into the nineteenth century as a tourist attraction.[34] Tombs of famous people are iconic images that are central to the forging and development of a city's cultural identity, to its rooting in a storied past and present.[35] Following the tradition of Parthenope's tomb, Rome's greatest poet was buried in Naples, embedded in its ground and its local traditions. In the *Silvae* Parthenope is always

---

31 Thomas (1988) *ad loc.*
32 Thomas (1988) 1. The approximate date for composition of the *Georgics* is between 36 and 29 BCE.
33 Cf. Donatus, *Vita Vergilii* 36, *ossa eius Neapolim translata sunt tumuloque condita qui est via Puteolana intra lapidem secundum* ("his bones were transferred to Naples and buried in a tomb which is on the Via Puteolana within the second milestone"). Virgil's epitaph cites "Parthenope" as his final resting-place, *Mantua me genuit, Calabri rapuere, tenet nunc / Parthenope* ("Mantua first gave me life, the Calabrians snatched me away, now Parthenope holds me"). See Bettini (1976) 439–443; Putnam (2016) 142–143.
34 Comparetti (1946) 57–61; Hendrix (2015).
35 Harrison (2002).

in a sense Virgil's Parthenope. But while she represents distinguished poetic and local traditions, she is also associated by Statius with new beginnings in a post-Vesuvian, imperial world.

3 Nostra Parthenope: *Silv.* 3.5

Parthenope's expanded role as a figure of both continuity and renewal is seen in *Silv.* 3.5, Statius' poetic epistle to his wife urging her to leave Rome and retire with him to Campania. He claims that cities are still populated and indeed flourish, even although Vesuvius remains restless:

> non adeo Vesuvinus apex et flammea diri
> montis hiems trepidas exhausit civibus urbes:
> stant populisque vigent ...
>   [...]
> nostraque nec propriis tenuis nec rara colonis
> Parthenope cui mite solum trans aequora vectae
> ipse Dionaea monstravit Apollo columba.
>
> (*Silv.* 3.5.72–74; 78–80)

> Vesuvius' summit and the flaming storm of the cursed mountain have not after all drained our fearful cities of their citizens: they stand and flourish with people ... our Parthenope is robust, not lacking in her own folk or in new settlers; to her Apollo with Venus' dove showed a gentle soil when she was conveyed across the sea.

Statius' optimism about the present state of the Bay of Naples is contrary to the despair expressed in Martial's epitaphic epigram, 4.44. In the penultimate line Martial claims, *cuncta iacent flammis et tristi mersa favilla* ("all things are destroyed by fire and buried in sad ash," 7). Statius' phrase, (*non*) *exhausit civibus urbes* (73), almost exactly echoes Lucr. 6.1138, *exhausit civibus urbem*, where Lucretius refers to the plague that devastated the city of Athens. But Statius' expression suggests that, unlike the Athenian Greeks, who succumbed to the plague, the people of Campania are standing strong, in fact flourishing in population, despite nature's assault.

Statius' reference to the myth of Parthenope here validates the right of the region for divine protection—and his own right to accommodate Virgil's Parthenope to his experimental, literary ends. The adjective *tenuis*, used here with negation to indicate the now robust population of the region, is a frequent term for refined, Callimachean-style poetry; for instance, it appears programmatically at the start of Virgil's *Eclogues* in reference to pastoral poetry, *tenui ... avena* (1.2).

Following Shackleton Bailey's text, the negation (*nec*) of *tenuis* in *Silv*. 3.5 elevates Parthenope to a heroic level beyond strict categories of gender and genre.[36] Statius too in part fashions himself here as a new type of hero, returning to the Bay of Naples to write epideictic poetry, praise of cities, against the backdrop of a still dangerous mountain; *Silv*. 3.5 concludes with detailed praise of the physical, moral and cultural attractions of Naples and the surrounding region (81–112). With the possessive pronoun *nostraque* (79), Statius appropriates Virgil's pastoral Muse for his own narrative of heroic recovery and literary re-foundation on the Bay of Naples.

Statius makes two alterations to the traditional foundation narrative of Naples. First, he conflates it with the founding myth of Cumae according to which Greek settlers from Chalcis in Euboea were guided to Cumae by an oracular dove (Vell. Pat. 1.4.1). Statius applies the Cumaean oracle of the dove directly to Naples and to its myth of the Siren, thus enhancing the city's founding legend with the inspiring presence of Apollo and Venus. This adaptation reflects the generic ambitiousness of his *Silvae*. The foundation of Naples is claimed as a divinely sanctioned event of symbolic significance for the city's identity as a continuing centre of poetry and creativity.

Second, the expression *trans aequora vectae* ("conveyed across the sea"), with its echo of Catullus' famous opening line of the lament for his drowned brother, *per aequora vectus* (101.1), represents Parthenope not, however, as a drowned Siren whose body was washed ashore but rather as a traveller by ship seeking refuge and a safe harbor. Parthenope is given a favourable passage to Italy thanks to an oracle. Apollo, god of poetry who emerges in Hellenistic poetry as also a god of city founding, guides her, accompanied by a dove which belongs to Venus, goddess of creative forces and mother of Aeneas.[37] Parthenope is thus brought into the literary orbit of Virgil's Aeneas. In *Aen*. 3.69–101, Delian Apollo gives Aeneas an oracle commanding him to sail to the land of his ancestral mother (96). As Angelova argues, Virgil "casts Aeneas in the mold of a Greek *oikist* from the age of colonization."[38] But the parallels with Rome's founding also accentuate the differences with the foundation of Naples. Parthenope's point of origin is not at stake, only the divine sanctification of her journey to Italy. On landing in Italy, she finds *mite solum*, "gentle soil" (79).[39] Aeneas, however, has

---

36 Cf. Courtney's (1990) text, *nostra quoque et propriis tenuis nec rara colonis*.
37 Cf. Callim. *Hymn*. 2 55–59, an early written testimony to Apollo as city founder. On Apollo's association with the refounding of Rome after Actium see Angelova (2015) 33–43.
38 Angelova (2015) 14.
39 Cf. Sil. *Pun*. 12.27–28, *mitis / Parthenope*, identifying the Siren with her physical environment.

a harrowing journey and on arrival in Italy finds conflict and war. The distinction between the two foundations is adumbrated in generic terms that admit the complexity of Statius' relationship with Virgil, on which we will now focus.

4 At Virgil's Tomb

The identity of Statius as both local and imperial poet is closely implicated with that of his city, its founder and its Virgilian legacy. Poetic succession is modeled topographically in *Silv.* 4.4, when Statius situates himself physically at Virgil's tomb:

> en egomet somnum et geniale secutus
> litus ubi Ausonio se condidit hospita portu
> Parthenope, tenues ignavo pollice chordas
> pulso, Maroneique sedens in margine templi
> sumo animum et magni tumulis adcanto magistri.
>
> (51–55)

> Look, pursuing sleep and the cheerful shore where welcoming Parthenope found refuge in an Ausonian haven, I strike the slender strings with idle thumb, and while I sit at the edge of Maro's shrine I take heart and sing out at the tomb of the great master.

As Putnam has noted, Statius here expresses his "deep allegiance" to Vergil, who is described here as Statius' *magister*, his teacher. The word *templum* implicitly deifies Virgil, in a reminiscence of the sphragis to the *Thebaid*, where Statius endows Virgil's epic poem with divine status as *divinam Aeneida* (*Theb.* 12.816). Here too Statius plays self-reflexively upon the sphragis to Virgil's *Georgics* (4.559–566) where Virgil reflects on his poetic achievements and acknowledges the nurturing, inspirational role of "sweet Parthenope" (*dulcis Parthenope, G.* 4.563–564). As Putnam argues, lines 54–55 suggest that Statius gains literary inspiration through physical proximity to Virgil's tomb, and by implication therefore from his writings.[40] Yet although Parthenope's tomb and cult are closely linked with the tomb and cult of Vergil in these lines, Virgil's *dulcis Parthenope* has an expanded role here. The verb *condidit* (52) refers in the first instance to the Siren's burial in Naples, but it also alludes to her close association with the city's foundation.[41] Since *condere* has the additional, common meaning of "to compose

---

40 Putnam (2016) 142–143.
41 On *condere* as a key, complex word of Rome's founding in the *Aeneid* see James (1995).

a literary work," the Siren with her beautiful song closely associates the city from its origins with the composition of great poetry.[42] She fosters both building in stone and building in words. As James reminds us, the word *condere* in the *Aeneid* is strongly marked from epic's start with the notion of Rome's violent foundation.[43] Its positive use in allusion to the cult of the Siren emphasises that the founding virtues of Naples are beneficent and poetic. The phrase *Ausonio ... portu* (52) is Virgilian and alludes to Helenus's prayer to the gods that Aeneas and his men may find the endpoint of their epic journey in "an Ausonian harbour" (*Aen.* 3.378).[44] But unlike Parthenope, who arrives from sea on "gentle soil" (*mite solum*, 79), they find in Italy terrible, protracted war.[45]

Statius describes Parthenope as *hospita* (52), rather than Virgil's *dulcis*. Coleman translates *hospita* as "refugee" but it can equally mean "hospitable, welcoming;"[46] Silius, for instance, describes Naples as a place whose *otium* is hospitable to the Muses, *hospita Musis / otia* (12.31–32). Statius associates the Siren's cult with the idea of Naples as both a physical refuge and a safe haven for the arts. *Hospita* also marks the Siren's shift in Neapolitan cult and Statius' myth-making from the fatal singer whose song drew passing sailors to their deaths to the protector of poets and poetry. In the post-Vesuvian landscape, the tombs of Parthenope and Virgil give material form to the region's continuing prestige in song. They are visible signs of endurance, continuity and also cultic protection that stand alongside the literary monuments of Virgil's *Eclogues* and *Georgics* and Statius' *Thebaid* and *Silvae*. At Virgil's tomb Statius establishes a Neapolitan genealogy of distinguished poetic succession from the Siren to Virgil to his own poetic self.

Like Virgil in the sphragis to the *Georgics*, Statius here reflects ironically and somewhat humorously on his own non-epic poetry, his *Silvae*. He describes them through the chiastic phrase *tenues ignavo pollice chordas* ("slender strings (struck) with idle thumb"), a probable allusion both to Virgil's ironically depreciatory classification of the *Eclogues* and *Georgics* as the product of *ignobilis oti* (*G.* 4.564), and to the programmatic *tenui ... avena* ("slender pipe") of Virgil's Tityrus (*Ecl.* 1.2), whose description of harmonious music-making opens the *Eclogues*. Indeed, Statius takes the pastoral trope of physical relaxation to an extreme by "pursuing sleep on a cheerful shore" (*somnum et geniale secutus / litus*,

---

42 *OLD* 14. Cf. e.g. Verg. *Ecl.* 6.7, *tristia condere bella*.
43 James (1995) 623–624.
44 *Ausonius* (Ausonian/Italian) first appears in Latin literature at Verg. *G.* 2.385.
45 Barchiesi (2015) 171, n. 7 observes that "the scale and moral intensity of the conflict are not justified by the existing traditions about the Aeneas legend."
46 Coleman (1988) 25, 147.

51–52); *genialis* is used programmatically by Ovid to describe his unwarlike, elegiac Muse, *Amores, imbelles elegi, genialis Musa* (*Am.* 1.15.19). But Statius proceeds to transgress the corresponding geographic and generic divisions articulated by the Virgilian sphragis, where Virgil in Naples is separated from Augustus Caesar's epic "thundering" on the Roman frontier (*G.* 4.561–563). Sitting on the verge of Virgil's tomb Statius gains epic inspiration, *sumo animum* (55); the phrase suggests an intensification of his poetic powers from the composition of *Silvae*.[47] He begins to plan a second epic, the *Achilleid*: *Troia quidem magnusque mihi temptatur Achilles* ("indeed by me Troy will be attempted and great Achilles", 4.4.94). Even as he pays homage to Virgil, he suggests that he will surpass Virgil's achievements.

Silv. 4.4 demonstrates Statius' creative resilience and that of his ancient city. Yet Stärk has argued that Statius at Virgil's tomb mourns the way of life represented by Virgil's *otium*.[48] Not only had the landscape been altered, so too political circumstances had changed. Indeed, whereas Virgil in his sphragis kept himself physically and generically separate from Caesar, Statius reveals that the emperor himself is prompting him for another epic, panegyrical, however, not the mythological epic that Statius plans (4.4.93–100). The addressee of *Silv.* 4.4 is Vitorius Marcellus, praetor in Rome in 95 CE; Quintilian dedicated his *Institutio Oratoria* to him the following year.[49] Although located in Parthenope, Statius associates himself in *Silv.* 4.4 with the wider imperial orbit of cultural relationships. At the same time, *otium* is dynamically reformulated in *Silv.* 4.4 to encompass a more ambitious, wide-ranging poetic agenda that includes the composition of epic poetry. And yet Virgil, not Domitian, is the higher master whom he will follow in cleaving to mythological epic. In paying homage to Virgil's tomb Statius is inspired with a design for the future—a second epic, a literary monument that will allow his career to surpass in productivity and ambition Virgil's own.

The accommodation of Parthenope to epic poetry as well as to *Silvae* is accentuated by another defining Neapolitan landmark, Mount Vesuvius, which Statius describes as still erupting, if intermittently, in wrath (4.4.78–87). An active volcano is the ultimate signifier of epic poetry. Scorning the touristic attractions of antiquities such as Greek paintings and sculptures, the anonymous author of the poem *Aetna* invites the reader to view the volcano as "the great work of nature

---

47 See for instance Ov. *Fast.* 1.147 (confronting a god), *sumpsi animum gratesque deo non territus egi*; Sen. *Ep.* 107.7.6–8, *magnum sumere animum et viro bono dignum, quo fortiter fortuita patiamur et naturae consentiamus*.
48 Stärk (1995) 142–143.
49 Coleman (1988) 135–138.

the artist" (*artificis ingens opus aspice*), with the implication that it is also the "great work of the poet," since volcanoes were the epic theme *par excellence*. Statius here suggests an element of literary rivalry with Virgil's description of Aetna (*Aen.* 3.570–587) and probably also with the sublime poetry of the *Aetna* when he writes of Vesuvius, *aemula Trinacriis volvens incendia flammis* ("rolling out fires that *rival* Sicilian flames," 4.4.80).[50] Silius Italicus likewise in his description of Vesuvius (Sil. *Pun.* 12.152–154) points to the challenges of literary secondariness with the phrase *Aetnae fatis certantia saxa* ("the deadly rocks that *rival* Etna's," 154).[51] By including this epic trope in his *Silvae*, Statius alludes not only to his status as epic poet; he also demonstrates his ambitious expansion of the literary canon of pastoral and georgic poetry established for Naples by Virgil's sphragis.

Statius' physical situation in *Silv.* 4.4, at Virgil's tomb with Vesuvius flaming in the background, gives topographical expression to his literary identity as poet of both epic and *Silvae*, of war and peace, of Naples and empire. Statius not only displays his *sang-froid* in continuing to sit at Virgil's tomb. Rather, the volcano's active presence has metapoetic implications. As Octavian "thundered" on the Euphrates in Virgil's sphragis (*G.* 4.560–562), Mount Vesuvius likewise thunders, but much closer to home for Statius: *necdum letale minari /cessat apex* ("not yet does the summit cease to threaten death and destruction," 4.4.84–85). In *Silv.* 4.4 the centre of epic composition has shifted from the Virgilian frontier of *Georgics* 4 to Naples. As a sign of genre, therefore, "Parthenope" is no longer confined to pastoral and agricultural poetry, as in Virgil's sphragis, but now accommodates epic poetry as well. In *Silv.* 4.4 Statius redraws and expands the geographically calibrated boundaries of the Virgilian system of genres. And through the poetic genealogy of the city suggested in this poem, the centrality of Naples to Roman literary culture is acclaimed, despite Vesuvius' continuing threats.

Tombs, as Alcock comments, are "landmarks and bulwarks of continuity" as physical sites of memory for a society, but their meanings can change over time.[52] Statius' location on the "margin of Virgil's tomb" symbolically models poetic reception in spatial terms as both poetic deference and poetic distance. As metonymy for the poet, Virgil's tomb is to be revered; as a memorial of the past, it is also an invitation to new poetic compositions, to poetic departures, and an expanded

---

50 Statius alludes directly to Virgil's description of Aetna (*Aen.* 3.570–587) at 4.4.79, *fractas ubi Vesuius erigit iras*; cf. *Aen.* 3.575–6, *avulsaque viscera montis / erigit eructans*. Lucretius' descriptive exposition of the eruption of Etna (6.680–702) became the *locus classicus* for ecphraseis of volcanoes.
51 Muecke (2007). Cf. the description of Vesuvius in Val. Fl. 4. 507–511, used to describe the terror the Argonauts felt at the Harpies.
52 Alcock (2002) 28–32; Fowler (2000) 206.

literary range for a new imperial age of heroic recovery and artistic excellence. Statius' location on "the margin of Virgil's tomb" symbolizes his dual status as poet of the *Silvae* and the *Thebaid*.

Strikingly, there is no allusion to Silius Italicus, epic poet and consecrator of Virgil's tomb, who, it seems, had purchased the land on which Virgil's tomb was situated (Mart. 11.48; 11.50) and which Statius in *Silv.* 4.4 occupies.[53] Silius worshipped Virgil's monument with religious devotion, "as if it were a temple" (Plin. *Ep.* 3.7.8). As senator, ex-consul, and owner of several villas in Campania (Plin. *Ep.* 3.7.8), Silius Italicus had considerable sociopolitical and material heft; Statius had to compete on literary grounds.[54] Underlying this poem is a silent conflict over who has the stronger claim as Virgil's successor. Statius' spatial location "on the margin" (54) of Virgil's tomb is a programmatic act of poetic aggression over the rights to Virgil's mantle. Sitting at Virgil's tomb in the shadow of Vesuvius, Statius presents himself as an innovative poet who surpasses Virgil (and Silius) in writing a second epic, and who accommodates Naples to the key Virgilian genre of epic as well as to the silvan Muse.

5 At the Tomb of Statius' Father

The role of Parthenope as both Statius' poetic Muse and symbol of the city's resilience emerges also in *Silv.* 5.3, where Statius situates himself at another tomb, his father's. In this poem, a funerary tribute, Statius praises his father as a distinguished Neapolitan poet and teacher.[55] Along with Virgil (*magni … magistri*, *Silv.* 4.4.55), he is named by Statius as his *magister*, who inspired him to greatness in epic: *te nostra magistro / Thebais urguebat priscorum exordia vatum* ("with you as my teacher our *Thebaid* pressed close upon the output of poets of old," *Silv.* 5.3.233–234). The line of poetic succession that Statius constructs for himself in the *Silvae* is thus extended to include Statius senior, an active intermediary between himself and Virgil.

This succession is marked by the invocation to Parthenope to perform the father's last rites. She is here addressed as a survivor and poetic mother, commanded to lift her head from the ashes for this final act of honouring her distinguished poetic devotee:

---

53 Hinds (2001) 255–257; Morgan (2007) 127–128.
54 Lovatt (2010).
55 On the distinguished literary and pedagogical career of Statius senior see *Silv.* 5.3.116–208; Hardie (1983) 2–14.

> exsere semirutos subito de pulvere vultus,
> Parthenope, crinemque adflato monte adustum
> pone super tumulos et magni funus alumni
> quo non Munychiae quicquam praestantius arces
> doctave Cyrene Sparteve animosa creavit.
>
> (5.3.104–108)

> Raise your half-ruined face from the sudden dust, Parthenope, and place on the tomb and body of your great foster son a lock of hair that has been singed by the breath of the mountain; neither the towers of Athens nor learned Cyrene or spirited Sparta created anything more distinguished.

Grief for the city is thus entwined with grief for the father. As Gibson points out, the architectural term *semirutos* ("half-ruined") neatly describes the physiognomy of the Siren while also evoking the physical condition of the city.[56] Although Naples suffered less than other cities in the region, Taylor argues that the eruption of 79 CE must have covered it with at least a metre of ash.[57] The chiastic phrase *crinemque adflato monte adustum* graphically describes the physical effects of the eruption, the mountain's poisonous "breath" of gases and its fires. At line 105, however, Gibson, prefers to read *solutum* ("disordered") over Heinsius' emendation *adustum* (for M's *sepultum*), on the grounds that a single burnt lock of hair is hardly a suitable offering.[58] Yet in this post-Vesuvian landscape references to ash and to fire, standard features in describing an eruption, vividly conflate the imagery of the poet's funeral and the city's ruin. If we retain Shackleton Bailey's reading *adustum*, then the Siren's offering of a singed lock of hair at the tomb of Statius' father evocatively links the two tragedies, the death of Statius' father, Parthenope's beloved poet, and the physical catastrophe that has befallen the region; the Siren mourns a double loss. But the image of Parthenope here, half-buried in ash and with burnt hair, is also one of resilience. Despite her dreadful circumstances, she performs the proper rites for her poet, who is ranked here among Greece's finest poets and is honoured by a new poem by the even more distinguished literary son; his poetic genius and successful new epic, the *Thebaid*, are celebrated later in the poem (209–238).

The term *alumni* applied to Statius' father (106) acknowledges that although he was not born in Naples, but rather the Roman *municipium* of Velia, he was made an honorary citizen of Naples (127–130), where he taught as a *grammaticus*

---

56 Gibson (2006a) 305.
57 Taylor (2015) 293. Cf. Mart. 4.4.7 *cuncta iacent flammis et tristi mersa favilla*, with Watson/Watson (2003) 335–336.
58 Gibson (2006a) 306. Courtney (1992) retains *sepultum*.

and had many successes in literary competitions as well as abroad (112–115).⁵⁹ The compliment to Statius' father extends to his inclusion within a distinguished genealogy of poets.⁶⁰ Comparison of Parthenope to Greek cities and regions associated with fostering literary excellence—Athens, referred to with the rare Greek adjective *Munychiae*,⁶¹ Cyrene, birthplace of the learned Hellenistic poet Callimachus, and Sparta, referred to here as possibly the home of the seventh-century poet Tyrtaeus, known for his innovative elegiac poetry—suggest that Naples is now a major literary rival in the Roman imperial world to the old Greek cities, with the elder and younger Statius major contributing factors to her eminence. Through the firmly Hellenic character of his father's poetry and his teachings—the poem provides the list of Greek texts that Statius senior assigned to his students (146–158)—Statius acknowledges an important feature of Neapolitan culture, its philhellenism. Yet as Bonadeo argues, Statius represents himself in *Silv.* 5.3 as going beyond the influence of his father by his successful engagement with Roman models also, in particular Virgil. As in *Silv.* 4.4, the tomb of a distinguished literary predecessor becomes the site for outlining a literary-historical process of "competitive mimesis" whereby new talents build upon their predecessors' achievements and surpass them.⁶² Despite the funerary imagery of this brief address to Parthenope, the positive connotations of *creavit* (108) acknowledge in gendered terms the continuing recreative powers of Naples' mythical founder for son as well as for biological and literary "fathers."

6 Moving Mountains

In *Silv.* 2.2 and 3.1, Statius expands the range of his "minor poetry" by engaging directly with a significant epic trope, domination of nature.⁶³ These two poems describe the villa of Statius' patrons and friends, the wealthy freedman Pollius Felix and his wife Polla, which was located on the rugged southern arm of the

---

59 Hardie (1983) 2–14.
60 Gibson (2006a) 306–307.
61 Attested in Greek inscriptions and a *hapax* in Ovid (*Met.* 2.709); see Bömer (1969) 405. An inscription found in Athens suggests that Statius senior had success in poetic competitions there; see Clinton (1973).
62 Bonadeo (2007).
63 The origins of the trope lay with the cutting down of oaks from Mount Ida for Patroclus' funeral (Hom. *Il.* 23.117–122).

Bay of Naples near Sorrento; it provided an important artistic refuge for Statius.[64] As Dufallo has argued, a particular feature of Flavian poetry is the patron's provision of an artistically stimulating environment that gives the poet the freedom to write in its praise. This, in addition to endorsement of the poet's work, is the patron's gift.[65] But unusual in *Silv.* 2.2 and 3.1 is the poet's representation of his patron as engaged in a heroic struggle to create that environment in a rugged and resistant landscape. As I have argued elsewhere, the construction of a villa on a rocky clifftop near Sorrento involves a new form of heroic conflict, one against a harsh, obdurate nature that is aided by technology and is directed to material and artistic ends.[66] Domination of nature takes on new urgency in the post-Vesuvian landscape and is given implicit licence by continuing proof of the volcano's arbitrary, destructive powers. The villa owner, Pollius, is represented as a soldier and farmer, heroically taming a harsh, rocky landscape to create from the wilderness an intellectual and artistic utopia that attracts the poet Statius, and even the Siren (*Silv.* 2.2.52–62; 3.1.117–135, 166–170). As described by Statius in *Silv.* 2.2 and 3.1, Pollius' villa provides a vivid example of a post-Vesuvian landscape where nature has been tamed and brilliantly transformed in harmony with social and cultural imperatives.

Pollius follows a long tradition of technological incursions into the rugged Campanian landscape, starting with the causeway traditionally built by Hercules.[67] Ambitious engineering works continued under various emperors, beginning with Augustus' Portus Iulius connecting Lake Avernus to the sea.[68] Imperial power was effectively expressed by the ability to reorganize and transcend nature. It could also easily be formulated in negative rhetorical terms as an example of imperial hubris. Caligula exploited the land and the imperial budget with his mania for building villas (Suet. *Cal.* 37.2–3); Nero attempted to build a canal from Campania to Rome, a failed experiment that to his own day, Tacitus remarks bitterly, left its marks of futility on the land (*Ann.* 15.42). Pollius resembles these imperial builders in that, like Caligula and Nero, he levels mountains for plains (*Silv.* 2.2.54; Suet. *Cal.* 37.3; Tac. *Ann.* 15.42), and he builds, like Caligula, with incredible speed (*incredibili ... celeritate*, Suet. *Cal.* 37.3; *Silv.* 3.1.134–138). Yet

---

[64] On the origins and career of Pollius Felix see Newlands (2011) 21, 153–154; on Pollius and his wife see Dewar (2015) 41–49.
[65] Dufallo (2013) 208.
[66] Newlands (2002) 154–198, (2012) 151–153.
[67] See note 16 above.
[68] Verg. *G.* 2.161–164; Leonard (2015) 142.

consistently Pollius' domination of nature in Statius' post-Vesuvian world is represented as beneficial and successful, directed to creating a safe, peaceful environment in line with the tenets of Epicureanism. Unlike Virgil's farmer of the *Georgics*, he consistently masters nature. His heroic endeavours are in close metaphorical alignment, moreover, with the poetics of the swiftly composed, yet elaborately descriptive *Silvae* which flowed with pleasant haste from Statius' pen (*quadam festinandi voluptate fluxerunt*, 1 *praef.* 3–4).

Significantly, although a fine view was an important aesthetic feature of a villa's design, Vesuvius itself is not mentioned in this description of Pollius' villa. Any visitor to the Bay of Naples today is struck by the dominance of Vesuvius from virtually any point of view on the Bay. But in Statius' description of Pollius' villa, which we are told has countless viewing points (*Silv.* 2.2.72–73), there is no visual evidence of the volcano. In the earlier process of leveling the ground for the building, "a mountain is ordered to retreat" (*iussumque recedere montem*, 2.2.59), a euphemistic expression for the blasting of a mountain by engineers that may well be a coded reference to the removal of Vesuvius, the dominating mountain of the region, from the view. [69]

The selective topography of *Silv.* 2.2 also involves an editing of Virgil's epic landscapes. Pollius' villa includes a view of the islands of Prochyta and Inarime (76), two of several sites in literary tradition where the giants, after their defeat by the gods, were restlessly imprisoned, creating volcanic activity. In a striking simile (*Aen.* 9.710–716), Virgil compares the crash of a slain warrior to the collapse of a harbour pier in the Bay of Naples, which makes the islands shudder (715–716): *tum sonitu Prochyta alta tremit durumque cubile / Inarime Iovis imperiis imposta Typhoeo* ("then at the crash lofty Prochyta trembles and Inarime, her rocky bed placed over Typhoeus by Jupiter's commands").[70] In Virgil's epic simile, the Bay of Naples appears as the site of gigantomachy and of overly ambitious engineering. In his pairing of the two islands Statius alludes to Virgil's simile, yet without mentioning volcanic or gigantic activity (2.2.76), *haec videt Inarimen, illinc Prochyta aspera paret* ("this one looks at Inarime, from here rugged Prochyta appears"). Virgil made low-lying Prochyta mountainous (*alta*) and thus more "epic." But Statius' Prochyta is simply "rugged." In this appropriation of Virgil's epic geography, the view from Pollius' villa remains ordered and attrac-

---

69 Cf. the "malignant mountain" that temporarily blocks Pollius' construction of a temple to Hercules on his estate, *solidus contra riget umbo maligni /montis* ("the solid mass of a malignant mountain protrudes, stiff and unyielding opposite you," *Silv.* 3.1.110–111).
70 On this simile see Hardie (1994) 223–224.

tive, a sign not only of superior technology but also of a poetic art that can accommodate the creative peace associated with pastoral poetry to a built, controlled environment.

The finest and most exclusive room in the villa, the *diaeta*, is oriented to a view north, thus avoiding the area of greatest volcanic devastation. It offers the most attractive view over the Bay, which is of Naples itself:[71]

> una tamen cunctis, procul eminet una diaetis
> quae tibi Parthenopen derecto limite ponti
> ingerit ...
>   [...]
> omnia Chalcidicas turres obversa salutant.
> macte animo, quod Graia probas, quod Graia frequentas
> arva ...
>
> (2.2.82–84; 94–96)

> One special room stands out, one room far above the rest which presents you with Parthenope by a straight line over the sea ... all the room's marbles face the Chalcidian (Neapolitan) towers in greeting. A blessing on your mind, that you favour Greek things and inhabit Greek country.

The *diaeta* is decorated with splendid, coloured marbles, transported from across the empire. This one small room is a metonym both of its wealthy, cultured owners and of the broader cultural traditions of imperial Naples. A brief but vivid catalogue of the marbles (85–93) forms the climax of Statius' ecphrasis of Pollius' villa, bringing into sharp focus the central theme of nature's domination while also reflecting the dynamic features of Statius' poetic art.

Coloured marbles were central to the discourse of imperial luxury, but they have a wider discursive function here.[72] Statius' elevated ecphrasis of coloured marbles exploits the intermedial relationship between the building and decorating of the villa and the composition of his elaborately descriptive *Silvae*. Statius here gives an epic dimension to epigram's attention to intricately wrought, sophisticated works of art. Like the gems described by the Hellenistic poet Posidippus, the marbles are characterized by light and a play of colour, but on a monumental scale:[73]

---

[71] Pollius' *diaeta* resembles Augustus' "Syracuse," a retreat at the top of his house; see Rimell (2015) 30.
[72] Bradley (2006).
[73] Elsner (2014) 156–7.

> Hic et Amyclaei caesum de monte Lycurgi
> quod viret et molles imitatur rupibus herbas;
> hic Nomadum lucent flaventia saxa Thasosque
> et Chios et gaudens fluctus aequare Carystos.
>
> (2.2.90–93)
>
> Here too is green marble hewn from the mountain of Amyclaean Lycurgus which imitates soft grass with its rocks; here gleam the yellow stones of Numidia and Thasus and Chios and Carystos that delights in rivaling the waves.

The marbles of Pollius' *diaeta* come from Egypt, from Africa, and from the Greek islands. Quarried from the harsh rock of mountains and transported long distances to Italy, marbles also represent a triumph of human technological skill and aesthetics within an imperial, global trade in luxury goods.[74] The world's geology is mapped onto the *diaeta* in an educated but playful discourse that mediates between art and nature.[75] Hard, immobile marble, for instance, resembles soft grass or the fluctuating waves of the sea. In the *Silvae* the metamorphosis of stone into beautiful, polished marble represents the ultimate domination and containment of wild, obdurate mountains. This small but microcosmic room demonstrates an imperial mastery of space and material wealth that works in tandem with a paradoxically exuberant "aesthetics of containment."[76]

Elsner, in a move away from Bourdieu's approach to art as primarily a mark of social distinction and cultural capital, coins the term "lithic poetics" to describe the epigrams on gems composed by the Hellenistic poet Posidippus.[77] By "lithic poetics" he refers to the forging of artistry—visual and literary—out of natural matter and the way in which stones mediate between nature and culture. The same term could apply here to Statius' catalogue of marbles, adapted to an imperial context. These grand, variegated marbles with their gem-like qualities reflect the penchant of Statius' new Silvan poetics for vivid and paradoxical effects. They demonstrate the imperial recasting of epigram on a grand scale—not tiny gems but great marble slabs or columns brought from all over the empire at great cost and effort and difficult to carve. As the most monumental of materials, marble has considerable semantic weight. Associated with permanence, its *gravitas* counteracts the smallness of the *diaeta* in which they shine, and the brevity of the poem in which they are celebrated. Marbles represent here not moral decadence but the power of human technology and of literary genius to make magical

---

74 On the challenges of transporting marble see Lapatin (2015) 220–222.
75 Bradley (2006) 3–5.
76 Rimell (2015) 30–31.
77 Elsner (2014); on Bourdieu and Statius see Zeiner (2005).

and beautiful the harshness of stone—to tame wild nature, creating physical and moral order, and, with wonderful swiftness and concise art, to make lasting poetry.

The spatial dynamics of the *diaeta* involve both an inward and outward movement. The marble room faces the "Chalcidian towers" of Naples in greeting (94), an expression of mutual regard for the Bay's long association with Greek culture. But the expression *Parthenopen ... ingerit*, which taken literally means "brings in Parthenope" (with characteristic slippage between city and Siren) also situates Pollius' villa in the dominant position of host. The wording suggests more than the primacy of the view of Naples or Pollius' philhellenism. The Siren Parthenope, who traditionally drew men to their deaths, is drawn to Pollius' villa in a metaphorical transfer of Virgil's Parthenope to new poetic traditions.[78] By bringing Parthenope into his opulent room through the view, Pollius' villa appears as an alternative "Parthenope", a centre of literary excellence in the post-Vesuvian imperial world. The Siren implicitly endorses Pollius' distinction both as a poet in his own right (2.2.113–115) and as a discriminating patron of Statius, many of whose *Silvae* were composed at Pollius' villa, *multos ex illis in sinu tuo subito natos* ("many of my poems were born suddenly in your lap," 3 *praef.* 3–4). As Parthenope nurtured the youthful Virgil, *Vergilium me ... dulcis Parthenope alebat* (G. 4. 563–564), so too Pollius, a successful freedman, has virtually assumed the role of Virgil's Parthenope as nurturer of one of the most prestigious poets of his day, a role that undoubtedly gives him the gift of great cultural prestige in turn. Elsewhere in the poem the Siren flies from her islands near Sorrento to hear "better songs" (116–117). The expression *Parthenopen ... ingerit* is a metaphor for a literary *translatio imperii* whereby Virgil's Parthenope has become truly imperial in her global perspective, with Greek and Roman culture, moreover, melded in the figure of her most distinguished native son, Statius.

7 Conclusion

To sum up, the local founding myth of Parthenope plays a key role in the *Silvae* both in the narrative of post-Vesuvian recovery and in Statius' self-positioning in Roman literary tradition. As a founding figure Parthenope is associated in the Neapolitan *Silvae* with the arts of peace, not the arts of war; in the post-Vesuvian landscape heroic energy is turned to rebuilding and regeneration. Gendered as

---

[78] See further Newlands (2012) 153–155.

female, Parthenope also represents both literary continuity and change. Through Parthenope, Statius interrogates Rome's cultural primacy and Virgil's confinement of Parthenope to non-epic work. In Naples Statius writes both epic poetry and new forms of "minor poetry" that experiment with epic tropes in a new socially and culturally fluid environment. In the *Silvae* Statius reflects his pride as a native son of Naples and inheritor of its distinguished Greek cultural traditions, while linking himself to his distinguished Roman predecessor, Virgil, and to Roman literary traditions. Thus in the *Silvae* Statius represents Naples as the centre not simply of "minor poetry," as it was for Virgil, but of a dynamic, hybrid, imperial culture.[79]

Bessone has argued that Statius "constructs himself as a living myth, an inspired *aoidos* invested with an outstanding social function: by recalling the mythic origins of the poet's trade, he ennobles the role he plays in imperial society."[80] Statius closely implicates this mythic, poetic self with his native city and its mythic, poetic founder who established a distinguished line of literary succession. Statius boldly bypasses Silius Italicus, his literary contemporary on the Bay of Naples, to assert his position as the most prestigious poet of his generation and as Virgil's rightful successor. At the conclusion of *Silv.* 3.2, a poem that Putnam has shown is deeply indebted to Virgil's *Aeneid*, Statius, finishing his *Thebaid* in Naples, refers to his epic as *laboratas ... Thebas* ("beaboured Thebes," 143).[81] Here then it seems is a response to Virgil's "ignoble leisure" (*ignobilis oti*, *G.* 4.564). Parthenope now inspires not only the generically ambitious *Silvae* but the highest, most challenging of genres, epic poetry.

Bibliography

Alcock, Susan (2002), *Archaeologies of the Greek Past, Landscapes, Monuments, and Memories*, Cambridge.
Angelova, Dilana (2015), *Sacred Founders*, Berkeley/Los Angeles.
Augoustakis, Antony (ed.) (2010), *Brill's Companion to Silius Italicus*, Leiden.
Augoustakis, Antony (ed.) (2014), *Flavian Poetry and its Greek Past*, Leiden.
Barchiesi, Alessandro (2015), *Homeric Effects in Vergil's Narrative*, Princeton.
Bessone, Federica (2014), "*Polis*, Court, Empire: Greek Culture, Roman Society, and the System of Genres in Statius' Poetry", in: Augoustakis (2014) 214–233.
Bettini, Maurizio (1976), "L'epitaffio di Virgilio", in: *Dialoghi di archeologia 9–10*, 439–448.

---

[79] On the "three hearts of Statius", Greek, Roman and Neapolitan see Rosati (2011).
[80] Bessone (2014) 215.
[81] Putnam (2017), esp. 134–137.

Bömer, Franz (1969), *P. Ovidius Naso*, Metamorphosen, *Buch I–III*, Heidelberg.
Bömer, Franz (1986), *P. Ovidius Naso*, Metamorphosen, *Buch XIV–XV*, Heidelberg.
Bonadeo, Alessia (2007), "I classici nella *paideia* di P. Papinio (Stat. *silv.* 5.3)", in: Bonadeo/Romano (2007) 160–176.
Bonadeo, Alessia/Canobbio, Alberto/Gasti, Fabio (eds.) (2011), *Fillenismo e Identità Romana in Età Flavia*, Pavia.
Bonadeo, Alessia/Romano, Elisa (eds.) (2007), *Dialogando con il passato*, Florence.
Bradley, Mark (2006), "Colour and Marble in Early Imperial Rome", in: *PCPhS* 52, 1–22.
Citroni, Mario (1989), "Marziale e la Letteratura per i Saturnali (poetica dell'intrattenimento e cronologia della pubblicazione dei libri)", in: *ICS* 14, 201–226.
Clinton, Kevin (1973), "Publius Papinius St[---] at Eleusis", in: *TAPhA* 103, 79–82.
Coleman, Kathleen (1988), *Statius*, Silvae *Book 4*, Oxford.
Connors, Catherine (2015), "In the Land of the Giants: Greek and Roman Discourses on Vesuvius and the Phlegraean Fields", in: *ICS* 40, 121–137.
Comparetti, Domenico (1946), *Virgilio nel Medio Evo*, II, 2nd ed. with Giorgio Pasquali, Florence.
Damon, Cynthia (2003), *Tacitus, Histories, Book 1*, Cambridge.
D'Arms, John H. (1970), *Romans on the Bay of Naples*, Cambridge, MA.
Dewar, Michael (2014), *Leisured Resistance*, London.
Dufallo, Basil (2013), *The Captor's Image: Greek Culture in Roman Ecphrasis*, Oxford.
Elsner, Jaś (2014), "Lithic Poetics: Posidippus and his Stones", in: *Ramus* 43.2, 152–172.
Fowler, Don (2000), *Roman Constructions: Readings in Postmodern Latin*, Oxford.
Frederiksen, Martin (1984), *Campania*, Rome.
Gibson, Bruce (2006a), *Statius*, Silvae *Liber 5*, Oxford.
Gibson, Bruce (2006b), "The *Silvae* and Epic," in: Nauta *et al.* (2006) 163–183.
Hardie, Alex (1983), *Statius and the* Silvae: *Poets, Patrons and Epideixis in the Graeco-Roman World*, Liverpool.
Hardie, Philip (1994), *Vergil,* Aeneid *Book IX*, Cambridge.
Harrison, Robert Pogue (2002), "Hic Jacet", in: Mitchell (2002) 349–364.
Hendrix, Harald (2015), "City Branding and the Antique: Naples in Early Modern City Guides", in: Hughes/Buongiovanni (2015) 217–241.
Heyworth, Stephen J. (ed.) (2007), *Classical Constructions*, Oxford.
Hinds, Stephen (2001), "Cinna, Statius, and 'Immanent Literary History' in the Cultural Economy", in: Schmidt (2001) 221–265.
Hughes, Jessica/Buongiovanni, Claudio (eds.) (2015), *Remembering Parthenope*, Oxford.
James, Sharon L. (1995), "Establishing Rome with the Sword", in: *AJPh* 116, 623–637.
Lapatin, Kenneth (2015), "Materials and Technique of Greek and Roman Art", in: Marconi (2015) 203–240.
Leonard, Amy (2015), "From *otium* to *imperium*: Propertius and Augustus at Baiae", in: *ICS* 40.1, 139–154.
Lo Cascio, Elio/Storchi Marino, Alfredina (eds.) (2001), *Modalità Insediative e strutture agrarie nell'Italia meridionale in età romana,* Bari.
Lovatt, Helen (2010), "Interplay: Silius and Statius in the Games of *Punica* 16", in: Augoustakis (2010) 155–178.
Marconi, Clemente (ed.) (2015), *The Oxford Handbook of Greek and Roman Architecture*, Oxford.
Mitchell, William J.T. (ed.) (2002), *Landscape and Power*, 2nd ed., Chicago.

Morgan, Llewelyn (2007), "*Natura Narratur*: Tullius Laurea's Elegy for Cicero (Plin. *Nat.* 31, 8)", in: Heyworth (2007) 113–140.
Muecke, Frances (2007), "Hannibal at the 'Fields of Fire': A 'Wasteful Excursion?' (Silius Italicus *Punica* 12, 113–57)", in: *MD* 58, 73–91.
Nauta, Ruurd R./Van Dam, Harm-Jan/Smolenaars, Johannes J.L. (eds.) (2006), *Flavian Poetry*, Leiden.
Newlands, Carole (2002), *Statius'* Silvae *and the Poetics of Empire*, Cambridge.
Newlands, Carole (2010), "The Eruption of Vesuvius in the Epistles of Statius and Pliny", in: Woodman/Miller (2010) 206–221.
Newlands, Carole (2011), *Statius'* Silvae *Book 2*, Cambridge.
Newlands, Carole (2012), *Statius, Poet between Rome and Naples*, Bristol.
Putnam, Michael C.J. (2016), "The Sense of Two Endings: How Virgil and Statius Conclude", in: *ICS* 41.1, 85–149.
Putnam, Michael C.J. (2017), "Statius *Silvae* 3.2: Reading Travel", in: *ICS* 42.1, 83–139.
Rimell, Victoria (2015), *Closure of Space in Roman Poetics: Empire's Inward Turn*, Cambridge.
Rosati, Gianpiero (2011), "I *tria corda* di Stazio, poeta greco, romano e napoletano", in: Bonadeo *et al.* (2011) 15–34.
Rutter, Keith N. (1979), *Campanian Coinages 475–380 BC*, Edinburgh.
Schmidt, Ernst (ed.) (2001), *L'histoire littéraire immanente dans la poésie latine*, Vandœuvres-Geneva.
Soricelli, Gianluca (2001), "La regione vesuviana tra secondo e sesto secolo d.C.", in: Lo Cascio/Storchi Marino (2001) 455–472.
Squire, Michael (2011), *The* Iliad *in a Nutshell: Visualising Epic on the* Tabulae Iliacae, Cambridge.
Szelest, Hanna (1972), "Mythologie und ihre Rolle in den *Silvae* des Statius", in: *Eos* 60, 309–317.
Stärk, Ekkehard (1995), *Kampanien als geistige Landschaft*, Munich.
Stocks, Claire (2014), *The Roman Hannibal*, Liverpool.
Taylor, Rabun (2015), "Roman Neapolis and the Landscape of Disaster", in: *JAH* 3.2, 282–326.
Thomas, Richard F. (1988), *Virgil, Georgics, Volume 1, Books I–II*, Cambridge.
Watson, Lindsay/Watson, Patricia (2003), *Martial, Select Epigrams*, Cambridge.
Woodman, Anthony J./Miller, John F. (eds.) (2010), *Proximis Poetis*, Leiden.
Zeiner, Noelle (2005), *Nothing Ordinary Here: Statius as Creator of Distinction in the* Silvae, London.

Neil W. Bernstein
Quantitative and Qualitative Perspectives on the Use of Poetic Tradition in Silius Italicus' *Punica*

I examine intertextuality in Silius' *Punica* from two complementary perspectives in this paper. These are the philological commentator's qualitative perspective on the poem's individual words and phrases, and the statistician's quantitative perspective on text reuse in the Latin hexameter tradition.[1] The goal of the paper is to understand Silius' relationship to the poetic tradition through both of these approaches: one involving new tools for computer-assisted word searching, the other employing the familiar tools of close reading and connoisseurship of Roman poetic tradition.

1 Quantitative Perspectives on Silius' *Punica* and the Latin Epic Tradition

The first part of the paper focuses on Silius' text reuse in the context of the hexameter tradition as a whole. My discussion summarizes a large-scale collaborative study of text reuse.[2] Using the *Tesserae* interface, my co-authors and I analyzed text reuse in 24 hexameter collections across seven centuries, from Lucretius through Corippus.[3] We tested each text against each of its predecessors,

---

[1] See Coffee and Gawley in this volume for a similar quantitative, macrophilological approach. Coffee and Forstall 2016 provided an earlier example of the methodology employed here in investigating large-scale comparisons of intertextual relatedness. They likewise began from Tesserae results in order to arrive at macro-scale conclusions. These include the following findings: a) that Statius in the *Thebaid* has a notably high number of parallels to the Aeneid which poets between Virgil's time and his left "unused"; and b) that Claudian's *De Consulatu Stilichonis* engages significantly more intensively with Lucan's *Bellum Civile* than does his *De Raptu Proserpinae*. The present chapter focuses on Silius' relationship to prior tradition and compares the actual incidence of shared language with the baseline of predicted occurrences.

[2] Bernstein *et al.* (2015).

[3] These collections include: Lucretius, *De Rerum Natura*; Virgil, *Eclogues, Georgics, Aeneid*; Horace, *Satires, Epistles, Ars Poetica*; Ovid, *Metamorphoses*; Manilius, *Astronomica*; Persius, *Satires*; Lucan, *Bellum Civile*; [Anonymous] *Ilias Latina*; Valerius Flaccus, *Argonautica*; Statius, *Thebaid*,

yielding 276 pairs of source and target texts. *Tesserae* (tesserae.caset.buffalo.edu) lists all matches of two-lexeme phrases in a large corpus of poetic and prose texts from the Greco-Roman literary corpus. A scoring feature then automatically assigns a score to each match by applying a formula accounting for the distance between the matched lexemes in the parallel contexts and the frequency of their occurrence in the source and target texts. Thus, for example, *Tesserae* matches the following passages:

> Stat. *Theb.* 4.260: audaci Martis percussus amore, "struck by a bold desire for warfare".

> Verg. *Aen.* 9.197: magno laudum percussus amore, "struck by a great desire for glory".

The *Tesserae* scoring system signals the potential interpretive significance of the match by assigning it a relatively high score. The version of the *Tesserae* scoring system available at the time assigned it a score of 8 on a logarithmic scale of 1–10; the current version uses a 15-point scale. Using the *Tesserae* Batch Processing option (http://tess-dev.caset.buffalo.edu/html/batch.php), we recorded the number of "hits" (phrases sharing at least two matching lexemes) in each of our 276 pairs of source and target texts.[4] Hits may include exact matches of inflected forms, such as Verg. *G.* 1.493 *exesa inueniet scabra robigine pila* ~ Stat. *Theb.* 3.582 *tunc fessa putri robigine pila* (lemmata: *robigo*, *pilum*). Matches may also occur among differently inflected forms of the same lexeme, such as Verg. *G.* 2.64 *solido Paphiae de robore myrtus* ~ Stat. *Theb.* 4.300 *hi Paphias myrtos a stirpe recuruant* (lexemes: *Paphius*, *myrtus*). False lemma matches also sometimes occur, such as Verg. *G.* 4.308 *ossibus umor* ~ Stat. *Theb.* 4.698 *ora ... umor*. Here *ossibus* ("bones") and *ora* ("faces") are inflected forms of two different lexemes, both of which share the lemma *os*. Since such false matches occur infrequently, we did not expect them to affect the results significantly.

We then weighted high scoring hits (*Tesserae* scores of 7 and above), normalized the results from texts of greatly differing lengths, and scaled the results to determine a baseline rate of text reuse among poems in the Latin hexameter tradition. The statistical method employed in this study is principal component analysis (PCA). It was developed by Wei Lin, a statistician in the Ohio University Mathematics department. The formula used to weight and scale the *Tesserae* results is as follows:

Achilleid; Silius Italicus, *Punica*; Juvenal, *Satires*; Juvencus, *Historia Evangelica*; Ausonius, *Mosella*; Claudian, *De Raptu Proserpinae*, *De Quarto Consulatu Honorii Augusti*, *De Bello Gildonico*, *De Consulatu Stilichonis*; and Corippus, *Iohannis*.

4 Searches were conducted by Chris Forstall on 2 May 2014.

- $C_{obs} = 0.057C_7 + 0.225C_8 + C_9 + 6.286C_{10} + 227.744C_{11}$ (observed count)
- $C_{exp} = -19.591 + 1.311w_s + 1.208w_t$ (expected count)
- residual count $(r) = C_{obs} - C_{exp}$
- C = weighted hit count. C_7 = *Tesserae* score of 7, C_8 = *Tesserae* score of 8, etc.
- w_s = word count of source
- w_t = word count of target
- r is determined by subtracting expected weighted count of *Tesserae* hits (based on length of texts) from actual weighted count.

We used this baseline to calculate measures of the relative intensity of text reuse (the residual, or r-value) for each of the 276 pairs of texts in the study. We expect pairs of long texts to produce a large number of meaningful hits and pairs of short texts to produce a small number of meaningful hits. So in determining that Silius Italicus' *Punica* reuses the *Aeneid* intensively, we take into account that both works are quite long. The r-value is a measure of the *intensity* of text reuse that takes into account the lengths of the source and target texts in each pair. Table 1 lists text pairs with high positive residual counts:

Tab. 1: Text pairs with high positive residual counts

Source text	Target text	Residual (r)	Standardized r
Verg. *G.*	Verg. *Aen.*	0.280	4.571
Ov. *Met.*	Auson. *Mos.*	0.073	3.830
Ov. *Met.*	*Ilias Lat.*	0.719	2.565
Verg. *Ecl.*	Verg. *G.*	0.603	2.153
Verg. *Aen.*	*Ilias Lat.*	0.594	2.119
Verg. *G.*	Ov. *Met.*	0.560	1.999
Verg. *Aen.*	Sil. *Pun.*	0.540	1.928

The text pairs with high positive r-values listed in Table 1 show far more reuse than we would expect from texts of comparable length, and so point to a marked interest in text reuse. Some examples include reuse by the same author, such as Virgil's reuse of the *Georgics* in the *Aeneid*. Other texts such as Ausonius' *Mosella* show an intense engagement with a privileged predecessor, in this case Ovid's *Metamorphoses*.

Pairs with r-value close to 0 show reuse at an expected rate—that is, neither greater nor lesser than any other two comparable pairs in our set. Thus Juvenal's

Satires, for example, do not show a particularly intense reuse of Horatian satire or the Horatian *Epistles*. Table 2 lists text pairs with residual counts close to 0:

Tab. 2: Text pairs with residual counts close to 0

Source text	Target text	Residual (r)	Standardized r
Verg. *Aen.*	Man. *Astr.*	0.011	0.039
Hor. *Ars P.*	Pers.	0.008	0.028
Hor. *Epist.*	Juv. *Sat.*	0.003	0.010
Verg. *Ecl.*	Val. Fl.	-0.003	-0.012
Ov. *Met.*	Val. Fl.	-0.006	-0.020
Hor. *Sat.*	Juv. *Sat.*	-0.007	-0.026
Verg. *Ecl.*	Claud. *Rapt.*	-0.009	-0.032

Pairs with high negative *r*-values show far less reuse than we would expect from texts of comparable length, and so point to a marked avoidance of text reuse. Satire, for example, uses pedestrian vocabulary and talks about everyday concerns. So it should not come as a surprise to see that the residual scores reflect the strong separation of this genre from the more elevated style and subject matter of epic. Table 3 lists text pairs with high negative residual counts:

Tab. 3: Text pairs with high negative residual counts

Source text	Target text	Residual (r)	Standardized r
Stat. *Theb.*	Juv. *Sat.*	-0.434	-1.548
Man. *Astr.*	Pers.	-0.468	-1.669
Hor. *Sat.*	Claud. *Rapt.*	-0.485	-1.731
Verg. *Aen.*	Pers.	-0.537	-1.917
Pers.	Claud. *Rapt.*	-0.579	-2.065

These calculations enable us to discuss text reuse in Silius in quantitative terms through the scores provided by the *Tesserae* program, and thus to compare the patterns of text reuse in the *Punica* with the other Roman hexameter poems.

Table 4 excerpts some of the residuals for Statius' *Thebaid* and Silius Italicus' *Punica* when paired with other texts:

Tab. 4: Residuals for selected text pairs involving the *Thebaid* and *Punica*

Source	Target	Residual (r)	Standardized r	Source	Target	Residual (r)	Standardized r
Verg. *Aen.*	Sil. *Pun.*	0.54	1.928	Verg. *Aen.*	Stat. *Theb.*	0.299	1.067
Verg. *G.*	Sil. *Pun.*	0.433	1.546	Verg. *G.*	Stat. *Theb.*	0.186	0.664
Ov. *Met.*	Sil. *Pun.*	0.146	0.52	Ov. *Met.*	Stat. *Theb.*	0.037	0.131
Luc. *BC*	Sil. *Pun.*	0.126	0.45	Luc. *BC*	Stat. *Theb.*	-0.075	-0.268
Val. Fl.	Sil. *Pun.*	0.076	0.272	Val. Fl.	Stat. *Theb.*	0.064	0.229
Stat. *Theb.*	Sil. *Pun.*	0.057	0.204		Stat. *Theb.*		
Man. *Astr.*	Sil. *Pun.*	-0.013	-0.046	Man. *Astr.*	Stat. *Theb.*	-0.189	-0.673
Lucr.	Sil. *Pun.*	-0.092	-0.329	Lucr.	Stat. *Theb.*	-0.363	-1.296
Hor. *Sat.*	Sil. *Pun.*	-0.205	-0.731	Hor. *Sat.*	Stat. *Theb.*	-0.387	-1.381

The *Tesserae* results provide some alternative perspectives on text reuse from the traditional scholarly assumptions. The intensity of text reuse of both the *Georgics* and *Aeneid* by the Valerius Flaccus' *Argonautica*, Statius' *Thebaid*, and *Achilleid* is indeed higher than average, falling between 0.160 and 0.299. But it is not as high as the intensity of reuse of any of Virgil's three works by the *Metamorphoses*, falling between 0.323 and 0.560. The Flavian poets accordingly reuse distinctive Virgilian phrases at a lower rate than Virgil's Augustan successor.

The notable exception is the *Punica* of Silius Italicus, which had much higher than average intensity of text reuse when paired with the *Georgics* ($r = 0.433$) and *Aeneid* ($r = 0.540$). Scholarly readers have assumed that Silius reuses distinctive Virgilian phrasing more consistently than any of his Flavian peers: the *Tesserae* data enable us to say how much. Please note, however, that r values simply measure the frequency with which a predecessor's text has been reused, not the originality or creativity of that reuse. For instance, a poet may quote a predecessor's words exactly, but in a completely different and original context. We may think of Aeneas' words to Dido in the Underworld: "unwillingly, queen, I left your shore" (*inuitus, regina, tuo de litore cessi*, *Aen.* 6.460), that echo in an unexpected context the words spoken by the lock of hair in Catullus' *Coma Berenices* ("unwillingly, o queen, I left your head," *inuita, o regina, tuo de uertice cessi*, Catull.

66.39).[5] *Tesserae* cannot distinguish between this highly creative reuse of Catullus' words and a putatively "uncreative" reuse by another poet; only a human reader can.

For each of our 24 chosen texts, we determined the mean value of *r* for all pairs involving that text (23 pairs each time), and sorted the texts by the results. We considered this to be a measure of the "centrality" of each of our chosen texts within the 24-text set: that is, how often each text reuses earlier texts and is reused by later texts. A text strongly influenced by its predecessors and influential to its successors would have a higher mean *r* than a text more peripheral to the literary tradition of Latin hexameter poetry. Table 5 shows Silius' position on the centrality table:

Tab. 5: Centrality scores for 24 hexameter texts: mean text reuse intensity for all 23 pairs involving that text

Text	Centrality score	Text	Centrality score
Verg. *G.*	0.279	Luc. *BC*	0.006
Ilias Lat.	0.186	Man. *Astr.*	-0.006
Verg. *Aen.*	0.133	Verg. *Ecl.*	-0.018
Stat. *Ach.*	0.117	Val. Fl.	-0.036
Claud. *Stil.*	0.105	Stat. *Theb.*	-0.096
Claud. *Rapt.*	0.088	Juvenc. *EH*	-0.102
Claud. *IV Hon.*	0.086	Juv. *Sat.*	-0.120
Coripp. *Ioh.*	0.078	Hor. *Ars P.*	-0.146
Ov. *Met.*	0.073	Lucr.	-0.151
Auson. *Mos.*	0.057	Hor. *Epist.*	-0.153
Sil. *Pun.*	0.044	Hor. *Sat.*	-0.187
Claud. *Gild.*	0.032	Pers.	-0.27

Virgil's *Georgics* top this list in part because of their brevity. Distinctive phrases from this short text recur frequently across the tradition, with the poet's own *Aeneid* as the first and most significant "receiver" of his earlier work. The works of the Roman satirists are found at the bottom of the list, again as we might expect given the difference of satire's diction from other hexameter genres.

We find Silius Italicus' *Punica* in the positive part of the table, above Lucan's *Bellum Civile* but below Ovid's *Metamorphoses*. These data confirm in objective

---

[5] See the classic discussion at Conte (1996) 88–90.

terms what readers familiar with Silius might have suspected. The Flavian poet reuses phrases from predecessors such as Virgil and Ovid, and is in turn reused by successors such as Claudian and Corippus. But Silius' rate of reuse of his predecessors is not so exceptional as to condemn him as a slavish imitator, and the pattern of reuse of the *Punica* by his successors shows that his distinctive phrases were avidly imitated by the Latin poets of later antiquity.[6]

This is a first step in algorithmic criticism of the hexameter "super-genre".[7] As observed above, *Tesserae* has some limitations which reflect its current state of development, and others which reflect the nature of Latin hexameter poetry. In this initial study, we confirm the value of the lexeme-matching approach by comparing it to the traditional critical narrative of relationships among Latin hexameter poems. Our goal is to model a system of relationships between texts that can frame critics' discussions of the role of individual poems within the tradition. As Johanna Drucker observes in *SpecLab*, "on the surface, a model seems static. In reality it is, like any 'form,' a provocation for a reading, an intervention, an interpretive act."[8] In Drucker's terms, *Tesserae* modeling is a dynamic rather than static approach to textual analysis. New data sets can easily be constructed, whether by using different *Tesserae* parameters or changing the texts in the group under analysis. These future analyses will produce new and different perceptions of the system of relationships among Latin literary texts in other genres, or between other genres and the hexameter super-genre. How we use such analytical tools inevitably alters the way in which we frame questions about intertextuality in the Roman poetic tradition. The following section discusses some examples of qualitative interpretation made possible by the *Tesserae* interface.

2 Qualitative Perspectives on Silius' *Punica* 2 and the Latin Epic Tradition

In this second part of the paper, I briefly discuss from a qualitative perspective some individual examples of text reuse discovered through the use of the *Tesserae* interface. I present two case studies of Silius' role as a mediator of poetic tradition developed from my commentary on *Punica* 2. Silius creatively adapts

---

6 See further Bernstein (2016b).
7 See Hutchinson (2013).
8 Drucker (2009) 16.

two characteristic images from the Roman epic tradition: i) a woman's bared arm and breast; and ii) the image of light wavering upon the water.

2.1 The bared arm and breast

Virgil describes Venus' huntress disguise when she meets Aeneas in Libya as follows:[9]

a) Verg. Aen. 1.320: *nuda genu nodoque sinus collecta fluentis*, "with her knee bare and her flowing robes collected in a knot."

Late in the *Aeneid*, Camilla the Amazon takes the battlefield with one breast bare:

b) Verg. Aen. 11.649: *unum exserta latus pugnae, pharetrata Camilla*, "quiver-bearing Camilla, one breast thrust forward for combat."

The use of the adjective *nudus* in the description of Venus and the accusatives of relation in both passages were noteworthy for Virgil's successors. Valerius combined both passages in his description of the war goddess Bellona:

c) Val. Fl. 3.61: [Bellona] *nuda latus passuque mouens orichalca sonoro*, "Bellona, her breast bare, her bronze weapons clanging as she moves."

The recombinant allusion links Valerius' Bellona to Virgil's Venus (as a goddess) and Camilla (as a warrior). A later description of an Amazon defeated by Hercules similarly recalls both passages:

d) Val. Fl. 5.135: *quae pelta latus atque umeros nudata pharetris*, "stripping the shield from her flank and the quiver from her shoulder."

At the conclusion of *Aeneid* 7, Virgil describes the Italian mothers marveling at Camilla's appearance:

e) Verg. Aen. 7.815–816: *ut fibula crinem / auro internectat*, "how the clasp entwines her hair with gold."

---

9 Adapted from Bernstein (2016c).

Silius' description of the Amazon Asbyte recombines elements of both the Virgilian Venus and Camilla, as well as the Valerian Bellona:[10]

f) Sil. *Pun.* 2.77–79: *religata fluentem / Hesperidum nodo crinem dextrumque feroci / nuda latus Marti*, "The Hesperides' golden gift tied back her flowing hair and her right side was bared for fierce combat."

Asbyte's hair (*fluentem ... crinem*) tied up in a knot (*religata ... nodo*) recalls the knot that collects the flowing robes of Virgil's Venus in (a): *nodoque sinus collecta fluentis*. The use of a golden clasp to tie back her hair recalls Camilla's *fibula* in (e): Silius' *Hesperidum nodo* is a calque on Virgil's *auro*. The second part of Silius' description both recombines aspects of Virgil's Venus and Camilla once more and shows the poet's awareness that his older Flavian contemporary had already done so. Silius adapts the key phrase *nuda latus* from Valerius' description of Bellona in (c) to make his Amazon evoke the war goddess of the *Argonautica* as well as the Amazon of the *Aeneid*.

Silius' description of the goddess Diana of the Aventine Hill, occurring some ten books later in the epic, may constitute self-allusion as well as another learned reuse of the distinctive phrases of Virgil and Valerius:

g) Sil. *Pun.* 12.715: *exsertos auide pugnae nudata lacertos*, "eagerly thrusting forward her bared upper arms for battle."

Nudata with an accusative of relation recalls Valerius' defeated Amazon *umeros nudata pharetris* (d). It is an instance of *oppositio in imitando*, however, as Silius' Diana is one of many gods who will successfully deter Hannibal from assaulting Rome.[11] *Exsertos auide pugnae*, meanwhile, aligns Diana with Virgil's Camilla, *exserta latus pugnae* (b).

Valerius recombines the images of the naked knees of Virgil's Venus with Camilla's bared breast in his descriptions of the war goddess Bellona and a defeated Amazon. Silius in turn recombines Camilla's bared breast with Venus' flowing hair to describe the Amazon Asbyte. In addition, he adapts Valerius' recombined phrase *nuda latus*, and like Valerius applies the phrase to an armed goddess, Aventine Diana. Silius' *Punica* features numerous examples of this distributive form of allusion. By applying the phrases to the same targets as Valerius (an Amazon

---

10 See Uccellini (2006).
11 See Chaudhuri (2014) 231–255.

and an armed goddess), he indicates that his reading of his predecessor has been exhaustive.

In his panegyric for Olybrius and Probinus, the consuls of 395, Claudian adapts words from each of his predecessors in a single remarkable line describing Rome armed in the image of the goddess Minerva:

h) Claud. *Ol. Prob.* 87: *dextrum nuda latus, niueos exserta lacertos*, "her right side bare, thrusting forth her snowy upper arms."

Claudian has recombined Valerius' *nuda latus* (c) with Silius' *dextrum* and *lacertos* (f, g). As the foregoing discussion has demonstrated, each of the Flavian poets' phrases is in turn a recombination of Virgilian motifs. Theme and context support Claudian's recombination of each of his predecessors' motifs in a description of an armed goddess that recalls Silius' Aventine Diana, Valerius' Bellona, Virgil's Venus, and the Amazon warriors of each poet.[12] Rome is a protector goddess like Aventine Diana; she is armed for battle like Bellona and the Amazons; and she is the mother of a race like Venus. Four centuries removed for Virgil, Claudian demonstrates his mastery of the intervening poetic tradition in his "first Latin commission."[13] Some elements of this poetic tradition could be assembled from commentaries; others depended on use of *Tesserae*. The interface enables the rapid collation and visualization of the interrelation between distinctive phrases employed by the Latin poets.

2.2 Light on water

Another characteristic image from the Latin poetic tradition, the wavering of light on the water,[14] provides a further example of qualitative appreciation of text reuse across the epic tradition enabled by the *Tesserae* interface. The Latin poets develop the image across a tradition that begins with Apollonius Rhodius' account of Medea's erotic distress:

---

[12] Taegert (1988) *ad loc.* identifies an echo in Prudentius' image of *Fides*: Prud. *Psych.* 22–23 *pugnatura Fides agresti turbida cultu / nuda umeros intonsa comas exerta lacertos*. Corippus' Rome recalls Claudian's, but transforms the Amazon's breast to a nourishing mother's breast: *In laud. Just.* 1.288–290: *addidit antiquam tendentem bracchia Romam, / exerto et nudam gestantem pectore mammam, / altricem imperii libertatisque parentem*.
[13] Ware (2012) 29. See also Berlincourt (2015) and Wheeler (2007).
[14] Adapted from Bernstein (2016a).

a) Ap. Rhod. *Argon.* 3.755–760
πυκνὰ δέ οἱ κραδίη στηθέων ἔντοσθεν ἔθυιεν,   755
ἠελίου ὥς τίς τε δόμοις ἔνι πάλλεται αἴγλη,
ὕδατος ἐξανιοῦσα τὸ δὴ νέον ἠὲ λέβητι
ἠέ που ἐν γαυλῷ κέχυται, ἡ δ' ἔνθα καὶ ἔνθα
ὠκείῃ στροφάλιγγι τινάσσεται ἀίσσουσα—
ὣς δὲ καὶ ἐν στήθεσσι κέαρ ἐλελίζετο κούρης.   760

Over and over the heart within her breast fluttered wildly, as when a ray of sunlight bounds inside a house as it leaps from water freshly poured into a cauldron or perhaps into a bucket, and quivers and darts here and there from the rapid swirling—thus did the girl's heart tremble in her breast. (tr. Race)

In his *Argonautica*, Apollonius described Medea's erotic confusion by comparing her shifting emotions to light rippling in water. The Latin poets eagerly adapted the motif. Virgil's comparison of Aeneas' *curae* as he travels up the Tiber to Pallanteum becomes formative for the tradition:[15]

b) Verg. *Aen.* 8.22–25
sicut aquae tremulum labris ubi lumen aënis
sole repercussum aut radiantis imagine lunae
omnia peruolitat late loca, iamque sub auras
erigitur summique ferit laquearia tecti.

As when in bronze bowls a flickering light from water, flung back by the sun or the moon's glittering form, flits far and wide over all things, and now mounts high and smites the fretted ceiling of the roof high above. (tr. Fairclough/Goold)

Ovid adapts *Aen.* 8.23 in the *Heroides*, where he evokes the erotic context of the Apollonian simile but removes the sense of anxiety or conflicted thought. Leander observes in his letter to Hero that the night was bright as he swam to her:

c) Ov. *Her.* 18.77
unda repercussae radiabat imagine lunae.

The wave shone with the image of the reflected moon.

Silius restores the Virgilian context of a leader's psychological conflict. When Fabius traps Hannibal near Gerunium, the narrator describes the commander's rapidly changing thoughts as he searches for an exit strategy in terms that recall Virgil's simile:

---

[15] For the resonance of the image in the *Aeneid*, see Lyne (1987) 127–130.

d) Sil. *Pun.* 7.143–145
sicut aquae splendor radiatus lampade solis
dissultat per tecta uaga sub imagine uibrans
luminis et tremula laquearia uerberat umbra.

Even so, when a sunbeam is reflected in water, the light flits to and fro through the room, quivering as the reflection moves, and strikes the ceiling with flickering shadow. (tr. Duff)

Silius obviously wished the Virgilian model to be recognized instantly. I have indicated through underlining where words have been repeated, sometimes in identical form and *sedes*. Yet by including verbal forms not used by Virgil, such as *dissultat*, *uibrans*, and *uerberat*, the Flavian poet newly emphasizes the anxiety in Hannibal's mind. One of these vocabulary items, *uibrans*, derives from a different source: the passage of Lucan's *Bellum Civile* which describes Caesar's fleet becalmed off Brundisium. The interrelation between these two passages can be confirmed by the fact that they are the only occurrences of the clausula *imagine uibra-* in classical Latin:[16]

e) Luc. *BC* 5.444–446
... pontusque uetustas
oblitus seruare uices non commeat aestu,
non horrore tremit, non solis imagine uibrat.

The sea forgets to keep its ancient alternations, and is not moved to and fro by the tides; no ripple ruffles it, nor does it twinkle with any reflection of the sun. (tr. Duff)

Silius adapts elements of Lucan's narrative in order to amplify Hannibal's anxiety. Like Aeneas, his thoughts also scatter like light in water, but he is not heading to a friendly city under divine protection. Rather, he must grapple with Fabius' successful guerrilla war, and so more closely resembles Lucan's becalmed Caesar, threatened by supply shortages and potential attack.[17]

At the end of *Punica* 2, Silius narrates the Carthaginian sack of Saguntum, which he relates structurally and thematically to Virgil's sack of Troy. After they despair of help from Rome, the Saguntines sacrifice themselves on an communal pyre to avoid capture and enslavement. The *Punica* describes the reflection of the pyre's light on the ocean as follows:

---

[16] Spaltenstein (1986) and Littlewood (2011) do not comment on the connection.
[17] For the contribution of Lucan's Caesar to Hannibal's characterization, see Marks (2010).

f) Sil. *Pun.* 2.663–664
ardent tecta deum. resplendet imagine flammae
aequor, et in tremulo uibrant incendia ponto.

The gods' dwellings are burning. The sea shines with the flame's reflection and the fires quiver on the tremulous water.

The key words *imagine, tremulo,* and *uibrant* link this motif to the earlier simile (d), which describes Hannibal's anxiety as he seeks to evade Fabius. This brief narrative motif vastly increases the scale of the reflection, from a pitcher to the ocean. The amplification of scale suggests the extent of the Saguntines' mental turmoil, as the Fury Tisiphone has just compelled these innocent victims to engage in mass suicide.

The motif also draws on the Virgilian sack of Troy in *Aeneid* 2. Virgil's Aeneas watches helplessly as the Greeks set fire to Troy, and observes the ocean reflecting the flames:

g) Verg. *Aen.* 2.310–312
... iam Deiphobi dedit ampla ruinam
Volcano superante domus, iam proximus ardet
Vcalegon; Sigea igni freta lata relucent.

Even now the spacious house of Deiphobus has fallen, as the fire god towers above; even now his neighbour Ucalegon blazes; the broad Sigean straits reflect the flames. (tr. Fairclough/Goold)

Contextualizing the allusion mobilizes a narrative of contrast. Virgil's Greeks invade Troy and burn it, while Silius' Saguntines destroy themselves before the Carthaginians can enter. Silius' narrator describes the fall of the city from an omniscient, distanced perspective, and sees far more (the *arx, litora,* and *tecta*) at once than a single viewer like Aeneas could see. The verb *resplendet* accompanying the phrase *tremulo ... ponto* (f) evokes a different, peaceful Virgilian scene, in which the Trojans sail to Latium past Circe's island:

h) Verg. *Aen.* 7.9
splendet tremulo sub lumine pontus.

the ocean shines beneath the trembling light.

As with the evocation of the fall of Troy, the goal is *oppositio in imitando*. Silius contrasts the Trojans' safe passage by Circe's island (*Aen.* 7.10–24) with the fire that destroys the helpless Saguntines. In this complex recombination, a careful reader may observe the contrast in narrative focalization, divine narrative, and the affective resonance of each seascape passage. Virgil's Trojans travel under Neptune's protection; at Silius' Saguntum, by contrast, hostile goddess conspire to destroy the city, and its divine benefactors Hercules and Fides cannot stop them. Silius's ocean reflects the fires that destroy the city at Tisiphone's instigation, while Virgil's peaceful sea evokes security and divine beneficence:

Silius' passage (f) additionally evokes a second, peaceful image of Troy, Valerius' celebrations among the Trojans as the Argonauts depart:

> i) Val. Fl. 2.582–583
> hinc unda, sacris hinc ignibus Ide
> uibrat et horrisonae respondent Gargara buxo.
>
> On one side the waves, on the other Mt. Ida flashes with sacrificial fires, and Gargara resounds to the fierce box-wood flute.

Valerius' passage similarly includes the verb *uibrare*, a verb beginning *resp-*, and an image of light reflected on the ocean. Like Virgil's Trojans (h), the Argonauts have also enjoyed a peaceful voyage to Troy along with a festival. Valerius puts the threat closer to the surface, however, than Virgil's Circe passage. Troy is still standing, but Laomedon's treachery will lead to Hercules' sack of the city. As observed above, Silius frames Saguntum as a second Troy, and Hannibal as a second Hercules. Valerius' offended Hercules stands behind Hannibal in this intertext.

To sum up: Virgil applies Apollonius' image of erotic distress to Aeneas' *curae*, which Silius in turn applies to Hannibal's deliberation. Silius also employs the image on an expanded scale to describe the reflection of fire on water as the city of Saguntum burns. As in the previous example of the bared arm and breast, Silius incorporates allusion to his older Flavian contemporary Valerius as well as the Neronian poet Lucan. These passages of his narrative, like many others, offer the careful reader a history of the first-century Latin epic tradition.

3 Conclusion: Algorithmic Criticism and Traditional Philology

The multitext search feature of *Tesserae* allows discovery of *loci similes* such as the ones assembled above, but interpretation of the significance of each parallel locus remains the task of the commentator. The mass of potential intertexts readily generated by *Tesserae* productively complicates the commentator's task of assigning meaning. It cannot be the case, as Farrell demonstrated a decade ago, that the Roman poets consciously intended to include every potential intertext in their work and controlled the interpretation of each intertext.[18] But neither can the reader idiosyncratically assign meaning to an instance of text reuse. A lengthy scholarly tradition, represented in philological commentaries and other critical works, frames the interpretation of intertexts. The ease of assembling instances of text reuse and other poetic features through tools such as *Tesserae* now shifts the bulk of the scholar's intertextual work from discovery to interpretation.

Bibliography

Augoustakis, Antony (2010a), *Motherhood and the Other: Fashioning Female Power in Flavian Epic*, Oxford.
Augoustakis, Antony (ed.) (2010b), *Brill's Companion to Silius Italicus*, Leiden.
Berlincourt, Valéry (2015), "*Innuptae ritus imitata Minervae*: une comparaison chez Claudien et ses connexions flaviennes", in: *Dictynna* 12, https://dictynna.revues.org/1118 (seen 10.07.2018).
Berlincourt, Valéry/Galli Milić, Lavinia/Nelis, Damien (eds.) (2016), *Lucan and Claudian: Context and Intertext*, Heidelberg.
Bernstein, Neil W. (2016a), "Light on the water in Silius Italicus' *Punica* and Claudian's *De Raptu Proserpinae*", in: *Mnemosyne* 69, 1050–1057.
Bernstein, Neil W. (2016b), "Revisiting Ovidian *Silius*, along with Lucretian, Virgilian, and Lucanian *Silius*", in: Fulkerson/Stover (2016) 225–248.
Bernstein, Neil W. (2016c), "Rome's Arms and Breast: Claudian *Panegyricus Dictus Olybrio et Probino Consulibus* 83–90 and its Tradition", in: *CQ* 66.1, 417–419.
Bernstein, Neil W. (2017), *A commentary on Silius Italicus, Punica 2*, Oxford.
Bernstein, Neil W./Gervais, Kyle/Lin, Wei (2015), "Comparative rates of text reuse in classical Latin hexameter poetry", in: *Digital Humanities Quarterly* 9.3, http://www.digitalhumanities.org/dhq/vol/9/3/000237/000237.html (seen 10.07.2018).
Chaudhuri, Pramit (2014), *The War with God: Theomachy in Roman Imperial Poetry*, Oxford.
Coffee, Neil/Forstall Christopher (2016), "Claudian's Engagement with Lucan in his Historical and Mythological Hexameters", in: Berlincourt *et al.* (2016) 255–284.
Coffee, Neil/Koenig, Jean-Pierre/Poornima, Shakthi/Ossewaarde, Roelant/Forstall, Christopher/Jacobson, Sarah (2012), "Intertextuality In the Digital Age", in: *TAPhA* 142, 383–422.
Conte, Gian Biagio (1996), *The Rhetoric of Imitation: Genre and Poetic Memory in Virgil and Other Latin Poets*, Ithaca.
Cristante, Lucio (ed.) (2005–2006), *Il calamo della memoria. Riuso di testi e mestiere letterario nella tarda antichità. Trieste, 27–28 aprile 2006. Atti del II convegno. Incontri triestini di filologia classica 5*, Trieste.
Dominik, William J./Newlands, Carole E./Gervais, Kyle (eds.) (2015), *Brill's Companion to Statius*, Leiden.

---

18 See Farrell (2005).

Drucker, Johanna (2009), *SpecLab: Digital Aesthetics and Projects in Speculative Computing*, Chicago.
Farrell, Joseph (2005), "Intention and Intertext", in: *Phoenix* 59, 98–111.
Fernandelli, Marco (2005-2006), "La maniera classicistica di Silio. Tre esempi dal libro VII", in: Cristante (2005–2006) 73–118.
Fulkerson, Laurel/Stover, Tim (eds.) (2016), *Repeat Performances: Ovidian Repetition and the Metamorphoses*, Madison.
Hutchinson, Gregory (2013), *Greek to Latin: frameworks and contexts for intertextuality*, Oxford.
Jockers, Matthew L. (2013), *Macroanalysis: Digital Methods and Literary History*, Urbana, Illinois.
Littlewood, R. Joy (2011), *A commentary on Silius Italicus' Punica 7*, Oxford.
Lyne, R.O.A.M. (1987), *Further Voices in Virgil's Aeneid*, Oxford.
Marks, Raymond (2010), "Silius and Lucan", in: Augoustakis (2010b) 127–153.
Marks, Raymond (2014), "Statio-Silian Relations in the *Thebaid* and *Punica* 1–2", in: *CPh* 109, 130–139.
Nelis, Damien P. (2001), *Vergil's Aeneid and the Argonautica of Apollonius Rhodius*, Liverpool.
Ripoll, François (2015), "Statius and Silius Italicus", in: Dominik et al. (2015) 425–443.
Scourfield, David J.H. (ed.) (2007), *Texts and culture in Late Antiquity: inheritance, authority, and change*, Swansea.
Spaltenstein, François (1986), *Commentaire des Punica de Silius Italicus (livres 1 à 8)*, Geneva.
Spaltenstein, François (1990), Commentaire des Punica *de Silius Italicus (livres 9 à 17)*, Geneva.
Stocks, Claire A. (2014), *The Roman Hannibal. Remembering the Enemy in Silius Italicus' Punica*, Liverpool.
Taegert, Werner (1988), *Claudius Claudianus, Panegyricus dictus Olybrio et Probino consulibus*, Munich.
Uccellini, Renée (2006), "Soggetti eccentrici: Asbyte in Silio Italico (e altre donne pericolose del mito)", in: *GIF* 58, 229–253.
Ware, Catherine (2012), *Claudian and the Roman epic tradition*, Cambridge.
Wheeler, Stephen M. (2007), "More Roman than the Romans of Rome: Virgilian (self-)fashioning in Claudian's *Panegyric for the consuls Olybrius and Probinus*", in: Scourfield (2007) 97–133.

Peter Heslin
Lemmatizing Latin and Quantifying the *Achilleid*

It is generally acknowledged that the style and tone of Statius' incomplete *Achilleid* is very different from that of his first epic, the *Thebaid*, and that this change reflects, in some sense, the imprint of an Ovidian sensibility on the new project. But there is no consensus around the implications of this observation for the nature of the *Achilleid* as a completed project. The question is whether the reader would have expected the epic to carry on in the same mode after the Scyros episode, or if a reversion to a grimmer atmosphere was inevitable once Achilles arrived at Troy and engaged with the enemy. This is an important question, which matters more than inconclusive speculation as to what particular episodes in Achilles' life Statius intended to include. The issue is fundamental for how we read the existing poem: as a lighthearted prelude to serious matters, or as the start of an alternate narrative of the most canonical epic biography imaginable. It also has consequences for the *Thebaid*, which ends with such a remarkable statement of literary filiation with respect to the *Aeneid*. Should we read that statement as a general manifesto of personal belief or as a rhetorical position determined by the particular ambitions of the *Thebaid* as a meditation on civil war, kingship and nationhood?

The Ovidian character of the *Achilleid* and the importance of the *Metamorphoses* in particular as a model for it have been emphasized by a number of scholars, especially Rosati and Hinds.[1] By contrast, Cameron and Fantuzzi have argued that the matters of parenthood, love and gender that dominate the existing part of the epic should be understood as a clearly demarcated parenthesis, and that the story of Achilles' life would inevitably have taken a serious turn after the point where our text ends.[2] A corollary of Cameron's position is to understand the Ovidianness of the *Achilleid* strictly in terms of amatory elegy. According to this view, the cross-dressed love-story on Scyros is fundamentally alien to heroic epic, an instance of generic *Kreuzung*. The existing episode becomes a self-contained foreign body in the epic as a whole.[3] It is true that Ovid's amatory poetry does have an influence on the Scyros episode, but my view is that the crucial Ovidian inter-

---

1 Rosati (1994) 25–30 and Hinds (1998) 135–144.
2 Cameron (2009), Fantuzzi (2012) 71–97.
3 On the influence of the *Ars Amatoria* on the *Achilleid*, see Sanna (2007).

text for the *Achilleid* as a whole is the *Metamorphoses*. This suggests a very different reading of Statius' epic in which the presence of Ovid introduces not just a delimited, temporary amorous interlude but suggests instead a wholesale subversion of the canonical Trojan epic tradition.

I have tried to emphasize the generic aporia of the ending of the *Achilleid*, whereby we are left uncertain as to whether the rest of the epic would follow the path of the *Iliad* or the *Metamorphoses*.[4] I still believe that is correct, but at the present moment what needs to be stressed is the programmatic significance of Ovid's epic. I recently returned to the subject in an article that shows how Statius adumbrates the possibility of an Ovidian Troy as one of the potential directions for his own poem, based upon Books 12 and 13 of the *Metamorphoses*.[5] A very un-Homeric answer to the question of what happens when Achilles arrives in Ilium is given by Ovid's narrative of Cycnus, which happens right after the Greek landing and the death of Protesilaus (*Met.* 12.67–69). The strange death of Cycnus prompts the Greeks, including Achilles, to wonder in amazement at the phenomenon of his invulnerability; this prompts Nestor to mention his encounter with the invulnerable Caeneus, which is the pretext for his lengthy narrative of the Lapiths and Centaurs. My argument is that Ovid hints, during Achilles' battle with Cycnus, at the possibility that Achilles himself is partially invulnerable, and that, unlike Cycnus, he dishonestly conceals it. This is why Apollo needs to guide the arrow of Paris when he kills Achilles at the end of the book (*Met.* 12.604–606). Ovid does not say where that arrow struck, but well-informed readers will have thought of Achilles' heel, thus making clear that Ovid was alluding to the story of Thetis dipping him in the Styx, even as he suppressed overt reference to it. The unstated organizing principle of Book 12 is therefore the limitations of corporeal invulnerability, from Cycnus at the start, through the story of Caeneus and the Lapiths and Centaurs in the middle, to the death of Achilles at the end.

Statius takes the next step by overtly referencing the story of Thetis' efforts to render her baby son invulnerable by dipping him in the Styx, and doing so no less than three times in the short text of the *Achilleid*.[6] Statius is not only referring to its lost, presumably Hellenistic, source, but also to its implicit presence behind Ovid's playful narrative of invulnerability at Troy.[7] Statius wants us to contemplate the question of what an epic narrating the story of the Trojan War would

---

[4] Heslin (2005) 84–86.
[5] Heslin (2016).
[6] *Ach.* 1.133–134, 1.269–270 and 1.480–482, on which see Heslin (2016) 94–96.
[7] On the ultimate source of the myth of Achilles' partial invulnerability, see Burgess (1995) and Heslin (2005) 166–169.

look like if Achilles enjoyed the advantage of near invulnerability that later tradition attributed to him, especially if the Trojans did not know about it. The tragic mortality of Achilles as framed by Homer would take on a very different complexion. This is not to say that Statius was committed to this development of Ovid's Trojan narrative, but he does carefully lay that out as one of his options.

In the light of my own view that the Ovidianness of the *Achilleid* goes deeper than its amatory content, I thought it might be interesting to generate some statistics on the extent to which its language might mark a departure or not from the *Thebaid* and possibly show an increasing influence of the *Metamorphoses*, especially Books 12 and 13. Does the *Thebaid* show a greater linguistic affinity with the *Aeneid*? Of course, questions of literary criticism cannot be reduced to statistical problems, but quantitative data can sometimes prompt a new way of looking at a text. Macroscopic analysis cannot replace close reading, but it can offer a fresh perspective on familiar texts.[8] To that end, I wanted to run a variety of tests for similarity on these four texts: the *Aeneid*, *Metamorphoses*, *Thebaid* and *Achilleid*. Of course, the vocabulary of mythological hexameter narrative is highly constrained, but my aim was to see if, despite that fact, the epics showed any statistical clustering that might be of interest from a literary point of view.

As we will see, the statistical information about Statius proved in the end to be not more than mildly interesting, and certainly not decisive. What occupied most of my effort and thought was the intermediate step of lemmatizing the texts. There is a great deal of open-source text-mining software available that makes it easy to generate statistics about language use; the first thing they require is that texts need to be lemmatized. In other words, morphological differences need to be excluded. This is fairly straightforward for an uninflected language like English, but, naturally enough, it proved to be more difficult for Latin. None of the existing tools I could find were satisfactory, so I made my own. I was also prompted to think about the next step forward in improving the necessarily imprecise output of automatic lemmatizers for Latin and Greek.

1 Lemmatizing Latin

Most lemmatizers for English take a fairly crude approach. Removing all suffixes, they reduce all the words in a family to a common root. So "analysis", "analyse",

---

[8] For secondary literature on the topic of text mining, macroscopic analysis and distant reading, see Coffee and Gawley in this volume.

"analytical" and so on are all reduced to "analy". This is an appropriate technique for topic modelling: for example, if a user enters one of those terms into a search engine and you want to match relevant documents, but it may be too crude an approach for literary studies. Furthermore, Latin, as a highly inflected language, poses particular problems. We can blithely throw away the morphosyntactic information contained in Latin word endings (this is called the "bag of words" model), since we are not doing any analysis of syntax but simply measuring word frequency. However, simply stripping off Latin suffixes will obviously lead to many cases where very different words are treated as the same, and where inflected forms of a single word are categorized as different. So the first step in applying quantitative analysis to Latin is to develop a more sophisticated model for lemmatization. No automated algorithm will be perfect, as there are many cases where a form could be resolved into different lemmata, and only an understanding of the context will enable a correct decision (and in some cases, even that may not be absolutely decisive).

There are, to my knowledge, three main projects that are designed to supply the need for the automated morphological analysis of Latin words: Morpheus, Collatinus and LemLat. Morpheus is part of the Perseus project and also serves as the morphological engine behind a number of other projects: PhiloLogic, Tesserae and Diogenes.[9] Where a form is ambiguous, Morpheus simply spits out multiple alternative parses. This is entirely appropriate when the output is designed to be read by a human. For example, my own Diogenes software does not attempt to disambiguate lemmata. When a user clicks on a word, it simply presents a list of possible parses from Morpheus and then the dictionary entries corresponding to each possible headword. The Tesserae project also bases its lemma-matching on the output of Morpheus.[10]

For Greek, it is possible to download XML versions of freely distributable texts which have been fully lemmatized by Morpheus and also by the Perseus under PhiloLogic project, which in some cases has refined the output of Morpheus.[11] To my knowledge, the same output format was not available for Latin, or I would have used it as my starting point, rather than using the Morpheus data from Diogenes. What all of these Morpheus-based projects have in common is that they do not attempt to distinguish between ambiguous forms; they produce output that designed to be interpreted, on some level, by humans, who may be

---

9 For the Morpheus code, see https://github.com/PerseusDL/morpheus.
10 For the code, see https://github.com/tesserae/tesserae. The file of interest is data/common/la.lexicon.csv.
11 https://github.com/gcelano/LemmatizedAncientGreekXML.

presumed to have the competence to weed out any spurious matches resulting from ambiguous parses. This poses a problem for automatic lemmatization, where we have to make a choice of what lemma to record for each word, however arbitrary that may be. I will return in a moment to the most important advantage of Morpheus, which is that its lemmata are keyed to the entries in a freely available lexicon.

Collatinus is another project that aims to produce a lemmatizer for Latin. In its source code, there is an interesting document which summarizes some of the difficulties of automated disambiguation and suggests a way forward.[12] The document points out that Collatinus at the moment simply outputs lemmata in the order it finds them (like Morpheus), so that the word *suis* is parsed first as the genitive singular of *sus*, before it is parsed as the dative or ablative plural of *suus*. As a solution to this problem, it suggests making use of the hand-tagged and lemmatized corpus of Latin texts from the Lasla project.[13] This corpus would provide the basis for a sophisticated probabilistic tagger, insofar as it would be possible to see which parses are more common in real usage, and potentially to do so on the basis of context.

While this article was being written, the developers of Collatinus announced a lecture on their Lasla-based probabilistic tagger, with the promise that it will soon be released.[14] The abstract of the paper indicates that it will be based upon a standard techniques for part-of-speech tagging in modern languages, called "Hidden Markov Models".[15] Such a tagger would be trained by looking in turn at each three-word sequence in the hand-tagged corpus and keeping track of how many times a given word is analysed as representing a certain form in that particular three-word context. It would then compute a set of contextual probabilities from those totals. The tagger is applied to a new text by assigning to each given sentence a sequence of tags that maximizes the total of all the three-word contextual probabilities for that sentence.

---

12 The document is NOTES_Tagger.md in the Biblissima project repository (https://github.com/biblissima/collatinus).
13 For Lasla, see http://web.philo.ulg.ac.be/lasla/textes-latins-traites/.
14 The talk was "Collatinus: Lemmatizer and morphological analyzer for Latin texts" by Yves Ouvrard and Philippe Verkerk, delivered at the conference "Digital Classics III: Re-thinking Text Analysis", Heidelberger Akademie der Wissenschaften, (11–13 May 2017), https://projet.biblissima.fr/en/collatinus-lemmatizer-and-morphological-analyzer-latin-texts.
15 From the abstract: "Then, for a sentence, we compute the probability for all the possible sequences of tags and we select the most probable one. The probabilities are extracted from the Lasla's corpus and consist simply in the number of occurrences for each succession of three tags. It is thus a probabilistic tagger based on a hidden 2nd order Markov model."

The obvious problem with applying such a model to Latin is that it is predicated on the assumption that word order is strongly correlated with meaning. There are aspects of Latin that are somewhat amenable to that assumption, such as prepositional phrases: if the word *caelo* appears immediately after the word *in*, it probably does not mean "I engrave" in that particular context. But it is not obvious that relying upon strict word-order to provide sematic cues is a sound general assumption for literary Latin of the classical period. Indeed, Latin would provide a useful test case for the limits of the applicability of Markov models for natural language processing. It would be important for the Collatinus developers to experiment with training their probabilistic tagger on part of the Lasla corpus and using the other part to validate the correctness of the output. It would also be interesting to experiment with other models and compare their accuracy. For example, one could imagine a model that segmented the training corpus into contextual phrases on the basis of punctuation. It would generate a table of lemmata-pairs recording the number of times the two words appear together in the same phrase, excluding common words. One could then tag an ambiguous form by choosing the lemma with the highest total of pairwise frequencies with the unambiguous forms in the same phrase.

Unfortunately, the Lasla corpus does not seem to be distributed under an open-access license, so experiments like this are not as easy as they might be; but there are other possibilities for acquiring such a corpus. Perseus has long encouraged users to vote on which parse they believe is correct in a given context, though I am not sure it provides an API to query that data easily. Perseus is also aggregating treebank data from the Arethusa project.[16] Arethusa can run texts through Morpheus as a preliminary step and then prompt the user to choose between its outputs or to provide another answer.[17] Once a large enough treebank of hand-tagged texts is available on an open-access license, it should be possible to leverage existing work on corpus linguistics to create a probabilistic tagger along the lines of that being developed by the Collatinus developers. We would feed the hand-tagged texts to a machine learning environment, which would be able to disambiguate the morphology of new texts based upon contextual similarity to the training set. But until such a corpus is available, automatic lemmatization remains stuck at the problem of choosing between ambiguous parses.

A third lemmatization project is LemLat. This is a project that appears to have a long history, having been implemented first in Lisp, then in C or C++, and now

---

16 https://github.com/PerseusDL/treebank_data.
17 http://www.dh.uni-leipzig.de/wo/projects/ancient-greek-and-latin-dependency-treebank-2-0/.

in Java.[18] The current version (3.0) has been released under a free software license and the code was recently uploaded to Github.[19] According to the documentation, the lemmata were drawn from the *Oxford Latin Dictionary*, supplemented by other sources, including Georges' *Ausführliches lateinisch-deutsches Handwörterbuch* and the Onomasticon of Forcellini's lexicon. This promises a lemmatization tool with much wider lexical coverage than Morpheus, which draws its lemmata from the lexicon of Lewis and Short. The *OLD* is in many respects a much better lexicon than Lewis-Short, so LemLat would seem a clear improvement on Morpheus. The problem, however, is that the *OLD* is not freely available in a digitized format, whereas the Perseus project distributes the digital L-S lexicon to which Morpheus is keyed. This might not seem an important consideration for a lemmatizer, but it turned out to be essential for my purposes.

The importance of having access to the lexicon from which the lemmatizer draws its lemmata became clear after considering the approach of another project, the Classical Language Toolkit (CLTK). This tool provides an infrastructure by which multiple lemmatizers can be combined in sequence, including those from Collatinus and Perseus. It has an interesting but flawed approach to disambiguation. The documentation says: "For ambiguous forms, which could belong to several headwords, the current lemmatizer chooses the more commonly occurring headword."[20] If we need to choose one headword from several possibilities, we clearly need some sort of heuristic.

The CLTK lemmatizer begins from a file borrowed from my Diogenes project; it records the output of Morpheus when run over a list of all of the inflected forms found in the Packard Humanities Institute CD-ROM database of Latin texts before 200 CE.[21] This approach permits Diogenes to offer the output of Morpheus when applied to the PHI texts without incurring the technological difficulties of distributing Morpheus itself. CLTK processes the Diogenes list and chooses the commonest headword in ambiguous cases.[22] If I understand that code correctly, however, CLTK chooses the commonest headword in the morphology file, which has no real relation to actual usage. Morpheus will produce all possible parses for a very rare word, which will make it loom much larger in the morphology file than it ever did in the language. For example, even very rare verbs tend to have many

---

18 See http://www.lemlat3.eu.
19 https://github.com/CIRCSE/LEMLAT3.
20 http://docs.cltk.org/en/latest/latin.html.
21 This is the file latin-analyses.txt, which CLTK misidentifies as coming from the Perseus project; that may be partly my fault for not identifying the source of the data more clearly.
22 The code is at https://github.com/cltk/latin_pos_lemmata_cltk/blob/master/transform_lemmata.py.

different morphological variants when compared with nouns, but this does not imply that, if a given form could be a verb or a noun, the verb is always more likely. If we look in the morphology file, a rare verb will have many more entries than a frequently used noun, which naturally has a more constrained morphology.

The CLTK approach prompted me to try to come up with an equally simple heuristic that might work a bit better. I adapted the same technique, but I substituted the lexicon for the morphology file, disambiguating parses by always choosing the word with the longer lexicon entry. For the purposes of this article, I created a lemmatizer that always chooses the headword that has the longest entry, in terms of characters, in the Lewis and Short lexicon. This is a quick-and-dirty tactic (I did not even bother to strip out XML markup from the lexicon), but it does a surprisingly good job on the important task of distinguishing common words from the uncommon. This approach might seem a bit simplistic, but it actually works reasonably well in practice. The reason for this is Zipf's law, which quantifies the observation that word frequencies decrease exponentially in all languages.[23] That is, in all languages there is a very small number of extremely common words and a very large number of relatively uncommon words. One important task for an automatic lemmatizer, therefore, is not to confuse one with the other. In other words, in the absence of any additional information, it is usually better to guess that an ambiguous term is a form of a common word rather than an obscure one.

This approach does mean, of course, that some uncommon words are misidentified as forms of the common word. In other words, sometimes *caelo* really does mean "I engrave", though my strategy will never identify it as such. By definition, rare words will not greatly impact the frequencies of common words, and missing out some uncommon words should not be a critical issue for our purposes. The bigger problem with this approach comes from forms that are ambiguous between two words of similar frequency. Should we label *oris* as a form of *os* or of *ora*, whose lexicon entries are of roughly similar length? Our heuristic will pick the word with the slightly longer lexicon entry and always use it. This will have the effect, in the case of words of similar frequency, of suppressing one and doubling the frequency of the other. My lemmatizer depends upon having free access to a digital version of the lexicon upon which the lemmatizer is based,

---

23 Whether this is a trivial or profound observation is disputed; see Ferrer i Cancho (2007) 131–133. On Zipf's law, see also Coffee and Gawley in this volume.

which currently means using Morpheus and Perseus' Lewis and Short.[24] In order to use LemLat, we would need to know the length of the corresponding *OLD* (or other) lemma for each analysis. The project might already have this information in some form; if so, it would be useful to expose it to the user.

A possible improvement on this idea, which I have not yet implemented, would be to switch from always choosing one lemma for a given inflected form to making a probabilistic decision. If we were to use the length of lexicon entry as a very rough indicator of root-word frequency, then we could generate a relative probability based on that. We would not want to use raw lexicon entry length as a metric, since even very rare words have a minimum length entry to give basic information. But lexicon entry-lengths above a certain threshold should give a rough indication of relative frequency. A problem with probabilistic lemmatization, however, is that it will produce different results every time the lemmatizer is run over the same text, which may not be what users expect.

A step further would be to look at not just the length but also the substance of the lexicon entries, which often contains numerous passages giving the context of the word in its various forms and meanings. This could be quite useful from the point of view of machine learning. One could imagine a process whereby an ambiguous parse was resolved by comparing the words in its immediate context with the words of context provided by the respective lexicon entries. In this way, the word *suis* would normally be parsed as a form of *suus*, unless it appeared in a clause where it appeared near a form of a word or words that appear prominently in the entry for *sus*, such as, say, *ferus*. One potential problem is that lexicon entries may cite passages illustrative of atypical or problematic usage more often than typical usage.

In order to generate the statistics below, I wrote a script that iterates over the file latin-analyses.txt from Diogenes, which contains the output of Morpheus when applied to all of the words in the PHI Latin database. For each analysis of a given word-form, it finds the corresponding entry in the Perseus digital version of Lewis and Short and notes the length. For each form, it writes a line to an output file with that form and the lemma with the longest lexicon entry. Then I wrote another script that read in the contents of that file and then iterated over a given Latin text, replacing each word-form with the corresponding lemma. The results, when applied to the beginning of the *Achilleid* (1.1–7), look like this:

---

24 I believe Collatinus also derives its list of headwords from Lewis and Short, but it is less tightly bound to it. For example, Morpheus uses the same numbering as Lewis and Short for identical headwords.

> magnanimus Aeacides formido tono
> progenies et patrium veto succedo caelum
> divus refero quisquam ago vir multus inclutus cano
> Maeones sed multus vaco nos eo per omnis
> sic amo sum heroum volo Scyros lateo 5
> Dulichium profero tuba neque in Hector traho
> sisto sed totus juvenis deduco Troius.
>
> (*Achilleid* 1.1–7)

This way of representing Latin text is certainly rather bizarre to look at; it demonstrates just how much meaning is conveyed by the word endings. There is also a measure of arbitrariness in this representation. When does a participle cease to be a form of the verb and become a substantive in its own right? The word *acta* (line 3) is represented as a form of *ago*, which may not be what all users expect. Reducing participles to root verbs is important, because all verbal forms consisting of a participle and an auxiliary are treated as separate words. The extra counting of forms of *sum* is not significant, since that word is removed as uninteresting.

One can immediately see a number of problems with my tool: in the phrase *sic amor est* in line 5, the word *amor* has been lemmatized wrongly as a form of the verb *amo*, as if it meant "I am loved". This is because, while the noun *amor* has a fairly long lexicon entry (16,596 characters), the entry for the verb *amo* is a bit longer (24,163). For similar reasons, *quamquam* (own lexicon entry: 6,513 characters) is analysed as a form of *quisquam* (7,607). Ironically, the only way *quamquam* would appear as a lemma is if it were printed in the text as *quanquam*. It is important to bear in mind the limitations of automatic lemmatization of Latin before making use of statistical data based upon it. But this is the kind of representation we need, if we are to feed it into text analysis software mainly designed for modern languages. As we will see in a moment, when I was digging further into the output, other problems with the lemmatization emerged.

2 Quantifying Statian Epic

Returning now to the matter at hand, we are in a position to use standard techniques for analysing word-frequency statistics in modern texts. I ran my lemmatizer over the *Aeneid*, *Metamorphoses*, *Thebaid* and *Achilleid* and input those into the R statistical environment, which has many tools available for studying word frequency. The next step was to remove the most frequent Latin words from the texts. There are various lists of Latin stopwords available online, including one from the Perseus project, but I found that these did suit my purposes.[25] All the lists I found were based on unlemmatized Latin, so they would include *est* but not *sum*. Furthermore, I found that some of the most frequent words in the lemmatized texts did not appear at all on the stopword lists. This is because, once the many forms of common verbs were converted into their headword (*possum, facio, do, dico, video*, etc.) their aggregate number pushed them high up the frequency list.

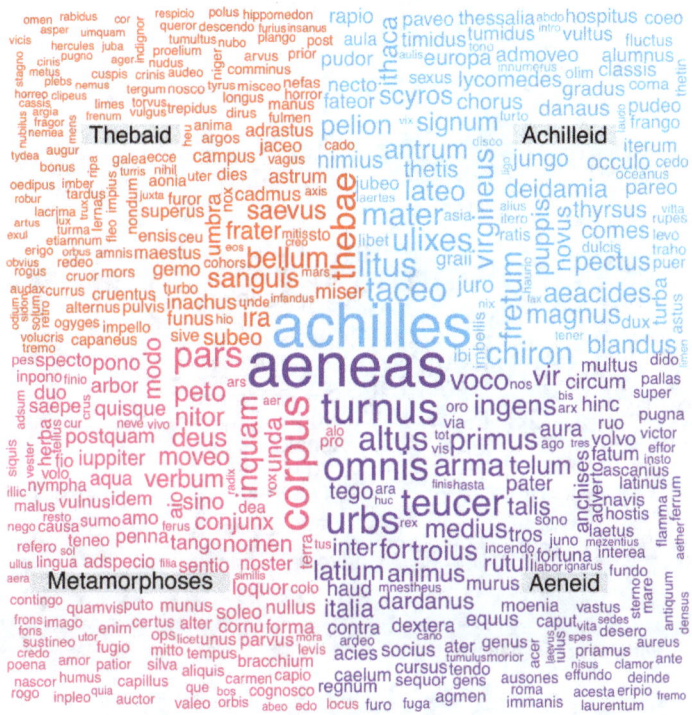

Fig. 1: Comparative word cloud showing the most distinctive words in four texts

A popular means of visualizing word frequencies is by means of "word-clouds", wherein words are shown at a size proportional to their incidence in the text(s). Figure 1 shows a word-cloud comparing relative word frequencies in the *Aeneid*,

---

25 See e.g. http://www.perseus.tufts.edu/hopper/stopwords.

Metamorphoses, *Thebaid* and *Achilleid*.[26] The largest words are those whose frequency in one text is much higher than in the corpus of four texts as a whole.[27]

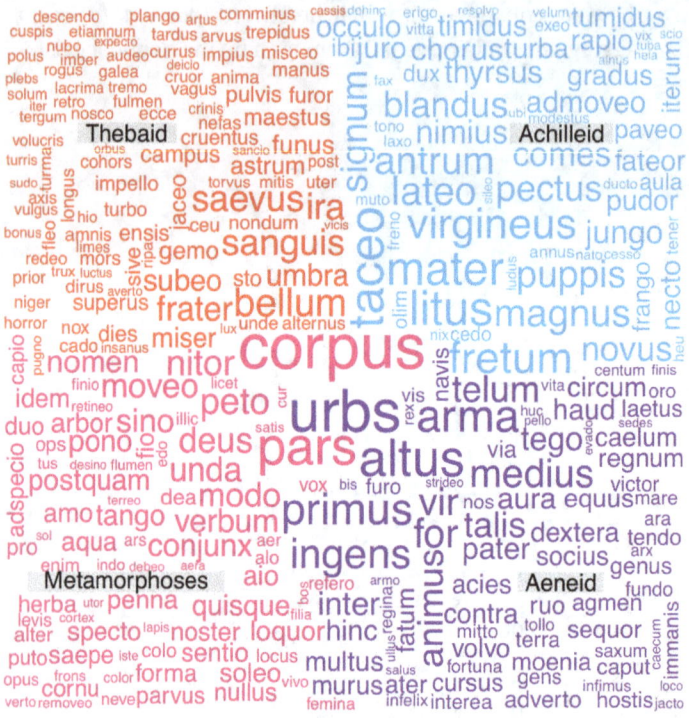

Fig. 2: As Figure 1, but without proper names

Unsurprisingly, the image is dominated by the names of Achilles and Aeneas in their respective epics. What is more interesting is the contrast with the other two poems. The *Metamorphoses* and *Thebaid*, though very different in many ways,

---

26 The image was generated with comparison.cloud function of the "wordcloud" package (version 2.5) for the R language for statistical computing. See https://cran.r-project.org/web/packages/wordcloud/wordcloud.pdf.
27 According to the documentation: "The size of each word is mapped to its maximum deviation ..., and its angular position is determined by the document where that maximum occurs."

are both collective epics that do not focus on the deeds of a single hero. Consequently, their commonest words (*corpus* and *Thebae*, respectively) are less dominant.

The comparative word-cloud of the *Achilleid* in particular is dominated by the names of its characters. We can eliminate those if we take all proper names out of the equation. I removed all words in all four texts beginning with a capital letter; after lemmatization, essentially all of the capitalized words in the text were proper names. This tells us a bit more about the themes of the epics; the result is in Figure 2. On this view, it is the thematic focus of the *Metamorphoses* and the *Aeneid* that emerge most clearly in the prominence of the words *corpus* and *urbs* respectively. The theme of the *Thebaid* is also readily apparent in its major words: *bellum, saevus, sanguis* and *frater*. One can also see aspects of the theme of the *Achilleid*: *mater, virgineus, taceo* and *lateo*. But these words are less dominant than the thematic words of the other three epics; they are mixed in with words incidental to the setting of the existing episodes: *litus, fretum, antrum, puppis*. This seems to be an effect of the fact that the *Achilleid* is much shorter than the other texts. This inequality is easily mitigated in the statistics, since word frequencies can be divided by the length of the text. But the issue remains that the content of this text necessarily has less variety in its setting and incident, so it is much more uniform than the others. Even after accounting for the different lengths of the texts, the *Achilleid* is always going to look different from a statistical point of view from the others.

The comparative word-cloud offers a nice visualization of the differences between our four texts, but we need another tool to investigate their similarities. One standard way of approaching this is to identify distinctive words, defined as words that are of relatively low frequency in the corpus, but which appear more often in one or more texts. This metric is called term-frequency/inverse-document-frequency or tf-idf, which measures words that are relatively infrequent in global terms but relatively frequent in particular documents.[28] The idea is that this might help to identify texts that share distinctive themes. A first effort at computing the tf-idf index for all words in our four epics runs into the same problem as our first word-cloud: the domination of proper names. Of the top 20 words in the corpus by tf-idf, 15 are names, starting with Aeneas and Turnus in the *Aeneid* and Deidamia and Lycomedes in the *Achilleid* (Achilles is down in 7th place, because he is not especially rare in the other texts). But looking at the other words on that list reveals a further problem.

---

[28] I began by using the tf-idf function of the quanteda package for R, but I eventually found the bind_tf_idf function of the tidytext package more convenient to use.

After removing proper names, the item with the highest tf-idf is the specious lemma *adspecio* in the *Metamorphoses*. It turns out that this is the product of editorial inconsistency. The PHI text of the *Metamorphoses*, unlike the other texts used here, sometimes, but not always, prints the verb *aspicio* in its unassimilated form, *adspicio*. In other words, for some reason the editors of this text have printed both *aspexit* and *adspexit* in different contexts.[29] This inconsistency in turn triggered a bug in Morpheus, whereby it resolved *adspexit* and similar forms in *adsp-* to a spurious lemma, *adspecio*. This then appears in the tf-idf list as one of the most distinctive words in the *Metamorphoses*.

Problems with inconsistently unassimilated verbal prefixes in the edition of the *Metamorphoses* also account for other words with high tf-idf. The editor of that text uses the form *inpono* (except for one instance) and the others use *impono*; once again Morpheus fails to unify these; there is a similar problem with the unassimilated forms of *inpleo* and *inpello*. The editor of the *Thebaid* prints forms of *expecto*, whereas the others use *exspecto*, and once again Morpheus fails to regularize. These errors highlight the fact that in Latin we rely on the lemmatizer to do a lot of work beyond morphological analysis, including the assimilation of orthographic variants (such as u/v and i/j) to a single form. Of course, Morpheus was not designed for the purpose to which I have turned it, so it is not surprising that it sometimes fails to regularize alternative forms. The editors of the *Metamorphoses* print the word *siquis* (sometimes, but not always), whereas the others print *si quis*. It is not obvious that it is the job of a lemmatizer to harmonize that sort of difference, but if it does not, *siquis* will appear to be a distinctive item of vocabulary in some texts.

What this reveals is that tf-idf is a metric that is very susceptible to variations in editorial practice from text to text (or even, in the case of F. J. Miller's *Metamorphoses*, within the same text). If a common word is spelled differently in one text, it will have a high tf-idf score, even though the only thing distinctive about it is its spelling. This is a particular problem with a language where the lemmatizer has to do a great deal of work. Once we pass over proper names and spurious words, finally, at number 24 on the list, we hit *navis* in the *Aeneid* and at 27 we get *sexus* in the *Achilleid*, both of which would seem to be genuinely distinctive. But the list as a whole is so full of proper names and oddities that is does not fill one with confidence as an indication of distinctive themes.

---

[29] The Packard Humanities Institute corpus has digitized the Loeb edition of the *Metamorphoses* edited by F.J. Miller and revised by G. Goold.

Another standard metric for measuring how close two texts agree in their vocabulary is a single number called cosine similarity. In order to explain the concept, imagine a language with only three words. Now imagine plotting their frequency by means of a point in a 3-dimensional space, with each axis corresponding to one of those three words. For a given text, if we measure the number of times each word is used and plot the result on the x, y and z axis, the resulting point represents the frequency of all of the words used in the text, which we can equally represent as an arrow drawn from the origin to that point. If we do that for another text, we have two arrows in three-dimensional space. The angle made by the intersection of the two arrows at the origin can serve as a measure of the overall difference between the two texts, in terms of how often each text uses those three words.

Of course, real languages have more than three words. So we have to imagine not two arrows in 3 dimensions but vectors in n-dimensional space, where n represents the total number of all vocabulary words in our corpus. It is hard to visualize vectors in more than 3 dimensions, but the formula for computing the angle between them is straightforward, even for large values of n. This metric is known as cosine similarity, since the output is the cosine of the angle between the two text-vectors, and it varies between zero and one. This metric has the advantage of being independent of the lengths of the two texts. If you make a text longer, but keep the proportions of the three words the same, the arrow will get longer but will still point in the same direction (for example, if we compare a text and itself doubled). In that case, the cosine of the angle will be one and their similarity is maximal. If, on the other hand, the two texts have no words at all in common, the arrows will be orthogonal and the cosine of the angle will be zero.

Tab. 1: Cosine similarities of the four lemmatized epics

	Achilleid	*Aeneid*	*Metamorphoses*
Aeneid	0.7319906		
Metamorphoses	0.7365669	0.8173574	
Thebaid	0.7961133	0.8467871	0.8241863

Text-mining software enables us to easily compute the cosine similarities of the four lemmatized epics.[30] Table 1 shows the results. Surprisingly, the *Achilleid* has less vocabulary in common with any of the other epics (similarity < 0.8) than each of them has with each other. One possibility is that this genuinely reflects the idiosyncrasy of Statius' epic, but it may be that this is another side-effect of the shortness of the *Achilleid* and its relative lack of variety of incident and hence of vocabulary. As a control against the effect of length, I ran the same test against individual books of the epics. I took the first book of the *Achilleid*, as it is the only complete book; the first book of the *Aeneid*, with which, as I have argued previously, the *Achilleid* has much in common; the twelfth and thirteenth books of the *Metamorphoses*, since those are the two books I think Statius was thinking of when contemplating an Ovidian Troy; and the first book of the *Thebaid*, which was chosen somewhat arbitrarily. The results of this test are given in Table 2. Overall, the level of similarity is significantly lower, which shows that, even though length is explicitly factored out of the cosine measure, it nevertheless affects the results. Presumably, there is more likelihood of idiosyncrasy in shorter texts. On this measure, the most idiosyncratic text is Book 12 of the *Metamorphoses*.

Tab. 2: Cosine similarities of selected individual books of the four lemmatized epics

	Achilleid 1	*Aeneid* 1	*Metamorphoses* 12	*Metamorphoses* 13
Aeneid 1	0.6242276			
Metamorphoses 12	0.5917354	0.5566238		
Metamorphoses 13	0.6633080	0.6250299	0.6687240	
Thebaid 1	0.6413900	0.6227937	0.5476565	0.5913332

As far as demonstrating the affinity of the *Achilleid* with the Trojan parts of the *Metamorphoses*, the results are interesting. The statistics show that *Achilleid* 1 has a particularly low similarity with *Metamorphoses* 12, but particularly high similarity with *Metamorphoses* 13 (almost as high as the internal similarity between those two books of Ovid's epic). This is borne out if we make a separate comparison of *Achilleid* 1 with each of the books of the *Metamorphoses* in turn. The cosine similarity sits in a narrow range from 0.5799212 at the lowest (for Book 1) to

---

[30] This was initially done using the pairwise_similarity function from the widyr package for R and the results were checked against the output of the textstat_simil function from the quanteda package, which is what is given in Tables 1 and 2.

0.6298531 at the highest (for Book 2), with the exception of Book 13, which stands apart at 0.6633080. One could argue that this is simply the accidental result of the content of that book. In his long speech, Ulysses embeds a miniature biography of Achilles in order to highlight his own connection to him as a reason for deserving his armour. Statius was certainly thinking of this text, for Ovid's Ulysses describes his trick on Scyros (*Met.* 13.162–170) and alludes to Achilles' draft-dodging again later, applying to him (ironically?) the epithet *magnanimus* (13.298), which Statius adopts as the first word of his epic.[31] Does the particularly high similarity score for Book 13 indicate that the influence of Ulysses' speech on the *Achilleid* goes beyond those passages that allude to Scyros? Statistics are rarely a convincing mode of literary criticism, but they might suggest fruitful places to look for influence.

3 Conclusion

The outcome of this attempt to use quantitative methods to answer an interpretive question has been equivocal, but I think the journey has been interesting and revealing. Latin is a language with a notably restricted lexis when compared with Ancient Greek or Modern English; like German, it tended to expand by extending the meaning of existing words by means of metaphor and calque. That makes it a good language for writing poetry, but less amenable to statistical differentiation between texts. The repertory of words that are metrically tractable and stylistically appropriate within the Latin hexameter is even smaller. Furthermore, the epics of Ovid and Statius are direct responses to the *Aeneid* and, even when they diverge thematically, their language is largely determined by Virgil's example. As a consequence, the corpus of post-Virgilian epic is more self-similar than different, and efforts to distinguish between texts statistically are hampered by the high level of overall similarity.

Efforts to evaluate the *Achilleid* against other, full-length epics are undermined by its comparative shortness and resulting lack of variety in incident. This is true even when, from a mathematical point of view, text length is eliminated as a factor. Other measures of statistical significance give results that are clearly impaired by the difficulties of lemmatization. The metric of tf-idf is dominated by proper names, which is not surprising and reflects the reality of the texts, but also

---

[31] For the other layers of meaning of this epithet, see Hinds in this volume.

by artefacts of editorial inconsistency and incomplete lemmatization. A prerequisite for any kind of statistical approach to quantifying Latin literature is better lemmatization. The ideal would be to have the corpus of classical Latin hand-tagged. This is not an unrealistic aspiration and it will surely happen one day, but not soon. In the meantime, we can hope for better probabilistic tagging based upon a smaller hand-tagged corpus. But my own crude efforts at automatic lemmatization by using lexicon data to choose among alternative parses suggests another possible approach.

The fact is that we already have a large corpus of hand-lemmatized Latin. In the *Zettelarchiv* of the *Thesaurus Linguae Latinae*, there are 10 million cards of Latin text, all hand-lemmatized and filed under the relevant lemma.[32] We may hope that the entire archive will at some point in the future be digitized for all to consult. Until then, we can turn to the published portions of the *TLL*, which reports a large portion of this data, and for some words, all of it. The *TLL* itself has been digitized, and it ought to be possible to search it in reverse, i.e. to look for a particular passage and output all of the lemmata under which it is cited. Currently, however, the on-line *TLL* is an expensive commercial product which does not offer that functionality.[33] Perhaps the archive can find a way to share the data generated by its massive exercise in hand-lemmatization without interfering with its publishing agreements. For the fact is, long before the advent of digital tools, lemmatization has always been the first step in analysing a language. We should not have to begin again from scratch.

Bibliography

Burgess, Jonathan S. (1995), "Achilles' Heel: the Death of Achilles in Ancient Myth", in: *ClAnt* 14, 217–243.
Cameron, Alan (2009), "Young Achilles in the Roman World", in: *JRS* 99, 1–22.
Fantuzzi, Marco (2012), *Achilles in Love: Intertextual Studies*, Oxford.
Ferrer i Cancho, Ramon (2007), "On the Universality of Zipf's Law for Word Frequencies", in: Grzybek/Köhler (2007) 131–140.

---

[32] For the process by which the cards were lemmatized (or "baptized", *getauft*), see the account at https://www.thesaurus.badw.de/ueber-den-tll/zettelmaterial.html.
[33] In a very welcome development since this paper was written, the *TLL* has recently released PDFs of many of its published volumes under a form of open access (http://www.thesaurus.badw.de/en/tll-digital/tll-open-access.html), though it is not clear how usable the OCR will be for the purposes of lemmatization. It is hoped that this may be a harbinger of the eventual digitization of the Zettelarchiv itself.

Fulkerson, Laurel/Stover, Tim (eds.) (2016), *Repeat Performances: Ovidian Repetition and the Metamorphoses*, Madison.

Grzybek, Peter/Köhler, Reinhard (eds.) (2007), E*xact methods in the study of language and text: Dedicated to Gabriel Altmann*, Berlin.

Heslin, Peter J. (2005), *The Transvestite Achilles: Gender and Genre in Statius'* Achilleid, Cambridge.

Heslin, Peter J. (2016), "Ovid's Cycnus and Homer's Achilles' Heel", in: Fulkerson/Stover (2016) 69–99.

Hinds, Stephen (1998), *Allusion and Intertext: Dynamics of Appropriation in Roman Poetry*, Cambridge.

Rosati, Gianpiero (1994), *Stazio*, Achilleide, Milan.

Sanna, Lorenzo (2007), "Achilles, the Wise Lover and his Seductive Strategies (Statius, *Achilleid* 1.560–92)", in: *CQ* 57, 207–215.

Neil Coffee/James Gawley
How Rare are the Words that Make Up Intertexts? A Study in Latin and Greek Epic Poetry

1 Introduction

Among the new approaches to literary criticism made possible by the digital humanities, macroanalysis has been perhaps the most popular and powerful. Digital tools have been used with considerable success to study authorship, textual influence, and stylistics, within large individual works and across multiple works.[1] In classics, macro-scale studies have begun to expand our understanding of intertextuality, further illuminating how ancient authors adapted and reused other texts. Classicists are beginning to identify large numbers of localized intertexts automatically, then look at the overall trends they contain, as exemplified by the contribution of Neil Bernstein to this volume.[2]

The notion of macroanalysis was developed as a digitally-enabled counterpart to microanalysis, or traditional "close reading" of individual literary passages.[3] This study employs digital methods to pursue a different form of microanalysis. "Micro" refers here not to the small number of words or works considered, but rather to linguistic features not readily evident in the course of the ordinary or even intensive reading of literature.[4] Through a microanalytical approach to intertextuality, we can begin to identify more robustly the formal features that make up localized intertexts. Theoretical discussions of intertextuality have long been concerned with the role of the author or reader in determining whether a particular piece of text recalled another, and so constituted an intertext. The formal study of intertextuality instead begins by studying intertexts recognized as such by scholars and studies their linguistic properties, such as

---

[1] Jockers (2013) 22.
[2] Coffee *et al.* (2012) offer an analysis of large-scale intertextuality within one work, Lucan's *Civil War*. The German eTRAP group has carried out some measurements of text reuse over a large corpus of classical Latin (Büchler *et al.* 2013).
[3] Moretti (2005) contrasts "close reading" with "distant reading," his term for what Jockers calls "macroanalysis."
[4] The linguistic reading of poetics had its earliest distinguished modern exponent in Jakobson (1960), esp. p. 351.

similarity of lemma, meaning or sound. In this way, we can determine what features make a text marked enough to constitute a meaningful intertext.[5]

In this article, we investigate the formal features of intertextuality using two sets of recognized parallels between classical epic poems. The first is a collection of 317 Latin-language parallels between Book 1 of Lucan's epic *Civil War* and the whole of Vergil's *Aeneid*, compiled from commentators and inspection of Tesserae search results.[6] The collection was edited to include only intertexts consisting of at least two lemmata shared among the two texts, where in each text the lemmata fell within the bounds of one sentence.[7] In previous work, such bigram lemma intertextuality has been estimated to account for 67% of the intertexts between *Civil War* book 1 and the *Aeneid* and so represent of a major type of intertextuality.[8] The second set consists of 376 ancient Greek parallels between Book 3 of the *Argonautica* of Apollonius Rhodius and the *Iliad* and *Odyssey* of Homer, compiled from Richard Hunter's commentary on *Argonautica* 3, also consisting only of minimum two-word parallels. The intertexts in these sets include instances of language that recalls other passages, whether to generate specific comparison of the two, or just as artistic repurposing.[9]

Within these sets, we focus one formal question: how common or rare are the words that make up intertexts? Word frequency was one important consideration in ancient poetic practice. In his treatise on *Poetics*, Aristotle advises poets to use rare words, but only occasionally. Vergil comes in for criticism in antiquity for creating a new kind of poetic affectation, or *cacozelia*, produced by using common words in uncommon combinations. Words could have marked poetic effects because they were rare in the lexicon overall. Or they could be rare within a certain literary register, as when prosaic words were used in epic poetry, or within a certain genre, as when words that Homer used only once, *hapax legomena*, were used by later epic poets like Apollonius.[10]

---

[5] Morgan 1977, 3, discussed by Hinds (1998) 19. Fowler (2000) 122 writes of "markedness" as one criterion for what makes up an intertext, along with "sense" (i.e., that someone has to recognize a piece of language as marked and make some sense of it for it to be an intertext). With digital methods: Büchler *et al.* (2010), Coffee *et al.* (2012), Büchler *et al.* (2013), Forstall *et al.* (2014).

[6] The full set is available at: http://tesserae.caset.buffalo.edu/blog/benchmark-data/. For more information on the methods used to obtain it, see Coffee *et al.* (2012).

[7] Where semicolons, in addition to the other usual marks of punctuation, were understood to mark sentence endings.

[8] Coffee *et al.* (2012) 415.

[9] That is, the sets include types 3–5 of the scale given in Coffee *et al.* (2012) 392–398.

[10] Aristotle *Poetics* 22 1458a – 1459a. Vergil's detractor is one M. Vipranius, quoted in Donatus's *Life of Vergil* section 44, available in Ziolkowski/Putnam (2008) 186. For prosaic words in Latin

The question of rarity appears elsewhere in this volume. Chiara Battistella and Lavinia Galli Milić focus on the way allusions shape characterization in Valerius Flaccus's *Argonautica*, but they acknowledge that previous scholarship has relied on rare words to identify some of those intertexts. Raymond Marks also relies on the importance of word-rarity as a marker of intertextuality in his study of Silius Italicus. In his quantitative study of Silius, Neil Bernstein's formula for measuring the rate of intertextuality between authors assumes that rare words close together distinguish allusions from other types of shared language. It is important to note that all of these studies involve Latin word rarity. Bernstein's contribution in particular assumes the importance of rarity based on evidence derived from previous analysis of Lucan's relationship to Vergil. As Stephen Hinds points out in his survey of scholarship on Flavian epic in this volume, we must be careful not to develop a Latin-only focus when we deploy quantitative tools to study Flavian intertextuality. To properly follow this advice, we must avoid importing assumptions about word rarity to the study of Greek intertextuality which were originally built upon studies of Latin literature. This chapter represents a first step in that direction, by comparing the intertexts of one Latin and one Greek epic poem.

Common sense suggests that intertexts are likely to be made of relatively rare words, since rare words stand out and can bring to mind the unusual passages in which they have appeared. Our results confirm this intuition, but also give it specificity, by showing the particular level of rarity of intertext words. They also reveal a contrast between Latin and Greek epic.[11]

These conclusions provide support for other work on intertextuality in this volume that relies, explicitly or implicitly, on rarity as a marker of significant intertexts in Latin, including the contributions of Battistella and Milić, Bernstein, and Marks. At the same time, our results provide a further, possibly corrective view, as Stephen Hinds warns may be necessary, by defining the difference in rare word usage in intertexts between Greek and Latin authors in the same genre.

---

poetry, see Axelson (1945). Wills (1996) 2 remarks upon word frequency as a marker of intertextuality, with reference to Vergilian *hapax legomena* referring to corresponding *hapax legomena* in Theocritus and Homer.

11 The intuition about word frequency and intertextuality has for several years been incorporated into the Tesserae Project website (http://tesserae.caset.buffalo.edu/), which scores highest the n-gram matches with words that are relatively rare and close together in their respective phrases.

2 Overall Word Frequency Comparison: Apollonius and Lucan Intertexts versus Random Words

To begin, we provide a picture of the frequencies of the words in the intertexts of *Argonautica* and *Civil War* compared to the frequencies of randomly chosen words from the poems. For the random sets, two-word phrases were chosen randomly amounting to the same number of instances as contained in the respective intertext sets. In each case, we calculated word counts by first identifying the lemma for each word in a bigram, then finding the number of times it appears in the Tesserae corpus. The counts for the words of each phrase were then averaged, to give a single number representing the whole phrase. The results are illustrated in Figure 1.

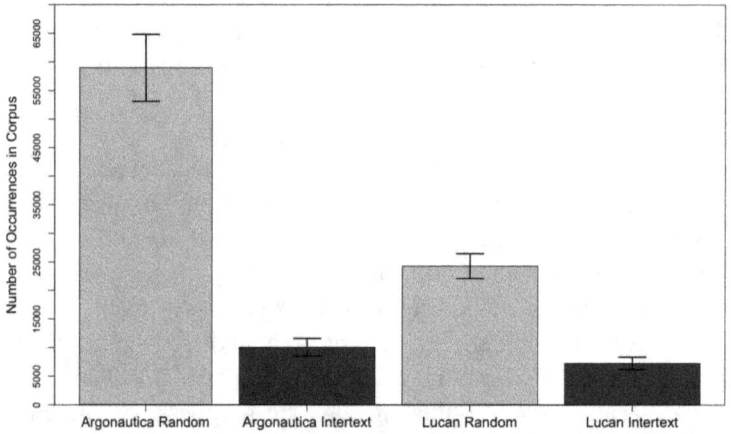

Fig. 1: Occurrences in respective Greek and Latin corpora of intertext vs. non-intertext words from *Argonautica* 3 and *Civil War* 1

The leftmost column represents the average number of occurrences in the Greek corpus of the random words from Apollonius' *Argonautica*, the second column the *Argonautica* intertext set, and so likewise for Lucan's *Civil War*. Whiskers represent the standard error measurement for these broadly distributed data sets. The words that make up intertexts are clearly rarer in the corpus than words that do not. Apollonius's intertext words occur less than a quarter as often as his non-intertext words. Lucan's occur less than half as often. Closer analysis will help to explain the difference between the intertextual practice of the two poets.[12]

3 Latin Epic: Lucan and Vergil

Figure 1 raises the question of what sort of distribution lies behind the average rarity of the intertext words of the poets. That is, given that the poet's intertext words are relatively rare overall, we might wonder whether this is because, for example, he uses many words that are at some point below the median frequency, or because he instead uses both very rare and very common words, whose frequency averages out to that point.

To answer the question, we can compare the frequencies of the individual bigrams that make up the intertext sets and random sets, in order from most common to most rare, as shown in Figures 2 and 3.[13]

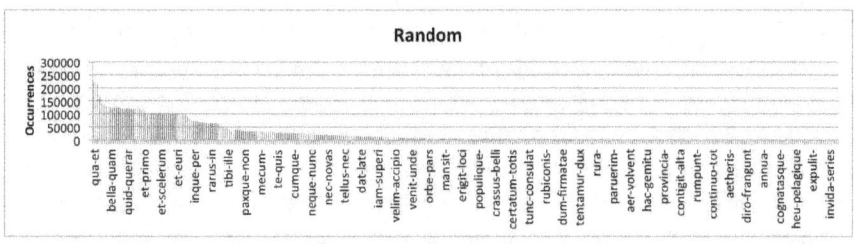

Fig. 2: Average number of appearances in Tesserae Latin corpus of words in bigrams randomly sampled from Lucan *Civil War* 1

---

12 The Tesserae Latin corpus is identical with the Perseus corpus, with a small number of additional texts. For its contents, see http://tesserae.caset.buffalo.edu/sources.php.
13 For the intertext sample, this meant dividing by two or more, depending upon the total number of words in the phrase. For the random sample, this always meant dividing by two, for the two random words selected.

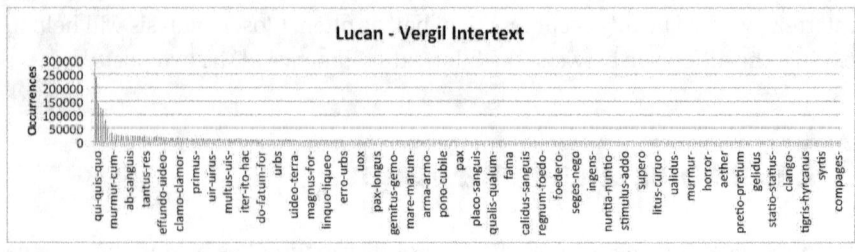

Fig. 3: Average number of appearances in Tesserae Latin corpus of words in n-grams in set of recognized parallels in Lucan *Civil War* 1 with Vergil *Aeneid*

Figure 2 represents the results for the random two-word phrases from *Civil War* 1. The y-axis shows the average number of occurrences of these words in the corpus. The x-axis lists the phrases in order from highest frequency on the left to lowest frequency on the right. A small number of phrases consist of words that are used very frequently, as shown in the left of the chart, while the majority of phrases consist of words are used relatively rarely and trail off to the right. Therefore the frequency pattern in our random sampling of Vergil is consistent with the commonly-cited analysis of Zipf, who posited that natural languages consist of a small number of words repeated often and a majority of words used rarely.[14]

Figure 3 shows the word frequencies of the *Civil War* 1 intertext phrases. The difference from Figure 2 is most evident on the left of the chart. The rapid flattening of the graph from left to right shows that intertext phrases in *Civil War* 1 are almost never made up of very common words, in contrast with random two-word phrases, which more often are. Figures 2 and 3 show that part of the rarity of Lucan's intertext vocabulary is caused by the absence of common words that occur elsewhere in his poem.

The scale of Figures 2 and 3 makes it difficult to see any difference between the rightmost part of their curves, which represents the rarest words. Figure 4 offers a closer look at this end of the frequency distribution.

---

14 Zipf (1949).

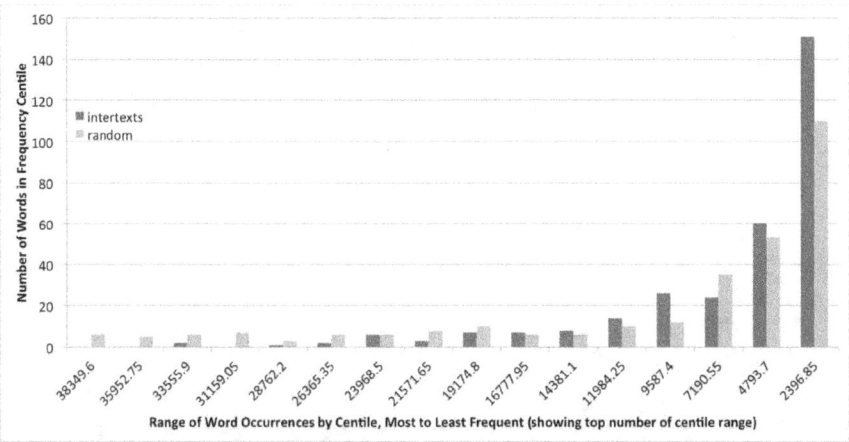

Fig. 4: Occurrences of Intertext and Random Phrases By Centile – Top 16 Centiles

Figure 4 represents the right end of the curves in Figures 2 and 3, but in a different way. Each two-word phrase, again, was given a number corresponding to the average number of occurrences of the words that made it up. These figures ran from the equivalent of 239,716 appearances in the corpus, the most frequent, to 31 appearances, the least frequent. This range was then divided into 100 equal parts. All the phrases that occur in the corpus between 239,716 and 237,289 times were counted and put into the first group, those that had occur between 237,288 and 234,890 times were counted and put into the second group, and so forth. Of these 100 groups, Figure 4 shows just the 16 with the rarest words, ending with the very rarest on the right. There are few words in Latin that occur frequently and many more that occur rarely. The graph in Figure 4 thus rises toward the right, reflecting the increasing number of words that occur only rarely.

The greater height of the rightmost column for Lucan's intertexts shows that Lucan makes use of rare words, particularly those in the 100th centile, more often than they occur randomly. So far, then, we can conclude that Lucan's intertexts with Vergil do indeed consist of words that are relatively rare, in that they show a reduced use of frequent words and increased use of rare words compared to a random sample. Put in terms of poetic technique, we would say that Lucan used relatively rare words, consciously or unconsciously, when creating intertexts with the *Aeneid*.

4 Greek Epic: Apollonius and Homer

As with Lucan, the frequency of random two word combinations from Apollonius follows a Zipf distribution, as illustrated in Figure 5.

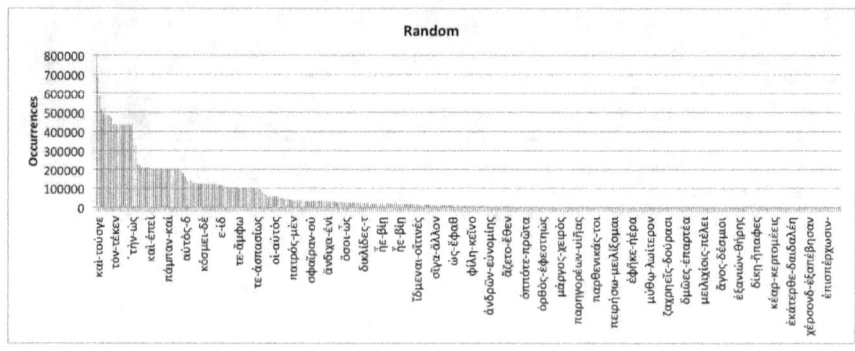

Fig. 5: Average number of appearances in Tesserae Greek corpus of words in bigrams randomly sampled from Apollonius *Argonautica* 3

As the larger range of the y-axis indicates, there are far more different words (types) in the ancient Greek lexicon than in the ancient Latin lexicon, a fact reflected in the Perseus corpora for both languages, from which the Tesserae corpus is primarily drawn. Apollonius also uses primarily Homeric language, while word frequencies were tabulated based on the entire Greek corpus.[15] Relative to each language, however, the distribution of random bigram combinations from Apollonius is similar to that for Lucan.

Likewise, the Apollonius intertext phrases also contain fewer very common words than the random sample, as illustrated in Figure 6.

---

15 On Apollonius using Homeric language, see Hunter (1989) 38 with further references.

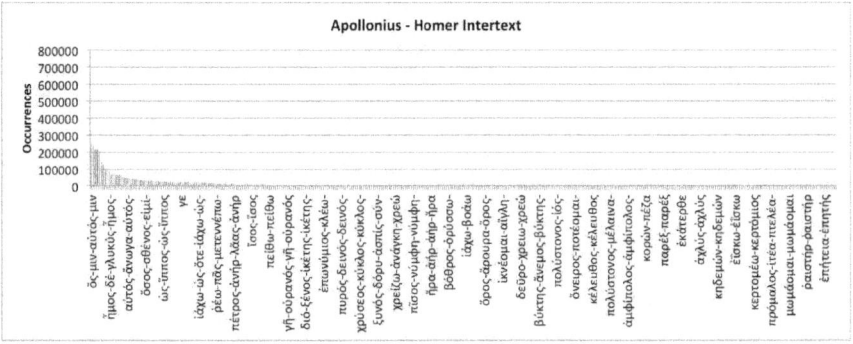

Fig. 6: Average number of appearances in Tesserae Greek corpus of words in n-grams in set of recognized parallels in Apollonius *Argonautica* 3 with Homer *Iliad* and *Odyssey*

Closer consideration shows that Apollonius prefers rare words even more than Lucan does. To begin with, none of the Apollonius parallels contain the very most frequent words, while at least a few of Lucan's do. The highest frequency words contained in Apollonius's parallels appear about 200,000 times in the Greek corpus, while the highest frequency words in our random sample of his poem appear about 400,000 times in the corpus. By contrast, the highest frequency words in Lucan's intertextual phrases appear roughly 240,000 times in the Latin corpus, while the highest frequency words in our random sample of his poem appear 220,000 times. In other words, even the most frequent words that appear in Apollonius intertexts occur only half as often as the most frequent words in his poem overall, while the most frequent words in Lucan's intertexts occur equally as often as the most frequent words in his poem overall.

We find an analogous difference if we consider the appearance of the rarest words in Apollonius's intertexts with Homer, as illustrated in Figure 7.

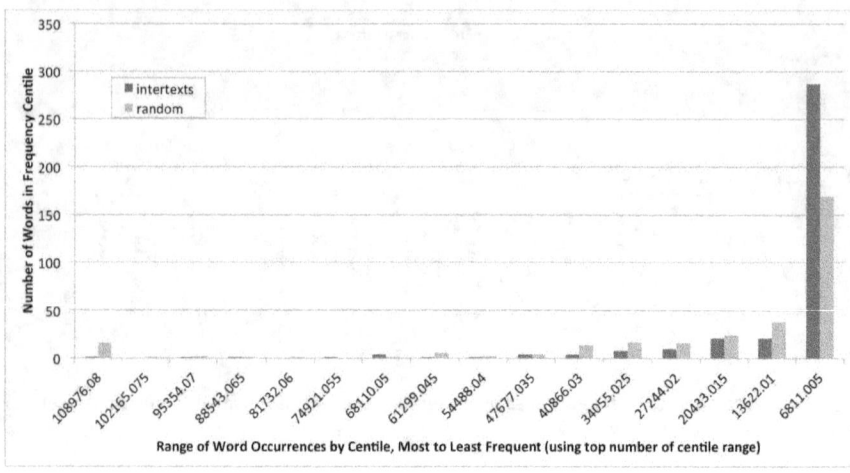

Fig. 7: Frequency Counts of Intertext and Random Phrases By Centile – Top 16 Centiles

The procedure for the creation of Figure 7 was the same as that for the creation of Figure 3, substituting the words of Apollonius for Lucan's. Once again the poet uses the rarest words more often in intertexts, which indicates that the difference in average word count seen in Figure 1 comes from two formal characteristics of intertexts: the appearance of fewer common words, and the more frequent use of extremely rare words.

In comparison to their respective random samples, the Apollonius parallels contain a greater number of words in the rarest centile than do the Lucan parallels. As comparison of the final paired columns in Figures 4 and 7 illustrates, there are only 137% more Lucan intertexts in the rarest centile than found in the random sample, while there are 170% more Apollonius intertexts in the rarest centile than found in the random sample. In this subset of rarest words, the intertextual data set is substantially larger than the randomly selected data set. This difference is larger than the analogous difference found when we compare the random and intertextual data sets in the rarest centile of words from Lucan.

5 Conclusions

The results of this study support the intuition that, for a phrase to be intertextual, it often consists of words that are relatively rare. This is not the case for every intertext. At the opening of Lucan's *Civil War*, at Book 1 line 8, his narrator asks "what madness" it was that drove Roman citizens to kill one another: *quis furor?* As commentators have observed, this is the same question asked by Ascanius in Book 5 line 670 of the *Aeneid*, deploring the madness of Trojan women burning their own ships in hopes of ending the miserable wanderings of their people. Although the word *quis* is among the most frequent in the Latin language, the phrase remains distinctive. Yet our results show that the words that make up intertexts are overall rarer than average. Furthermore, this average level of occurrence results from a particular distribution, in which the rarest words in the language appear more often and most frequent words less often. Our study also demonstrates that the intertexts of Apollonius are more strongly marked by rarity than those of Lucan. The difference might be explained by the poets' distinctive approaches to epic. Our study did not account for Apollonius's fondness for Homeric *hapax legomena*, but his frequent use of these rarest of words shows the Hellenistic-era poet had a general preference for recherché Homeric language, which extended into this longer intertexts.[16]

Lucan likewise forms his intertexts with rare words, but two factors likely kept him to a more common dictional register overall. Vergil had provided an authoritative model within the Latin epic tradition for making marked tropes from common words, his special form of *cacozelia*. Lucan may have picked up this habit in re-using the language from Vergil's epic.[17] Lucan also wrote historical, rather than mythical epic, and accordingly employed more prosaic words than Vergil did.

Alternatively, the stronger pattern of rarity in the intertexts of Apollonius might reflect a more general difference between Greek and Latin epic. Future work should replicate the current study using new benchmark sets for comparable works in each language. If intertexts appear more strongly marked by word rarity in multiple works of Greek epic, then another level of explanation will be necessary beyond the artistic choices of individual authors.

---

16 For Apollonius's use of Homeric *hapax legomena*, see Fantuzzi (1988), chapter 1 and Kyriakou (1995).

17 See Roche (2009) 51–53. This study did not consider phrase frequency, or how often two words occur together, beginning instead from the frequency of individual words that make up two-word phrases and employing as an index the average of their frequencies. Measuring phrase frequency instead could yield different results, since, as in Vergil's practice, it might be most unusual to find certain common words used together.

Bibliography

Axelson, Bertil (1945), *Unpoetische Wörter, ein Beitrag zur Kenntnis der lateinischen Dichtersprache*, Lund.

Büchler, Marco/Geßner, Annette/Eckart, Thomas/Heyer, Gerhard (2010), "Unsupervised Detection and Visualization of Textual Reuse on Ancient Greek Texts", in: *Proceedings of the Chicago Colloquium on Digital Humanities and Computer Science* 1.

Büchler, Marco/Geßner, Annette/Berti, Monica/Eckart, Thomas (2013), "Measuring the Influence of a Work by Text Re-use", in: *BICS Supplement* 122, 63–79.

Coffee, Neil/Koenig, Jean-Pierre/Poornima, Shakthi/Ossewarde, Roelant/Forstall, Christopher/Jacobson, Sarah (2012), "Intertextuality in the Digital Age", in: *TAPhA* 142.2, 381–419.

Fantuzzi, Marco (1998), *Ricerche su Apollonio Rodio: diacronie della dizione epica*, Rome.

Forstall, Christopher/Coffee, Neil/Buck, Thomas/Roache, Katherine/Jacobson, Sarah (2014), "Modeling the Scholars: Detecting Intertextuality through Enhanced Word-Level N-Gram Matching", in: *Literary and Linguistic Computing* 10.1093/llc/fqu01.

Fowler, Don (2000), *Roman Constructions: Readings in Postmodern Latin*, Oxford.

Hinds, Stephen (1998), *Allusion and Intertext: The Dynamics of Appropriation in Roman Poetry*, Cambridge.

Hunter, Richard L. (1989), *Apollonius of Rhodes*, Argonautica, book III, Cambridge.

Jakobson, Roman (1960), "Closing Statement: Linguistics and Poetics", in: Sebeok (1960) 350–377.

Jockers, Matthew L. (2013), *Macroanalysis: Digital Methods and Literary History*, Champagne, IL.

Kyriakou, Poulheria (1995), *Homeric hapax legomena in the Argonautica of Apollonius Rhodius: A Literary Study*, Stuttgart.

Moretti, Franco (2005), *Graphs, Maps, Trees: Abstract Models for a Literary History*, London/New York.

Morgan, Kathleen E. (1977), *Ovid's Art of Imitation: Propertius in the Amores*, Leiden.

Roche, Paul (2009), *Lucan, De bello civili. Book 1*, Oxford.

Sebeok, Thomas A. (ed.) (1960), *Style in Language*, New York.

Wills, Jeffrey (1996), *Repetition in Latin Poetry: Figures of Allusion*, Oxford.

Ziolkowski, Jan M./Putnam, Michael C.J. (2008), *The Virgilian Tradition: The First Fifteen Hundred Years*, New Haven.

Zipf, George K. (1949), *Human Behavior and the Principle of Least Effort: An Introduction to Human Ecology*, Cambridge, MA.

Stephen Hinds
Pre- and Post-digital Poetics of 'Transliteralism': Some Greco-Roman Epic Incipits

The distinctive nature of this volume's collaboration gives it a dual identity: as a study of Flavian epic which happens to make use of some digital tools for intertextual analysis; and as a study of digital tools for intertextual analysis which happens to take Flavian epic as its case study.[1] My own contribution to the 2015 conference in Geneva, as the sole non-technologist in the digital technology panel, put me somewhere between these identities. My brief, as an intertextualist whose habits were largely formed in the pre-digital age,[2] was to consider digital pattern-recognition as an idea good even for a non-digital person to *think with*: a human approach, if you like, to a 'tessellating' sensibility.

Modern theoretical reassessments of Latin literature have tended to ground themselves disproportionately in the texts of Roman epic, so that, in practice, the questioning of established norms of literary history has brought with it some reconfirmation and reinscription of age-old ideas of canon and hierarchy. No surprise, then, that as the theory and practice of digital text-matching advances, Roman epic should be a preferred laboratory here too.

No less in line with recent developments, however, is the fact that, for two leading-edge digital projects,[3] that choice has also involved a shift of attention *within* the epic canon from the Augustans to the Flavians, until recently second-

---

1 For conviviality and for intellectual stimulation at the colloquium on Intertextuality in Flavian Epic Poetry held at the Fondation Hardt in May 2015 I am grateful to hosts and fellow-participants alike. In writing up my own piece I received valuable input from Denis Feeney and Antony Augoustakis. For generous subsidy of my travel I thank the University of Geneva, as also the Department of Classics at my own university; for support of the longer-term project of which this paper forms part I am indebted to that great institution (long may it prosper), the National Endowment for the Humanities.
2 "... largely formed ...": but I am of course a long-time user of the TLG and PHI data-bases, first via David Packard's Ibycus system and in recent years via the indispensable Diogenes tool of Peter Heslin.
3 The Tesserae project is well represented in this volume. For the Fīlum tool of the Quantitative Criticism Lab (the nomenclature is more recent than the article cited), see Chaudhuri *et al.* (2015), esp. par. 3 and n. 4 for the Flavian turn. Peter Heslin too (see prev. n.) has longstanding Flavian poetic interests, which in these pages find new convergence with (and visualization in!) his digital work.

https://doi.org/10.1515/9783110602203-020

class citizens in the modern academic polity of ancient epic. In the early to mid-twentieth century, the very survival of multiple epics from one late first-century CE generation seemed to militate against the kind of appeal to exceptionalism characteristic of the evaluative criticism of those years, an appeal that could, in the absence of extant peers, have boosted the stock of (say) Statius. Instead, the precious opportunity to measure epic contemporaries alongside one another proved as fertile in generating dispraise as praise. Statius – Valerius – Silius. *sunt qui Silium malint*, as it were … In the past two or three decades, however, a growing interest in literary *system* has boosted the stock of the Flavian epicists at large, for that same reason of their multiple survival; and this is the context within which the current interest of digital humanities specialists is to be understood. But alongside this embrace of Flavian intertextual system come new *caveats* about methodological narrowness.

Outside the digital realm, a sense has been developing that Flavian epic criticism should spend more time outside its own and Latin epic's capacious (for antiquity) textual boundaries: witness the cultural and cultural materialist turn of many recent collections, and, alongside this, the call in Augoustakis (2014) to pursue more strenuously the *Greek* intertexts of Flavian epic system.[4]

There was a time (as recently as the 1970s and early 1980s) when it was an article of faith that the Augustan achievement of a native high-poetic canon in Latin had caused interest in Greek poetic intertexts to atrophy among the 'Silver' Latin poets. Not so, as we now know, thanks to advances on many fronts, culminating in Augoustakis' Hellenic manifesto.[5] However, an odd consequence of increasing attention to digital text-matching is that the ready availability of Latin data sets may be skewing curiosity about Flavian epic intertextuality towards Latin-only textual systems and away from Greek, thus unintentionally promoting a back-slide towards silver epic monoglottism. (Beyond this lies the broader risk that the digital data will drive a resurgent hyper-formalism, and thus deflect Flavian epic study from its promising cultural turn.)

Such dangers are avoidable. Provided that we understand what textual concordances can and cannot do for a poetic text, the advantages of ever-closer analysis of words, phrases and *topoi* enabled by Tesserae and kindred technologies

---

4 Augoustakis (2014), esp. 1–3; that volume's conversations resonate with many of the chapters in this volume.
5 Earlier advances: Juhnke (1972), monumentally; more recently, e.g. Lovatt (2005).

are very considerable.⁶ In the final analysis, what digital text analysis at its innovative best can do is to challenge us all, technologists and non-technologists alike, to increase our scrutiny of textual phenomena within, beyond *and* perhaps at the very limits of its interpretative reach.

Hence, without leaving the realm of *tessera* by *tessera* literalism, necessarily at the centre of this volume, let me in this short piece commit to the *cross-linguistic* turn, a current Holy Grail in the world of digital text-recognition. By way of encouraging the technologists' still-provisional experiments in Greek-Latin matching,⁷ let me offer some readings towards a future in which a digital search can perform to human standards in finding or recognizing a Latin 'match' for a Greek text, not just word by word but (with an eye for idiom beyond the basics of first-generation translation software) phrase by phrase and *topos* by *topos*; a future which may, by the time of publication, already be upon us.

What follows are some treatments of negotiation between Greek and Latin in epic proems, at a point of heuristic intersection between the study of translation (or quasi-translation) and of digital text-matching: a set of snapshots of what I shall term poetic *transliteralism*. Snapshots or, better, virtual screen grabs; but unlike other contributors to this technological sequence of chapters I offer no actual digital data for analysis.

My focus on epic proems, mostly pre-Flavian, effects an opportunistic intersection between the present volume's agenda and an ongoing project of my own on 'poetry across languages'.⁸ The rather disparate case-studies here will be unified by a recurrent emphasis upon the cross-linguistic *turn* (to lay emphasis upon that word): in each case the decisive (and decisively human?) interpretative move occurs at the moment that a translinguistic match is understood to be *self-reflexively aware* of its status *as* translation.

---

6 Cf. the programmatic opening paragraph of the chapter by Federica Bessone, in this volume: like her I accept the challenge to embrace "intertextual microanalysis ... (with all the associated risks)."

7 Tesserae's (for now) prototype Greek-Latin function is at http://tesserae.caset.buffalo.edu/cross.php. The program of the Geneva conference included a paper by Chris Forstall and James Gawley titled 'Digital approaches to Greek-Latin intertextuality', which offered a progress report on work in this area.

8 *Poetry across languages: Studies in transliteral and transcultural Latin, in antiquity and since* (working title).

1 Begin the Begin

How *do* Latin poets thematize and editorialize on cross-linguistic intertextuality? The question should send us back to revisit the very first verse in Roman epic tradition, Livius Andronicus, *Odussia* 1:

> virum mihi, Camena, insece versutum.
>
> Tell me, Camena, of the man, a turned one.

Given the achievement (not quite yet …) of a digital text-matching system capable of matching these words to Homer, *Odyssey* 1.1:

> ἄνδρα μοι ἔννεπε, Μοῦσα, πολύτροπον …
>
> Tell me, Muse, of the man of many turns …

an achievement dependent (of course) upon a wealth of pre-digital philological learning, what kinds of further post-digital story remain here for the human commentator to tell?

That is, what kind of cultural reprocessing is necessary to recreate the third century BCE *surprise* of *Camena* as a match for Μοῦσα? What kind of tweak does it take to recognize that Livius' *Camena* does not so much *reflect* a cultural match here as *create* one? To see *insece* not just as a translation of ἔννεπε but as a comparative philological essay upon it? And, if the technologist should insist that these higher interpretative moves are themselves within the potential reach of digital replication, what kind of Cartesian consciousness would the search engine have to acquire to go beyond locating *versutum* as one among many viable Latin matches for πολύτροπον and to see it as a self-annotating match, a 'turning' of the Greek word into the Latin one?[9]

Stepping back from such matters of word-by-word matching, what would it take for the machine to identify Liv. Andron. *Od.* 1 as a privileged *locus* of cross-linguistic 'tessellation' *because* it is the *incipit* of an epic, and epic *incipits* are

---

9 With this paragraph's questions see Hinds (1998) 58–62 (with refs.), esp. 61: "*Vertere* is the technical term *par excellence* for 'translation' in early Latin literature (as in *Plautus vortit barbare*); and here … our poet introduces a Ulysses in whom the very linguistic switch to which he owes his textual existence has been made part of his proverbial versatility, has been troped into his πολυτροπία". For more on the cultural 'turn' in *versutum* cf. now Bettini (2012), esp. 37–44, 55–57, 116; Feeney (2016) 53–56.

(and will continue through early modernity to be) privileged and self-reflexively concentrated sites for the negotiation of such 'tessellation'? And what kind of account is necessary to explain why this intertextual nexus is available in the first place? Why does a Tarentine speaker of Greek, perhaps (or perhaps not) a freed prisoner of war, produce this summary translation of the *Odyssey*, in Rome, in Latin, in Saturnians, for an Italian readership?[10] Of such stuff are literary histories made (see now Denis Feeney's *Beyond Greek*, a transformative work):[11] all that this page has done is to offer a less familiar slant on some very familiar questions of early Latin (pre-) hexameter poetics.

2 Aratology

ἐκ Διὸς ἀρχώμεσθα, τὸν οὐδέποτ' ἄνδρες ἐῶμεν
ἄρρητον. μεσταὶ δὲ Διὸς πᾶσαι μὲν ἀγυιαί ...

(Aratus *Phaen.* 1–2)

From Zeus let us begin; him do we mortals never leave unnamed. Full of Zeus are all the streets ...

The corpus of Latin translations or versions of the *Phaenomena* of Aratus will always have something to offer to any enquiry into 'transliteralism', whether analogue or digital. Here, recurrently available in ancient literary history, is a cross-linguistic nexus rich in opportunities for a digital program to 'learn' a repertoire of words, phrases and *topoi* self-consciously aligned between Greek and Latin verse idiom; here, recurrently, is another provocation to consider what may be at stake when Roman writers display their poetic virtuosity in Greek (why so often with one text, and why with *this* text ...?).

Take the *Aratea* of Germanicus Caesar, an intervention datable to the early first century CE. Alongside Aratus' own *incipit* (above), let me quote the opening lines (1–4):

ab Iove principium magno deduxit Aratus.
carminis at nobis, genitor, tu maximus auctor,

---

10 Excellent framing of these questions in McElduff (2013) 43–54; cf. 10 on the scope and scale of the *Odussia* (twenty-four Homeric books 'chopped' down to one, closer to epitome than to full-scale translation).
11 Feeney (2016), esp. 53–56 (already cited), 62–66 and 77–79.

> te veneror tibi sacra fero doctique laboris
> primitias. probat ipse deum rectorque satorque.
>
> From Jove, the great one, Aratus drew his beginning. But you, sire, are the greatest author of song for me. You are the one that I reverence; you are the one to whom I bring sacred gifts, the first fruits of my learned labour. The ruler and begetter of the gods himself approves.

As with Livius, it may be heuristically useful to apply (or to imagine applying) the emergent technology of digital Greek-Latin text-matching to this well-known case of cross-linguistic equivalence. A 'tessellating' mindset will allow the last word of Germanicus' opening sentence, *Aratus* (1), to be described not just as a specification of his poetic source, not just as a post-Alexandrian 'gloss' of Aratus' own sphragistic pun in the enjambed ἄρρητον (1–2),[12] but (another way of describing the same thing) as a *near-transcription* of that final word in the Alexandrian poet's opening sentence.

Character-by-character transliteralism, then, from the Greek alphabet to the Roman, spelling out the name of an author at the Latin line-end. Not, however, the author of this poem itself. In his sphragistic and apparently self-reflexive juxtaposition of *Aratus* and *auctor* at the ends of the first two hexameters, what Germanicus has done, in fact, is to associate his poem with *two* 'authors' other than himself: Aratus in line 1, Tiberius or Augustus—that is, the poet's adoptive father or grandfather—in line 2.[13]

To dig a little deeper into these opening lines, let me quote and then supplement a representative critical paraphrase of German. *Arat*. 1–16:[14]

> "... Although the two poems begin with the same phrase (ἐκ Διὸς ἀρχώμεσθα = *ab Iove principium*), they quickly diverge: Aratus' Stoic Zeus [*Phaen*. 1–18] is left behind in favour of imperial panegyric [Germ. *Arat*. 2–16]."

Yes indeed; but the qualification needs to be qualified. The literalism which matches those *incipit*-phrases encodes *within itself* an ideologically-freighted pun: even before the divergence in dedicatees described in the quotation, the

---

[12] Bing (1990), with Possanza (2004) 107.
[13] While taking as read Germanicus' authorship of the poem, I need not here go into the matter of whether Augustus or Tiberius is to be understood as the addressee (*genitor* in line 2 is honorific on one interpretation, literal on the other): see Possanza (2004) 219–243, esp. 227–233; Caldini Montanari (2010); Volk (2015) 277, n. 54. For apparent reinforcement of the imperial address by an etymologizing gesture in *auctor* to 'Augustus' (a title applicable to either emperor) see Possanza (2004) 107, n. 6; cf. n. 33 below.
[14] Schroeder (2005), reporting Possanza (2004) 105–109.

Latin 'beginning' in *principium* already foreshadows the switch from Zeus to, precisely, a *princeps* (whether Tiberius or Augustus). From the outset, Germanicus' translation has reconfigured the Stoic primacy of Zeus for the vocabulary of Roman rule, has found the ἀρχή in ἀρχώμεσθα …

Even more than those of Aratus, Germanicus' opening verses loop in upon themselves to *thematize* beginnings: at close quarters, what are the *doctique laboris / primitias* offered to the Caesarian addressee in lines 3–4 but, in particular, the poem's *primi versus*? An apt emphasis in a proem which begins by Latinizing ἐκ Διὸς ἀρχώμεσθα, a proem whose opening words (appropriately for a poet joining a succession of Roman translators who have competitively rendered these lines) constitute a meditation on how to render the idea of ἀρχή into Latin—'first fruits' indeed.[15]

German. *Arat.* 15 *haec ego dum Latiis conor praedicere Musis* …, "While I attempt to give notice of these things with my Latin Muses …": the Aratean tradition at Rome was always available, it seems, as a laboratory for cross-linguistic text matching, a centuries-long insiders' conversation about poetic literalism between Greek and Latin, from Cicero and Varro Atacinus to Ovid, Germanicus and beyond.[16] More than that, the 'Aratean moment' seems to have operated as a trope for cross-linguistic and cross-cultural interaction not just when Romans were actually translating the *Phaenomena* but when they were talking about it. Most famously in Cinna's neoteric epigram about a deluxe gift copy of the *Phaenomena* imported to Italy on a Bithynian boat,[17] and in a host of allusions (direct and oblique) by Virgil, Ovid and other poets; but in more impalpable instances too, such as an anecdote in the *Attic Nights* of Aulus Gellius (2.21) in which, as I plan to argue elsewhere, Aratus' *Phaenomena* lurks as an implicit subtext when a group of Hellenophile Romans and Romanophile Greeks sails through the night

---

15 It is a feature of competition in the Aratean tradition that it can often appear to be *de minimis*. In the felicitous suggestion of Katz (2009) 79–84, Cicero's rendition of the initial ἐκ Διὸς as *a Iove*, rather than *ab Iove*, with omission of the 'b', allows *his* version of Aratus to begin by sounding out all five vowels, *aioue*, in a gesture of pure language-processing (Cic. *Arat.* 1 ap. *Leg.* 2.7 <u>A Iove</u> *Musarum primordia*); much more *ad loc*. And what Germanicus' imperializing *principium* does in the pun proposed above is not to add new wording to the repertoire, but to give new force to some *existing* wording: Verg. *Ecl.* 3.60 *ab Iove principium Musae: Iovis omnia plena*, "From Jove is the beginning of my song: of Jove all things are full" (a famous amoebean 'sample' of Aratus; cf. Clausen (1994) *ad loc.*, and Calp. *Ecl.* 4.82 later).

16 And a conversation about much else too: (differently) rich treatments in Gee (2013) and Volk (2015).

17 Hinds (2001) 224–236, esp. 224–227.

from Aegina to the Piraeus gazing at the stars and weighing their Greek and Roman names and back-stories.[18]

3 The wrath of Juno

'Transliteralism' is just one specialized subset of the traffic across languages that defines Roman poetry at every level, from the *Aeneid* on down. The *Aeneid* is of course famous for *not* being Livius' *Odussia*, or indeed Germanicus' (or Cicero's, or anyone else's) *Aratea*: this is a Roman epic which 'translates' both the *Iliad* and the *Odyssey* without literalism, a spacious and successful act of literary and cultural mediation between Greek codes and Latin.

And yet, the *most literal* case of intertextual transcription in Roman epic has been uncovered by modern (but pre-digital) criticism in the opening words of the divine character who drives the *Aeneid*'s plot of 'anger':

> cum Juno, aeternum servans sub pectore volnus,
> haec secum: 'Mene incepto desistere victam,
> nec posse Italia Teucrorum avertere regem?
> quippe vetor fatis …'
>
> (Verg. *Aen.* 1.36–39)

> … when Juno, nursing an everlasting wound deep in her breast, spoke thus to herself: 'What! I resign my undertaking, vanquished, and fail to turn from Italy the Teucrian king? The fates, doubtless, forbid me …'

In the formulation of Don Fowler, building upon the insights of William Levitan and Denis Feeney, "'… The poet [of the *Aeneid*] is already looking forward to the eventual end which Jupiter will impose on the poem, and on the anarchy of Juno, who, as befits the deity of the Kalends, has dominated the beginning: her second word is 'beginning' (*incepto*, 1.37).' Indeed, it has been argued that her first word is also a beginning: in *mene incepto desistere victam* … it is possible to hear the angry echo of the first word of the *Iliad*, μῆνιν."[19]

Let us use a 'tessellating' sensibility to revisit this nexus. What would it take to configure a digital search engine to 'find' a cross-linguistic pun like *men(e) in-*?

---

18 Gell. *NA* 2.21, esp. 1–2, to be treated in my projected *Poetry across languages* (mentioned earlier).
19 Fowler (1997) 9 = (2000) 291–292: pun from Levitan (1993); quotation within the quotation from Feeney (1991) 137–138.

Not a lot; and yet, in another way, a great deal. Five letters out of six, and negotiation across non-identical word breaks complicated by elision: a digitally programmable hit, to be sure;[20] but, for all that, a needle in a haystack among all the false positives. Note that true sound-matching technology is not (yet) in play: many 'heard' echoes would be less hospitable than this one to character-by-character on-page tracking.

A needle in a haystack: it must fall to the human commentator, surely, to find and to press this pun, picking up the 'reflexive annotation' of *men(e) in-* by *incepto*, so delicately delineated in Fowler's account above, and, on a larger arc, picking up the speech-opening as one of the *Aeneid*'s many re-performances of its own *incipit* sentence: *Aen.* 1.4 ... *saevae memorem Iunonis ob iram*. In 1.37 Juno's *ira* is indeed 'mindful' (sc. of its Iliadic origins), and 'speaks' its memory (*memor* again) by uttering those first two syllables of Homer's originary epic.

More tendentiously, Juno's pun 'answers' the imperative in that opening command of Greek literature (duly decontextualized): μῆνιν ἄειδε, θεά ..., "goddess, sing '*menin*'". Here at *Aen.* 1.37 a goddess *does* sing '*menin*' (or at least '*men(e) in-*'); and she declares her disinclination to let go of the word. It is worth registering that, before resorting to cross-linguistic punning, Juno has already (in Virgil's reportage) exhausted the available Latin lexicon of wrath a few lines above (1.23–29):

> ... veterisque memor Saturnia belli,
> prima quod ad Troiam pro caris gesserat Argis –
> necdum etiam *causae irarum saevique dolores*
> exciderant animo: manet *alta mente* repostum
> iudicium Paridis spretaeque *iniuria* formae,
> et genus *invisum, et* rapti Ganymedis honores.
> his *accensa* super ...

> ... The daughter of Saturn, mindful also of the old war which previously she had fought at Troy for her beloved Argos—not yet, too, had the causes of her anger and her bitter sorrows faded from her mind: deep in her heart remain the judgment of Paris and the outrage to her slighted beauty, her hatred of the race and the honours paid to ravished Ganymede. Inflamed hereby yet more ...

---

20 The Tesserae program does indeed have a 'sound' feature under 'advanced search', thus far limited to searches *within* Latin or Greek, which "returns sets of parallels between texts where the matched words *share three-letter sequences*" (http://tesserae.caset.buffalo.edu/help_advanced.php).

What now remains for the transcultural goddess, as direct speech begins, but to use her Latin to reach back for the originary Greek term?[21]

However plausible or implausible such a plot of metatranslation may be thought to be, it looks likely to elude the protocols of digital measurement. And yet ... for a critic with computational interests there *is* a consideration, measurable but quirky, that may nudge this particular pun towards intelligibility: an appeal to so-called stichometric intertextuality.[22] One reason the inspired intuition about *men(e) in-* must be right is that it moves the *incipit*-word of the *Iliad* into a shadow 'delayed proem' position 37 lines into *Aeneid* 1: and that positioning just happens to anticipate the *locus* into which Virgil will famously move the *actual* delayed proem of his epic's second—Iliadic—half, 37 lines into *Aeneid* 7: *nunc age, qui reges, Erato ...*, "Come now, Erato, who were the kings ...". In a world of digital text measurement, stichometric number-crunching has the potential to get completely out of hand: but in the present case it is hard to resist this equivalence of positional displacement, whether it be discerned through an ancient technology of line numbering in the physical margin,[23] through a modern technology of searching *by* line number, or just through the heightened awareness which any writer or reader of epic brings to anything associated with a proem, or with a *proemio al mezzo*.

4 Iliades Latinae (1)

Not just in Virgil but elsewhere in Latin too, the *incipit* of the *Iliad* is an inherently privileged nexus for any cross-linguistic poetic enterprise. If anyone was in a position to understand this, it was Statius, native of the bilingual Bay of Naples, and

---

21 So similarly O'Hara (1996) 115, citing also *Aen.* 1.11 *tantaene animis caelestibus irae?*, "Can such great anger reside in heavenly spirits?".
22 The idea of the 'precise stichometrical equivalent' first received systematic discussion from Llewelyn Morgan in connection with certain intertextual effects in the *Georgics*: Morgan (1999) 23–27 and 223–226; cf. Hinds (1998) 92 and n. 80 on Stat. *Theb.* 10.445–448 and Verg. *Aen.* 9.446–449; Smith (1990) on Ov. *Met.* 10.475 and Verg. *Aen.* 10.475. In the present case one might more properly speak of stichometric *intra*textuality.
23 "Running, current, partial or marginal stichometry is a way of describing the practice of numbering the lines of a text by ascending letters of the alphabet, often between two horizontal bars, or else by a series of dots, normally every hundred lines or the prose equivalent ... The evidence [from papyri] is entirely Greek": Morgan (1999) 223–226 at 223 and n.1.

Latin poetic son of a Greek poetic father.[24] Here (to touch for one time only upon an indubitably Flavian epic text) are the opening words of the *Achilleid* (1.1–3):

> magnanimum Aeaciden formidatamque Tonanti
> progeniem et patrio vetitam succedere caelo,
> diva, refer ...

In response to Statius' overt characterization of this new epic as a kind of supplementary reworking of the *Iliad—Ach.* 1.3–4 *quamquam acta viri multum inclita cantu / Maeonio (sed plura vacant)*[25]—it may be a worthwhile exercise to read these opening words *as if* they were the start of a direct Latinization of the Homeric poem, a latter-day counterpart to the *Odussia* of Livius Andronicus.

In the Flavian poet's incipitatory naming of the epic hero, we can register an approach to the opening verse of the *Iliad*:

> μῆνιν ἄειδε, θεά, Πηληιάδεω Ἀχιλῆος
>
> The wrath sing, goddess, of Peleus' son Achilles

No actual verbal 'hit' between the patronymic words, but *Aeaciden does* precisely complete the three-generation genealogy set in motion by Πηληιάδεω Ἀχιλῆος— a reachable and teachable match, perhaps, for a digital search engine. Indeed, this kind of pattern-recognition must be a medium-term *sine qua non* for digital text-matching in classical poetry, whether within Greek, within Latin, or cross-linguistically: clusters upon clusters of genealogically and geographically associated names and epithets await tagging. Achilles = Pelides = Aeacides ...[26]

To continue for a moment the experiment of seeking post-Iliadic literalism in Statius' first words,[27] the *Achilleid* begins with a calque on a Homeric epithet (*magnanimum* ~ μεγάθυμον) followed by a Greek (and Greek-inflected) name (*Aeaciden* = Αἰακίδην).[28] But also the beginning and end of Statius' opening *sentence*,

---

24 In the felicitous formulation of Rosati (2011), then, a poet with *tria corda*: Greek, Roman and Neapolitan. Cf. Newlands (2012), esp. 136–159, and anew in this volume.
25 See below for full quotation of *Ach.* 1.1–19, with English translation.
26 Neil Coffee draws my attention here to the relevance of current prosopographical initiatives like SNAP-DRGN (Standards for Networking Ancient Prosopographies) and their integration by Recogito (an on-line platform for collaborative document annotation).
27 A single match registers on a search using Tesserae's prototype Greek-Latin digital function: *Ach.* 1.3 *diva ... cantu* and *Il.* 1.1 ἄειδε, θεά.
28 The combination of patronymic Αἰακίδης and epithet μεγάθυμος is not found in Homer, but the epithet itself is a very common one in the *Iliad* (over sixty occurrences); it is applied to Achilles at 20.498 Ἀχιλλῆος μεγαθύμου, 23.168 μεγάθυμος Ἀχιλλεύς; 21.153 Πηλείδη μεγάθυμε; 17.214,

> magnanimum Aeaciden ... diva, refer

can be read as a near-to-literal translation of the *Iliad*'s opening *line*: *Aeaciden* renders Πηληιάδεω Ἀχιλῆος (as just noted); *diva, refer* renders (and indeed 'brings back') ἄειδε, θεά;[29] and in each case the opening word names the hero's and epic's governing emotion. The μῆνιν of Achilles is redescribed by Statius as a 'mightiness' of *animus* (spirit, pride, anger, all of the above ...) in the compound adjective *magnanimum*; and, perhaps, this equivalence is helped a little by an element of phonetic convergence between the epics' opening syllables: *menin* > *mañan*, as it were.

Be that as it may, searches both digital and pre-digital have of course traced the Roman allusive genealogy of the *Achilleid*'s *incipit*-word *magnanimum* within Latin poetry itself: an epithet repeatedly applied by Virgil to Aeneas, from *Aen.* 1.260 on; an epithet applied by Ovid to Achilles himself at a suggestively 'pre-Statian' moment in *Met.* 13.298;[30] but also an epithet most recently applied to Domitian (*magnanimus ... Caesar*) just seven lines 'earlier' in Statius' own epic output—at the very end of the *Thebaid*.[31]

Domitian: let us shift our attention at this point to the *politics* of the epic's set-up. Here is the *Achilleid* proem in its entirety, a proem whose wealth of nuance has in recent years been so well elucidated, not least by contributors to the present volume:

> magnanimum Aeaciden formidatamque Tonanti
> progeniem et patrio vetitam succedere caelo,
> diva, refer. quamquam acta viri multum inclita cantu
> Maeonio (sed plura vacant), nos ire per omnem –
> sic amor est – heroa velis Scyroque latentem   5
> Dulichia proferre tuba nec in Hectore tracto
> sistere, sed tota iuvenem deducere Troia.
> tu modo, si veterem digno deplevimus haustu,
> da fontes mihi, Phoebe, novos ac fronde secunda
> necte comas: neque enim Aonium nemus advena pulso   10
> nec mea nunc primis augescunt tempora vittis.
> scit Dirceaus ager meque inter prisca parentum
> nomina cumque suo numerant Amphione Thebae.
> at tu, quem longe primum stupet Itala virtus

18.226 and 19.75 μεγαθύμου Πηλείωνος (19.75 μῆνιν ἀπειπόντος μεγαθύμου Πηλείωνος, "... since the great-hearted son of Peleus had renounced his wrath"). Cf. Heslin (2005) 71, n. 38.
29 "... brings back": I owe this self-allusive read of *refer* to Denis Feeney, *per litteras*.
30 Excellently unpacked by Heslin (2005) 71–72; cf. Dilke (1954) *ad loc.*
31 *Theb.* 12.814: cf. Penwill (2013) 45–46.

Graiaque, cui geminae florent vatumque ducumque   15
certatim laurus – olim dolet altera vinci –,
da veniam ac trepidum patere hoc sudare parumper
pulvere. te longo necdum fidente paratu
molimur magnusque tibi praeludit Achilles.

(*Ach.* 1.1–19)

Of mighty-spirited Aeacides and the offspring feared by the Thunderer and forbidden to succeed to his father's heaven, goddess, relate. Although the hero's deeds are much famed in Maeonian song, more are yet to celebrate: be it your pleasure that I (so I desire) traverse the whole hero, bringing him forth by Dulichian trumpet as he hides in Scyros, and that I not stop at Hector's dragging, but lead the warrior down through Troy's whole story. Only do you, Phoebus, grant me new founts if I have drained the old one with a worthy draught, and bind my hair with propitious leafage; for indeed as no stranger do I knock at the Aonian grove, nor are these the first fillets to magnify my temples. The land of Dirce knows it, and Thebes numbers me among her forebears' ancient names along with her own Amphion. But you, the wonder of Italian and Greek manhood first by far, for whom the twin laurels of bard and commander flourish in rivalry (one of the two is long since sad to be surpassed), give me good leave; suffer me in my trepidation to sweat awhile in this dust. On you I work in long and not yet confident preparation, and mighty Achilles is the prelude to you.

Alongside the overt citation of Homer as code model (3–4 *cantu / Maeonio*), alongside the cross-linguistic metapoetic pun in *Dulichia … tuba* (6), whose island epithet trumpets an epic both 'long' (δολιχ-, δουλιχ-) and Odyssean, while also combining with *tota iuvenem deducere Troia* (7) to revisit Ovid's *perpetuum deducite … carmen* (*Met.* 1.4), Statius has included in these opening lines a passage that overtly thematizes the idea of bilingual and bicultural competence (14–16):

at tu, quem longe primum stupet Itala virtus
Graiaque, cui geminae florent vatumque ducumque
certatim laurus …

The competence here is of course not the poet's but the emperor's. And yet, in the larger context of the preface, the emperor's bilingual and bicultural credentials— his appeal to the admiring gaze of Greek and of Italian 'manhood'—model and mirror the poet's.[32] The presentation of the emperor *as* a poet allows Statius not just to defer to the emperor but to *double* him, not least as a player across languages and cultures, and indeed (bold claim for any Roman poet) as a claimant

---

[32] Fundamental here is Bessone (2014) 216–221, esp. 221 on the relationship between *Theb.* 12.814–815 and *Ach.* 1.14–16; also 218–219 on the implication in *Ach.* 1.12–13 that the *Thebaid* has made Statius into an 'honorary citizen' of Thebes and hence, at the start of the *Achilleid*, "already a 'naturalized' Greek" (221 again).

on a Greek-speaking *audience* as well as a Latin-speaking one. Just above, the poet's brows are magnified—*augescunt* (11)—by his latest epic enterprise; but the crowning of that enterprise is enabled and guaranteed by the ultimate giver and receiver of 'increase', Caesar Domitianus *Augustus*.[33]

Unlike in Germanicus' case in the *Aratea* proem, this coming together of the projects of poet and of *princeps* is not a family matter.[34] However, the conceit of cross-cultural reach as a shared goal of epic and imperial enterprise is an enduring one, to be emblematized in stone at a later point in antiquity through a part-Latin and part-Greek inscribed monument in Trajan's Forum, jointly dedicated by a western and an eastern emperor to Claudian, a distinctly post-Statian poet, "the mind of Virgil and the Muse of Homer in one man."[35]

The *Achilleid* preface synecdochically performs the full richness of Flavian epic intertextuality, sorting in new ways the relations and interrelations of myth, literary history, poetic career, and geopolitical ideology. But also, specifically, the first impression of the opening words as a meta-translation of a Homeric Greek proem remains in play; and this is reinforced by the closing clause, which, after nineteen lines, reinscribes the idea of a Statian doubling of the *Iliad incipit*,

> ... magnusque tibi praeludit Achilles

a doubling which has now been redoubled in the intervening verses. This proem reperforms the proem of the *Iliad*; but also it *pre*performs the prelude to an epic about Domitian; and in a sense it annexes not just its own Achilles-preface but *any* Achilles preface—including Homer's in *Iliad* 1—as the prelude to a Statian epic about Domitian.

A confident prediction of future achievement. However, the proem's much-studied thematics of secondariness and succession are fraught with anxiety too (a quality hard to measure digitally, let it be said).[36] The extraordinary opening sen-

---

[33] On the repertoire of words associated with the title 'Augustus' in ancient etymologizing, including *augere/auctus*, see Suet. *Aug.* 7.2, Ov. *Fast.* 1.609–16, and Maltby (1991) s.v. 'augustus'.
[34] But the parallel is a suggestive one: Rosati (2002), esp. 242–243, is surely right to make Germanicus central to such conversations about the interplay of poetic and imperial inspiration.
[35] ΕΙΝ ΕΝΙ ΒΙΡΓΙΛΙΟΙΟ ΝΟΟΝ ΚΑΙ ΜΟΥΣΑΝ ΟΜΗΡΟΥ: on the Claudian monument (*CIL* 6.1710; a Latin prose dedication culminating in a Greek elegiac distich) set up at the command of the brother-emperors of West and East, Honorius and Arcadius, and on Claudian as a poet with extant works in both languages, see Hinds (2013) 171–174 and refs.
[36] "... secondariness and succession": I pick up, *inter alia*, my own previous discussion at Hinds (1998) 95–98.

tence in 1–3 presents Achilles not just as a great-spirited hero but as the (not-) offspring of Jove who is so feared by that powerful father as to cause him to deny, or rather to forestall, his paternity. Political readings of the *Achilleid*, as of the *Thebaid*, are ready to weigh the epics' Greek myths of fraught succession against the dynastic anxieties of Flavian Rome; but the potential reverberations of the succession plot for *Statius' own* poetic and linguistic inheritance are worth considering too. Is the Hellenizing *Achilleid* a worthy successor to the Hellenizing *Thebaid? But also,* is it—as an Achilles epic—the natural offspring of the original Hellenic and Homeric *Iliad*, or rather a successor that poses some kind of threat to the parent tradition, a *progenies* of problematic paternity? To all the other succession anxieties here should one add, *even after all these years*, the anxiety (for readers as well as for poets, in one language as well as in the other) of the canonical turn from Greek into Latin, newly and uniquely urgent for a poet of Statius' own bicultural background and paternity?

5 *Iliades Latinae* (2)

But I close with a more direct Latinization of the *Iliad*'s *incipit*, once regarded as Flavian but more likely datable a long generation before the *Achilleid*, and hence as good a text as any to put at the boundary of a volume on Flavian epic intertextuality. Here are the opening lines of the *Ilias Latina*,[37] the probably Neronian poem which served for the Middle Ages as a make-do surrogate for the *Iliad*, just now beginning to receive due attention as a *tour de force* of meta-translation, and a suggestive text for the emerging study of the poetics of epitome;[38] also, incidentally, a poem which short-circuits Latin literary history through a sense of structural affinity with Livius' *Odussia*:

> iram pande mihi Pelidae, diva, superbi,
> tristia quae miseris iniecit funera Grais
> atque animas fortes heroum tradidit Orco
> latrantumque dedit rostris volucrumque trahendos

---

37 *Ilias Latina*: fundamental is the edition and commentary of Scaffai (1982); cf. the succinct edition of Kennedy (1998), with English translation (self-published and hard to obtain); also Tilroe (1939), an old dissertation from the University of Southern California. For the vexed beginning of line 7 (on which more below) I adopt the emendation of Kilpatrick (1992); translation after Kennedy, with minor adjustments.
38 I draw attention here to the multi-year project (2015–2019) on 'Epitome in Late Latin Literature' at the University of Ghent (principal investigator Marco Formisano).

illorum exsangues, inhumatis ossibus, artus.   5
confiebat enim summi sententia regis,
obtulerant ex quo discordia pectora pugnas,
sceptriger Atrides et bello clarus Achilles.
quis deus hos ira tristi contendere iussit?

(Ilias Lat. 1–9)

Inform me, goddess, of the anger of Peleus' haughty son that brought grim deaths upon the wretched Greeks and sent brave souls of heroes to the underworld, leaving their bloodless limbs to be torn by the jaws of dogs and birds; in open fields their bones unburied lay, consequent upon the will of heaven's king unrivalled, from the time when discordant hearts provoked a quarrel: those of the sceptered son of Atreus and Achilles famed in war. What god ordered them in grievous rage to contend?

More than the rest of the *Ilias Latina*, which has fewer than 1,100 lines in which to encapsulate the 15,000-plus of the *Iliad* itself, these opening verses track their Homeric original line by line and even word by word. Digitally, then, like the Aratean poems, an opportunity for a text-matching program to 'learn' pattern-recognition between Latin and Greek, and indeed specifically to learn a range of *topoi* and turns of phrase which can 'educate' such a program to match Roman epic idiom with its Homeric models and analogues.[39] For the ancient author and his readers, probably already a 'laboratory' for thinking intertextually about poetry across languages, about epic between Greek and Latin. And for the modern post-digital intertextualist, another cue to *use the idea* of pattern-recognition to 'tessellate', to read and to scrutinize with the sense of closeness and minuteness required of those who design digital text systems.

In particular, the framework of 'transliteralism' established by the opening words—*iram pande mihi Pelidae, Diva* = μῆνιν ἄειδε, θεά, Πηληιάδεω etc.—has the effect of sharpening the reader's awareness of every discernible departure in the wording of the *Ilias Latina* proem from its Homeric original. Take the bodies which are "[made] to be the spoil for dogs and birds" in lines 4–5:

latrantumque dedit rostris volucrumque trahendos
illorum exsangues, inhumatis ossibus, artus

... αὐτοὺς δὲ ἑλώρια τεῦχε κύνεσσιν
οἰωνοῖσί τε πᾶσι ...

---

[39] A comparison between the opening lines of *Iliad* 1 and of the *Ilias Latina* using the prototype of Tesserae's Greek-Latin function disappoints, perhaps inevitably: idiomatic and genre-sensitive pattern recognition will come only with further programming.

An expansion, to be sure: *inhumatis ossibus* renders explicit an anxiety about deprivation of burial which was already inherent in the Iliadic original. Not just an expansion, however, but also an epitomator's conflation. *dedit ... trahendos / illorum exsangues ... artus* elaborates αὐτοὺς δὲ ἑλώρια τεῦχε; but it is an elaboration which assimilates these generalized Greek heroes' limbs to the fate of one particular hero on the opposing side, Hector (of course), whose limbs will so famously be 'dragged' (not in this case by scavenging dogs or birds) at the opposite end of the epic here encapsulated. A 'thematic' allusion beyond the reach of digital text-matching? Well, in this case, no; because when towards its conclusion the *Ilias Latina* offers its précis of the dragging of Hector's body (997–999),

> ... hunc animi nondum satiatus Achilles
> deligat ad currum pedibusque *exsanguia membra*
> ter circum muros victor *trahit* ...

Achilles, his anger not yet full, ties him to his chariot and by his feet drags his bloodless limbs in victory thrice around the walls.

the *inter*textual correspondence with Book 22 of the *Iliad* also turns out to be an *intra*textual correspondence (marked by my italics) with lines 4–5 of the *Ilias Latina* itself.

In the systems of first-century CE Roman epic intertextuality (as every reader of Flavian *epos* knows), to be post-Homeric is almost by definition to be post-Virgilian; and the *Ilias Latina* is no exception. The axiom may even extend to those very first words, in which the Homeric original is tracked so closely:

> iram pande mihi Pelidae, diva ...

> μῆνιν ἄειδε, θεά, Πηληϊάδεω ...

In terms of cross-linguistic matching, a little latitude is granted to transliteralism in *pande mihi* ('open up for me') = ἄειδε; and it is a specifically Virgilian kind of latitude. In a pattern that a digital search will prioritize only if Muse-invocation is tagged as a privileged nexus, the changed nuance of the invocatory verb Virgilianizes the *Iliad-incipit* by drawing, not on the *incipit* of the *Aeneid*, but on a call to poetological action *within* the *Aeneid*, the start of the catalogue of Italian forces (7.641–642):[40]

---

[40] *Aen.* 7.641 is repeated *verbatim* by Virgil at *Aen.* 10.163; the context there (Etruscan catalogue, balancing *Aen.* 7's Latin catalogue) is not inimical to the connotations suggested here.

> *pandite* nunc Helicona, *deae*, cantusque movete,
> qui bello exciti reges ...

> Open up Helicon now, goddesses, and mobilize poetic strains, telling what kings were roused to war ...

Perhaps (to press the allusion, if such it is) the poet of the *Ilias Latina* accesses not Virgilian Muse-invocation language *tout court* but Virgilian Muse-invocation language as the marker of a *specifically Italian* epic project:

> ... quae quemque secutae
> complerint campos acies, *quibus Itala iam tum*
> *floruerit terra alma viris, quibus arserit armis.*
>
> (*Aen.* 7.642–644)

> ... what battle lines followed each one, filling the plain; with what manhood even then did the nurturing land of Italy bloom, what armed forces kindled her to flame.

An intertextual stretch, perhaps: yet this new *incipit* is one with a very special kind of investment in 'Italianness', even beyond (say) the Latinizations of Homeric combat in *Aeneid* 7–12. The *Ilias Latina* is a Greek epic converted into Latin; more than that, it is a Greek epic whose *incipit* proclaims the Italianness which is its *raison d'être* through a particular device of book-production (*Ilias Lat.* 1–9 again, typographically enhanced):

> **I**ram pande mihi Pelidae, Diva, superbi,
> **T**ristia quae miseris iniecit funera Grais
> **A**tque animas fortes heroum tradidit Orco
> **L**atrantumque dedit rostris volucrumque trahendos
> **I**llorum exsangues, inhumatis ossibus, artus.   5
> **C**onfiebat enim summi sententia regis,
> **O**btulerant ex quo discordia pectora pugnas,
> **S**ceptriger Atrides et bello clarus Achilles.
> quis deus hos ira tristi contendere iussit?

Yes, in *this* importation of the *Iliad* proem, the literal Latinization of Homer's *incipit* is annotated and thematized by ... incipitatory acrostic. And *I-T-A-L-I-C-O-S* in the opening letters of *Ilias Latina* 1–8[41] is not just any incipitatory acrostic but

---

41 Or, as transmitted, I-T-A-L-I-C-*-S. The acrostic escaped detection until 1875 (Seyffert) because of the fact that in the great bulk of the manuscripts (45 are consulted by Scaffai) line 7 begins *protulerant ex quo* (PW, the oldest witnesses) or *pertulerant ex quo* (most others; occasionally reversed as *ex quo pert.*). Modern editorial work has addressed the resultant crux

an incipitatory acrostic across languages: whether it identifies the epitome's author as a certain Baebius Italicus (as specified in the superscript of one humanist manuscript),[42] as the more famous Silius Italicus (as was once thought), or as another poet named Italicus, it also, no less importantly, spells out the *Italianness* of this 'Latinized Iliad'—*nomen omen*—, contributing anew to a pattern of geopoetic negotiation characteristic of Roman epic prologues at large.

As we shall see shortly, the 'signature' will be completed more than a thousand lines later, with a book-ending acrostic in the epilogue—*scripsit* 'wrote'— to pick up and balance the initial *Italicos*.

The actual retelling of the *Iliad* concludes, however, just before that epilogue:

stant circum Iliades matres manibusque decoros
abrumpunt crines laniataque pectora plangunt:
illo namque rogo natorum funera cernunt.
tollitur et iuvenum magno cum murmure clamor   1055
flebilis: ardebat flamma namque Ilion illa.
inter quos gemitus laniato pectore coniunx
provolat Andromache mediosque immittere in ignes
se cupit Astyanacta tenens, quam iussa suarum
turba rapit. contra tamen omnibus usque resistit,   1060
donec conlapsae ceciderunt robora flammae
inque leves abiit tantus dux ille favillas.

(*Ilias Lat.* 1052–1062)

The Ilian matrons stand about and with their hands tear their fine hair and beat their lacerated breasts: for on that pyre they look upon the funerals of their sons. A tearful cry of youths is raised with a mighty murmur, for in that flame was burning Ilium. Among the lamentations, Hector's wife Andromache rushes forth, tearing her breast, and seeks to throw herself amidst the flames while holding Astyanax, but the crowd of her companions under orders holds her back. She continues to resist them all until the strength of the flames dies completely down and that leader in his greatness has departed into unsubstantial ash.

The *Ilias Latina* nears its end, just like the original *Iliad*, with the funeral of Hector and the despair of the Trojans (cf. *Il.* 24.707–804); a despair marked in this case,

---

through a variety of solutions which replace the initial P with an initial U/V or, in the case of Kilpatrick (1992), followed here, initial O; cf. Scaffai (1982) 11–13 and ad *Ilias Lat.* 6–8. Kennedy (1998) reproduces the acrostic in his version of 1–8; I disguised it earlier by abandoning his stichic form. (Contrast my layout of 1063–1070 below.)

42 The attribution to 'Baebius Italicus' in the title of an 'otherwise undistinguished' 15th century manuscript was noticed in 1890 (i.e. a few years after the detection of the acrostic): Schenkl (1890), with Kennedy (1998) 10–11. The resultant eclipse of the initial attribution to Silius Italicus is traced in Scaffai (1982) 11–18, esp. 15–18.

however, with some extra prophetic hindsight. In the *Iliad* the mourners' laments are charged with a foreboding that this funeral is the beginning of the end of Troy itself; in the *Ilias Latina* that foreboding has become a *locus* for *recollection* of the intervening tradition *of poetry about* the end of Troy, especially (since the epitomator is writing in Latin) poetry by Virgil. Especially but not exclusively: digital searching confirms some intertextual privileging of a previous exercise in Latin epitome, the potted history of the Trojan War and its aftermath in Books 12–14 of Ovid's *Metamorphoses*.

To the poet of the *Ilias Latina* the flame of Hector's pyre is, in anticipation, the burning of Troy itself (1056 *ardebat flamma namque Ilion illa*). That anticipation is also a recall of a summary set-up phrase at Ov. *Met*. 13.408, *Ilion ardebat*, a link confirmed by additional convergences of phrasing in the preceding and succeeding lines: with *Ilias Lat*. 1053 *laniataque pectora plangunt* (Trojan women anticipate their own sons' deaths) and 1057 *laniato pectore* (of Andromache) compare *Met*. 13.491–493 (Hecuba, after the actual fall of Troy) *consuetaque pectora plangit ... laniato pectore*, "she beats the breasts habituated to the blows ... tearing her breast."

Epitome begets epitome: but also, this small subplot of 'tessellation' can serve as a reminder of a larger principle important for the Flavian texts studied in this volume, namely that, no matter how post-Homeric or post-Virgilian the overall agenda, Ovid is always central to later first-century epic tradition too. As Scaffai notes *ad loc*., the very end of Hector's story, in the final narrative verse of the *Ilias Latina* before the closing sphragis and acrostic, reads as a post-Ovidian metamorphic fade (1062):

> *inque leves abiit* tantus dux ille *favillas*

Compare Meleager, in the myth at the midpoint[43] of the *Metamorphoses* (8.524–525):

> *inque leves abiit* paulatim spiritus auras
> paulatim cana pruinam velante *favilla*.

> ... his life's breath gradually departed into unsubstantial air as white ash gradually veiled the glowing coals.

---

[43] Meleager as *Met*. midpoint: Hinds (1985) 22 = (2006) 430.

More pervasively (to return from Ovid to Virgil), the *Iliad's* anticipation of the fall of Troy in the closural laments for Hector becomes in the *Ilias Latina* a (p)refiguration of the *Aeneid*'s own version of the Fall of Troy in the mythological future and literary past. Thus (in a sentence mined above for Ovidian resonance) the Trojan women at Hector's funeral, thinking ahead to future deaths,

> *stant circum Iliades matres* manibusque decoros
> abrumpunt crines ...
>
> (*Ilias Lat.* 1052–1053)

'are' the later/earlier Trojan women who stand around under the gaze of Aeneas in an affectively unfinished hexameter near the end of *Aeneid* 2 (766–767)

> ... pueri et pavidae longo ordine *matres*
> *stant circum* [line breaks off]
>
> boys and in long array trembling matrons stand about

and who cluster at the tomb of Polydorus, with hair unloosed, near the start of *Aeneid* 3 (65):

> et *circum Iliades* crinem de more solutae
>
> and about them Ilian women, with hair untied in the customary way.

Within the literary-mythological system, the *Ilias Latina* retells a story that has always already been retold: the Virgilian *de more*, like Ovid's *consueta* above at *Met.* 13.491, is itself a reflexive annotation of the Greco-Roman '*Troades*' tradition.

Strikingly, indeed, the meta-Virgilian momentum at the end of the *Ilias Latina* carries over from the narrative proper into the first line of the concluding sphragis (1063–1070; tr. after Kennedy):

> **S**ed iam *siste gradum finemque impone labori*,
> **C**alliope, vatisque tui moderare carinam,
> **R**emis quem cernis stringentem litora paucis,
> **I**amque tenet portum metamque potentis Homeri.
> **P**ieridum comitata cohors, summitte rudentes
> **S**anctaque virgineos lauro redimita capillos
> **I**psa tuas depone lyras. ades, inclita Pallas,
> **T**uque fave cursu vatis iam, Phoebe, peracto.
>
> **S**tay now your step and put an end to the labour,
> **C**alliope, and as I approach the shore with a few oars

Restrain your poet's barque.
I reach my port, the goal of powerful Homer.
Pierian Muses in attendance, let loose the cables of my sails.
Sainted one whose virgin locks are bound with laurel,
Inhibit now your lyre. Be present, glorious Minerva.
Turn, O Phoebus, a favouring look upon a poet's voyage ended.

Here in the '*explicit*', the Trojan narrative has been left behind, except that the initial line of this poetological address to Calliope embeds two cento-like moments of Virgilian heroic action (1063, with my italics).[44] The closural *siste gradum* quotes Aeneas' last words to Dido in the Underworld (*Aen.* 6.465), whatever is to be made of that.[45] But even more clearly Virgilian is the injunction in *finemque impone labori*, a 'quotation' from the *Aeneid*'s own Trojan book (2.619–620):

> eripe, nate, fugam *finemque impone labori*;
> nusquam abero et tutum patrio te limine sistam.

> Hasten your flight, my son, and put an end to the labour. Nowhere will I leave you but will set you safely on your father's threshold.

Amid the conflagration of Troy, Venus promises to set Aeneas down safe at his father's home, *patrio ... limine*, in a *microcosm* of the safe conduct she will give him in his larger voyage throughout the *Aeneid*. So too, under Calliope's guidance, the poetic ship of Italicus is about to come to shore at a safe destination (1066):

> iamque tenet portum metamque potentis Homeri.[46]

This epitomator comes 'home' to his poetic father—on a journey (across language and across epic tradition) which has been both post-Homeric and post-Virgilian;

---

44 Noted by Scaffai (1982) *ad loc.*; but the interpretation is mine.
45 *Aen.* 6.465 *siste gradum teque aspectu ne subtrahe nostro*, "stay your step and withdraw not from our view." Oddly parallel to Statius' sphragistic recasting of Aeneas' last instruction to Creusa at Troy (*Aen.* 2.711), in the epilogue of the *Thebaid*: 12.817 *sed longe sequere et vestigia semper adora*, "... but follow at a distance and ever adore her footsteps"; on that allusion ('*Thebais*' to follow '*Aeneis*' at a respectful distance) see Malamud (1995) 26–27.
46 The v. l. *patentis Homeri*, favoured in early editions and championed by Wernsdorf (1785), is not unattractive: "vult enim, se magnum opus Homeri, tanquam patens mare, nunc emensum esse": cf. Verg. *G.* 2.41 *pelagoque volans da vela patenti*, "and spread your sails to speed over an open sea", also poetological. Noted by Tilroe (1939) *ad loc.*, but not by Scaffai.

a journey self-reflexively marked at its close by the book-bracketing *ductus* (which we can now register) of the acrostic S-C-R-I-P-S-I-T.

Tessellated intertextualities, inscribed in the horizontally *and* vertically readable bookends of the *Ilias Latina*. This is the place to mention Vollmer's proposed (and then withdrawn) embellishment of the opening acrostic with a medial P-I-E-R-I-S in lines 1–6, yielding (between *Ilias Lat.* 1–7, 1b–6b and 1063–1070) *Italice Pieris scripsit*, "The Muse wrote in the Italian tongue":[47] on this reconstruction (dependent upon a different approach to the crux in line 7) a poet's name is lost but a cross-linguistic agenda becomes fully explicit. Penthemimeral acrostics …: a dangerous enticement to the digital programmer; too dangerous, perhaps.

All in all the *Ilias Latina*, inventive yet delimited, offers within its compass a range of detailed opportunities and challenges for that intertextual cyborg of our time, the digitally equipped historian of Greco-Roman literature. And so back to the larger project: to put man and machine into collaboration in coding and decoding the texts and contexts of Roman imperial epic at large … and to do so with a continuing sense that the *sistema letterario* will sometimes, but not always, work for us like an operating system.

Bibliography

Augoustakis, Antony (ed.) (2014), *Flavian Poetry and its Greek Past*, Leiden.
Bessone, Federica (2014), "*Polis*, court, empire: Greek culture, Roman society, and the system of genres in Statius' poetry", in: Augoustakis (2014) 215–233.
Bettini, Maurizio (2012), *Vertere: un'antropologia della traduzione nella cultura antica*, Turin.
Bing, Peter (1990), "A pun on Aratus' name in verse 2 of the *Phainomena*?", in: *HSPh* 93, 281–285.
Bonadeo, Alessia/Canobbio, Alberto/Gasti, Fabio (eds.) (2011), *Filellenismo e identità romana in età flavia*, Pavia,
Caldini Montanari, Roberta (2010), "L'inno proemiale di Germanico ad Augusto", in: *Paideia* 65, 9–48.
Chaudhuri, Pramit/Dexter, Joseph/Bonilla Lopez, Jorge (2015), "Strings, triangles, and go-betweens: intertextual approaches to Silius' Carthaginian debates", in: *Dictynna* 12, http://dictynna.revues.org/1117 (seen 06.08.2018)
Clausen, Wendell (1994), *Virgil*, Eclogues, Oxford.
Dilke, Oswald (1954), *Statius*, Achilleid, Cambridge.

---

47 1b–6b *Pieris* (= 'Muse'; cf. *Ilias Lat.* 1067) from P̲elidae I̲niecit hE̲roum R̲ostris I̲nhumatis S̲ummi; the adverb *Italice* from a different solution to the line-beginning crux in 7 (in a few MSS *pertulerant ex quo* is reversed as *ex quo pertulerant*: n. 41 above). See Scaffai (1982) 13–14 for discussion of this proposal by Friedrich Vollmer, offered in 1898 and withdrawn in 1909.

Feeney, Denis (1991), *The Gods in Epic: Poets and Critics of the Classical Tradition*, Oxford.
Feeney, Denis (2016), *Beyond Greek: The Beginnings of Latin Literature*, Cambridge, MA.
Fowler, Don (1997), "Second thoughts on closure", in: Roberts *et al.* (1997) 3–22.
Fowler, Don (2000), *Roman Constructions: Readings in Postmodern Latin*, Oxford.
Fuhrer, Therese/Erler, Michael (eds.) (2015), *Cosmologies et cosmogonies dans la littérature antique*, Vandœuvres-Geneva.
Gee, Emma (2013), *Aratus and the Astronomical Tradition*, Oxford.
Heslin, Peter (2005), *The Transvestite Achilles: Gender and Genre in Statius' Achilleid*, Cambridge.
Hinds, Stephen (1985), "Booking the Return Trip: Ovid and *Tristia* 1", in: *PCPhS* 31, 13–32.
Hinds, Stephen (1998), *Allusion and Intertext: Dynamics of Appropriation in Roman Poetry*, Cambridge.
Hinds, Stephen (2001), "Cinna, Statius and 'immanent literary history' in the cultural economy", in: Schmidt (2001) 221–265.
Hinds, Stephen (2006), "Booking the Return Trip: Ovid and *Tristia* 1", in: Knox (2006) 415–440 [reprint of Hinds (1985)].
Hinds, Stephen (2013), "Claudianism in the *De Raptu Proserpinae*", in: Papanghelis *et al.* (2013) 169–192.
Jamison, Stephanie/Melchert, Craig/Vine, Brent (eds.) (2009), *Proceedings of the 20th Annual UCLA Indo-European Conference*, Bremen.
Juhnke, Herbert (1972), *Homerisches in römischer Epik flavischer Zeit*, München.
Katz, Joshua (2009), "Wordplay", in: Jamison *et al.* (2009) 79–114.
Kennedy, George (1998), *The Latin Iliad*, Fort Collins, CO.
Kilpatrick, Ross (1992), "The 'Ilias Latina' acrostic: a milder remedy", in: *Latomus* 51, 857–859.
Knox, Peter (2006), *Ovid*, Oxford.
Levitan, William (1993), "Give up the beginning? Juno's mindful wrath (*Aeneid* 1.37)", in: *LCM* 18, 14.
Lovatt, Helen (2005), *Statius and Epic Games: Sport, Politics and Poetics in the Thebaid*, Cambridge.
Malamud, Martha (1995), "Happy birthday, dead Lucan: (p)raising the dead in *Silvae* 2.7", in: *Ramus* 24, 1–30.
Maltby, Robert (1991), *A Lexicon of Ancient Latin Etymologies*, Leeds.
Manuwald, Gesine/Voigt, Astrid (eds.) (2013), *Flavian Epic Interactions*, Berlin.
McElduff, Siobhan (2013), *Roman Theories of Translation: Surpassing the Source*, New York/London.
Morgan, Llewelyn (1999), *Patterns of Redemption in Virgil's Georgics*, Cambridge.
Newlands, Carole (2012), *Statius, Poet between Rome and Naples*, London.
O'Hara, James (1996), *True Names: Vergil and the Alexandrian Tradition of Etymological Wordplay*, Ann Arbor.
Papanghelis, Theodore/Harrison, Stephen/Frangoulidis, Stavros (eds.) (2013), *Generic Interfaces in Latin Literature*, Berlin.
Penwill, John (2013), "Imperial encomia in Flavian epic", in: Manuwald/Voigt (2013) 29–54.
Possanza, Mark (2004), *Translating the Heavens: Aratus, Germanicus, and the Poetics of Latin Translation*, New York.
Roberts, Deborah/Dunn, Francis/Fowler, Don (eds.) (1997), *Classical Closure: Reading the End in Greek and Latin Literature*, Princeton.

Rosati, Gianpiero (2002), "Muse and power in the poetry of Statius", in: Spentzou/Fowler (2002) 229–251.
Rosati, Gianpiero (2011), "I *tria corda* di Stazio, poeta greco, romano, e napoletano", in: Bonadeo *et al.* (2011) 15–34.
Scaffai, Marco (1982), *Baebii Italici Ilias Latina*, Bologna.
Schenkl, Heinrich (1890), "Zur *Ilias Latina* des Italicus", in: *WS* 12, 317–318.
Schmidt, Ernst (ed.) (2001), *L'histoire littéraire immanente dans la poésie latine*, Vandœuvres-Geneva.
Schroeder, Chad (2005), Review of Mark Possanza, *Translating the Heavens*, in: *BMCR* 2005.05.20.
Smith, Alden (1990), "Ov. *Met.* 10.475: an instance of 'meta-allusion'", in: *Gymnasium* 97, 458–460.
Spentzou, Efrossini/Fowler, Don (eds.) (2002), *Cultivating the Muse*, Oxford.
Tilroe, Welcome (1939), *The Ilias Latina: A Study of the Latin Iliad, including Translation, Commentary, and Concordance*, diss. University of Southern California, Los Angeles.
Volk, Katharina (2015), "The World of the Latin *Aratea*", in: Fuhrer/Erler (2015) 253–283.
Wernsdorf, Johann (1785), *Poetae Latini Minores*, IV, Altenburg.

Digital resources (all seen 15.9.2017)

Diogenes: https://community.dur.ac.uk/p.j.heslin/Software/Diogenes/
PHI (Packard Humanities Institute: Classical Latin Texts): http://latin.packhum.org
Quantitative Criticism Lab: https://qcrit.org/home
Recogito: http://recogito.pelagios.org
SNAP-DRGN (Standards for Networking Ancient Prosopographies: Data and Relations in Greco-Roman Names): https://snapdrgn.net/about
Tesserae: http://tesserae.caset.buffalo.edu
TLG (Thesaurus Linguae Graecae): http://stephanus.tlg.uci.edu

List of Contributors

Antony Augoustakis is Professor of Classics at the University of Illinois at Urbana–Champaign (USA). He is the author of *Statius, Thebaid 8* (Oxford, 2016), *Motherhood and the Other: Fashioning Female Power in Flavian Epic* (Oxford, 2010) and *Plautus' Mercator* (Bryn Mawr, 2009). He has edited several volumes, most recently, *Campania in the Flavian Poetic Imagination* (Oxford, 2019), *Epic Heroes on Screen* (Edinburgh, 2018), the *Oxford Readings in Flavian Epic* (Oxford, 2016). He is in the final stages of a commentary on Silius Italicus' *Punica* 3, co-edited with Joy Littlewood. He serves as editor of *The Classical Journal*.

Chiara Battistella is Associate Professor of Latin language and literature at the University of Udine. Her interests lie mainly in the field of Augustan poetry and Senecan drama. Amongst her publications, there is a commentary on Ovid's *Heroides* 10 (2010) and articles on Vergil, Ovid, and Seneca's tragedies (especially the *Medea*).

Thomas Baier is Professor of Classics at Würzburg University. His main areas of research are Roman Epic, Roman Comedy, Hellenistic Philosophy and Neolatin Studies. His major current project is a commented bibliography of Joachim Camerarius the Elder. In this context, he takes a special interest in the function and development of literary genres from Antiquity to Renaissance.

Neil W. Bernstein is Professor in the Department of Classics & World Religions at Ohio University. He is the author of *Silius Italicus, Punica 2* (Oxford, 2017); *Seneca: Hercules Furens* (Bloomsbury, 2017); *Ethics, Identity, and Community in Later Roman Declamation* (Oxford, 2013); and *In the Image of the Ancestors: Narratives of Kinship in Flavian Epic* (Toronto, 2008).

Federica Bessone is Professor of Latin language and literature at the University of Turin. She studied at the Scuola Normale Superiore and the University of Pisa. She is the author of *P. Ovidii Nasonis Heroidum Epistula XII. Medea Iasoni* (Florence, 1997) and of *La 'Tebaide' di Stazio. Epica e potere* (Pisa/Rome, 2011).With Marco Fucecchi, she co-edited *The Literary Genres in the Flavian Age: Canons, Transformations, Reception* (Berlin/Boston, 2017) and, with Sabrina Stroppa, *Lettori latini e italiani di Ovidio* (Pisa/Rome, 2019). She has published on Augustan and Flavian poetry, Seneca, Petronius; she is co-editor of the series "Millennium" (Alessandria, Edizioni dell'Orso), and a member of the scientific committee of *Eugesta*, *MD* and *RCCM*.

Neil Coffee is Professor of Classics at the State University of New York at Buffalo. His interests include Latin epic poetry, Roman social history, Hellenistic philosophy, and digital approaches to literary and intellectual history. He is the author of *The Commerce of War: Exchange and Social Order in Latin Epic* and *Gift and Gain: How Money Transformed Ancient Rome*. He founded and directs the Tesserae Project, an effort to use digital methods to trace intertextuality, which has been supported by the National Endowment for the Humanities, the Swiss National Science Foundation, and the Fondation Maison des sciences de l'homme. He founded and serves as Co-Chair of the Digital Classics Association.

Michael Dewar is Professor of Classics at the University of Toronto. He is the author of *Statius. Thebaid IX. Edited with An English Translation and Commentary* (Oxford, 1991), *Claudian. Panegyricus De Sexto Consulatu Honorii Augusti. Edited with Introduction, Translation, and Literary Commentary* (Oxford, 1996), and of *Leisured Resistance: Villas, Literature and Politics in the Roman World* (London/New York, 2014). He has also published numerous articles and bookchapters on Virgil, Ovid, Lucan, Statius, Claudian, Sidonius Apollinaris, Venantius Fortunatus, and Corippus.

Chris Forstall is Assistant Professor of Classics at Mount Allison University in New Brunswick, Canada. He previously held positions as a post-doctoral researcher in Computer Science at the University of Notre Dame, Indiana, USA, as a post-doc in Classics at the University of Geneva, Switzerland, and as lead programmer for Tesserae at the University at Buffalo, SUNY, USA. He has a PhD in Classics from the University at Buffalo, where he wrote his dissertation on Homeric poetics. He is a digital classicist with interests in Greek and Latin poetry, computational stylometry, cognitive science, and oral-formulaic theory.

Marco Fucecchi is Associate Professor of Latin Language and Literature at the University of Udine (Italy). He specializes in Augustan and early imperial poetry, especially epic. He has published several articles and chapters on Virgil, Ovid, Lucan, Silius, Statius, and Valerius Flaccus, as well as a commentary on Valerius' *Argonautica* 6 in two volumes (Pisa, 1997 and 2006). He is currently working on Virgil *Aeneid* 3 as well as Silius' *Punica* 17. Together with Federica Bessone, he is editor of *The Literary Genres in the Flavian Age: Canons, Transformations, Reception* (Berlin, 2017). He is member of the committee of the *Epic Poetry Network* and member of the *Réseau de Recherche sur la poésie Augustéenne*.

Lavinia Galli Milić is Lecturer in Latin at the University of Geneva and SNSF Research Associate. She is the author of *Blossii Aemilii Dracontii Romulea VI-VII* (Florence, 2008), a critical edition and commentary. Her researches focus on 1st c. CE epic poetry (Lucan, Valerius Flaccus, Statius) and Late Latin (Dracontius, the *Anthologia Latina*, Venantius Fortunatus). She is currently collaborating on the project *Towards a digital edition of the Achilleid of Statius*, funded by the Swiss National Science Foundation (SNSF) and led by Damien Nelis.

James Gawley is a PhD candidate in the Classics Department of the University at Buffalo. He studies idea transmission in the ancient world, with a particular focus on epic intertextuality. His approach combines philology with computational linguistics and cognitive science. His work has been published in *Digital Scholarship in the Humanities* and *Mouseion*.

Mark Heerink is Associate Professor of Latin literature at the University of Amsterdam and VU University Amsterdam. He is the author of *Echoing Hylas: A Study in Hellenistic and Roman Metapoetics* (Madison, 2015) and co-editor of *Brill's Companion to Valerius Flaccus* (Brill, 2014). He is currently revising J.H. Mozley's 1934 edition and translation of Valerius Flaccus' *Argonautica* for the Loeb Classical Library.

Peter Heslin's research interests lie in Latin poetry and its reception, Roman topography and material culture, and digital humanities. He is the author of three monographs: *The Transvestite Achilles: Gender and Genre in the Achilleid of Statius* (Cambridge, 2005); *The Museum of*

Augustus: The Temple of Apollo in Pompeii, The Portico of Philippus in Rome, and Latin Poetry (Los Angeles, 2015); and *Propertius, Greek Myth, and Virgil: Rivalry, Allegory, and Polemic* (Oxford, 2018). He is the developer of *Diogenes*, a widely-used open-source software package that provides access to legacy databases of classical texts. He is Professor of Classics and Ancient History at Durham University.

Stephen Hinds is Professor of Classics at the University of Washington, Seattle. He is the author of *The Metamorphosis of Persephone: Ovid and the Self-Conscious Muse* (Cambridge, 1987) and *Allusion and Intertext* (Cambridge, 1998); many of his articles focus on Ovid and the ancient Ovidian tradition. With Denis Feeney, he co-founded and co-edited the Cambridge book series Roman Literature and its Contexts (14 volumes between 1993 and 2016). A current project, with the working title *Poetry across languages: Studies in transliteral and transcultural Latin, in antiquity and since*, explores cross-linguistic and intercultural relations of Latin literature both in antiquity and between antiquity and (early) modernity; more longstanding commitments include a commentary on Ovid, *Tristia* 1.

Alison Keith teaches classics and women's studies at the University of Toronto, where she is currently Director of the Jackman Humanities Institute. She has written extensively about the intersection of gender and genre in Latin literature and Roman society, and published books on Ovid, Latin epic, Propertius, and Virgil, as well as a commentary on selections from Latin epic. She has edited or co-edited volumes on Latin elegy and Hellenistic epigram, Latin epic, the medieval and early modern reception of Ovid's *Metamorphoses* (with Stephen Rupp), Roman dress and Roman literary cultures (with Jonathan Edmondson), and women and war in antiquity (with Jacqueline Fabre-Serris).

Helen Lovatt is Professor of Classics at the University of Nottingham and has published on Flavian epic, including *Statius and Epic Games* (Cambridge, 2005) and *The Epic Gaze* (Cambridge, 2013). She has edited a volume on classical reception in children's literature (with Owen Hodkinson, I.B. Tauris, 2018) and is currently working on a project on the cultural history of the Argonaut myth.

Raymond Marks is Associate Professor at the University of Missouri. He has published extensively on Silius Italicus and is the author of *From Republic to Empire: Scipio Africanus in the Punica of Silius Italicus* (2005). His current research focuses on the reception of Ovid among post-Augustan epic poets.

Damien Nelis has been Professor of Latin in the University of Geneva since 2005. Before that, he held the Chair of Latin (1870) in Trinity College Dublin. He works mainly on Latin poetry, with a special interest in its Hellenistic background. He is currently writing a book on Vergil's *Georgics*.

Carole Newlands is College Professor of Distinction in Humanities at the University of Colorado Boulder. Her research interests include classical and medieval Latin literature and cultural and reception studies. She is the author of over forty articles on classical and medieval topics, and she has published several books: *Playing with Time: Ovid and the Fasti* (Cornell University Press, 1995); *Statius' Silvae and the Poetics of Empire* (Cambridge, 2002); *Statius' Silvae Book*

II (Cambridge Greek and Latin series 2011); *Statius: A Poet between Rome and Naples* (London, 2012); *Ovid: an introduction* (London, 2015). She is also co-editor of the *Wiley-Blackwell Companion to Ovid* (Oxford, 2014); *The Brill Companion to Statius* (Leiden, 2015); and *Ancient Campania: Poetics, Location, and Identity* (Illinois, 2015).

François Ripoll is a Former Pupil of the Ecole Normale Supérieure of Paris and Docteur ès Lettres of the University of Paris-Sorbonne. He is Professor of Latin Language and Literature at the University of Toulouse. His main field of research is Flavian Epic, about which he has published two books: his doctoral thesis, *La morale héroïque dans les épopées latines d'époque flavienne : tradition et innovation*, and a Commentary of the *Achilleid* (in collaboration with Jean Soubiran). He has also written several articles about Flavian epicists, Virgil, Lucan, Petronius, Q. Curtius, Martial and the Younger Pliny.

Gianpiero Rosati is Professor of Latin Literature at the Scuola Normale Superiore (Pisa), where he is currently Dean of the Faculty of Humanities. He worked on Augustan poetry, in particular on Ovid (with essays, editions and commentaries), literature of Neronian and Flavian age (Seneca, Statius, Martial), and Latin narrative (Petronius, Apuleius). He is currently working on a project on the interaction between poetry, material culture, and visual arts in the Flavian culture.

Tim Stover is Associate Professor of Classics at Florida State University in Tallahassee, Florida. He specializes in Latin literature, with a particular interest in epic poetry. In addition to articles on Lucretius, Vergil, Lucan, Valerius Flaccus, and Statius, he is the author of *Epic and Empire in Vespasianic Rome: A New Reading of Valerius Flaccus' Argonautica* (Oxford, 2012). He is also the co-editor, along with Laurel Fulkerson, of *Repeat Performances: Ovidian Repetition and the Metamorphoses* (University of Wisconsin Press, 2016). He is currently working on a book tentatively entitled *In the Wake of Argo: Valerius Flaccus and Flavian Epic*, which examines the influence of the Roman *Argonautica* on Statius' *Thebaid* and Silius Italicus' *Punica*.

Index Locorum

Apollonius Rhodius
1.311–316	217 n.47
1.332–362	57
1.440–447	307
1.466–468	289
1.1043	174
1.1284–1286	44
1.1286–1289	44
1.1289–1295	44
1.1296–1301	45
1.1310–1320	45
2.720–3.212	67
2.720–900	67
2.858–900	68
2.862–863	68
2.899–900	69
2.901–910	71
2.901–1259	67, 71
2.911–961	71
2.962–1000a	71
2.1000b–1008	71
2.1009–1245	71
2.1256–1257	71–72
2.1260	75
2.1260–1270	74
2.1260–1278	72
2.1260–1285	67
2.1264–1265	75
2.1265	75
2.1271–1272	78
2.1271–1275	74, 76
2.1273	77
2.1273–1275	78
2.1276–1280	76
2.1277–1280	74
2.1281–1283a	78
2.1281–1285	76
2.1282	76
2.1285	74
3.1–5	67, 74, 79, 80
3.6–7a	80
3.6–166	67
3.7b–166	81
3.167	81
3.167–212	67
3.213–248	323 n.1
3.215–241	246 n.10
3.250–252	228
3.253	216 n.40
3.275–298	215 n.39
3.478	229
3.528–530	229
3.616–635	209, 210 n.25
3.616–636	210
3.755–760	383
3.878–884	211
3.919–923	218
3.956–961	218
3.958–959	221 n.57
3.975–1145	215 n.38
3.1030–1036	229
3.1211	229
4.54–65	226
4.55–56	227
4.63–65	226
4.246–247	225 n.68
4.1021–1022	224 n.67

Aemilius Macer
6 Courtney = 54 Hollis	110 n.8

Aeschylus
Septem contra Thebas
427–431	289 n.15
529–530	288–289
752–756	151 n.54

Apollodorus
Bibliotheca
1.8.3	49
3.13.8	256 n.61

Epitome
3.7	245 n.7

Aratus
Phaenomena
1–2	425, 426
1–18	426

Aristotle
De anima
403a   308
Poetica
22 1458a–1459a   410 n.10

Augustus
Res Gestae
19   325

Ausonius
Mosella
276–279   125

Bacchylides
5.68–70   48
5.69   48
5.71   49
5.127–129   49
5.129–135   49
5.165–166   49

Callimachus
Hymn 2, to Apollo
55–59   357 n.37

Calpurnius Siculus
Eclogues
3.55   98 n.23
4.82   427 n.15

Cassius Dio
66.22–23   350

Catullus
1.4   107
16.5–8   110
64.14–15   113 n.14
64.59   113 n.14, 155
64.105   155
64.340–341   155 n.67
64.341   113 n.14
66.39   157, 377–378
68.133   142 n.35
101.1   357

Cicero
Aratea
Fr. 1   427 n.15
De divinatione
2.98   95 n.17
De legibus
1.40   142 n.34
Epistulae ad Atticum
2.8.2   349
5.6.2   274 n.33
7.2.1   107 n.1
Epistulae ad Brutum
24.3   153 n.62
Epistulae ad familiares
1.9.4   274 n.32
6.9.2   274 n.33
8.15.1   274
8.16.1   274 n.33
10.12.2   257 n.68
Epistulae ad Quintum fratrem
2.1.1   274
In Pisonem
46   142 n.34
In Verrem
2.2.142   274 n.32
Pro Caelio
14   247 n.20
Pro Murena
70   257 n.68
Pro Sexto Roscio Amerino
67   142 n.34

Corpus Inscriptionum Latinarum
6.1710   434 n.35

Cinna
1 Courtney = 6 Hollis   114–115
1.3 Courtney = 6.3 Hollis   116
1.4 Courtney = 6.4 Hollis   116
2 Courtney = 2 Hollis   123
5 Courtney = 17 Hollis   110
6 Courtney = 10 Hollis   112
11 Courtney = 13 Hollis   117

Claudianus
De consulatu Stilichonis
1.318   116 n.20

De raptu Proserpinae
1.115	263 n.14

Panegyricus dictus Probino et Olybrio consulibus
87	382

Columella
De re rustica
8.16.9	179 n.34

Corippus
In laudem Justini Augusti Minoris
1.288–290	382

Cornificius
2 Courtney = 96 Hollis	120, 121

Diodorus Siculus
4.45–46	224 n.67

Dionysius Halicarnassensis
De imitatione
2.7	293

Donatus
Vita Vergilii
36	355
44	410 n.10

Elegiae in Maecenatem
2.153–154	268
2.159–163	268–269

Ennius
Annales
414 Sk.	143 n.38
467 Sk.	53

Medea exul
216	154

Euripides
Medea
395–400	233
789	233

Phoenissae
1533–1535	140
1543–1545	140

Skyrioi
5 Jouan	254 n.56
6 Jouan	254 n.56

Supplices
163–192	297
301–302	298

Gellius
Noctes Atticae
2.21	427
2.21.1–2	428
13.23.14	146 n.44

Germanicus
Aratea
1	426
1–4	425–426
1–16	426
2	426
3–4	427
15	427

Gospel of Mark
1.14	318
8.22–26	317
8.27–30	318
10.46–52	317
15.39	318

Homer
Iliad
1.1	429, 431, 431 n.27, 436, 437
1.4–5	436
1.161–162	158–159
5.639	48
5.677–678	173 n.16
5.677–680	173
6.152ff.	14
9.410–416	250
10.180–217	244
10.213–232	245
10.218–253	250
10.242–247	244
10.296–298	245
11.420–427	173
12.322–328	294

12.328	294	9.344	285 n.4
13.32ff.	14	9.373–374	285 n.4
13.701–708	149, 150	9.452–453	286 n.10
13.703–704	150	9.456–457	286 n.10
13.704	151	10.476–481	246 n.13
13.704–705	150	11.267	48
13.706	150	11.566–567	245 n.9
13.708	150	12.31–35	246 n.13
17.214	431 n.28	12.39–54	352
17.611–614	173	12.165–200	352
18.226	431 n.28	18.343	246 n.11
19.58	159	19.336–342	246
19.75	431 n.28	20.1–97	246 n.13
20.498	431 n.28	20.301	253 n.53
21.153	431 n.28	21.371	253 n.53
22.25–32	219	23.111	253 n.53
22.30–31	221 n.57		
22.38–76	294	**Horace**	
22.82–89	294	*Ars Poetica*	
23.117–122	364 n.63	141–142	251 n.48
23.168	431 n.28	*Carmina*	
24.448–456	323 n.1	1.2.34	142 n.35
24.707–804	439	1.3.2	123 n.34
Odyssey		2.5.21–24	163 n.87
1.1	424	2.16.10–12	142 n.31
1.3	245 n.9, 251	3.30.6–7	267 n.23
5.55–74	14	*Epistulae*	
6.25–40	210 n.25	1.2.19	247, 251 n.48
6.102–108	211	*Epodi*	
6.107–108	212 n.32	11.14	274
6.110–114	329	*Sermones*	
6.141–148	249	1.9.59	257 n.68
6.148	215	2.1.58	143
6.150–185	215	2.1.71	274
6.168	251		
6.232–235	218	**Ilias Latina**	
6.259–322	329	1	437
7.133–134	246	1b–6b	443, 443 n.47
7.311–314	251	1–7	443
8.370–380	251	1–8	438 n.41
9.116–566	285	1–9	435-436, 438
9.118–135	285 n.5	4–5	436, 437
9.128–129	285 n.6	6–8	438 n.41
9.269–271	285	7	443, 435 n.37, 438 n.41, 443, 443 n.47
9.273–278	285		
9.288–293	285 n.4		
9.311	285 n.4	997–999	437

Index Locorum — 455

1052–1053	441	1.92–93	153 n.59
1052–1062	439	1.123–124	153 n.59
1063–1070	438 n.41, 441–442, 443	1.135	271
		1.136–143	271
1053	440	1.356–386	57
1056	440	1.366	148
1057	440	1.674–695	307
1062	440	2.79–80	142 n.30
1063	442	2.725–731	272 n.29
1066	442	3.1–7	272 n.29
1067	443 n.47	3.9–11	276
		3.14–15	276 n.36

Isidorus
Origines

		3.30–32	276 n.36
		4.212–213	148 n.50
8.11.54	325 n.13	5.444–446	384
		5.503	278 n.43

Josephus
Bellum Judaicum

		5.654–660	264
		5.659–660	264 n.16
4.618	318	5.665–666	265
4.658	318	5.668–671	265
		5.771–775	269

Livy

		6.179	95 n.18
1.6.4	153 n.62	7.7–19	274
1.17.1	153 n.62	7.19–24	274
8.22.5–6	352 n.21	7.23–24	272 n.29
21.10.4	153 n.62	7.24b–44	274
22.56.2	99 n.28	7.29–36	274–275
23.42.12	274 n.33	7.772–773	278 n.44
30.20.4	273 n.30	7.776	276, 278 n.44
30.20.7	273, 271 n.28, 273 n.30	7.781–783	276
		8.257–258	278
30.30.29	262 n.11	8.258	264 n.17
40.8.18	153 n.61	8.339	278
		8.449–450	271 n.27

Livius Andronicus
Odusia

		8.505–509	278 n.44
		8.622–635	266
1	424	8.627	267
		8.629–631	266, 279

[Longinus]
Peri Hypsous

		9.549	53
		9.966–969	17
13.3	292	9.980–986	268 n.24
		9.985–986	267 n.23

Lucan

1.4	153 n.59	**Lucilius**	
1.8	418–419	1276	179 n.34
1.51–59	331		
1.72–74	263		

Lucretius

1.146	141
1.146–148	141 n.26
1.199	146 n.44
2.7–13	153 n.61
2.12–13	153 n.61
2.59–61	141 n.26
3.91–93	141 n.26
4.1046	153 n.62
4.1090	153 n.62
6.39–41	141 n.26
6.680–702	361 n.50
6.1138	356

Lycophron
Alexandra

712–736	352
721	353

Macrobius
Saturnalia

1.17.33	325 n.13
6.5.13	120–121

Manilius
Astronomica

1.840	18

Martial
Epigrammata

1.7	112
2.64.1–2	160 n.80
2.64.9	160 n.80
2.64.9–10	159–160
4.4.7	363
4.44.7	356
7.14.3–6	112
7.63	87 n.2
8.50[51].14	90 n.8
8.81.2	129 n.40
9.28.2	98 n.23
9.pr.11	98 n.23
10.48.1	129 n.40
10.53.1	98 n.23
11.48	342–343, 362
11.48	87 n.2
11.50	362
11.50[49]	87 n.2

Spectacula

5.1[4.5]	275 n.34

Moschus
Europa

51	128 n.39

Musonius

8.65	316 n.48

Ovid
Amores

1.2.1	189 n.7
1.2.9	191 n.14
1.5.25	165 n.93
1.10.47	147
1.15.19	360
1.15.21–22	107
1.15.29–30	107
1.15.41–42	267–268
1.15.42	269
2.1.2	98 n.23
2.16.1	89
2.19.5	191 n.14
3.8.23	98 n.23
3.8.38	274
3.15.8–10	104
3.15.11	89

Ars amatoria

2.355	247 n.21
2.451	98 n.23
2.452	98 n.23
3.635	129 n.40

Epistulae ex Ponto

1.2.33	98 n.23
1.2.34	98 n.23
1.2.129	98 n.23
1.2.131	98 n.23
1.2.136	98 n.23
1.6.41–44	100
1.9.21–22	100
3.2.101–102	275
3.3.42	91
4.3.11	98 n.23
4.3.13	98 n.23
4.3.15	98 n.23

4.3.16	98 n.23	232	96
4.3.17	98 n.23	237–242	94
4.8.85–86	275	238	95
4.14.35	247 n.21	239	95
4.14.49	89	241	95
Fasti		243	95, 97
1.147	360 n.47	243–248	94
1.609–16	434 n.33	243–250	97
2.195–242	88 n.5	244	95
3.505	98 n.23	245	95
3.523–710	88	246	95, 97
4.77–82	92	246–247	97
4.81	89	247	97, 98
4.82	93	493–494	100
4.190	90	502	183 n.49
4.247–348	88 n.5	593–594	99
4.273–274	254 n.54	611–614	100
6.259	90	*Metamorphoses*	
6.693–710	90	1.1–2	341
6.707	90	1.4	433
Halieutica		1.57–60	152
96		1.60	152
Heroides	179 n.34	1.323	90
1.28	95 n.17	1.452–465	30 n.20
1.41	148 n.50	1.583–746	119
3.89	159	1.622–721	128 n.38
12.21	145 n.41	1.634	119
12.105	98 n.23	1.668	129 n.41
16.107–110	254	1.757	98 n.23
16.246	98 n.23	2.1–4	326
16.320	70 n.13	2.1–18	323 n.1
18.77	383	2.1–30	325
19.83	90	2.2	330
21.232	95 n.17	2.3	326
Ibis		2.4	330
1–2	103 n.33	2.5	332
5–6	90 n.9	2.5–7	327
9–10	103 n.33	2.8-16	333
14	96	2.8–11	331
17–18	99, 100	2.8–18	333
39–40	95 n.19, 103 n.33	2.17–18	327–328, 333
45–54	103 n.33	2.22–24	326, 330
135–140	103 n.33	2.25–32	327
147–148	99	2.67–69	334–335
209–250	94	2.150–158	335
221–222	96	2.153	335
229–231	96	2.311–318	335–336

2.340–343	334	8.217–220	340
2.342	334	8.227–230	340
2.346	334	8.372	212 n.32
2.347	334	8.437	49
2.364–366	334	8.524–525	440
2.398	336	8.741–776	253
2.398–400	336	9.4–5	164 n.92
2.401–408	328	9.149–151	50
2.524	129 n.41	10.475	430 n.22
2.709	364 n.61	12.67–69	390
2.719	143 n.36	12.162–163	164
3.1	341	12.163–164	164 n.92
3.182	219	12.306	180 n.40
3.619	53, 53 n.32	12.334–335	179
4.64	221	12.547–548	302
4.213	116	12.604–606	390
4.226	98 n.23	13.1–381	243 n.1
4.317–328	217 n.43	13.34–42	245 n.7
5.46	248 n.24	13.45	52, 53
5.264–268	101	13.102–170	254 n.56
5.268–272	101	13.162–170	405
5.268–293	101	13.166–170	254
5.273–274	101	13.168	255
5.274–293	101	13.170–180	256
5.289–293	101	13.256–262	172–173
5.293	101	13.258–259	173
5.319–331	302	13.260–261	173
5.348	297 n.32	13.298	405, 432
5.362–384	30 n.20	13.408	440
5.375–376	214	13.491	441
5.385–395	213–214	13.491–493	440
5.391–392	231	13.761	285
5.394	214	13.904	125
5.395	214	13.904–14.69	120
5.409–412	184 n.52	13.904–906	124
6.382–400	90	13.956–957	165
6.400	90	14.80	341
6.472–473	141	14.330	181 n.43
6.587–600	141 n.25	14.381	95 n.17
6.652	141, 141 n.25	14.457	181 n.41
7.1–424	233 n.90, 235 n.99	14.507	143 n.36
		14.512	181 n.41
7.177–178	228 n.79	14.617	181 n.42
7.500	182 n.45	14.778	245 n.8
7.854	145	15.500	98 n.23
8.200–202	340	15.879	267
8.201–202	340		

Remedia amoris		3.7.8–9	355
402	146 n.42	4.14.5	110
753	90		
Tristia		**Propertius**	
1.1.56	90 n.9	1.1.33	189 n.7
1.2.14–16	272 n.29	1.5.10	189 n.7
1.5.5	100	1.6.13–14	115 n.18
2.2	90 n.9	1.7.19	189 n.10
2.171	143 n.36	1.10.17	189 n.7
2.207	88, 90 n.9, 100, 103	1.11.1–5	351 n.16
		1.11.5	189 n.7
2.208	103 n.33	1.15.21–22	297
3.3.74	90 n.9	2.7.11	189 n.7
3.14.6	90 n.9	2.8.35	159
4.5.12	98, 98 n.23	2.15.1	70 n.13
4.10.1	98 n.23	2.18.21	189 n.7
4.10.3	89	2.20.1	158 n.76
4.10.43–44	109	2.31.1	325 n.12
5.7b.55	98 n.23	2.31.1–2	326
		2.31.3	325 n.12
Petronius		2.31.6	325 n.12
Satyrica		2.31.8	325 n.12
39.3	162	2.31.9	325 n.12, 326
		2.31.9–12	325
Phaedrus		2.31.11	326
4.26	274	2.31.12	325 n.12, 326
		3.1.3–4	190
Pindar		3.1.19–20	189
Nemean 3		3.3.5	274
53–54	155 n.67	3.7.19–20	267 n.23
		3.15.1	274 n.33
Plautus		3.17.4	189 n.7
Amphitruo		4.1.61	189 n.8
601	98 n.23	4.9.38	98 n.23
Pliny the Elder		**Prudentius**	
Historia Naturalis		*Psychomachia*	
3.62	352 n.20	22–23	382
3.108	89		
16.172	90 n.8	**Quintilian**	
37.118	110	*Institutio oratoria*	
		10.1.62	292–293
Pliny the Younger		10.1.87	109, 110 n.9
Epistulae		12.10.64	248 n.28
1.16.5	111		
3.7.6–8	343	**Rhetorica ad Herennium**	
3.7.8	87 n.2, 362	4.60	274

Sallust
De Catilinae coniuratione
5.4 247
Historiae
4.69.5 = 4.67.5 McG. 153 n.62

Sappho
22.11–12 Voigt 142 n.35

Scholia ad Homeri Iliados libros
11.604 207 n.12

Scholia in Lucani bellum civile
9.701 110 n.8

Seneca the Elder
Controversiae
7.1.27 108

Seneca the Younger
Agamemnon
463 15, 18
De beneficiis
7.25.2 145
De clementia
2.3–4 316 n.46
De ira
3.3 308
Epistulae
56.5–6 108–109
56.6 108 n.4
107.7.6–8 360 n.47
122.14 141 n.27
Hercules furens
340 314
Medea
12 213 n.34
46–47 224 n.65
88–89 219
99–101 219
185 232
270 232
301–363 235
362 235
516 232
549–550 233
577–578 233
603–669 235
607–615 213 n.34
652–653 183
670 232
670–739 233
674 232
738 232
740–840 233
740–848 232
750–842 220
751 232 n.89
752 233
771 233
773 233
785 234
785–786 233
786 234
797 233
797–810 234
800 233
801–802 233
804 233
806 233
812–816 234
814–816 234
817 233
833–839 220 n.55
840–841 234
840–842 220
843–848 233
849–851 154
872 232
889–890 221, 222
982–985 213 n.34
995 231
Oedipus
39–41 221 n.58
971 140 n.23
999 140
1001 140 n.23
1012 140
Phoenissae
9–10 140 n.23
46–48 140 n.21
245–253 140 n.22
358–362 140 n.22

Thyestes
84–85	153

Servius
In Vergilii Aeneidem *commentarius*
3.359	89
11.235	342

In Vergilii Georgica *commentarius*
4.563	352 n.21

Silius Italicus
1.58	291
1.99–119	260 n.7
1.324	180
1.437–439	179–180
2.77–79	381
2.663–664	385
2.696–707	277 n.38
2.700–701	277 n.40
2.701–702	278 n.42
2.704–705	276 n.35
2.705–707	277 n.39
3.40–42	121
3.61–65	278
3.61–162	261
3.344	248 n.24
3.584–590	266 n.20, 266 n.22
3.618–621	87
4.175–177	180–181
4.181–188	180–181
4.454–460	262 n.12
5.323	180 n.36
7.38–65	88 n.5
7.143–145	384
7.413–414	113 n.14
7.598–616	181–182
7.606–608	264 n.16
8.25–43	88
8.44–201	88
8.54–70	90 n.10
8.70	99 n.26
8.158–159	90 n.10
8.202–241	88
8.242–283	88
8.244	96
8.249	96
8.262	96
8.284–348	88
8.290–291	97, 97 n.21
8.301	96
8.332–333	96
8.349–355	88
8.356–621	88
8.404–411	87
8.451	182 n.48
8.495–497	89
8.495–510	88
8.498–501	89
8.502	90
8.502–504	89
8.503	90, 93 n.14
8.504	90
8.505–509	89
8.509–510	89
8.510	89
8.535	181
8.591–595	87
8.622–767	91
9.1–65	91
9.9–14	91
9.56–65	94, 96, 97
9.57–58	95, 97
9.58	95
9.60	95
9.60–61	95 n.17
9.61	95, 97
9.62–63	95
9.65	95
9.66	103
9.66–69	93
9.66–177	91
9.70–76	92
9.77–82	93
9.128	97
9.128–130	96
9.134	93
9.134–141	93, 97
9.135	93
9.136–140	93
9.139	93
9.148	103
9.173–177	99
9.174	102

9.174–175	97	12.347	180 n.38
9.175	91, 103 n.33	12.387–419	87
9.178–243	91	12.715	381
9.244–266	91	13.86	116 n.21
9.260	103, 103 n.33	13.86–89	115
9.260–261	103	13.779–791	87
9.261	103, 103 n.33	13.868–893	277
9.262–266	100–101	13.874–875	277 n.41
9.263	101	13.879–880	277–278
9.266	97, 101, 102, 103	13.881–882	278
9.267–277	91	13.886–890	278
9.278–286	91	13.890–892	277 n.39
9.350–351	266 n.22	14.473	184
9.350–353	266 n.20	14.515	184
9.548	95 n.17	14.567–579	183
9.637–639	96 n.20	15.59	98 n.23
9.649–655	100	15.61	98 n.23
10.146	291	15.571	53
10.260–275	98	15.723	182 n.47
10.267–273	99	16.17–19	271 n.26
10.269	99 n.27	16.366	180 n.36
10.270	99 n.27	17.1–47	88 n.5
10.271	99 n.27	17.149–150	270
10.276–291	98	17.149–291	270
10.287–291	98	17.150–151	270–271
10.289	98, 98 n.23	17.160–163	276 n.35
10.303–305	98	17.203–211	271 n.28
10.318–325	99	17.211–212	271 n.28
10.346–347	128	17.213–217	271
10.608–612	99	17.218–235	272
11.177	98 n.23	17.221–224	273
11.180	98 n.23	17.223	276
12.27–28	357 n.39	17.225–229	273 n.30
12.31–32	359	17.230–231	273 n.30
12.85	338 n.36	17.258	272 n.29
12.85–86	337, 338, 339	17.260–267	265 n.18
12.85–101	338–339	17.566	262
12.89	339	17.606–607	263
12.90	339	17.606–610a	263
12.92–95	340	17.606–615	262–263
12.95	340, 341	17.610b–615	263, 267
12.96	341	17.611–612	269
12.99–101	340	17.612	263–264, 267,
12.143–146	351 n.16	268	
12.152–154	361	17.613–615	265 n.19
12.154	361	17.614	264
12.212–222	87		

Solinus
1.8	89
2.6	89 n.6

Sophocles
Oedipus Tyrannus
260	151 n.54
371	141
371–374	141 n.28
374	141
459–460	151 n.54
471–472	142
477–482	142
1183	140 n.23
1256–1257	151 n.54
1271–1274	140 n.23
1316–1318	141
1334–1338	140 n.23
1347	141
1371–1390	140 n.23
1389–1390	141
1409–1412	140 n.23
1424–1431	140 n.23

Statius
Achilleis
1.1–3	431, 435
1.1–7	397, 398
1.1–19	431 n.25, 432–433
1.3	431 n.27
1.3–4	431, 433
1.4–5	250
1.5	398
1.6	433
1.7	257, 433
1.11	434
1.12–13	433 n.32
1.14–16	433, 433 n.32
1.19	434
1.43	156 n.70
1.49	136 n.11
1.60–62	249 n.44
1.63–64	248 n.34
1.71–74	135 n.10
1.73	136
1.94	251
1.133–134	390 n.6
1.189–192	155
1.193	156
1.250	156 n.71
1.255–258	163 n.87
1.269–270	390 n.6
1.321–322	162 n.84
1.335–337	163 n.87
1.403–404	249 n.37
1.475–476	256 n.62
1.476–482	256 n.62
1.480–482	390 n.6
1.491–513	136 n.14
1.493	136
1.493–496	136 n.13
1.526–536	257 n.64
1.536–559	250
1.538	245
1.538–559	244
1.539–545	244
1.542	246
1.544–545	248 n.24, 257 n.65
1.546–547	244
1.549	245, 256 n.60
1.560	164 n.89
1.577–579	156 n.69
1.619–639	249
1.624	249 n.45
1.632–633	249 n.45
1.650	98 n.23
1.652–655	157
1.655–656	158 n.76, 249 n.45
1.689	246
1.698–699	247
1.704–708	245
1.709–725	253
1.712–717	253
1.718	253
1.726–818	250
1.728–802	248
1.741	246
1.742–746	246
1.748	246
1.761–762	246
1.761–766	246

1.766	246	2.60–62	253
1.780–782	161	2.60–78	248 n.35
1.780–783	251	2.94–95	164
1.784	247, 249 n.42	2.94–167	156 n.69
1.785–787	251	2.110–116	155 n.67
1.785–793	249	2.111–112	113 n.14
1.788	249 n.36, 249 n.37	2.166–167	165
		Silvae	
1.791–793	248 n.33	1.praef.3–4	366
1.792–802	249	1.2.197–198	112
1.794	246	2.praef.15–16	349
1.796	248 n.31, 249 n.45	2.1.29	145 n.40
		2.2.1	352 n.24
1.797	249 n.45	2.2.23–24	352
1.799	249 n.45	2.2.42–44	336 n.33
1.800–802	249, 257 n.66	2.2.46	15, 18
1.801	248 n.33	2.2.52–62	365
1.802–805	248 n.26	2.2.54	365
1.806	249 n.43	2.2.59	366
1.810	251	2.2.72–73	366
1.811	249 n.41	2.2.76	366
1.816–817	246	2.2.79	366
1.817	248	2.2.82–84	367
1.819–840	251	2.2.85–93	367
1.846–847	162, 247, 252	2.2.90–93	368
1.856	160 n.82	2.2.94	369
1.866–876	249 n.38	2.2.94–96	367
1.867–874	248, 254–255	2.2.113–115	369
1.868–869	248 n.31	2.2.116–117	352 n.24, 369
1.869–871	248 n.32	2.3.22	113 n.13, 113 n.14
1.872	159, 255	2.6.24–25	113 n.13
1.908–909	161	2.7.77	109
1.952–955	162 n.84	3.praef.3–4	369
1.953	159 n.78	3.1.64	352 n.24
1.956–957	159 n.78	3.1.110–111	366 n.69
1.960	113 n.14, 155	3.1.117–135	365
2.12	257 n.67	3.1.134–138	365
2.32	256	3.1.163–186	352
2.32–33	248 n.32	3.1.166–170	365
2.32–83	248	3.2.8–11	124
2.35	248 n.30	3.2.35–41	122
2.41–42	255–256	3.2.101–103	127
2.48	249 n.36, 249 n.37	3.2.102	128
		3.2.143	370
2.49–83	253	3.4.101	145 n.40
2.55–57	155	3.5.72–74	356
2.57	248 n.32	3.5.73	356

3.5.78	357	1.59	145
3.5.78–80	356	1.60	145
3.5.79	357, 359	1.60–61	146
3.5.81–112	357	1.66–71	144
4.3.76	98 n.23	1.68–69	146
4.4.51–52	359–360	1.70	146
4.4.51–55	358	1.73–74	144
4.4.52	358, 359	1.88–122	22
4.4.54	362	1.118	135 n.7
4.4.54–55	358	1.118–122	135 n.8
4.4.55	360, 362	1.123–130	153
4.4.78–86	351	1.123–141	22
4.4.78–87	360	1.123–196	23
4.4.79	361 n.50	1.127–128	153
4.4.80	361	1.128–129	153 n.59
4.4.84–85	361	1.129	153
4.4.93–100	360	1.129–130	153 n.61
4.4.94	360	1.130	151
4.6.25–26	118	1.131–138	149
4.8.6	353	1.133	152
5.3.104–108	363	1.137	151
5.3.105	363	1.142–164	23
5.3.106	363	1.164–196	23
5.3.108	364	1.165–168	23 n.11
5.3.112–115	364	1.197–302	23
5.3.116–208	362	1.250–255	126
5.3.127–130	363	1.251	126
5.3.146–158	364	1.251–255	128
5.3.209–238	363	1.252	126
5.3.233–234	362	1.275	17
5.5.38	98 n.23	1.298–313	26, 27–28, 39
5.5.40	98 n.23	1.303	29
Thebais		1.303–311	23, 25
1.1–45	22	1.304	30
1.2	116 n.21	1.310	32 n.25
1.7	116 n.21	1.312	25
1.16–17	151	1.312–313	33
1.41–45	288	1.312–377	23
1.46	145 n.41	1.316–319	146–147
1.46–52	139	1.319	147
1.46–88	22	1.377–427	23
1.49	140	1.428–720	23
1.49–52	140	1.448	127
1.53–54	145	1.453	300
1.54	144	1.457–459	121
1.55–56	144	1.459–460	300
1.58–62	144	1.467	127

1.488–490	300	7.41–43	17
1.533	32 n.25	7.44–45	18
1.542–543	126–127	7.45	15
1.557–668	23	7.46–47	18
1.613	178 n.32	7.185–186	135 n.8
1.696–720	23	7.333–337	122, 130
2.1–5	37	7.369	178 n.32
2.214–215	113 n.14	7.477	146 n.43
2.219	127	7.537	127, 148 n.50
2.339	153 n.61	7.546–547	148 n.50
2.513	32 n.25	7.711–719	177
2.613	116	7.746	30 n.22
3.13	178 n.32	7.789	30 n.22
3.74–77	142 n.33	8.31	263 n.14
3.293	30 n.22, 32 n.25	8.71	300
3.398	183 n.49	8.228	116, 116 n.21
3.399–400	183	8.277	32 n.25
3.582	374	8.476	178 n.32, 180 n.40
3.598	288		
3.600–602	291	8.478	300 n.36
3.602	288	8.484	182 n.45
3.604–605	289	8.530	300 n.36
3.611–613	290	8.599	30 n.22
3.615–616	288	8.666	98 n.23
3.659–661	290	8.762–766	300
4.176	289	9.1	300 n.36
4.260	374	9.184	300
4.271	113 n.14	9.221	30 n.22
4.300	374	9.252	178 n.32
4.407	248 n.24	9.272	30 n.22
4.589	127	9.328	125
4.597	178 n.32	9.328–331	122
4.698	374	9.333	116
5.16	17	9.434	98 n.23
5.34	98 n.23	9.545	300 n.36
5.78	153 n.61	9.548–550	289
5.162	153 n.61	9.744–769	170–171
5.163	143 n.37	9.758–759	170
5.220–230	178	9.764	180 n.37
6.165	135 n.7	9.764–769	170
6.245	175	9.820	135 n.7
6.290–293	116, 117	9.831	30
6.531–547	39	9.831–833	31
6.813	32 n.25	9.834	32 n.25
6.887	32 n.25	10.313–315	170 n.4
7.39	15	10.381–382	142 n.29
7.40–63	14	10.445–448	430 n.22

10.628–631	31	12.816–817	118
10.636	31	12.817	442 n.45
10.827–836	288		
10.834	291	**Stesichorus**	
10.845–846	291	6 Curtis = 17 Davies/Finglass	294
10.847	290	7 Curtis = 15 Davies/Finglass	294
10.849–852	290, 299 n.34	12.15–17 Curtis = 19.45–47	
11.1	291, 292	Davies/Finglass	293
11.7–8	291		
11.9–11	292	**Stobaeus**	
11.51	53	*Florilegium*	
11.110	127	4.7.67	316 n.48
11.123–124	292 n.21		
11.165	98 n.23	**Strabo**	
11.201	159 n.79	1.2.12–13	352 n.24
11.425	135 n.7	5.4.5–6	351 n.16
11.472	31	5.4.7	352
11.557–560	148		
11.655–656	153 n.61	**Suetonius**	
12.117–121	300	*Divus Augustus*	
12.120–121	301	7.2	434 n.33
12.121–123	301	16.10	350
12.127–128	301	29.3	342
12.175	313 n.34	*Divus Julius*	
12.267	145 n.40	59.1	310 n.19
12.331–332	126 n.37	*Divus Titus*	
12.465	127	8.3–4	350 n.12
12.481	313	*Divus Vespasianus*	
12.499–505	313	1.2	314
12.501	314	4.5	319 n.58
12.543–586	297	*Domitianus*	
12.546–551	298	1.1	314
12.547–548	300	12.1	314 n.40
12.552–562	298	20	342
12.553–554	299 n.34	*Gaius Caligula*	
12.557	299	37.2–3	365
12.562	299	37.3	365
12.575–577	300	*Nero*	
12.575–579	299	53	331 n.26
12.730	179		
12.741–746	179	**Tacitus**	
12.800–802	301	*Annales*	
12.803–804	301	13.5	342
12.810–812	118	15.42	365
12.814	432 n.31	*Dialogus de oratoribus*	
12.814–815	433 n.32	21.1–2	111
12.816	267 n.23, 358		

Historiae
1.2	312 n.33
1.76.1	57
2.1–2	350
2.86.2	56
3.1–3	58
3.49	58
3.49.2	57
3.52–53	58
3.53	58
3.74	59
3.74.1	59, 314 n.40
4.11	58
4.13.6	28 n.17
4.39	58
4.68	58
4.80	58
4.80.1	60
4.81	312, 312 n.30

Terence
Phormio
101	274

Tertullian
Apologeticus
50.7	147 n.48

Tibullus
1.2.76	189 n.7
1.4.65–66	267 n.23
1.5.9	98 n.23
1.6.31	98 n.23
2.4.11	189 n.7
2.5.16	95 n.17
2.5.109	191 n.14

[Tibullus]
3.4.72	98 n.23
3.7.203	95 n.17

Turpilius comicus
Fragmenta
30 Ribbeck	274

Ulpianus
Digesta
4.3.1	247 n.20

Valerius Flaccus
1.7–21	55
1.28–29	306
1.60–63	209
1.71	58
1.71–74	306
1.73	306
1.76	310
1.79–80	310
1.81–90	306
1.130–132	209 n.22
1.130–148	207
1.184–254	306
1.198	308
1.205–239	307
1.224–225	206 n.9
1.235–236	307
1.244	309
1.244–245	307–308
1.246–247	309
1.338	180 n.40
1.394	182 n.45
1.398–399	59
1.399–401	59
1.433–435	50
1.434–435	50, 58
1.505–527	331 n.24
1.531–567	201, 310
1.537–554	55
1.545–546	310
1.546–548	206 n.7
1.547	209 n.22
1.555–560	55
1.634–635	48
2.101–106	217–218
2.115–119	193
2.131–132	193
2.196–215	192
2.216–241	192
2.242–305	194
2.265ff.	194 n.27
2.311–312a	217 n.48
2.311–331	217 n.48

Index Locorum — **469**

2.311–427	194	3.736	200
2.356	196 n.32	4.13–14	206 n.9
2.373	196 n.34	4.25	200
2.373–374	196 n.34	4.32	52, 53
2.380–382	196	4.138	15
2.391–392	197	4.181–186	14
2.408–418	195	4.244–245	50
2.419–424	195	4.344–421	119
2.423–424	195 n.30	4.357	128
2.424	195 n.30	4.372	119
2.544–545	50	4.378–379	119
2.579–583	72	4.379	119
2.582–583	386	4.507–511	361 n.51
2.654	59 n.55	4.662–671	209–210
3.61	380	5.1–72	66
3.124–137	178 n.32	5.1–328	66
3.198–206	174	5.2–3	183
3.559–560	18	5.43	95 n.17
3.587–591	200	5.63	68
3.598–725	43, 58, 61	5.63–72	68
3.601–603	58	5.69b–71	69–70
3.615–627	44	5.69–72	69
3.617–622	45	5.70	70 n.13
3.629–631	58	5.73–176	66, 71
3.637	51	5.82–119	71
3.637–645	44	5.107–108	71 n.17
3.644	51	5.120–139	71
3.645–689	44, 46-47	5.135	380
3.646	48	5.140–141	72
3.646–647	48	5.140–146	71
3.648–649	60	5.147–153	72
3.649–689	58	5.168–170	72–73
3.651	52	5.177–180a	74
3.656–660	52	5.177–182	74–75
3.670–671	49	5.177–216	66, 74
3.670–672	56	5.179	75 n.21
3.672	48	5.180	76 n.23
3.676–678	48	5.184	75
3.677–678	58	5.184–209	74
3.679–681	50, 58	5.185–186	76
3.688–689	58	5.190	76
3.690–691	58	5.190–191	77
3.697	55	5.192	78
3.697–714	44	5.194–209	78
3.699–701	57	5.198	76 n.23
3.715–725	45, 58	5.205	222
3.717–718	45	5.210b–216	74

5.210–212a	78	5.350	222
5.215–216	78	5.351	213
5.216	78	5.352	209 n.22
5.217	77, 80	5.358	209 n.22
5.217–221	74, 80	5.359–360	217 n.44
5.217–277	66, 79	5.363–372	218
5.218	80	5.366–367	220
5.219–221	206 n.7	5.367	219 n.51
5.222–277	80	5.368	220
5.231–40	81–82	5.369	221
5.231–240	311	5.370	220
5.232–233	311	5.371–372	221
5.238	82 n.26	5.373	209 n.22
5.244	311	5.375	208, 215
5.257–258	82	5.376–377	208, 215
5.260	311	5.378–384	214–215
5.264–265	311	5.378–390	205 n.2
5.276–277	83 n.27	5.391	209 n.22
5.278–295	66	5.392	209 n.22, 222
5.278–296	80	5.397	222
5.296–328	66	5.397–398	222
5.297	80	5.399–454	329
5.325–328	217 n.48	5.403–406	329
5.325–398	217 n.48	5.403–456	329
5.329	207	5.404–406	329
5.329–331	209 n.21	5.406	329 n.22
5.329–398	207, 208	5.407–410	330
5.331	18	5.407–454	222
5.332	222	5.408–409	330
5.334	211	5.409	329 n.22, 330
5.334–340	210	5.410	330
5.335	209 n.22, 211, 217	5.410–415	330–331, 333
		5.415	332
5.336–337	211	5.415–454	207
5.338	211	5.416–418	332
5.338–340	211	5.418–432	333
5.339	209 n.22	5.418–451	333
5.341	222	5.427	222
5.343–349	211	5.429	334
5.343–352	211–212	5.429–432	333
5.344–345	214	5.431	334, 335, 336, 336 n.33
5.346	212, 214		
5.346–347	212	5.432	336
5.347	213	5.433–434	332
5.348	212	5.433–451	333
5.348–349	212	5.433–454	207 n.18
5.349	212, 213	5.451–452	332

5.455	332, 332 n.28, 333 n.29	7.249–250	207 n.18
		7.309–311	207 n.18
5.455–456	332–333	7.339–340	207 n.18
5.456	333 n.29	7.440	211 n.27
5.532	335	7.485–486	207 n.18
5.973–981	71	7.501–510	207 n.18
6.43–47	207 n.18	8.77	207 n.18
6.372–380	175	8.108	207 n.18
6.402–409	201	8.159	224 n.67
6.427–431	198	8.204–206	207 n.18
6.427–494	224	8.217–219	222 n.60
6.439–440	198	8.232	53
6.439–448	209 n.22	8.236	207 n.18
6.449	224	8.248–251	207 n.18
6.467ff.	197 n.37	8.256	222 n.60
6.477–506	197	8.259–317	199
6.490–506	230–231	8.265–266	209 n.22
6.492	213 n.35	8.316–317	207 n.18
6.492–494	231	8.318–368	199
6.494	231	8.385–404	199
6.495	228	8.392–393	209 n.22
6.495–502	207, 223, 224–225, 234	8.420–422	207 n.18
		8.459–461	207 n.18
6.496	228	8.467	199
6.497–502	207 n.18		
6.498	209 n.22	**Varro**	
6.499	228	*De lingua Latina*	
6.500	225	7.4.5	274 n.33
6.500–502	235	*Saturae Menippeae*	
6.501	225, 229 n.80, 235	fr. 552.1	146 n.44
6.501–502	226	**Varro Atacinus**	
6.502	225	10.1–2 Courtney = 129.1–2 Hollis	108
6.575–601	197	10.2 Courtney = 129.2 Hollis	108–109
6.584–586	207 n.18		
6.600–620	198 n.41	**Velleius Paterculus**	
6.636–642	176	1.4.1	357
6.651	182 n.46		
6.657–680	197	**Virgil**	
6.674	231	*Aeneid*	
6.681	231	1.1–2	33
7.141–152	210 n.25	1.4	126, 429
7.182–185	230	1.11	430 n.21
7.192	235 n.98	1.12	25
7.210–291	197	1.23–26	28
7.238	225 n.69	1.23–29	429
7.238–239	225 n.69	1.25	28

472 — Index Locorum

1.36–39	428	1.689–690	30
1.37	428, 429, 430	1.695	26
1.50	152 n.57	1.723	26
1.52–57	152	1.753–756	26
1.55–56	152	2.25–30	271 n.28
1.60–62	152	2.42–44	162
1.69–70	135 n.10	2.43–44	247, 252
1.81	25	2.82	116, 126 n.37
1.85	152 n.57	2.90	53 n.34
1.94–101	265 n.18	2.97–99	53 n.34
1.122	18	2.122	136
1.124–125	25	2.122–144	136 n.13
1.147–156	25	2.125	53 n.34
1.157	25	2.164	53 n.34
1.174–179	35	2.261	251 n.49
1.180	25	2.310–312	385
1.180–181	35	2.335–360	245
1.203	165 n.93	2.360	143 n.37
1.223	25	2.413–419	152 n.57
1.254	253 n.53	2.594–595	308
1.254–296	201	2.601–203	308
1.260	432	2.601–625	136 n.11
1.279	26, 310 n.21	2.602	136
1.297–309	26, 39-40	2.619–620	442
1.305	26	2.711	442 n.45
1.305–313	247	2.762	251 n.49
1.320	380	2.766–767	441
1.326–334	216	3.1–5	33
1.415–417	26	3.10–12	272 n.29
1.418	26	3.65	441
1.448–449	15	3.69–101	357
1.455–456	333 n.29	3.96	357
1.494–495	246 n.10, 333 n.29	3.141–142	221 n.58
		3.207	32 n.25
1.495	215	3.378	359
1.496	212 n.32	3.444	95 n.17
1.496–508	329	3.548	32 n.25
1.498–504	211	3.570–587	361, 361 n.50
1.501	214 n.37, 219	3.575–576	361 n.50
1.503	212	3.619–620	285
1.613	215–216, 216 n.41	3.621	285 n.5
		3.622–627	285 n.4
1.631–632	24 n.12	3.660–661	286
1.633	24 n.12	3.672–674	285 n.3
1.637	24 n.12, 38	3.675–679	285 n.6
1.657	26	3.677–678	285 n.6
1.689	30	3.679	285 n.6

Index Locorum — **473**

4.1	38	5.778–796	136 n.11
4.1–9	210, 210 n.25	6.9–33	337–338
4.68	200	6.9–75	337 n.34
4.68–73	190	6.13	338
4.69–73	215 n.39	6.14	339
4.150	219 n.51	6.14–33	332, 339
4.169	192	6.14–35	342
4.173–195	193	6.32–33	339–340
4.193–194	193	6.69–70	342
4.259–264	14	6.69–76	337 n.34
4.265–267	148 n.50, 160	6.149–152	69
4.265–295	196	6.162–235	69
4.267	160 n.81	6.177	32 n.25
4.280	160 n.82	6.453–454	217 n.46
4.293–294	52	6.460	157, 377
4.317–318	145	6.465	442, 442 n.45
4.320–323	158	6.529	52 n.31, 53, 53 n.34
4.325–330	195–196		
4.327	159 n.78, 161 n.83	6.860–866	143 n.37
		6.866	143
4.327–330	161	7.1–4	69
4.331–332	159 n.78	7.1–6	76 n.23
4.340–344	52	7.1–7	68
4.361	308–309	7.1–285	68
4.377–378	30 n.21	7.7b–9	69
4.393–394	159 n.78	7.7–9	70
4.465–470	34	7.8	70 n.14
4.473	142 n.32	7.8–24	68
4.532	51-52	7.9	385
4.551	191 n.15	7.10	71 n.17
4.553	191	7.10–24	385
4.560	255	7.15	72
4.569	159, 160 n.81, 255	7.23–24	74
		7.25–26	75
4.569–570	160	7.25–36	68, 74, 75, 77
4.600	156 n.70	7.28	75–76
4.610	142 n.32	7.29–30	76
4.645–647	195	7.30–32a	75
4.653	264 n.16	7.36	75, 76
5.1–6	272 n.29	7.37	80, 81, 430
5.140	32 n.25	7.37–45a	79
5.230	147	7.37–105a	77
5.368	32 n.25	7.37–106	68
5.372	182 n.45	7.41	80
5.458	32 n.25	7.44	80
5.670	419	7.45b–101	81
5.749	32 n.25	7.53	82–83

7.58–101	81	7.645	165 n.93
7.59–70	81	7.647–654	287
7.71	82 n.26	7.648	289
7.71–80	81	7.653–654	297
7.81–103	81	7.710–186	14
7.87	82	7.712	181 n.43
7.95–98	82–83	7.815–816	380
7.98	311	8.7	289
7.102–106	77, 81	8.9	181
7.105–106	78, 83 n.27	8.22–25	383
7.107–115	78	8.23	383
7.107–147	68, 77	8.26–27	108
7.107–285	81	8.57–58	29
7.113	78	8.107–110	247
7.120	76 n.23	8.201–204	295
7.133	78	8.293–295	121
7.135–140	78	8.294	180 n.40
7.136–137	77	8.422	327
7.141–147	77, 78	8.485–488	286
7.145	76 n.23	8.499	95 n.17
7.146–147	78	8.612–613	332 n.27
7.148–285	68	8.618	332
7.156	32 n.25	8.625–728	332
7.170	15, 323	8.628	327
7.170–191	323 n.1	8.724	332
7.174	342	8.727	182 n.47
7.225	135 n.7	8.730	332
7.286	81	8.791–793	287–288
7.308–309	156 n.70	8.811–812	287
7.323–405	194	8.812	297
7.335–336	151 n.55	9.38	160 n.81
7.461	153	9.85–89	254
7.481–482	191	9.184–185	153 n.62
7.483–492	188	9.197	374
7.489	189	9.201	175 n.22
7.493–502	191	9.206	147 n.48
7.500	191	9.321–323	29
7.501	191	9.360	181 n.42
7.516	135 n.7	9.446–449	288, 430 n.22
7.516–518	135 n.8	9.593	181 n.42
7.517	181 n.43	9.602	53 n.34
7.525–539	190 n.13	9.630	135 n.7
7.535–539	180 n.36	9.647	182 n.45
7.575	180 n.36	9.710–716	366
7.641	437 n.40	9.715–716	366
7.641–642	437–438	9.769	174
7.642–644	438	10.1	37

Index Locorum — **475**

10.118	37	12.829	253 n.53
10.163	437 n.40	12.845–852	142 n.33
10.190	334	*Eclogues*	
10.272–275	221 n.58	1.2	356, 359
10.356–361	152 n.57	2.49	189
10.417	95 n.17	3.60	427 n.15
10.446	215	4.3	349
10.453	30	4.60	156 n.71
10.475	430 n.22	6.7	359 n.42
10.697–700	177 n.31	6.47	107 n.2
10.773–774	289	6.62–63	334
10.815–820	297	8.16	15
10.860–866	286–287	8.47–48	154
10.900–902	295	10.41	189
10.907	295	*Georgics*	
11.1	37	1.36–37	153 n.62
11.182–183	38	1.135–144	309
11.234–235	342	1.493	374
11.242	181 n.41	1.493–497	151 n.56
11.336–337	51	2.41	442 n.46
11.500	30	2.64	374
11.649	380	2.161–164	365 n.68
11.675	178 n.32	2.385	359 n.44
11.690	182 n.45	2.495–498	151
11.713	32 n.25	2.510–513	151 n.56
11.742	181 n.41	3.153	128
11.785–867	228 n.75	3.267–268	124 n.35
11.794	135 n.7	4.308	374
11.803–804	176 n.24	4.350–351	113 n.14
11.836–849	227	4.425–428	221 n.58
11.837	228	4.471–474	232 n.86
11.840	228	4.559–562	354
11.845	228	4.559–566	358
12.14–15	135 n.8	4.560	361
12.49	147, 147 n.46	4.561	354
12.75	183 n.49	4.561–563	360
12.149–150	163 n.87	4.563	354
12.355	30	4.563–564	358, 369
12.445–447	170 n.6	4.563–566	351, 352, 353, 354
12.457–458	170 n.6		
12.469–472	180	4.564	359, 370
12.476	170 n.6		
12.539	170 n.6	**[Virgil]**	
12.546	17	*Aetna*	
12.553	32 n.25	600	360–361
12.646	148	*Ciris*	
12.696–698	170 n.6	46	118

409	98 n.23	414	98 n.23
411	98 n.23